KidsHealth®
Guide *for* Parents

KidsHealth®
Guide *for* Parents
PREGNANCY TO AGE 5

Steven A. Dowshen, M.D.
Neil Izenberg, M.D.
Elizabeth Bass

Contemporary Books

Chicago New York San Francisco Lisbon London Madrid Mexico City
Milan New Delhi San Juan Seoul Singapore Sydney Toronto

Library of Congress Cataloging-in-Publication Data

Dowshen, Steven A.
    Kidshealth guide for parents : pregnancy to age 5 / Steven A. Dowshen, Neil
Izenberg, and Elizabeth Bass.
        p.   cm.
    Includes index.
    ISBN 0-8092-9872-4
    1. Children—Health and hygiene.   I. Izenberg, Neil.   II. Bass, Elizabeth
R. (Elizabeth Ruth), 1951–   .   III. Title.

RJ101 .D69   2001
613'.0432—dc21   2001028837

3-8-02
$19.95

Contemporary Books

A Division of The McGraw·Hill Companies

1 2 3 4 5 6 7 8 9 0   AGM/AGM   0 9 8 7 6 5 4 3 2 1

ISBN 0-8092-9872-4

This book was set in Bembo
Printed and bound by Quebecor Martinsburg

Cover photographs: top © www.comstock.com; bottom © Elyse Lewin/Image Bank
Interior design by Nick Panos

McGraw-Hill books are available at special quantity discounts to use as premiums and
sales promotions, or for use in corporate training programs. For more information, please
write to the Director of Special Sales, Professional Publishing, McGraw-Hill, Two Penn
Plaza, New York, NY 10121-2298. Or contact your local bookstore.

Important note: All information in *KidsHealth Guide for Parents: Pregnancy to Age 5* is for
educational purposes only. For specific medical advice, diagnoses, and treatment, consult
your child's doctor.

This book is printed on acid-free paper.

Authors

Steven A. Dowshen, M.D.
Neil Izenberg, M.D.
Elizabeth Bass

Contributors

Jennifer Buccigrossi, M.D.
Susan E. Cheeseman, M.S.N., R.N.P., N.N.P.
Kate Cronan, M.D.
Jennifer Hanlin-Xenakes, M.Aud., C.C.C.-A.
Wayne Ho, M.D.
Sharon S. Lehman, M.D.
Robert G. Locke, D.O.
John Loiselle, M.D.
Michael L. Spear, M.D.
Rhonda Walter, M.D.

Editorial Consultants

Joseph DiSanto, M.D.
Jessica Donze, R.D., C.D.N.
Karen Ginther Harbut, R.Ph.
William Houston, M.D.
Patrick Jarvie, M.D.
Joel Klein, M.D.
Stuart R. Levine, Pharm.D.
Francis Montone, D.O.
Kim A. Rutherford, M.D.
Susan Bee Stine, M.D.

To children everywhere and the parents who love them

Contents

chapter twenty-nine **Signs and Symptoms**

chapter thirty **Childhood Infections**

A Word from the Authors

Parenthood can be an amazing, life-changing experience—but one with its share of stress and tears, of course.

As pediatricians and child health educators, we have learned firsthand what concerns parents have. You've told us—by your words and actions in office visits and in telephone conversations. You've told us in the emails that you have sent to us at KidsHealth.org—our Web site for parents, kids, and teens. It's amazing how the same questions and concerns keep coming up again and again—not only from parents in this country, but from parents around the world.

More than a generation ago, pediatrician Benjamin Spock revolutionized the world of parenting when he advised parents to "trust themselves" to know what was best for their babies. At that time, doctors regularly gave parents a set of rigid instructions about eating, sleeping, and just about everything else involving baby care. By suggesting that parents follow their own instincts, Dr. Spock led the way in establishing a view that now seems second nature: Parents and medical professionals need to work together to meet the differing needs of each child.

More than half a century later, a lot has changed. The world is more complex—and knowledge about children's growth, development, and health increases every day. Sure, parents are more likely to trust their instincts now, but they also are hungry for information to test their instincts against.

The Nemours Foundation, where we work, is one of the nation's largest not-for-profit children's health organizations, founded in 1936. Since 1993, at the Nemours Foundation's Center for Children's Health Media, we've worked to help families learn about children's health through our videos, books, and Web sites (www.KidsHealth.org and www.TeensHealth.org). In fact, KidsHealth.org has become the most visited and most linked-to site of its kind on the Internet.

We've written *KidsHealth Guide for Parents* the way we'd speak to our non-health-care-professional friends. And we've jam-packed the *Guide* with lots of in-depth, practical information about prenatal care, feeding decisions, choosing and working with doctors, routine health care, signs and symptoms of illness in children, chronic conditions and childhood infections, health information on the Web, health insurance and managed care—and much, much more.

The first parts of *KidsHealth Guide for Parents* begin with pregnancy and preparing for your new arrival. We move through the birth and early months of your child's life and follow with discussions on the health and behavioral aspects of your child's journey through the toddler and preschool years. We hope you'll find the first parts of the book so helpful you'll want to read them through completely to get an overall perspective on your child's health and development.

The final parts of the book are for reference—really a collection of comprehensive "mini-encyclopedias" on first aid and emergencies, infections, health problems of young children, and interpreting your child's signs and symptoms. Although you will find that the information on our Web site is a useful and continually updated complement to the book, the vast majority of the content in *KidsHealth Guide for Parents* was newly and specifically written for this book.

But we didn't do it alone. We asked you (via our Web site and through our practices) to tell us what you wanted to know, what you wished you had known, what worked, and what didn't work for you as a parent. A sampling of your thoughts and observations is included in the book. We'd like to include even more of your comments in future editions of *KidsHealth Guide for Parents*. Email us at Guide@KidsHealth.org with suggestions and comments.

One important note: The information in our book is meant to be used to support the individualized advice of your child's doctor—not to take the place of it. If you're concerned about your child's health, nothing takes the place of an evaluation by your child's doctor.

So enjoy this book—and enjoy being a parent. It's a special time—and we're glad you invited us along with you on your journey through parenthood.

Steven A. Dowshen, M.D.
Neil Izenberg, M.D.
Elizabeth Bass

About the Authors

Steven A. Dowshen, M.D., F.A.A.P., is a board-certified pediatrician and subspecialist in pediatric endocrinology practicing at the Alfred I. duPont Hospital for Children in Wilmington, Delaware. Long interested in helping children and families learn about health, Dr. Dowshen is medical editor of The Nemours Foundation's Center for Children's Health Media, where he oversees the medical review process of KidsHealth.org, a Web site with health information written for parents, kids, and teens. He is also the associate editor-in-chief of Charles Scribner's Sons' *Human Diseases and Conditions* (2001), a three-volume encyclopedia for middle and high school students. Dr. Dowshen directed the establishment of the hospital's statewide system of primary care pediatric practices, created to expand access to health care for medically underserved children in Delaware. Prior to joining the staff at the Alfred I. duPont Hospital for Children, Dr. Dowshen was director of the pediatric residency training program at the Albert Einstein Medical Center in Philadelphia. Dr. Dowshen received his B.S. from Pennsylvania State University and his M.D. from Jefferson Medical College of the Thomas Jefferson University. He completed his pediatric residency and fellowship training in pediatric endocrinology and metabolism at St. Christopher's Hospital for Children. He is a fellow of the American Academy of Pediatrics. Dr. Dowshen lives in Philadelphia with his wife and two daughters.

Neil Izenberg, M.D., F.A.A.P., is a board-certified pediatrician at the Alfred I. duPont Hospital in Wilmington, Delaware. Dr. Izenberg is founder and chief executive of The Nemours Foundation's Center for Children's Health Media and editor-in-chief of the KidsHealth Web site. A pediatrician specializing in adolescent medicine, Dr. Izenberg is the editor-in-chief of Charles Scribner's Sons' *Human Diseases and Conditions* (2001) and author of a number of books on children's health topics, including *How to Raise Non-Smoking Kids* (Pocket Books, 1997). He is also cocreator of Not So Scary Things, a board game for children ages four to eight years. A recipient of the American Academy of Pediatrics' Education Award, Dr. Izenberg has written and/or produced more than 25 nationally distributed award-winning video programs for both children and parents on a variety of health issues. Dr. Izenberg received his B.A. from Columbia University and his M.D. from the Robert Wood Johnson Medical School. He received his pediatric training at the Schneider Children's Hospital and his fellowship training (in Pediatric Diabetes/Endocrinology and in Adolescent Medicine) at Children's Hospital of Philadelphia. A fellow of the American Academy of Pediatrics, Dr. Izenberg lives in Philadelphia.

Elizabeth Bass is a writer and editor who specializes in making health information clear and practical for general readers. As science and health editor at *Newsday* for six years, she supervised projects that won top awards in their fields, including the Pulitzer Prize. She was an associate editor of Charles Scribner's Sons' *Human Diseases and Conditions* (2001) and has taught at the Columbia Graduate School of Journalism. Now senior projects editor at *Newsday*, she lives on Long Island with her husband and their young son.

About KidsHealth and the Nemours Foundation

KidsHealth, a project of the Nemours Foundation's Center for Children's Health Media, is one of the largest resources for medically reviewed pediatric information on the Web. The site has a physician-directed, professional editorial staff specializing in developing age-appropriate content for three distinct audiences—parents, kids, and teens. All content is reviewed extensively by pediatric generalists and specialists. KidsHealth was voted "Best Health Care Content" at the eHealthcareWorld Awards, and Netmom® Jean Amour Polly declares it, "The Best Health Site on the Net for and About Kids" in her *Internet Kids & Family Yellow Pages* (McGraw-Hill Professional Publishing, 2000).

The Nemours Foundation's Center for Children's Health Media also creates a range of useful printed materials, including guides for parents, health resource books, and children's books. Recent publications include *First-Aid Tips for Parents, How to Raise Non-Smoking Kids* (Pocket Books, 1997), and Charles Scribner's Sons' *Human Diseases and Conditions* (2001), a three-volume encyclopedia for middle and high school students. Additionally, the Center produces broadcast-quality pediatric video programs, which are distributed to families by physicians and hospitals as a key aspect of patient education.

The Nemours Foundation is one of the largest nonprofit organizations devoted to children's health and is the nation's largest physician practice delivering subspecialty pediatric care. It operates the world-renowned Alfred I. duPont Hospital for Children in Wilmington, Delaware, and Nemours Children's Clinics in Delaware and Florida. The Foundation was established and funded by a trust in Alfred duPont's will in 1940.

Acknowledgments

With a book like this, there are many people to thank—those who reviewed (and re-reviewed) our writings, those who contributed to the content with their special expertise, those who edited and (hard as it is to believe!) even improved our words, and those who have always been there for us: our families, friends, and colleagues.

Thanks to D'Arcy Lyness, Ph.D., and Jennifer Brooks for their support and inspiration. To Robert A. Doughty, M.D., Ph.D., and Jeff Wadsworth at The Nemours Foundation for their support of the Center for Children's Health Media. And to the many Alfred I. duPont Hospital for Children staff and community physicians who generously shared their knowledge and experience with us.

Thanks to Kristen Kirchner, Cathy Ginther, Gwyneth Finnell, and Amy Sutton for their excellent editing and managing skills. To Shirley Morrison and Diane McGrath for keeping us and the Center organized. To Judith McCarthy, Michele Pezzuti, Marisa L'Heureux, Pam Juarez, Susan Moore-Kruse, Nick Panos, and Dawn Shoemaker at Contemporary Books for their enthusiastic support of this project. And to the entire talented team at KidsHealth, especially Jennifer Lynch, Karen Riley, Annie Hill, and Elaine Chan, for their editorial assistance.

More personally, Steve Dowshen thanks his wife, Arlene, for her love, support, and patience while he worked on this book; his grown-up daughters, Nadia and Beth, who are living proof that his wife (mostly) and he must have done something right as parents; and Florence and Albert Dowshen and Jean Lucker for being the best role models a couple of young parents could have. Elizabeth Bass gives special thanks to (and for) her husband, Joseph Masci, M.D.; their son, Jonathan; and her mother, Beatrice Bass, for their patience, inspiration, and love. Neil Izenberg gives personal thanks to parents Jim and Shirley Izenberg and to family members Seth, Paul, Karen, Lisa, Rebecca, Ben, Karlin, Josh, Jake, and Lia.

Guide *for* Parents

PART ONE

Special Delivery!
Pregnancy, Birth, and
Your Baby's First Months

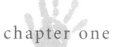

chapter one

Prenatal Care

Getting off to a good start

"We're going to have a baby!"

First—congratulations!

You've started on one of life's great adventures, an epic journey into new worlds of love, excitement, endurance, and, occasionally, fear.

One thing all parents will tell you: Your life will never be the same. It's true, because you'll be seeing the world through new eyes—the eyes of a parent (and sometimes through the eyes of your child).

If you're like most parents-to-be (and why wouldn't you be?), you're excited, nervous, and thrilled, all at once. At the same time, these feelings may be mixed with an occasional nagging concern: Will your baby be healthy?

So let's start with the good news: In most cases—in fact, in the overwhelming majority of cases—babies are born healthy and vigorous. So the odds are good that your baby, too, will be healthy and vigorous. More good news: By doing or not doing just a few things—eating well, taking folic acid, getting medical care, and avoiding cigarettes, alcohol, and drugs—a pregnant woman can dramatically improve the odds that her baby will have a healthy beginning.

Of course, "taking care of yourself" is not only for pregnant women. It's also important for fathers-to-be, for men and women planning to adopt a child, and for those intending to conceive someday. For all future parents, practicing good health habits can help your child grow up healthier. For instance, if no one in your home smokes, your child is less likely to have asthma, bronchitis, ear infections, and other illnesses. If your whole family eats well and gets exercise, your child will learn these habits that will help her for a lifetime. For couples, building good health habits is much more fun if you do it together than if one person tries to do it alone. The father-to-be can help by joining his partner in eating well, being physically active, and keeping any shared temptations—especially cigarettes and alcohol—out of the house.

What if you're a woman who is already well along in pregnancy and you haven't been taking care of yourself the way you should? The old saying "better late than never" really does apply here. No matter how far along your pregnancy is, if you're drinking alcohol or smoking, stop now—for both your sakes. But don't beat yourself up about the past. The odds are still good that your baby will be fine.

What if you're already taking care of yourself? Waiting for a baby—whether through pregnancy or adoption—can be an anxious time. But worrying now about every possible risk will not help your baby or you. Once you've taken care of the things you can control, try to relax and savor this unique period of waiting and anticipation.

The truth about pregnancy is, you get no guarantees when it comes to health. Just as most babies are born healthy no matter what you do, some will have problems no matter what you do. In most cases, if a problem occurs, there is no way the parents could have prevented it. In other words, it is nobody's fault. That's important for everyone in your family to remember.

All you can do by acting wisely is improve the odds in your baby's favor. But that's a lot.

The advice in this chapter aims to help you reach that goal. It's divided into two sections:

1. Healthy living, which includes tips on nutrition, exercise, rest, and vitamins and advice about work, sex, and avoidance of harmful substances
2. Medical care, which includes information on choosing a health care provider, getting tests, getting care if you don't have insurance, and knowing when to call your doctor

If You Are Planning to Become Pregnant

Doing—or not doing—a few things in advance can help your baby get a healthy start.

1. Take folic acid (a B vitamin) daily. Begin at least a month before you start trying to get pregnant, and continue throughout the first three months of

pregnancy. This simple act can help prevent many cases of spina bifida and other neural tube defects (birth defects that affect the brain and spinal cord). The recommended dose of 0.4 to 0.8 milligram (mg) is found in most multivitamins.

2. If you smoke or drink alcohol (even moderately), stop.

3. If you are severely overweight or underweight, work toward achieving a healthier weight before you attempt to get pregnant. This can reduce your risk of many prenatal problems.

4. If you have a chronic illness or suspect you have a sexually transmitted disease, see your doctor and get treatment before you become pregnant.

5. Do not take oral prescription drugs called retinoids (synthetic variants of vitamin A); they can be dangerous to your fetus. The most commonly prescribed form of this drug is the acne drug Accutane (isotretinoin). This drug can be particularly damaging early in pregnancy, before a woman may even realize she has conceived. Related drugs Soriatane (acitretin) and Tegison (etretinate), used to treat psoriasis, may damage a fetus even after a woman has stopped taking them. If you have ever taken these drugs, talk to your doctor.

   (Some skin creams, such as Retin-A or Renova, contain a related substance called tretinoin or retinoic acid. In studies so far, these do not appear to cause problems. But until more research is done, it may be wise to avoid retinoic acid creams before and during pregnancy.)

Dealing with potential problems ahead of time can make life better for you and your baby. That's one reason doctors advise that women or couples have a "preconception visit" with a health care provider months before a planned pregnancy (we discuss this visit later in this chapter).

Healthy Living During Pregnancy

Eat Well

It's best to eat a balanced diet that includes lots of whole grain breads, pasta, and cereal; plenty of fruits and vegetables; and smaller amounts of low-fat dairy products and protein-packed foods such as poultry, fish, meat, dry beans, and nuts. The "Food Guide Pyramid," designed by the U.S. Department of Agriculture, is a good basis for such a diet (see Figure 1.1). As the guide suggests, it's better to avoid empty calories—foods like candy, chips, and soda that are high in calories but low in nutrients.

During pregnancy, keep in mind a few more food tips.

- Eat a little more. A woman of moderate weight will need to add an average of 300 extra calories a day to her diet. Three hundred calories is not a lot of food—a low-fat eight-ounce yogurt and an apple will do it, or half a turkey sandwich and a glass of 1 percent milk. Nutritious foods like these are a good way to get the extra calories (although the occasional late-night pint of ice cream is one of the time-honored perks of pregnancy).

- Gain weight. The National Academy of Science has recommended that women of normal weight gain 25 to 35 pounds during pregnancy. Overweight women should gain less (15 to 25 pounds), and underweight women should gain more (28 to 40 pounds). If your doctor thinks your fetus is growing well, don't worry about exactly how much weight you're gaining; most women who fall outside this range still have healthy babies. But don't try a weight-loss diet while you're pregnant. Wait until after your baby is born.

- Drink a lot of water. During pregnancy, a woman needs extra fluid. The amount of blood in her body increases by an average of almost 50 percent. The fetus, placenta, and amniotic fluid all require water. Dehydration can deepen fatigue early in pregnancy and lead to premature contractions later on. Aim to get eight eight-ounce glasses of fluids a day; make as much of it from water as possible.

- Don't eat raw or undercooked meat, raw eggs, raw (unpasteurized) milk, or cheese made from raw milk. Such foods can carry microorganisms, such as *Listeria monocytogenes* or the parasite that causes toxoplasmosis, that can harm a fetus. Order meat well done in restaurants; at home cook it to an internal temperature of 160 degrees Fahrenheit. If you handle raw meat, wash your hands and utensils immediately afterward. Wash raw fruits and vegetables before eating. In general, practice good food safety techniques to prevent infections; get information at www.foodsafety.gov or call (888) SAFEFOOD. The Food and Drug Administration suggests that pregnant women avoid eating swordfish, shark, king mackerel, and tilefish because of possible high mercury levels.

- Be sure you get enough iron and calcium. The recommended dose of iron is 30 mgs a day to prevent anemia in the mother (increased to 60 to 100 mgs if the woman is large or carrying twins). This is especially important later in pregnancy when the fetus, the placenta, and the mother's expanding blood supply can easily use up her stored iron.

The recommended dose of calcium is 1,200 mgs a day for pregnant women. Prenatal vitamins, which are commonly recommended by doctors, typically contain only 200 to 300 mgs of calcium because taking more can interfere with the absorption of iron in the supplement. If you wait a few hours, however, this is no longer a problem. So, unless you get a lot of calcium in your diet, you may want to take your prenatal vitamin in the morning and a calcium tablet at night.

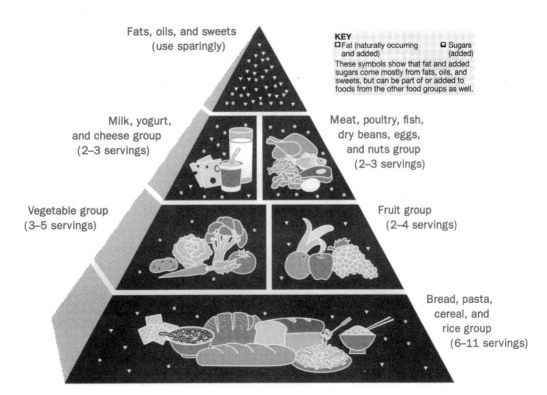

Figure 1.1. Food Guide Pyramid. The USDA's Food Guide Pyramid is helpful in planning a properly balanced diet during pregnancy—and afterward for your entire family. Talk with your doctor, nurse midwife, or a dietitian about special nutritional requirements during pregnancy. (*Source: U.S. Department of Agriculture/U.S. Department of Health and Human Services*)

KidsHealth Tip

A Is for Avoid (Excess Vitamin A)

Don't take herbal or vitamin supplements, especially in megadoses (amounts above the Recommended Daily Allowance) unless your doctor OKs it. Large amounts of vitamin A pose a particular risk (although it is safe to take beta-carotene, a substance that is converted by the body into vitamin A).

In one study, women who took more than 10,000 IU of vitamin A a day were more likely to have a malformed fetus. Many multivitamins contain 5,000 IU of vitamin A. So taking a double dose of them could put you into the danger zone.

Sleep and Rest a Lot

You may be surprised at how tired you are in the first few months of pregnancy—when you don't even look pregnant yet. Most women feel less tired midway through the pregnancy, and then weary again at the end. If you feel tired, don't fight it. Take a nap, or put your feet up, close your eyes, and listen to music. If you're working outside the home, try to find a place where you can lie down for a few minutes during the day. Go to bed early, even if it means cutting back on activities or getting your partner to do more around the house (or leaving it undone). Take a personal day.

Get Some Exercise

If your doctor approves, get moderate, regular, low-impact exercise, such as walking, swimming, or pedaling a stationary bike. Twenty to 30 minutes of exercise at least three times a week is recommended for most pregnant women. If you're already a well-conditioned runner or workout star, you'll probably be able to continue, perhaps at a lower intensity. If you're out of shape, you shouldn't try anything too strenuous during pregnancy. Some women should not exercise at all

KidsHealth Tip

Prenatal Sleeping

As your belly begins to grow, you should try to lie on your left side as much as possible when you rest or sleep. This prevents the growing uterus from pressing on large blood vessels and restricting blood flow to your placenta (and therefore your baby). It can also help prevent swelling that might occur in your legs.

during pregnancy. So whether you're a triathlete or a couch potato, you should discuss exercise with your doctor first.

As you get further along in your pregnancy, your sense of balance may be thrown off and your ligaments will get looser. (It's a hormonal thing.) Because of these changes, many doctors advise against sports where falls are likely, such as skiing, cycling, and horseback riding. Waterskiing, surfing, and scuba diving are considered especially dangerous and should be avoided.

Take frequent breaks while exercising, and drink plenty of fluids. Limit exertion during hot, humid weather—you don't want to get overheated. Avoid exercise that requires you to lie flat on your back after the first three months of pregnancy; the uterus may press on large blood vessels, restricting blood flow to your heart. Even if you are in good shape, do not push yourself anywhere near your limit. It appears that it may be safer if your heart rate (the number of beats per minute) stays below 140.

In addition to aerobic exercise, strengthening and stretching exercises can help prevent backache and other pregnancy discomforts. Try the pelvic tilt and Kegel exercises for starters.

The Pelvic Tilt

Start on your hands and knees. Relax your back, then breathe out and tighten your abdominal muscles while tucking your buttocks down. Your back will naturally arch upward. Hold for a count of five or ten. Repeat. You can also do it standing against a wall: When you tighten your abdomen and tuck in your buttocks, your lower back will flatten against the wall.

Kegel Exercises

Kegel exercises are like internal calisthenics. They strengthen the pelvic floor muscles (the muscles around the vagina and anus). This may make childbirth and recovery easier and help prevent the leaking of urine that new mothers sometimes experience. (Because they tighten vaginal muscles, they may even improve your sex life!)

To do Kegels, tense the muscles around the vagina and anus as if trying to stop the flow of urine. Hold them tight for several seconds, then relax. Do 10 to 20 contractions three or four times a day, and try to work up to holding each contraction for 10 seconds. You can do this exercise when you're sitting, standing, or lying down. Any time you're waiting—at a red light, in a store, or at the doctor's office—you can get in a few Kegels.

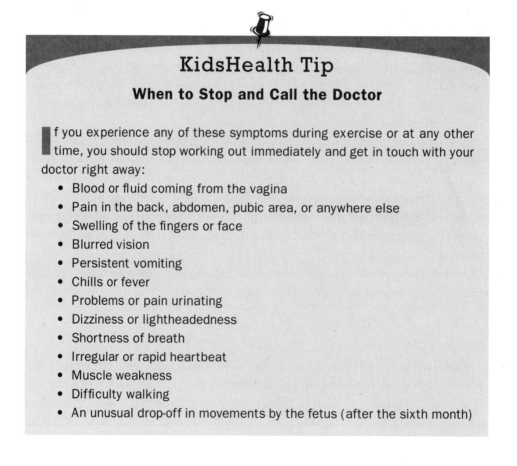

KidsHealth Tip

When to Stop and Call the Doctor

If you experience any of these symptoms during exercise or at any other time, you should stop working out immediately and get in touch with your doctor right away:

- Blood or fluid coming from the vagina
- Pain in the back, abdomen, pubic area, or anywhere else
- Swelling of the fingers or face
- Blurred vision
- Persistent vomiting
- Chills or fever
- Problems or pain urinating
- Dizziness or lightheadedness
- Shortness of breath
- Irregular or rapid heartbeat
- Muscle weakness
- Difficulty walking
- An unusual drop-off in movements by the fetus (after the sixth month)

The Big Don'ts During Pregnancy

A few precautions are worth taking.

Don't Drink Alcoholic Beverages

Heavy drinking (five or six drinks a day) throughout pregnancy can cause fetal alcohol syndrome, which is a set of severe, lifelong problems that include mental retardation, facial deformities, and heart problems. (For more information, see Chapter 26, "Medical Issues in Adoption.") But even moderate drinking (one or two drinks each day) or occasional "binge" drinking (five or more drinks at a sitting) increases the risk of miscarriage, premature birth, low birthweight, and growth and development problems that continue after the child is born. Recent studies indicate that binge drinking early in pregnancy significantly increases the risk of cleft lip and palate in the infant. Because it's not known whether a "safe" level of drinking exists, it's safest for pregnant women not to drink alcohol at all.

Can One Drink Hurt?

Warnings against drinking during pregnancy often leave even light drinkers worrying about alcohol they consumed before they knew they were pregnant. Other women wonder whether there's any harm in having a glass of wine to celebrate a special occasion while they're pregnant. There's no evidence that an isolated drink or two will harm your fetus, and there's no advantage in worrying about what you did before you knew you were pregnant. But whether you're trying to become pregnant, or already are, avoiding alcohol altogether is safest. If you do decide to have a special-occasion drink, be sure that one drink does not lead to another, and don't find repeated reasons to "celebrate."

Don't Smoke

Don't smoke, and don't spend a lot of time around people who do. Smoking contributes to many cases of low birthweight, miscarriage, and premature birth. Secondhand smoke can affect babies as well. If people in your home or office cannot stop smoking, ask them to step outside for their nicotine fix. If, for some reason, they can't do this, ask them to confine their smoking to one room, and stay out of it.

Don't Consume Too Much Caffeine

Caffeine has been linked to an increased risk of miscarriage and low birthweight when consumed in large amounts. Some experts think it's OK for a pregnant woman to have up to 200 to 300 mgs a day, which is about the amount in one or two small cups of coffee. (Of course, if you drink coffee, make sure you don't get additional caffeine from soda or other sources.) Others think it's wisest to avoid caffeine altogether. Caffeine has other drawbacks: It promotes loss of fluid and calcium, which pregnant women can't afford to lose. It also can make frequent urination, a typical annoyance of pregnancy, even more frequent. Caffeine is found mostly in coffee, some teas, cola, and some other sodas; these drinks have little or no nutritional value.

Don't Use Illegal or Recreational Drugs

Cocaine, crack, heroin, and PCP can all endanger your fetus's health as well as your own. So can taking "uppers" (amphetamines) and "downers" (tranquilizers) or sniffing glue.

Take Care with Medications

Don't take any medications—whether they're prescription or over the counter, synthetic or "natural," high-tech or herbal—unless your doctor says it's all right. When there's a choice, as with less serious illnesses, it's better to use nonmedicinal remedies: chicken soup and a vaporizer rather than a cold tablet, for instance. For morning sickness, avoid products that claim to be remedies; instead, try eating frequent small snacks of bread or crackers.

The National Institutes of Health recently recognized acupuncture as an effective treatment for nausea and vomiting during pregnancy. Speak with your doctor about this if your symptoms are severe.

Don't stop taking any medication or cut the dosage without consulting your doctor. If you hear or read something that worries you about a drug you are taking, discuss it with your doctor. The reports you hear may be incomplete or based on unconfirmed data. And, in some cases, the risks of not treating the health condition may outweigh the possible risks of taking the drug. Of the big three over-the-counter medications for fever and pain, acetaminophen is generally considered

KidsHealth Tip

Look Out for Hidden Caffeine

Some non-cola soft drinks, such as Mountain Dew, can have as much caffeine as colas or even more. And watch out for super-sized beverages. The 20-ounce bottles of soda sold in many vending machines contain two and one-half servings; a large takeout coffee is far bigger than the 5-ounce or 6-ounce cup of coffee used in most "caffeine-per-cup" listings.

safer in pregnancy than aspirin or ibuprofen. But don't take any medication without consulting your doctor.

Avoid Raising Your Body Temperature

Don't sit for long in a hot tub, bake in a sauna, or soak in an extremely hot bath. In general, it's better not to do anything that could raise your body temperature to above 102 degrees Fahrenheit.

Avoid Exposing Yourself to Toxic Chemicals

During pregnancy, it's smart to stay away from toxic chemicals, such as pesticides, carbon monoxide, lead, or organic solvents (such as toluene, tetrachloroethylene, glycol ethers, and other chemicals used primarily in manufacturing). Although the risks are not always clear, such chemicals have been linked to increased chance of miscarriage, among other problems. For information on occupational risks in pregnancy, call the National Institute for Occupational Safety and Health (NIOSH) at (800) 35-NIOSH, or check its Web site, www.cdc.gov/niosh. Also check out the U.S. Occupational Safety and Health Administration (OSHA) Web site, www.osha.gov. If you suspect hazards in your workplace, talk to your union (if you have one), your employer, and your doctor. In many states, you can find a union-funded Committee for Occupational Safety and Health that may be able to help. For a listing of these groups, see the Web site of the New York Committee for Occupational Safety and Health at www.nycosh.org.

Many cancer chemotherapy drugs can be harmful to a developing fetus. If you require treatment for cancer, be sure to seek your doctor's advice about planning or continuing a pregnancy.

Be Careful with X-rays

Medical or dental X-rays for diagnosis can be done safely, but before getting any X-ray you should make sure that doctors, nurses, and technicians know that you are or may be pregnant. Higher doses of X-rays, such as those used to treat cancer, can cause problems.

Avoid On-the-Job Exposure to Viruses and Bacteria

Exposure to viruses and bacteria is a hazard primarily for people who work in the medical field or with young children. Discuss recommended immunizations or precautions with your doctor.

Don't Go Near the Litter Box

If pregnant women voted for their favorite piece of advice, this "don't" would probably top the list: Don't change the cat litter; get someone else to do it. This advice is standard because contact with cat feces is one of the major ways people can get toxoplasmosis. (Other ways you can get toxoplasmosis include eating raw or undercooked meat, raw eggs, or raw goat's milk.) This parasitic infection can cause miscarriage or serious birth defects if a woman gets infected during pregnancy. You can be tested for toxoplasmosis before pregnancy to see if you were previously infected and therefore are immune. Discuss this with your doctor. If you are not immune or were not tested, you should be extra careful. You can also have your cats tested to see if they have an active infection. To make cat infection less likely, keep cats indoors and don't let them eat raw meat. Also, make sure the litter box is changed daily because the feces get more infectious with time. If you must do the job yourself, wear disposable rubber gloves and wash your hands thoroughly afterward.

Whether you have cats or not, always wear gloves when gardening because outdoor soil can be contaminated with the parasite; for the same reason, avoid sandy soil and sandboxes. Never eat raw or undercooked meat, and wash hands immediately after touching raw meat. Always remember to wash raw fruits and vegetables before eating.

What About Working?

Most women in low-risk pregnancies can continue working during pregnancy, right up to the day of delivery, if they choose to. Although you should discuss this with your doctor, in most cases the decision to stop or continue working is based on comfort (you're just too big, heavy, and tired to go on) or practical considera-

Sighs of Relief

Over the years, people have worried that certain common activities—using a microwave oven, drinking diet soda, or using hair color—might not be safe during pregnancy. But so far studies have not shown that these activities cause any damage to the fetus. Some women still feel more comfortable avoiding microwave radiation, cosmetic chemicals, and aspartame (the sweetener in most "diet" products), given that these things are optional. But they do not appear to be risky. And for the millions of women who work at computer terminals each day (a far less optional activity for many), studies of computer terminals in the workplace have not shown a link to miscarriage as was once feared.

tions (you don't want to use up any of your maternity leave before your baby arrives).

If your job is physically strenuous, involving bending, lifting, or long hours of standing, your doctor may advise cutting back on your hours or stopping work a few weeks or months before you are due to deliver. Some studies suggest that strenuous work or standing for hours each day late in pregnancy may increase the chances of high blood pressure in the mother or low birthweight in the baby. This is more of a concern if you are underweight or carrying twins.

If your doctor thinks you are at high risk for premature labor or if complications have developed during the pregnancy, you may be advised to stop working and get more rest. Round-the-clock bed rest may even be prescribed, but this is uncommon.

What About Sex?

In a smooth, low-risk pregnancy, it is usually considered safe to engage in sexual intercourse as long as you feel like it. If there's a risk of premature labor or other complications, the doctor may advise abstaining.

If you are having sex, beware of sexually transmitted diseases (STDs). Because these can threaten a pregnancy and severely harm the fetus, women are routinely tested and, if necessary, treated for any STDs early in the pregnancy. But if a woman acquires an STD after getting pregnant, it may go undetected and untreated. To prevent infection, use a condom or don't have sexual relations with anyone you think may have been exposed to a sexually transmitted disease. If you think you may have been exposed to one, tell your doctor. Such diseases often cause no symptoms.

Medical Care

How many times in this chapter have we advised you to consult your doctor about what's best for you personally? Please don't count—it would take too long. Clearly, you're likely to have a lot of contact with this person, especially if you're older than 35 or have other factors that raise pregnancy risks (see box on page 17).

Finding a doctor may be simple—you may want to stick with the doctor who has been giving you gynecological or family health care, provided he or she also does obstetrics and deliveries. Less pleasantly, your insurance may limit you to a short list of choices. Or, you may have friends or relatives who recommend someone they like. Typically, people get recommendations from their regular doctor or from a medical center in the area. Nurses who work in labor and delivery may be particularly good sources. When choosing a doctor, here are some things to consider.

Different Kinds of Health Care Providers

Professionals who provide medical care during pregnancy and delivery come in three basic types.

Obstetrician-Gynecologists

OBs, as they're called for short, are surgeons who, after medical school, have had at least four years of training in women's health and reproduction. They deliver about 90 percent of babies in the United States. They can handle complicated pregnancies and can also perform cesarean sections. If you have pregnancy risk factors, your doctor probably should be an obstetrician.

Look for obstetricians who are "board certified," meaning they have passed an examination by the American Board of Obstetrics and Gynecology. If doctors are described as "board eligible," it means they have the training to take the exam but either haven't taken it yet or haven't passed it yet. If your preferred doctor is board eligible, you could ask about the specifics of his or her situation.

Some board-certified obstetricians go on for further training in high-risk pregnancies. These physicians are called maternal-fetal specialists or perinatologists. In most cases, your regular doctor would refer you to such a specialist if needed.

What Is a High-Risk Pregnancy?

There is no official definition of a high-risk or low-risk pregnancy. But conditions like the ones listed here are signs of increased risk. A pregnancy with even one of these features, and certainly with two or three, would be considered high risk by many health care providers. That need not be as scary as it sounds. It often just means a woman may need to take extra precautions or get close medical monitoring. If none of these apply to you, most likely you can consider your pregnancy low risk.

Risk is raised if the woman:

- Has had a problem pregnancy in the past
- Is younger than 15 or older than 35 (some doctors would say 40)
- Is carrying twins or triplets
- Has a serious medical problem such as diabetes; high blood pressure; epilepsy (a seizure disorder); or heart, lung, or liver disease
- Has a sexually transmitted disease or other serious infection
- Smokes, drinks alcohol, or takes illegal drugs
- Has multiple sexual partners
- Does not get prenatal care
- Gains little or no weight
- Experiences vaginal bleeding after the first three months of pregnancy
- Develops pregnancy-related high blood pressure (called preeclampsia)

Risk is raised if the fetus:

- Has an abnormal heartbeat
- Shows signs of growing less than expected (a condition called intrauterine growth restriction, or IUGR)

Certified Nurse-Midwives

Certified nurse-midwives (CNMs) are registered nurses who have a graduate degree in midwifery, meaning they are trained to handle normal, low-risk pregnancies and deliveries and have passed a certifying exam. Nurse-midwives generally practice under the supervision of a physician, an arrangement called a collaborative practice, and should always have a physician on call in case backup is needed. Most CNMs deliver babies in hospitals or birthing centers, although some do home births. Part of their role is being able to recognize complications and refer women to physicians, when needed.

The use of CNMs has increased in recent years. Generally, they do an excellent job of providing lower-cost, prevention-oriented health care for pregnant women. Studies have shown they achieve results as good as, or better than, obstetricians do when managing uncomplicated pregnancies ending with a routine vaginal delivery.

Other Kinds of Midwives

In some states, you will hear of certified midwives (CMs) or certified professional midwives (CPMs). These midwives are not required to be nurses. CMs take training courses and must pass the same exam as certified nurse-midwives. CPMs, who are accredited by a different group, may be trained through apprenticeship; they are encouraged to do home deliveries and not work with doctors. Not all states allow such midwives to practice. In terms of the quality of their work, these kinds of midwives have not been studied in the same way as certified nurse-midwives.

Family Practitioners

Family practitioners (also called family practice physicians) are medical doctors whose post-graduate training mixes adult medicine, pediatrics, obstetrics-gynecology, and other fields. The modern version of the old GP, or general practitioner, these doctors offer medical care for the whole family. Some deliver babies, particularly those in rural areas, but many do not. (In a survey by the American Academy of Family Physicians, fewer than one-third of the doctors responding said they had ever delivered a baby in their practice, although the numbers were higher in the West.) Some family practitioners handle only normal pregnancies and refer complicated cases to obstetricians. Family practitioners, too, should be board certified or board eligible.

Which Kind of Health Care Provider Is Best for You?

Health professionals, like other people, are so unique that it's risky to generalize which one is right for you. But taken as a group, each type of practitioner tends to have its strong and weak points.

Obstetricians clearly should be your choice if you have a chronic illness, are carrying twins, are older than 40, or have reason to think your pregnancy might be complicated. If you are a medically oriented person who wants to know as much as possible about the baby before it is born and wants to use the latest in medical technology, you are likely to find a kindred spirit in the ranks of OBs. If you want a low-tech, "natural" delivery with little medical intervention, it may be harder to find an obstetrician who shares your approach.

Feel Free to Change

Your gynecologist may also be an obstetrician, but don't feel you must stay with this doctor. The person who prescribed your birth control or cured your yeast infections may not be the person you want to see you through your pregnancy. Spending nine months with a doctor who will deliver your baby is different than the once-a-year, hello–good-bye relationship you may have now with your doctor. Take your time and think about what kind of doctor you really want. It's OK to change doctors at this point.

Certified nurse-midwives tend to spend more time with patients and to focus more on emotional support, nutrition, and other aspects of healthy living. This can be particularly helpful if you are a single parent or lack support at home, or if you are having trouble doing the things you know you should, such as quitting smoking or eating healthy meals.

In labor and delivery, CNMs may pay more attention to helping you avoid medical interventions, such as induction of labor, a cesarean section, or an episiotomy (an incision in the vagina to widen the opening for delivery). On the other hand, nurse-midwives have less training than obstetricians do in recognizing complications. If a problem does arise, they will have to refer you to a doctor. Collaborative practices, in which doctors and certified nurse-midwives work together, can mix the strengths of both traditions. If your pregnancy is going smoothly, you may see the midwife for most of your prenatal visits. But if a problem is suspected, a doctor you know will be on hand.

Family practitioners generally treat birth as a family event. If your family doctor also provides your pregnancy care, he or she may know both parents-to-be, which can make it easier for the father to be involved in the process. The same doctor can also care for your child into adulthood, providing continuity and familiarity. If serious complications arise during pregnancy, however, a family practitioner may refer you to an obstetrician. That means that at an anxious moment you may find yourself with a new doctor.

KidsHealth Tip

Labor Assistants

Studies have found that having a labor assistant—an experienced and skilled person who provides continuous emotional and physical support during labor—may make labor shorter and easier. If your health care provider is a midwife, the midwife may fill this role. If not, you may want to line up an additional labor assistant or doula. For more information, see Chapter 3, "Your Baby's Birth."

Other Factors to Think About When Choosing a Health Care Provider

Location of Delivery

When you choose a health care provider, you'll want to know where he or she does deliveries. Here are some questions to consider:

- Is the hospital or birth center easy to get to?
- How is it equipped to handle emergencies?
- What is the nurse-to-patient ratio? (A ratio of 1:2 is considered good during low-risk labor; a 1:1 ratio is best in complicated cases or during the pushing stage.)
- What procedures does it follow after birth?
- Can your baby and the father stay with you in your room round-the-clock if you desire?

- If you're interested in a warm, comfortable atmosphere, does the hospital have homelike birthing suites or even an in-house birth center? We discuss different birth settings in more detail in Chapter 3, "Your Baby's Birth."

Size of the Practice

If you choose a solo health care provider, you may develop a close relationship with this one person. But if he or she is on vacation or delivering another baby, you can find yourself with a backup person you've never met. If you go with a solo health care provider, find out who the backup person is.

If you choose a group practice, you're likely to see one person most of the time, but some of your appointments may be with other members of the practice. With this arrangement, if your health care provider can't deliver your baby, at least you'll know the person who does. If the group practice is large, however, you may not meet all of its members before the day of your delivery.

Convenience

When choosing a health care provider, be sure to ask questions about practical matters. How close is the practice to your home or office? What are its hours? Its procedures for calling in with questions? Its billing practices?

The Cost/Insurance Equation

Having a baby in the United States is expensive. For a normal pregnancy and birth, charges for doctors and the hospital together can average around $7,000; for a cesarean section, add about $4,000 to that. If you're a member of a health maintenance organization (HMO), you'll probably have to use an HMO doctor to get costs covered. (To learn more about insurance, see Chapter 27, "The Health Care System for Children.") With other forms of health insurance, you'll probably have to choose your health care provider from a list in order to get as much of the cost covered as possible. Often you can use someone not on the list ("out of network," it's often called), but you'll have to pay more out of pocket. Sometimes you can get a health care provider added to the list, especially if your employer is large and others in the company also want to use that person. But even if that works, it will take time—you'd have to start the process well in advance of a pregnancy.

Don't hesitate to discuss the fees in detail with your health care provider before you sign up. If you are going to be paying for the care without insurance, you may be able to negotiate discounted fees or a plan that allows you to pay in installments over time. You may need to have the same discussion with the hospital where you'll deliver your baby because hospitals may want payment in advance.

Check Out Your Insurance

If you're planning a pregnancy, check ahead of time to see what your insurance covers. Here are some questions to ask:

- Will there be co-payments for prenatal visits? These are out-of-pocket payments (often $5 to $20) you must make at the time of each visit.
- Will there be a deductible for your hospital admission? This is an amount you must pay before the insurance picks up the rest. Deductibles can range widely, from perhaps $50 to several thousand dollars.
- Does the insurance company pay for routine tests? Some policies may cover certain tests or kinds of care only in "high-risk" pregnancies. Because there is no standard definition of this term, it's important to know how the insurer defines it. Your doctor may think you need high-risk care, but your insurer may not agree.
- Will your insurance cover such things as childbirth education, genetic counseling, a labor assistant, epidural pain relief, a lactation (breast-feeding) consultant, or help at home after the delivery?
- When and how should you notify your insurer when you go into the hospital for delivery? (Without timely notification, an insurer may try to deny your claim.)

If you are uninsured and can afford to get insurance, do it before you become pregnant.

If the insured person (you or your partner) is planning to change jobs, check out the insurance situation first. If the new employer's insurance has a waiting period before it kicks in, you could find yourself uncovered for part of your pregnancy or even for delivery.

No Insurance, Not Enough Money

If you are uninsured, you may be eligible for free or reduced-cost prenatal care. The largest source of such care is Medicaid, a joint federal-state program for people with low incomes. Although eligibility varies from state to state, all states must offer Medicaid coverage for prenatal care to pregnant women whose family income is below 133 percent of the federal poverty guidelines (about $15,000 for a couple, based on year 2000 figures). Most states offer it to those with incomes below 185 percent of the poverty level (about $20,000 for a couple), and some go higher.

For a listing of Medicaid phone numbers and hotlines for each state, see the Health Care Financing Administration Web site at www.hcfa.gov/medicaid /mcontact.htm.

Other programs offer reduced-cost prenatal care to women who have incomes too high for Medicaid; such programs often have a sliding scale for fees, based on the woman's income. In California, for example, Access for Infants and Mothers (AIM) serves some women with incomes two or three times as high as the poverty level. (See www.mrmib.ca.gov/MRMIB/AIM.html.)

Here's how to find out about other reduced-cost programs:

- Call your state, county, or local health department or check their Web sites.
- Try the federal Healthy Start hotline at (800) 688-9889. In some states, this number will connect you to a state or local hotline offering information about getting prenatal care. In some places, it will connect you to a local clinic that is funded under the federal Healthy Start program, which aims to reduce infant mortality.
- Call local hospitals.
- Call Planned Parenthood at (800) 230-PLAN, or check its Web site, www .plannedparenthood.org. Although best known as a birth control provider, Planned Parenthood does offer sliding-scale pregnancy care in some of its many clinics.

Routine Prenatal Care

Routine prenatal care can begin even before your pregnancy does, and it should continue throughout pregnancy.

The Preconception Visit to a Health Care Provider

For women or couples who are planning to become pregnant, doctors recommend a preconception visit. Your health care provider will talk with you about your medical history, about any previous pregnancies you have had, and about illnesses that run in your family. Based on this information, as well as your age and your ethnic background, your health care provider may suggest that you get genetic counseling or testing now or after conception. (These procedures are described later in this chapter.) This is also a good time to raise any questions you may have.

Your doctor should discuss your lifestyle, asking about smoking, drinking, and drug use as well as what you eat and whether you exercise. If you are over- or underweight, he or she may encourage you to move toward a healthier weight before getting pregnant. Your doctor may suggest ways to increase your chances of getting pregnant and may suggest that you keep a menstrual calendar to help pinpoint the date of conception. Knowing exactly when pregnancy began can help your doctor judge how well your fetus is growing.

It's routine at a preconception visit for a doctor to do a Pap test (to check for signs of cervical cancer) and to draw blood that will be used to screen for syphilis and hepatitis B, as well as for general signs of infection or other illness. Testing for HIV (the AIDS virus), gonorrhea, and chlamydia is recommended.

At this visit, you should be tested for immunity to rubella (German measles), a disease that can cause birth defects if contracted during pregnancy. If you're not immune, you should get a rubella vaccine at least three months before becoming pregnant. If you've never had chicken pox, you might ask about getting vaccinated for that as well. Your doctor may also suggest other immunizations, including one for hepatitis B.

If you have a cat or live in an area where cats roam, discuss with your doctor whether you should be tested for immunity to the parasite that causes toxoplasmosis, described earlier. If you aren't immune, you can take extra precautions.

KidsHealth Tip

Speaking Frankly

To get the best medical care, it's important to be honest about your personal habits and your medical and sexual history. If your partner will be accompanying you to the doctor, make sure you talk with him ahead of time about any sensitive issues. This isn't the time to surprise him at the doctor's office or conceal something from the doctor. If there are things you feel you just can't tell your partner, you may be better off going to your doctor alone, at least for the first visit.

The First Prenatal Visit

As soon as you think you are pregnant, it's wise to see your doctor. By then, you'll probably have tried a home pregnancy test—or two or three—just to be sure. But don't wait longer than the second missed period to see your doctor.

If you didn't have a preconception visit, your doctor will do the same sort of questioning, advising, and testing mentioned earlier (although it's too late for rubella and chicken pox vaccines). At this visit, your doctor will confirm the pregnancy with an obstetrical exam. He or she may even use ultrasound (described later in the section) to give you your first, unforgettable image of your fetus: After six or seven weeks of a normal pregnancy the fetus looks like a lima bean with a heartbeat. The baby's heartbeat is a milestone—it means the chances of miscarriage in the pregnancy are greatly reduced.

At this visit, and all other prenatal visits, you'll be asked to leave a urine sample to be tested for signs of two of the more common complications of pregnancy: gestational (pregnancy-related) diabetes and preeclampsia (pregnancy-related high blood pressure).

The Numbers Are with You

Good news: About 90 percent of babies are born at full term (37 to 42 weeks of gestation) and have a birthweight of over five and one-half pounds (or 2,500 grams). Fewer than 2 percent have a very low birthweight of under three and one-third pounds (or 1,500 grams). An estimated 3 to 5 percent of babies are born with serious birth defects—which means that 95 to 97 percent are not.

Later Prenatal Visits

The traditional prenatal schedule calls for a visit every four weeks until week 28 of pregnancy, then every two weeks until week 36, then weekly until the birth. In recent years, studies have suggested that the number of visits often can be safely reduced, especially during the first six months.

Prenatal checkups often are brief visits during which your blood pressure and weight are checked. Your doctor or nurse-midwife will keep track of the size of your uterus as it expands and will listen for the fetal heartbeat. With a special stethoscope, the heartbeat usually can be heard between 16 and 19 weeks. It is fast—usually 120 to 160 beats a minute—and has been described as sounding like a watch ticking under a pillow. (Around the same time, or a little later, a woman usually will feel the first light, fluttering movements of the fetus, called "quickening.")

From the doctor's point of view, one important goal of the prenatal visits is to determine as accurately as possible the age of the fetus. This will help him or her decide how to interpret symptoms or treat problems if they arise later.

From the parents' point of view, routine prenatal appointments can be a time to gain reassurance, get answers to questions, and seek advice on dealing with discomforts. As the pregnancy proceeds, the doctor or nurse-midwife may refer you to childbirth educators, parents' groups, baby nurses, doulas, or breast-feeding experts. They can also give you suggestions or other help in choosing a doctor for your baby after delivery. (See Chapter 12, "Choosing and Working with Your Child's Doctor.")

Genetic Counseling and Testing

Doctors usually recommend genetic counseling or testing before conception for people in these groups:

- People of African ancestry, because they may be carriers of the gene for sickle-cell anemia
- People of Italian, Greek, or other Mediterranean or Asian descent, because they may be carriers for the gene that causes thalassemia
- People whose ethnic background is Eastern European Jewish, French Canadian, or Cajun, because they may be carriers for the gene that causes Tay-Sachs disease

If both parents are carriers of the gene for these diseases, there is a one in four chance that any baby they have together will have the disease. In such cases, parents might choose to take the risk, might choose not to conceive, or, if they are already pregnant, might decide to have the fetus tested. If the fetus is found to be affected, the couple will then learn ahead of time what challenges may lie ahead if they decide to continue the pregnancy. In some cases, they may choose to terminate the pregnancy. There's no getting around it—making any of these choices can be difficult and painful. When that's the case, couples can get advice and other help from doctors, counselors, and support groups.

Testing may also be recommended for these groups:

- People with a personal or family history of certain conditions such as cystic fibrosis, Duchenne muscular dystrophy, Huntington disease, mental retardation, or cardiac or other birth defects
- Couples who have had several miscarriages in a row

Testing During Pregnancy

Just as a growing number of risks to the fetus can now be detected before conception, a growing number of problems in the fetus can be detected before birth. Tests for these come in two varieties: screening tests and diagnostic tests. Screening blood tests are recommended for all women. Diagnostic tests are recommended for women who have a positive screening test for women with other risk factors, including those who will be 35 or older when their child is born because they are at higher risk of having a child with Down syndrome or other chromosomal disorders.

Screening Tests

Screening tests are easy and have no side effects because they require only a blood sample from the mother. But they cannot tell if the fetus actually has a problem (or doesn't have one). They can tell you only if your fetus may be at higher than normal risk of having a problem. If the fetus is found to be at higher risk, then diagnostic testing is usually recommended. (In most cases, the diagnostic testing brings good news: The fetus is not affected.) These are the recommended screening tests:

- The alpha-fetoprotein test (full name: maternal serum alpha-fetoprotein screening test, or MSAFP). This tests the mother's blood level of alpha-fetoprotein, a protein made by the liver of the fetus. If the level is abnormally high, the fetus may be at increased risk of having a neural tube defect, such as spina bifida, or several other problems. If it is abnormally low, the fetus may be at increased risk of having Down syndrome or other chromosome problems. But abnormal levels can also reflect harmless conditions, such as the weight of the mother or the presence of twins.
- The triple screen (or multiple marker screen). This test, an enhanced version of the alpha-fetoprotein test, has become the standard screening test recommended by most health care providers. It's generally done between 15 and 20 weeks. It measures alpha-fetoprotein and two other body chemicals: human chorionic gonadotropin (hCG) and estriol. (Another version, the double

screen, does not include estriol.) The double or triple screen is more accurate in identifying Down syndrome risk than the alpha-fetoprotein test alone. Even so, these tests are far from perfect: They generally identify about 50 percent of Down syndrome cases and about 85 percent of spina bifida cases. One in 20 women has a false-positive response, indicating possible Down syndrome when the fetus does not actually have the condition. And remember: Usually when the results are abnormal, the fetus turns out to be normal after all.

Diagnostic Tests

Diagnostic tests can detect a wide variety of illnesses, diseases, and disorders. The most common tests are the ultrasound, the non-stress test, amniocentesis, and chorionic villus sampling.

Talking to Your Doctor About Prenatal Tests

Prenatal tests can be stressful. Because many women who have abnormal tests end up having healthy babies, and because many of the problems that are detected cannot be treated, some women decide to forgo some of the testing.

One important thing to consider is what you will do if a birth defect is discovered. Implicit in much of this testing is that you can make a decision to terminate the pregnancy based on the results. But even if that's not an option for you, you may want to know about health problems in advance. That way, you can prepare emotionally and medically to deal with the issues you might face when your child is born. Your obstetrician or a genetic counselor can help you establish priorities, give you facts, and discuss your options.

It's important to remember that tests are *offered* to women—they are not mandatory. You should feel free to ask your doctor why he or she is ordering a certain test, what the risks and benefits of the test are, and most important, what the results will—and won't—tell you.

If you think that your doctor isn't answering your questions adequately, you should say so. You don't have to accept the answer, "I do this test on all of my patients."

Ultrasound (Sonogram). Ultrasound uses sound waves to form a moving picture of the fetus. As a wandlike transducer, which produces sound waves, is passed over the belly, fuzzy images of the fetus appear on a TV screen. Early in pregnancy, the transducer may need to be inserted into the vagina to produce an image; this is called transvaginal ultrasound.

Painless and considered safe for both woman and fetus, ultrasound is increasingly used to provide information on normal pregnancies, as well as to diagnose problems. A blurry sonogram photo is often baby's first picture added to the family album or shown to friends in a ritual of modern pregnancy. Doctors and studies differ about whether it's worth offering all women a routine sonogram even if their pregnancy has no risk signs. But many doctors do offer them, usually at 18 to 20 weeks. Even in a normal pregnancy, doctors like to have the extra information an ultrasound provides, and they know the parents-to-be are likely to be moved and reassured by seeing their baby moving in the womb.

In a high-risk pregnancy, an ultrasound of more complexity may be done repeatedly to track the fetus's growth and development. Ultrasound may also be used to create a "biophysical profile," which tries to assess the fetus's overall health by measuring its movements and the amount of amniotic fluid. This is usually combined with monitoring of the fetal heartbeat through a non-stress test, described later.

> ## The Voice of Experience
>
> *"Picking names is one of the most fun things you and your partner do over your pregnancy. My husband and I like to narrow down our name choices to two for a boy and two for a girl before the baby is born. The final decision is made after the baby is born so we can take into account his or her appearance and personality. Somehow it just seems more personal if the name is a reflection of who they are and not something that was decided months before without their 'input.'"*
>
> —FROM THE KIDSHEALTH PARENT SURVEY

These are some problems that ultrasound can diagnose:

- An ectopic pregnancy—a pregnancy in which the embryo starts growing outside the uterus
- Fetal death or miscarriage
- Many birth defects, such as missing limbs, malformations of the heart or urinary tract, and sometimes cleft lip or spina bifida
- Some cases of Down syndrome or other chromosome abnormalities

- Abnormally slow fetal growth (called intrauterine growth restriction, or IUGR)
- Positions of the fetus or placement of the placenta that might require special precautions or a cesarean section at birth

In a normal pregnancy, ultrasound can reveal the presence of multiple fetuses (twins, triplets, and so on) and help the doctor better estimate the due date and size of the baby. And often, but not always, it can reveal the sex of the baby.

The Non-Stress Test. During a non-stress test a fetal heart rate monitor is placed on the woman's belly for about half an hour, and she is instructed to push a button whenever she feels the fetus move. If the fetal heart rate speeds up when the fetus moves, it is considered a sign of health. This test can be used to monitor fetal well-being after about 26 weeks' gestation. It may be done several times a week or even daily in high-risk pregnancies, especially if the woman has severe high blood pressure or diabetes, or if the fetus does not seem to be growing properly. In these cases, abnormal results may lead a doctor to recommend delivering the baby early. But because the test is open to a wide range of interpretations, the doctor's judgment is key.

Amniocentesis. Using ultrasound to see inside the uterus, a doctor performs an amniocentesis test by inserting a thin needle through the woman's abdomen and withdrawing a small amount of amniotic fluid from the uterus. Because the fetus has been floating in this fluid, it contains fetal cells. These cells are then grown in the laboratory and can be tested for Down syndrome and other chromosome problems, as well as a wide range of genetic problems. Amniocentesis can also help diagnose spina bifida and other neural tube defects by measuring the alpha-fetoprotein level in the amniotic fluid.

"Amnio," as it is often called, is usually done 15 to 18 weeks after a woman's last menstrual period; it usually takes a week or two to get the results. This test is considered more than 99 percent accurate in diagnosing chromosome abnormalities such as Down syndrome. But it is not recommended for all women because it carries a small risk of miscarriage—estimates of the risk of miscarriage range from 1 in 200 to 1 in 400, or less than half of 1 percent. (If the procedure is done earlier in pregnancy, at 11 to 14 weeks, the risk may be somewhat higher.)

Although not required, amniocentesis is recommended for women who will be 35 or older when their baby is born because, for them, the risk of Down syndrome

The Other Strep

When you think of a strep infection, you probably think of a painful sore throat that you had as a child. Chances are you were given antibiotics, and it went away without a problem. A different type of streptococcal disease, however, sometimes can cause a serious, even deadly, illness in infants around the time of birth. This type of strep infection is caused by group B streptococcus (GBS) or *Streptococcus agalactiae*, a type of bacteria that may inhabit a woman's gastrointestinal tract and vagina. About 10 to 30 percent of women have GBS in the vaginal or rectal areas. Spread of GBS to a newborn around the time of labor or delivery can result in the infant's developing a severe blood infection or meningitis (infection of the lining covering the brain). To minimize the risk of such a newborn infection, your doctor may take a culture of your vagina toward the end of your pregnancy to determine if you have GBS. About 10 to 30 percent of women will have a positive culture; most, though, will have a negative culture. Although most babies born to culture-positive mothers will do well, the potential for a serious problem is there. If the culture is positive, your doctor may recommend antibiotic treatment for you before or at the time of delivery depending on a number of factors such as whether your membranes rupture (water breaks) early, whether you experience premature labor, and whether you have a fever. Medical approaches to the management of GBS during pregnancy vary. Speak to your doctor about your options.

is higher. (The risk of Down syndrome rises with the mother's age. It is estimated to be 1 in 1,400 if the mother is 20, 1 in 250 if she is 35, 1 in 75 if she is 40, and 1 in 20 if she is 45.) Be sure to discuss any questions or concerns you might have about this test with your doctor.

Doctors may also offer amnio if the couple has had a previous pregnancy with a birth defect, if certain genetic defects run in their families, or if neural tube defects are suspected, based on the previously mentioned screening tests. Amnio accurately reveals the sex of the fetus, although it should not be done for that purpose alone unless a sex-linked medical problem is suspected.

Chorionic Villus Sampling. In chorionic villus sampling (CVS), a small sample of tissue is taken from the chorion, the fetal membrane. To get the sample, a thin needle is inserted either through the cervix or through the abdomen. CVS is recommended for the same reasons as amniocentesis and is similarly accurate except that it cannot test for neural tube defects. Its advantage over an amnio is that it can be done earlier in pregnancy, generally 10 to 12 weeks after the woman's last menstrual period. If you might end a pregnancy because of a problem with the fetus, it's safer and may be less emotionally traumatic to find out sooner rather than later. It can also be a huge relief to find out early that there is no problem, which is the good news the test usually delivers.

The disadvantage of CVS is that the risk of miscarriage after this test is about 1 to 2 in 100, somewhat higher than after amniocentesis. In addition, some studies suggest that CVS may cause a slight increase in the number of fetuses born with shortened or missing fingers or toes. That risk may be around 1 in 3,000 births. Other studies, however, have found no increased risk of malformation.

For both amniocentesis and CVS, the risk of miscarriage may be lower if the practitioner is highly experienced at doing the test.

Having Fun at the Doctor's (We're Serious)

Pregnant or not, people often feel tense when they go to the doctor. And the kinds of tests and screenings we've described in this chapter may heighten the tension for some people, at least temporarily.

But if you're like many women, pregnancy may bring a surprise: For the first time in your life, you may actually enjoy going to the doctor.

First of all, you're not sick. Usually you feel fine, and some women feel better than ever. If you're lucky, the office is cheerful, filled with women your age, some of whom you might like to know. You can spend a few minutes chatting or reading magazines. Then you are seen by a (usually) solicitous nurse-practitioner, midwife, or doctor. You get to ask all the questions and describe all the strange and wonderful sensations that are beginning to bore your friends. Chances are, you will walk out with reassuring news about your baby and helpful suggestions about any discomforts you feel.

Thanks to a special stethoscope, you get to hear your baby's heartbeat earlier than you otherwise could. And you may even see your baby moving, kicking, and sucking her thumb on a routine sonogram. You feel more and more like a parent.

All in all, it's not a bad way to spend an hour.

No Guarantees

Although testing before and during pregnancy can rule out many problems, it cannot detect all possible problems or guarantee that your baby will be healthy. And although amniocentesis and chorionic villus sampling are highly accurate in detecting Down syndrome and some other chromosome problems, ultrasound results and fetal monitoring tests are often difficult to interpret. If you get a test result that concerns you, it's wise to get a second opinion—if possible, from a maternal-fetal medicine specialist or another physician who is skilled and experienced at dealing with high-risk pregnancies. Getting an expert second opinion is especially important if you are considering terminating the pregnancy based on abnormal test results.

Need More Information?

Check the Index and Appendix C, "Resource Guide." And of course, consult your doctor.

chapter two

Preparing Your Home and Family

All you need is love (plus diapers, a crib, a car seat . . .)

Preparing your home for a baby can be an important part of preparing yourself to be a parent. Your child-to-be, and your new role, will begin to seem more real. Whether you're pregnant or adopting, getting ready will help you pass the time until your baby arrives and will make your life easier afterward. Plus it can be a lot of fun!

In this chapter, we'll discuss how to prepare the members of your household—including you, your partner, and your toddler if you have one—for a new arrival. We'll also explain how you can make your home safe and comfortable for your new baby. And finally, we'll give you the lowdown on stocking your home with baby gear essentials; it's never easier to fall prey to slick marketing and pushy salespeople than when you're a new parent shopping for your first baby. We'll show you how to prioritize—and what you'll never miss.

Preparing the Members of Your Household

Everyone in your home needs to get ready for your new baby. Start with yourself.

Six Useful Things to Do to Get Started

1. Use the time before your baby arrives to talk with your partner. Talk about your hopes for your child, your parenting approach, your view of your role

in the family, and your own experiences as children—good and bad. You'll get to know each other—and yourself—better, and you may become aware of sensitive areas that you'll want to keep thinking and talking about. Reading books or articles about raising children or talking with friends who have kids can help spark these discussions. But don't try to work out every hypothetical issue (should Alex play soccer?) in advance. You don't know your child yet, and you'll need to be flexible so you can respond to your child's particular needs and nature.

2. Take a class in infant cardiopulmonary resuscitation (CPR), the life-saving first-aid procedure used if a person stops breathing. Courses are available through hospitals, the American Red Cross, schools, and rescue squads. You might never need to perform CPR, but it's better to be safe than sorry.

3. Line up potential help for after the baby comes, whether you think you'll need it or not. Help can range from friends and support groups for new parents to paid or volunteer baby nurses, breast-feeding coaches, or housekeepers. If you can afford it, a few days of professional help can help you settle in, especially if you'll be breast-feeding for the first time or having a cesarean section. If you will be relying on friends or family, be realistic: If your sister is a know-it-all who drives you crazy, think twice before you invite her to move in for two of the most emotional weeks of your life.

4. If you're going to need full- or part-time child care within a few months of the baby's arrival, or think you may, start your search now. (For more on choosing child care, see Chapter 25, "Choosing Child Care.")

5. If you haven't been planning for your family's financial future, this is a good time to start. Make a will. Get financial advice about saving for your child's college tuition. Check out life insurance options.

6. Choose, buy, and install a car seat. (See The Crucial Car Seat later in this chapter.)

Big Brother (or Sister) Is Watching

Although some experts say that sibling rivalry is inevitable, young children vary widely in how they respond to sharing the nest. Children age five or older, for instance, often seem to enjoy helping with a baby, at least some of the time. But at any age, preparing a child seems to help make the transition to sister- or brotherhood easier.

KidsHealth Tip
Sibling Preparations

Before your child knows there's a baby on the way, talk about the concept of families, and point out the siblings of your child's friends or cousins. This will assure your child that siblings are a common part of life and not a diabolical plot you invented as a form of torture.

No matter how young your child is, tell her ahead of time that your family is getting a new member. If your child is old enough to understand (say, age three or four), tell her at the same time you tell the rest of your family. You don't want your child to hear the big news from someone else or suspect there's a big secret in the house. Because most children have trouble understanding time, put the arrival date in terms she'll understand, such as "when it gets hot again," or "just after your birthday." This is also usually a good chance to explain—with more or less detail, depending on your child's age—where babies come from.

When you talk about the new baby's arrival, try to be both reassuring and honest. Don't tell your child that nothing will change or that the newborn will be his baby. (If it's his, after all, he could give it back!) Don't give the impression that a newborn will be a fun playmate. Instead, emphasize the things that truly will not change ("You'll still go to nursery school and visit Grandma on Tuesdays"). Try not to make promises you may not be able to keep ("I will still read to you before bed every night"). Emphasize that in the beginning the baby will be too small to play or to do the interesting and exciting things your older child knows how to do.

Arrange things so there will be as few changes as possible in the older child's life when the baby is born. If you plan to move the child from one room to another, do it months before the baby comes. (And don't say, "You have to move out of this room because the new baby needs it.") For other major changes—such as moving from crib to bed, weaning, learning to use the toilet, or starting preschool—do it well ahead of time, if your child is ready. If your child is not ready, however, don't rush things. Instead, wait until well after the baby arrives.

In many families, one parent, usually the mother, has had the main responsibility of caring for the child. When a new baby arrives, the other parent often takes on more of the older child's care. That's why the arrival of a sibling can be a time for the father and an older child to deepen the bonds between them. Once again, it's good to start this change well before the baby's arrival so your child can get used to having a different person put him to bed, feed him, and dress him. If your child is old enough, it's also good to encourage him to dress himself and do more things independently.

As you prepare for the new baby, take your cues from your child in terms of how much he wants to help. If he's interested, let him choose some things you buy for the baby from acceptable alternatives (for instance, the mobile with teddy bears rather than the one with bunnies). Talk about what he liked when he was younger, and ask his advice about what the baby might like.

Many books are available to help prepare siblings for the birth of a new brother or sister. In addition, many hospitals offer sibling preparation classes. These may include learning about how to hold, talk to, or diaper a baby (with practice on dolls); watching films about babies; touring the hospital to see the labor and delivery rooms; and looking at the newborns through the nursery window.

If you will be in the hospital more than a day, let your child visit as soon as possible, preferably when no other visitors are there. Then, when you and your newborn arrive home, make a special effort to be sure your older child gets extra attention for the first few weeks. Try to spend some one-on-one time doing things your child enjoys. You might want to bring a present home from the hospital and

KidsHealth Tip

Who Will Take Care of Me?

Make sure your child knows in advance who will stay with her when Mommy goes to the hospital. Children often assume that Daddy will stay home, and they can get upset if they wake up one morning and find an aunt or neighbor there. You should also let your child know whether you will wake her to say good-bye if you have to leave for the hospital during the night. Discuss issues like these well in advance in case your baby arrives ahead of schedule.

stash away some small gifts to pull out if visitors bring gifts only for your new baby. You might also ask a favorite relative to pay special attention to big brother or sister during this time.

Encourage visitors to relate to your older child on his own terms. Talk about his friends, his toys, and his likes or dislikes, rather than only about the baby. Asking about his new trike may be better than asking about his new sister.

Let your child help you take care of the baby, if he wants to. Even a very young child can hand you a diaper or a baby blanket. A child who is a bit older can help you wash the baby or hold him while sitting on the floor. Show him diplomatically how to treat the baby gently and speak softly, but don't leave your baby and child alone. Safety has to be your first consideration.

Coping with Your Child's Reaction

Despite your best efforts to prepare your child and consider her feelings, the arrival of a newborn in the house is likely to shake up your child's world. Some children will regress a bit. They may go back to needing diapers, for instance, even though they have been using the potty for a while. Don't be surprised if your big boy or girl acts like a baby for a few weeks, clinging to your side, wetting the bed, or demanding to breast-feed or have a bottle.

If this happens, it's wisest to let your child regress, at least for a while, humoring him through it while reminding him of all the things he can do that the baby can't. The child-care author Penelope Leach put it this way: "You want him to feel that while the baby gets a lot of things he does not normally get, she is not getting anything he cannot have, but only things which he has grown out of."

When a baby arrives and changes her life, a child can also feel—and directly show—anger and jealousy. If the child is old enough to speak, help her to talk about how she feels. Let her know that her feelings are important, and help her distinguish between acceptable and unacceptable ways of expressing her feelings. In other words, drawing a family picture that leaves out the baby is fine, but yelling at the baby—or at Mommy or Daddy—is not. You may need to summon all your energy to find the gentle patience that can help your older child adjust.

Preparing Your Pets

- If your cat or dog is used to sleeping on your bed and you expect to share your bed with the baby even some of the time, teach the animal to sleep elsewhere before the baby arrives.

- If you have an untrained or unruly dog, consider taking him to obedience school, or get a good book and work at training him yourself.
- In the same way you help an older child adjust to a newborn, be sure to pay extra attention to your pet the day you bring the baby home and for a few weeks afterward.

Preparing Your Home

The most important part of preparing your home is making it safe for your new baby. The following suggestions will make any house or apartment safer—whether a baby lives there or not. But knowing you will be bringing a baby home gives you an extra incentive to get this work done.

- Install smoke alarms. You should have at least one on each floor in or near the bedrooms and the kitchen. If you already have alarms, make sure they're working. Test them and change the batteries regularly. (Fire officials advise doing this each spring and fall when you adjust the clocks for daylight savings or standard time. It's helpful to mark a calendar to remind you.)
- Set your water heater below 120 degrees Fahrenheit to prevent scalding.
- Make sure you have working fire extinguishers in several places in your home.
- If your home has a second floor, get an escape ladder for the upstairs rooms.
- Get window guards to prevent falls from upstairs windows. (In some cities, landlords are required to install these in apartments where young children live.)
- Ban smoking in your home and your car. Not only is smoking a fire hazard, but children's exposure to cigarette smoke has been linked to ear infections, asthma, pneumonia, and other respiratory conditions. It also has been linked to "crib death," or sudden infant death syndrome (SIDS), a rare but terrible condition in which apparently healthy babies are found dead after being put down to sleep.
- Check for fire hazards, and correct any you find. Common ones include overloaded electrical sockets, electrical wires running under carpets, frayed wires, and lamps, nightlights, or electric heaters that are near or touching curtains or

other fabric. Be particularly careful with halogen lights. Appliances that spark, overheat, or smell like they're burning should be fixed or replaced. Have your chimney cleaned regularly, especially if you frequently use the fireplace.

- If you have oil or gas heat, install a carbon monoxide detector. Oil and gas furnaces can give off this odorless gas, which can cause illness and death. Babies are especially susceptible. Have your furnace checked each year to make sure it is working properly.

- Post emergency numbers prominently near each phone. These should include numbers for fire, police, rescue, doctor, poison control center, and neighbors who might help you in a crisis.

- If your house, apartment, or car needs important repairs, make them now, if possible. Spending money to fix the roof, repair the furnace, or get new tires may seem mundane compared with decorating the baby's room to magazine-level perfection. But from the baby's point of view, being safe and warm beats being color-coordinated.

- If you do plan to redecorate, do it in plenty of time to allow fumes from new carpet, wallpaper, or other furnishings to fade before the room will be used.

- If you use well water and have any reason to suspect it is polluted or contaminated, have it tested.

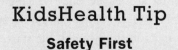

KidsHealth Tip

Safety First

Don't forget that even the gentlest and most beloved pet can hurt a frail newcomer by accident. For this reason, *never* leave an animal alone with a baby. (And make sure your pet does not have access to your baby when you are asleep.)

Reptiles, including snakes, lizards, and turtles, should not be kept in a household where children younger than five live, according to the U.S. Centers for Disease Control and Prevention. That's because they are frequently infected with salmonella, a kind of bacteria that can be particularly dangerous to young children.

- Consider testing your home for radon. Long-term exposure to high levels of this radioactive gas, a natural product of rocks and soil, contributes to lung cancer, particularly in people who smoke. It's estimated that about 6 percent of U.S. homes have radon levels high enough to be worth fixing.

"Babyproofing" Your House

"There's no such thing as babyproofing," a wise mother told us on one of our KidsHealth surveys. She meant that, try as you might, you can't make a house totally safe for an inquisitive child—you still have to supervise the baby. But you can prevent a lot of injuries by making a few simple changes in your household. (If it can't be babyproof, at least it can be baby-resistant.) Try this "babyproofing" checklist for starters:

- Survey your house for hazards twice, once walking slowly through it and once crawling to get a baby's-eye view. You should repeat this process every time your baby moves up in mobility—when she starts to crawl, walk, run, and climb.
- Move all sharp objects, including knives, forks, vegetable peelers, and sewing or hobby implements, out of reach, or get latches and locks for their drawers and cabinets. Drawer latches of various designs are widely available through stores, catalogs, and Web sites that sell baby products.
- Move anything that could be swallowed into high or locked cabinets or closets. This includes medicines, vitamins, cleansers, cosmetics, detergents, stain removers, air fresheners, candles, and pet food. Regular human food can also choke a baby and should be kept out of baby's reach.
- If you have drawers that can be pulled all the way out, without stopping, install latches or stops so baby doesn't pull them out onto herself.

- Block unused electric sockets with outlet covers or plugs.
- Check for hanging wires, blind cords, or the like that could be pulled down or could strangle a baby.
- Move objects that could break or fall.
- Move high-risk furniture or make it safe. Tall bookcases and dressers should be secured to the walls with brackets so that if a child climbs on them they won't tumble over on top of her. You can buy elasticized padding to put around the hard edges of tables that might be in a toddler's path.
- Be prepared to install gates to block off staircases. (Use the kind that mounts to the wall with hardware.)

Lead Paint Alert

If your house or apartment was built before 1978, after which lead was banned from house paint, and if paint is chipped or peeling anywhere in the house, have your home checked for lead paint. Lead paint is seductively sweet. If young children eat paint chips or inhale lead dust, they can suffer lead poisoning. Even milder forms of lead poisoning have been associated with learning problems. Severe cases can cause mental retardation and many physical problems. If lead paint is found in your home, ideally it should be removed or covered with paneling or plasterboard before your baby arrives. Lead paint is best removed by professionals who know how to contain the lead dust it produces. (See Chapter 14, "Health Screening Tests," for the details about testing babies for lead poisoning, and see Chapter 32, "Health Problems in Early Childhood.")

KidsHealth Tip

Five Safety Items Your Home Should Have

1. Smoke detectors
2. Fire extinguishers
3. Carbon monoxide detectors
4. Flashlights
5. Escape ladder

It is especially important to know about lead paint if you plan to renovate rooms because such work can create and spread lead dust.

If you are a renter and your landlord refuses to have your apartment checked for lead, contact your local health department. Rules vary from place to place about if and when landlords can be required to remove or cover over lead paint.

Stocking Your Home with Baby Gear (or, How Much Stuff Does One Baby Need?)

Stores, catalogs, and Internet sites teem with gear and gadgets for the youngest among us. Much of it is unnecessary, especially in the beginning, when your infant is fully engaged in eating, sleeping, and encountering his body and the few inches of world just beyond it. But well-chosen baby gear can make parenthood more pleasant for you and safer for your baby.

Much of the gear will be used only briefly and can be borrowed or bought secondhand at yard sales and school fairs. But be careful—older items may not meet current safety standards or may be damaged in dangerous ways. In many cases, it's better to pass up the bargain. Two key items in particular—car seats and cribs—should be purchased new if at all possible.

Before you go out and buy anything, however, it's wise to do some comparison shopping. Consumer Reports' ratings can be very helpful. Try its Web site, www.consumer reports.org, or its book *Consumer Reports Guide to Baby Products* (sixth edition, 1999). Parenting sites with active message boards, such as www.parents place.com or www.parentsoup.com, can also be helpful sources of feedback about products you may be considering.

> ### The Voice of Experience
>
> "Never underestimate the importance of basics! Sure it's fun to buy and receive fancy baby clothes, but in reality most newborns hate to be manipulated into fussy clothes. After your baby screams and cries while you try to put him in a complicated getup, you'll find yourself grateful to have front-opening T-shirts and other clothes that don't have to go over the baby's head. One-pieces that have drawstring bottoms or button-down fronts as opposed to pant legs will also be much appreciated by your newborn. Remember, clothes in and of themselves are an adjustment for newborns."
>
> —FROM THE KidsHealth PARENT SURVEY

KidsHealth Tip

Certification Savvy

Car seats and full-size cribs are covered by federal safety regulations. For some other items—including highchairs, playpens, strollers, and gates—manufacturers can choose to have their products tested by the American Society for Testing and Materials and certified by the Juvenile Products Manufacturers Association. Such certifications, which will be noted on the label, don't guarantee safety but certify that the products perform up to certain standards.

The Basic Baby Shopping List

Let's start with the essentials. Here's what you'll need early on to take care of your baby:

- Car seat
- Crib, bassinet, or other safe sleeping place
- Changing table of some sort (a pad on the floor or on a dresser can work well)
- Diapers and diaper bag
- Clothing and receiving blankets
- First-aid and grooming supplies
- Cloth baby carrier
- Stroller
- Nursing or feeding gear (See Chapter 9, "Breast-Feeding," and Chapter 10, "Bottle-Feeding," for information.)

You may also want to consider these handy extras (in fact, some people say they couldn't live without them):

- Baby bathtub
- Baby monitor
- Indoor seat or swing (quickly calms some crying babies!)
- Toys
- Playpen or play yard

Now we're clearly entering the nonessential amenities list—items that you'll be glad to have, but you can certainly live without:

- A portable phone, for convenience, sanity, and safety (Why safety? Because being able to take the phone with you around the house means you won't be tempted to leave the baby unattended while you answer a call. It can also help in an emergency.)
- A tape or CD player and recorded music for your baby's room
- A rocking chair or glider for your baby's room
- A supply of frozen meals, homemade, purchased, or donated
- A washer and dryer

Six Things to Avoid

1. Soft bedding, such as pillows, quilts, sheepskins, or soft mattresses. Keeping the crib or bassinet free of such objects appears to lower the risk of SIDS.
2. Stuffed animals or other soft toys in the crib or bassinet. They, too, should be banished from your baby's sleeping place to lower the risk of SIDS.
3. Tub seats. These are intended for use in a bathtub by babies old enough to sit up, but experts advise against using them: They may tempt a parent to leave the baby alone in the tub, which can be extremely dangerous.
4. Walkers. These seats on wheels (designed for children six months and older) send nearly 30,000 kids a year to the emergency room. Injuries happen when babies in walkers hurtle down stairs, knock into hot stoves, or grab dangerous objects normally out of their reach. Contrary to popular belief, they don't help children learn to walk. A safe substitute includes the Exersaucer, a seat with a saucer base that rocks and rotates but doesn't move across the floor. Substitutes are generally called "baby exercisers" or "baby entertainers."
5. Talc (baby) powder. If inhaled, it can irritate the lungs.
6. Latex balloons. Uninflated or broken, they pose a choking risk.

The Crucial Car Seat

If your child is going to be riding in a car—yours, a friend's, Grandma's, or a taxi—you're going to need a car seat. This absolutely vital piece of baby equipment must be the proper size, properly installed, and used *every* time your baby is in the car (see Figures 2.1a–c). Car accidents are by far the leading killer of U.S. children. More than 600 children younger than age five die in crashes each year, and most of them are not belted into car seats. The U.S. Department of Transportation has estimated that correctly using car seats on every trip would not only save lives but could prevent 50,000 injuries each year to children younger than five.

If you'll be driving your newborn home from the hospital or birthing center, you'll need a car seat right from the start. Many hospitals will not let you leave without one. In fact, hospitals often provide free or low-cost car seats to people who can't afford the full price, which ranges from about $40 to more than $100. Many children's hospitals will provide car seats even for babies born elsewhere.

Car seats should be bought new, if possible, safety experts say. That way you get up-to-date safety features, and you can register ownership in case there's a recall. Plus, you won't risk getting a seat that has been damaged. Most car seats have a life span of five to eight years, depending on the model. If you are going to borrow one from a friend, be sure it's a recent model and hasn't been in an accident or otherwise battered. Get all the instructions that came with the seat; if the instructions are not available, call the company for another copy. Also, if you choose to accept a used seat, call the manufacturer to find out if the seat was ever recalled. Recalls happen occasionally, and the manufacturer may be able to provide you with a replacement part or new model.

You should check your car manual before you buy; it may tell you which car seats are best for that particular car. Buy early and install the car seat before you actually need it. This lets you practice using it and gives you time to check for problems. (Check the store's return policy before you buy.)

The Three Stages of Car Seats

As your baby grows, you'll need to buy two or three different car seats.

Stage one: Until babies are at least one year old and weigh at least 20 pounds, they should ride in a rear-facing car seat installed in the backseat. You can get an infant seat, which is used only during this period, or a convertible seat, which can be turned around to face forward when your child gets large enough.

Stage two: From 20 to 40 pounds (up to about age four), toddlers can use a forward-facing seat in the backseat, either the convertible seat mentioned previously or a forward-facing toddler seat. Convertible seats are bucket-shaped with sides that (sometimes) can cradle a sleeping baby's head. Forward-only toddler seats (sometimes called child seats or child seat/boosters) have high backs but no sides. Some newer car models have built-in forward-facing child seats.

Stage three: At 40 pounds, preschoolers can graduate to a booster seat, also in the backseat. Booster seats position children higher so they can use the regular shoulder/lap seatbelt without it pressing on neck or belly. Some forward-facing toddler seats have removable straps and can double as booster seats when your child gets large enough. These seats, which have high backs, provide more protection than backless booster seats.

For parents, moving from one kind of car seat to another can seem like a big event, a milestone of growth. But the more "grown-up" the car seat, the less protection it provides. So until your child truly outgrows a seat, don't rush to "move up" to the next level. This is especially important when you are switching from a rear-facing seat to a front-facing one. Your child should be both at least one year old and at least 20 pounds.

Backseat Driver

In all cases, the car seat should be installed in the backseat, preferably in the middle. But don't expect to pop your newborn into a car seat and drive off footloose and carefree. Your newborn needs an adult companion in the backseat to keep her head from lolling from side to side (or whipping to the side on a turn) and to make sure she doesn't slump forward, which can hinder breathing. Remember, your newborn will be in the backseat facing away from you. Without an adult back there, you will have no way of making sure that your baby is OK. Until your baby can control her head and sit up, it's best to keep drive time to a minimum and provide a backseat companion.

KidsHealth Tip

Car Seat Warning

Don't confuse car seats with lighter infant seats made for indoor use. All car seats should have labels saying they meet or exceed Federal Motor Vehicle Safety Standards (sometimes abbreviated as FMVSS 213). No other kind of seat should ever be used in a car.

2.1a. Rear-facing infant-only car seat with "T" strap.

2.1b. Rear-facing convertible car seat (with handle) with adjustable crotch strap. **Note:** Children should not face forward in a car seat until they are at least a year old and weigh 20 pounds or more.

2.1c. Front-facing toddler car seat. The seat belt running through the seat should be snug, not loose.

Figures 2.1a–c. Car seat safety.

Choosing a Car Seat for Your Newborn

Here are some things to consider when you are deciding whether to get an infant seat or a convertible seat for your newborn.

For the first few months, in particular, an infant seat will fit your baby better. Infant seats are cheaper (around $50) and lighter, with handles so they can serve as carriers or as seats indoors. Ease of carrying varies a lot, so check it out. Some infant seats are made to be part of a "travel system," which means they can be removed from the car and snapped onto a matching stroller. With this type, you won't have to wake your baby to move her from car seat to stroller. (This is particularly convenient if you're going to be making a lot of short trips.)

Warning: If you do use an infant car seat indoors, don't leave your baby alone in it, especially on an elevated surface. If it tips over, it could injure or smother your baby.

If you expect to do little driving with your brand-new baby (a good plan, if you can stick to it), convertible seats can save you the expense of buying an infant seat. In addition, some convertible seats can be used in the rear-facing position for children up to 25 or 30 pounds (check the model before you buy). Because facing the rear in a crash is safer for babies' spinal cords, this is a good feature. It is especially helpful with big babies because they may reach 20 pounds before they are one year old, but they still need the protection that comes with facing the rear. Convertible seats start around $50, with many models more than $100.

Your convertible seat should have a tether to secure its top to the car's backseat and attachment points at the bottom, as required of all seats made after September 1999. By September 2001, all new cars should have built-in anchor points to accommodate such seats. If your car is older, contact the manufacturer about modifying it. The new system is supposed to make seats safer and easier to install.

Car Seats for Small or Premature Babies

Because most infant seats are designed for babies who weigh at least seven pounds, they will be too big for the littlest passengers. Some babies, especially those born prematurely or very small, may have trouble getting enough oxygen when they are in the semiupright position that car seats require. For this reason the American Academy of Pediatrics recommends that premature babies (born before 37 weeks' gestation) be checked in a car seat before they are discharged from the hospital. Car seats for premature or small babies should not have abdominal pads, armrests, or a plastic shield over the straps. One infant car seat, the Cosco Dream Ride, folds down so your baby can lie flat while traveling, which can make breathing easier. And once you get to Grandma's, it can double as a bassinet. (Another car restraint, the Graco Cherish, is a bed only; it is intended for babies up to nine pounds.)

Checking Installation

Some studies have found that about 80 percent of car seats are installed or used incorrectly. The most common error is attaching the seat to the car too loosely or strapping the baby in too loosely.

Read and follow the installation instructions that come with the car seat, as well as the instructions in your car manual. Then, each time you use the seat, test first to see if it is strapped in tightly enough. On a rear-facing seat, if you grip the top edge, you should not be able to push it from a semireclining angle to a reclining position. It may, however, swivel a few inches to the left or right. On a forward-facing seat, you should not be able to tip it more than an inch to the side or forward.

Often hospitals have people trained to check that a car seat is properly installed. In addition, some car dealers host car seat checkup sessions as part of the National Safe Kids Campaign. For information on such sessions in your area, call the campaign at (202) 662-0600, or see www.safekids.org.

KidsHealth Tip

Front-Seat Safety

If you absolutely must put the child in the front seat—for example, if you must use a car that has no backseat—move the front seat as far away from the windshield as possible. And if you have front airbags, **never** put your child's car seat in the front seat. If the airbag opens, it can severely injure or kill your baby or child. Under certain conditions, you can have a switch installed to turn your airbag system on and off, and some newer cars have this capability.

Car Travel Accessories

You might want to buy a sunshade to protect your baby's eyes and skin (some seats come with one built in). Bolsters are available to wedge your small baby into a big seat and stabilize your baby's head, or you can use rolled-up towels or blankets. Such padding should be used only on the sides of your baby, not between your baby and the straps. Either way, the watchful eye and helping hand of an adult is preferable.

Car Seats and Air Travel

Dragging a car seat through endless airport corridors and down narrow airplane aisles is a hassle that might tempt you to leave the car seat at home. And many parents tend to rationalize that if there were a plane crash, a car seat wouldn't help their child. But people do survive plane crashes. And your baby's chances of survival are better in a car seat than in your lap. In addition, using a "child restraint system" (or CRS, in airline lingo) can prevent injuries during turbulence or emergency landings, which are more common occurrences. On long plane trips, a car seat may even allow you to nap or read. And once you arrive, your baby will have a familiar seat for car travel. The Federal Aviation Administration recommends using child restraints on airplanes. Most car seats are approved for airplane use, but check the label to make sure.

For More Information

Check the American Academy of Pediatrics "Family Shopping Guide to Car Seats" (www.aap.org/family/famshop.htm or 141 Northwest Point Boulevard, Elk Grove Village, IL 60007-1098). To find out if a car seat has been recalled or to get permission to disengage an air bag, check the U.S. Department of Transportation's Auto Safety Hotline at (888) DASH-2-DOT or www.nhtsa.dot.gov. A nonprofit organization called SafetyBeltSafe U.S.A. also offers a wealth of detailed information about car seat use and installation. Check its Web site (www.carseat.org), or call its hotline at (800) 745-7233. Its recall list includes a picture gallery so you can identify your model even if you don't have the model number. (For more information on car safety, see Chapter 24, "Child Safety.")

KidsHealth Tip

Look Out for Hot Metal

After a few hours in the sun, the buckles of a car seat can be hot enough to hurt your baby. Keep a towel or sheet in the car to cover the car seat on hot days. You can also buy a reflective car seat cover that keeps the whole seat noticeably cooler. At the least, tuck the buckles under the seat to shield them from the sun when you get out of the car.

Although children younger than two can fly free in their parent's lap, to be sure you can use your car seat, you must buy a ticket for your baby. If you haven't bought a ticket and the plane has empty seats, the airline may (or may not) allow you to use your car seat. It pays to check with the airline first, asking whether they offer discounts for babies younger than two, whether you can use a car seat in a vacant seat, and which flights are likely to have vacancies.

Car Seats and Car Rentals

If you're going to rent a car, arrange ahead of time to get a car seat, usually available at a small extra charge. Be clear and specific about how big your baby is and what kind of seat you need.

Cribs

Schools of thought vary on whether newborns should sleep in a crib from the start, in a bassinet in their parents' room, or even in their parents' bed. We discuss these questions in Chapter 21, "Sleep." But despite variations in sleeping arrangements, almost all families eventually get a full-size crib and use it at some point.

At the least, a crib should be a safe place where your baby can be left alone. In fact, a crib is the only place in the house where your baby is likely to spend many hours with no one watching. Like car seats, cribs are federally regulated for safety. If you get one made after 1990, it should meet federal standards. Buying a new crib, rather than a used one, ensures that the model hasn't been recalled or damaged in a way that might compromise safety.

If you do get an older crib, make sure it has these features:

- The slats are no more than 2⅜ inches apart. This will prevent your baby's head from becoming trapped between the slats (see Figure 2.2).
- The crib has no cutouts in the headboard or footboard that can trap baby's head.
- The side rails that lower have a locking mechanism that will prevent your toddler from releasing them.
- The side rails, when raised, are at least 26 inches above the mattress support at its lowest position.
- The side rails, when lowered, are at least 9 inches above the mattress support.
- The crib has no corner posts (or finials), which can catch a child's clothing and possibly strangle him.
- The crib doesn't have lead paint. A crib built before 1978 or one that has been repainted by previous owners may have lead paint, which can cause lead poisoning if your baby chews on the rails. The paint must be removed and the crib repainted.

Whether your crib is new or used, make sure that it is not rickety and that all of its hardware and slats are tightly in place. Make sure you can lower the side rail without too much difficulty. Cribs are supposed to have childproof locking mechanisms, but some seem to be adult-proof as well.

Federal safety rules have established standardized crib sizes so that any mattress you buy should fit snugly in a recently manufactured crib, which prevents your baby's head from becoming trapped between the mattress and crib bars. But double-check if you have an older crib—you should not be able to put two fingers between the mattress and the sides of the crib. Either way, the mattress should be firm to minimize the risk of suffocation. Be sure you remove any plastic wrapping from the mattress.

Bassinets and Cradles

For the first few months, many parents like to use a bassinet, which is a small, portable bed that can be placed beside the parents' bed at night and rolled into other rooms during the day. If you use a bassinet, take a few precautions:

- Be sure the mattress is firm and fits tightly, to prevent suffocation.
- Be aware of the bassinet's weight limit and stop using it before your baby reaches that weight.

- Be sure the legs lock open to avoid possible collapses.
- Don't use a bassinet if pets or other children could accidentally topple it.

Cradles are small beds that have an additional feature: They rock. These beds have rocked infants to sleep for centuries, but today safety experts worry that a baby may get rocked against the side, blocking his ability to breathe. If you use a cradle, be sure it has a locking pin that prevents it from rocking more than five degrees.

In addition to bassinets and cradles, here are other small-bed options:

- A portable crib that can be used like a bassinet but is generally more stable and lower to the ground. New ones are light and fold up for traveling.
- A cosleeper, sidecar, or bedside sleeper—all three-sided beds. The fourth, open side should line up with your bed to make middle-of-the-night nursing easier while still giving your baby a safe space of his own. The catch is that the sleeper must be exactly level with the bed and securely connected to it to avoid falls.

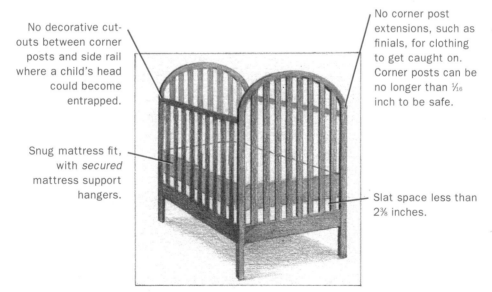

No decorative cut-outs between corner posts and side rail where a child's head could become entrapped.

No corner post extensions, such as finials, for clothing to get caught on. Corner posts can be no longer than 1/16 inch to be safe.

Snug mattress fit, with *secured* mattress support hangers.

Slat space less than 2⅜ inches.

Figure 2.2. Crib safety. Make sure that your baby's crib meets all recommended specifications to prevent accidental strangulation, suffocation, and falls. This illustration is an example of a proper crib design that meets safety requirements, as described in detail in the text. Note that slats should be no more than 2⅜ inches apart.

Bedding and Accessories

For your baby's crib, bassinet, or cradle, you'll want safe bedding and accessories. Look for these:

- A crib bumper. This is a padded length of fabric that runs around the inside of the crib and ties onto the bars. Trim the ties to six inches to prevent a choking risk. Once your baby can stand, remove the bumper so your baby can't use it as a stepping-stone to climb over the bars.
- Three or four fitted bottom sheets for the crib or the bassinet. These should fit tightly, for safety's sake.
- Two to six waterproof pads, for use under the sheet and elsewhere in the house.

The American Academy of Pediatrics recommends you consider using a sleeper (a warm sleep outfit) instead of a blanket to avoid having anything in the bed that might cover your baby's face, causing suffocation or increasing SIDS risk. If you do use a blanket, choose a thin one. Place your baby's feet toward the foot of the crib, and tuck the blanket around the foot of the mattress so it reaches only to your baby's chest.

Changing Tables

You can change your baby on any safe, flat surface, including a crib mattress when the railing is down. But you will be changing your baby so many times in the next few years that you'll probably want a safe place that makes things easier for you.

KidsHealth Tip

Changing Table Purchases

When buying a changing table, look for sturdiness, stability, and storage space. Railings should be two inches high. If you use a chest with a fold-down platform for diapering, be especially careful because these usually do not have a guardrail.

For many parents, that safe, convenient place is a changing table with a railing, a vinyl-covered pad, a safety strap, and shelves or drawers to store supplies so you can reach them easily and your baby can't reach them at all.

Wherever you change your baby, be sure everything you need is at hand. This will make it easier for you to abide by the number-one safety rule of baby changing: Keep at least one hand on your baby at all times. (Follow-up rule: If you have to go get something, take your baby with you.) Falls from changing tables are avoidable.

Diapers

You may plan to use disposable or cloth diapers (with or without a diaper service) or some combination of both. Whatever your choices, you can plan on your newborn going through 10 or more diapers a day.

Whichever kind of diaper you use, it pays to buy some cotton diapers for nondiapering chores, such as protecting shoulders and sheets from spit-up and drool, mopping up spills, and blocking sunlight. You might want to get one pack of thicker diapers and one pack of the gauzy kind. If you're also using cloth diapers as diapers, mark your "household" diapers so you can tell them apart.

The Voice of Experience

"Baby clothing sizes are very deceptive. For many newborns, the three-month size may be good for only a couple of weeks. Unless you know your baby will be small, you'll probably need the six-month size very soon, so plan ahead."

—FROM THE KIDSHEALTH PARENT SURVEY

Baby Clothes

These days, it's easy to find cute outfits that are everything baby clothes should be:

- Easy to get on and off. That means shirts that snap down the front, rather than pull over the head, or ones that have ample neck openings. Babies have big heads, and many hate having clothes pulled over their heads.
- Easy to open for diaper changes. The one-piece stretchy suits that are a staple of babywear should have snaps from foot to neck. Avoid annoying hybrids like outfits whose snaps end at a knitted cuff.
- Soft and stretchy. Avoid crisp fabrics, rough or protruding seams, and sharp-edged vinyl appliqués, even if they look cute.
- Machine washable. What more needs to be said?

- Safe. Avoid clothing that ties at the head or neck, or remove or shorten the strings to eliminate any risk of strangling. Snaps are preferable to zippers, which can catch the skin, or to buttons, which can fall off and be swallowed or choked on. Sleepwear should be fire-resistant (check the label). Check the toes of footed sleepers, and remove any loose threads that could get wrapped around a tiny toe (yes, it happens and it's painful).

Here are some basics to have on hand when you bring the baby home:

- Three to six undershirts, long- or short-sleeved, depending on the season. Many parents prefer "onesie" undershirts, which snap at the crotch and never ride up.
- Three to six stretchies or more for a winter baby. For many babies, these one-piece, long-sleeved, footed suits are the basic garb day and night. They can be worn with or without an undershirt, depending on the temperature.
- Three to six rompers or more for a summer baby. These are a cross between stretchies and onesies. They usually have short sleeves and snap at the crotch, with either short legs or no legs.
- Three to six nightgowns. These gowns enclose the legs in a sack with an elasticized opening at the bottom, making diaper changes easy. Some parents use them instead of stretchies at night; others use them over stretchies, like a lightweight sleeping bag. Some babies seem to love them; others seem to find them annoying against the legs. Note: These are not good for use with car seats because you need to put a strap between your baby's legs.
- Two or more bibs. Even though baby won't be eating solid food right away, bibs are good for drool and spit-up.
- One to three sweaters or sweatshirts. Beware of loosely knit sweaters that can catch on baby's fingers. Hooded, zip-up-the-front sweatshirts, while less traditional, are a good choice. If the hood has a drawstring, pull it out to avoid any risk of strangulation.
- One to three hats, either knit caps for winter or one knit cap and two sun hats for summer.
- Three to six pairs of socks or booties.
- One snowsuit bag or bunting for winter babies. Look for something usable in a car seat.
- Three to six receiving blankets. For newborns, receiving blankets—those small, flannel squares that hospitals wrap babies in—are more like clothes than bed linens. Well wrapped around your baby in a warm room, they can take

the place of everything but the diaper. Plus they can serve as bolsters, washcloths, and the like.

- Two to three terrycloth towels with hoods.
- Three to six baby washcloths.

Grooming and First-Aid Supplies

When it comes to creams, oils, and soaps, the current wisdom is less is better. In
the beginning, you can wash your baby with lukewarm water alone; later you can
use a mild, unscented soap and a no-tears baby shampoo. Most babies do not need
skin lotion or oil, and some may even develop a rash from mineral oil (baby oil).
If your baby's skin seems dry, you can use an unscented moisturizing lotion. All
you need in the way of grooming products are a baby brush and comb and curved
baby nail scissors or a baby nail clipper. For newborns, some people prefer to use
emery boards instead of clippers or scissors; they can be safer for such tiny nails—
and just as easy to use.

You will, however, want to have some first-aid and "daily care" products. So
you can find them fast, it's best to pack them together in a box. If you spend a lot
of time in the car or at a relative's house, you may want to have a second box for
your home-away-from-home. On the cover, tape emergency phone numbers,
including your child's doctor, the local poison control center, the local rescue
squad, fire, and police, as well as any neighbors who might help in a crisis.

In Chapter 28, "First Aid and Emergency Care," we list the items a general first-
aid kit should have. Here are some additional items to include for the care of your
newborn:

- Diaper-rash ointment containing zinc oxide.
- Infant acetaminophen (such as infant Tylenol), a fever-reducing medication.
  You should use this only after talking with your child's doctor. Until your
  baby is about four months old, any fever should be reported to your child's
  doctor.
- Syrup of ipecac. This is an emetic, which means it causes vomiting and can
  be used as a first-aid measure in some cases of poisoning. In some kinds of
  poisoning, however, it can do more harm than good, so it should be used only
  at the instruction of a poison control center or your child's doctor.
- Petroleum jelly (such as Vaseline) and alcohol wipes for lubricating and cleaning your thermometer if the thermometer you pack in your first-aid kit is a

rectal one. (A rectal thermometer is recommended for at least the first three months, when accuracy is most important.) See Chapter 29, "Signs and Symptoms," for advice on how to take your infant's temperature.

- Nasal aspirator, a bulb device for removing mucus from the nose.
- Calibrated spoon or oral syringe for giving medication.

Although it may not fit in your first-aid kit, it's good to have a bottle of baby rehydration fluid (such as Pedialyte) in your house. Your baby's doctor may recommend using this in cases of severe diarrhea or vomiting. Note the expiration date; it doesn't last forever.

Soft Cloth Carriers

Many a parent's sanity has been rescued by finding just the right baby carrier to wear. The price tag—about $25 to $80—may seem high for what amounts to a few bits of fabric and padding that strap onto your body. But anyone who has slipped a baby into one of these contraptions and has seen a crying jag melt into peaceful sleep knows they can be priceless. Slings and other carriers meet babies' almost universal desire to be held and carried for hours at a time while allowing their parents at least partial use of their arms and hands. In many cases, especially with slings, babies can be nursed or bottle-fed while in the carrier.

Strollers

If you've been at gatherings of young families, you may have seen a knot of new dads gathered around the latest stroller discussing its special features in terms that seem more suited to a hot new car. Upscale strollers do have some nice refinements, including lightweight materials and nifty folding mechanisms that make them easier to carry up a flight of stairs or stow in a car trunk. Can built-in stereo systems and heated seats be far behind?

Strollers range in cost from $15 for bare-bones umbrella strollers (not for newborns) to several hundred dollars for some plush carriage/strollers or lightweight imports. Some strollers come as part of "travel systems." You buy a matching infant car seat that fits into the stroller; when your child outgrows the car seat, you use the stroller alone.

Here are some tips for choosing a stroller:

- If you plan to use a stroller before your baby can sit up, make sure the stroller fully reclines. With adult supervision, such a stroller can double as a portable bed for use indoors or in the park; just make sure your baby lies on his back and is belted in. The safest belt design is a T-buckle: a crotch strap and waist belts that connect together.

- Umbrella strollers—lightweight cloth slings with thin metal frames that fold like an accordion—do not provide enough support for newborns and usually don't recline. But they can be fine for short jaunts with your toddler.
- Make sure your stroller has a canopy to block the sun.
- Check for weight, ease of steering, and ease of folding. Weigh the stroller down with 20 or 25 pounds, and then push it around the store. Try pushing with one hand—you should still be able to steer the stroller in a straight line. Try folding and unfolding it.
- For stability, the wheelbase should be wide and the seat low in the frame. The stroller should resist tipping backward when you press lightly down on the handles.
- A roomy underseat bin can save your shoulders and back from the strain of carrying heavy bags.

Safe Carrying Tips

Follow these precautions when using a sling or other baby carrier—especially in the beginning:

- Until you get used to the carrier, have another adult help you put it on and get your baby in. Do it on a bed in case your baby slips out.
- At first, keep your arm curved around your baby's back as you walk to avoid knocking her into door frames, walls, and the like. Soon, you'll have a sense of how much space you need to maneuver.
- Lower yourself by bending your knees, not by bending from the waist. If your baby is on your back, he can be pitched out of the carrier. (This will also save wear and tear on your back.)
- Try to avoid sudden, twisting movements.
- Don't cook, drink hot liquids, smoke, or go near a hot stove when you're carrying your baby.
- Don't carry your baby in a soft cloth carrier on a bicycle; while running, skating, sledding, or doing any other sport; or while in the car (always strap your baby into a car seat instead).

Strolling with Two

Strollers for two come either in tandem style, where one child sits behind the other, or side by side. Not all side-by-sides can fit comfortably through a standard doorway, so check before you buy. Tandems are generally easier to maneuver, especially if you have riders of unequal weight—an infant and a toddler—rather than twins. They're also more compact when folded. But side-by-side transports allow both users to recline more comfortably at the same time. And being side by side may be more fun for them (or you can try a tandem in which your children can face each other).

Jogging Strollers

These carriages, also called sports or running strollers, are designed to be pushed as you run or jog. Because of the shaking that comes with higher speed, it's best not to run or jog while pushing your baby until your child is about one year old. Even then, look for routes that are smooth underfoot.

Some Nonbasic Gear to Consider

Baby Bathtub

It's often said that you can bathe an infant in any plastic tub, or in the sink, or in the bathtub with a towel under him to prevent slipping. Although this is true, bathing your young baby is a slippery business, and a specially molded baby bathtub can be a big help, especially if you are not practiced in the arts of baby handling.

The tub should be made of plastic that is heavy enough not to bend under the weight of a full load of water. It should have a plug for draining the water. It should have a slip-resistant bottom, and it should be shaped so it holds your baby in a semi-upright position on a slip-resistant surface. For a longer period of usefulness, get a tub good for infants and toddlers. Indentations to hold washcloths, soap, and a cup (for rinsing) are nice features.

Whatever you choose, don't use the tub or submerge your baby's belly into water until she's a couple of weeks old and the umbilical cord stump has healed.

Until then, just use a washcloth or sponge for daily cleaning. For more on bathing, see Chapter 11, "Baby-Care Basics."

Baby Monitors

Baby monitors let you eavesdrop on your baby's cries, sighs, and breathing when she is out of sight. They consist of a transmitter placed near your baby and a portable receiver that can be placed in another room or carried around. Volume is adjustable, and some have visual cues, such as red lights that go on when a sound registers. Having a monitor can be reassuring if you're a heavy sleeper and your baby sleeps in another room or if you have a large house and want to be alerted when your baby wakes from a nap.

Warning: Baby monitor transmissions can be picked up on cell phones as well as on neighbors' baby monitor receivers. So be careful what you say in the baby's room—many a parent has had an embarrassingly frank conversation before remembering the transmitter was on.

Baby Seats and Indoor Swings

Not to be confused with car seats (which have a heavy plastic shell), indoor seats are usually lightweight. They may be hammocklike devices of fabric hung from a springy frame that jiggles when your baby moves, or they may have thick padding and a motor that makes them vibrate. Either kind should have a seat belt, which should always be used, and the base should have a nonskid surface. The seats can be used for children up to 20 or 30 pounds (check the label).

Baby swings are semireclining seats that hang on rigid arms from a four-legged frame. Electric or windup versions are available. Babies differ widely in their reaction to these: The same swing that terrifies one baby and bores another may bring bliss to a third (yours, if you're lucky). So it's best to try them out before buying, especially because they take up a lot of floor space.

Toys

A newborn doesn't need toys, especially the candy-colored stuffed animals they are likely to accumulate as gifts. In fact, it's safer to keep an infant's crib and play area free of toys.

Some toys, however, are worth considering:

- A windup or electric mobile visible from the crib can give your baby something interesting to look at while he's lying on his back. Many mobiles also play music. Be sure the mobile is securely fastened, is out of your baby's reach, and is not hanging directly over the crib (just in case it falls). Crib mobiles should be removed by the time your child is able to get on hands and knees, usually when he is about five or six months old. A mobile visible from the changing table can also help keep baby amused during diaper changes.

- Once your baby can grasp something, he'll probably love rattles, especially if they have parts that move. Of course, they need to be smooth and unbreakable.
- Padded play mats, often with segments that crinkle or squeak, are fun for babies who cannot yet crawl. They should be placed on the floor.
- Floor gyms provide things for babies to grab and bat while they lie on their backs on the floor.

(For information about toys for different ages, see Chapter 18, "Play Time.")

Highchairs and Booster Seats

Unlike baby seats and swings, which can be used from birth, highchairs are for babies who can sit up well on their own, usually at age six months or older. Look for a stable chair that won't tip over readily, is easy to clean, and has a tray that removes for quick cleaning. Check how easy it is for you to remove the tray. If the highchair has wheels or folding legs, make sure they lock. Always use the crotch seat belt to keep young babies from slipping out and older babies from standing up.

Although some parents find their highchair becomes a mainstay of daily living for a good two years, others end up using it only briefly before switching to a booster seat. This seat, not to be confused with a booster seat used in a car, is usually a lightweight, unpadded plastic shell that straps onto a regular kitchen chair. The stability of the chair largely determines how safe the booster seat is. Boosters often have a snap-on tray that can be removed so your baby can eat at the table. Because booster seats offer less support and security, they are better suited to a baby who is thoroughly experienced at sitting up. Their chief advantages are that they take up no extra space, are easily portable, and please babies who want to feel "grown-up."

Playpens and Play Yards

Some parents swear by playpens; others never use them. It may be wise to wait until your baby has been home a while before you rush out and buy this piece of baby equipment. If you do use one, be sure an adult always remains in the room with your baby. Standard playpens and smaller travel play yards both have raised floors and mesh walls.

When buying a playpen, look for thick padding on the top rim and padding on the metal frame of the pen. To minimize suffocation hazards, the floor pad should be firm and the sides of the pen should not lower. Do not use a damaged playpen, because babies can get entangled in torn mesh or can choke on bits of vinyl from chewed-on padding.

Travel play yards are simply playpens that fold. Avoid older models that have hinges in the center of the top rail on each side because they can pose a strangulation hazard. As with playpens, the floor covering should be firm and fit tightly in the frame.

In addition, you can find floorless play yards—plastic walls that snap together and can be arranged in various shapes on the floor. These can be a less restrictive way of confining your baby. You can carve out a safe zone in a room that isn't babyproofed. Or, instead of confining your baby, you can confine a hazardous object, such as a decorated Christmas tree. As with other playpens, however, a play yard should be used only if an adult is watching.

Need More Information?

Check the Index and Appendix C, "Resource Guide." And of course, consult your doctor.

chapter three

Your Baby's Birth

The main event

"A friend told me to look as my baby came out. It was the best advice ever—a magical moment I'll never forget!"

"I cut the cord at my son's birth—it was important for me as the father to be involved in the birth, to share in this whole process in ways that I could. I'll absolutely never, ever forget watching my wife hold him for the first time."

"Giving birth was the hardest thing I've ever done in my life—and the most amazing. Not everything went as I'd planned, but that's OK—we have the most beautiful daughter I could have ever dreamed of, and I can't wait to do it again."

Happily, almost all births in the United States today end with a healthy mother and baby. And what a miracle it is! Medical professionals continue to work hard to make childbirth as safe as possible and to foster an environment that's nurturing, supportive, and family friendly. But doctors and nurses aren't the only ones calling the shots today. In part, your birth experience will be shaped by your baby's needs—and in part, by the decisions you make prior to the big day.

This chapter focuses on the experiences and options you may have with the birth of your child. These include the people who will help you through pregnancy and delivery, the birth settings you may consider, the stages of labor and delivery, the possibility of a cesarean delivery, and the options in pain management. It also details common medical procedures that accompany labor, delivery, and after-birth baby care.

Getting Help

As you prepare for the birth of your child, build a support team for yourself. You will encounter many people who can help make the experience a healthy and satisfying one.

- Take a childbirth class. A trained professional who has lots of experience with labor and birth will teach you what to expect when the soon-to-be mom goes into labor and also how both partners can actively participate in the birth of the child. You will learn the details of labor and delivery, as well as breathing, relaxation techniques, and other ways of managing pain and fatigue. If the expectant dad doesn't plan to attend the birth, the woman should take the course with a friend or relative who can serve as a labor coach and be there through the process if possible.

- Try to choose a health care provider you like and trust and who shares your approach to childbirth. If you are eager to give birth without pain medications or induced labor, your chances of getting your wish are better if your doctor or midwife supports your feelings on these issues. On the other hand, if your priority is to have as swift or painless a childbirth as possible, choose a health care provider who will be supportive of this choice. Many experts advise writing up a "birth plan," which is a statement about your preferences on such matters. Although this may be worth doing, you can't anticipate everything that may happen or how you may feel when you actually give birth. You need a health care provider whose judgment you trust. For more about the different kinds of health care providers, see Chapter 1, "Prenatal Care."

- Consider hiring a labor assistant. Studies indicate that getting continuous support during labor from a trained and experienced woman, such as a midwife or doula, can have benefits: shorter labor, less medication, less chance of needing a cesarean, and a more positive feeling about the labor when it is over. The labor assistant provides reassurance, advice on managing pain, and physical contact such as giving backrubs or holding the woman during a contraction. She does not take the place of the father, but she can help reassure him, as well as free him to provide the kind of support he finds most comfortable. If your health care provider is a midwife, she may fill this role or you may want another aide. (For more information about doulas, see Chapter 9, "Breast-Feeding.")

  To find a labor assistant, talk to your health care provider or childbirth educator. Or you can contact DONA (Doulas of North America), www.dona

.org, 13513 North Grove Drive, Alpine, UT 84004, (801) 756-7331; or the Association of Labor Assistants and Childbirth Educators (ALACE), www .efn.org/~djz/birth/add695/alacegen.html, P.O. Box 382724, Cambridge, MA 02238, (617) 441-2500.

Another helpful tip: Forget about trying to have the perfect birth. This is good practice for parenthood when you will have to forget about other notions of perfection (your own as a parent and your child's). If you have specific ideas of how childbirth should go, be prepared to have it go some other way. You may find you need to be flexible as circumstances change. Choose people whose judgment you trust to be with you on this important day; make your plans, and then keep your eyes on the prize—a healthy baby.

Plan Ahead to Get Dad or a Close Friend Involved

Talk with your doctor or labor assistant about ways that your baby's father—or a close friend—can participate in the birth (if they choose to do so). Certainly Dad should not be forced to do anything that would make him uncomfortable (yes, sometimes men do pass out in the labor room these days!). But, for example, many dads today treasure the memory of cutting the baby's umbilical cord, holding a mirror so that his wife can see the baby come out, and helping in other ways in the labor room. Don't wait until the last minute to talk with your partner and doctor about ideas. Many men, if prepared for what to expect in advance, are eager to get involved!

The Birth Setting

The place where you give birth—the hospital or birth center—can influence the kind of birth your baby has. Both types of settings have similarly low rates of infant and maternal mortality, but birth centers handle only low-risk pregnancies and are relatively scarce.

> ### *The Voice of Experience*
>
> *"Make sure to include a camera when you pack your 'it's-time-to-go-to-the-hospital bag.' Whether you want to bring a video camera or just a still camera, the pictures you have of you and your partner with your minutes-old child will be ones you will treasure forever, and of course it's a moment that can never be recaptured."*
>
> —FROM THE KIDSHEALTH PARENT SURVEY

The Voice of Experience

"Make sure to review with your doctor when you should call and go to the hospital after the onset of labor. The old TV sitcom scenes of a woman feeling the first pangs of labor and the bumbling husband struggling to remember to bring his wife as he speeds off to the hospital aren't realistic. You can be in labor for many hours before the contractions are frequent and regular enough for your doctor to want you to report to the hospital. It can be a big emotional letdown to be sent home from the hospital because you were in false labor."

—FROM THE KIDSHEALTH PARENT SURVEY

The Voice of Experience

"The best experience was the birth of our son! The hospital did everything they could to make sure that my wife was comfortable and had anything she needed. That's really important to me."

—FROM THE KIDSHEALTH PARENT SURVEY

Hospitals

About 99 percent of American women give birth in hospitals. The main advantage of this choice is knowing that professional medical help will be on hand in the event that you or your baby needs it. When investigating hospitals, find out if they are equipped to safely handle high-risk deliveries as well as low-risk births (not all hospitals are). The hospital should have the capacity to do an emergency cesarean section within 30 minutes of your doctor's decision that one is needed. The hospital also should be able to resuscitate your baby, if necessary, and provide intensive care or quickly transfer him to a place that can provide it. To do those things, the hospital should have an obstetrician, an anesthesiologist, and a pediatrician available.

If you have pregnancy risk factors (some are listed in Chapter 1, "Prenatal Care"), it may be safest to deliver in a hospital with a level III neonatal intensive care unit (NICU) designed to deal with the smallest and sickest babies. A 1996 study found that high-risk babies had a 38 percent lower chance of death if they were born in such a hospital. If you know your baby is likely to be very premature or have another serious problem, it's worth checking that the NICU is a busy, long-established one so that you know the staff has a lot of experience with babies like yours. Such NICUs tend to be found in major medical centers.

Different Approaches

Hospitals approach childbirth in different ways, but most do have an approach—a set of steps (called protocols) that staff are expected to follow. Whether you are choosing among hospitals or are limited to one hospital by your health insurance, find out the approach your hospital takes. You should know what to expect when you arrive in labor. If you would like something that isn't standard, you could try to negotiate that in advance.

Here are some approaches you can look for:

- Traditional medical model. Obstetricians are clearly in charge here and often intervene in (or "manage") labor for comfort and convenience as well as health reasons. Inducing labor, for instance, may be common. The woman may be required to lie flat throughout labor, to refrain from eating or drinking, and to deliver in a certain position. The staff may encourage the use of drugs for pain, do continuous electronic monitoring on all fetuses, and take the baby from the mother soon after birth. The setting is medical, and the woman will move from a labor room to a delivery room.
- Modified or relaxed medical model. Starting in the 1970s, some women's health advocates argued that birth should be treated as a natural event, not a medical problem, and they set up alternative birth centers with this orientation. In response, many hospitals have modified their approach for low-risk births. They may have rooms with homelike settings where women can labor, deliver, and recover without being moved. They may take their cues more from the laboring woman, allowing labor to proceed more slowly and without intervention if all seems to be going well. They may welcome the assistance of midwives and labor assistants as well as use nondrug pain management if requested. Women may be able to sip water, walk around, take a warm bath, and assume any position that seems to help during labor and delivery. Not just the father, but children, grandparents, and friends may be allowed to attend the birth. After birth, babies may remain with their mother longer. In its fullest form, this less medical approach is sometimes called family-centered care. Most hospitals fall somewhere in the wide spectrum between the strict medical model and family-centered care.
- In-house birth center. This is a low-tech birth center located within a hospital for use by women with low-risk pregnancies only. It is likely to be staffed by certified nurse-midwives and to have some of the features of a freestanding birth center.

Freestanding Birth Centers

Freestanding birth centers have been described as "maxi-homes rather than mini-hospitals." A woman labors, delivers, and recovers in the same homey room, where family and friends, including siblings, may come and go. There is usually a kitchen, and the mother is generally allowed to eat during labor. The woman is supposed to be in control of the birth, with the midwife assisting but following the mother's lead rather than setting the pace.

A doctor is seldom present, and medical interventions are rarely or never done. Pain control is based on massage, whirlpool baths, relaxation exercises, and other techniques. Drugs are usually not available. If complications develop during labor or if a woman wants anesthesia for pain, she is taken to a hospital. This happens in 10 to 25 percent of labors and is especially common in first births.

At birth centers, women usually go home less than 12 hours after birth, with follow-up care at home. Not surprisingly, a birth-center delivery is generally much less expensive than a hospital birth.

Birth centers are an option for women with low-risk pregnancies who have already given birth without any problems and who are psychologically committed to the idea of having a low-tech, more natural childbirth. Although this may involve more preparation, especially in pain-management techniques, many women find this empowering. But freestanding birth centers may be hard to find; at the time of this writing, more than a dozen states had no accredited birth center.

Most states license birth centers. National accreditation is done by the Commission for the Accreditation of Birth Centers, an agency of the National Association of Childbearing Centers. Accredited centers are listed on NACC's Web site (www.birthcenters.org).

At Home

A small fraction of U.S. women give birth at home, usually with a midwife. Midwives who attend births at home are less likely to be certified nurse-midwives than those who work in hospitals or birth centers. (See Chapter 1, "Prenatal Care," for a description of different kinds of midwives.) Although most home births turn out fine, we don't recommend them because they lack options for medical aid if something goes wrong. First-time mothers, who are more prone to birth complications, should be especially wary. If you are experienced at childbirth and want to consider a home birth, be sure your birth attendant is skilled and experienced and that she has made advance arrangements with a nearby hospital and emergency transport service in case you need help.

An Extra Checkup

If you are considering an out-of-hospital birth, either at a birth center or at home, it's a good idea to have a sonogram late in pregnancy even if all seems to be going well. This painless, noninvasive test, also called ultrasound, can alert you to certain problems such as breech (feet-first) position of the baby or a fetal abnormality that might make an out-of-hospital birth difficult or unwise. For more on ultrasounds, see Chapter 1, "Prenatal Care."

When to Call the Doctor or Midwife

As the big day approaches, your health care provider will generally give you detailed instructions about when to call with signs of labor. Most want to hear from you as soon as you think you are in labor (even if it turns out you're not). Unless you've been instructed otherwise, call your health care provider day or night if any of the following occur:

- Your contractions are getting closer together and more intense.
- Your contractions are less than 10 minutes apart and are uncomfortable.
- You are less than 37 weeks along and are feeling persistent contractions.
- You are experiencing vaginal bleeding.
- Your amniotic membrane has ruptured (your water has broken). The fluid may trickle out, or it may gush. If the fluid is greenish, brown, or red, call immediately.
- The fetus is moving less frequently than usual.

If you can't reach your health care provider in these situations, go to the hospital.

Stages of Labor and Delivery

Labor and delivery are divided into stages and phases. The following descriptions of how labor usually progresses will give you an idea of what to expect. But remember: The lengths of time given here are averages only. Labor can take much more or less time and still be perfectly normal.

First Stage

The first stage of labor lasts from the start of contractions to full dilation (or opening) of the cervix (the open end of the uterus that protrudes down into the vaginal canal). It has three phases:

1. Early or latent labor. Contractions start out being short (30 to 45 seconds each) and infrequent (every 5 to 20 minutes). They gradually become longer (60 to 90 seconds each), more intense, and more frequent (less than 5 minutes apart). This phase lasts an average of about 8 hours in a first birth (up to 20 hours is normal, though) and less in subsequent births. But the time range is wide, and it's often hard to know exactly when this phase begins. In fact, some women go through much of it without realizing it has begun. Others know it's happening but can remain at home for much of it, walking, sleeping, and eating lightly before going to the hospital.

   During this early phase, the soon-to-be mother may have a "bloody show," the discharge of a blood-tinged mucous plug from the cervix. The amniotic membranes may rupture, releasing a rush (or a trickle) of amniotic fluid. During this phase, the cervix dilates to three or four cm and becomes fully effaced (or thinned).

2. Active phase. Contractions occur every three to five minutes and last about 40 to 60 seconds, as the cervix dilates to seven to nine cm. This phase usually lasts five to eight hours in first births and three to six hours in later births. Pain and discomfort usually intensify. By the start of this phase, the woman should be in the hospital. If the membranes have not ruptured, the doctor may rupture them. During active labor, women may begin to feel the need for pain relief. They may use massage, breathing exercises, and other techniques learned in childbirth classes, or they may ask for pain medication.

3. Transitional phase. This is a shorter, more exhausting phase. During the first stage of this phase, the contractions become more intense, coming every two to three minutes, lasting 60 to 90 seconds each, with much of that time spent at peak contraction intensity. Some women may feel like the contractions never completely end in this phase. The almost no-longer-pregnant woman is likely to feel strong pressure in the lower back, the rectum, and the perineum, the area between the vagina and rectum. (She may feel as if she has

to have a bowel movement. In fact, she may expel some stool during the pushing stage. Delivery staff are used to this and clean it up immediately.) If the cervix is not fully dilated, the woman may have to restrain an urge to begin pushing the baby out. This is the point when some women feel they've had it—they may feel angry, frustrated, and discouraged. If a woman screams "shut up" or something less polite at her partner or labor coach, odds are she's in transitional labor. By the end of this time—which usually lasts 15 minutes to an hour—the cervix is fully dilated to 10 cm.

Second Stage

During the second stage of labor, the woman actively pushes the baby out. It averages about an hour in first births and 20 minutes in later ones. But it can go longer, especially if she's had an epidural (a form of pain relief described later). The health care provider usually helps guide her in pushing, which can be exhausting. Once the baby's head is visible between contractions, the medical staff prepares for delivery. In many hospitals, this may mean moving the mother to a delivery room; in others, it may mean removing part of the labor bed. Once the baby's head is out, it usually takes only a few pushes to deliver the rest of the baby.

Third Stage

After the birth of the baby, the third stage of labor and delivery is yet to come. "What's left?" you might ask. The placenta is still inside and needs to be delivered. This usually takes about 15 minutes of weaker contractions. Not surprisingly, women tend to pay little attention to this stage. The baby is here, and the afterbirth is just an afterthought.

> ### The Voice of Experience
>
> *"Nothing really prepares you for the birth of your first child. It is an uplifting and spiritual experience but also a very stressful and deeply traumatic event. And this is just speaking from the husband's point of view! My wife has had two deliveries without medical intervention or pain medication. Very rarely does one see one's partner in such pain, and, frankly, you may not be prepared for the amount of blood and tissue even normal childbirth produces. In retrospect, however, it is a momentous occasion that I would not have wanted to miss. (My wife has a different opinion, though, and frequently reminds me that next time, it should be my turn!)"*
> —FROM THE KIDSHEALTH PARENT SURVEY

3.1a

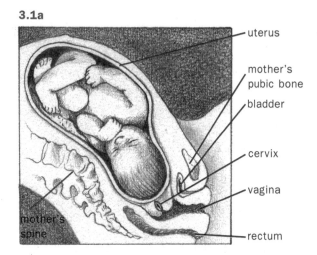

uterus

mother's pubic bone

bladder

cervix

vagina

mother's spine

rectum

3.1b

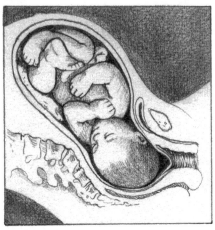

3.1c

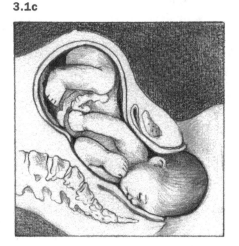

3.1d

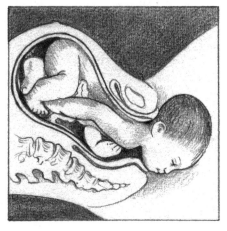

Figures 3.1a–d. Vaginal delivery overview. The position of the baby as it travels down the birth canal during a normal vertex (baby's head first) vaginal delivery is illustrated here.

Cesarean Delivery

About one in five American babies are delivered by cesarean section (c-section), an operation in which the obstetrician makes incisions in the abdomen and the uterus and then lifts the infant out.

Cesarean deliveries undoubtedly save the lives of many babies and save many women from severe birth injuries. But experts have said for years that many unnecessary cesareans are being performed. Federal health officials set a goal of reducing the cesarean rate to 15 percent by the year 2010. In recent years, the c-section rate did fall but only from 22.8 percent (in 1989) to 18 percent (in 1998).

The difficulty with reducing unnecessary cesareans is knowing which ones are unnecessary. If a doctor isn't sure one is needed in a given case, he or she may choose to err on the side of caution, preferring to do the operation rather than taking any chance with the health of the mother or baby. Most parents would endorse this decision. If it is not an emergency, you can ask for a second opinion. In the end, you most often need to rely on the judgment and good faith of the doctors.

Reasons for Cesareans

In some cases, cesareans clearly are needed. If your doctor knows you have one of these conditions, a c-section should be done before labor begins.

- Placenta previa. The placenta blocks the cervical opening. If labor begins and the fetal head presses against the placenta, massive bleeding can result.
- Placental abruption. Much of the placenta has separated from the wall of the uterus.
- Active genital herpes infection in the mother. Doing a cesarean can prevent the baby from getting infected while in the birth canal.
- Prolapsed umbilical cord. If the amniotic membranes rupture early, the umbilical cord sometimes is flushed through the cervix and into the vaginal canal while the baby is still in the uterus. Pressure on the cord by the baby's head could cut off the baby's oxygen supply.

KidsHealth Tip
What About "VBAC"?

Doctors have learned that most women who have had a cesarean can safely deliver their next baby vaginally. If you have had a c-section, talk to your doctor about vaginal birth after cesarean, or VBAC (pronounced v-back).

In other cases, when a baby needs to be delivered promptly for medical reasons, the doctor usually tries to induce labor. But if it takes too long or causes fetal distress (abnormalities in the heart rate), a cesarean may be necessary. Here are some cases in which this might happen:

- Preterm delivery is needed because of preeclampsia (pregnancy-related high blood pressure) or diabetes in the mother.
- The baby is showing signs of intrauterine growth retardation (its growth seems to have stalled) but is mature enough to be delivered.
- The fetus is two weeks or more past the due date. Conditions in the uterus may start to deteriorate, endangering the fetus.
- Your water breaks, but labor doesn't start on its own within a specified period of time, generally within 24 hours. (Longer delays may raise the risk of infection.)

The most common reasons for cesareans, however, are none of the above. They are typically done for the following reasons:

- The woman had a cesarean before.
- The baby is in a breech position (buttocks or feet first) or lying transverse (shoulder first). Such babies sometimes can be turned before labor or can be delivered vaginally, although forceps and anesthesia may be necessary.
- Labor has come to a standstill or failed to progress at a certain rate (a condition called labor dystocia). In some cases, labor stalls because the baby's head

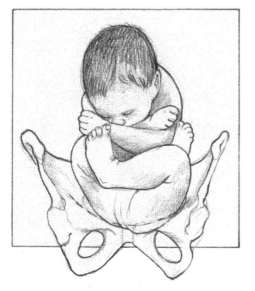

Figure 3.2. Breech position. When the fetus is in a breech position, it moves into the mother's pelvis and birth canal buttocks first. In some cases, the doctor can press on the mother's abdomen and turn the baby into a deliverable position. Otherwise, the baby must be delivered by cesarean section.

is too big to go through the mother's pelvis (a condition called cephalopelvic disproportion).

• Monitoring of fetal heart rate (and sometimes of fetal blood oxygen levels) indicates fetal distress. This is a catchall term for signs that the fetus may be in danger. Such signs are often difficult for doctors to interpret accurately. Some doctors use the term "nonreassuring heart patterns" instead. In other words, the doctors are not reassured by what they hear or see—they're concerned, simple as that.

The last two reasons—failure to progress in labor and fetal distress—are the most controversial, in part because they are subject to interpretation. There is evidence that the routine use of electronic monitors, which continuously track the fetal heartbeat, have led doctors to overestimate fetal distress. This, in turn, has led to some unnecessary cesareans without improving the outcome for babies or mothers. And some childbirth experts argue that many cesareans performed due to "lack of progress" could be avoided in various ways: by using pain-control techniques to allow longer labors, by using oxytocin to spur labor, and by simply waiting.

Why C-Sections Are Worth Avoiding

Cesareans are reasonably safe operations, but they are surgery and do have risks. Babies usually suffer no ill effects, but some may have temporary respiratory problems that require closer observation and treatment in the hospital nursery. Women

KidsHealth Tip

Baby Blues

In the weeks after a baby joins the family, many new mothers—and fathers as well—have periods of sadness and anxiety, and some have serious depression. If talking with family and friends doesn't help, look for professional help right away. The health care providers who helped you during pregnancy should be able to recommend someone to help you deal with postpartum depression. In an emergency, call 911 or go to a hospital emergency room.

are more likely to get infected or have bleeding that requires transfusion than with a vaginal birth, and recovery takes longer. Although the maternal death rate is very low, it is higher than with vaginal births. And cesareans, especially if a woman has more than one, increase the risk of serious complications in future pregnancies.

Cesareans are often done with epidural or spinal anesthesia, which numbs the woman from the waist down but leaves her fully conscious. She can hear her baby's first cry and hold him right away, and the father usually can be present. The scene can be as joyful as any birth. But in an emergency, general anesthesia may be required because it works faster. As a result, the woman is not conscious, and, as often occurs in an emergency, the father is not allowed to be present.

C-sections can be a big disappointment to couples who have prepared to have a vaginal birth. They can also make the newborn period more difficult for the new mother. She has more pain and may have trouble lifting the baby. Breast-feeding may be uncomfortable. Some women feel depressed, especially if they invested a lot of themselves in preparing for a "normal" birth and went through hours of labor only to have a c-section under general anesthesia.

Managing the Drawbacks of C-Sections

Although no one can promise you that a cesarean will be easy, there are a few things you can do to minimize the drawbacks:

- If you know or suspect your baby will be born by cesarean, talk to your doctor ahead of time about any concerns you might have. For instance, if it's possible, the mother might want to be conscious, the father might want to be present, and you both might want to hold your baby immediately after birth. If the father cannot be present, you might want to have someone in the delivery room take pictures of your baby.
- Check on your doctor's usual surgical practices: If he or she does a low horizontal incision in the uterus, as most obstetricians routinely do, chances of delivering vaginally next time will be better. If he or she does a low or "bikini" incision in the abdomen, the scar will be largely hidden by pubic hair. (Separate incisions are made in the abdomen and the uterus.)
- Get extra help from family, friends, or paid workers to help you physically in the first week or two after you come home. During this time, you should have nothing to do except hold and feed the baby and rest (which can seem like plenty!). In the excitement over the baby, it's easy for loved ones to forget that you are recuperating from major surgery.
- Remind yourself that how your baby came out of your body says nothing about what kind of parent you will be or what kind of relationship you will

Looking on the Bright Side (or Pollyanna's Guide to C-Sections)

Cesarean deliveries are worth avoiding if possible. But if you know in advance that one will be necessary for medical reasons, you might as well focus on the positives (politically incorrect as it may be to mention them). If the c-section is not planned but follows a hard labor, these may not apply.

- With a planned cesarean, you know exactly when your baby will be born. You have none of the pain of labor, and you can usually be awake and well rested for the birth.
- Your baby's first pictures may be cuter because her head will be round rather than molded (temporarily misshapen) by squeezing through the birth canal.
- You won't have incontinence (of urine, gas, or feces), which can occur temporarily in some women after vaginal births.
- When you are ready to resume sexual activity, intercourse is likely to be more comfortable for you than if you had a vaginal birth.

have with her. But if you do feel bad, don't feel guilty about it. You can love your baby and still have regrets about the way she was born. You can feel grateful and lucky and still sometimes angry or sad.

Pain Management

Pain in childbirth varies a great deal; so do the techniques for dealing with it. Explore all your options with your doctor well before the delivery date approaches.

Delivery Without Drugs

Studies have shown that the perception of pain in childbirth can be reduced when women know what to expect, have confidence in themselves and their health care providers, have loved ones at hand, and have the support and encouragement of skilled labor assistants such as midwives or doulas. Pain-management techniques without drugs include relaxation and breathing exercises, as taught in many child-birth classes; hypnosis or self-hypnosis; massage; counterpressure; changes of position; and immersion in warm water. In many cases, a woman needs to start learning and practicing these techniques months or weeks before she gives birth.

Narcotics

To dull the pain of contractions or cervical dilation, drugs related to morphine can be injected every two to four hours or given intravenously. These include meperidine (Demerol) or newer variants such as fentanyl (Sublimaze), butorphanol (Stadol), or nalbuphine (Nubain). Because these drugs can cause nausea, they are often given with an antinausea drug. Other possible side effects to the mother include drowsiness, vomiting, and a drop in blood pressure. (Women differ widely in how much pain relief and how many side effects they experience from these drugs.)

The effects of narcotics on the baby—including sleepiness that can make immediate nursing difficult—depend on how large the dose is and how close to delivery it is given. In rare cases, these drugs may cause a baby's breathing to be weak so that oxygen and breathing assistance are needed, but their effects can be quickly reversed by the injection of another medication.

Epidurals and Other Regional Anesthetics

Epidurals are the most commonly used form of pain relief; in some hospitals, 80 to 90 percent of women get them. This method of anesthesia numbs the woman below the waist but leaves her fully conscious. Unlike narcotics, which are simple to give, epidurals require a thin plastic catheter to be inserted through a needle into the woman's lower back and then into the epidural space just outside the membrane covering the spinal cord. Drugs—usually local anesthetics—flow through the catheter and temporarily numb the nerves that provide feeling below the waist. Because this procedure requires a trained anesthesiologist, not all hospitals offer it.

Epidurals can slow second-stage labor and make it harder for a woman to push strongly. In several studies, women who had epidurals were more likely than other women to have cesarean sections or vaginal deliveries that required forceps or vacuum extractors. But it's not clear if the surgery was needed because of the epidurals or if the surgery and the epidurals were both needed because of some underlying problem.

It is often said that a skilled anesthesiologist can minimize an epidural's effects on labor by varying the anesthesia used and by giving it at the right moment (generally after labor is well established but well before pushing begins).

Although epidurals are the most commonly used of the regional anesthetics, others exist:

- Spinal block. Similar in effect to an epidural, this is often used for cesareans.
- Saddle block. This blocks pain to a smaller area, chiefly the vagina and perineum, and is often used for forceps-assisted deliveries.
- Pudendal block. In this procedure, anesthetic is injected inside the vagina, with relief only to the vagina and perineum. This may be used for vaginal deliveries, including some forceps deliveries, and for performing and repairing an episiotomy.

General Anesthesia

General anesthesia, which makes a person unconscious, once was commonly used in childbirth, but it's now usually reserved for emergency cesareans and some vaginal births that require forceps. Not only does it provide total pain relief, but it works rapidly. The anesthesia is usually inhaled, the woman becomes unconscious, and an endotracheal tube is inserted into her throat to keep her airway clear.

The woman is usually unconscious only for the few minutes it takes to deliver the baby, but she awakes groggy and sometimes nauseated. The fetus can become sedated, too, but this can be minimized by giving the anesthesia at the last possible moment and delivering the baby before much of the drug has had time to get into his body.

Most often women are not allowed to eat while in labor because if it becomes necessary for the woman to receive general anesthesia, vomited food particles from the stomach can be inhaled into the lungs. Antacids may also be given before general anesthesia is used to neutralize stomach acid that also could be thrown up and inhaled while the woman is unconscious.

Other Common Medical Procedures

During labor and delivery in a hospital, several other medical procedures are common. Here's an overview of the ones you're most likely to encounter.

Fetal Monitoring

Some form of fetal heart monitoring is used in virtually all births. The low-tech version is called intermittent auscultation, which means simply on-and-off listening. A health care provider, usually a nurse, listens to the fetal heartbeat with a special stethoscope or Doppler device (which lets you hear the baby's heartbeat, too) every 5, 15, or 30 minutes, depending on the case and the stage of labor. Studies have found that such monitoring produces results as good as those with the higher-tech electronic monitoring described later. Of course, hospitals must have enough nurses—in some cases a 1:1 nurse–patient ratio—to do this reliably.

In recent decades, however, most hospitals have embraced electronic fetal monitoring for all or most laboring women. Electronic monitoring comes in external and internal forms. In external monitoring, the woman wears a belt (or two) around her abdomen. The monitor registers contractions and the way the fetal heartbeat reacts to them. It prints out a record for health care providers to review; in some cases it may also sound an alarm. (Don't panic if you hear one; false alarms are common.) The monitor may be used continuously, or readings may be taken at set intervals.

For internal monitoring, an electrode on the end of a tube is passed through the cervix and attached to the scalp of the fetus. To do this, the amniotic membrane must have previously broken and the cervix must be at least somewhat dilated. Internal monitoring may be used if greater accuracy is needed or if there is difficulty registering the heartbeat externally.

One drawback of electronic fetal monitoring, as previously mentioned, is that there is evidence that in some cases, it can lead to unnecessary cesareans for fetal distress.

Amniotomy

One of the most common procedures in obstetrics is the artificial rupturing of the membrane containing the fetus and the amniotic fluid. Amniotomy, or breaking the waters, is often done to induce labor, to speed up its pace, or to allow closer monitoring of the fetus through a needle inserted in her scalp. The health care provider breaks the membrane with a little plastic hook during a vaginal exam. Once the membrane is broken, artificially or naturally, it's wise to keep internal exams to a minimum because they can promote infection.

Induction of Labor

Labor is often induced (or artificially started) if mother or baby is thought to have a condition that requires speedy delivery. Some of these conditions were discussed earlier in this chapter in the section on cesarean delivery.

Some health care providers will also perform "elective inductions"—in other words, they will induce labor if the mother wants it for nonmedical reasons. For instance, if she lives far from the hospital and has difficulty arranging child care for her older children, she may want to know as precisely as possible when her labor will occur. Some health care providers, however, will not induce labor for such reasons, believing it's wiser to let nature take its course unless medical reasons make that dangerous.

Inducing labor is not like turning on a faucet. If the body isn't ready, induction may fail, and, after hours or days of trying, a woman may end up having a cesarean delivery. This appears to be more likely if the cervix is not yet "ripe," which means soft, thinned out, and dilated.

To induce labor, medical staff may take the following actions:

- Insert a gel or tablet of prostaglandin into the vagina to help ripen the cervix if it is not yet ripe. This is typically done overnight in the hospital.
- Rupture the membranes (an amniotomy, as described earlier), which alone will sometimes induce labor.
- Give the hormone oxytocin (Pitocin) intravenously to stimulate contractions. The drug is started in a small dose, and the fetus and uterus need to be closely monitored. When contractions start, they are usually more frequent and regular than in a labor that starts naturally. Oxytocin is also used frequently to spur labor that is going slowly or has stalled. (In one recent year, more than a quarter of U.S. births involved either induction of labor or use of oxytocin to augment labor.)

Forceps or Vacuum Extraction

An estimated 10 percent of U.S. women have "operative vaginal deliveries." These are deliveries in which the doctor turns the baby or gently pulls him out with either forceps (a pair of curved paddles) or a vacuum extractor (a suction device with a cap that goes on the top of the baby's head). Forceps deliveries once had a fearsome reputation, but now the riskier forceps procedures (high forceps and most midforceps deliveries) have been replaced by cesarean sections.

Today, in most cases, forceps and vacuum extractors are used only when the baby's scalp is already visible (called outlet forceps) or shortly before (called low forceps). In these cases, side effects to the baby are rare and temporary; these may include swelling under the scalp, marks on the head, facial bruising, and an

increased likelihood of jaundice in the infant. The mother may be more likely to
have injury to the birth canal and perineum with forceps than with a vacuum
extraction or a spontaneous birth. A local anesthetic is used in most cases, but some
require regional or general anesthesia. If a forceps or vacuum extraction fails, the
obstetrician should be prepared to do a cesarean.

Operative vaginal deliveries are done when the mother or the baby shows signs
of physical trouble that could be relieved by a speedier birth. This might include
fetal distress, premature separation of the placenta, heart or lung problems in the
mother, exhaustion in the mother, or pushing that lasts more than two or three
hours. Another common reason is to turn a baby whose current position would
make delivery difficult.

Obstetricians vary in how they feel about forceps and vacuum-extraction deliveries and how experienced they are at performing them. As a result, some may do
a c-section where others would use forceps or vacuum extraction.

Episiotomy

Just before birth, when the baby's head is straining and stretching the perineum, it
used to be standard practice for obstetricians to make an incision—called an episiotomy—to widen the vaginal opening. The idea was that the episiotomy would
prevent uncontrolled tearing that might do more damage and be more difficult to
repair.

But studies have not confirmed such benefits in routine vaginal births. Instead,
they found that midline episiotomies (the kind most often done in the United
States) can sometimes lead to tearing that damages the muscles of the anus. This
can cause severe pain, as well as temporary problems controlling gas or, more
rarely, bowel movements. As a result, medical experts no longer recommend routine episiotomies. If tearing occurs, as it often does, it is usually not serious and is
surgically repaired. Episiotomies are often needed, however, in complicated births,
such as in breech births or forceps deliveries, or if the health care provider thinks
a more serious tear will otherwise occur.

Health care providers differ widely in how frequently they do episiotomies and
in whether they favor routine incisions. Some, especially midwives, often make it
a priority to help a woman emerge from childbirth with her perineum intact. So
if you have concerns about episiotomies, discuss this procedure with your health
care provider long before the due date.

Checking Out Your Baby

Immediately after birth, your baby will be tested and examined to assess her health and to determine if she does or does not need extra medical attention.

The Apgar Score

The minute your baby is born, she will be evaluated using the Apgar score to see if she needs help breathing. Developed in 1952 by anesthesiologist Virginia Apgar, this tests and rates five factors: heart rate, breathing, color, muscle tone, and reflex response. The doctor or midwife gives each factor a score from zero to two and adds the five numbers together. A score of 7 to 10 is considered normal. A lower score means oxygen or other special measures may be needed to help your baby.

The Apgar score is done at one minute after birth and again at five minutes after. Although it reflects your newborn's immediate condition, it does not accurately predict long-term health or illness. If your baby has a score below seven, it does not mean she will not be healthy and "normal." Premature babies in particular may score lower.

Just After a Normal Birth

In the delivery room or sometimes in the nursery, the medical staff or midwife generally will do the following:

- Clear your newborn's nasal passages with a bulb syringe so she can breathe easily.
- Weigh her, measure her length and head circumference, take her temperature, and estimate her gestational age.
- Put antibiotic ointment or drops in her eyes to prevent infection.
- Take her footprints or palm print for identification, and give her and you ID bracelets or anklets. (The nurse will check these IDs each time your baby is brought to you after being out of your sight.)
- Dry her, wrap her in a blanket, put a tiny knitted cap on her head, and perhaps place her in a warmed bassinet (or on your chest), to prevent heat loss. (Newborns cannot regulate their temperatures as well as adults can.)

Bonding

Within minutes, if all is well, he will be in your arms. (Both Mom and Dad should have an opportunity to hold the new baby.) Once you have adjusted to this amazing fact (at least a little), you can begin to get to know him. Just after birth, most babies are quiet and alert for about an hour, looking calm and wise beyond their minutes. Then they usually become sleepy for hours or even days. The alert period is the best time to begin breast-feeding, even though he may get very little of the thin, yellow colostrum the breast produces at first. If you stroke his cheek, he will probably turn in that direction, ready to suck. (In studies, babies who were laid on their mother's belly immediately after birth rested for about 30 minutes and then began to suckle at the breast.)

Young as he is, your baby will use all his senses, including smell and touch, to identify and become attached to you. He may turn or react to the sound of your voice. Although his vision is blurry, he can see anything that's up to about two feet away, and he is likely to study faces—especially yours if it's close enough. He will grab onto your finger if you place it in his palm. He's just been through a lot and he needs to rest, but at the same time, he seems to want to take everything in.

The quiet-alert period after birth is sometimes referred to as the bonding period. The term was popularized in the 1970s, when some pediatricians theorized that the mother would be more likely to love the baby and have a better relationship with him later if she held the baby skin-to-skin and interacted with him in the first hour after birth.

This theory, or misinterpretations of it, has caused a lot of anguish in parents who for various reasons could not hold their baby until hours, days, or weeks after birth. Moreover, it has never been proved—and common sense argues against worrying about it. After all, millions of parents—including many parents of premature, ill, or adopted children—form the strongest bonds of love and attachment without being able to "bond" just after birth. In fact, many parents "bond" with their children during pregnancy or while waiting for adoption, where bonding is based only on an idea or sometimes a picture of the loved one. And many others, even if they cradle the baby at birth, do not feel loving attachment for days or even weeks.

Bonding, in truth, is a long process. Love, trust, and attachment are built day by day as you care for your child, respond to his needs, and learn to interpret his cries and actions. Cuddling and nursing your baby just after birth is a wonderful thing— do it if you can. But if you can't—or if you are too exhausted by the birth to even want to cuddle or nurse—try not to worry about it. Any parent who cares enough about his or her child to read this book is unlikely to have any problems bonding with him.

Next Steps

In many hospitals, after a period with the mother and father, the baby is taken to the nursery, perhaps accompanied by the father, while the mother rests and is moved to her room (unless the birth took place in a combination labor-delivery-recovery room). If you are in a birth center, immediate postbirth care is likely to be done at your bedside so you and your baby are not separated.

In the hospital nursery, the staff will do the following:

- Give your baby an injection of vitamin K to help the blood clot properly. This crucial vitamin does not cross the placenta well from mother to fetus, so babies usually are born low in K.
- Possibly give your baby a first injection of hepatitis B vaccine. If not, your baby's doctor will do it after discharge. A total of three shots are required in the first six months to protect against hepatitis B, a virus that can cause long-term liver damage and cancer.
- Bathe your baby.

The hospital staff will call the doctor you have chosen to care for your child to announce the arrival of his or her newest patient (unless the doctor was already called to attend the delivery). If you haven't arranged for a doctor beforehand (see Chapter 12, "Choosing and Working with Your Child's Doctor") or if your child's doctor isn't on staff at the hospital where you had your delivery, the hospital will either supply one who is on staff or suggest one for you to contact.

Bonding, Statistically Speaking

In one study, 97 mothers were asked when they first felt love for their baby. Forty-one percent said during pregnancy, 24 percent said at birth, 27 percent said during the first week, and 8 percent said after the first week.

The doctor will do the following:

- Examine your baby thoroughly, listening to her heart and lungs, moving her limbs, feeling her abdomen, and checking that certain reflexes are present.
- Order blood tests, done by pricking your baby's heel. Some newborn screening tests are performed in all states unless you withhold your permission. These generally include tests for phenylketonuria (PKU) and hypothyroidism (low thyroid function), both disorders that can cause mental retardation if not treated promptly. Your child may also be checked for sickle-cell anemia.
- Possibly order additional blood tests or X-rays if problems are suspected.

Banking Cord Blood

In recent years, cutting-edge parents have faced a new quandary: Should they save blood from their baby's umbilical cord? Cord blood contains valuable stem cells. These are immature cells that theoretically can make new bone marrow in a person who needs a bone marrow transplant but can't find a marrow donor who matches. So some parents save their baby's cord blood in case someday it may be used to help a family member, or their baby himself, with a serious illness.

If you already have a child who has leukemia, lymphoma, or another illness that may require a bone marrow transplant, you should consider banking your newborn's cord blood. Talk to your child's doctor about it.

For others, the chances of needing the stem cells may be small. It is not clear how long the cells can be stored or whether the technique will prove as useful as some medical professionals hope. Some proponents who run cord-blood-banking companies say it offers "biological insurance" for your newborn. But if your newborn developed an illness that required stem cells, his own cord blood might not be helpful because it might contain the same defect that caused the illness.

Harvesting the blood causes no harm or pain; it's taken from the umbilical cord after the cord is clamped, shortly after delivery. The main drawback is cost: Private banking costs around $1,500 initially, with a yearly storage fee of $100.

Another option—which is free—is to donate your newborn's cord blood to a public cord-blood bank, where it might save the life of some other person or be used in lifesaving research. For some families, making such a precious gift might seem a wonderful way to honor a birth. As with regular blood donations, the donor has no special claim on the blood once it is given. Cord blood is collected by many nonprofit blood banks, including some affiliated with the American Red Cross or university hospitals.

For either public or private banking, your obstetrician or nurse-midwife must be willing to collect the blood, and you need to get a kit from the blood bank in advance, ideally by week 30 of your pregnancy. For more information on this evolving field, the UCLA Umbilical Cord Blood Bank's Web site (www.cord blood.med.ucla.edu) is a good place to start.

If There's a Problem at Birth

The scenario of birth we outlined in this chapter is the common one that ends in exhaustion and joy at the arrival of a healthy newborn. However, a small number (3 to 5 percent) of newborns have a significant abnormality that requires specialized medical care.

Some birth defects, genetic diseases, and chromosomal problems can be diagnosed prenatally, especially if the mother has had an ultrasound or amniocentesis performed. (See Chapter 1, "Prenatal Care," for more information about these tests.) These conditions include spina bifida (in which the spinal cord doesn't close properly), Down syndrome, some heart malformations, and cleft lip or palate. Many of these conditions are described in Chapter 32, "Health Problems in Early Childhood."

If a birth defect was discovered prenatally or if a serious problem was suspected before birth, your obstetrician will prepare you for what will happen after delivery. In this case, you will need to make sure that your baby is delivered at a hospital that can provide the best care for him. In cases of serious congenital problems or extreme prematurity, the best facility is almost always a tertiary care hospital with a neonatal intensive care unit (NICU) or special care nursery. (See Chapter 6, "Premature Babies," for more on prematurity.)

If you know your baby will need special care after his birth, you can visit the NICU or special care nursery in advance and meet the team that will care for your child. The team may include a neonatologist (a pediatrician specializing in care of newborns), a pediatric anesthesiologist, and a pediatric surgeon, as well as neonatal nurses and nurse-practitioners. A social worker should also be available to help you find services your child may need, and counselors may be able to help you with the emotional turmoil, grief, or fear you may be feeling.

Sometimes, however, birth defects are not detected before birth, or the baby may suffer a complication during birth, such as meconium aspiration—a potentially serious condition that occurs when the baby has a bowel movement while still in the uterus and inhales some of it with his first breath. And most cases of prematurity are also unexpected.

In these cases, parents must grapple with shock, as well as grief and fear about the future. They may have to be separated from the baby for long periods. When this happens, experienced and caring hospital staff can do a great deal to help parents find their way.

Thinking It Over

This chapter has given you a lot of information about the options available for your baby's birth. Take your time to think carefully about who will help you during the pregnancy and delivery, as well as where your baby will be born. Familiarize yourself with the stages of labor so you can participate in the birth process with confidence. Well in advance of the delivery, talk to your doctor about pain-management options. Be knowledgeable about cesarean deliveries and other common medical procedures you may encounter. Knowledge about the birth process can give you a sense of empowerment and relieve fears that accompany the unknown. Your baby's birth is indeed a miracle!

Need More Information?

Check the Index and Appendix C, "Resource Guide." And of course, consult your doctor.

chapter four

Looking at Your Newborn

"He definitely has your ears . . ."

In birth scenes on TV, the mother-to-be, often a famous actress in full makeup and with her hair only fashionably mussed, "delivers" a baby after a few token grunts and groans. Seconds later, the doctor presents the glowing parents with a picture-perfect, cooing, neatly combed and scrubbed, several-month-old infant, who, if he were any older, probably could walk out of the delivery room on his own.

Contrast that picture with how a baby really looks just after emerging from the womb: bluish, waterlogged, covered with blood and cream-cheesy glop, and battered as though he had just been in a fistfight—and lost. Not a pretty sight.

The fact that your newborn doesn't resemble one of those Hollywood "stand-ins" shouldn't come as any great surprise. Remember that the fetus develops immersed in fluid, folded up in an increasingly cramped space inside the uterus. The whole process usually culminates with the baby being pushed forcibly through a narrow, bone-walled birth canal, sometimes with the aid of metal forceps or suction devices.

When you first look at your baby, however, remember that the features that make a newborn look strange usually are temporary. As you examine him closely—every crease, curve, and bulge—it may help to know how full-term newborns normally look. (Premature infants may look and act differently; see Chapter 6, "Premature Babies," for more information.) Despite all the glop and other less comely newborn features, we think that nothing could be more beautiful—and when it's your baby, we're sure you'll feel the same way!

The Head

Birth leaves its mark mostly on an infant's head—the largest part of a newborn's body and the part that has usually led the way on the journey through the birth canal. The newborn's skull is made up of several separate bones, allowing the large head to squeeze through the narrow, rigid-walled birth canal. Because of this tight squeeze, the heads of infants born by vaginal delivery often show some degree of molding (see Figure 4.1c), which is when the skull bones shift and overlap, making the top of the infant's head look elongated, stretched out, or even pointed at birth. This somewhat bizarre appearance will go away over several days as the skull bones move into a more rounded position. The heads of babies born by cesarean section or breech delivery (buttocks or feet first) usually will look round from the start.

Because of the separation of your newborn's skull bones, you will be able to feel (go ahead . . . you won't harm anything) two fontanels, or soft spots, on the top of the head. The larger one located toward the front of the head is diamond-shaped and usually about one to three inches wide. A smaller, triangle-shaped fontanel is found farther back on the head, where a beanie might be worn. Don't be alarmed if you see the fontanels bulge out when the infant cries or strains, or if they seem to move up and down in time with the baby's heartbeat—this is perfectly normal. The fontanels will eventually disappear as the skull bones close together—usually by about 6 months of age for the back and by about 12 to 18 months of age for the front fontanel.

KidsHealth Tip

Predicting Eye Color

If you're wondering what color eyes your child will have, here are the rules that generally apply: If a baby's eyes are brown at birth, they will remain so. This is the case for most African American and Asian infants. Most white infants are born with bluish-gray eyes. But the color may gradually darken until the permanent eye color is reached around age three or six months.

A newborn's head may look not only elongated but also lumpy as a result of the trauma of delivery. Caput succedaneum is a circular swelling and bruising of the scalp usually seen on top of the head toward the back (which is the part of the scalp most often leading the way through the birth canal). This will fade in a few days.

You might also see a cephalohematoma; this is a lump caused by blood collecting under a membrane that covers one of the skull bones. It's usually caused by the head's pressing against the mother's pelvic bones during birth. The lump is confined to one side of the top of the baby's head and, in contrast to caput, it may take a week or two to disappear. When the collected blood breaks down, these infants may become somewhat more jaundiced than others over the first week of life.

It is important to remember that both caput and cephalohematoma occur due to trauma outside the skull—neither indicates any injury to the infant's brain.

The Face

The appearance of a newborn's face can look quite puffy due to fluid accumulation and the battering it takes on the way out. In some cases, a newborn's facial features can also be distorted as a result of positioning in the uterus and the squeeze through the birth canal; when the baby moves quickly through the birth canal, the face may even get bruised. Not to worry, though—that bloated face, flattened nose, or crooked jaw usually comes back into place over time.

The Eyes

A few minutes after birth, when some of the commotion has subsided, most infants open their eyes and start to look around at their environment with a quiet intensity. Newborns have good vision, but they probably don't focus very well at first, which is why their eyes may often seem out of line or crossed during the first two to three months. (This is normal in a very young infant, but by age three months, crossed or drifting eyes should have corrected themselves. If they haven't, consult your child's doctor.) Because of the puffiness of their eyelids, some infants may not be able to open their eyes widely right away—to the disappointment of their adoring parents. But you can encourage eye opening by taking advantage of the "doll's-eye" reflex—babies tend to open their eyes more when held in an upright position.

Parents are sometimes startled to see that the white part of one or both of their newborn's eyes appears completely blood red. Called subconjunctival hemorrhage, this scary-looking condition occurs when a tiny bit of blood leaks from under the covering of the eyeball due to the trauma of delivery. It is a harmless condition similar to a skin bruise that goes away after several days. It generally doesn't indicate that there has been any damage to the infant's eyes.

The Ears

A newborn's ears may be distorted by the position he was in while in the uterus. Because the baby has not yet developed the thick cartilage that gives firm shape to an older child's ears, it is not unusual for newborns to emerge with temporarily folded or otherwise misshapen ears.

The Nose

Small amounts of fluid or mucus in a newborn's nose can cause her to breathe noisily or sound congested even though she doesn't have a cold or other problem. This happens because newborns tend to breathe through their noses, and their nasal passages are narrow. Talk with your baby's doctor about using saltwater nose drops and a bulb syringe to help clear the nasal passages if necessary. Sneezing is very common in newborns. This is a normal reflex and is not due to an infection, allergies, or other problems.

KidsHealth Tip

When Breathing Pauses

It is normal for young infants to breathe irregularly. It is common for them to occasionally stop breathing for about 5 to 10 seconds and then start up again on their own. These are known as apneic spells, and they are more likely to occur while an infant sleeps. If the pauses last longer than 10 to 15 seconds, tell your child's doctor right away.

The Mouth

When your newborn opens his mouth to yawn or cry, you may notice some small white spots on the roof of his mouth, usually near the center. These are small collections of cells called Epstein's pearls. These spots, as well as fluid-filled cysts, sometimes occur on the gums and will disappear over the first few weeks of life.

In some infants, the frenulum, the membrane that connects the tongue to the floor of the mouth, appears short. This may seem to limit the baby's ability to stick out his tongue. Concerns about being "tongue-tied," as it was called, were common in the past; both doctors and parents worried that a short frenulum would interfere with sucking or speaking. This is almost never the case, and the once-common surgical "clipping" of the frenulum is rarely performed today.

Occasionally, infants are born with one or more teeth already present in the mouth. An X-ray may be done to determine if the teeth are really "extra" ones or, as is more commonly the case, are regular baby teeth that have come through the gums early. Newborn teeth may need to be removed, particularly if they are loose and present a choking hazard to the baby.

The Chest

Both boys and girls usually are born with enlarged breasts. This happens because the female hormone estrogen is passed from the mother to the fetus during pregnancy. You may feel firm, disc-shaped lumps of tissue beneath the nipples, and, occasionally, a small amount of milky fluid (called "witch's milk" in folklore) may be released from the nipples. Almost always, the breast enlargement will disappear over the first few weeks of life. Despite what some parents think, you should not squeeze the breast tissue—this will not cause the breasts to shrink any faster.

Because an infant's chest wall is thin, you may easily feel or observe your infant's upper chest move with each heartbeat. This is normal and no cause for concern.

The Belly

It's normal for an infant's belly to appear somewhat full and rounded. When the baby cries or strains, the skin over the middle of the abdomen may protrude between the strips of muscle making up the abdominal wall on either side. This almost always stops happening over the next several months as the infant grows.

The umbilical cord stump and surrounding skin are usually blue because of an antibacterial dye used in most nurseries. (See Chapter 11, "Baby-Care Basics," for information about how to care for the umbilical cord stump.)

KidsHealth Tip

Sounds like a Baby

Although he won't be talking until later on, your newborn will produce a symphony of noises—grunts, moans, high-pitched squeaks—in addition to the obligatory crying. Sneezing and hiccups occur frequently and don't indicate infection, allergies, or digestive problems in newborns.

The Sexual Organs

The sexual organs, or genitalia, of both boys and girls may appear relatively large and swollen at birth. This is caused by hormones produced by the mother and fetus, bruising and swelling related to birth trauma, and the natural course of development.

In girls, the outer lips of the vagina (labia majora) often appear puffy. The skin of the labia may be either smooth or somewhat wrinkled. Sometimes, a small piece of glistening pink tissue may protrude between the labia—this is a hymenal tag and of no medical concern; it will eventually recede into the labia as the genitals grow. Most newborn girls will have a vaginal discharge consisting of mucus and sometimes some blood that will last a few days. This "miniperiod" is normal and represents menstrual-type bleeding from the infant's uterus that occurs as the estrogen passed to the infant by the mother begins to disappear. If you see swelling in the groin of an infant girl, it can indicate the presence of an inguinal (groin) hernia, although this condition is much more common in boys.

In boys, the scrotum (the sack containing the testicles) often appears swollen. This is usually due to a hydrocele, a collection of fluid that usually disappears over the first few months of life. The testicles of newborn boys may be difficult to feel because the scrotum is swollen and the muscles attached to the testicles pull them up into the groin briskly when the genital area is touched or exposed to a cool environment. Normal infant boys experience frequent penile erection, often just before they urinate. You should consult your child's doctor if you notice swelling or bulging in your son's scrotum or groin area that persists beyond three to six months or seems to come and go. This may indicate the presence of an inguinal hernia, which usually requires surgical treatment.

The end of an uncircumcised newborn's penis is usually completely covered by the foreskin. The foreskin remains attached to the tip of the penis in infancy, so you shouldn't attempt to pull it back to clean underneath. (By about the age of five years, the foreskin of nearly all uncircumcised boys will have become retractable. At this point the boy can be taught to slide the foreskin back and clean the tip of the penis.) The opening in the foreskin should be large enough to allow the infant to urinate with a forceful stream. Consult your baby's doctor if your son's urine dribbles out.

More than 95 percent of newborns will pass urine within the first 24 hours of life. If your baby is delivered in a hospital, nursery personnel will want to know if this occurs while the infant is with you. Many times, the first urination seems to be delayed, but the infant actually peed right after delivery and nobody noticed (remember, the baby's born soaking wet, so it's easy to miss a little urine).

Ten Things That Concern Parents About Their Newborn That Are Usually Nothing to Worry About

1. Elongated, pointed head
2. Curved legs and feet
3. Blue hands and feet
4. Enlarged breasts
5. Vaginal discharge or bleeding
6. Frequent sneezing
7. Frequent hiccups
8. Peeling skin
9. Trembling when crying
10. Crossed eyes (After two to three months, eyes should be straight most of the time. If they aren't, consult your child's doctor; see Chapter 15, "Hearing and Vision," for more information.)

Arms, Hands, Fingers, Knees, and Toes

The arms and legs of full-term newborns generally are all scrunched up—flexed and held close to the body—just as they were in the cramped uterus. The hands are usually tightly closed, and it may be difficult for you to open them. Touching or placing an object in their palms triggers a strong grasp reflex.

Immediately after birth, many parents perform a quick finger and toe count—and usually there are 10 of each. However, extra digits can form on the hands and feet. This occurs in about 10 percent of African American infants and less frequently in other racial/ethnic groups. Most often, the extra digits are little more than pieces of skin with partially formed nails that are dangling from a thin stalk attached to the side of the infant's normal pinkie finger or little toe. These are of no medical concern and tend to run in families. Your baby's doctor can usually remove them by simply tying a suture tightly around the thin stalks, which cuts off the blood supply to the extra digits. They will usually wither and drop off within a few days.

Don't be concerned about the curved appearance of your newborn's feet and legs. The usual position of the fetus in the womb during the final months of pregnancy keeps the hips flexed and knees bent, with the legs and feet crossed tightly up against the abdomen. It's no surprise that a newborn's legs and feet tend to curve

Suck, Grasp, Startle: The Newborn Reflexes

Infants are born with instinctual responses to stimuli, such as light or touch. These primitive reflexes, as they are called, gradually disappear as the baby matures. Primitive reflexes include these:

- The sucking reflex. The infant sucks on any object put in her mouth.
- The grasp reflex. The infant tightly closes her fingers when you touch the inside of her hand.
- The Moro reflex or startle response. The infant suddenly throws her arms out to her sides and then quickly brings them back toward the middle of her body whenever she has been startled by a loud noise, bright light, strong smell, or sudden movement.

KidsHealth Tip

Scratch Alert

Newborns' fingernails may be long and can scratch their skin as they bring their hands to their faces. If this is the case, you can carefully trim your baby's nails with a small scissors. If you can't do that at the moment, you can slip an infant sock over the baby's hand for temporary protection.

inward. These are not rigid deformities, however. Usually, you can easily move your newborn's legs and feet into a "walking" position, and this will happen naturally as your infant grows and begins to stand.

The Skin

There's little doubt about why we say that inexperienced people are "still wet behind the ears." It's because newborns are wet behind the ears—and every other body part, too. They emerge from their mother covered with various fluids, including amniotic fluid and often some blood (the mother's, not the baby's). Newborns are also coated with a thick, pasty, white material called vernix caseosa (made up of skin cells and secretions from the fetus), most of which will be washed off during the baby's first bath.

The color patterns of a newborn's skin may be startling to some parents. Mottling of the skin, a lacy pattern of small reddish and pale areas, is common because of the normal instability of the blood circulation at the skin's surface. For similar reasons, a newborn's hands and feet may be blue, especially in a cool setting; this is called acrocyanosis. When bearing down to cry or have a bowel movement, an infant may turn beet red or bluish-purple temporarily. Red marks, scratches, bruises, and petechiae (tiny specks of blood that have leaked from small blood vessels in the skin) are all common on the face and other body parts. They are caused by the trauma of squeezing through the birth canal or by the pressure from forceps used during the delivery. These will heal and disappear during the first week or two of life.

Fine, soft hair, called lanugo, may be present on a newborn's face, shoulders, and back, especially in premature babies. This hair will disappear over the first few weeks after birth.

The top layer of a newborn's skin will peel off during the first week or two. This is normal, and no special skin care is needed. The skin may be already peeling at birth, particularly in babies who are postterm—that is, born past their due date.

Birthmarks

Not all babies are born with birthmarks, but many are. Some are temporary; others are permanent:

- Pink or red areas, sometimes called salmon patches (see Figures 4.1a–b), are common. Most frequently found on the back of the neck or on the bridge of the nose, eyelids, or brow (hence the nicknames "stork bite" and "angel kiss"), they can occur anywhere on the skin and are especially noticeable in light-skinned infants. They generally disappear within the first year.

- Strawberry or capillary hemangiomas are raised red marks caused by collections of widened blood vessels in the skin. These birthmarks may appear pale at birth and then become red and enlarge over the first months of life. They usually shrink and disappear over the first few years without treatment.

- Port-wine stains, which are large, flat, reddish-purple birthmarks, will not disappear on their own. Although they are usually not associated with other medical problems, concerns about appearance (particularly if present on the face) may require the attention of a dermatologist as the child gets older.

- Café-au-lait spots, so called because of their "coffee with milk" light brown color, are common. These may deepen in color (or may first appear) as the child grows older. They are usually of no concern. If they are very large, however, or if a child has six or more spots measuring more than one-half inch, they may indicate the presence of other medical conditions.

- Flat patches of slate blue or blue-green color that resemble ink stains may occur on the back, buttocks, or elsewhere (see Figure 4.1d). They are found in more than half of African American, Native American, and Asian infants and less often in white babies. These spots are of no medical concern and almost always fade and disappear over the first few years of life.

- Common brown or black moles, known as pigmented nevi, may be present at birth or may appear or deepen in color as the child gets older. Larger moles

Figures 4.1a–d. Normal skin variations.

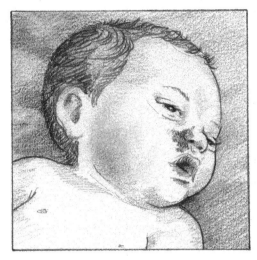

4.1a. Salmon patches commonly occur on the lower forehead (often called an "angel's kiss") and next to the nose. Most salmon patches disappear by one year of age.

4.1b. If a salmon patch appears on the back of the baby's neck, it is often referred to as a "stork bite."

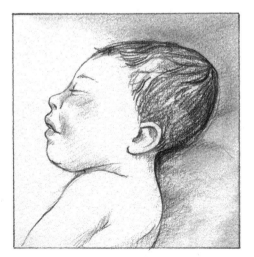

4.1c. A newborn's head often assumes an elongated shape from squeezing through the birth canal. The baby's head returns to a normal, rounded shape within a few days.

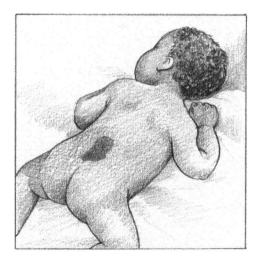

4.1d. It's common for newborns to have patches of blue or blue-gray pigmentation on their lower back, as well as elsewhere on their skin. These usually fade with time.

Pick Your Baby's Term

- Full term: a baby who is born within the period of two weeks before and two weeks after the "due date" in a 40-week pregnancy
- Preterm: a baby who is born at or before week 37 of the pregnancy
- Postterm: a baby who is born at or after week 42 of the pregnancy

or those with an unusual appearance should be brought to your child's doctor's attention because they may require removal.

For more information about birthmarks and moles, see Chapter 32, "Health Problems in Early Childhood."

Skin Rashes

Several harmless rashes may be present at birth or appear during the first days and weeks of an infant's life.

- Milia are tiny, flat, yellow or white spots on the nose and chin. They are caused by the collection of secretions in skin glands. These will disappear over the first few weeks.
- Miliaria are small, raised, red bumps that often have a white or yellow "head"; they are sometimes called infant acne because of their appearance. Although this harmless condition often occurs on the face and large areas of the body, it will go away over the first several weeks of life with normal skin care.
- Erythema toxicum, despite the frightening sound of its name, is also a harmless newborn rash. It consists of red blotches with pale or yellowish bumps at the center, which give the rash a hivelike appearance. It usually blossoms during the first day or two of life and disappears within a week.
- Pustular melanosis is marked by dark brown bumps or blisters scattered over the neck, back, arms, legs, and palms that disappear without treatment. This rash is present at birth mainly in African American infants.
- Sucking blisters may be present on a newborn's fingers, hands, or arms. These occur because the fetus can suck while still in the uterus.

Jaundice

Jaundice is the yellowish discoloration of the skin and white parts of the eyes that occurs in about 60 percent of newborns. It normally doesn't appear until the second or third day of life and disappears within one to two weeks. (See Chapter 5, "Common Newborn Medical Conditions," for more information.)

Need More Information?

Check the Index and Appendix C, "Resource Guide." And of course, consult your child's doctor.

chapter five

Common Newborn Medical Conditions

What they are—and how they're handled

Aside from looking battered and blotchy from the strenuous journey of birth, many newborns have medical conditions that require monitoring and perhaps treatment. The medical terms may sound unnerving, but conditions such as jaundice and thrush are quite common and usually easily managed. In most cases, these are nothing to worry about—your baby will be just fine in no time!

But just the same, if you're like most new parents, you'd probably like to at least be informed about the most common newborn conditions. So here's a quick overview to get you up to speed.

Jaundice

Jaundice means yellowing of the skin and whites of the eyes. It's seen in about 60 percent of full-term babies and 80 percent of premature infants and usually goes away by itself without doing any harm. It typically starts in the face and can move to the torso and limbs as it gets more pronounced.

Jaundice is caused by a buildup in the blood of bilirubin, a substance produced by the normal breakdown of red blood cells. Usually bilirubin passes through the liver and is excreted through the intestines in bowel movements. But sometimes it builds up faster than a newborn can pass it from her body. In most cases, the baby's liver simply is not mature enough to do the job fast enough. In other cases, more bilirubin than normal is being made or too much of it is being reabsorbed from the intestines before the baby gets rid of it in her stool.

How high is too high for a bilirubin level in a newborn? The answer depends on several factors, primarily the baby's size, degree of maturity, and medical condition. A level considered safe in a healthy full-term infant might be risky in a premature or ill baby. If your baby's doctor thinks that the bilirubin level is approaching a number that may put your child at risk, he or she will discuss treatment options with you.

Treatment with phototherapy begins before potentially dangerous levels are reached. The baby is placed unclothed under blue or broad-spectrum white light until bilirubin levels fall. The light alters the bilirubin so that it is more rapidly disposed of by the baby's body. If significant jaundice is noticed while the baby is still in the hospital, she may be treated there. If the baby is already home when it emerges, she may be treated at home with a portable light unit, or she may need to return to the hospital.

In rare cases, the baby may need an exchange transfusion in which her blood is exchanged for donor blood.

These are the most common kinds of newborn jaundice:

Physiologic (Normal) Jaundice

Seen in most newborns, this jaundice occurs because of the immaturity of the baby's liver. It generally appears when the baby is between two and four days old and disappears when she is between one and two weeks of age.

Breast-Feeding Jaundice

In 10 to 15 percent of breast-fed babies, physiologic jaundice is intensified because they get less milk than formula-fed babies do in the first week. This usually can be addressed by more frequent nursing or by improving breast-feeding technique; it is rarely a reason to stop breast-feeding.

Breast Milk Jaundice

This rarer condition, seen in 1 to 2 percent of breast-fed babies, usually starts later, after the first week of life, and lasts 3 to 10 weeks. Its cause is not clear, but it appears that the breast milk contains a substance that prevents these babies from excreting bilirubin as rapidly. If bilirubin levels get worrisome, feeding the baby formula instead of breast milk for one or two days usually causes a speedy drop. Then breast-feeding can be safely resumed.

Blood Group Incompatibility Jaundice

If a baby and mother have different blood types, the mother may produce antibodies that destroy some of the infant's red blood cells. This can create a buildup of bilirubin in the baby's blood, as well as anemia. Incompatibility jaundice usually begins during the first day of life and can rapidly become severe. One form of incompatibility—between an Rh-negative mother and an Rh-positive baby—can cause particularly severe jaundice, but jaundice due to Rh incompatibility is generally preventable and has become uncommon.

When to Call Your Child's Doctor About Jaundice

Call your child's doctor immediately if any of these conditions occur:

- Jaundice is noted during the first 24 hours of life.
- The jaundice involves your baby's arms or legs (rather than just the face and trunk).
- Your baby develops a fever higher than 100.4 degrees Fahrenheit (rectal temperature).
- Your baby is very lethargic, isn't feeding well, or otherwise looks or acts sick.
- The yellow color of your baby's skin deepens after day seven.
- The jaundice is not gone by day ten.
- Your baby has no wet diapers for more than six hours.
- You are concerned about the amount of jaundice.

KidsHealth Tip

Jaundice Tip

Frequent feedings of breast milk or formula help prevent bilirubin levels from rising in the blood.

Umbilical Hernia

Umbilical (or navel) hernias are common in newborns, particularly in African American infants. They occur because a circular hole exists in the wall of the abdomen at the site of the umbilical cord (the future navel). The size of the hole is usually between the width of a dime and the width of a quarter (or sometimes larger). The baby's intestine protrudes through the hole when she cries or strains, causing the overlying skin to bulge outward.

These hernias are generally harmless and not painful to the infant. The large majority of them close on their own and disappear over the first few years of life. Simple surgery can fix the hernia if it doesn't close on its own. Home remedies for umbilical hernias that have been tried through the years (such as strapping and taping coins over the area) should not be attempted. These techniques are ineffective and may result in skin infections or other injuries.

Thrush

Thrush is an infection of the mouth with a yeastlike fungus called *Candida*. It causes cracks in the corners of the mouth and what looks like white or yellowish curds of milk on the lips, tongue, palate, and inside of the cheeks. If you brush the patches away, you may see pinpoints of blood. The mouth rash may be the only symptom, or your baby may seem fussy and eat less than usual. Thrush occurs in 2 to 5 percent of normal newborns, developing as early as 7 to 10 days after birth. Mild cases may need no treatment. For others, the child's doctor may prescribe an antifungal drug.

Candida is found in the gastrointestinal and vaginal tracts of many healthy adults, and babies pick it up in the vaginal canal during birth. In healthy people, it is usually kept in check by other microbes and by the immune system, so no illness results. But even healthy newborns often get thrush, and it may occur later if they have been treated with antibiotics, which can upset the balance of microbes in their bodies. If thrush persists or keeps coming back, your baby should be checked by your child's doctor to make sure he has no other health problem that is making him susceptible.

Candida can cause other conditions besides thrush. In healthy newborns, the most common form of candidiasis (candida infection) is a diaper rash. Skin in the diaper area becomes red and tender, especially inside skin folds and creases. Small circular, red, scaly patches are commonly seen on the skin surrounding the main rash. It can be treated with an antifungal ointment applied to the skin.

Candida infections can be very serious in premature infants and in children with cancer, HIV infection, or any weakness of the immune system. In these children, candida infection may spread through the blood to attack the lungs and other organs. This is called systemic candidiasis. (For more information, see Chapter 30, "Childhood Infections.")

Other Common Conditions in Newborns and Young Infants

Infants in the first few months of life may develop other conditions you've probably heard of, including these:

- Gastroesophageal reflux disease (GERD)—excessive spitting up (also commonly referred to as "reflux")
- Apnea—pauses in an infant's breathing
- Colic—excessive crying and fussiness
- Eczema—a skin condition that may be allergy related
- Inguinal (groin) hernia—part of the intestine pushing through an opening or weak area in the wall of the abdomen
- Undescended testicle—one or both testicles fail to drop into the scrotum during development

For more detailed information about these conditions, see Chapter 29, "Signs and Symptoms," and Chapter 32, "Health Problems in Early Childhood."

Need More Information?

Check the Index and Appendix C, "Resource Guide." And of course, consult your child's doctor.

chapter six

Premature Babies

Special care for small packages

When a woman unexpectedly goes into premature labor, she and her partner are usually completely unprepared for this change in plans. They have a baby who just can't wait to be born, but no one is ready just yet for his arrival! It can be a scary time, one full of unanswered questions and uncertain outcomes.

Fortunately, the prognosis for babies born after 28 weeks in the uterus has improved dramatically in just the past few years. New procedures, equipment, and medications and a wealth of research and knowledge have all combined to give these babies an excellent survival rate and outlook. This chapter will give you an overview of the special care that you can expect will be given to your premature baby to promote his health and continued growth.

Who Is the Premature Baby?

A full-term pregnancy is 40 weeks long—sort of. The standard method counts a pregnancy as beginning on the first day of the mother's last menstrual period, although most often the baby is not conceived until at least two weeks later. So when a baby is born at full term at 40 weeks, he has probably really been in existence for only 38 weeks. What this means is that when your doctor counts your baby's age to determine the degree of prematurity, he or she may give you a number that does not coincide with your own calculations based on the date of conception.

Based on this method of age determination, a premature birth is one that occurs between weeks 20 and 37 (the possibility of infant survival really begins at 23 weeks). Babies born within this period are called preterm and may need the help of the special care nursery (SCN) staff to support and protect them while they continue to grow and mature.

SGA Babies

A small-for-gestational-age (SGA) baby weighs less than expected for the number of weeks that have passed since he was conceived. This newborn may be a full-term baby who is very small at birth or a premature baby who is smaller than he should be for the time he has spent in the womb. An SGA baby, like a premature baby, may require special attention after birth.

Degrees of Prematurity

Premature babies' expected size, weight, special needs, and survival rate vary depending on how early they were born. (The following survival statistics exclude babies born with birth defects that are not directly related to prematurity.)

An infant born between 35 and 37 weeks' gestation is considered borderline premature. She looks like and may even weigh as much as a baby born at term. Most often these babies weigh between three pounds twelve ounces and seven pounds eight ounces, and on average they are 17 to 18 inches long. The survival rate for these babies is 98 to 100 percent.

Infants born between 30 and 34 weeks' gestation usually weigh between about two pounds three ounces and five pounds eight ounces, and on the average they are 14 to 18½ inches long. Their survival rate is greater than 98 percent.

The further from term your baby is born, the more immature his physical development will be. The more immature your infant is, the more difficulty he may have breathing, eating, and regulating his body temperature. Your baby has a lot of growing to do before his physical appearance (and internal organs) can be compared to that of a full-term baby. Don't let that bother you; your baby looks exactly as he should for his gestational age, and that makes him beautiful. (Gestational age is the number of completed weeks of pregnancy at the time of birth.)

An infant born at 26 to 29 weeks' gestational age (14 to 11 weeks early) is very premature. Most often these babies weigh between one pound eight ounces and three pounds eight ounces, and on average they are 12 to 17 inches long. Their survival rate varies: Those born closer to 26 weeks and who weigh about two pounds have a 90 to 95 percent chance of survival. Those born at 28 to 29 weeks have a 98-plus percent chance of survival.

Infants born at less than 26 weeks' gestational age (more than 14 weeks early) are extremely premature. Most often these babies weigh less than one pound 10½ ounces, and on the average they are less than 12 inches long. Fewer than 5 percent of premature infants fall into this category, and their survival rate varies: Those born closer to 26 weeks and who weigh about one pound 10½ ounces have as much as a 50 percent chance of survival. Those born much before 25 weeks have a much lower chance of survival. The health risks are great, and the babies require intensive medical support.

Why Are Babies Born Prematurely?

In most cases the reason for premature delivery remains unknown. It is known that premature delivery is more likely to occur in these situations:

- There is a multiple pregnancy—twins, triplets, etc.
- There are structural abnormalities of the cervix or uterus.
- There is abnormal bleeding from the placenta that is covering the cervix (placental previa), or the placenta separates early from the uterine wall (placental abruption).
- The mother has pregnancy-induced hypertension (PIH), intrauterine infection, or a chronic illness like diabetes, heart disease, or hypertension.
- The mother is younger than 20 years or older than 40 years.

Overwork, smoking, heavy drinking, drug use, poor nutrition, and inadequate weight gain may also have an influence, but remember that many women deliver at term with one or more of these factors. It's different for every mother-to-be.

In some cases, through an ultrasound examination or other screening test, it may be determined that a baby is not growing adequately or that the baby has a medical condition that makes early delivery advisable. In many cases, however, premature delivery occurs in pregnancies where women have been in good health and have taken good care of themselves. The premature birth of their baby comes as a complete surprise.

Special Care During Pregnancy

If your pregnancy is complicated by any condition associated with premature delivery, your obstetrician may have you see a perinatologist (a doctor who specializes in the complications of high-risk pregnancy) and a neonatologist (a doctor who specializes in the care of newborns with special needs). The perinatologist, along with your obstetrician, will follow your progress through your pregnancy, seeing you periodically while performing necessary tests and procedures. The neonatologist can provide you with information about caring for an infant born prematurely. In addition, if you are at risk for a premature delivery, you should arrange to have your baby in a hospital that can provide you and your baby with immediate and intensive care. Infants born very early may need the specialized care and support provided only by the intensive care nurseries of selected hospitals.

You're in Premature Labor. Now What?

Delivery may be the best option, especially if labor has progressed rapidly or if you have complications like high blood pressure, infection, or bleeding.

If it seems appropriate to stop the labor, you may be placed on bed rest and given fluids to determine if rest and hydration will ease your labor. If labor persists, your doctor may try using medication to suppress further progress. In preparation for the possibility of an early delivery, your obstetrician may give you a steroid medication such as betamethasone (Celestone) to speed up your baby's lung development and thus improve her chances of survival. (This is most effective if it is given more than 24 hours before delivery.) But despite the best medical care, premature labor cannot always be stopped.

Preparing for Early Delivery

While you are in early labor, your obstetrician may ask a member of the special care nursery (SCN) team to speak to you about the care your baby may need if delivered early. This person can give all the information that's available at that time:

- Of course, you will want to know the chances for your baby's survival—but before delivery, this is difficult to determine. Many factors must be considered. The most important of these are the baby's gestational age and weight, the severity of breathing problems, the presence or absence of diseases and infection, and the presence of birth defects.

- You will also want to know what the chances are that your baby will have a disability or handicap. Common minor disabilities associated with prematurity include short attention span, learning problems in school, and poor coordination. Significant handicaps include mental retardation, inability to walk without assistance, blindness, and deafness. Full-term infants can also be born with these problems, but the likelihood and severity of disabilities and birth defects increases the further from full term the child is born. For any infant it is impossible to predict ahead of time the likelihood of a significant handicap. However, some factors increase the risk of these handicaps. Infants born extremely premature, especially at 22 to 24 weeks' gestation, infants who are very sick at birth and remain sick for several weeks, and infants with brain abnormalities occurring before birth or as a complication of their prematurity are at risk for significant handicap.

- You will want to ask questions concerning the early delivery such as: Who will care for your baby in the delivery room? Does the hospital have a nursery and the medical staff to care for an infant born prematurely, or will your baby need to be transferred to another hospital? What are some of the common procedures performed in the SCN? You'll feel more comfortable having answers to questions like these.

Special Care for Your Special Delivery

Many professionals work together to care for infants who are born prematurely. Infants requiring special care after delivery are placed in the SCN, also called the neonatal intensive care unit (NICU) or intensive care nursery (ICN). A neonatologist will care for

The Voice of Experience

"I loved the NICU nurses. Both our boys spent their first week in the hospital, and the nurses were so caring and understanding of all the emotions my husband and I were going through. Also, the care our boys received was outstanding. They both came home 'early!'"

—FROM THE KIDSHEALTH PARENT SURVEY

your newborn in the ICN. This is the person with whom you can discuss the specific plan of care for your baby based on his circumstances.

The neonatologist works closely with other medical staff to ensure the best care for your baby. In fact, many different professionals may help care for your baby in the ICN, including the following:

- The neonatal fellow is a pediatrician in training to be a neonatologist.
- The pediatric residents are doctors training to be pediatricians.
- Physician assistants and neonatal nurse-practitioners have received additional training in newborn intensive care and perform many of the same tasks as doctors in the ICN.
- The primary nurse does most of the hands-on care for your baby, develops your baby's nursing care plan, and teaches you to care for your baby.
- The social worker will help you with nonmedical issues such as insurance, transportation, and so on. The social worker also provides emotional support and counseling.
- The respiratory therapist has special training in the care and management of the oxygen, breathing machines, breathing treatments, and so on.
- The occupational therapist, physical therapist, and speech and language therapist in the ICN have special training in infant development and can teach you about supporting your baby's growth and development.

If your baby has a particular problem, another physician specialist may be called in, such as a cardiologist for heart problems, a neurologist for brain and nervous system problems, and an ophthalmologist for eye problems. (For more information about specialists you may encounter, see Chapter 27, "The Health Care System for Children.")

KidsHealth Tip

Keeping Track

Often, there are many health care providers involved in the care of a premature baby. You may find it helpful to write down the names of the people with whom you will interact the most.

Neonatal Transport Team

When a premature birth is expected, delivery arrangements are made in advance at a hospital that has an intensive care nursery. But when the early arrival is a surprise and occurs in a hospital that is not equipped to care for infants born prematurely, your baby should be transported immediately to a larger facility that can best handle his special needs.

The neonatal transport team from the referral center, along with a physician or nurse-practitioner, nurse, and respiratory therapist, will transport your infant by helicopter, airplane, or ambulance to the designated regional center. In most cases, you will be able to visit and touch your baby before he is transferred, and you will meet and talk with the medical staff from the referral center who will be caring for your baby during the transport. They will give you information about the referral center and provide you with directions and phone numbers to keep you in touch with the staff caring for your baby. If possible, the nursery nurse will take some pictures of your baby before he is transferred. The baby's father or other family members cannot accompany the infant to the referral center, but they can follow behind and be close by throughout the medical evaluations and treatments.

> ### The Voice of Experience
>
> *"When my five-year-old son was born six weeks early at a small country hospital and had to be MedEvaced to an NICU unit, we were scared to death. But the staff and doctors were very supportive and encouraging. His initial promised three-week stay lasted only eight days. And he has been going strong ever since."*
>
> —FROM THE KIDSHEALTH PARENT SURVEY

Of course, it is difficult to stay behind while your newborn is moved to another hospital. But you will find that the support of the staff and your family will help you cope during this difficult time.

Getting to Know Your Premature Infant

When you visit your baby in the SCN, you will find her surrounded by all the medical technology needed to keep her alive and thriving. She will be sleeping on a special bed that keeps her warm. She will be "wired" to a cardiorespiratory monitor or heart monitor that shows her heart rate, heartbeat pattern, breathing rate, and breathing pattern. A coated wire on your baby's skin measures her temperature and is connected to the overhead warmer or isolette to regulate how much heat is provided for your baby. You may see a tiny light attached to your baby's palm, foot, finger, toe, or wrist by a piece of adhesive elastic. A cord travels from the light to a machine called the pulse oximeter, which continuously measures your baby's blood oxygen. She may have a small catheter placed into one of the veins in her hand, foot, or scalp that is attached by tubing to a container of fluid. This is called an intravenous infusion (IV). The IV is used to deliver fluids, medications, and nutrients to the baby. Your baby may also have an umbilical venous catheter (UVC) or an umbilical artery catheter (UAC), which is a small piece of tubing threaded into your baby's artery or vein in the umbilical stump. In addition to delivering fluids, medications, and nutrients, the catheter allows blood to be withdrawn painlessly for laboratory testing. The doctors and nurses caring for your baby will carefully explain all these bells and whistles. Although at first they appear alarming, you'll soon find them comforting, knowing they are keeping track of every breath your baby takes.

Your premature baby's appearance may shock or surprise you. But try to remember that you are not looking at a full-term infant; you are looking at an infant born early who is continuing to grow and develop outside the womb. Your baby will look just as she would if she had not been born yet. Your premature infant's head looks large in comparison to her body. She has thin skin, which appears wrinkled and has a red-purplish tinge. She may appear "skinny" because she has not yet developed insulating layers of fat. And a fine hair called lanugo covers your baby's back and the sides of her face.

In an extremely premature infant, the skin has a gelatin-like transparency that makes the surface arteries and veins clearly visible. Her ears will not spring back if folded down because they haven't developed enough firm cartilage yet. Her chest may look small, and the ribs stand out. She has neither breast nipples nor breast tissue under the skin. The areola (the dark circle of skin around the nipple) is just visible. The newborn has just the beginning buds of finger- and toenails and has few if any creases on the soles of her feet.

Even in the extremely premature infant, the male and female genitalia are clearly differentiated. The male's testes may not be descended into the scrotum, which will appear smaller and smoother than in an older baby. The female's clitoris will appear prominent because the outer folds of protective skin have not yet fully developed. The baby has very little muscle tone, which makes it difficult for her to pull her arms and legs in close to her body in the common fetal position. The immature nervous system makes the baby's movements jerky.

Although the premature baby's appearance may be surprising at first, most parents marvel that their baby, even their extremely premature baby, has arms, legs, genitals, fingers, toes! The baby opens her eyes, blinks at a bright light, and is startled by a loud noise. The baby stretches and yawns, sneezes, and hiccups. She can cry and even make efforts to suck. The early beginning of a premature life is truly a miraculous event.

Overwhelming Emotions for Parents

Having a premature baby is one of the most stressful experiences a parent can have. If you deliver prematurely, you may be in shock initially, completely occupied by the problems surrounding your baby's early delivery. It may be difficult for you to think clearly and remember what has been said. You may need to hear the same information repeated several times. You may experience feelings of denial, not wanting to believe the whole event is occurring. You may wish you could just wake up from this bad dream. You may feel angry that your baby is sick and feel sad that you did not deliver the full-term baby you had planned for and dreamed about.

It's common for families to experience symptoms of anxiety and depression during this time. Some parents turn to their extended family, friends, and clergy or seek professional help. The doctors, nurses, and social workers in the newborn special care unit can be wonderful sources of support as well. Many units have parent support groups comprised of parents who have already experienced what you are going through. Advice from a veteran parent can be comforting. The doctor you have chosen to care for your baby after discharge can also be a source of support to you while your baby is in the special care nursery. You should not be shy about seeking out professional help to deal with anxiety and depression.

What Can You Do for Your Premature Infant?

Along with all the care your baby will receive from professionals, there are things only you can give your baby to help him thrive.

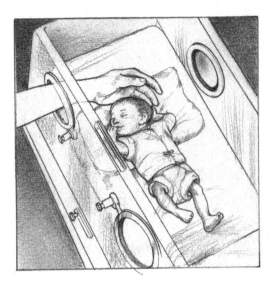

Figure 6.1. Premature baby in isolette. Even when premature infants need to be in an incubator or other controlled environment for a time, they can greatly benefit from the gentle and soothing touch of their parents. Regular contact calms the baby and helps him thrive.

Breast-Feeding

There are many advantages to breast-feeding your premature infant. In addition to all the advantages breast milk can give any baby (see Chapter 8, "Breast or Bottle," and Chapter 9, "Breast-Feeding," for more details), it contains higher amounts of certain nutrients that premature infants need. The early breast milk, called colostrum, is especially rich in antibodies and cells that help fight infection. Mother's milk is better tolerated by the premature baby and may reduce the risk for necrotizing enterocolitis, a serious disorder of the immature bowel. Even small amounts of mother's milk in the early days or weeks after birth can provide premature babies with health benefits. So if you are uncertain about breast-feeding, you may want to consider providing breast milk for your infant for just a few weeks or while he is in the hospital.

In the beginning, breast-feeding your premature infant will take patience, time, and some equipment. Many premature babies are not able to feed at the breast for many days or weeks after delivery. When this is the case, you can express or pump milk from your breast that can be collected, stored, and given to your baby through a small tube that is threaded through his nose or mouth into the stomach. You should begin expressing, or removing, milk from your breasts as soon as possible after your baby's birth and continue to do so at regular intervals in order to establish your milk supply. As your baby matures, he will gradually develop the skills he needs to feed at the breast.

Skin-to-Skin Care

Whether you breast-feed or bottle-feed, you and your baby will benefit from skin-to-skin contact. Skin-to-skin contact, also termed "kangaroo care," is a special way of holding your baby. The baby, dressed only in a diaper, is placed between the mother's breasts or in the center of the father's chest, with skin-to-skin contact. The baby's head is turned to the side so that the baby's ear is against the parent's heart. Ventilator tubing and wires are taped to the parent's clothing, and blankets are placed over the baby and parent's chest for warmth. While the nurse monitors your baby's heart and respiratory rate and temperature, you can sit in a rocker or recliner next to your baby's bedside and enjoy this special close time with your baby.

In addition to the way skin-to-skin holding can make you feel emotionally, there are many other benefits that occur even if it happens for only a few minutes each day. The baby's temperature, heartbeat, and breathing tend to stabilize. Babies gain more weight, feed better, sleep longer, and cry less as a result of this type of holding. Also, breast-feeding mothers who provide kangaroo care are more likely to produce adequate amounts of milk.

Developmental Care

Your participation in your infant's developmental care program will greatly influence her physical and mental development. Developmental care is a process in which caregivers, including parents, learn to interpret the infant's subtle responses, or cues, so they can identify her likes and dislikes as well as appreciate her individual needs.

Each premature infant is a unique individual with a distinct personality. Your premature baby will have his own well-defined responses to his environment and to the care he receives. These responses are grouped into "stable cues" and "stress cues." Stable cues, such as relaxed posture, smooth movements, and focused attention, can indicate a baby likes what is happening or is ready for interaction. Stress cues, such as hiccups, twitches, and irritability, can identify dislikes or discomfort. Stress cues often signal the need for a break from the current activity. Developmental care has been shown to decrease the length of time the babies stay in the hospital, decrease complications and interventions, and improve long-term developmental abilities.

While your baby is in the hospital and most vulnerable, you will want to keep light and noise levels moderate. Helping your baby to get into a flexed position with blanket rolls or other commercially available products will help him be more comfortable and encourage appropriate motor development. Providing undisturbed periods of sleep will give your baby the rest he needs to heal and grow. As your infant matures and becomes more stable physically, you will want to provide opportunities for interaction when he is awake.

Common Medical Problems and Procedures

Your premature baby's medical care is individualized to meet his special needs. The professionals involved in your baby's care will give you in-depth explanations of his medical needs and all necessary procedures and treatments. However, babies born prematurely do experience some common medical problems and require certain procedures that you should be familiar with. It's helpful if when health care providers start talking, you have some knowledge of what they're talking about.

Body Temperature Control

Premature babies do not have adequate layers of insulating tissue and fat to allow them to maintain their body temperature. Your premature infant needs an artificial heat source, like an open bed with an overhead heater or an isolette, to help her stay warm. Your baby's temperature and the temperature around your baby are constantly monitored to ensure proper heat control. As your baby grows and matures, she will be able to maintain her temperature in an open crib or bassinet bundled in blankets.

Breathing Problems

Some infants born prematurely are able to breathe without any respiratory assistance, but most often, the lungs are not mature enough to work effectively on their own. This immaturity can cause a number of medical problems that require special medical care.

Respiratory Distress Syndrome
Respiratory distress syndrome (RDS) is the most common lung disease of premature infants. This respiratory condition occurs in preterm babies because of immature lung development. The more premature he is, the more likely your baby is to

have this problem, caused by having an inadequate amount of surfactant in the lungs. Surfactant is a soaplike substance produced by the lungs that spreads like a film over the tiny air sacs, allowing them to stay open.

A baby with RDS may need extra oxygen or the administration of oxygen under pressure called continuous positive airway pressure (CPAP), which helps keep the air sacs open. If the surfactant deficiency is more severe, your baby may need to have a breathing tube (endotracheal tube, or ETT) inserted into his windpipe (trachea), and he may be placed on a breathing machine (respirator or ventilator). Your baby may be given an artificial surfactant, which is a medication instilled right into the lungs by way of the breathing tube. If your baby is extremely premature or if your baby has more severe disease, the recovery can be slow.

When RDS has been severe or there have been other complications, your baby may have injury and scarring of the lungs called bronchopulmonary dysplasia (BPD). BPD is a reaction of the premature lung to its disease and to the oxygen and mechanical ventilation that were needed to treat the infant's lung disease. A baby with BPD needs extra oxygen and medications for the lungs for a few weeks or months, occasionally for up to a year.

Apnea of Prematurity

Apnea is a respiratory condition in which there are periodic pauses in breathing that may be accompanied by bradycardia (slowing of the heart rate) or changes in your baby's color, causing him to appear pale, purplish, or blue. Premature babies have immature respiratory control centers in the brain. They normally have irregular breathing patterns—bursts of big breaths followed by shallow breathing or pauses. Apnea of prematurity may be treated with medications such as caffeine, theophylline, and aminophylline. Some babies may need oxygen delivered under pressure—CPAP—through little tubes placed in the nose. Others may be placed on a ventilator. Apnea of prematurity generally goes away as your infant grows and matures.

Hypoglycemia

Hypoglycemia, or low blood sugar, is common in premature infants. They may not have had enough time in the womb to store up the glucose (sugar) they need to do the work of newborns—breathing, crying, and waving their arms and legs. Your baby's blood sugar is monitored closely in the hours following delivery. An intravenous infusion of sugar water will give your baby the sugar she needs for energy.

Feeding and Nutrition Challenges

A few days after delivery, premature infants are given a special fluid called hyper-alimentation solution through an IV or umbilical catheter, which will provide fat and protein, along with vitamins and minerals in addition to sugar. Then, when your premature baby is strong enough, feedings of pumped breast milk or formula may be started. Depending on gestational age, your premature infant may not yet be able to coordinate sucking, swallowing, and breathing. Therefore, the initial feedings may need to be given through a feeding tube placed in your baby's mouth or nose and threaded down to the stomach. The feeding may be given as a slow constant drip, called a continuous feed, or a small amount may be given every few hours, called gavage or bolus feeding. Either way, the feedings are slowly increased as the intravenous infusion is decreased.

During tube feedings, your baby may be offered a pacifier or the breast that is empty of milk to encourage and satisfy the infant's desire to suck. You may be concerned about your baby using a pacifier because you've heard that in full-term infants the use of pacifiers in the first few weeks of life may lead to breast-feeding difficulties. In the premature baby, however, nonnutritive sucking (sucking without taking milk) is calming to the infant, helps digestion, and improves weight gain.

Gradually, as your baby recovers and matures, he will learn to breast-feed or bottle-feed. Around 34 weeks' gestation, most infants' suck-swallow-breathing pattern becomes coordinated enough to begin breast- or bottle-feeds. (Some infants will be ready at 32 weeks, although others may not be ready until 36 weeks' gestation.) At first your baby will be offered breast- or bottle-feeding just once a day. The number of breast- or bottle-feedings per day will be gradually increased as your baby becomes more skilled. Coordinating this feeding by mouth is one of the most difficult skills a growing premature infant must learn before he can be discharged from the hospital.

Jaundice

Jaundice is the yellow skin color that is commonly seen in the first few days after birth in both premature and full-term babies. It is usually managed with light treatment called phototherapy, which is explained in Chapter 5, "Common Newborn Medical Conditions."

Infection

Premature babies are at risk for infection because they have an immature immune system. Often your baby's doctor will obtain samples of blood, urine, and spinal fluid for analysis to help detect infection in your infant. If an infection is found, it will be treated with medication. Common infections in premature babies include these:

- Generalized infection or infection of the bloodstream (called sepsis)
- Pneumonia, which is an infection in the lungs
- Meningitis, which is an infection of the fluid that surrounds the brain
- Urinary tract infection (UTI)
- Infections of the skin or infections under the skin (called abscesses)

Infections are among the most serious threats to a premature baby's health and long-term well-being.

Anemia

Anemia is an abnormally low concentration of red blood cells—the cells that carry oxygen to all the tissues of the body. Most premature infants experience some degree of anemia for one reason or another. Your premature baby with anemia may show signs of poor feeding, poor weight gain, and an increased heart rate as he tries to compensate for the lack of oxygen reaching the tissues. The condition is treated with transfusions of red blood cells.

Patent Ductus Arteriosus

The ductus arteriosus is a blood vessel connecting the main artery leading to the lungs (pulmonary artery) with the main artery carrying blood to the body (aorta). Normally the ductus narrows and closes in the first few hours or days after birth. In the premature infant, however (especially those with respiratory distress syndrome), the ductus stays open and the baby's lungs get too much blood, making breathing more difficult.

If the ductus is small, your baby's doctor may wait to see if it closes on its own. While the ductus is open the doctor might decrease the amount of fluid the baby is receiving and administer a medication, called a diuretic, to decrease the fluid in the lungs. To treat the patent ductus arteriosus (PDA), the doctor may use a medication that causes the ductus to narrow so less blood flow can go through it. If the ductus does not close with medication, the PDA may be tied off (ligated) surgically through an incision in your baby's chest.

Necrotizing Enterocolitis

Necrotizing enterocolitis (NEC) is a serious bowel disorder that can result in the destruction of part of the intestine. The bowel in premature infants is sensitive to changes in blood flow that can alter the normal activity of bacteria in the bowel. This can lead to infection in the wall of the intestine, which causes irritation, swelling, and destruction of the bowel.

Why any one baby develops NEC is not clear. NEC occurs more often in the very premature infant and the baby who has been very sick since delivery. Babies who receive breast-milk feedings are less likely to develop NEC.

Because NEC is life-threatening, premature infants are monitored closely for the condition. If your baby's doctor thinks your baby is developing NEC, his feedings will be stopped, and fluids will be given through a small plastic catheter placed in a vein. A tube will be placed into the stomach from the nose or mouth to drain air and fluid from your baby's stomach and intestines. Your baby will be started on antibiotics and will be monitored closely with blood tests and frequent X-rays of the intestines.

Some babies will require surgery to remove the diseased portion of bowel. The end of the bowel above the portion removed will be brought to the surface of the skin, through an opening called an ostomy. The baby will pass stool into a bag on the abdomen. When the baby recovers and grows, the healthy ends of the bowel can be rejoined.

Most babies who recover from NEC do not have additional problems. Some babies can have scarring and narrowing of the bowel causing a blockage of the bowel. When a large portion of the bowel is removed, the remaining bowel may not be sufficient to absorb all needed nutrients for optimal growth.

Retinopathy of Prematurity

Retinopathy of prematurity (ROP) is an abnormal growth of blood vessels in a baby's eye. In normal development, blood vessels arise in the back of the eye and grow around in all directions toward the front of the eye. This process is completed a few weeks before delivery at term. In premature infants the process can go off course and the vessels grow and branch abnormally. The smallest and sickest premature infants are at the greatest risk of developing ROP. Premature infants at risk for ROP will have an eye exam by an ophthalmologist (an eye doctor) around four to six weeks of age with regular follow-up every one to two weeks until the eye vessels have completely grown to the edges of the retina.

The ophthalmologist will examine your baby's eyes for orderly growth of the blood vessels. Babies with stages I and II ROP do not usually need any treatment, and the abnormal growth corrects itself. Close follow-up is needed. Stage III cases may need treatment with laser therapy (destroying the vessels with heat) or cryotherapy (freezing the vessels). Without treatment the abnormal growth of blood vessels can cause scarring and distortion of the retina, even retinal detachment and blindness. Treatment of ROP decreases the chances of blindness but cannot always prevent it. Myopia (nearsightedness), amblyopia ("lazy" eye), and strabismus ("crossed" eyes) can develop as a result of ROP.

Intraventricular Hemorrhage/Hydrocephalus

The blood vessels in and around premature infants' brains are fragile and prone to break or rupture. In most intensive care nurseries, babies born before 32 to 34 weeks' gestation are routinely screened for intraventricular hemorrhage (IVH), which refers to bleeding into the normal fluid spaces (ventricles) within the brain.

Ultrasonography is the most reliable and easiest way to diagnose intraventricular hemorrhage. The ultrasound scan (also called a sonogram) is performed right in the nursery at the baby's bedside.

The more premature or the sicker the baby is, the greater the risk for IVH. IVH is categorized into four grades, or degrees, of severity. In grade I, the mildest form, a small amount of bleeding is confined to an area of the brain that has a lot of blood vessels and grows rapidly during fetal life. In grade II, a small amount of blood is also in the ventricles. The blood is usually slowly absorbed by the body. Neither grade I nor grade II hemorrhages have any adverse consequences for long-term development and growth.

In grade III, a large amount of blood in the ventricles causes the ventricles to enlarge, sometimes only temporarily. The body can slowly reabsorb the blood. However, the large amount of blood in the ventricles can block the flow of cerebrospinal fluid and interfere with the absorption of the cerebrospinal fluid around the brain. This leads to hydrocephalus, which means there is too much fluid in the ventricles. This extra fluid may cause the baby's head to grow more rapidly than normal and puts pressure on the baby's brain. The majority of infants with grade

III IVH do not develop hydrocephalus. Babies who need surgical treatment to relieve pressure on the brain are at very high risk for developmental disability.

Grade IV is a hemorrhage within the brain tissue. Often this is accompanied by large amounts of blood in the ventricles and is complicated by hydrocephalus. This is similar to an adult who has had a stroke. These babies are at high risk for permanent brain damage and severe developmental disability. Another type of brain injury is periventricular leukomalacia (PVL). This refers to an injury to the portion of the brain that controls movement. This type of injury is associated with the development of cerebral palsy (see Chapter 32, "Health Problems in Early Childhood").

Your baby's doctor will give you information about IVH as it applies to your baby. Additional screening or follow-up ultrasounds may be performed as your baby grows. It is important to know that a normal brain ultrasound does not mean that a baby will have a normal neurologic outcome. Although brain imaging studies can help your child's doctor tell you the risks, currently there is no accurate method to predict how an infant will do after discharge from the nursery. Factors such as genetics, future health problems, and home environment all influence growth and development. Only follow-up over several years can provide an accurate picture of how your child will do.

Taking Your Infant Home

Most babies can go home when they are able to keep their body temperature normal in an open crib, take all their feedings by breast or bottle, and gain weight steadily. The average baby meets these criteria about two to four weeks before the original "due date," but this varies greatly, especially for the smallest and sickest premature infants.

As the time to go home approaches, the staff at most nurseries will allow you to "room in" for several nights at the hospital to become more comfortable with your infant. Often, the nursery staff will arrange for a visiting nurse before and after your discharge; the nurse will help you and your baby settle in at home. You will need to know the date and time of the home visit or who will be contacting you to set this up.

Before discharge you will want to learn to properly position your baby in a car seat. Many nurseries monitor premature infants in car seats before discharge. Once you have selected which physician will be caring for your baby after discharge, you will want to make an appointment to see the doctor shortly after discharge. Your baby may have additional appointments with other specialists or services, such as the early intervention program or a neurologist, a doctor who specializes in problems of the brain and nervous system. If your baby is a boy, decide if you want him circumcised. You will want to learn the results of all routine screening tests performed in the nursery and find out if repeat testing is needed. Routine screening includes a hearing test, metabolic screen, eye examination, and head ultrasound. Inquire about immunizations. Obtain a record of all immunizations given.

Every parent should learn infant cardiopulmonary resuscitation (CPR). Most hospitals or communities have instructional programs. If yours does not, contact the American Heart Association. If your infant is going home on an apnea monitor, complete monitor training. Learn important phone numbers for problems or emergencies.

Most parents are surprised when they feel anxious and sad about discharge. After all, taking the baby home is all they have thought about since the baby was born. But this is a natural reaction. Taking home this tiny baby who has had intensive, round-the-clock care can be a little frightening. Don't worry—the doctors, nurses, and social workers will continue to give you plenty of support for the tremendous change your family is about to experience. By the time your baby is ready to go home, you'll be nervous but ready. And your baby will love being home with you.

Need More Information?

Check the Index and Appendix C, "Resource Guide." And of course, consult your child's doctor.

chapter seven

Circumcision

The issues, the decision

If you've eagerly flipped to this chapter looking for the definitive medical rec-ommendation on whether to have your son circumcised, sorry, you won't find the answer here. In almost all cases, circumcision is an entirely personal decision to be made by parents. However, this chapter will provide you with information that may help you in making that choice.

What Is Circumcision?

Circumcision is the surgical removal of the cuff of skin (called the foreskin) that surrounds and covers the end of the penis (the glans). The removal of the foreskin exposes the tip of the penis.

It's difficult to know how often circumcision is performed on infant boys in the United States because most ritual circumcisions are performed outside the hospital. Circumcision rates also vary widely among racial, ethnic, and socioeconomic groups. The most recent estimates indicate that about two-thirds of all baby boys born in the United States underwent the procedure in 1995.

Circumcision of a newborn generally takes no more than a few minutes, and complications are rare when the procedure is performed by a skilled physician (usually an obstetrician, family physician, or pediatrician) or mohel (a Jewish rit-ual circumciser). The skin of the penis usually heals within a few days, and little care is needed following the procedure. (See Chapter 11, "Baby-Care Basics," for information on care of the penis after circumcision.)

Making the Decision

If you know you will be having a boy, you should decide whether to have him circumcised before the birth. You'll probably have enough on your mind with the excitement of your new arrival without having to make this decision as well.

For parents of certain religious faiths, the decision may be simpler and based on a tradition of ritual circumcision that has been performed for thousands of years. In the Jewish and Moslem religions, circumcision is considered an important expression of the child's relationship to God. In other cases, circumcisions in the United States are performed based on social and cultural custom—"his father is circumcised" or "so he won't feel different from the others"—or aesthetic or hygienic considerations. In some cases, the decision is made based on false notions, such as the mistaken belief that circumcision decreases the urge to masturbate.

The toughest decisions are when the mother and father disagree, especially if they are from different religious or cultural backgrounds. There's no easy answer. If both parents learn more about the question and discuss together what they've read (including this chapter), it may help them reach a decision they both feel OK about. Sometimes one partner (typically the father) will feel far more strongly about circumcision—pro or con—than the other. If that's true in your family, you may want to follow the wishes of the person who cares more deeply about the decision.

Whatever you decide, it may help to keep in mind that, circumcised or not, most boys grow up healthy and happy. How you resolve this dispute—whether it brings you closer together or leaves bitterness between you—may have more impact on your son's happiness than what you actually decide.

Here are some issues that you may want to consider in making your choice.

Task Force on Circumcision

"Existing scientific evidence demonstrates potential medical benefits of newborn male circumcision; however, these data are not sufficient to recommend routine neonatal circumcision."

(The 1999 policy statement of the Task Force on Circumcision of the American Academy of Pediatrics)

Urinary Tract Infections

There is now fairly convincing medical evidence indicating that urinary tract infections are more common during the first year of life in uncircumcised boys than in circumcised boys. It should be noted, however, that infections occur in about only 1 in 100 uncircumcised male infants (versus about 1 in 1,000 circumcised male infants). The infections are treatable, and the long-term effects of having had a urinary tract infection in infancy are uncertain.

Balanitis, Phimosis, and Hygiene Considerations

In newborn males, the foreskin usually has not separated completely from the end of the penis, making it impossible to fully retract or pull back the foreskin to expose the glans. It may take months or years before the foreskin becomes retractable, which allows the boy to clean the area of the penis under the foreskin. (This occurs in about 90 percent of uncircumcised boys by five years of age.) Infection of the glans and foreskin, called balanitis, is more common in uncircumcised males, but this is usually avoidable by teaching boys to regularly clean the area once the foreskin has become retractable.

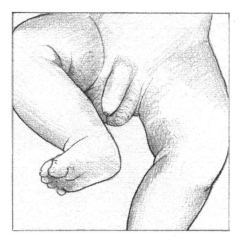

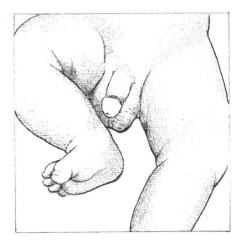

Figure 7.1. Uncircumcised penis. The uncircumcised penis of a newborn has a collar of skin, known as the foreskin, that surrounds the head of the penis.

Figure 7.2. Circumcised penis. In the circumcised penis, the foreskin has been surgically removed to reveal the head of the penis.

In about 5 to 10 percent of uncircumcised boys, the foreskin remains tightly wrapped around the glans or cannot be retracted easily, a condition known as phimosis. In some cases, phimosis can cause increased risk of balanitis, pain when the penis becomes erect, and blockage in the outflow of urine. (Even uncircumcised infants should have a forceful urine stream—consult your child's doctor if your son's urine only dribbles out.) These conditions may require circumcision surgery, which after the newborn period is a more formal surgical procedure performed under general anesthesia.

Penile Cancer and Sexually Transmitted Diseases

Although the risk of penile cancer appears to occur more frequently in uncircumcised men, the condition is rare, affecting only about 1 in 100,000 males in the United States. Whether there is an increased risk of cervical cancer in the sexual partners of uncircumcised men is also uncertain.

Some research has indicated that uncircumcised men have a higher risk of syphilis and HIV infection, but the results of these studies are too conflicting and complex to yield a definite conclusion.

Sexual Function and Sensation

Anecdotal reports have stated that circumcision may either heighten or decrease penile sensation. Scientific studies have not demonstrated any differences in this regard.

Appearance and Social Acceptance

Many parents make their decision about circumcision based on their feelings that being circumcised (or not being circumcised) will enhance their son's appearance to others or will promote social acceptance. Having a child look like Dad or like most of the other guys in the locker room is important to some parents. Some, however, raise the ethical concern that social preferences alone are not enough to justify operating on an infant.

The Pain of Circumcision

Until fairly recently, the pain associated with circumcision and other newborn procedures was given little attention. Research studies have now documented that infants show signs of feeling significant pain and stress when circumcision is performed without the use of pain-control medicines and techniques. Although the pain of circumcision doesn't last long, the Task Force on Circumcision of the American Academy of Pediatrics recommends using one of the currently available safe and effective pain-control methods. Both topically applied and injected medications can reduce the pain associated with circumcision. A recent study indicated that one of the techniques, known as a ring block, which involves injecting pain-control medications around the base of the foreskin, appears to provide the greatest degree of pain control during the procedure. Ask the person who will be performing the circumcision on your infant about this and other pain-control options.

When Should the Circumcision Be Performed?

If you have decided to have your son circumcised, it's best to have it done in the first two to three weeks of life. After that age, circumcision becomes a more involved and formal surgical procedure performed in an operating room. General anesthesia is usually required. Also, in contrast to newborn circumcision, stitches are routinely needed to close the wound and control bleeding.

Possible Complications of Circumcision

Complications associated with newborn circumcision are uncommon when an experienced circumciser performs the procedure. Excessive bleeding, the most common of these complications, occurs in about 1 in 1,000 circumcisions. Usually, this is easily controlled and the infant doesn't require a blood transfusion.

To avoid complications, circumcision should not be performed under some circumstances. It should be performed only when it is clear that the infant is in stable medical condition, usually after the infant has reached 12 to 24 hours of age. Circumcision should not be done in the delivery room. The procedure should also be delayed if your child's doctor feels the infant might have a bleeding problem or if certain abnormalities of the penis are present because the foreskin may be needed for use in future surgical repair of the defect.

Although evidence suggests that circumcision may have some medical benefits, currently most believe it is not medically necessary. You should be fully informed about the potential benefits and risks involved before making a decision. If you choose to have your newborn circumcised, make sure that an experienced circumciser performs the surgery when the infant is in healthy and stable condition and that appropriate pain control is used.

Need More Information?

Check the Index and Appendix C, "Resource Guide." And of course, consult your child's doctor.

chapter eight

Breast or Bottle

What's best for your baby and your family?

If human milk were developed by scientists, packaged by conglomerates, and sold in six-packs in the supermarket, it would be considered a miracle food. It provides balanced nutrition; prevents diarrhea, ear infections, and other illnesses; needs no heating, cooling, or preparation; and is free for the taking. That's some product!

The American Academy of Pediatrics (AAP), the World Health Organization, the American Dietetic Association, and the American Medical Association strongly concur that breast-feeding is best for most babies. The AAP puts it this way: "Human milk is uniquely superior for infant feeding."

But deciding how to feed a newborn—breast or bottle—is not always so simple. The decision is often a deeply emotional one. When we surveyed parents, we heard from many who said breast-feeding was the best decision they ever made, a unique source of joy, pleasure, and satisfaction. We also heard from women who stuck with it because of its benefits to the baby but found it confining or difficult. And we heard from women who said they were made to feel guilty because they couldn't breast-feed or didn't want to. Some said that advice to breast-feed "no matter what" had made their baby's first weeks a struggle, and they expressed bitterness at breast-feeding advocates who they felt were unreasonable or overzealous.

> ### *The Best Advice I Got Was . . .*
>
> "*. . . to take a class on breast-feeding. Do it even if you're just thinking about it. It's so rewarding when you know what you're doing. It can be so frustrating and traumatic when you don't!*"

Breast-feeding and bottle-feeding each has advantages and disadvantages. The final decision is a personal one that only the mother and her partner can make, based on what they think is best for their family. Either way, you can have a healthy, happy, well-adjusted baby. Either way, you can be good, loving, nurturing parents who will bond with your baby. Either way, you should not feel guilty about your choice. Only you know what is best for yourself and your family. It's your decision and no one else's.

Having said that, we must make one point clear. Medical evidence strongly supports the exceptional benefits of breast milk for infants, and this is the choice we strongly encourage. Even if they encounter some difficulties at first, most new mothers can breast-feed successfully, especially if they get the support they may need.

But we understand that medical and personal circumstances sometimes can make it difficult or impossible for a mother to breast-feed; in these situations, bottle-feeding is a safe, nutritious option. If, however, you have the freedom to choose breast-feeding or bottle-feeding, we strongly encourage you to breast-feed. As you will learn in this chapter, it provides the perfect nourishment for an infant.

If you're not sure what you want to do, consider giving breast-feeding a try. After all, you can always switch if you don't like it. But if you start out on the bottle and later want to try breast-feeding, you may not be able to get the milk flowing. Besides, even a few weeks of breast milk can help protect your baby from illness at a time when his immune system is not yet fully functioning. If you try, you may find it easier than you expected and more rewarding than you imagined.

Making Your Choice: Breast or Bottle?

Let's look at some of the issues concerning infant feeding. If you're undecided how to feed your baby, this information may help you choose. If you've already decided, it may help you to accentuate the positive and minimize the negative of whichever method you've chosen. That should make your feeding experience as happy and healthy as possible.

Nutrition

Human milk is uniquely suited for human babies. For most babies, it meets all nutritional needs in easily digested form. It also provides antibodies and live immune-system cells that protect babies from disease. Moreover, each mother's milk is uniquely suited to her baby; its makeup varies, for instance, with the baby's age. Many of the elements in human milk have not been identified, let alone duplicated. Good as formula may be, all baby formulas "differ markedly" from human milk, according to the AAP.

On the other hand, millions of healthy, well-nourished babies—most U.S. babies, in fact—have been raised on commercial formula, which is safe and nutritious. The content of formula sold in the United States is regulated by the U.S. Food and Drug Administration.

Health

Many studies have confirmed the health benefits of breast-feeding. There is strong evidence that babies who are breast-fed for the first six months are less likely than bottle-fed babies to get certain illnesses including diarrhea, lower respiratory infections, ear infections, and urinary tract infections. Most of the studies looked at the first six months of life, when the protection against infection is thought to be most important; after that, babies' immune systems have matured, and they are more able to fight infections on their own.

> ### The Best Advice I Got Was . . .
>
> "*. . . to keep trying. After about two weeks of breast-feeding, the baby and I were getting frustrated. I spoke to a friend who told me not to give up. She told me to hold on at least a month to six weeks. I took her advice, it did become easier, and I've been doing it for seven months.*"

Development of Jaws and Teeth

The sucking motions used in breast-feeding—which are different from the motions of sucking a bottle—may help promote proper development of the jaws and teeth.

KidsHealth Tip

Health Benefits for Mom

Breast-feeding mothers also enjoy health benefits. The uterus shrinks back to its usual size more quickly, and postpartum bleeding is usually reduced. Breast-feeding appears to cut the risk of ovarian cancer and of early (premenopausal) breast cancer. It may also improve bone mass, making hip fractures less likely later in life.

There is also evidence, although not as strong so far, that breast-feeding may help protect babies against sudden infant death syndrome (SIDS), as well as possibly help protect them later in life against diabetes, obesity, allergies, and chronic digestive diseases such as Crohn's disease and ulcerative colitis.

Although breast-fed babies as a group do have a health advantage, we all know that many bottle-fed babies sail through childhood as healthy as can be. Many do not suffer any more cases of diarrhea, respiratory infections, or ear infections than breast-fed babies do. And some breast-fed babies get sick, develop allergies, and have long-term health problems. Clearly, breast-feeding does not guarantee good health, and bottle-feeding does not promise illness. What breast-feeding can do is improve the odds that a baby will avoid illness.

Exceptions to the Rule

If the mother is infected with HIV (the AIDS virus) or has untreated, active tuberculosis, she should not breast-feed because she could pass the infection on to the baby. (Women who have hepatitis B or C should consult their doctor.) Breast-feeding should also be avoided in these cases:

- If the mother uses illegal drugs or drinks heavily
- If the mother must take certain medications such as cyclosporine or anticancer drugs (If you are taking any medications, check with your child's doctor about whether they are safe to take during nursing.)
- If the mother is severely malnourished or has a chronic illness so serious that nursing would endanger her health or tax her strength

• If the baby is born with galactosemia (Babies with this condition cannot handle galactose, a sugar found in milk.)

A few other conditions may prevent breast-feeding, but you usually won't know for sure until you try. For instance, if you have had breast surgery, especially near the nipple, the milk ducts may have been severed. Finally, a small percentage of women may produce very little milk. But this is rare. In most cases, when mothers fear their milk supply is too small, either they are mistaken or they can increase their supply by taking steps we describe in Chapter 9, "Breast-Feeding."

If Your Baby Is Premature

Some newborn conditions can require special measures to make breast-feeding possible. If a baby is premature, breast milk may need to be pumped, fortified, and fed to the baby through a tube until he matures enough to suck adequately (see Chapter 6, "Premature Babies"). If a baby is born with cleft palate, a mouth appliance and caregiver training may be needed to help the baby feed effectively.

Although in such cases breast-feeding may be difficult, the health benefits of breast milk can be all the more important to babies born with health problems.

Intelligence

There is debate over whether feeding methods affect intelligence. Some studies have found that children who had been breast-fed did better in tests of intelligence by a small but significant amount and performed slightly better in school than children who had been formula-fed. The greatest effects generally were seen in low-birthweight babies who were exclusively breast-fed. Not all studies, however, agree on this: Some did not find a cognitive (or intelligence) benefit at all. Others found a benefit but linked it to social factors rather than to breast-feeding. (In these studies, the mothers who breast-fed tended to be better educated and more affluent than those who didn't. Children who have educated, affluent mothers tend to do better in school, whether or not they were breast-fed.) Nonetheless, the evidence at least suggests a benefit, especially for low-birthweight babies.

Bonding and Family Ties

Mothers who have happily breast-fed often say it helped them bond with their infant, strengthened their love, and helped them learn about their infant's needs and personality. But, of course, mothers—and fathers—who bottle-feed also bond with their infants, know them deeply, and feel transforming, transfixing love.

Advocates sometimes talk as though it's obvious that breast-feeding promotes bonding more than bottle-feeding does. In fact, it is not known whether this is true, and few studies have tried to find out. One study, done in New Zealand, found that when breast-fed babies grew into teenagers, they were no better adjusted psychologically or socially, and no less likely to use drugs or get into trouble with the law, than bottle-fed babies. But the longer they had been breast-fed, the more likely they were to perceive their mothers as caring.

Of necessity, breast-feeding mothers spend a lot of time in intimate contact with their babies. Bottle-feeding parents can do the same—cradling the baby, looking into his eyes, cuddling with bare skin—but they have to make more of an effort. With breast-feeding, the contact is built in.

When it comes to bonding between baby and father (or baby and other family members), bottle-feeding may make things easier. With bottle-feeding, the father can share equally in the most basic part of child care in a way that is impossible with breast-feeding. This may help the father develop a closer, more nurturing relationship with his baby and prevent him from feeling excluded from this

> ## The Voice of Experience
>
> *"To nurse my children was the best advice. The quiet times I shared with each of my three children during nursing times reinforced my deepest emotions and love for my kids."*
> —FROM THE KidsHealth PARENT SURVEY

> ## The Voice of Experience
>
> *"Breast-feeding is not the only way to nurture your baby. To feed a baby a warm bottle as he cuddles in your arms is just as satisfying and rewarding as breast-feeding."*
> —FROM THE KidsHealth PARENT SURVEY

> ## I Wish Someone Had Told Me . . .
>
> *". . . motherhood can lead to intense feelings of guilt over issues like feeding, working, etc. If you don't breast-feed, it doesn't mean that you are any less a mother."*

intimate experience. Older siblings, grandparents, and other relatives can also play a more important role in the infant's life. This can be especially helpful in nontraditional families—for instance, if the father stays home with the baby while the mother goes to work or if a grandparent helps raise the baby.

With breast-feeding couples, of course, the father can play an important role by helping the mother or giving an occasional bottle. And he can interact with his baby in other ways. But couples may need to pay more attention to making sure he doesn't feel excluded.

Freedom and the Mother's Lifestyle

The bottle-feeding mother can more easily leave her baby with someone else while she goes out for chores, recreation, exercise, or the like. More important for many women, she can return to work without having to worry about pumping and saving milk. She can work as much as she wants, and sleep as little, without depleting her baby's food supply. She can travel for her job more easily.

The bottle-feeding mother can wear whatever she wants, while the nursing mother needs to stick to washable clothes with easy access for the baby. If the bottle-feeding mother is out in public and hears a baby cry, she doesn't have to worry that her milk will start to flow (seeing or hearing a baby can trigger the release of milk). If she needs medical tests or treatments, she can have them without considering how they might affect her milk.

Will Breast-Feeding Help You Lose Weight?

Breast-feeding burns calories, so you may lose weight without cutting back on calories. It also shrinks the uterus, which can make you look more svelte (if that word can be used without irony for the mother of a newborn). On the other hand, bottle-feeding mothers can try some exercises and weight-loss diets that are not advisable when you're starting to breast-feed. Either way, it's wise to assume that it will take you nine months to a year to get back to your prepregnancy weight. While breast-feeding, a woman of normal weight should lose no more than one to two pounds a month.

But compared to all the life-altering changes that come along with any baby, the extra limitations on nursing mothers are relatively minor and last only a few months. For most women, no dietary changes are needed, for instance. Leaving a newborn home requires planning, no matter how you feed her, and breast milk can be saved in bottles to allow Mom time away from the baby for work or play. Besides, breast-feeding mothers generally find it easier to take their infants with them on outings because they don't need any feeding paraphernalia!

Juggling nursing and full-time work outside the home can be a more challenging problem—it's one of the main reasons women stop breast-feeding. We offer some suggestions on making it work in Chapter 9, "Breast-Feeding."

Stress on the Parents

In the first few weeks after birth, feeding an infant can be exhausting for any parent. Breast-feeding round-the-clock can be extra tiring for the mother, especially if she had a difficult birth or is having trouble getting her milk flow established. Because human milk is digested more quickly and easily than formula, breast-fed babies generally eat more frequently, wake more frequently at night, and begin to sleep through the night later than bottle-fed infants. Although they tend to sleep less overall, breast-fed infants can be taught to sleep for longer periods at night by using the techniques discussed in Chapter 9, "Breast-Feeding." With bottle-feeding, the father, another relative, or a paid helper can share round-the-clock feeding duties or take them over entirely if the mother needs rest.

Another source of stress for many parents is the worry that a newborn is not eating enough. With bottles, you can keep track of every ounce at every feeding. For parents who are worried about this issue, that can be a big relief.

Whatever stress breast-feeding may bring, however, it's usually limited to the first few weeks and can be eased if someone offers a helping hand. With help, the breast-feeding mother may be able to spend a week or two mostly in bed if she wants, doing nothing but nursing and resting. Similarly, weight checks and the attentions of a concerned doctor can help parents be sure their baby is getting enough milk.

Once nursing is going well, breast-feeding can be more relaxing than bottle-feeding. If your baby sleeps in your room, you won't have to get up for a bottle. Travel with your baby is simpler. And many women report that nursing triggers deep feelings of relaxation and well-being (perhaps linked to hormonal changes).

It's important to remember, too, that for some families, nursing is as easy as bottle-feeding right from the start—the milk flows and the baby grows.

Convenience and Cost

Breast-feeding moms never run out of milk and don't incur the expense of buying formula. Those who breast-feed exclusively and stay at home with their baby don't have to wash or sterilize bottles, cool or heat formula, carry feeding supplies along on every outing, or run to the kitchen in the middle of the night.

But if breast-feeding mothers begin to leave their baby at home, things begin to even out. They have to express and store milk, invest in equipment, and prepare and clean bottles.

For bottle-feeding, convenience is closely tied to cost. Powdered formula that is mixed with water is relatively inexpensive but takes time and care to prepare. Single-serving, ready-to-eat formulas in disposable bottles are simple but much more expensive. There are also options in between. As a bottle-feeder, you will also need a kitchen full of bottles, nipples, bottle brushes, and maybe a sterilizer. And you will need an insulated bag to cart all these things wherever you go.

Emotions, Embarrassment, and Sex

Breast-feeding is (check one): (a) a turn-on, (b) a turn-off.

People are sometimes reluctant to discuss the sexual aspect of breast-feeding, but it is a concern for many couples. You and your partner may want to discuss how you feel about the sexual and emotional sides of breast-feeding (although it's not always easy to predict how you'll feel once you're doing it).

Some women are repelled by the idea of handling their own breasts in a matter-of-fact way and think their partners will be repelled at seeing them do it, too. They may be uncomfortable about the whole idea of breast-feeding and embar-

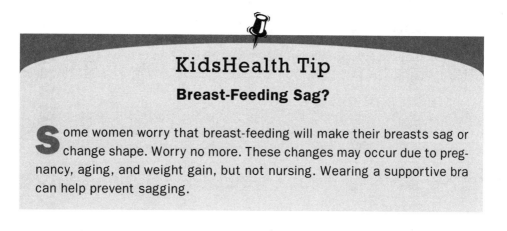

KidsHealth Tip
Breast-Feeding Sag?

Some women worry that breast-feeding will make their breasts sag or change shape. Worry no more. These changes may occur due to pregnancy, aging, and weight gain, but not nursing. Wearing a supportive bra can help prevent sagging.

rassed at the prospect of doing it in public (even though, with practice, it can be done while revealing nothing). Some men have similar feelings about their partner's breasts being used for a nonsexual purpose. Other men and women find these prospects sensual and exciting. Be honest about how you feel.

Studies do suggest that breast-feeding women tend to be less interested in sexual activity in the first few months after birth. Fatigue may be a factor, along with the feeling some women get of being physically used up by breast-feeding—"all touched out." Others complain of vaginal dryness caused by low estrogen during lactation, a problem that can be helped by using a lubricant.

But even when negative feelings do exist, they often fade after breast-feeding becomes established. Some women say that breast-feeding improved their sex life by making them more comfortable with their bodies and more responsive. Some couples find they are aroused by the milk, which may leak or spray during sexual activity. For some women, the act of suckling an infant itself causes feelings of sexual arousal. More commonly, it causes pleasurable, comfortable feelings that aren't erotic. Either reaction is normal.

If you bottle-feed your baby, this choice should have no effect on your sex life (beyond whatever effect parenthood itself might have).

If You're Still Not Sure

If you're still undecided, read more in Chapter 9, "Breast-Feeding," and in Chapter 10, "Bottle-Feeding," and talk to people who have done both—it may help you make up your mind.

Need More Information?

Check the Index and Appendix C, "Resource Guide." And of course, consult your child's doctor.

chapter nine

Breast-Feeding

Nature's way

Breast-feeding may be natural and good for your baby, but it's not always easy. In recent years, most American mothers were breast-feeding their infants when they went home from the hospital, but many switched to bottles in the first few weeks. By six months, only about 20 percent were still nursing. To make breast-feeding easier to maintain, start preparing before your baby is born:

- Learn about breast-feeding and line up people to help you if problems or worries occur. Books are useful (we list some in Appendix C, "Resource Guide"). But nothing beats talking to people who have been there. Check with your hospital to to see if it offers breast-feeding instruction or can refer you to a lactation consultant. If you don't know any experienced breast-feeders, you can find some through the local chapter of La Leche League, an organization that promotes breast-feeding. Check the Web site at www.lalecheleague.org or call (847) 519-7730. If you are going to hire someone to help you after the birth, look for a person with breast-feeding expertise.

- Be sure you and your partner are emotionally prepared for the round-the-clock commitment of breast-feeding, especially in the first couple of weeks. Doing it—and getting enough rest and food so that she can do it comfortably—may consume most of a new mother's waking moments. The new father, too, will have adjustments to make as he tries to keep the household running while struggling with sleep deprivation himself. His efforts, his support, and his encouragement can be crucial.

- Make sure your child's doctor is knowledgeable about breast-feeding and sees it as part of his or her job to help you carry it out, as long as it is in your baby's best interest. Most doctors are likely to say they favor breast-feeding—it's gospel these days. But as with any group of people, doctors vary in how much they know or care about this subject. Some will help you find a way to work around problems; others will encourage you to switch to the bottle long before other options have been exhausted. Many pediatric practices have a lactation consultant on staff, and some physicians have been certified themselves as lactation consultants.

- Prepare a comfortable place (or several spots around the house) for nursing. Many women favor a rocker, glider, or other cozy chair with arms, a footstool, and pillows to help prop their baby into a comfortable position. You may want a telephone and a radio within arm's length, as well as a place to put drinks and snacks for you and cloths for burping your baby. An adjustable light is a nice touch. If you have a toddler, add a stash of toys, books, or games for a special play time while you nurse your baby.

Getting Equipped for Nursing

Nursing doesn't require much gear, but a few things gathered ahead of time can help make it easier:

- Nursing bras. A well-fitting supportive bra will make you more comfortable and prevent sagging. Nursing bras have a flap on each cup that opens for nursing. Look for an all-cotton bra without an underwire, with cups that are easily opened with one hand. It should not be tight or compress the breasts. In the first weeks of nursing, most women go up in bra size temporarily.
- Nursing pads. Some nursing bras come with removable nursing pads. These should be either disposable or washable cotton; you can make your own from cotton diapers or handkerchiefs. They are worn inside the bra to absorb leaking milk, especially in the first weeks, and should be changed as soon as they get wet. Do not use plastic-lined pads.
- Purified lanolin ointment (such as PureLan or Lansinoh). This thick ointment helps heal sore, cracked nipples, according to the testimony of many women. Its big advantage is that it does not have to be washed off before nursing. It's sold at maternity shops, large drugstores, and online.
- Clothing. All you really need are loose, washable tops that can be pulled up or unbuttoned from the waist up, for discreet nursing. Maternity stores and child-care catalogs also sell nursing clothes, typically with pleats or flaps on the top that conceal slits that allow access to the breast. This is helpful if you

want to wear a one-piece dress while nursing. Some women also like to drape a shawl or wide scarf over the baby for privacy while nursing away from home.

• Breast pumps. If you need to express milk occasionally, you can do it by hand. But if you will need to do it daily for a long period—typically, because of your job or your baby's prematurity—you'll probably want to use a breast pump. A pump can also help stimulate your milk supply if it is low or help relieve engorgement (this happens when the breast gets uncomfortably full of milk). Although you can wait to see if you need a pump, it's best to learn about them ahead of time, so you won't find yourself running into a drugstore and buying the first one you see, which may not be the best for you.

The most efficient and, for many women, the most comfortable breast pumps are hospital-grade electric pumps that are rented for home use, generally through a lactation consultant or hospital. In some cases, medical insurance may cover the cost if your doctor can show that it's medically necessary for your baby.

You can also find smaller electric pumps, battery-operated pumps, and various kinds of manual pumps. Among the manual types, many experts counsel against buying the kind shaped like a bicycle horn, which are often sold in drugstores, because they're less effective at emptying milk from the breast. A La Leche League leader or a lactation consultant may help you find a pump that meets your needs. The major pump makers are Medela (www.medela.com) and Ameda (www.hollister.com).

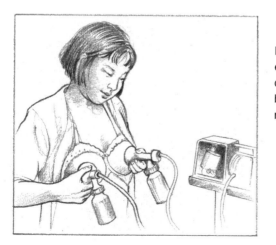

Figure 9.1. Breast pumps. An electric-powered breast pump can make collecting and storing breast milk faster and easier for moms-on-the-go.

Two Kinds of Helpers

Many nursing women get advice and help from their mothers, sisters, and friends. But others lack a support circle of women experienced in breast-feeding. Often, women now seek help from two fairly new kinds of practitioners: lactation consultants and doulas.

Lactation Consultants

Lactation consultants, or LCs, teach couples about breast-feeding and help solve problems that may arise. They may be nurses, nutritionists, childbirth educators, midwives, or lay people with training. Some work out of hospitals or childbirth centers; some are affiliated with pediatric practices; some have independent practices or work for lactation centers. The most widely recognized credential is certification as an International Board Certified Lactation Consultant (abbreviated I.B.C.L.C. after the person's name). Usually, hospital staff or your child's doctor can recommend a lactation consultant, or you can get names from the International Lactation Consultant Association, (919) 787-5181. Ask about a consultant's training and experience. If your child's doctor refers you to a consultant, it may improve the chances that your insurance will cover it, but don't count on it.

Doulas

Unlike baby nurses who take care of the baby, doulas take care of the mother and other family members so that the mother can concentrate on taking care of the baby. Doulas can support the mother's breast-feeding by seeing she eats well, rests, and relaxes. They may do the housework or take care of an older sibling. Traditionally, a female relative or friend has filled this role. But in recent years, professional, paid doulas have become more common. Friends or health care providers may be able to provide referrals. Or you can try to find one through national registries including Doulas of North America (DONA) and the National Association of Postpartum Care Services Inc.

> ### The Voice of Experience
> ───────⊘───────
>
> *"When you are breast-feeding, keep a basket of necessities with you (cordless phone, burp cloth, paper, pen, emery boards, a book). It's easy to just hook it on your arm and tote it around, so wherever you sit it will be with you."*
>
> —FROM THE KIDSHEALTH PARENT SURVEY

(NAPCS). Because a doula will fill an intimate role in your family, you want to find someone whose personality is a good fit, who can be reassuring and supportive but not domineering or guilt-tripping.

Preparing Your Breasts

Late in pregnancy, you should stop using soap or other cleansers on your nipples to avoid drying them out. You should also check to see if your nipples are flat or inverted, conditions that are not always obvious. Place your thumb and fingers on opposite sides of the areola (the dark area around the nipple) and squeeze. If your nipple gets flatter or burrows into your breast, rather than poking out, consult a lactation expert. Most babies can nurse anyway, but it may help to use a breast pump first. Sometimes women are advised to wear breast shells over the areolas during the last few months of pregnancy or between nursing sessions once their baby is born. The plastic shells are thought to help make the nipples protrude, but their use is controversial. It's not clear if they help, and having to wear them may needlessly discourage some women from breast-feeding. Only in rare cases do inverted nipples make it impossible to breast-feed.

"Toughening" the nipples—by rubbing them with a towel, for instance—is not necessary and may make them more prone to crack.

Getting Started

Your baby should be put to your breast soon after birth—ideally in the delivery room. When the nipple touches your baby's lips, even a newborn will usually lick and suck a little. At this point, you're just meeting your baby—don't worry about technique.

Mother's milk usually comes in on the third or fourth day, but it can happen sooner or later. Until then, your baby will be sucking small amounts of colostrum, a yellowish fluid that is rich in antibodies that help protect your baby from disease.

During this period, you should nurse your baby frequently—about every two hours. It's easiest if your baby "rooms in" with you—that is, stays in your hospital room round-the-clock. If that is impossible, try to arrange for your baby to spend most of the day with you.

Once your milk comes in, expect to nurse 8 or 12 times in each 24-hour period. Each session may take only 15 minutes (if your baby's an efficiency expert) or closer to an hour if he dawdles, dozes, and likes to finish up with so-called non-nutritive sucking—sucking for comfort.

Unless there is a medical reason, your baby should not be given bottles of water, sugar water, or formula (as is sometimes done in hospital nurseries). Besides making him less hungry, sucking on a bottle requires different mouth motions than breast-feeding. If the baby learns bottle-sucking, which is usually easier, he may be reluctant to switch to the breast, a phenomenon sometimes called "nipple confusion." For similar reasons, he should not be given a pacifier in the nursery unless there are medical reasons; you don't want his sucking urge to be filled by anything but the breast. Talk to your child's doctor and the nurses to make sure you're all in agreement on this. Premature babies may be a special case. See Chapter 6, "Premature Babies," for information.

The Early Checkup

After a short hospital stay, most women take their babies home before their milk comes in. Nursing advocates advise first-time nursers to see a lactation consultant a couple of days after coming home, just to check their technique. A nurse or doctor expert in feeding techniques can also fill this role when you bring the baby in for his first checkup. In most cases, that checkup should occur two to three days after you come home, according to the American Academy of Pediatrics (AAP).

How to Hold Your Baby for Breast-Feeding

There are several ways to comfortably hold your baby while breast-feeding (see Figures 9.2a–c). Whichever hold you use, make sure that your baby's neck is straight, not bent.

The Cradle Hold

This hold is easiest when you're sitting up, with pillows behind your back for comfort. Cradle your baby in one arm, with his head at your elbow and his buttocks in your hand. Turn him on his side so his belly is facing yours. Raise him up to breast level, then place pillows on your lap to support the weight of your baby and your arm. If you try to hold him rather than rest him on pillows, your back will soon start aching. For the same reason, don't lean over and lower your breast to your baby. Sit comfortably upright and raise your baby to your breast, holding him close against your body. It may help to put your feet up on a footstool.

In the beginning you may find the lying cradle hold more comfortable, especially if you have had a cesarean section. Lie on your side, with your head propped on pillows so your neck stays straight. Put your baby on his side facing you, cradled in your lower arm. Move him to your breast.

The Crossover or Cross-Cradle Hold

This is similar to the cradle hold except that you hold your baby in the arm opposite the breast you are using. Lie on your side, put your baby on his side facing you, and hold him with your top arm so his neck rests in your hand, with your thumb and fingers supporting the back of his head and your arm supporting his back. Then lift him to your breast. Because you have more control over your baby's head, this hold can be helpful with babies who are having trouble latching on (taking the breast into their mouth in the proper way).

The Clutch or Football Hold

This hold sometimes works better with small babies or large breasts, and it may be more comfortable if you have had a cesarean because your baby doesn't rest on your belly. Sit with a pillow behind your back. Put a pillow next to you, and place your baby with his head on top of your knees. Put your arm around him, with your hand supporting his head and neck. Lift him to your breast and once he begins nursing, put pillows under his back to support his weight and the weight of your arm.

The Importance of Latching On

Nursing experts agree that the way your baby latches on (positions her mouth on the breast) is the key to comfortable, productive nursing. Your baby should take as much of your areola (the darker circle around the nipple) into her mouth as possible, with her gums resting not at the base of the nipple but at least an inch down the areola (see Figures 9.3a–c). Milk is stored in reservoirs under the surface of the areola. When your baby sucks, her tongue presses the areola against the roof of her

9.2a. A proper feeding position when the mother is sitting.

9.2b. The double "football carry" position when breast-feeding twins.

9.2c. A proper feeding position when the mother is lying on her side.

Figures 9.2a–c. Proper breast-feeding positions.

KidsHealth Tip

Feed on Demand

Whether you feed your baby by breast or bottle, feed a newborn whenever he shows signs of hunger, says the American Academy of Pediatrics (AAP). Such signs include increased alertness or activity, mouthing objects, or rooting with the mouth. Crying, notes the AAP, is a late sign of hunger; by the time a baby is howling, he's already been hungry for a while. Newborns should be nursed 8 to 12 times in every 24 hours, each time until they don't want any more. Pediatric experts and many other child-care professionals fear that some newborns may not grow as well as they should if they are put on strict feeding schedules, as advocated in some recent books. Newborns should set their own schedules.

mouth, which drives milk into your nipple and then into her mouth. Your baby should suck the areola, not the nipple.

Sucking the nipple can cause several problems. The baby gets less milk, which causes the mother's body to produce less. At the same time, the nipples are likelier to become painful and cracked. The pain—and the mother's anticipation of pain as she prepares to nurse—further inhibits the flow of milk. That leaves the baby hungry and crying, and the mother suffering and anxious. She may decide that she just can't make enough milk, when a relatively simple change in technique could have solved the problem.

Latching On Properly

The first step in a proper latch-on is to wait until your baby's mouth opens wide. Holding your breast with your thumb on top and your fingers under your breast, brush your baby's lips with your nipple until his mouth opens, not just a little but as if yawning. Then pull your baby toward you and onto your breast. If you don't move quickly enough, the baby's mouth may be half-closed by the time he latches on. If this happens, it's better to break his suction by slipping your finger between his gums and your nipple and start over. You may need to compress your breast with your fingers, so more of it will fit in his mouth; if you do, keep your fingers well back of the areola. It may also help to squeeze out a few drops of milk, to give your baby an enticing taste from your nipple or a finger.

Once your baby is latched on, both of his lips should be turned out as they press against your breast. If not, use your finger to turn them out. Otherwise, he may be sucking his lip, not your breast.

Watch for a steady rhythmic motion of your baby's cheeks as he sucks; once the milk comes in, you should also be able to hear him swallow. With experience, mothers can distinguish between so-called nutritive sucking (nursing to get milk) and the more relaxed, nonnutritive sucking (nursing for comfort) that often follows.

A Typical Nursing Session

Let your newborn nurse as long as she wants on one breast, then burp her and switch her to the other breast. Because your baby is likely to nurse more from the first breast, alternate the breast you start with. You can keep track by moving a safety pin or piece of ribbon from one strap of your nursing bra to the other. Some of the parents who responded to our survey recommended switching a watch from wrist to wrist to keep track.

Once your milk comes in, you will want to continue to make sure that your baby empties at least the first breast each session, rather than taking a little from each breast. That's because the first milk out of the breast, called the foremilk, has less fat in it than the milk at the end, called the hindmilk. You want your baby to get enough hindmilk to grow well.

In most cases, let your baby nurse as long as she wants. Usually she will stop on her own or fall asleep while sucking. If she seems to suck endlessly—more than an hour in each session—check with your child's doctor to make sure she is getting enough milk. If your baby is nursing and growing well a month or two after birth but still wants long periods of nonnutritive sucking, you can consider trying a pacifier. But don't introduce one until breast-feeding is well established. Early use of a pacifier makes it less likely that a mother-baby pair will continue breast-feeding.

If you need to take your baby off the breast, don't just pull away—it'll be painful. Instead, break her suction by putting your pinkie between her gums in the corner of her mouth.

Figures 9.3a–c. The latching-on process.

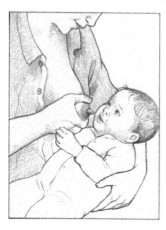 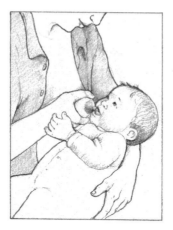

9.3a. Stimulate rooting reflex. Once your baby is in the proper position, use your thumb and forefinger to grasp your breast just behind the nipple and touch the baby's cheek to stimulate the rooting reflex.

9.3b. Latching on. Your baby will respond by turning his head to "latch on." To help the baby take all of the nipple into his mouth, you should use your thumb and forefinger to compress your breast slightly just behind the nipple.

9.3c. Proper feeding position. Note that the entire nipple is in the baby's mouth, which ensures good milk flow for the baby and prevents sore nipples for the mother.

How Can You Tell if Your Baby Is Getting Enough Milk?

This is one of the major concerns of new parents, especially if their baby was born small or premature. It is normal for a baby to lose up to 7 to 10 percent of her birthweight in the first week of life and to regain it by the end of the second week. The dip in weight, however, may increase parents' anxiety.

If you have any doubts about whether your newborn is getting adequate nutrition or if your baby does not show the reassuring signs listed next, bring your baby to his doctor for a weight check. This is a common practice; a doctor may ask to see a premature or small baby two or three times a week for the first couple of weeks. In rare cases, the doctor may even want to weigh the baby before and after a feeding to check how many ounces he has taken. With a newborn, you should not delay seeking help if you think your baby is not getting enough milk.

Because you can't measure breast milk the way you measure formula, here are other ways of telling if your baby is getting enough milk:

- Once your milk comes in, your baby should have six to eight wet cloth diapers or five to six wet disposable diapers per day, with clear or very pale urine. It can be hard to be sure how wet disposable diapers are. For that reason, you may want to use cloth, at least in the beginning. Or you can put a piece of tissue into the diaper and check whether it's wet.
- Your baby should have two to five or more bowel movements a day. For the first couple of days, the stool will be dark. Once your milk comes in, the stool should be soft and yellowish. After a month, breast-fed babies usually have fewer bowel movements and may not have one every day.
- Your baby should seem alert and content. Talk to your child's doctor if your baby sleeps more than four hours at a time during his first couple of weeks or if he nurses for long periods but cries, frets, and seems restless as soon as he stops.
- Your baby should gain weight at a healthy rate. He should regain his birthweight by two weeks after birth, then gain at least five to seven ounces a week during the first three months. During this time, breast-fed and bottle-fed babies should gain weight at the same rate. After three months, weight gain usually slows in breast-fed babies. Between three or four months and six months, infants typically gain three to five ounces a week; after six months, weight gain usually slows further. Your baby should be weighed on his doctor's baby scale; home scales for adults are not accurate enough to track a baby's weight.

Stimulating the Milk Supply

In most cases, the more milk that is sucked from a breast and the more frequently it is sucked, the more will be produced. That's why you usually can increase your milk supply by increasing how often and how long you nurse. Other strategies you might try to increase your milk supply include the following:

- Eat well and drink plenty of fluids. Have an extra glass of milk, water, juice, or a yogurt drink before or during nursing.

- Rest more. Sleep when your baby does, even if work goes undone.
- Try to relax before and during breast-feeding. Try meditation or visualization techniques (you may have learned these in childbirth-preparation classes), take a warm bath, listen to music, or chat with a friend.
- Have skin-to-skin cuddling contact with your baby while you are nursing.
- Do breast massage before nursing. Starting at the top of the breast and moving toward and around the areola, use your fingers to press with a circular motion, then move on to the next spot. Stroke the breasts from the top and sides to the nipple.
- If milk supply is still a problem, express or pump your milk after or between feedings, including during the night; this increased demand should lead to an increased supply. Save the milk in the refrigerator or freezer, as described later, to be used as a supplement if necessary.

> ## The Voice of Experience
>
> *"You should prioritize your work at home, because when you breast-feed, you need a lot of rest and good nutrition. That's more important for your baby than keeping the house neat and getting stressed out."*
> —FROM THE KIDSHEALTH PARENT SURVEY

What Is Letdown?

Letdown is a reflex in which milk is squeezed out of the milk glands (where it was made) and along the ducts that lead to the nipple. Without it, there's little or no milk available to the baby. This process, also called the milk ejection reflex, is triggered by release of the hormone oxytocin from the mother's pituitary gland. It usually happens more than once during a feeding.

In the first couple of weeks of nursing, a baby usually must suck for several minutes to stimulate letdown. If a baby tires easily at first, pumping the breast to trigger letdown can save him from getting tired or frustrated.

Later on, letdown usually occurs quickly. In many women, it happens as soon as they settle into their usual nursing chair with their baby in their arms; in some, it happens if they see any baby or hear one cry. Women who pump their breast milk each day often can condition their letdown to occur simply by looking at a picture of their baby.

For many women, letdown causes a tingling, pins-and-needles sensation in the breasts or a feeling of fullness. There are other signs, too: While your baby nurses from one breast, milk may drip from the other. Or you may feel abdominal cramps because oxytocin, the hormone involved in letdown, also causes the uterus to contract. Many women, however, do not feel anything during letdown, and new mothers may worry that it is not occurring. If your baby seems to be getting enough milk, as described earlier, letdown is occurring, whether you feel it or not.

Supplementation

In some cases, a newborn may need supplemental feedings until the mother's milk supply increases or the baby gets big or strong enough to nurse properly. A supplemental feeding system that uses a tube or syringe may make it easier to breast-feed later than if you use a bottle. In some systems, sometimes called nursing trainers, the baby sucks milk from the breast and from the tube at the same time. Consult a lactation consultant about such systems.

Supplementing with a bottle, however, may be easier, and doctors may prefer it, especially if the baby is very small and weak. Using a bottle temporarily doesn't necessarily mean the end of breast-feeding if the parents are committed to continuing. Some babies seem to have little trouble switching from one to the other; others can be persuaded with patience. Some mothers, whose milk came in late or took longer to build up, have had good results by nursing as usual, then giving a bottle of formula, either immediately or after waiting a few minutes. In other cases, a bottle (of expressed breast milk or formula) may be substituted for one feeding a day. If milk supply is a problem, however, you should stimulate the supply by pumping each time you bottle-feed. When your milk supply increases, you can stop the bottle.

> ### The Voice of Experience
> *"Watch your baby, rather than clocks and books, for cues. Feed on demand, not by the clock."*
> —FROM THE KidsHealth PARENT SURVEY

In general, breast-feeding advocates warn against supplementing with a bottle before breast-feeding is well established, usually after six weeks. But if the alternative is letting your baby go hungry, which can be hazardous to a young baby's health, or quitting breast-feeding altogether, then supplementing with a bottle is worth trying.

Once mother and baby have breast-feeding down pat, many parents use an occasional bottle for reasons of convenience—to let Mom sleep uninterrupted or to spend a few hours away from the baby. The baby may be more accepting of the bottle if it is offered fairly early—at seven or eight weeks, perhaps—and by Dad or someone else other than Mom. The nursing mother can express or pump her milk and freeze it for future use.

When mothers work full time outside the home, supplementing with bottles of formula or breast milk is necessary (unless you can take your baby to work or have on-site day care). Daily breast pumping usually becomes part of the routine.

Expressing or Pumping Breast Milk

Before you begin expressing or pumping milk, take a few minutes to prepare. First, wash your hands. Then massage your breast from the base toward the nipple. Try to induce letdown by thinking about your baby and nursing. Then begin. If you are expressing by hand or using a manual pump, it can take 15 to 30 minutes to drain both breasts; electric pumps usually are quicker.

Expressing Milk by Hand

To express milk by hand, place your fingers on your areola, with your thumb above your nipple and your index and middle fingers beneath it. Press back toward your chest, then roll your thumb and fingers forward, as though you were being fingerprinted. Repeat this, compressing different parts of the areola. Let the milk drip into a clean, wide-mouthed container, ideally one in which it can also be stored. At first, you may get only a few drops. But eventually you probably will be able to get several ounces at a time. Some mothers become quite good at hand expressing milk.

Pumping Milk with a Breast Pump

If you are pumping milk with a breast pump, the details of the process depend on the kind of machine you are using. Be careful to scrupulously clean the machine, carefully following the instructions that come with it.

Storing Breast Milk

Breast milk can be stored in the refrigerator in screw-top bottles or special, heavy bags made for this purpose, not regular plastic bags. You can refrigerate it for up to 72 hours before discarding, but freezing is preferable unless you know you will use it within 24 hours. Freeze breast milk in two-ounce or four-ounce servings so you don't waste it. Date the containers and keep them in the coldest part of the freezer (not the door). In a freezer at zero degrees Fahrenheit, breast milk should keep three to six months. If your refrigerator has a freezer compartment without a separate outer door, it may keep only two to three weeks.

Thaw frozen milk in the refrigerator. Or, for quicker thawing, place the container in a bowl of warm water. It's better not to use a microwave oven because it heats food unevenly, resulting in hot spots that can burn your baby's mouth. If you feel you need to use a microwave oven, make sure that the milk is well mixed to eliminate hot spots—and always check the temperature of the milk before feeding it to your baby.

Returning to Work

Many women continue nursing after returning to their prebaby jobs. Use the following tips to help prepare for your return:

- Practice expressing or pumping milk while you are still at home so that you get comfortable and efficient at doing it. Freeze the milk for use later.
- Introduce your baby to the bottle, using expressed breast milk. Ideally you should do this after your baby has been successfully nursing about six weeks and a week or two before you go back to work. Babies often seem to accept a bottle better if it is offered by someone other than their mother—by Dad or the person who will be caring for them while the mother is away. If your baby takes one bottle a day for a few days before you go back to work, you will be reassured that she'll eat while you're gone.
- Try to find caregivers for your child who will help you in your efforts to continue nursing. For instance, if possible, your baby should not be fed for a couple of hours before you arrive home, so he can nurse right away.
- If possible, ease into your work schedule. Return to work on a Wednesday or Thursday or start with a few half days.

If you want to continue nursing for many months while you work, try to maximize nursing during the time you are home. Wake earlier and nurse without hurrying before you get ready for work; breast-feed exclusively on the weekends. Although most parents are eager (even desperate) for their babies to sleep through the night, night nursing can help keep your milk supply up.

Taking Care of a Nursing Mother

A nursing mother should eat the same healthy, balanced diet that is recommended during pregnancy. (If you ate a lot of high-fat or sugary foods when you were pregnant, now would be a good time to improve your way of eating.)

The Food Guide Pyramid eating plan described in Chapter 22, "Healthy Eating," is healthy for children and will be just as healthy for you. Just eat more servings: six to eleven servings from the grain group of foods, three to five servings of vegetables, two to four servings of fruit, and three servings of meat, eggs, nuts, or dry beans. Load up on foods from the dairy group to keep up your supply of calcium. If you do not eat dairy products, make sure you get enough calcium. Try calcium-fortified orange juice or cereal, or take a supplement.

If you are a vegan (a vegetarian who eats no animal or dairy products at all— no meat, eggs, or cheese), take care to get enough calories (typically 2,200 to 2,700 a day) and enough protein and vitamin B_{12} in particular.

Drink plenty of caffeine-free fluids each day, about six glasses. Drink water before and during nursing.

KidsHealth Tip

Keep It Cool

If you will be pumping or expressing milk at work, keep it in a closed clean container in an insulated cooler or a refrigerator.

What About "Problem Foods"?

Proteins and other substances from foods you eat can be passed on to your baby in your breast milk. If there are allergies, asthma, or eczema in the family, your doctor may advise you to drink little or no milk while nursing. He or she may suggest that you avoid other foods that are most likely to cause allergies, such as peanuts, soy, fish (including shellfish), egg whites, and wheat.

But if allergies or asthma do not run in your family (and you don't have any yourself), you can eat just about anything you enjoy, including spicy foods. To minimize trouble, eat a variety of foods in moderate amounts rather than eating the same thing every day or having huge helpings of a single food. If you suspect your baby is reacting to something you ate, becoming fussy or refusing to eat, try eliminating the food for a few days or a week. If the symptoms disappear, try eating the food and see if they recur. The foods you eat may flavor your milk, and some babies may simply like or dislike certain flavors.

Some mothers find that eating broccoli, brussels sprouts, or cabbage seems to give their babies gas. And some babies seem to get restless or irritable because of caffeine, which can build up in a baby's system over a period of weeks. Although most nursing women can have a cup or two a day of coffee with caffeine (four- to six-ounce cups), beware of hidden caffeine in soft drinks, tea, chocolate, and over-the-counter medications. You may be consuming more caffeine than you realize.

Of course, if your baby has a rash, diarrhea, or vomiting, symptoms that can be signs of allergies or illness, consult his doctor.

Alcohol, Cigarettes, and Medication

Alcohol gets into breast milk, which means it gets into your baby—so be careful. But one beer, one shot of whiskey, or one glass of wine will not harm a breast-feeding infant. If you sometimes have several drinks in a row or have a drinking problem, discuss this with your baby's doctor. You should not breast-feed if you drink excessively.

If you are a smoker, you can breast-feed. A smoker's baby is more prone to illness whether he is fed by breast or bottle, so he might as well get the health benefits breast-feeding can provide.

Most—but not all—medications are considered safe to take while breast-feeding, so it's important to check with your doctor. Be sure any doctor who prescribes medications for you knows that you are breast-feeding.

KidsHealth Tip

You Can Get Pregnant if You Breast-Feed

Plenty of nursing mothers get pregnant. Breast-feeding stimulates prolactin, a hormone that can suppress the hormones needed to get pregnant. But prolactin levels vary and may fall low enough to allow conception, especially if a woman is not breast-feeding exclusively. After giving birth, some women ovulate and become fertile before they resume having menstrual periods. Don't rely on breast-feeding or the absence of your period for birth control.

Most over-the-counter medications (including acetaminophen, ibuprofen, aspirin, antihistamines, and decongestants) are also considered safe for occasional use. If you need to take them for more than a couple of days, consult your doctor. In general, try to handle minor conditions without drugs, and don't take more drugs than you need (in other words, don't take a multisymptom cold medicine if all you have is a cough).

Don't assume that herbal remedies are safe because they are "natural." Some herbs can be dangerous to you and your baby if taken in large amounts and can harm your milk supply. In addition, depending on the source of the herbs, it can be hard to know exactly what's in them. To be safe, check with your baby's doctor before taking any herbal remedies.

How to Deal with Common Problems

Be prepared to deal with a few problems as you and your baby learn how to breast-feed. There's no reason to panic or quit if these occur.

Engorgement

When your milk comes in, your breasts may become engorged—swollen and hard to the touch. They can be so firm that your baby may have a hard time latching on. You can express or pump a little milk until your breast is softer. Warm showers or warm moist towels wrapped around your breast a few minutes before a feeding also seem to get the milk flowing more easily. Some women find that using cold packs after a feeding makes them more comfortable. But the basic treatment for engorgement is to nurse frequently, at least every two to three hours.

Painful Nipples

Mild soreness of the nipples is common during the first few days of nursing. But severe or persistent pain is not normal, experts say, and you should not try to tough it out. Usually pain is caused by the baby's latching on to the nipple rather than the areola or by some other problem of technique. If you think you and your baby are doing everything right and you still have pain, have a lactation consultant or other breast-feeding expert watch you nurse.

Meanwhile, you can try expressing a few drops of milk and letting it dry on your nipples after nursing as a protective coating. Or try soothing the nipples with medical-grade purified lanolin, mentioned earlier, which does not have to be washed off before nursing. You can also try different feeding positions, express some milk at the start of a feeding to speed things up, and take an over-the-counter painkiller like acetaminophen or ibuprofen before nursing.

Sometimes, nipple pain occurs when a nipple is infected by candida—a type of yeast infection. Candida can cause white spots in the baby's mouth (called thrush) and burning or stabbing pain in the woman's nipples and deeper in the breast during and after nursing. Although most nipple pain occurs in the early days of nursing, pain caused by candida infection can occur after weeks of comfortable breast-feeding. Consult your doctor if you think you may have a nipple infection or if you think your infant has thrush. (See Chapter 29, "Signs and Symptoms," for more information regarding candida.)

Clogged Milk Duct

A breast has 15 to 20 ducts carrying milk to the nipple. If one gets plugged, it can cause a hard, sore lump to form. If left clogged, this can lead to a breast infection (mastitis). To solve the problem, nurse often, especially on the affected side. Apply warm moist heat, and gently massage the blocked area just before nursing to encourage milk flow. If your baby doesn't empty the affected side, it may help to pump that breast. If a lump lasts more than a few days, consult your doctor.

Infected Breast (Mastitis)

Mastitis is an infection of the breast, usually caused by bacteria. It is not harmful to the baby but can cause pain, heat, and swelling of part or all of the breast and may also cause fever and an achy, generally sick feeling in the mother. Consult your doctor if you have such symptoms. Mastitis typically is treated with antibiotics. It's usually possible to keep nursing despite the infection. Bed rest is often advised, along with moist warm compresses applied to the breast before nursing.

Jaundice

Jaundice, a yellowing of the skin, is extremely common in newborns. See Chapter 5, "Common Newborn Medical Conditions," for an explanation of breast-feeding jaundice and breast milk jaundice.

Refusing to Nurse

Sometimes after several months, a baby will suddenly refuse to nurse without any apparent reason. If you keep trying to nurse, the typical "nursing strike" is often over in a day or two. Nursing a sleepy baby in a dark, quiet room often seems to work. Meanwhile, you can express the milk and offer it in a spoon or a cup. In some cases, if your baby is six months or older, she may be telling you she's ready for weaning.

Nursing Twins and More

The mother who plans to breast-feed twins needs help right from the start. Early on, most mothers nurse each baby separately, so the mother is basically nursing (or napping) all the time and needs another set of hands to care for the baby who is not being nursed at the moment. Later, when both babies are breast-feeding well, mothers generally nurse them together, one on each breast, swapping breasts if one baby is a stronger nurser than the other. Simultaneous nursing of twins means that "feeding on demand" is very demanding.

Because twins often are born early, get prepared early. Besides using the sources of help mentioned earlier, you can contact the National Organization of Mothers of Twins Club to find a local support group for mothers of twins and other multiples; call (877) 540-2200, or check their Web site, www.nomotc.org.

Exclusively breast-feeding higher multiples—triplets or more—is hard and often impossible. Some mothers breast-feed two at each feeding while someone else bottle-feeds the rest so that all the babies are breast-fed some of the time but none is breast-fed all of the time.

Nursing an Adopted Infant

With a large investment of time and effort, some women can produce some breast milk for an adopted infant, a process called "induced lactation." This involves using a hospital-grade electric pump to pump the breasts every few hours for weeks before the baby arrives. It may also involve taking hormone-stimulating drugs.

Even women who have breast-fed in the past generally do not produce enough milk from these methods to meet a baby's nutritional needs, so supplementing is necessary. Many women produce little or no milk under these circumstances. In such cases, some advocates say nursing with a supplemental system and formula still helps build closeness. ("The production of milk, if it happens, is a pleasant side effect of the goal of a happy nursing relationship," according to La Leche League International.)

Others may feel that going to such lengths to breast-feed gives too much weight to the biological aspects of parenthood and adds tension to the adoption process. Parents who are adopting, especially after a difficult period of infertility, need to remember that millions of people revel in parent-child love, closeness, and bonding without breast-feeding. It doesn't take breast-feeding to make a "real" mother.

Weaning

The American Academy of Pediatrics, which represents most U.S. pediatricians, recommends that in most cases, babies need nothing but breast milk for the first six months of life. After that, as solid food is added, breast-feeding should continue until the baby is at least one year old, then for as long as both mother and baby desire. Most experts today feel that there is nothing wrong with nursing into the toddler or even the preschool years if mother and child are both comfortable with it. On the other hand, a mother shouldn't pressure a child to keep nursing if he no longer wants to.

KidsHealth Tip

Nipple Care

- Keep your nipples dry between feedings. Change nursing pads or your bra as soon as it is damp. Use a cotton bra without any kind of plastic liner, which can trap moisture. Open the flaps of your nursing bra to allow nipples to air-dry.
- Be sure your bra is supportive but not tight.
- Don't use soap or other drying cleansers on your breasts.

Babies generally start eating some solid food by six months (for more information, see Chapter 22, "Healthy Eating"), but usually they are about 9 to 12 months old before they are eating enough to make a difference in their hunger for breast milk. At this age, many babies start to lose interest in breast-feeding, and mothers start to replace breast-feeding sessions with food and drink from a cup.

Ideally, weaning is gradual. One daily breast-feeding session is dropped, then a week or so later another session is dropped. This lets both the mother's breasts and the child adjust to the change. Usually, the first feeding to go is the midday session, which tends to be smallest and least convenient. The last feeding before bed is usually the last to go, and some mothers continue this pleasant good-night ritual months or even longer after their baby is eating solid food.

Another approach to weaning is to leave it up to your child entirely. Once your child is eating three meals and several snacks a day of solid food, stop offering the breast and nurse only when your child asks for it. With this approach, some babies continue to "snack" on breast milk long after they are eating solid food. Unless mothers pump, their milk may dry up in such a situation.

Whether you drop nursing sessions or try the "nursing by request only" approach, you can ease the transition for your baby. Offer a well-liked snack, a fun play activity, or a special outing at a time when your baby usually nurses. Avoid sitting in your usual nursing spots or wearing your usual nursing clothes. If there are some "big kid" things your toddler has been hankering to do, try doing them to emphasize the pleasures of growing up.

No matter how or when you wean, make sure you offer plenty of loving attention to reassure your baby that mother's love will not wane when nursing ends.

Weaning Earlier than One Year

Despite the experts' recommendations, most women stop breast-feeding before their child is one year old. This is an issue you must decide based on what's best for your baby, your family, and you. If you wean from the breast well before the child is one year old, you will need to switch to formula—before a baby is one, he should get formula, not regular cow's milk. If your child is close to one, you may want to try switching to formula and a cup, rather than a bottle. If you do switch to formula, be sure to read the next chapter, which is full of tips for making bottle-feeding nourishing and healthy.

ⓘ Need More Information?

Check the Index and Appendix C, "Resource Guide." And of course, consult your child's doctor.

chapter ten

Bottle-Feeding

A parent's guide

If you've decided that you want to bottle-feed your baby, do it with confidence, and pay no attention if anyone tries to make you feel guilty about not breast-feeding. This is your baby, your body, and your decision. Enjoy it, and watch your newborn grow into a strong and healthy child.

If you wanted to breast-feed, but you or your baby had problems with it, you may be feeling some disappointment, however. Try to turn from such thoughts. Even if bottle-feeding wasn't your first choice, it is now the best choice for you and your baby. And thank goodness this safe, nutritious choice exists. Embrace it (and your baby) with love, and don't look back.

Bottle Basics

Feeding time should be a nurturing experience that gives you a chance to focus your full attention on your baby. Here are some pointers for happy bottle-feeding:

- Settle yourself in a comfortable chair, preferably in a quiet place. Or prop yourself up in bed. Cradle your baby against your body, with his head resting on the inside of your elbow and his bottom held in your hand. You can also feed your baby while he is in a baby sling or a front holder facing you. To reduce spitting up, your baby should be semierect, with his head higher than his feet (see Figure 10.1).
- To simulate the breast-feeding experience, you can open your shirt so you and your baby have skin-to-skin contact.

- Gently place the nipple between your baby's lips. Keep the bottle tilted so that the nipple is always filled with formula. This prevents the baby from swallowing air, which can cause discomfort.
- Midway through the feeding, remove the bottle and burp your baby (for details, see Chapter 11, "Baby-Care Basics"). Burp him again at the end.
- Look in your baby's eyes while he's eating, and talk to him quietly.
- When your baby is finished, hold him in a semiupright position for a while to reduce spitting up. Bottle-fed babies tend to eat more quickly than breast-fed babies, but they should get just as much cozy contact. So hold, cuddle, or rock your baby after he has eaten. But be gentle. If you bounce him around after a meal, it's likely he'll spit his meal right back at you.
- Never prop a bottle up so your baby can eat on his own. This deprives the baby of the loving contact he needs, and it can be dangerous if the baby chokes.
- Don't put your baby to sleep with a bottle. This can lead not only to spitting up and choking, but it can also promote ear infections and severe tooth decay.
- If other family members or hired helpers will be feeding your baby, make sure they know and follow these tips.

Choosing a Formula

Ask your baby's doctor to recommend a formula. The American Academy of Pediatrics' Committee on Nutrition recommends using a formula that is based on cow's milk and fortified with iron. In such formulas, the cow's milk has been modified to be more digestible and somewhat more like human milk. If a baby is fussy, gassy, or colicky, with daily crying spells that seem to have no cause, parents often suspect an allergy or intolerance to formula, but studies have shown that such intolerances are uncommon. Sometimes, however, a baby may prefer one milk-based formula to another. It may be just a matter of taste.

In recent years, as vegetarianism and soy foods have become more popular, more parents have chosen formulas based on soy protein. Most doctors, however, do not recommend using soy formula unless a baby is truly allergic to milk-based formula or cannot tolerate the milk sugar lactose (lactose intolerance is rare in infants). Soy formulas are even less like human milk than cow's-milk-based formulas. One major difference is that soy lacks lactose, which helps with calcium absorption.

Figure 10.1. Proper bottle-feeding technique. Note that the bottle is held with the bottom angled upward. This keeps the nipple filled with formula and helps prevent the baby from swallowing excessive amounts of air while sucking.

Unfortunately, infants who are allergic to cow's-milk-based formula often are allergic to soy formula as well. For these babies, formulas based on hydrolyzed (predigested) protein are generally used. Other special formulas are available for specific medical conditions. If you think your baby may need a soy-based or hydrolyzed formula, you should check with your child's doctor first.

Whatever type of formula you choose, stick with commercially prepared formulas for an infant. Plain milk, soy milk, and evaporated milk are not good substitutes; nor are homemade formulas. Occasionally, formula "recipes" may circulate on the Internet or among parents of babies with medical conditions. These may be nutritionally inadequate or contain dangerous or untested ingredients; it is safer not to use them. And don't change a commercial formula by diluting it (which can leave a baby malnourished), by making it more concentrated (which can tax a baby's kidneys), or by adding anything to it (which can be dangerous). If you think your baby needs a change, discuss it with your child's doctor.

Packaging Choices

Formulas come packaged in a variety of ways. Here we list them from the least expensive (and generally least convenient) to the costliest and easiest:

- Powdered formula, which you mix with water (sterilized if water comes from a well), in large cans or individual packets

- Concentrated liquid formula, which you dilute with water (sterilized if water comes from a well)
- Ready-to-feed liquid formula in large cans (Once opened, these must be refrigerated and used within a day or two or discarded—check the label.)
- Ready-to-feed formula in single-serving cans, which you pour into a bottle
- Ready-to-feed formula in disposable bottles

Whichever kind you generally use, you may want to keep some single-serving cans or bottles in the house. They are convenient if you and your baby need to go somewhere on short notice or if you miscalculate and run out of your usual formula in the middle of the night.

Once your baby seems happy with a certain kind of formula, you can save money by buying it in cases at discount groceries or shopping clubs. Just be sure to check the expiration dates: You don't want it to expire before you have a chance to use it all. Wherever you buy formula, be sure you always keep enough on hand to last at least several days.

KidsHealth Tip
Getting Help

Whether breast-feeding or using formula, U.S. parents who have trouble affording nutritious food for mother and child may be able to get help from the federal feeding program called Special Supplemental Nutrition Program for Women, Infants, and Children (WIC). In most states, the program is run through the state health department and serves mothers and young children in families whose gross income (before taxes) is no more than 185 percent of the federal poverty level. (For example, the year 2000 income limit was $25,678 for a family of three in most states.) WIC serves almost half of all babies born in the United States each year. Find out more at www.fns.usda.gov/wic, or call your state health department.

KidsHealth Tip

Safe Shopping Tips

- Always check the expiration date on formula (and on any other dated baby products) before you buy it.
- If you see outdated cans for sale, be a good citizen and tell the store staff so they will pull the product off the shelf.
- Don't buy cans that are dented or bulging.

Types of Baby Bottles

Bottles come in various types; which ones you choose will be a matter of your own and your baby's preference. You can try a few types, if necessary, and then stock up on the ones your baby prefers.

Typically, bottles come in four-ounce and eight-ounce sizes. If you are bottle-feeding from birth, you'll probably want four to six of the small bottles and six to ten of the larger ones. Or, to economize, you can use the big bottles from the start, but put in just a few ounces of formula at first.

Each size can be found in three versions:

1. Straight style. This is the standard, classic bottle—nothing fancy.
2. Bent neck. The bent neck allows you to hold the bottle at a more comfortable angle while still keeping the nipple filled with formula; this prevents your baby from swallowing air. Filling bent-neck bottles, however, requires more care to avoid spills.
3. Straight with disposable liner. Bottles with disposable, sterilized liners—the Playtex Nurser is the classic—free you from sterilizing bottles and also are supposed to minimize air swallowing. The drawback is that you must keep buying new liners.

You'll also see bottles with novelty shapes—hourglass shapes, footballs, loops, and handles that make holding the bottle easier for a baby. For an infant, however, you want a bottle that is easy to clean (without a lot of odd-shaped crannies) and has easy-to-read markings (so you can see how much formula is left). Your newborn will not be feeding herself, so the handles are unnecessary.

Some baby bottles are still made of glass, but most are made of plastic. Rigid, clear plastic bottles are usually made of polycarbonate. Softer tinted plastic bottles and disposable liners are usually made of polyethylene or polypropylene.

In 1999, controversy arose about polycarbonate bottles when Consumer Reports advised against their use. At issue are experiments in which liquid was boiled in those bottles for 30 minutes and minuscule amounts of a substance called bisphenol-A leached out of the plastic into the liquid. Other experiments, however, have not found this kind of leaching to occur. In addition, scientists differ over whether there is evidence that bisphenol-A does harm, even if it does leach into formula. The U.S. Food and Drug Administration has said the bottles are safe for normal use. If you use clear plastic bottles, you can minimize any chance of leaching by sterilizing and cooling the bottles before they are filled. (For more information on sterilizing bottles, see Do You Need to Sterilize Bottles, Nipples, and Water? later in this chapter.)

Types of Nipples

Nipples generally come in three shapes: the standard bell shape; the "orthodontic," which is longer and flattened on one side; and the flattened nipple, which comes with disposable nursers. Both the orthodontic and the flattened nipple are supposed to promote a sucking action more like the one used by breast-feeding

Shopping List for Bottle-Feeding

- Four-ounce bottles
- Eight-ounce bottles
- Nipples
- Bottle brush
- Nipple brush (or combined bottle/nipple brush)
- Can or bottle opener
- Jar to hold clean nipples
- Insulated bag and ice pack for outings
- Possibly, tongs for sterilizing, sterilizer, bottle warmer

babies, but there is no consensus that they are better for the baby's oral development than the standard type.

Nipples also vary in the size of the hole, which helps determine how hard your baby must work to get food. Too small and your baby may become frustrated and exhausted, too large and your baby may start to choke on a gush of formula. A general rule of thumb says that when you turn the bottle upside down, formula should drip at one drop a second for a few seconds and then stop. If you need to enlarge a hole or make additional holes as your baby grows, you can do this with a hot sewing needle or pin.

You can also adjust the flow by adjusting the ring that holds the nipple on the bottle. If you loosen the ring a bit, air enters the bottle and the liquid flows more readily; if you tighten the ring, the flow is reduced.

Nipples are made out of either latex (the tan ones) or silicone (the clear ones). Latex may grow sticky or clogged or start to break down after a couple of months of use. With silicone, it's easier to see if the nipples are clean. Silicone nipples do not get sticky or deteriorate—but they may tear.

Whatever kind of nipples you use, check them frequently for wear, and keep extras in reserve for replacements. You don't want your baby chewing a piece off a damaged nipple.

Do You Need to Sterilize Bottles, Nipples, and Water?

Talk to your baby's doctor about sterilizing bottles, nipples, and water. Some doctors recommend sterilizing bottles and nipples for the first three months of your baby's life. Others think this is not necessary if your water comes from a municipal water supply that is chlorinated, but they recommend sterilizing if you use well water or another nonchlorinated water supply. In addition, whatever your water supply, package labels often recommend sterilizing before a new item—a nipple, bottle, pacifier, or teething toy—is used for the first time.

If you do want to sterilize bottles, you should rinse them well immediately after use, getting rid of all visible formula. Then you can sterilize in various ways:

- Use a dishwasher with hot water and a hot drying cycle.
- Submerge them in a pot of water and boil for 20 minutes with the pot covered. If you use glass bottles, put a washcloth or dishtowel on the bottom of the pot to cushion them.

- Use a stovetop sterilizer, which is a pot with a rack to hold bottles and other implements while you steam them.
- Use an electric sterilizer. Its chief advantages are that you can use it anywhere there's an electric outlet and it turns itself off.
- Use a microwave sterilizer, which goes into a microwave oven. It allows you to avoid heating up the kitchen and also turns itself off.

If you are sterilizing bottles, you should sterilize everything you use to prepare them. Depending what formula you use, this could include can openers, measuring cups or spoons, bottle rings and caps, jars for storing clean nipples, and jars for mixing formula.

If you use powdered or concentrated formula, you'll need to mix it with clean water—either tap water (from the cold tap) or bottled water. If your child's doctor thinks your baby needs sterilized water, boil it for five minutes, whether it's bottled or tap water. (Bottled water is generally not sterile unless it is intended for medical use and is labeled sterile.) Don't boil water so long that a lot of it boils away; that could concentrate any chemicals that might be present.

Keeping Things Clean

If you don't sterilize, you should still pay attention to keeping things clean:

- Wash bottles, nipples, bottle rings, and caps in hot soapy water. Use a bottle brush on the bottles. Use a nipple brush on the nipples, and squeeze soapy water, followed by clear rinse water, through the holes.
- If you use formula from a can, wash the top of the can with soap and hot water and dry it before opening. (If you're sterilizing, rinse with boiling water.)
- Set aside a can opener to use on formula cans, and wash it as carefully as you wash the bottles after each use.
- Let bottles, nipples, and the rest air-dry thoroughly on a clean dishtowel or paper towel. Special bottle-drying racks can make things neater.

How to Prepare Formula

Wash your hands before you start. Follow the directions on the label carefully about how to mix formula, whether to shake it, how to store it, and how long you

KidsHealth Tip

Feed on Demand

Newborns should be fed at the first sign of hunger and allowed to eat as much as they want at each feeding. Feed your newborn whenever he shows signs of hunger, says the American Academy of Pediatrics (AAP). Early signs of hunger include increasing alertness or activity, mouthing objects, and rooting with the mouth. Don't assume that if your baby is not crying, he's not hungry. Crying is a late sign of hunger—by the time a baby is howling, he's already been hungry for a while. Plus, crying may be a sign of many other problems as well—or of no problem at all!

The AAP and many other child-care professionals fear that some newborns may not grow as well if they are put on strict feeding schedules.

Because formula takes longer to digest than breast milk, formula-fed babies generally go a little longer between feedings than breast-feeders. For the first month or so, a formula-fed baby will usually eat every three to four hours, round-the-clock. In the first week or if your baby is particularly small, she may eat even more frequently. If your baby sleeps longer than four or five hours between feedings, wake her up and offer her a bottle.

During the first few days of life, babies may eat very little, a teaspoonful or less. For the next month, babies typically take two to four ounces at a feeding. A rule of thumb says that in each 24-hour day, newborns drink two to three ounces of formula for each pound of their body weight. For example, a seven-pound baby would take 14 to 21 ounces.

As the months pass, babies take more at a sitting and eat less frequently, usually settling into a fairly predictable routine. By the time they reach 12 pounds, many can take enough to sleep through the night. By six months, babies typically are taking formula four or five times a day, consuming 7 to 8 ounces at each feeding, or up to 32 ounces (one quart) in a 24-hour day. At that point, they should start to get an increasing share of their nutrition from solid food. They can also start drinking from a cup (see Chapter 22, "Healthy Eating," for more information).

The best guide to whether your baby is eating enough is how well he is growing. But if your baby is eating far more or far less than the amounts outlined here—or if you have any other feeding concerns—consult your baby's doctor.

can keep opened containers before discarding. With liquid formula, double-check whether it needs to be diluted. It is important not to make formula stronger or weaker than it is supposed to be. If you change brands or types, check the label; the directions may be different.

Prepare no more than a day's worth at a time. You can either fill the bottles, cap them, and refrigerate them or prepare the formula in a clean (or sterilized) jar, refrigerate it, and fill the bottles as you need them. Do not freeze formula.

Once your baby has drunk from a bottle, discard whatever is left. If your baby dozes off while eating and wakes in a few minutes, it's OK to keep using the same bottle, but don't save leftovers for a later feeding. The formula may have become contaminated with bacteria.

If you're taking filled bottles on an outing, pack them in an insulated bag with an ice pack, ice cubes, or a frozen juice box. To be safe, the formula should still feel cold to the touch at the time you use it. A safe alternative is to take along unopened single-serving cans and clean, capped bottles. Then fill a bottle just before feeding.

Most babies seem to do fine with formula whether it is cold (straight from the refrigerator) or slightly warmed (to room temperature or to body temperature). Babies may have individual preferences or may become used to a certain temperature. Follow these directions to warm refrigerated formula:

- Hold the bottle for a few moments under warm running water, or put it in a bowl of warm water.
- At night, you may want to use an electric bottle warmer. These devices are usually kept at the bedside. They keep a bottle cold until you need it, then rapidly warm it, saving you a trip to the refrigerator.

KidsHealth Tip
Offer a Little Extra

How much should you put in your baby's bottle? An ounce or two more than she usually eats. That way, if she's extra hungry or her appetite is growing, she'll still get enough. If you give her only what she eats, so that she always empties the bottle, you'll never know if she would have taken more if it had been available.

- Do **not** use a microwave to warm a bottle. The bottle may feel cool to the touch but still have hot spots inside that can burn your baby.
- Do **not** let a bottle sit at room temperature to get warm for more than a few minutes.
- Test the temperature of the formula by dripping a few drops onto the inside of your wrist. It should feel neutral, neither cold nor warm.

Common Feeding Problems

Your baby may experience a few common feeding problems such as spitting up, vomiting, and food allergies. For tips on dealing with these problems, see Chapter 11, "Baby-Care Basics."

Weaning

Many pediatricians and dentists recommend weaning from the bottle at one year, largely to avoid tooth decay. In reality, however, many formula-fed babies, like many breast-fed babies, do not seem ready at 12 months to give up their comforting source of sucking. Others may still find drinking from a cup a struggle. It is common for children of two or even three years to want a bottle, especially before bed, just as many breast-fed children of that age still want the breast. You needn't feel guilty or embarrassed about this. But there are some ways you can prevent the bottle from becoming a problem:

- Do not let your child take a bottle to bed. Falling asleep with a mouthful of formula, milk, or juice can cause severe tooth decay—the dreaded "baby bottle caries"—as well as increase the likelihood of ear infections. Even taking water to bed will reinforce your child's association between the bottle and sleeping; this is not a good idea.
- Do not let your child carry a bottle around all day as a pacifier. Restrict its use to certain times and places—at the table during mealtimes, for instance, or in the rocking chair just before bed.
- Don't suggest the bottle if your child doesn't ask for it.
- Try not to let your child drink so much milk or formula from the bottle that she has no appetite for solid food. This can be a balancing act: If your child

eats very little or has trouble with gagging or choking on solid food, you may welcome the bottle as a way of providing some sure nourishment until your little one gets more skilled or enthusiastic about eating. The trick is not to rely on it so heavily that your child is discouraged from eating.

Eventually, most children either lose interest in the bottle or, spurred by peer pressure, reject it as babyish. If you are weaning before that happens, do it gradually, with a week or so of adjustment time between steps. Here are some methods you can use:

- Drop one bottle-feeding a day, substituting formula or milk in a cup and a solid snack. A week or so later, drop another session. Usually, the midday session is the easiest to drop first, and the bedtime feeding is the last to go.
- Gradually decrease the amount of formula at each bottle-feeding, then drop the feedings one by one, substituting milk in a cup.
- Switch from formula to water in the bottle, then drop the feedings one by one, substituting water in a cup.

No matter how you wean, you can ease the transition for your baby by offering a well-liked snack or a fun activity at a time when your child usually has a bottle. If there are some "big kid" things your toddler has been wanting to do, try doing them to emphasize the pleasure of growing up. And make sure you offer plenty of loving attention to reassure your child as she gives up the bottle, a source of comfort and security.

Need More Information?

Check the Index and Appendix C, "Resource Guide." And of course, consult your child's doctor.

chapter eleven

Baby-Care Basics

A how-to manual for daily care

"Relax!" "Enjoy!" That's what many experienced parents told us when we asked them for the best advice they ever got about taking care of their new baby. Wonderful advice, you may say—if only you could do it. You and your partner may be thrilled about being parents, and you may pass the first weeks with your newborn in a blissful haze of love and gratitude (made hazier by lack of sleep). But this period of adjustment, joyful as it may be, is also likely to include moments of self-doubt, times of concern, and flashes of absolute terror. "I have a baby! What do I do now?" These feelings—the good and the bad—are perfectly normal. With some guidance from more experienced moms and dads, and help (if you need it) from health professionals, you're more than likely to get through this time with a happy, healthy baby (and some wonderfully sweet memories!).

If you feel insecure, remember that you're not alone. If you're having problems, reach out: Ask questions, ask for help, and seek support. Although your hospital stay is likely to be short, take advantage of the expertise around you while you are there. Many hospitals have feeding specialists who can help you get started nursing or bottle-feeding. Nurses can show you how to hold, burp, and change your baby. Friends and more experienced parents can tell you about local parenting centers, playgroups, or sources for babysitters.

For more extended help, you might want to hire a doula or a baby nurse to help you for a week or two after your baby is home. Ask the hospital staff or your baby's doctor for referrals, and make sure you interview each woman in person. Are you comfortable with her? Is your baby? Ask for references, and contact each one. Above all, trust your instincts. (For more information about doulas, see Chapter 3, "Your Baby's Birth," and Chapter 9, "Breast-Feeding.")

Don't forget to tap into the kindness of relatives. They may be eager to help and, although you may disagree on certain things, you shouldn't dismiss their experience. Having your mother or mother-in-law on hand for the first several weeks can also be a way of connecting through the generations in a special way.

Whether you have help or not, focus on your baby's needs and your own, without worrying about whether your house is clean or your guests are fed. Invite only those visitors who will help—either by lending a sympathetic ear or by doing the laundry. Don't ask anything of yourself beyond caring for your baby and building your new family.

When you're not sure about the "right" way to do something for your baby, remember that there's no one way to do things. As long as you and your baby are safe and healthy and it works for you, it's right. As one mother told us in our KidsHealth survey: "Listen to everyone's advice, and then do what you feel comfortable doing. Parenting is not a perfect science. Follow your instinct."

In the very beginning, your baby's world is not too complex. She will spend most of the day and night eating or sleeping, and you should let her do these things on her own schedule. If you haven't had experience with a newborn, you may be surprised how little else she does at first. We discuss feeding in Chapters 8 through 10 and sleep in Chapter 21, "Sleep." In this chapter, we'll focus on the other basics—including handling, soothing, diapering, and bathing—that will be part of this unique period in your life—and your baby's.

Handling Your Newborn

It's true—you don't have to handle your newborn like a piece of fragile glassware. But you should be careful to support his head. Because a very young infant hasn't developed head control, he needs to be carried so that his head doesn't flop from side to side or snap back to front. Cradle the head when carrying your baby in a lying position, and support his head when carrying him upright or when you lay him down.

Be careful not to shake a newborn, whether in play or in frustration. Shaking can cause brain damage, even death. If constant crying, for instance, has you on the verge of losing control and no help is available, put your baby down in a safe place and walk out of the room. If you need to wake an infant, don't shake him—instead, tickle his feet or blow gently on his cheek.

When he's traveling, make sure he's securely fastened into his carrier, stroller, or car seat. Limit car rides and any other activity that would jounce him around.

Whatever you do, do it gently. A newborn is not ready for rough play, such as being jiggled on the knee or thrown up in the air. Instead, begin building bonds between parent and child by holding the baby, looking at him, stroking him, and talking and singing to him.

Soothing and Connecting with Your Baby

Infants know they are cared for when they are held, caressed, massaged, and kissed. In most cases, they love attention. Cradle your baby in your lap, and gently stroke her in different rhythmical patterns. This simple bit of love and attention can reap great benefits: Studies have shown that babies who are seldom touched don't grow or develop normally. If you and your partner both hold and touch your infant a lot, she will soon come to know the difference between Mommy's and Daddy's ways of touching.

Premature babies and those with medical difficulties may especially respond to infant massage. Many books and videos cover the subject; discuss with your child's doctor which one you think might work for you and your baby. Be careful, however; babies are not as strong as adults are and can't take anything like the pressure or manipulation of a regular adult massage.

Babies usually love sounds, so talk, babble, sing, and coo away in the first months. Most babies also like everyday sounds like pots and pans rattling and the sounds of other children playing and laughing. Take advantage of your baby's own "talking"; repeat whatever sounds she makes and wait for her to make more. These "conversations" teach lessons about tone, pacing, and taking turns when talking to someone else. Touch and name all the parts of your baby's body as she watches. Make a game out of it by moving your hands from her foot to her hands and back again.

> ### The Best Advice I Got Was . . .
>
> ". . . from my oldest son's pediatrician. He told me that there are many opinions as to what is right and wrong when raising a child, but as long as common sense and love always come first, I could not do anything to hurt him."

> ### The Voice of Experience
>
> "No one loves your baby like you! So love him up now! There will never again be a time when it is just you and him."
> —FROM THE KIDSHEALTH PARENT SURVEY

Your baby probably will also love listening to music. Try out a variety of types and see what she seems to like best. Baby rattles and musical mobiles are other good ways to stimulate your infant's hearing. If your baby is being fussy, try singing, reciting poetry and nursery rhymes, or reading to her as you rock gently in a rocking chair. Or put on some calming music. Hold your baby's face close to your own and gently sway to the tune. It might calm you both. Take your baby for a walk in a stroller, baby carrier, or sling, and sing to her when she's being fussy.

Some babies, especially premature ones, may be unusually sensitive to touch, light, or sound. Such a baby may startle and cry easily, sleep less than you might expect, or turn her face away when you speak or sing to her. Try to keep noise and light levels moderate, and move slowly and calmly when you interact with her. Watch her reactions closely, and back off if she seems stressed.

Many babies like to be carried and held *all* the time. The closer you can come to meeting this need (perhaps by carrying your baby on your chest in a cloth carrier or sling), the easier it may be for you both.

The "Blues" and Depression

It's estimated that "baby blues" strike about 50 percent of all new mothers in the first week after birth, and they strike many fathers and adoptive mothers as well. Usually lasting only a few days, the blues may bring anxiety, sadness, irritability, and insomnia. You may swing from joy to weepiness and back again for no apparent reason. Don't let these feelings worry you. They are normal and will pass.

In rare cases, however, serious postpartum depression can occur, sometimes two or three months after a birth. Fortunately, it is very treatable. If you are depressed most of the time for two weeks or more, you should get medical help promptly. Some signs of depression include losing interest in activities you usually enjoy, sleeping too little or too much, feeling jittery or drained of energy, feeling worthless or guilty, and being unable to concentrate. If you have thoughts about death, suicide, or harming your child, get help right away. You can start by calling your doctor. In an emergency, call 911 or go to a hospital emergency room.

Make Room for Daddy

When both parents are involved in your baby's life right from the beginning, it's good for your child and for everyone in your growing family. But fathers sometimes feel left out—especially if the mother is breast-feeding—or feel nervous about caring for the baby. If that's the case in your family, you both may need to make an effort to involve Dad in every aspect of your child's life. Both parents can carry your baby, diaper him, play with him, take him for walks, rock him, sing to him, read him stories, and bathe him. (Even when Mother and Baby are nursing, Dad can be there to keep them company and share the moment.) There's plenty for everyone to do.

Diapering

Cloth diapers and disposable ones both have advantages: Cloth diapers are "natural," can be less expensive than disposables in the long run, are softer to the baby's skin, and breathe better. If you use a diaper service, cloth diapers can be almost as easy to use as disposables. On the other hand, disposables are convenient and require no washing or pickup service. Some people use a diaper service in the first few weeks and then switch to disposables. Some use cloth diapers at home and disposables when the baby has an outing. Whichever you use, you will need about 10 diapers a day, or about 70 a week.

Diapers and the Environment

There's been lots of discussion about the environmental effects of reusable and disposable diapers, making it hard to know what's best. Most experts agree that reusable diapers require more water and generate more waterborne wastes as a result of the laundering process. In addition, home laundering uses more energy than commercial laundering (which can also be expensive!).

So what's the downside of disposable diapers? Manufacturing them requires more raw materials, and they are the third largest source of solid waste—the average baby will go through 70 a week! Although some diapers are touted as biodegradable, the lack of oxygen in landfills means disposable diapers can take a long time to break down.

Getting Rid of Diaper Rash

Most babies have at least a few bouts of diaper rash, and some have rashes so frequently that it becomes a constant irritation. To help prevent or heal diaper rash, try this:

- Change your baby's wet or soiled diaper promptly, especially after she's had a bowel movement.
- After cleaning the area with mild soap and water or a prepackaged wipe, apply a diaper cream. Creams with zinc oxide are recommended because they form a barrier against moisture.
- If you use cloth diapers, launder them in dye- and fragrance-free detergents, and avoid drying them with scented dryer sheets.
- Let your baby go undiapered for part of the day, lying on top of a couple of open cloth diapers. (If you have a boy, place another cloth diaper over him when he's on his back to avoid his spraying you, the walls, and everything else in range.)

If the diaper rash continues for more than three days, call your child's doctor—it may be caused by a fungal infection that needs a prescription ointment.

In weighing your choice, you may want to consider the environmental challenges in your local area; for example, if you live in an area prone to droughts and water shortages, disposable diapers may be the better choice.

Getting Ready

Before diapering a baby, make sure you have all supplies within easy reach. Never—not even for a second—leave your baby unattended on the changing table. As one of our readers enthusiastically told us, "Never underestimate your baby's ability to roll!"

To change a newborn, you need the following items on hand:

- A clean diaper and fasteners if a cloth diaper is used
- Diaper ointment or petroleum jelly, especially if your baby has a rash

- Cotton balls and a small basin with lukewarm water and a clean washcloth (Or you can use commercial diaper wipes as long as your baby is not sensitive to them.)

What do you do next? Remove the dirty diaper by gently lifting your baby's legs and feet and sliding it out from under the buttocks. Use the water, cotton balls, and washcloth or the wipes to gently wipe your baby's bottom area clean. When removing a boy's diaper, do so carefully because exposure to the air may make him urinate right then and there. When wiping a girl, wipe her bottom from front to back to help avoid urinary tract infection. If your baby has a rash, apply ointment. (Some parents like to apply ointment to the diaper area routinely to prevent the development of a rash.) Remember to wash your hands after changing a diaper.

If using disposable diapers, remember the following tips (see Figures 11.1a–b):

- Open the diaper and, gently lifting your baby's legs and feet, slide the diaper underneath. Then attach, using tape on both sides.
- Bowel movements should be emptied into the toilet before the diaper is put into the garbage. Garbage should be emptied regularly to prevent a health hazard.

11.1a

11.1b

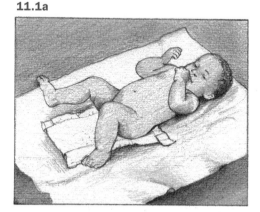 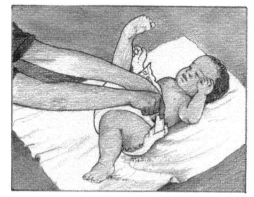

Figures 11.1a–b. Diapering with disposable diapers. First place the open diaper underneath your baby with the back (or top part with adhesive strips) about level with your baby's navel. Then bring the front (or bottom) part of the diaper up between your baby's legs and onto his belly. Fasten snugly with the adhesive strips.

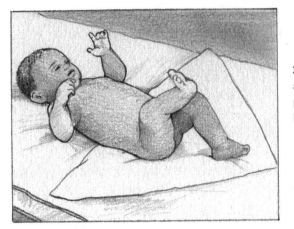

11.2a. Diapering your infant with a cloth diaper is a three-step process. First, fold the diaper in half to form a triangle, and place it under your baby as shown in (a).

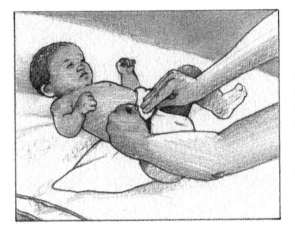

11.2b. Bring the bottom corner up between the legs and onto your baby's belly, and then fold one side corner over and across to the middle of the belly so that it overlaps with the bottom corner (b).

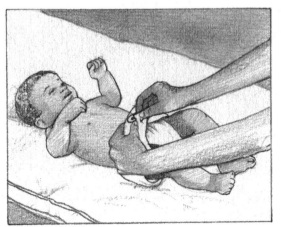

11.2c. Last, fold the remaining side corner to overlap with the other two corners on your baby's belly. Fasten all three corners together with a safety pin, being careful not to prick your baby with the pin (c). You can also choose to secure a cloth diaper on both sides—like a disposable diaper with adhesive strips—by using two safety pins.

Figures 11.2a–c. Cloth diapering technique.

If you are using cloth diapers, keep these helpful tips in mind (see Figures 11.2a–c):

- Cloth diapers usually come prefolded or in a square that you can fold into a triangle to fit your child. Initially, you will probably need to fold about a third of the diaper down from the end so that it's not too long. If the diaper has extra padding, place it in the front for boys and in the back for girls.
- Place your baby in the diaper by gently lifting your baby's feet and legs as little as possible and sliding the diaper under. If using a rectangular fold, bring the diaper through the middle and fasten on both sides. If using a triangle, bring the center corner up through the middle; then bring one and the other ends together, and fasten in the middle.
- If using pins, use oversize pins with plastic safety heads. To prevent pricking your baby, keep your hand between the pin and his skin. If this makes you nervous, use diaper tape that comes in a dispenser.
- If you are washing the diapers yourself, wash them separately from other laundry, using a mild baby detergent. Don't use fabric softener or antistatic products, which can cause rashes on sensitive baby skin. Use hot water and double rinse each wash.

Swaddling

When you first see your baby in the hospital nursery, she will probably look like a well-wrapped package. Her body will be swaddled in a receiving blanket that keeps her arms close to her body and her legs securely bound. During the first few weeks, your baby can spend much of her time wrapped in a receiving blanket. Not only does this keep her warm, but the slight pressure also seems to give most newborns a sense of security and comfort. Here's how to swaddle your baby (see Figures 11.3a–d):

1. Spread the blanket out flat.
2. Lay your baby face up on the blanket with her head at a corner.
3. Wrap the bottom corner over her body, and hold it over her belly.
4. Bring one of the side corners onto her belly up over her feet.
5. Wrap the other side corner around her.

That's it! Your baby is now securely swaddled.

11.3a

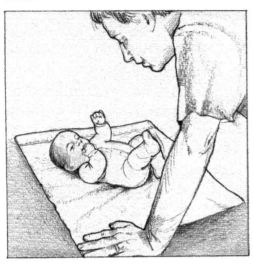

11.3b

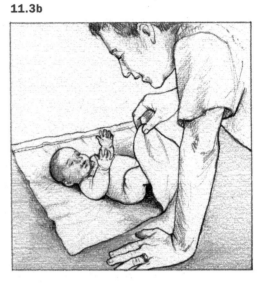

11.3c

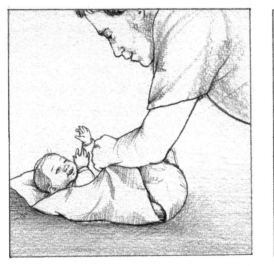

11.3d

Figures 11.3a–d. Swaddling. To swaddle your baby, first place the infant on a square or rectangular blanket, as shown in (a). Next, fold the bottom corner over your baby's body. Then fold one of the side corners onto the belly. Then, bring the remaining side corner over and wrap it snugly around your infant's body, covering the other corners.

Pacifiers

A child's need to suck her thumb or a pacifier comes from a normal reflex that is present at birth. These behavioral forms of sucking do not indicate emotional problems in your baby. In fact, about 80 percent of children suck at times other than feedings. Many seem to need to suck to comfort or quiet themselves, and this behavior will often increase as breast- or bottle-feeding decreases. Most babies discontinue this extra sucking around age one.

Because your baby's need to suck is natural, you won't want to stop her. Both thumb and pacifier have their advantages. The thumb never gets lost in the middle of the night or left behind at Grandma's; the pacifier is within the parents' control and can be removed at a later age. It's hard to say which is better.

If you prefer pacifiers, they should be introduced in the first eight weeks (but if you're nursing, wait until breast-feeding is well established, usually by six weeks, to avoid "nipple confusion"). Use only pacifiers made from one piece of rubber; avoid those that can come apart. Once your baby decides on a certain type, it's smart to buy a few extra you can pull out when one ends up on the floor or is chewed by the dog.

Don't coat the pacifier with sugary sweeteners; this habit can cause cavities later on. Never tie the pacifier to a string that is then tied around your child's neck. This could cause strangulation. Remove the pacifier from the crib before bed or naps so your baby doesn't become dependent on it for going to sleep. A pacifier can gradually be taken away between ages 6 to 12 months before the baby grows to depend on it. Also, the findings from a recent study suggest that pacifier use may be associated with an increased risk of ear infections. (For information on pacifier use by toddlers, see Chapter 19, "Temperament, Behavior, and Discipline.")

Crying and Colic

All infants cry in the first few weeks. The first cry in the delivery room fills the newborn's lungs with air and expels any fluid. Babies cry because they are tired, hungry, bored, wet, uncomfortable, or for no apparent reason at all. After a while, you will be able to tell one kind of cry from another. If your baby cries, it usually doesn't mean you are doing anything wrong. But don't hesitate to pick up a crier; when a parent responds quickly to a baby's cry in the first few weeks of life, the newborn feels nurtured and reassured.

By two to three weeks of age, infants typically start to develop a type of fussy crying. Most babies have a fussy spell between 6:00 and 10:00 P.M. (just when you are apt to feel most frazzled), and sometimes it worsens as the evening goes on. You may try all kinds of things to stop the crying: feeding, walking, rocking, putting him in the swing or infant seat, singing, taking him for a ride, and so on. And you'll find that sometimes these work for a short while or don't work at all. But be assured that the fussy spell will end, and when it does, your baby probably will have his best feeding of the day and then go off to sleep for his longest sleep of the day.

Twenty-five years ago, Dr. T. Berry Brazelton studied crying patterns in newborns and found that the typical newborn cries about two and one-quarter hours a day for the first seven weeks of life. The crying reaches a peak at six weeks of life, approaching three hours a day. Of course, all babies are individuals, so your baby may cry much less (or even more).

Sometimes when babies cry, parents worry they have colic, but a fussy spell does not equal colic. Colic is usually defined as inconsolable, continual crying that lasts three or more hours a day for weeks. The baby may seem to be in pain, flailing and screaming, with tense legs drawn up to his belly. The crying is not due to hunger, a wet diaper, or other visible causes, and the child cannot be calmed down. This condition—which can be extremely difficult on parents—occurs in perhaps 10 percent of babies and goes away on its own, usually by three months.

When trying to determine if your baby has colic, the first thing to do is rule out illness as the cause for the crying. Colicky babies have a healthy sucking reflex and a good appetite. Usually, babies who are ill won't have the same strong sucking reflex, and they'll drink less milk. Colicky babies usually like to be cuddled and handled. Ill babies may not like to be handled despite their fussiness. Colicky babies may spit up from time to time, but if your baby is actually vomiting or otherwise seems sick, you should call your child's doctor. Even if your baby doesn't have symptoms of illness,

The Best Advice I Got Was . . .

"*. . . when my wife was pregnant. Our OB-GYN, who has three of her own, said that at the end of the first year, you will remember nothing of the bad things and all of the great things. She was also the only one who told us to expect extreme ranges of emotion with respect to our child and whether it was worth it, especially at 3:00 A.M. when she was colicky. That was important because most new parents don't or won't talk about their feelings toward the child who is colicky. But, as our doctor said, you won't remember any of the bad from the first year!*"

KidsHealth Tip

Calming with Vacuum Cleaning

When a baby with colic cries, it sometimes seems like nothing will soothe him. Try running the vacuum cleaner—its humming noise tends to calm a colicky baby. If this works, tape the noise and you'll be able to bring your "vacuum cleaner soundtrack" wherever you go.

check with the doctor about excessive crying, just to be sure there is no medical cause.

The cause of colic is unknown—it may be a mix of things or different things in different babies. Contrary to popular belief, doctors believe that colic is rarely, if ever, caused by a milk allergy or reactions to other food. Still, if you're breast-feeding and think you notice some relation between what you eat and your baby's colic, you could try dropping the suspect foods from your diet to see if it helps. If your baby is on formula, you could consult with her doctor about trying a different kind.

Doctors also think that gas is rarely the cause of colic. They suggest that more often than not, a colicky baby who has gas swallowed too much air during his crying spells. (In other words, the crying caused the gas, rather than the other way around.) As a result, antigas medication has not proved to be very effective in treating colic.

Many doctors think that colic may be caused by differences in the way babies' nervous systems develop. In other words, some babies just take a little longer to get adjusted to the world. This is normal and is not cause for worry—even if the noise drives you to distraction. The colic will go away—just keep repeating those words to keep yourself calm!

Meanwhile, during those crying spells, try to comfort your baby. Try feeding, walking, rocking, putting him in the swing or infant seat, singing, placing him across your lap on his belly, and rubbing his back. Some parents find that carrying their baby next to their stomach in a baby sling helps. Putting him in a car and going for a ride also can work.

Dealing with a fussy baby can be the most exhausting part of early parenting. It can leave a parent or other caregiver feeling helpless and like a failure, or frustrated and enraged, possibly even setting the stage for child abuse. If there's no help at hand and you feel at the end of your rope, it's better to put the crying baby in a safe place and leave the room, rather than risk shaking or hitting the baby.

But it's best to get some relief before the crying pushes you to the edge. If a spouse can't help, ask a relative to help you, or hire someone for a few hours a day and get out of the house. Join a mothering center or parenting group; often, the support of other parents—or honest discussion and sympathy between you and your partner—is all you need to get through these tough weeks. Try to take advantage of those times when your baby is asleep and rest yourself.

KidsHealth Tip

Reassure Siblings

When parents bring a new baby home, older children may be surprised or worried about how much a newborn cries. Two-week-old babies normally cry for about two hours every day. At six weeks, they cry even longer—almost three hours. By the time they're twelve weeks old, they're down to about an hour each day. Babies' favorite crying time is usually between 3:00 and 11:00 P.M. Reassure an older brother or sister that the new baby can cry and still be all right.

Bathing

An infant doesn't need much bathing if you wash the diaper area thoroughly during diaper changes. During her first week or two, until the stump of her umbilical cord falls off and the navel heals over, your newborn should have only sponge baths. Then, a bath two or three times a week in the first year is sufficient. More bathing may dry out her skin.

Sponge Baths

Before you bring your baby to the bathing area for a sponge bath, gather together a clean washcloth, mild baby soap, one or two towels or blankets, and a basin of

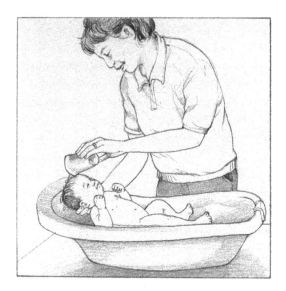

Figure 11.4. Bathing safety. When bathing your baby, never leave him unattended—even for a second.

warm water. To test the water temperature, stick your elbow in it; it should feel warm, not hot or cold.

Pick a warm room and any surface that's flat and comfortable for you both, such as a changing table, floor, or counter next to the sink. If the surface is hard, lay down a towel or blanket. If your baby is not on the floor, use a safety strap or keep one hand on her **at all times** to make sure she doesn't fall.

Undress your baby and wrap her in a towel. Keep her wrapped in a towel, exposing only the part of her body you are washing at the moment. First, wash her face with a dampened washcloth without soap. Then wet the cloth again and wash the rest of her body. Pay special attention to creases under the arms, behind the ears, and around the neck and the genital area. Once you have washed those areas, make sure they are dry.

Tub Baths

Once the umbilical cord stump has fallen off and the navel has healed, you can try placing your baby directly in the water. Her first baths should be gentle and brief. If she seems miserable, go back to sponge baths for a week or two, then try the tub bath again.

Many parents like bathing their newborn in a special baby tub (see Figure 11.4), the sink, or a plastic tub lined with a clean towel. Whatever type of tub you use,

KidsHealth Tip

No Daily Baths

When it comes to skin and hair, babies don't have to contend with some of the hygiene issues that adults do: They don't perspire under their arms, they don't work out, and they don't have hair that gets overly greasy. Instead of bathing your baby every day, which can result in dry skin, limit baths to two or three a week. On off days, just wash your baby's face, hands, and diaper area.

before you put your baby in, add two inches of warm water, testing it with your elbow. If you're filling the basin from the tap, turn the cold water on first and off last to avoid scalding the baby or yourself. Make sure your hot water heater is set no higher than 120 degrees Fahrenheit.

Have your supplies on hand and the room warm before you bring in your baby. You will need a clean washcloth, mild baby soap, and one or two towels, plus a cup for rinsing with clean water. If your baby has hair, you may want to have baby shampoo, too.

Once you've undressed your baby, place her in the water right away so she doesn't get chilled. Use one of your hands to support her head and the other to guide her in, feet first. Talk gently to her, and slowly lower the rest of her body until she's in the tub. Most of her body and face should be well above the water level for safety, so you'll need to pour warm water over her body frequently to keep her warm.

Use a soft cloth to wash her face and hair, shampooing once or twice a week. Massage her scalp gently, including the area over her fontanels (soft spots); don't worry, this won't hurt her. When you rinse the soap or shampoo from her head, cup your hand across her forehead so the suds run toward the sides, not into her eyes. If you do get soap in her eyes, take the wet washcloth and wipe her eyes with lots of lukewarm water until the suds are gone and she will open her eyes again.

When your baby comes out of the bath, wrap her in a towel, making sure her head is covered. Baby towels with hoods are handy for this move.

If you have forgotten something or need to answer the phone or door during the bath, take the baby with you. **Never** leave your baby alone in a bath.

Care of the Penis

In a newborn, the uncircumcised penis is usually completely covered by the foreskin. The foreskin remains attached to the tip of the penis in infancy, so you shouldn't attempt to pull it back to clean underneath. (By about the age of five years, the foreskin almost always has become retractable. At this point the boy can be taught to slide the foreskin back and clean the tip of the penis.) The opening in the foreskin should be large enough to allow the infant to urinate with a forceful stream. Consult your child's doctor if your son's urine only dribbles out.

If you decide to have your son circumcised (see Chapter 7, "Circumcision," for more information), it is best to have it done in the first few weeks of life. Immediately after the circumcision, the tip of the penis is usually covered with gauze coated with petroleum jelly. This dressing usually will come off when your baby urinates. It is probably not necessary to apply a new dressing as long as the area is gently wiped clean with soap and water when the diaper is changed. Healing is rapid, and any redness or irritation of the penis should subside within a few days. Complications are quite rare, but if the redness or swelling increases or if pus-filled blisters form, infection may be present and you should call your child's doctor immediately.

Care of the Umbilical Cord Stump

Don't be surprised if your baby's umbilical cord stump is blue. The color comes from an antibacterial dye used in many hospitals. To help prevent infection, swab the area with rubbing alcohol periodically until the cord stump dries up and falls off, usually in 10 days to three weeks. The infant's navel area shouldn't be submerged in water during bathing until this occurs. The withering cord stump will change color, from yellow to brown or black—this is of no significance. But you should consult your baby's doctor if the navel area becomes reddened or if a foul odor or discharge develops. Sometimes, after the cord stump falls off, the navel area doesn't completely heal over with skin on its own, and blood-tinged fluid may ooze out, staining the diaper just over the navel. To treat this, the doctor will swab the area with a small amount of the cauterizing chemical silver nitrate.

Limiting the Guest List

About 10 percent of infants experience infection, a cold, or other illness in the first month of life. Yet serious infections are rare if there are no other risk factors, such as low birthweight.

Because your baby's immune system is immature, it's a good idea to limit his exposure to lots of visitors in the first weeks. Ask your child's doctor when it is appropriate to take your baby into crowds, such as taking a trip to the shopping mall. If a friend or relative has an infection, it only makes sense for that person to delay visiting until he or she is better. If a member of your household becomes ill, limit his or her contact with the baby. (Make sure this person doesn't cough in your baby's face or kiss your baby until he or she is recovered.) Everyone in the household should, as always, practice good hygiene, washing hands thoroughly before touching your baby.

Early Outings

Fresh air and a change of surroundings are good for you and your baby, even in his first month, so take him out for walks if the weather is nice. Be careful to dress him properly for any outings. Until he is about a year old, an infant has more difficulty than other people do in maintaining his body temperature when he's exposed to excessive heat or cold. In general, your baby should wear one more layer (of clothing or a blanket) than you do when it is cold. But don't overdress your baby in warm or hot weather; dress him as you dress yourself to feel comfortable.

An infant is also extremely sensitive to sun and sunburn during the first six months, so keep him out of direct and reflected sunlight (such as sun reflected off concrete, water, or sand), especially during the peak sunlight hours of 10:00 A.M. to 4:00 P.M. Dress him in lightweight, light-colored clothing with a bonnet or hat to shade his face. If he's lying or sitting in one place, make sure it is in the shade, and adjust his position when the sun moves. If you must take him into sunlight, use sunblock to protect his skin (see Chapter 24, "Child Safety," for more information about sun safety).

If it is uncomfortably cold, keep your baby inside if possible. If you have to go out, dress him in warm sweaters or bunting bags over his other clothes and use a

Things to Expect in the First Weeks of Your Baby's Life

Bad things:

- Expect to be sleep deprived.
- Expect that your "normal routine" will no longer exist. There will be days when getting yourself dressed and cleaning the breakfast dishes will seem heroic.
- Expect that your child will probably cry at just the time in the day when you feel like crying yourself.
- Expect that establishing a feeding routine—whether breast-feeding or bottle-feeding—will take time.
- Expect that establishing a sleeping routine will also take time.
- Expect that, as a mother, you probably won't feel very romantic and fear you will look like a hag the rest of your life. Expect that, as a father, your partner won't feel very romantic and may seem constantly occupied with taking care of the baby.
- Expect that lots of people will have advice for you that may or may not be in line with your own thinking.
- Expect to make mistakes.

Good things:

- Expect from the beginning that your baby will respond to you and look to you for comfort and love.
- Expect that you will quickly learn to know your baby's needs, desires, and personality through his sounds and movements.
- Expect to have moments of closeness, when you hold and feed him, that are deeply satisfying.
- Expect your baby's first smile in the first month.
- Expect that you will watch him grow from week to week, from a helpless newborn to an infant whose vision, hearing, smell, touch, and muscle strength and coordination are changing almost daily.
- Expect that your sense of what it is to be part of a family and community will deepen.
- Expect that those who are close to you will embrace this new person.
- Expect that you will learn from your mistakes.

warm hat over his head and ears. You can shield his face from the cold with a blanket when he's outside, but hold it far enough from his nose and mouth so he can breathe easily.

To check whether your baby is clothed warmly enough, feel his hands and feet and the skin on his chest. His hands and feet should be slightly cooler than his body but not cold. His chest should feel warm. If his hands, feet, and chest feel cold, take him into a warm room, unwrap him, and hold him close so the heat from your body warms him.

Burping

Babies often swallow air during feedings and can get fussy and upset. When this happens, it's better to stop the feeding and burp her and then go back to feeding. If you don't, she may swallow more air, which will increase her discomfort and make her spit up.

A good strategy is to burp her frequently even if she isn't fussy. The pause and change of position will slow her gulping and reduce the amount of air she takes in. If she is bottle-feeding, burp her every two to three ounces. If she is nursing, burp her each time she switches breasts.

There are several ways to burp a baby (see Figures 11.5a–c). Try these and you'll soon figure out which works best for you both:

- Hold your baby upright with her head on your shoulder, supporting her head and back while you gently pat her back with your other hand. A diaper or towel on your shoulder is a good idea in case she spits up.
- Sit your baby on your lap, supporting her chest and head with one hand while patting her back with the other. A bib, diaper, or towel on her front is a good idea.
- Lay the baby on your lap with her back facing up. Support her head so it is higher than her chest, and gently pat or rub your hand on her back.

If your baby hasn't burped after several minutes, continue feeding her. When she's finished, burp her again and keep her in an upright position (on your shoulder is fine) for 10 to 15 minutes so she doesn't spit up.

Coughing

If your baby eats fast or is trying to drink water for the first time, she may choke and cough, but the cough should stop as soon as she adjusts to a familiar eating pattern. If she coughs consistently or chokes routinely during feedings, consult your child's doctor. If she makes wheezing, grunting, or "barking" sounds or appears to

11.5a

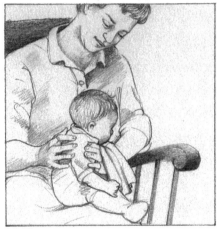

11.5b

Figures 11.5a–c. Positions for burping your infant: (a) over the shoulder, (b) sitting, (c) lying on belly. To help your baby bring up bubbles of air swallowed during feeding, gently pat or massage your baby's back and rock her. Make sure you place a cloth diaper or hand towel under your baby's mouth in case she spits up.

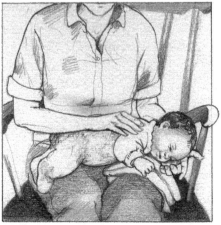

11.5c

be having a hard time breathing—she is breathing rapidly, the skin of her chest sucks in with each breath, her nostrils are flaring, or her skin is bluish—call your child's doctor immediately. These are signs of respiratory distress.

Spitting Up

When a baby spits up, food comes back up without effort or warning; the baby usually is not upset and may want to eat again immediately. This is common in the first year of life, especially when babies are burping or drooling, and some babies do it much more than others do (although rarely so much that it interferes with getting enough food). It is sometimes part of gastroesophageal reflux (or GERD, discussed in detail in Chapter 32, "Health Problems in Early Childhood"), which occurs when the muscle between the stomach and the esophagus is not fully developed enough to prevent backflow. Time usually cures this, but if your baby spits up very frequently, talk to his doctor about it. The doctor may recommend changing your baby's sleeping position or modifying his feedings.

Although you can't stop the spitting up altogether, these suggestions should decrease its frequency:

- Keep each feeding calm, quiet, and leisurely.
- Burp your baby at least every three to five minutes during feedings.
- Feed your baby when he is in a semiupright position, rather than lying down.
- Keep your baby in a semiupright position for an hour or so after eating.
- Do not jostle or play vigorously with your baby right after he's eaten.
- Try to feed him before he gets frantically hungry.
- If bottle-feeding, make sure the nipple hole is neither too big (which causes formula to flow out) nor too small (which causes him to gulp air). If the hole is the right size, a few drops should come out and then stop when you invert the bottle.

Vomiting

Unlike spitting up, which most babies don't seem to notice, vomiting is forceful and usually causes distress and discomfort for the baby. Vomiting generally occurs soon after a meal and produces greater volume. Babies may vomit after a hard bout of crying or coughing. Occasionally, they may vomit for no apparent reason. But more often than with spitting up, vomiting may be a sign of food intolerance or illness. This is especially true if the baby vomits after every feeding or is not gaining weight. If your baby vomits more than once or shows other signs of illness, such as listlessness, a rectal temperature of 100.4 degrees Fahrenheit or above, a marked change in his stools, lack of interest in feeding, persistent crying, or an unwillingness to be held, call your baby's doctor.

> ## The Voice of Experience
> ———————
> *"Enjoy them while they are little because they don't stay that way for long."*
> —FROM THE KIDSHEALTH PARENT SURVEY

Constipation

Most infants have one or more stools daily. However, young infants can sometimes go for several days between bowel movements. Usually, this is normal. Constipation in infants is the difficult passage of hard stools. Even with normal bowel movements, infants will sometimes grunt, turn red in the face, and appear to strain. However, if your infant appears to be experiencing discomfort or crying while straining, and is only passing small, hard "balls" of stool, he is probably constipated. In some cases, the hard stools may be streaked with blood due to an anal fissure (a crack in the anal skin resulting from the passage of hard stool).

Measures that can help relieve constipation include giving one teaspoon of dark corn (Karo) syrup twice a day (or adding it to the baby's bottle), or two to three ounces of apple or prune juice twice daily (only for infants over two months of age). Infants who have become constipated after switching to cow's milk feedings before 12 months of age may benefit from switching back to formula. Older infants can eat strained fruits or vegetables that are high in fiber. Do **not** give your infant laxatives, rectal suppositories, or enemas. Call your baby's doctor if your infant appears to be in increasing discomfort or cannot pass stool, or if you see blood in the stool or diaper.

"Cradle Cap" (Seborrheic Dermatitis)

Seborrheic dermatitis, or "cradle cap," is commonly seen in younger infants, often in the first few weeks of life. Greasy-appearing white or yellowish scales and plaques may cover the entire scalp. Redness and scaling can also involve the eyebrows, the skin behind the ears, and the creases in the neck and armpits. The scales may be thick and difficult to remove and may make combing the infant's hair difficult. The scalp itself underneath the crusting can become inflamed and reddened.

The cause of cradle cap is not known, although the baby's exposure to pregnancy hormones probably plays a role. Routine shampooing and massaging of an infant's scalp twice a week to loosen and remove any crusts usually prevent the condition from becoming a problem. Cradle cap almost always goes away by itself eventually, but this may take several months. If your infant develops severe cradle cap, you can try the following routine:

- Loosen scalp "crusts": Put warm (not hot) mineral oil, baby oil, cocoa butter, or olive oil on the scalp to help soften the crusts. Massage the scalp well when applying. Leave in for one to two hours, then shampoo.

- Shampoo: When first treating severe cradle cap, use a gentle nonprescription, selenium-containing, antidandruff shampoo once a day. Lather the scalp/hair thoroughly, then use a fine comb, soft brush, or washcloth to massage the scalp and help remove the now-softened crusts. Then rinse completely, massaging the scalp gently, making sure to get out all oils and soap. After about a week, when the cradle cap should be greatly improved, switch to regular baby shampoo and use it twice weekly.

  If the scalp is red and inflamed under the scales or if the rash isn't limited to your baby's scalp, your child's doctor may prescribe a mild steroid cream (hydrocortisone) to reduce the inflammation. In a few infants, the inflamed skin beneath the cradle cap becomes infected and antibiotic treatment is required.

Need More Information?

Check the Index and Appendix C, "Resource Guide." And of course, consult your child's doctor.

PART TWO

Routine Medical Care: Staying Healthy

chapter twelve

Choosing and Working with Your Child's Doctor

A partner you can trust

Parents-to-be often have an image of the ideal doctor. Warm, wise, knowledgeable, and unhurried, this pediatric paragon would mix the best of Einstein and Oprah. Although you may not find this perfect creature, it's worth looking for someone whose personal style, attitudes, and approach to child rearing mesh well with yours. You'll find it easier to work with such a person, and you'll feel more secure about entrusting your child's health to him or her. If you're lucky, your child's relationship with this doctor may last 10 or even 20 years, longer than some marriages. You want someone you can rely on, in sickness and in health.

Considering Your Options

Although factors such as where you live and the type of health plan you have may limit your choices in the type of doctor you select for your child, you will usually have several options, including a pediatrician, a family physician, and a pediatric nurse-practitioner.

Pediatrician

Pediatrics is the medical specialty fully focused on the physical, emotional, and social health of children from birth through adolescence. Pediatricians complete four years of medical school, followed by three years of pediatric residency training. To become board certified, a pediatrician must pass a written examination given by the American Board of Pediatrics. Pediatricians who completed training after 1988 must recertify by taking examinations every seven years. This means pediatricians must keep up to date on changes in children's health care. A pediatrician also must take a certain number of hours of continuing medical education each year to be eligible for license renewal in the state where she or he practices. (Women now outnumber men in the ranks of pediatric trainees.)

Some pediatricians have additional training in a subspecialty area such as critical care medicine. These subspecialists usually have completed one to three years of training after their residency and may be certified in their subspecialty.

Family Physician

Today's family physicians must complete three years of residency after medical school. This makes them eligible to take the certifying examination of the American Board of Family Medicine. They are also required to earn continuing medical education credits and take periodic recertification examinations.

Family medicine residencies include training in pediatrics and several other areas such as internal medicine, orthopedics, and obstetrics and gynecology. This prepares the family medicine physician to deliver care to a wide range of patients of all ages. Family physicians receive several months of specific training in the health care of children, far less than the three years that pediatric trainees complete, so family physicians generally do not have the same depth and breadth of knowledge about pediatrics. In some cases, particularly in areas where pediatricians are plentiful, family physicians may see few children or exclude younger children from their practice, so it's important to ask about these age policies. An advantage of enrolling your child in a family practice is the ability to have one doctor provide for the primary medical care for all members of the family. The family physician will know the details of the medical histories of all family members and, in some circumstances, may be more aware of the health, emotional, and social issues within your family that can affect your child's health and well-being.

Pediatric Nurse-Practitioner

The pediatric nurse-practitioner (PNP) generally has earned a master's degree in nursing and has special training in obtaining medical histories, performing physical examinations on children, making medical diagnoses, and providing counseling and treatment. Like pediatricians, PNPs may receive training in a specialized

KidsHealth Tip

Avoid the "Doc-Hop"

If you're on the move to a new city, don't wait until you need a pediatrician to let your fingers do the walking. Be prepared for that eventual ear infection or rash by choosing your doctor well in advance. Ask other parents or your new neighbors for their recommendations. And before you move on, check with your current doctor, who may have some suggestions.

area of care such as neonatology or endocrinology. PNPs work closely with pediatricians in hospitals, clinics, and private practices, and their numbers have been growing.

In our experience, some parents may feel somewhat reluctant to have their child receive care from a pediatric nurse-practitioner; perhaps they are concerned that the PNP is less extensively trained in the health care of children than the pediatrician is. These feelings are largely unwarranted. In fact, the presence of PNPs in the practice can have advantages that most parents will appreciate. Parents often find that these nurse-practitioners spend more time with them than the pediatrician does discussing child care and explaining how to handle illnesses. If the pediatric nurse-practitioner encounters a more complex medical problem with your child, he or she is trained to consult the pediatrician, when necessary. Most practices, however, will honor your request if you wish to see only the pediatrician or if you feel that the pediatrician should be consulted after a pediatric nurse-practitioner has seen your child.

Starting the Search for Your Child's Doctor

Babies can come earlier than planned, and you'll want to have time to do the research needed to find a doctor whose style and personality will complement your own. A good time to begin your search is about three months before your baby is due.

If you're in a managed health care plan (see Chapter 27, "The Health Care System for Children"), your choice of doctors may be limited to those on the list of participating physicians in your health plan who provide primary health care for children (pediatricians and family practitioners). In that case, your first step should be to obtain a copy of this list. These paper lists, however, often are outdated. If you are interested in a doctor who is not on the list, call your health plan or the doctor's office to check if he or she is a participating provider.

In some cases, the list of primary care providers may be limited, with few or no pediatricians. If you feel you need an out-of-network doctor (perhaps if your child has complex health care needs), you may be able to persuade your health insurance provider to make special arrangements.

Once you know the limits imposed by your health plan, compile a list of candidates from people you trust—your relatives, friends, neighbors, and coworkers who share your parenting philosophies. Your family physician, obstetrician, or nurse-midwife can also be good sources for recommendations.

If you've recently moved to a new area, you may not have the personal or social connections to ask for doctor referrals. In this case, you may want to contact area hospitals or medical schools for recommendations or ask the pediatric residents or nurses where they take their children.

> ## The Voice of Experience
> ————————
> *"It's imperative to find a pediatrician who agrees with your style of raising children and will use the parent as an ally, not an adversary, in treating your child."*
> —FROM THE KidsHealth PARENT SURVEY

Checking Out a Doctor

You've gathered recommendations from people you trust. Is there any way to check out those doctors before you decide to interview one or two? It's not easy to assess doctors, but you may be able to at least find out if a doctor has been found to have a serious problem. In each state, a medical board investigates complaints against doctors and may take disciplinary action, ranging from citing a doctor to suspending or revoking his or her license to practice medicine. In some cases, a doctor may be required to get more training or supervision or to undergo therapy for substance abuse if needed. Such disciplinary actions are quite rare, and information about them is generally public. In most states, the medical boards post lists of disciplined doctors on their Web site.

To find your state medical board's Web site, try a good general search engine, such as www.google.com. You can find links to some, but not all, state board Web sites at www.docboard.org, a site run by a group of state medical board directors, or at www.healthcarechoices.org, a useful site run by a New York nonprofit group.

A warning on disciplinary information: State practices vary widely. In some states, doctors may have been cited for minor administrative lapses, such as failing to pay certain fees on time. Or they may be cited automatically if they are convicted of any crime—even failing to file an income tax return. Listings can be erroneous; rulings can be overturned later.

> ## The Voice of Experience
> ———❦———
>
> *"It's OK to take control of your child's health. Question a doctor if your gut says to, ask a lot of questions, and educate yourself about child health concerns. We're with our child for 24 hours a day; the doctor sees him for 5 to 10 minutes and makes an educated decision."*
>
> —FROM THE KIDSHEALTH PARENT SURVEY

Sources of Basic Information

Basic information about doctors is available in directories found in many large public libraries, including *The Directory of Physicians in the United States* and *The Directory of Board-Certified Medical Specialists*. These tell you where and when doctors went to medical school and trained as residents, which hospitals they admit patients to, and whether they are certified as specialists. Similar information is available on

KidsHealth Tip

Do Your Homework

Need to find a doctor? You can get lists of doctors in your area from the American Academy of Pediatrics (www.aap.org), the American Academy of Family Physicians (www.aafp.org), local hospital "nurse line" referral services, the local medical society office, medical directories in public libraries, and the yellow pages of the phone directory. Although they usually can't provide specific information about the doctor's practice style or characteristics, they're a great place to start.

many Web sites. The American Board of Medical Specialists (www.abms.org) can tell you which specialties, if any, a doctor is certified in. The American Medical Association's (AMA) Physician Select (www.ama-assn.org/aps/amahg.htm) lists medical schools and other training for virtually all doctors; those who are members of the AMA can describe their approach and list office hours, if they like. In a growing number of states, the state's medical board Web site also includes basic background information.

What You Should Ask the "Finalists"

Once you have compiled a list of doctors, you are ready to begin interviewing. A prenatal appointment is an excellent opportunity for parents to ask questions, see how convenient the office is, and get acquainted with the office staff. Some pediatricians offer group classes for expectant parents to learn about the practice and discuss newborn care. Many insurance companies encourage these prenatal appointments or classes and will cover the cost. To avoid surprise costs, however, be sure to check with the pediatrician's office and your health plan about charges for "meet-and-greet" sessions.

During the interview, you should learn the ground rules about how the practice works. Making a checklist will help you organize your thoughts and be thorough. The following are some key issues to consider:

1. What are the office hours? You may prefer a physician who offers weekend and evening hours. Do daytime office hours begin early or end late enough for you to get your child there before or after work?

2. Is this a solo or group practice? In a solo practice, you know that your child will be seen by the same doctor for most visits and that you will be dealing with the personality and philosophy of only one physician. But, if your child needs attention at night or on weekends, you may often have to deal with an unfamiliar doctor who is providing coverage for your doctor when he or she is not on call. If you are considering a solo practice, find out the details about these coverage arrangements, including the qualifications of the covering physicians.

   Group practices are becoming increasingly common. In some, your child may see only one doctor in the group for routine care; in others, your child's care may rotate among the members of the group so that all the doctors become acquainted with you and your child. Although some parents like the opportunity to see the differing approaches of multiple doctors, other parents may find this confusing. In any case, group practices tend to offer more extended office hours than solo practices, and you are likely to receive care from one of the doctors in the group when your child is ill at night or on a weekend.

3. Does a pediatric nurse-practitioner (PNP) work in the office? If so, how does the PNP fit into the practice arrangement?

4. Which hospital(s) is the doctor affiliated with? Will your doctor come to the hospital to examine your baby when she is born? If your child requires admission to the hospital, what type of facility is it? Will your doctor care for your hospitalized child or will someone else?

5. How does the practice handle telephone questions during and after hours? This is one of the most important (and potentially frustrating) aspects of the practice. Is there a "telephone hour" or special time set aside for parents to call in with questions, or is there an open advice line (usually staffed by a "phone nurse") during regular office hours? How are after-hours calls handled? How quickly can you expect a call back from the doctor on call after you have contacted the answering service? Are after-hours calls routed to a telephone triage or "nurse-on-call" system?

    Nurse-on-call systems are rapidly spreading through the United States. They employ a staff of nurses who are trained to give advice to parents about handling most common childhood illnesses. Records of the encounter are relayed to your child's doctor by the next day. If your child's illness is thought to be possibly serious in nature, the nurse will transfer the call to your child's doctor or a covering physician or refer you directly to the emergency room. Although some physicians and parents were initially skeptical about this type of call triage, studies indicate that these systems have received high satisfaction ratings from both parents and doctors.

6. Is email an option for communicating with the doctor and office? If you would find this convenient and helpful, ask about it and read Chapter 34, "Finding Health Information on the Web."

7. Will your child's doctor handle emergencies, or will your child be referred to an emergency room or urgent care center? Are these facilities staffed and equipped to handle pediatric emergencies effectively?

8. Is laboratory testing done in the office? Most offices can perform some basic tests, such as blood counts, urine testing, and rapid strep tests, rather than sending samples out to a laboratory. This may save both time and money (depending on your payment plan).

9. What are the office policies concerning payment? This question is most important if you do not have prepaid health coverage. What are the fees? Are you expected to pay in full at the time of the visit? Are discounted or adjusted fee schedules available? Can payment plans be arranged if you are unable to pay in full at the time of the visit?

10. What are the policies regarding referrals to specialists in the event that your child needs additional care? Is the doctor financially penalized by your health plan for referring patients to specialists, and if so, will this influence the physician's referral practices? Will the doctor refer your child to pediatric subspecialists or those with extensive experience caring for children, as opposed to those who primarily treat adults? If you are a member of an HMO, it is important to ask how the doctor handles out-of-network referrals.

Get the Feel of the Office Environment

At the interview, you can see how well the office functions, particularly if you schedule your visit during regular office hours when the practice is operating at full steam. Observe the reception area—how many children are waiting? More than a handful may mean schedule overbooking. A crowded waiting room, however, is not necessarily a sign of practice problems. Sometimes the backup may mean the doctor is spending extra time with a patient who unexpectedly required it. You might appreciate this departure from the schedule if it is your child who needs the additional attention. Conversely, an empty waiting room doesn't guarantee the office is efficient. It may conceal the fact that patients may be waiting for long periods to see the doctor after being taken back into examination rooms. Is there a place where sick children can be separated from those who are there for a well visit? Is the area clean and child-friendly? Reception areas should be filled with a variety of age-appropriate playthings to occupy the waiting children.

Throughout your visit, observe the staff interacting with children and families. Are they polite, considerate, and caring? Or are they angry, impatient, and stressed? How were you handled on the telephone when you called to schedule your visit?

While you are waiting, talk to other parents to find out if they are satisfied with the care their child is receiving. Are they and their child comfortable with the doctor and staff? Do the parents feel confident the physician is thorough and competent? The overall atmosphere in the waiting area can give you valuable information about what the practice is like.

Save Your Research

Once you've chosen a doctor, don't throw out the information you've collected about the other finalists. Things can change—especially if your insurance changes—and you may find yourself looking for a new doctor. Or it may take a couple of tries to find a doctor you're happy with. This is not unusual. As you become a more experienced parent, you will be better able to assess the doctor's skills and behavior. And let's face it, some people are great in interviews (like a great first date) but not so great in real life.

The Doctor's Personality and Approach

Some parents are more comfortable with placing their trust in a doctor who takes a firm and directive approach, without much attention to detailed explanations or the pros and cons of alternative ways of doing things. In our experience, more parents want a physician who is a good listener, welcomes questions, explains things carefully, is comfortable with saying "I don't know," and collaborates with parents in the care of their child rather than acting as a superior.

In addition to getting a feel for these aspects of the doctor's personality during the interview, you will want to consider other issues. Are the doctor's age and gender important to you? Are your attitudes and parenting style consistent with the doctor's with regard to issues such as circumcision, breast-feeding, discipline, and the use of antibiotics and other medications? Is the doctor's philosophy focused on preventive care, including immunizations and guidance regarding child safety and proper nutrition? Is the doctor's attitude toward issues such as vegetarianism in childhood or the use of alternative therapies important to you? Will the doctor be supportive if you request a second opinion? Do you sense that the doctor is responsive to your concerns and genuinely cares for children?

Establishing a Good Relationship with Your Child's Doctor

It's 8:00 A.M. and 10-month-old Beth is the first patient through the door at the pediatrician's office. Beth had awakened coughing and crying twice during the night, and she is still irritable and congested. "Looks like she has a cold," the doctor says after examining her, "probably just a virus." Tired and frazzled, Beth's mother shakes her head and talks about how exhausted she feels and how worried she is that she will soon run out of sick days at her job. The doctor writes out a prescription for an antibiotic and hands it to Beth's mother with some basic instructions. In a few minutes Beth and her mother are on their way.

This kind of encounter occurs thousands of times each day in doctors' offices around the country. On the surface, it seems like the system worked pretty well—Beth was examined, diagnosed, and treated. But not really. The doctor was right when he said that viruses cause colds. But he was wrong when he prescribed an antibiotic—antibiotics work against bacteria, not viruses. So the "treatment" was worthless. Unfortunately, it may not have been harmless: The media are filled with reports about how antibiotics are often prescribed inappropriately, causing unnecessary side effects and encouraging the rise of antibiotic-resistant "superbugs" (germs that can't be treated by existing antibiotics).

So why did this knowledgeable doctor prescribe the antibiotic for Beth?

In many cases, this kind of situation occurs because of a basic problem in doctor-patient communication. In this section, we'll discuss how you can help ensure the best medical care for your child by establishing a good working relationship with your child's doctor.

The Changing Doctor-Patient Relationship

Although many patients are unaware of it and many doctors may be reluctant to admit it, today's patients can have a greater impact than ever before on the care they receive from their physicians. In most situations, this is a good thing—after all, as a parent, you have the ultimate responsibility for your child's health. But sometimes the doctor's perception of what the parent expects, as well as the demands of our current health care system, can pressure the doctor into making care decisions that are not necessarily in your child's best interests.

Take Beth's case, for example. The doctor might have interpreted Beth's mother's comments about exhaustion and her job worries to mean she expected him to do something (such as prescribing medication) to get Beth well faster, although that might not have been her intention at all. The doctor may have felt that if he didn't meet the mother's expectations and write the prescription, he might risk losing Beth as a patient. Pressed by health insurers to see more patients in less time and knowing that patients would be backing up in the waiting room, the doctor may have been reluctant to get into a discussion about how antibiotics are ineffective in treating viral infections.

Tips for Building a Better Partnership

You can become a more effective advocate for your child's health by following certain ground rules in working with your child's doctor and the practice's office staff:

- Let the doctor know that you trust him or her to make recommendations regarding your child's health care based solely on what is best for your child. This doesn't mean that you are giving up your rights and responsibilities as a parent. But it's a good idea to inform the doctor up front that you don't want his or her care decisions to be influenced by a perceived need to please you. Make it clear that you expect antibiotics or other treatments to be prescribed only when they will help your child, not you, feel better.
- Beware of "information overload." In recent years, the development of the Internet, along with the proliferation of print, cable television, and other media resources, has given people access to an avalanche of health information (see Chapter 34, "Finding Health Information on the Web"). Although some of this information is accurate and useful, some of it is incorrect or biased and may be misinterpreted or blown out of proportion.

  Today, it is not uncommon for parents to present their child's doctor with piles of articles downloaded from the Internet or copied from various publications. It is unrealistic to expect the physician to read and comment on such materials within the time limits of the typical office visit. In addition, it may be difficult for even the doctor to determine the true source and reliability of much of the medical information from the Web. And even if the findings are accurate, doctors may not know if other research on the same topic has produced contradictory results. It's amazing how many early studies don't hold up through time.

If you feel you need to get your child's doctor's opinion about an article on a child health issue, it would be better to mail, email, fax, or drop off a copy to the doctor *before* the office visit or phone call you make to discuss it so that the doctor has time to review the material in advance. It is also a good idea to ask the office staff about handouts or other resources that your child's doctor recommends on the topic. Reviewing these first may help give you a broader perspective on the subject.

- Learn the ground rules of the practice and try to follow them. Show up on time for appointments (or a few minutes early—you may be seen sooner if the office groups visits in hour or half-hour blocks). Call ahead if you are running late. This gives the office staff time to work you into the schedule or to save you a wasted trip if they can't. If possible, always give at least 24 hours' notice if you must cancel an appointment. Avoid developing a reputation for frequent cancellations. Many offices will double or triple book such patients with other patients or allot less time.

Try to give the office sufficient lead time when scheduling appointments—and let the office staff know the nature of the visit so they can schedule ample time for you. For example, if you know that your child will need a checkup before preschool starts, don't wait until two days before the deadline to set up the visit. Once you're at the office, stick to the reason for your visit; a visit scheduled for a cold, for example, is not the time to bring up behavioral issues that will take much longer to evaluate. An unexpected change in visit plans can put your doctor in an awkward position and make other patients wait longer than they should.

KidsHealth Tip

"The Office Is Closed for Vacation"

Even doctors need a break now and then, but do you know who will cover for your doctor when he or she takes a well-deserved vacation? Is it the same doctor as last year? Are you comfortable with him or her? Will your health insurance cover the fees?

Check into your doctor's vacation coverage before the answering service surprises you with an unfamiliar name and phone number.

- Facilitate the flow of information. Call the office in advance to make sure that any medical records, lab test reports, or other information needed for your child's appointment have been received. If they haven't, try to make sure they get there, or arrange to bring them with you. Make sure that you bring all needed insurance, billing, and referral information or forms to be filled out at the visit.

- Make sure that you understand, remember, and follow the instructions given to you. It is always a good idea to repeat the instructions to be sure you have heard them correctly. Taking notes or asking for printed handouts or written instructions can also be helpful. This is particularly important when the instructions are complicated or if your child is ill and you are upset or sleep deprived enough to forget some of what you heard. If you think you will have difficulty following the instructions for any reason, let the doctor know right then and there. Usually, the doctor will be able to adjust the plan to make sure your child gets the appropriate treatment.

- If possible, leave other young children at home. An office visit can be difficult and frustrating for both you and your child's doctor if you are distracted by your other children. It is unrealistic to expect most young children to sit quietly and behave while waiting in a doctor's office.

  Equally important, if you or your partner can't make it to an appointment to address a complex issue, such as behavioral or developmental concerns, it's better to reschedule the appointment than to send your child in with Grandma or a caretaker. Often, they can't answer the doctor's in-depth questions, making the visit an exercise in futility.

- Use good judgment about telephone questions. If you know the matter is not urgent, save the question for your child's next office visit or call during the daily "telephone hour" that many practices set aside to answer such questions.

> ## The Voice of Experience
>
> *"Always make sure you get all the answers to your questions from your child's physician. You have to understand what is going on with your child to be able to help him."*
> —FROM THE KIDSHEALTH PARENT SURVEY

> ## The Voice of Experience
>
> *"Never hesitate to call your child's doctor about something that is bothering you. He or she is there to help you and to take care of your child, in sickness and in health."*
> —FROM THE KIDSHEALTH PARENT SURVEY

As questions come to mind, write them down and save them for your office visit. Avoid calling for nonurgent questions on weekends or evenings. In many practices, you are likely to reach a covering physician who doesn't know your child or an after-hours "nurse-on-call" who is geared to handle emergencies or urgent problems only.

- Follow the payment policies of the practice and your health plan. Managed care plans frequently require a cash copay at the time of the visit, and the participating doctor's office is expected to collect this payment. If you cannot pay in full, speak to the office staff in advance to make any arrangements such as payment schedules or discounted fees you may be eligible for, and provide them with any supporting financial information needed.

Need More Information?

Check the Index and Appendix C, "Resource Guide." And of course, consult your child's doctor.

chapter thirteen

Routine Medical Care

An ounce of prevention . . .

What kind of care should your child get at the doctor's office, clinic, or health maintenance organization (HMO)? This chapter explains the services you can expect and provides tips to help you ensure that your child receives the best possible care. It will first look at routine checkups and then give you information about how to get prompt medical care when your child is ill. And don't skip over the final sections—there you'll learn how to calm your child's fears and how to use a favorite bit of advice from parents: Trust your instincts.

Childhood Checkups

Regular checkups help give your child the best possible start in life. They allow the doctor to monitor your baby's growth and development—physical, mental, and emotional.

These checkups also will alert you to any problems that may be better treated if caught early. Because your baby's body and brain are still not fully formed, early treatment can completely correct some potential problems. But if treatment is delayed, problems may be permanent. For instance, a child with a lazy eye (amblyopia) often can achieve full vision if the condition is treated early, usually by covering one eye with a patch temporarily. Otherwise, the child may have permanent vision loss in one eye that glasses can't correct.

In addition to problems that need treatment right away, a checkup may reveal an abnormality that the doctor will keep watching at future visits to see whether it resolves on its own or eventually needs treatment.

When no problems are found, checkups provide welcome reassurance—and a chance to glow as you talk about how well things are going. When parents feel more comfortable and less anxious, it's good for the whole family.

At a checkup, your child's doctor also can assess your child's feeding and sleeping patterns, observe your interaction with your child, and encourage healthy patterns. You can ask any questions you have about your child's health or behavior or about more general parenting issues. Often parents feel shy about calling with a routine question—perhaps it seems too simple—but feel comfortable asking it in person "as long as we're here." In addition, doctors and nurses who care for young children can often refer you to good sources of information and services—from books to playgroups to child-care centers.

Well-Child Visits: How Often?

Even the healthiest child should become a familiar face at the doctor's office. The American Academy of Pediatrics (AAP) recommends more than a dozen routine checkups (and even more immunization shots) by the time your child enters kindergarten, with most clustered in the first year.

These are the routine visits recommended by the AAP:

- Before your newborn is discharged from the hospital
- Within 48 to 72 hours of discharge if your baby left the hospital within 48 hours after birth
- For breast-fed infants, three to four days after birth
- For both breast- and formula-fed infants, around two to four weeks of age
- During the first year of life at 2, 4, 6, 9, and 12 months of age
- During the second year of life at 15, 18, and 24 months of age
- Yearly at age three, four, and five

The Voice of Experience

"When my son was about a month old, he had been crying all day and wouldn't take a nap. I was tired and frustrated, too. The next day, we went for a regular checkup, which found no problems. I asked why my son was crying so much. My doctor, placing his arm around my shoulder, said in the sweetest, most understanding way, 'Babies do that.' It was a simple comment that made me realize that there was nothing wrong with me or my baby. We were perfectly normal."

—FROM THE KidsHealth PARENT SURVEY

If your baby is small or premature or was born with a health problem, you are likely to visit the doctor even more often. And then, of course, there may be random visits for a cold, fever, rash, or ear infection and follow-up visits to check on a problem found earlier.

What Happens at a Well-Child Visit?

You can expect a well-child visit, also called a "health supervision visit," to include the following things:

A Health History

Your child's doctor will ask about your child's and your family's health history. The family history may be discussed before your baby is born, if you have a prenatal visit, or at an early checkup. This can help the doctor determine whether your child should have certain screening tests because he might be at increased risk for genetic, infectious, or environmental health problems. Other information, such as heights of parents and other close relatives, can help the doctor diagnose a growth problem in your child more readily. At each well-child visit, you should tell the doctor about any health problems your child has had since the last visit and about any new developments in your family medical history.

KidsHealth Tip

Picasso at the Pediatrician's Office

Waiting for the doctor to come into the exam room can be stressful for kids (and adults!). To help distract and relax your child, try bringing a few crayons or colored pencils to the doctor's office. The paper that covers the examining room table can become your child's canvas, and because the paper is thrown away after each patient visit, coloring does no harm to the table.

Monitoring of Growth

At each well-child visit, your child's weight and length or height should be recorded and plotted on a standard growth chart for comparison. Head circumference, which reflects the growth of the brain, is also usually measured at each routine visit until age 24 months.

Assessment of Development

Children who show delays in their physical, emotional, behavioral, or social development may have treatable medical conditions that need attention. That's why your child's doctor will check for these things during routine checkups.

Screening for Developmental Progress

Many types of developmental screening tests are available. The most commonly used in a primary care office is called the Denver-II. It includes questions for the parent about the child's skills, knowledge, and behavior. (See Chapter 17, "Growth and Development," for more information.) Parents may be asked to fill out pre-screening forms to answer some of these questions. The doctor or nurse will also observe as your child performs certain tasks (hopping on one foot, drawing, etc.) or responds to questions ("Which line is longer?").

KidsHealth Tip
Keep a Health Record

Keep your own record of your child's measurements, along with other data such as immunization dates and screening test results. Some doctors give you a small booklet for this purpose. If there's an emergency and you're too stressed to think clearly, a written record can help medical staff make better decisions. This booklet also can come in handy if you call your child's doctor for advice on the phone (when the office records won't be immediately at hand) or any time your child sees a new doctor. For a sample health record, see Appendix A.

It is important to remember that none of these screening tests is perfect. A child may "fail" an item on the test just because he is tired or uncooperative that day. Your child's performance on these tests over time is a much more reliable indicator of developmental health than the findings at one visit. And many children who show a delay in one or more developmental areas on the screening test turn out to have no significant problem on subsequent follow-up. On the other hand, even if your child shows no abnormalities on the screening tests, you should be sure to let the doctor know if you have any specific concerns about your child's development or behavior. Your observation or sense that "something isn't right" with your child can prove to be more accurate than a screening test.

If your child's doctor feels that your child might have a problem, he or she may refer your child for evaluation by a neurologist, developmentalist, audiologist, ophthalmologist, psychologist, or other specialist, depending on the type of problem suspected.

A Physical Examination

The elements of the physical exam, and the order in which they are done, will vary based on your child's age. With infants and young children, observation is particularly important: Your child's doctor can learn much about your child's health from her overall appearance, activity, responsiveness, and interactions with her environment.

When it comes to touching your child, the doctor might start by doing the things that are least threatening, such as listening to the heart with a stethoscope. The parts of the exam that tend to be more distressing to young children, such as looking in the ears and throat, are generally saved for last.

With older infants and toddlers, who are naturally somewhat fearful of strangers and too young to understand the need to be cooperative, parents (or others familiar to the child) can be of great assistance. The doctor may wish to perform much of the exam with your child on your lap or in your comforting arms. You may also be asked to help by gently restraining your child as the doctor performs parts of the exam that require the child to be still. Bringing along a favorite toy or other object can help in creating a distraction to make the exam go more smoothly.

Screening for Vision, Hearing, and Dental Problems
Beginning with your newborn's first examination, your child's doctor will be looking for signs of existing or potential vision and hearing problems. Share with your

child's doctor any concerns you may have. A parent's observations in this regard can be extremely helpful in diagnosing a problem early. For further information on evaluation of your child's vision and hearing, see Chapter 15, "Hearing and Vision."

Even before teeth begin pushing their way through your baby's gums, your child's doctor will be examining your infant's mouth at well-child checkups looking for signs of infection (such as thrush) or other oral health problems. He or she will give you advice about teething and tooth care and may refer you to a pediatric dentist for a checkup or treatment if a problem is suspected. When it comes to routine visits to the dentist, the AAP recommends starting them around three years of age (if problems aren't picked up before then), but various dental societies recommend starting by 12 months. For further information about your child's oral and dental health, see Chapter 23, "Dental Care."

Other Screenings

The doctor may screen your child for tuberculosis, lead poisoning, high blood cholesterol level, or anemia if he or she thinks your child may be at risk for these problems. For more information about screening tests, see Chapter 14, "Health Screening Tests."

Counseling and Guidance

One of the major reasons for well-child visits is so you can receive advice and information to help you raise a healthy, happy child. You should expect your child's doctor, nurses, and other staff to devote a sizable portion of the well-child visit to providing you with this information. They should thoroughly and clearly answer any specific questions you have about your child's health. Although this is mainly accomplished through face-to-face conversations, most practices and clinics will also have printed information sheets, pamphlets, booklets, and the like. These can give you more detail, offer suggestions about how to find additional information (such as books, reputable Web sites, and support groups), or help you remember

Check Us Out on the Web

Speaking of Web sites, check out ours at www.KidsHealth.org, and let us know what you think!

KidsHealth Tip

Be an Informed Parent

Take advantage of doctor's visits to ask parenting, health, and other late-night worry questions—and don't worry about asking what you might think is a "dumb" question! Keep a little piece of paper taped to the fridge so that you can write questions down as you think of them. Then, bring the paper to your next office visit so you won't forget anything.

what was said after you leave the office. Some practices and clinics offer group sessions at which parents of similar-aged children can discuss health, developmental, or behavioral topics with health care personnel.

The topics covered at your child's visits should include what pediatricians call "anticipatory guidance." This means telling you about physical and emotional changes you are likely to see in your child before they happen. You'll talk about things like how to prevent accidents, what foods are best for your child, and how to encourage your child's natural curiosity. Such guidance can help you know what to expect and give you more confidence as a parent. It can also help you keep your child safe from injury as he becomes more mobile. It can prepare you to deal with difficult but normal developments such as the appearance of separation anxiety. It may prevent some health or behavioral problems from occurring in the first place. And it can help you encourage, nurture, and fully enjoy your child's growing abilities.

In practice, some doctors may rush past the advising and counseling aspects of a visit. Sadly, in these days of managed care, doctors may be under pressure to spend as little time as possible on each visit. If your child is healthy, the doctor may be particularly eager to move on to the next patient. If that's the case with your child's doctor, it may help if you prepare for a visit, as explained later in this chapter. And you can let the doctor know in a polite way if you don't feel comfortable with the amount of time allotted or with your ability to get your questions answered. If things don't improve, you may want to look for a doctor who is less pressed or more communicative. On the other hand, if you trust the doctor's medical judgment and don't feel the need for more counseling, you may want to stick with the doctor you have.

Immunizations

The schedule of health visits for infants and young children is built in part around the timing of immunizations. The development of highly safe, effective vaccines to prevent a range of potentially fatal and crippling diseases has been a towering human triumph. Making sure your child gets these immunizations is one of the most important things you can do to ensure your child's health. Work with your child's doctor to make sure that your child not only gets all recommended vaccines but also gets them on schedule. Delays in immunization can leave your child unnecessarily vulnerable to illness. (See Chapter 16, "Immunizations," for all the details.)

Other Office Services and Referrals

Larger group practices and hospital-based clinics may offer other services at routine checkups:

- A social worker may help families with financial or insurance problems, help coordinate care with other providers or agencies, assist in obtaining special supplies or equipment, or address issues related to family problems or child abuse or neglect.
- A psychologist, counselor, or other mental health professional may help with emotional, behavioral, or learning problems.
- A dietitian or nutritionist may be available for counseling children with special dietary needs.

Your child's primary care physician should play the role of "quarterback" in coordinating referrals and care delivered to your child by other specialists. This is particularly important if your child has complex medical problems or special needs. If your child is enrolled in a managed health care plan, you should work closely with the doctor's office staff and the health plan to complete the procedures and paperwork that may be required to authorize lab tests, X-rays, or specialist referral for your child.

Making the Most of an Office Visit

To get the most out of an office visit, it helps to be prepared. This is especially true if your child's doctor is pressed for time or if you must see an unfamiliar person.

- Keep a list of questions and concerns as they come up between visits. Before the visit, go through the list and put them in order of priority. Ask the important ones first. (Studies have shown that people often save the questions that really matter to them until the end of a visit. By then, your child's doctor may be halfway out the door.) Don't be shy about reading from your written list.

- Remind the doctor of your child's medical history, especially if she has had any problems such as asthma or seizures. Be sure to mention any medications, prescription or nonprescription, that your child is taking. Don't count on the doctor remembering or having just reviewed the medical record.

- Bring along paper and write down any important instructions (or any useful notes, for that matter). If you don't understand something or think you might not be able to follow the doctor's instructions, tell him or her. Bring your child's health record, and update it as needed (see Appendix A for a health record).

- Bring things to keep your child entertained in case you have to wait a while. If your child is cranky or screaming by the time the doctor gets to you, it's not only unpleasant for you and the child but also harder for the doctor to do a thorough exam.

- If possible, don't bring other children to the appointment so you won't be distracted.

- If you have questions after the doctor leaves the room, tell the office staff you would like to speak to the doctor again. If that's impossible at the moment, call later to ask your question.

- If you go home and follow the doctor's instructions for dealing with some problem and it doesn't work out the way it was supposed to, be sure to call and let the doctor know, so he or she can adjust the plan or work out a different way to manage your child's problem with you.

When to Call the Doctor About Your Child

Back home, after a visit to your child's doctor, you may remember a question you wanted to ask the doctor but forgot. Should you call and ask it now? What if after getting a glowing health report, the next morning your child won't eat? Should you call? All new parents go through this should-I-call-or-should-I-wait routine. Here are some tips to help you decide.

Routine Calls

For routine questions, many doctors have phone hours each day when parents may call. Often, a nurse or nurse-practitioner handles most of these calls. Don't hesitate to call with your concerns, no matter how small they may seem. Of course, if you suspect your baby is ill and may need prompt attention, don't wait for phone hours—call the doctor immediately.

Calls for Illness

Any sign of illness in a baby less than three months old requires immediate attention because a newborn's condition can quickly deteriorate. The younger and smaller the baby, the more vulnerable she is.

Even a serious illness in a newborn may have seemingly minor symptoms, such as fussiness, drowsiness, or a fever that would be considered mild in an older child. If you are in doubt about your young baby's health, it's better to err on the side of caution even if it means calling an emergency number in the middle of the night or taking your baby to the emergency room. And never give your newborn medication, even infant Tylenol or other over-the-counter products, unless your child's doctor OKs it.

As your baby gets older and you get more experienced, it will become easier for you to make judgments about how ill your child is. You'll know when you should call the doctor versus when your baby just needs your time and a little TLC. You don't want to drag her to the doctor for every sneeze and sniffle. Still, no matter how old your child is, if you feel worried that something just isn't right, don't hesitate to call the doctor. And if you are worried, don't feel you have to hide your feelings to avoid seeming like a hysterical parent. A parent's level of concern can help a doctor determine how sick a baby is.

> ### I Wish Someone Had Told Me . . .
>
> ". . . not to be afraid to call your child's doctor about anything. That's what they are there for, and I guarantee that if you feel you are annoying them, there's always someone out there who annoys them more!"

Getting Medical Care When Your Child Is Ill

For most children, routine checkups account for only about one-third of all doctor's visits. Most visits are for acute illnesses and follow-up of acute and chronic health problems. Your child's primary care physician's office should be home base for sick care as well as preventive care.

Office or ER?

If your child is severely injured or shows signs of potentially life-threatening illness, you should go directly to an emergency room (ER), usually by ambulance or other emergency medical transport.

In most cases, however, you will be able to manage your child's illnesses on your own or with your child's doctor's help. If you need medical advice or think your child may need to be seen, you should contact your child's doctor, explain the situation, and ask if you should bring your child to the office or to the emergency room. (For more information about dealing with emergencies and everyday injuries, see Chapter 28, "First Aid and Emergency Care.")

The Office Sick Visit

Most office sick visits are similar to well visits except that the evaluation is focused on the child's illness. After you arrive at the office, a nurse or medical assistant will usually weigh your child and take her temperature, heart rate, breathing rate, and, in some cases, blood pressure. If your child appears seriously ill to the nurse, the doctor will be notified immediately so she can be seen right away. The medical history and physical examination performed by the doctor will focus on the aspects relevant to your child's illness. For some illnesses, this may take more time and require more detailed questioning and examinations than is usual at a well visit.

After your child has been evaluated, the doctor should give you a thorough explanation of the findings and recommendations. Depending upon the problem, this might include lab tests, X-rays, a variety of treatments in the office, prescription of medications, a visit to the ER, or admission to the hospital. Many offices will be able to give you starter doses of medications for your child to tide you over until you can get the prescriptions filled. Some practices may even be able to fill the prescriptions from their office pharmacy for some commonly prescribed medications (the cost of these in-office prescriptions, however, may not be covered by your child's health plan).

If your child is sent home after the visit, make sure that you understand all of the doctor's and nurse's instructions completely, including trouble signs you should watch for with your child's condition. Take notes or ask for written instructions if you think there is any chance you might forget what has been said. If you think you will have any problems following the treatment plan for your child, tell the doctor and staff before leaving the office so that alternative plans can be made.

Special Health Care Needs

Children with chronic conditions and complex medical needs often require services from physician specialists, therapists, and other providers. But the child's primary care physician usually has the responsibility for managing and coordinating the overall treatment plan for the child. In addition to providing the preventive care that all children require, often the primary care doctor will schedule additional visits to monitor and manage the child's chronic condition. For example, if a child has moderate to severe asthma, the primary care physician might see him several times a year to review the symptoms since the last visit, adjust his medication, if necessary, test his breathing function, and review the correct way to use an inhaler. If the child is in a managed health care plan, the primary care doctor may act as a "gatekeeper"—the person responsible for authorizing requests for special tests, supplies, equipment, and referrals to specialists. (For more information about chronic conditions and health problems, see Chapter 32, "Health Problems in Early Childhood." For more information about caring for a child with special health needs, see Chapter 33, "Caring for Your Child with Special Health Care Needs.")

Working the Phones

When you call your child's doctor because your child seems ill, it helps to be specific and focused, especially if you are calling at night or on the weekend.

- Remind the doctor of your child's age, any past or current medical problems (including low birthweight or prematurity), and any medications, including over-the-counter drugs or supplements, that he is taking.
- Describe the symptoms that led you to call. Say when the symptoms started, how they have changed, and how you have handled them so far. Be as specific as possible. "He usually wakes up to eat every four hours, but we've had to wake him for the last three feedings" is a description that tells the doctor more than if you just say the baby is unusually sleepy.

- Spell out what you are concerned about. "His cough seems to be getting worse, and now that it's bedtime, I'm worried he'll have trouble breathing during the night." "He has some red spots on his legs. I thought they were mosquito bites, but his cousin, who visited last week, just came down with chicken pox."

- Mention all the symptoms that concern you, but don't mix in routine issues that could be dealt with some other time, such as whether to use a pacifier or start solid food.

- With a newborn, take the baby's temperature before you call and write it down, along with the time it was taken.

> ### The Voice of Experience
>
> *"First of all, trust your instincts. If something does not seem right to you about your child, it is better to keep seeking an answer rather than to let something go, even if it means confronting your child's doctor. . . . Find the best doctor or health care professionals you possibly can for your child. Don't be afraid to ask a lot of questions and offer your observations of your child's health condition. A lot of times, parents can recognize changes in their child's condition that a doctor who does not see them on a daily basis would not detect. A good doctor knows this and takes a parent's observations seriously."*
>
> —FROM THE KIDSHEALTH PARENT SURVEY

- If your baby has vomited or had diarrhea, be prepared to describe when, how often, and what it looked like.

- Try to notice whether your baby is urinating as much as usual. If he isn't, be sure to tell the doctor.

- Have a pad at hand to write down instructions. Have your baby's health record available. (See Appendix A for information on how to make a health record.)

- Have the name and number of your pharmacy available in case the doctor wants to call in a prescription.

Children's Fears About Medical Exams

Going to the doctor's office can be a frightening experience for a young child. The office may be loud, busy, and full of strangers. Unfamiliar people poke and prod all body parts, and sometimes they do things that really hurt. It's not surprising that your child may scream even as you enter the door, so try to be understanding and help your child overcome his fears.

Reasons for a Child's Fear

If you can understand why your child is afraid of a medical visit, you'll be better able to calm his fears. The following are a few common reasons your child might cling and scream when he sees the doctor:

- Separation. Children often fear that their parents may leave them in the examining room and wait in another room. This fear is most common in children under age seven.
- Pain. Children may worry that a medical procedure will hurt—sometimes it does!
- The doctor. Unfortunately, a doctor's manner may upset a child. To a child, and sometimes to a parent as well, a doctor's speed, efficiency, or detached attitude may come across as sternness, dislike, or rejection.
- The unknown. Most children are apprehensive about the unknown. Not knowing exactly what's going to happen to them when the doctor comes into the examining room can be terrifying.

Things You Can Do to Help

You can help your child manage her fear by encouraging her to express her feelings. Don't say, "Oh, there's nothing to be afraid of. Don't cry." Instead try, "I know that visiting the doctor sometimes makes you cry, but I will stay right next to you the whole time to help you feel better." Always use words that she understands, and focus on the positive. Before you arrive at the office, take some time to prepare your child. The following tips will help.

Explain the Purpose of the Visit

If the upcoming visit is for a periodic health assessment, you might say something like, "The doctor wants to help you stay healthy. He's going to be happy to see how you are growing stronger and taller. He will look at every part of your body to make sure each part is healthy. He will ask you questions about how you feel, and you can ask him questions about your health, too." Stress that all children go to the doctor for such visits.

If the visit is to diagnose and treat an illness or other condition, explain in nonthreatening language that the doctor "needs to see you to help you feel better."

Equally important, if your child is going to receive a shot at the visit, be sure to tell him up front—and that it might hurt a little bit. Not telling a child will only violate his trust, resulting in a more lasting "pain" that will affect how he handles future visits to the doctor.

Address Any Guilty Feelings Your Child Might Have

If your child is going to the doctor because of an illness or other condition, he may have unspoken guilty feelings about it. Discuss the illness or condition in simple, neutral language, and reassure him that it is not his fault: "This is not caused by anything you did or forgot to do; illnesses like this happen to many children," and "Aren't we lucky to have doctors who can find the causes and who know how to help us get well?"

If you or other relatives or friends had (or have) the same condition, share this information if you can. Knowing that you and many others have been through it will help relieve your child's feelings.

If your child has been ridiculed or rejected by other children (or even by adults) because of a medical problem, you need to double your efforts to relieve feelings of shame and blame. Head lice, embarrassing scratching caused by pinworms, and daytime wetting are examples of conditions that are often misunderstood by others. Even if you have been very supportive, you need to reassure your child again, before the visit to the doctor, that the condition is not his fault, that the doctor knows it is not his fault, and that many children have had this problem.

Of course, if your child has suffered an injury after disregarding safety rules, you need to point out (as matter-of-factly as possible) the cause-and-effect relationship between the action and the injury. But you should still try to relieve guilt. You could say, "You probably did not understand the danger in doing that, but I am sure you understand now, and I know you will not do it that way again." If this is a repeated pattern, that's more worrisome and may require more thought as to what's going on and how to change the behavior.

In any of these cases, be sure to explain, especially to your young child, that going to the doctor for an examination is not a punishment. Be sure your child understands that adults go to doctors just as all children do and that the doctor's job is to help people stay healthy and help them get well if they are sick.

Tell Your Child What to Expect During Routine Exams

If the examination is a routine one, you can use a doll or teddy bear to show your young child how the nurse will measure height and weight. Show how your child's doctor will look at his eyes, into his ears, and in his mouth (and may need to hold his tongue down with a special stick for just a few seconds to see his throat). Show how he will listen to his chest and back with a stethoscope. Explain that the doctor may press on his tummy to feel what's inside. And show your child how the doctor may tap on his knee and look at his feet.

Be sure to mention that the doctor may also look at his "private areas" to make sure they are healthy. Let your child know that what you have taught him about the privacy of his body is still true but that doctors, nurses, and parents must sometimes examine all parts of the body. These people are exceptions. Incidentally, be aware that doctors are comfortable using such words as *penis* and *vagina* and other anatomically correct terms with children. And if your child will be receiving a shot, tell him before you go, or it will violate his trust.

Tell Your Child What to Expect During Sick-Child Exams

If your child is going to the doctor because of an illness or medical condition or is going to visit a specialist, you yourself may not know what to expect during the examination.

When you are calling to make the appointment, you can ask to speak to the doctor or a nurse to find out, in a general way, what will take place during the office visit and exam. Then you can explain some of the procedures and their purpose in gentle language, appropriate to your child's age level. Your child (and you) will feel more secure if he understands what is going to take place and why it is necessary.

Be honest, but not brutally honest. Let your child know if a procedure is going to be somewhat embarrassing, uncomfortable, or even painful, but don't go into alarming detail. Reassure your child that you will be beside him and that the procedure is truly necessary in order to fix—or find out how to fix—the problem. If the pain or discomfort will last for only a few moments, tell your child that. Children can cope with discomfort or pain more easily if they are forewarned, and they will learn to trust you if you are honest with them.

Admit to your child if you lack knowledge of this illness or condition, but assure him that you will both be able to ask the doctor questions about it. Write down your child's questions.

If a blood sample will be taken, be careful how you explain this. Some young children worry that "taking blood" means taking *all* their blood. Let your child know that the body contains a great deal of blood and only a little bit of it will be taken for testing and that her body will make more blood to replace it. (Blood tests usually take only a few drops. Even the tests that collect blood in a tube require only about a teaspoon or so of blood.)

Above all, make certain that your child understands that the visit, with its embarrassing or uncomfortable procedures, is not a punishment for any misbehavior or disobedience.

Involve Your Child in the Process

Don't overlook your child's interest in her own medical care. If she is involved, she will be less frightened. If the situation is not an emergency, allow your child to contribute to a list of symptoms that she will give the doctor. Include all symptoms you both have observed, no matter how unrelated they may seem to the problem at hand. You can also ask your child to think of questions that she would like to ask the doctor. Write them down and give them to the doctor; if your child is old enough, let her write down and ask the questions herself.

Choose a Doctor Who Relates Well to Children

Because your child's doctor is your best ally in helping your child cope with health examinations, you need to select the doctor carefully. Of course, you want a doctor who is knowledgeable and competent, but you also want a doctor who understands children's needs and fears and who communicates easily with children, in a friendly manner and without talking down to them. If your child's pediatrician or family doctor seems critical, uncommunicative, remote, or unsympathetic, do not be afraid to change doctors. For more information about choosing a doctor for your child, see Chapter 12, "Choosing and Working with Your Child's Doctor."

Trust Your Instincts

Many parents who responded to our KidsHealth survey told us the same thing: Trust your instincts. If you think something is wrong with your child, get help. If you aren't comfortable or confident with what your child's doctor has told you, get a second opinion. If you are really worried and have nowhere else to turn, take your child to a hospital emergency room, especially at a children's hospital or a major medical center.

Some of the parents who responded to our survey thought a doctor had taken too long to recognize the severity of their child's acute illness until another physi-

A Mother's Story

When my daughter was a baby, she threw up almost everything she consumed. I was terribly worried, and I took her to the doctor. He told me that she had an underdeveloped valve in her esophagus (which is common in newborns) and that when she was about nine months old, the vomiting would stop. He also said not to worry, she was still growing and hydrated (getting enough fluid). I didn't understand how he could possibly be right. Well, he was! Almost to the very day of her nine-month birthday, she completely stopped throwing up.

cian made the right call. Other parents said their child had a chronic illness that went undiagnosed for months as doctors told them not to worry, the child wasn't sick or would outgrow the problem. "If you think something is wrong, it probably is," several parents said.

But that isn't *always* true. Many (perhaps most—who knows?) of the things that worry parents really are nothing to worry about. Most children do outgrow them. Most children do not have serious chronic illnesses. Several parents told us they had grave doubts about their doctors' reassurances, only to be delighted when the doctor turned out to be right.

So what's a parent to do? Go ahead and trust your instincts. If you think something is wrong, call your child's doctor. If you think the doctor is ignoring a problem, take it up with him or her, and, if necessary, get a second opinion or even a third. Trust your instincts not only about your child but also about the doctor. Do you think he or she is careful, competent, and concerned? Can he or she explain his or her reasoning and the evidence behind it to you? If a problem persists despite treatment, does he or she try a different approach or refer you to a specialist? If the answers are yes, your instincts may tell you to trust the doctor's judgment. If the answers are no, your instincts may tell you to find a new doctor.

Need More Information?

Check the Index and Appendix C, "Resource Guide." And of course, consult your child's doctor.

chapter fourteen

Health Screening Tests

Which ones should your child have?

When it comes to health measures, screening tests are humble heroes. They seem so simple, usually taking only a few drops of blood or urine. But they can shout a warning about hidden medical conditions that could harm your child if not diagnosed and treated early. Not surprisingly, screening tests are an important part of pediatric preventive care—care that aims to keep your child healthy and developing normally.

Two major types of screening tests are commonly used:

- Universal screening tests are recommended for all people. All newborn infants, for example, are screened for phenylketonuria (PKU), a serious metabolic disease.
- Selective screening tests are recommended only for individuals who are thought to be at higher risk for having a particular problem, such as tuberculosis, lead poisoning, high blood cholesterol, and anemia.

Like all heroes, screening tests have their weaknesses. In many cases, an abnormal result on a screening test does not mean that a child definitely has the particular condition. Further evaluation, including more specific and accurate testing, is often necessary to be sure. For example, many premature infants may show results that are outside the usual range for other newborns when they are screened for the disorder congenital hypothyroidism. These abnormalities are generally temporary and don't mean that the infant has the condition. But the screening test lets the doctor know there's something that needs checking out.

Some of the screening tests commonly done in childhood are discussed in this chapter.

Newborn Screening for Hereditary and Metabolic Diseases

Each state in the United States and most developed countries in the world have programs that test newborns for certain hereditary and metabolic diseases. The number of conditions for which infants are tested varies from state to state.

Two of the most commonly performed newborn screening tests are for congenital hypothyroidism and PKU, conditions that can result in severe mental retardation if not recognized and treated within the first few weeks of life. (To learn more about these conditions, see Chapter 32, "Health Problems in Early Childhood.") These tests, as well as other tests that may be offered in your state, are performed by taking a small amount of blood from your baby (usually by a heel prick) and sending it to a laboratory for analysis. The blood specimen is usually drawn before your baby leaves the nursery.

Another blood sample may be taken at your child's first visit to the doctor's office, depending on various factors. For example, the initial test results may be unreliable for some conditions if your baby is premature or if your infant's blood was drawn before 24 hours of age. Because the results of newborn screening tests can take several days to come back from the laboratory, make sure that the hospital knows how to contact you and your baby's doctor after discharge.

A recently developed technique called "tandem mass spectroscopy" has made it possible to screen newborns for a much larger number of metabolic diseases than was previously possible from a small blood sample. At the time of this writing, most states have either begun offering this test or are considering adding it. If the test is not yet available routinely from their state program, some parents are electing to pay for the test themselves. Speak with your child's doctor about your options regarding this test.

Tuberculosis Screening

Think back to childhood—do you remember getting your forearm pricked with a little four-pronged device that looked like a round plug? That was the periodic tuberculosis (TB) test you probably got at your doctor's office or at school. Although TB continues to pose a significant health threat for some groups of children, universal screening (testing every child) is no longer recommended for U.S. children. The American Academy of Pediatrics (AAP) now recommends testing

TB Testing for High-Risk Children

Should your child be tested for tuberculosis? These children should be tested for TB immediately:

- Children in contact with persons with confirmed or suspected infectious TB
- Children with symptoms or lab or X-ray results suggesting TB infection
- Children immigrating from countries where TB is common (such as countries in Asia, Africa, the Middle East, and Latin America)
- Children who have traveled to or who have been in contact with people who have been living in these countries

These children should be tested annually:

- Children who have HIV infection or who live in a household with a person with HIV

These children should be tested every two to three years:

- Children exposed to the following persons: HIV-infected persons, homeless persons, residents of nursing homes, institutionalized or incarcerated adolescents or adults, illicit drug users, and migrant farmworkers

These children should be considered for testing at four to six years of age:

- Children whose parents immigrated from regions of the world where TB is common
- Children without other risk factors but who live in a neighborhood where TB is more common (Check with your child's doctor or public health department about the prevalence of TB in your neighborhood.)

These children should also be considered for testing:

- Children with certain chronic medical conditions or those who are about to begin treatments that suppress the immune system only children considered to be at higher risk for TB infection. Some states, schools, and child-care programs, however, may require TB testing of all children.

The four-pronged plug, however, is outmoded. The current TB test, the Mantoux test, uses a small needle to inject an extract of the TB germ *Mycobacterium tuberculosis* into the skin of the forearm. The test is read by looking for swelling at the injection site two to three days later. To ensure accurate interpretation, only a trained health care provider should read the test. If your child's test is positive, the doctor will make sure that your child gets any additional testing or treatment necessary.

Cholesterol Screening

Researchers have known for many years now that atherosclerosis (hardening of the arteries) and the heart attacks, strokes, and other health problems associated with it often have their roots in childhood. High blood cholesterol (along with smoking, obesity, lack of exercise, diabetes, and untreated high blood pressure) is a major

Blood Cholesterol Screening Recommendations

Does your child need cholesterol screening? These risk factors indicate a need for blood cholesterol screening:

- A child's parent or grandparent had coronary catheterization (an invasive heart test) at age 55 or younger and was found to have coronary atherosclerosis; this includes those who have undergone balloon angioplasty or coronary artery bypass surgery.
- A child's parent or grandparent had a heart attack, angina, peripheral vascular disease, stroke, or sudden cardiac death at age 55 or younger.
- A child's parent has an elevated blood cholesterol level (240 mg/dL or higher).

Also, consider screening a child whose parental health history is unknown, especially if the child has other heart disease risk factors (such as obesity).

risk factor for developing atherosclerosis at an early age. Like adults, children with high cholesterol can often reduce those cholesterol levels significantly by changing their eating habits—and most likely can lower their risk of future heart disease by doing so.

Cholesterol screening usually is not done until age 24 months, because strict dietary fat restriction is not considered to be safe before this age. The doctor will help decide whether your child should have a total cholesterol level measured or whether a lipid profile should be done, which also looks at the levels of HDL ("good") cholesterol, LDL ("bad") cholesterol, and triglycerides (another fat in the blood that can play a role in heart disease). The results of these tests will help guide you and your child's doctor in deciding whether dietary changes are needed and how your child should be followed over time.

Lead Screening

Although fewer U.S. children today have elevated blood lead levels than in past decades, lead poisoning continues to be a significant health threat in many communities. Urban children living in poverty are more likely to be exposed to lead,

Recommendations for Screening of Blood Lead Levels

A blood lead test is recommended at 9 to 12 months (and possibly again at 24 months) if your child lives in a high-risk community (as determined by local health authorities). Your child is also considered at high risk if the answer to one or more of the following questions is yes:

1. Does your child live in or regularly visit a house or child-care facility built before 1950?
2. Does your child live in or regularly visit a house or child-care facility built before 1978 that is being or has recently been renovated or remodeled?
3. Does your child have a sibling or playmate who has or had lead poisoning?

but rural children and those from middle- and upper-income families can also be at risk. Research studies have documented the toxic effects of lead exposure on the developing brain and nervous system of young children, resulting in lowered intelligence and perhaps other neurologic and behavioral problems as well. (See Chapter 32, "Health Problems in Early Childhood," for more information about lead poisoning.)

The U.S. Centers for Disease Control and Prevention recommends universal screening only for children who live in high-risk communities. Other children need to be screened only if they have other risk factors. Some states, schools, and child-care programs may require blood lead screening of all children, no matter their risk factors.

Guidelines for Anemia Screening

- Test (at 9 to 12 months, 6 months later, then annually from ages two to five years) all children in high-risk categories (such as children from low-income families, migrant children, and recently arrived refugees).
- Test (at 9 to 12 months and 6 months later) these children:
  - Premature or low-birthweight infants
  - Infants fed a non-iron-fortified formula for more than 2 months
  - Infants fed cow's milk before age 12 months
  - Breast-fed infants who didn't receive iron-containing foods after age 6 months
  - Children who drink more than 24 ounces of cow's milk daily
  - Children who have certain special health care needs as determined by a doctor

Anemia Screening

The most common cause of anemia among infants and young children is iron deficiency, caused by a lack of iron in the child's diet. (The body needs iron to produce hemoglobin to carry oxygen in the blood.) The U.S. Centers for Disease Control and Prevention recommends testing only for babies and children considered to be at high risk for iron deficiency.

Again, you should be aware that some school and child-care programs might require a test for anemia, even for children at low risk.

Need More Information?

Check the Index and Appendix C, "Resource Guide." And of course, consult your child's doctor.

chapter fifteen

Hearing and Vision

Taking care of your child's special senses

Imagine as your child grows how she will thrill at the sound of the wind and the beauty of the sunset. Can you see her squealing with joy at a joke and reading through her favorite book? Chances are she will be able to do these things and a million more if you make sure that her medical care includes attention to two vital senses: hearing and vision. This chapter focuses on how you, your child's doctor, and specialists can work together to safeguard these senses.

Your Child's Hearing

It is estimated that up to 3 infants per 1,000 born in the United States have significant hearing loss. Studies have shown, however, that significant hearing problems present at birth are often not diagnosed until the child's second or third year of life. This is unfortunate because the earlier a hearing loss is recognized and treatment is begun, the better the outlook for the child's learning and for development of speech and language skills.

Because of this situation, it is now recommended that all newborns be given early hearing evaluations. At the time of this writing, many states are in the process, or have completed the process, of passing legislation to mandate such screening. Many hospitals have already instituted newborn hearing screening programs. This is a big step forward toward meeting the goal of early detection and treatment of hearing problems.

Signs of a Possible Hearing Problem

Screening for hearing problems should be a part of your child's regular checkups right from the start. Before your child is old enough to cooperate with more formal hearing tests, your child's doctor will be looking for other signs that might indicate a hearing problem. Some of the signs that you and the doctor should look for include the following:

- Your newborn doesn't startle or jump in response to sudden loud noises.
- Your infant doesn't turn to the source of a sound or seem to recognize your voice by three to four months of age.
- Your infant babbles and coos in the first few months but then stops making speech sounds.
- Your infant tends to make only vibrating or gargling sounds.
- Your child doesn't imitate some sounds or say some single words like *Mama* or *bye-bye* by 12 months of age.
- Your child's speech is delayed or difficult to understand.
- Your child's development is delayed in other areas such as sitting and walking.
- Your child seems to hear certain types of sound but not others.
- Your child has trouble telling where a sound is coming from.
- The quality of your child's voice is unusual.
- Your child doesn't notice when people enter the room unless he sees them.
- Your child doesn't respond when you call or doesn't listen to your instructions.
- Your child has problems with learning or attention.
- Your child seems to need to watch people's lips when they speak.
- Your child turns the TV volume up very high.

KidsHealth Tip

Noise Worries

Many new parents are concerned that loud noises will damage their infant's ears. But the normal noises that occur in any house—like a dog barking or a television playing—will not do any harm at all. In addition, many babies have no trouble sleeping with this type of normal background noise, so it isn't necessary to tiptoe around the house.

The doctor will also give particular attention to hearing tests if your child has any of the following risk factors for hearing impairment:

- A history of childhood hearing loss in a family member
- A mother who had a rubella (German measles) or CMV (cytomegalovirus) infection during pregnancy
- A premature birth or severe medical problems at birth
- A history of meningitis (infection of the covering of the brain)
- Frequent ear infections, certain genetic syndromes, or birth defects, particularly those that involve the ears, face, skull, or brain (such as cerebral palsy)

If your child's doctor suspects your child may have a hearing problem or be at risk for one, of course you'll want to know why. Your child's doctor may be able to determine if the problem is congenital (present at birth) or if it developed later as the child grew. Hearing impairment may be hereditary or related to certain pregnancy problems (infections, drugs), prematurity, severe medical problems at birth, meningitis or other infections, repeated ear infections, traumatic injuries to the ears or brain, and certain genetic syndromes or birth defects. Whatever the cause, early detection and treatment are what's most important.

Managing Ear Infections

Ear infections in young children are common. If your child has symptoms (see the section on ear infection in Chapter 30, "Childhood Infections"), his ears will be examined. This will also be done at routine checkups. If an ear infection is detected, usually an antibiotic is prescribed. Your child may be examined again after the course of medication is completed to make sure the infection has cleared.

If, after treatment, your child's ear examination findings have not returned to normal as expected, your child's doctor may perform a test called a tympanogram to evaluate how well the eardrum and the middle ear are functioning. To perform a tympanogram, the person doing the test places the soft rubber tip of the testing device in your child's ear to deliver air pressure and sound into the ear. The goal is to see how much of the tone is absorbed or reflected off the eardrum as the pressure changes. This test causes a sensation like the "clogged ears" feeling when going up in an airplane, but it is not painful. An abnormal test result may indicate that there is a persistent collection of fluid behind the eardrum and that the infection may not have cleared completely. If, despite treatment with different doses and/or types of antibiotics, the test result remains abnormal over several weeks, the doctor may refer your child to an ear, nose, and throat (ENT) specialist.

Hearing Specialists

If your child's doctor thinks that your child might have persistence of fluid in the ear or recurrent infections that might interfere with your child's hearing, he or she will probably refer your child to a pediatric audiologist or ENT specialist for further evaluation.

An ENT specialist is a medical doctor who specializes in the treatment of ear, nose, and throat problems. The doctor will take a medical history and will examine your child to determine if your child is at risk for hearing problems.

> ### The Voice of Experience
>
> *"I found that my child got fewer ear infections if I fed him in an upright position."*
> —FROM THE KIDSHEALTH PARENT SURVEY

About 85 to 90 percent of the children seen by an ENT specialist for recurring or persistent ear problems are also referred to a pediatric audiologist for further testing. Pediatric audiologists are experts in the testing of hearing of infants and children.

Hearing Tests for Children

There are several methods of testing a child's hearing. The method chosen depends in part on the child's age, development, and medical status. Here's an overview of the tests used for screening and evaluating hearing problems at different ages.

Screening Tests for the Newborn

The technique most commonly used to screen a newborn's hearing today is called an otoacoustic emissions (OAE) test. This test can be performed shortly after birth as part of the routine newborn screening process. But because some newborns fail due to wax or debris in the ear canal, it's best to wait until just before discharge from the hospital to perform this test on a newborn.

Another newborn screening test used at some hospitals is an automated auditory brainstem response (ABR) test. The ABR is a bit more thorough than the OAE in that it tests a larger part of the infant's hearing pathway from the ear to the brain. However, some hospitals do not use it because the results can be more difficult to interpret.

Hearing Tests for Children Ages Three to Six Months

If your three- to six-month-old has a suspected hearing problem, she may be given either or both of the two tests mentioned in the section for newborns. If necessary, she may be sedated with medication for the ABR if she will not fall asleep on her own or stay asleep long enough to complete the test.

Hearing Tests for Children
Ages Six Months to Two and One-Half Years

At this age, the testing gets to be fun for the child. Children this age enjoy animation and various stimuli, so these things are used as part of the test. As your child sits on your lap in a sound booth, he hears sounds that come from speakers located on opposite sides of the sound booth. Animated toys placed between the speakers are used to keep the child's attention focused away from the speakers themselves. When the child turns to the source of the sound, he is rewarded by an automated puppet that lights up or moves.

Hearing Tests for Children
Ages Two and One-Half to Four Years

If your child needs a hearing test at this age, "games" will be used to test how well she hears and understands speech. For example, toys or picture cards are placed on a table in front of your child while she is wearing headphones. Then she is asked to point to the toy or picture that the audiologist requests.

KidsHealth Tip

Turn Down the Sound

Many kids who wear portable headphones set the volume too high when listening to music, which can potentially lead to hearing loss. A good way to tell if your child's music is too loud is to stand nearby and listen while he is wearing his headphones. If you can hear the music, turn down the sound.

Hearing Tests for Children Ages Four Years and Older

Your child's hearing should be screened routinely at well-child visits starting at the four-year-old health supervision visit. At this time and onward, she can be tested as adults are tested—by repeating two-syllable words and by raising her hand or pushing a button in response to a sound produced by a testing device.

Your Child's Vision

Your baby watches every move you make. When she sees you smile, she smiles. This visual interaction teaches your baby how her world works. To make sure your child is able to see all the things her world offers, her doctor should routinely screen her vision during childhood so that problems can be detected early.

The Development of Vision

How does vision develop? These guidelines are useful in judging progress:

Age	Early Visual Milestones*
0–1 month	Has limited ability to focus on someone's face or an object; sees light and form
1–3 months	Has longer periods of focusing; follows objects; learns to use eyes together
3–5 months	Explores environment; reaches for objects
5–8 months	Improves hand-eye coordination; shifts focus
8–15 months	Looks for hidden objects; imitates faces
2–2½ years	Shows improved attention to distant objects and visual memory

* These milestones may occur later in premature infants and children with developmental delay. If normal progress is not noted, special tests or treatment may be necessary.

If you believe that your child's visual development is lagging behind, you should talk to her primary care doctor to determine whether vision testing or other evaluation is needed.

Vision Screening Guidelines

The American Academy of Ophthalmology recommends the following schedule for screening vision:

- Newborns should receive a general eye check in the newborn nursery by the primary care doctor (pediatrician or family doctor).
- Premature infants, infants with obvious eye problems, and infants with a family history of eye problems (cataracts, eye tumors) should be examined by an ophthalmologist (doctor specializing in the medical and surgical treatment of eye problems).
- By six months of age, all infants should have an eye screening by the primary care doctor with a referral to an ophthalmologist if a problem is noted.
- At about age three to three and one-half years, children should have an eye screening, including a test for vision by the primary care doctor with a referral to an ophthalmologist if a problem is noted.
- At about age five, children should again have their vision and eye alignment checked by the primary care doctor with a referral to an ophthalmologist if a problem is noted.

Common Eye Problems

Several eye problems may be noticed by parents or discovered at screenings. Here's an overview of some of the most common problems.

Amblyopia

Amblyopia (or "lazy eye") is poor vision (usually in one eye) caused when a diminished or different image from each eye is presented to the brain. Because the brain cannot put the different images together, brain cells that work with one of the eyes will shut down to avoid confusion. Crossed eyes or a difference in near- or farsightedness between the two eyes are common causes of this condition. Amblyopia can cause permanent vision loss if not properly treated. It is most easily treated before the age of five or six years, although treatment should be considered up to age nine years. Treatment often includes wearing a patch over one eye temporarily, wearing glasses, or both. Surgery may be necessary if the amblyopia is caused by a droopy eyelid (ptosis) or by lens clouding (cataract).

Figure 15.1. Strabismus. In this child with strabismus, her right eye turns in toward her nose while her left eye looks straight ahead. Early treatment of this condition is essential to prevent amblyopia ("lazy eye").

Strabismus ("Crossed" or Drifting Eyes)

Strabismus is a misalignment of the eyes and can result in amblyopia if it's chronic. It is common in newborns, but by the time your child is three months old, any crossing of the eyes should be gone. After that age, you should not assume your child will "outgrow" crossed or drifting eyes. Glasses or surgery may be necessary. For more information about strabismus surgery, see Chapter 32, "Health Problems in Early Childhood."

Refractive Errors

Refractive errors cause nearsightedness, farsightedness, and astigmatism. These problems result when the eye is improperly shaped, causing a blurry image. Amblyopia and eyestrain can result. Glasses may be needed if the refractive error is significant.

Eye Problems in the Family

Some eye problems are more significant and require immediate attention and treatment. Alert your child's primary care doctor if there is a family history of any of these eye problems:

- Retinoblastoma is a malignant tumor that develops in the eye during the first few years of life. Loss of vision, drifting of the affected eye, or a white or abnormal appearance of the pupil may be noted. Multiple forms of treatment are available, depending upon the extent of the disease.

- Cataracts are a clouding of the lens of the eye and may be present at birth or develop in early childhood. Observation, patching, glasses, and surgery are possible treatments, depending upon the severity of the lens clouding.
- Congenital glaucoma is a rare condition in which the drainage system of the eye does not develop properly. Poor drainage can result in high pressure in the eye and can damage a child's vision. Surgery is often necessary, although medications may also be used.

KidsHealth Tip

The Better to See You With

If your child needs eyeglasses, you can help make getting them a positive experience.

- Point out to your child all the people he knows who wear glasses (sunglasses count, too!).
- If you are upset about the glasses, be careful not to convey this feeling to your child. Try to remember that glasses are a wonderful thing because they help your child see better and fully experience the world.
- Let your child practice wearing your sunglasses or his own to get used to the feel of glasses before you go shopping.
- If possible, ask your child's eye doctor or others you know to recommend an optician who has a lot of young customers. An optician who is good with kids can make the process more fun for everyone.
- Make sure the frames fit properly. Your child won't be comfortable if the frames are too tight and put pressure on his face or are too loose and slide down his nose.
- Choose polycarbonate lenses. This blended-plastic material is scratch-resistant, lightweight, and hard to shatter.
- Be certain your child is happy with the style of the frames. He's more likely to wear his new glasses if he feels confident.

KidsHealth Tip

Tiny Tot Computer Users

By the age of four or five, many kids would love to stay glued to a computer for hours at a time, thanks to enticing software. But the American Academy of Pediatrics recommends that you limit your child's screen time—the total time he spends looking at TV, videos, and computers—to no more than an hour or two per day. For preschoolers, it makes sense to set the limit at the low end of this range. If your child logs on, he should be pried loose every 30 minutes or so for a 5-minute break that includes walking around, moving his hands, and looking at faraway objects to rest his eyes.

Signs of Vision Trouble

- Poor focusing
- Poor following of objects
- Abnormal alignment or movement of the eyes (such as "crossed" eyes or a drifting eye) after three months of age
- Constant eye rubbing
- Extreme light sensitivity
- Chronic redness or cloudiness of the eyes
- Chronic tearing of the eyes
- A white pupil instead of black

Evaluation by a Pediatric Ophthalmologist

If a problem is identified, your child will probably be referred to a pediatric ophthalmologist. This is a physician who treats medical and surgical diseases of the eyes and has special training in the evaluation and treatment of eye diseases affecting children.

An Eye Examination

During eye exams, your child's doctor will look for the following:

- Visual acuity. The ability of each eye, individually and together, to fixate and follow objects will be observed. Older children will be asked to identify symbols or match symbols.
- Eye alignment. The doctor will shine a light toward your child's eyes and examine the alignment by observing where the light reflects off the front of the eyes. In older children, alignment may be tested by covering one eye and then the other while the child views an object (cross cover test).
- Depth perception and color vision. Older children may have depth perception and color vision testing.
- Eye structure. The structure of the eye is examined. Eyedrops are used to dilate the pupils to look for farsightedness, nearsightedness, or astigmatism. The doctor also checks the structure of the optic nerve and retina.

> ### *The Voice of Experience*
>
> *"When the doctor said my two-and-a-half-year-old needed glasses, I was afraid he'd be teased. It was a relief to find out young children seem to have no negative feelings about people who wear glasses. (Ironically, the one child who said something mean—"four eyes"—got this insult from a well-meaning book aimed at helping kids adjust to glasses. Neither he nor my son knew what it meant—and my son didn't even realize it was an insult.)*
>
> *"When he was a little older, kids would be curious and ask, 'Why do you wear glasses?' We prepared the simple answer, 'They help me see really, really well,' and that seemed to satisfy everyone."*
>
> —FROM THE KIDSHEALTH PARENT SURVEY

Visual Impairment

In some cases, children have poor vision that cannot be improved, due to problems such as albinism and retinal degeneration. Your pediatric ophthalmologist can help you understand the problem and make a plan to help your child reach his full potential. Visual impairment alone does not limit a child's ability to learn. For more on visual impairment, see Chapter 32, "Health Problems in Early Childhood."

ⓘ Need More Information?

Check the Index and Appendix C, "Resource Guide." And of course, consult your child's doctor.

chapter sixteen

Immunizations

Shots that save lives

Immunization programs have been one of the greatest public health success stories in history. In the words of the American Academy of Pediatrics (AAP), "Immunization continues to be the most effective method of preventing disease, disability, and death in children." In fact, childhood diseases that can be prevented by vaccines are at their lowest levels in history in the United States.

Vaccines protect your child by introducing a small amount of a killed or weakened disease-causing germ or substance into his body. This causes your child's immune system to build up antibodies and other defenses to fight the disease. These defenses that are developed in response to a vaccine remain with your child and enable him to fight off the disease if he is ever exposed to it. In this way, he becomes immune to the disease.

But despite the success of vaccination programs, outbreaks of serious childhood illnesses still occur: In 1989 and 1991, measles epidemics hit the United States, even though there is a vaccine to prevent the disease. As a caring and loving parent, it is your responsibility to have your child vaccinated according to the schedule your child's doctor will give you. (For more information on vaccine-preventable diseases, see Chapter 30, "Childhood Infections.")

Why Some Children Aren't Immunized— Even When They Should Be

Immunization works only if everyone participates. The U.S. Centers for Disease Control and Prevention still considers the immunization rate in this country to be

KidsHealth Tip

A Gift for Newborns

Newborn babies have temporary partial natural immunity to some serious childhood diseases, a gift from their mothers in the form of antibodies passed through the placenta. Breast-feeding continues to boost the infant's antibodies. Breast-feeding, however, is not a substitute for vaccines. Breast milk does not completely protect a child against all diseases, and, in any case, the natural immunity eventually wears off, making vaccinations just as important for breast-fed children.

too low. In 1998, only 79 percent of children ages 19 to 35 months had received a complete series of vaccines. This puts all children at risk. Let's take a look at some of the reasons kids aren't immunized—even when they should be.

Mistaken Belief That the Danger Is Gone

Often parents believe it isn't necessary to immunize their children because almost everyone else in the United States has gotten shots and so there is no one to spread the disease. We live in a global environment today, however, where we and people from other nations move freely around the world. Diseases move just as freely. As long as diseases such as polio or measles exist anywhere on the globe, your child is at risk and vaccinations are necessary. Potential epidemics are just a plane ride away. And in the case of tetanus, even vaccinating every other child on the planet won't protect your child from getting this disease. That's because tetanus is caused by bacteria in soil that can contaminate a wound.

Fear of Contracting Disease from the Vaccination

Another common misconception that keeps some parents from getting their children vaccinated is the belief that a vaccine will give the child the disease it is intended to prevent. The truth is, it is impossible to get the disease from a vaccine that is prepared with dead bacteria or viruses or that is made with only a part of the bacteria or virus. The only risk of contracting disease from a vaccine comes from vaccines made from live or weakened viruses, like the oral (but *not* the injectable) polio vaccine and the chicken pox vaccine (varicella). But even this risk is very small: For every 2.4 million oral polio vaccinations given each year, there is approximately one reported case of the disease resulting from the vaccine. But the U.S. Centers for Disease Control and Prevention now recommends that a vaccine carrying only the killed polio virus be used—entirely eliminating the risk of children contracting the disease from the vaccine. The few blisters and mild fever that may occur in some children who receive the chicken pox vaccine are much less of a threat than the more serious complications that can occasionally occur if a child gets the disease itself; these include pneumonia, meningitis, serious blood infections, and even death.

Fear of Injections

Some parents may skip scheduled vaccinations because they're worried the injection will hurt their children. But these parents should remember that the pain and distress of disease is far worse than the brief pain of an injection.

Fear of Bad Reactions

Some parents worry that their child may have a bad reaction to the vaccination. While some children have minor reactions—including redness and swelling where the shot was given, fever, and sometimes rash—more severe problems rarely occur. As with any medicines, a child can have a serious allergic reaction to a vaccine, but this is rare. A small number of children may have a brief seizure due to a fever caused by vaccines (just as can happen in children with a high fever from any cause), but this does not cause any permanent harm to the child. Although the risk

KidsHealth Tip

A Little Help

To guarantee that all American children can receive childhood immunizations on time, the U.S. government has dedicated money for free vaccines for those who can't afford to pay. For information on free immunizations in your area, call the National Immunization Hotline toll free at (800) 232-2522 (English) or (800) 232-0233 (Spanish).

Four Types of Vaccines

1. An attenuated virus vaccine, like the measles, mumps, and rubella (MMR) vaccine, is made with weakened live viruses.
2. The injected inactivated poliovirus vaccine (IPV) uses killed virus.
3. Toxoid vaccines, like those for diphtheria and tetanus, contain a deactivated (making it harmless) form of the toxin produced by the bacteria.
4. Biosynthetic vaccines, such as the *Hemophilus influenzae* type b (Hib) vaccine, contain part of the killed bacteria attached to another substance that helps trigger a stronger immune response, making the vaccine work well even in young infants.

of serious side effects from common vaccines is very low, you should always call your child's doctor if you have any questions or if your child experiences problems after receiving the vaccine.

Reports linking vaccines to multiple sclerosis, sudden infant death syndrome, and autism have not been substantiated by scientific studies.

Vaccines Commonly Given to Children

Today, children are immunized before school age against 11 different diseases. There are other vaccines, such as the influenza vaccine, that are also recommended for some children. Your child's doctor will tell you when the vaccines are due and if your child needs additional protection in certain circumstances. (See page 274 for the recommended immunization schedule for children.)

Hepatitis B Vaccine

Hepatitis B is a virus that infects the liver; people with the illness can develop serious problems such as cirrhosis (liver disease) or liver cancer. People can also become chronic carriers of the disease, infecting others. The vaccination gives children a long-term immunity to hepatitis B, reducing the increased risk of developing liver cancer and chronic liver disease that follows infection with the hepatitis B virus.

KidsHealth Tip

Taking the Tears Out of Vaccines

If your child is like most, he probably cries when he's given vaccinations at the doctor's office. To take the sting out of shots, ask your child's doctor about new methods of controlling vaccine pain. A topical anesthetic cream and spray are both being explored as ways to cut crying time at the doctor's office and may be available to your child now or in the near future.

A hepatitis B vaccine (HBV) will probably be your child's first immunization. The vaccine is given in three rounds. If an infant's mother is a hepatitis B carrier, the baby must receive the first shot within 12 hours of birth, along with an injection of hepatitis B immune globulin (HBIG) to help fight infection of the infant at birth. Otherwise, the first immunization is usually given either in the hospital before the newborn goes home or delayed until the baby is four to eight weeks old.

The second and third shots are usually given with the other routine childhood immunizations. If the first shot is given shortly after birth, the second is given at one to two months, and the final dose is given at six months. If the first shot is given at four to eight weeks, the second dose is usually given at three to four months, and the final dose is given when the child is six to eighteen months old.

Your child may develop fever or redness and soreness at the site of the injection. There are few serious problems associated with the HBV.

The vaccination should be delayed if your child is sick with anything other than a minor illness or cold or if he has had a severe allergic reaction to baker's yeast. If he develops a severe allergic reaction after a dose of HBV, talk to your child's doctor. Further doses may not be given.

Diphtheria, Tetanus, and Pertussis (DTaP) Vaccine

DTaP vaccine protects against diphtheria, tetanus, and pertussis:

- Diphtheria is a severe throat infection that can block the airway. It can also cause potentially life-threatening complications involving the heart and nervous system.

- Tetanus, which causes lockjaw, affects the nervous system and occurs when tetanus bacteria contaminate an infected wound. Because tetanus can occur at any age, even adults should receive a booster every 10 years.
- Pertussis is a respiratory illness, known as whooping cough because of the sound a child makes breathing following the severe bouts of coughing. Young infants are at greatest risk of developing complications from this disease. In severe cases the disease can cause brain damage or death.

The DTaP vaccination is given in five injections, usually at 2 months, 4 months, 6 months, 15 to 18 months, and 4 to 6 years. Later, at age 11 or 12, a child should be given a Td booster, for tetanus and diphtheria, if at least 5 years have elapsed since the last DTaP dose. This Td booster should then be given every 10 years.

Sometimes a child will experience mild side effects after DTaP is given, such as fever, soreness, crankiness, drowsiness, and loss of appetite. The pertussis portion of the vaccine causes most of these reactions. These problems were seen more frequently in the past with the previously used version of the vaccine (DTP). Today, the AAP recommends the use of the newly developed form of the vaccine (DTaP), which contains only certain parts of the pertussis cell instead of the entire killed

KidsHealth Tip

International Travel

If you are planning to travel out of the country, check with your child's doctor about which immunizations may be needed. Requirements vary according to the country you are traveling to, and immunizations usually should be given at least a month or more before your travel. Special vaccines required for some areas of the world are not routinely available in doctors' offices, so plan ahead in case you need to find a travel medicine office or your doctor needs to special order doses. The U.S. Centers for Disease Control and Prevention publishes a booklet titled *Health Information for International Travel*, which lists the requirements for each country worldwide. Contact the agency or visit its Web site, www.cdc.gov/travel, for more information. Take a copy of your child's immunization records with you if you plan to travel outside the United States.

cell. The resulting vaccine, the acellular pertussis vaccine, has resulted in fewer problems.

The large majority of children tolerate the vaccine without significant problems. But rarely, severe complications occur after DTaP is given. They can include allergic reactions and seizures in 1 out of 2,000 children. Although these are a rare occurrence, you should always call your child's doctor if your child has a severe reaction.

Your child's doctor will probably advise delaying or not giving the vaccine if any one of the following is true:

- Your child experienced very high fever, prolonged crying (more than three hours), or other worrisome symptoms following a DTaP vaccine in the past.
- Your child is ill with an infection causing more than a cold or mild fever.
- Your child has an *uncontrolled* seizure disorder or some types of neurological disease.

Hemophilus Influenzae *Type B (Hib) Vaccine*

Children who receive the Hib vaccine are protected against meningitis, pneumonia, and other infections caused by the *Hemophilus influenzae* type b bacteria.

KidsHealth Tip

Needle-Free Vaccines

You know how important it is to immunize your child, but your heart aches when the shot causes fears and tears. If only there were a way to immunize your child without needles, it would be so much easier, right? Researchers are currently working on needle-free injection devices that would not only reduce the amount of pain involved but would also be able to deliver multiple vaccines at once. The most common type of needle-free device is the jet injector, which works by using compressed gas or a spring that delivers a vaccine in a stream that's fast enough to penetrate the skin.

The vaccine is given at ages 2 months, 4 months, and 6 months. At ages 12 to 15 months, a child receives a booster shot. The possible side effects include fever and soreness at the site of injection. Your child's doctor will probably advise delaying the vaccine if your child is sick with anything more serious than a cold or if she experienced an allergic reaction after an earlier Hib dose.

Pneumococcal Vaccine

Pneumococcus (*Streptococcus pneumoniae*) is the most common cause of severe bacterial diseases such as meningitis, bloodstream infection, and otitis media (middle ear infection). Until recently, the only available pneumococcal vaccine worked only for those over age two, leaving many of the children at highest risk for these infections without an effective vaccine to protect them. However, a newly developed biosynthetic pneumococcal vaccine, trade name Prevnar, was recently released and has been recommended by the AAP for routine immunization of infants and children.

The recommended schedule includes four doses given at 2 months, 4 months, 6 months, and 12 to 15 months. If your child is over two years old and has a chronic illness (such as a lung condition or sickle-cell anemia), consult your child's doctor to see if your child might benefit from this vaccine.

Inactivated Poliovirus Vaccine

The inactivated poliovirus vaccine (IPV) is given as protection against polio—a gastrointestinal viral infection that can affect the nervous system and cause permanent paralysis.

IPV is given by injection at 2 months, 4 months, 6 to 18 months, and four to six years. The possible side effects include fever, soreness at the site of injection, and rash. However, the vaccine should not be given to people who are allergic to the antibiotics neomycin, streptomycin, or polymyxin B because these are used in the preparation of the vaccine.

Measles, Mumps, and Rubella (MMR) Vaccine

Measles, mumps, and rubella were common childhood illnesses until the development of vaccines (now usually given in combined form) effective against these viral infections:

- Measles (rubeola) causes runny nose, cough, high fever, and conjunctivitis (pinkeye). After three to four days, a rash develops on the forehead and spreads downward over the body. Complications can include ear infection, pneumonia, and encephalitis (infection of the central nervous system).
- Mumps causes swelling, pain, and tenderness of one or both parotid glands (salivary glands located between the ear and the bottom of the jaw). Pain with swallowing, mild fever, headache, and loss of appetite are other typical symptoms. Complications can include encephalitis, inflammation of the pancreas causing abdominal pain, and inflammation of the testicle that can permanently damage its ability to make sperm.
- Rubella (German measles) causes swollen lymph nodes (glands) in the neck and behind the ears, rash, and mild fever. The major health impacts of rubella are the severe effects (miscarriage, stillbirth, mental retardation, major birth defects) on the fetus if a pregnant woman becomes infected with the virus.

The MMR vaccine is given by injection in two doses: one at 12 to 15 months and the second at four to six years. It gives 90 percent of children protection against these childhood illnesses.

Some children develop a rash and occasionally a slight fever about a week after vaccination; it usually goes away in a few days. Your child's doctor may recommend delaying or not giving the MMR vaccine if your child has more than a minor illness; has a serious allergy (more than just a mild rash) to neomycin; has received gamma globulin in the past three months; has immune system problems related to cancer, leukemia, or lymphoma; or is taking steroids (such as prednisone). In the past, doctors sometimes worried about giving measles vaccine to individu-

KidsHealth Tip

Helping Your Child Cope with Vaccine Injections

You can help make vaccinations less stressful for your child. Prepare your child by telling her it's OK to cry, and make sure you're calm yourself. Consider distracting your child with a favorite toy or by singing a song. Plan something fun, perhaps a trip to the playground, afterward.

KidsHealth Tip

Rotavirus Vaccine Reevaluation

The recently developed vaccine to protect against rotavirus (a virus that can cause severe diarrhea and dehydration in infants and toddlers) has been withdrawn from use. At the time of this writing, the rotavirus vaccine is undergoing further evaluation because infants who received it had an increased risk of getting a type of bowel obstruction called intussusception.

als who were allergic to eggs. Experts now believe, however, that the risk of a serious allergic reaction to MMR vaccine is low in this group.

Varicella Vaccine

The varicella vaccine protects children against chicken pox—a common viral illness that almost all children came down with in the past. Varicella causes the characteristic itchy, blistering rash and fever. Complications of the infection can include secondary bacterial skin and bloodstream infections, pneumonia, and encephalitis. Prior to the introduction of the vaccine, chicken pox was a major cause of missed school for children and missed workdays for their parents.

The vaccine is given between ages 12 and 18 months. It prevents chicken pox in 70 to 90 percent of children, and if a child still does get the disease after receiving the vaccine, it's usually a mild case.

Serious reactions are rare, although a child may experience soreness, fever, fatigue, and a rash, which may occur up to a month after vaccination and will go away on its own.

Immunization should be delayed if your child has more than a mild illness, has a serious allergy (more than a slight rash) to neomycin or gelatin, has received gamma globulin or a blood or plasma transfusion in the past three months, or has immune system problems.

Special-Case Vaccines

Other childhood vaccines may be recommended by your child's doctor. Some children with asthma, cystic fibrosis, sickle-cell anemia, diabetes, or other chronic conditions may receive influenza vaccine to protect against the complications that could result if a child with one of these conditions gets the flu.

Rabies vaccine may be necessary if your child is bitten by an animal that is rabid or might possibly have rabies, or if the animal's rabies vaccination record is unknown. Dogs, skunks, raccoons, foxes, coyotes, and bats are most commonly infected. If your child is bitten by an animal, call your child's doctor or the health department for advice about rabies vaccine.

Hepatitis A vaccine is recommended for children who are traveling to or living in areas in which infection with the hepatitis A virus is common.

There is a modified schedule for immunizing HIV-infected children and those who have other disorders of the immune system.

Need More Information?

Check the Index and Appendix C, "Resource Guide." And of course, consult your child's doctor.

Recommended Childhood Immunization Schedule
United States, January–December 2001

Vaccines[1] are listed under routinely recommended ages. Bars indicate range of recommended ages for immunization. Any dose not given at the recommended age should be given as a "catch-up" immunization at any subsequent visit when indicated and feasible. Ovals indicate vaccines to be given if previously recommended doses were missed or given earlier than the recommended minimum age.

Age ▶ / ▼ Vaccine	Birth	1 mo	2 mos	4 mos	6 mos	12 mos	15 mos	18 mos	24 mos	4–6 yrs	11–12 yrs	14–18 yrs
Hepatitis B[2]	Hep B #1	Hep B #2			Hep B #3						Hep B[2]	
Diphtheria, Tetanus, Pertussis[3]			DTaP	DTaP	DTaP		DTaP[3]			DTaP	Td	Td
H. influenzae type b[4]			Hib	Hib	Hib	Hib						
Inactivated Polio[5]			IPV	IPV	IPV[5]					IPV[5]		
Pneumococcal Conjugate[6]			PCV	PCV	PCV	PCV						
Measles, Mumps, Rubella[7]						MMR				MMR[7]	MMR[7]	
Varicella[8]						Var					Var[8]	
Hepatitis A[9]									Hep A—in selected areas[9]			

Approved by the Advisory Committee on Immunization Practices (ACIP), the American Academy of Pediatrics (AAP), and the American Academy of Family Physicians (AAFP).

1. This schedule indicates the recommended ages for routine administration of currently licensed childhood vaccines, as of 11/1/00, for children through 18 years of age. Additional vaccines may be licensed and recommended during the year. Licensed combination vaccines may be used whenever any components of the combination are indicated and its other components are not contraindicated. Providers should consult the manufacturers' package inserts for detailed recommendations.

2. *Infants born to HBsAg-negative mothers* should receive the first dose of hepatitis B (Hep B) vaccine by age 2 months. The second dose should be at least 1 month after the first dose. The third dose should be administered at least 4 months after the first dose and at least 2 months after the second dose, but not before 6 months of age for infants.

   Infants born to HBsAg-positive mothers should receive hepatitis B vaccine and 0.5 mL hepatitis B immune globulin (HBIG) within 12 hours of birth at separate sites. The second dose is recommended at 1–2 months of age and the third dose at 6 months of age.

   Infants born to mothers whose HBsAg status is unknown should receive hepatitis B vaccine within 12 hours of birth. Maternal blood should be drawn at the time of delivery to determine the mother's HBsAg status; if the HBsAg test is positive, the infant should receive HBIG as soon as possible (no later than one week of age).

   All children and adolescents who have not been immunized against hepatitis B should begin the series during any visit. Special efforts should be made to immunize children who were born in or whose parents were born in areas of the world with moderate or high endemicity of hepatitis B virus infection.

3. The fourth dose of DTaP (diphtheria and tetanus toxoids and acellular pertussis vaccine) may be administered as early as 12 months of age, provided 6 months have elapsed since the third dose and the child is unlikely to return at age 15–18 months. Td (tetanus and diphtheria toxoids) is recommended at 11–12 years of age if at least 5 years have elapsed since the last dose of DTP, DTaP, or DT. Subsequent routine Td boosters are recommended every 10 years.

4. Three *Hemophilus influenzae* type b (Hib) conjugate vaccines are licensed for infant use. If PRP-OMP (PedvaxHIB® or ComVax® [Merck]) is administered at 2 and 4 months of age, a dose at 6 months is not required. Because clinical studies in infants have demonstrated that using some combination products may induce a lower immune response to the Hib vaccine component, DTaP/Hib combination products should not be used for primary immunization in infants at 2, 4, or 6 months of age, unless FDA-approved for these ages.

5. An all-IPV schedule is recommended for routine childhood polio vaccination in the United States. All children should receive four doses of IPV at 2 months, 4 months, 6–18 months, and 4–6 years of age. Oral polio vaccine (OPV) should be used only in selected circumstances. (See MMWR May 19, 2000/49(RR-5); 1–22.)

6. The heptavalent conjugate pneumococcal vaccine (PCV) is recommended for all children 2–23 months of age. It also is recommended for certain children 24–59 months of age. (See MMWR Oct. 6, 2000/49(RR-9); 1–35.)

7. The second dose of measles, mumps, and rubella (MMR) vaccine is recommended routinely at 4–6 years of age but may be administered during any visit, provided at least four weeks have elapsed since receipt of the first dose and that both doses are administered beginning at or after 12 months of age. Those who have not previously received the second dose should complete the schedule by the 11- or 12-year-old visit.

8. Varicella (Var) vaccine is recommended at any visit on or after the first birthday for susceptible children, i.e., those who lack a reliable history of chicken pox (as judged by a health care provider) and who have not been immunized. Susceptible persons 13 years of age or older should receive two doses, given at least four weeks apart.

9. Hepatitis A (Hep A) is shaded to indicate its recommended use in selected states and/or regions, and for certain high-risk groups; consult your local public health authority. (See MMWR Oct. 1, 1999/48(RR-12); 1–37.)

For additional information about the vaccines listed, please visit the National Immunization Program Home Page at http://www.cdc.gov/nip/ or call the National Immunization Hotline at (800) 232-2522 (English) or (800) 232-0233 (Spanish).

PART THREE

Your Baby Grows Up: The Joys and Challenges of Parenting

chapter seventeen

Growth and Development

Measurements and milestones

From the moment you brought your new baby home, you've been eagerly watching his progress. But what exactly are you watching for, and how do you know if your child is growing and developing properly?

This chapter will guide you through childhood growth and development as they are measured by the physical and developmental milestones that most children reach at each age level. These milestones include increases in height, weight, and head size, as well as development of cognitive skills (the ability to perceive, think, and remember), motor skills (movement, strength, balance, and coordination), and social and language skills.

Physical Growth

A newborn infant is a wonder to behold. It is particularly astonishing to think that this cuddly creature started out in the womb as a microscopic fertilized egg just a few months earlier. Although your infant will undergo tremendous changes during the first year of life, the most rapid and important phase of a child's physical growth occurs before birth. The detailed "construction plans" for the developing embryo are encoded in the genetic material provided by the parents' egg and sperm cells. Genes play the major role in determining most of the physical and chemical characteristics of your child—hair and eye color, whose nose she'll have, and even whether she's likely to have a high cholesterol level. Similarly, your child's physical growth pattern is largely preprogrammed from the start, although his growth can be affected by nutritional factors, illness, and certain factors in the womb.

A special note: The information about physical growth in this chapter will deal with babies who were carried to term. Infants born prematurely will be smaller at birth. (For more information about premature babies, see Chapter 6, "Premature Babies.") Current standard growth charts for U.S. children can be found in Appendix B.

Weight

In the United States, the average weight of a full-term infant is about seven pounds (90 percent of newborns weigh between five and a half and nine pounds). Lower birthweights are seen in premature infants and term infants who are small for their gestational age due to genetic conditions or medical problems during the pregnancy. Infants who are large for their gestational age are often those born to mothers with diabetes during pregnancy.

Don't be surprised if your newborn starts to lose weight immediately after birth. During the first week of life, many infants will lose up to 10 percent of their birthweight as they get rid of some of the extra body fluid that the fetus accumulates while in the uterus. This weight loss tends to be greater in breast-fed infants and those infants who take in less fluid in their initial feedings. By age two weeks, your baby should be back at birthweight or above, and she should gain about one ounce per day through the rest of the first month. The rate of weight gain then slows, reaching a rate of about six ounces per month at age five years.

Weight gain in the first year is amazing—most infants will double their birthweight by three or four months and triple their birthweight by twelve months! Toddlers, on the other hand, usually grow at about one-third that rate. That "fussy" two-year-old at the dinner table is probably just telling you that he doesn't need to eat as much as he used to. (See Chapter 22, "Healthy Eating," for more information about feeding toddlers.)

It's important to remember that, despite the smooth appearance of the curves on the standard growth charts, individual children do not grow at a steady pace.

Infants characteristically experience growth spurts during which they eat ravenously and gain weight rapidly for a week or two. Or a toddler may not gain any weight for a month or two through a rough winter stretch of colds and ear infections. When this happens, don't worry. The large majority of infants and children will gain weight and grow in a pattern that is normal for them as they are well fed, are well loved, and have a stimulating environment.

It is cause for concern if your baby is significantly underweight or fails to gain weight at the expected rate. This is called "failure to thrive" (explained in more detail in Chapter 32, "Health Problems in Early Childhood," in the section on growth disorders). Although growth in height may also be slowed, the poor weight gain is usually more prominent. This condition is often the result of inadequate nutrition and/or environmental deprivation or neglect, but doctors will also evaluate a child experiencing failure to thrive for other underlying medical problems that can interfere with his ability to gain weight.

In the United States and other developed countries where food is plentiful, excessive weight gain and obesity are much more common than failure to thrive. Normally, infants have a higher percentage of body fat than older children do—most "chubby" babies don't become obese children. However, approximately 30 percent of U.S. children are overweight, and that figure appears to be rising. Studies show that about one-third of adult obesity starts in childhood. It follows that prevention of obesity in childhood might prevent obesity in adults, which is linked to many health risks. Recent research indicates that genetic factors play a major role in determining whether a child will become overweight. It is likely, however, that a child's eating habits and physical activity also have an important influence. Parents should be aware that children under the age of two years shouldn't be put on a restrictive diet, which can be dangerous at this age. If your child seems to be gaining too much weight, speak with your child's doctor for advice. (For more information on obesity, see Chapter 32, "Health Problems in Early Childhood.")

Growth and Body Mass Index (BMI) Charts

Want to learn more about how your child compares to other children her age? Then check out the growth and body mass index charts provided in Appendix B.

Length and Height

In the United States, the average length of a term infant at birth is about 20 inches (90 percent of newborns will be between 18 and 21½ inches long). Children grow approximately 10 inches in the first year of life, 5 inches in the second year, and then about 2½ inches per year until they enter puberty.

Don't get too caught up in following your child's growth on a standardized growth chart. A child's growth in length/height is not completely smooth and constant. Some healthy children may not increase their height for weeks or months and then go through a "catch-up" period of more rapid growth. Some research indicates that children's growth rates may be seasonal—they seem to grow a bit faster in the spring.

A child's rate and pattern of height growth are largely genetically determined and will follow that hard-wired course unless something interferes with it, such as chronic illness, malnutrition, environmental deprivation, or neglect. Although some parents may be tempted to try, giving a well-nourished child extra vitamins, minerals, or calories will *not* cause the child to grow any taller than his genetic potential.

Normal Variations

It's not uncommon for healthy children (particularly during the first two years of life) to temporarily grow faster or slower than most other children their age and to change their position on the standard growth charts. For example, infants of

KidsHealth Tip

The Difference Between Length and Height

Length refers to the distance between the bottom of your child's feet and the top of his head measured lying down. Your child must be lying flat on a table or measuring device with his legs fully extended in order to obtain an accurate measurement. After children reach age three years, they will usually cooperate for measurement of a standing height.

Big Boys

Did you know that boys tend to be a bit larger at birth? Firstborns and multiple-birth infants (twins, triplets . . . and beyond!) tend to be smaller.

mothers with diabetes and those born to mothers who gained large amounts of weight during the pregnancy tend to be larger at birth, but these babies usually grow more slowly over the first few months of life until they settle back down into a growth channel consistent with the sizes of their parents. On the other hand, infants of tall fathers who are carried in the small uterus of a petite mother may be smaller at birth than one would expect. These babies may grow quickly over the first few months of life and "catch up" to their genetically predicted growth channel.

Children with short parents will usually start out small at birth, usually below the 5th percentile, and stay in about the same growth channel throughout childhood and adolescence. They will enter puberty at an average age, and generally they will reach an adult height similar to that of their parents.

Another normal growth pattern found in some children is called constitutional growth delay. These children are usually of average size at birth, and their parents are usually average in height. After initially growing at a normal pace, these infants will grow more slowly, usually starting in the second half of the first year of life. This slow growth continues until about 18 to 24 months of age. By then, the children often will have dropped below the 5th percentile line on the growth chart. From then on, they will grow about two and a half inches per year, which is similar to the growth rate of other children their age. Children with constitutional growth delay remain short through childhood. They begin their adolescent growth spurt at a later-than-average age (hence the term "late bloomer"). Because they continue growing after most of their peers have stopped, they "catch up" and reach an average final adult height similar to that of their parents. In many cases, a parent or other close relative of these children will have followed a similar growth pattern.

Children who are extremely short or who have a persistently slow rate of growth may need evaluation for a possible growth disorder. This may involve referral to a pediatric endocrinologist or other specialist. (For more information on related growth disorders, see Chapter 32, "Health Problems in Early Childhood.")

Head Growth

You've probably noticed that normal infants have relatively large heads. This is because most of the growth in the size of the brain takes place before birth, and brain growth is the major stimulus for growth of the head. At birth, the average baby's head circumference (the distance around the head, measured just above eyebrow level) is 13½ inches (34 centimeters), which is about two-thirds of its adult size.

After birth, head growth continues at a rapid pace for the first year of life. From then on, the rate of growth slows, with the head and brain reaching near adult size around age 10 years.

Your child's doctor will monitor your child's head (and brain) growth closely over the first two years by plotting head circumference measurements on a standard growth chart at each checkup. Small head size or slower-than-expected head growth can occur in infants with a variety of problems, including birth defects of the brain, intrauterine infections or exposure to toxins, abnormal growth of the skull bones, and a number of nutritional, genetic, and metabolic conditions. An overly rapid increase in the size of an infant's head can be a sign of excessive buildup of fluid and pressure within the head, as seen in the condition hydrocephalus. (For more information, see Chapter 32, "Health Problems in Early Childhood," and the head circumference charts in Appendix B.)

Development

What parents don't get excited and glow with pride when their little one takes her first steps at an earlier age than anyone else in the family? And what parents don't get a bit concerned if their son continues to merely point and grunt when he wants something, while all the other kids in the playgroup seem to be adding new words to their vocabularies every day? Comparing a child's developmental progress to that of other children is a popular pastime of parents and grandparents.

Although it's human nature to make these comparisons, there is great variation in the way normal infants and children grow physically, and their rates and patterns of development differ widely as well. You should rely on your child's doctor to assess and track development at his regular checkups. A child who isn't keeping pace with his peers developmentally may have a problem that needs attention, as discussed later in this chapter.

Measuring Your Child's Developmental Progress

Although many tools are available, a screening test commonly used by primary care doctors to track a child's developmental progress from birth through the preschool years is the Denver II, which is a modified version of the earlier Denver Developmental Screening Test. This and other similar screening tools help the doctor evaluate your child's development in four general areas or dimensions:

- Gross motor skills. These skills involve control and movement of the trunk and large muscle groups, such as holding the head up, sitting without support, pulling to a stand, and walking.
- Fine motor skills. These skills involve fine movements of the arms and hands requiring eye-hand coordination, such as reaching for objects, transferring objects from one hand to the other, and building a tower of blocks.
- Language skills. These are skills such as making the first speech sounds, understanding and saying specific words, using gestures and other nonverbal types of communication, forming sentences, knowing colors, counting, and developing complex verbal expressions.
- Personal/social skills. These involve activities such as brushing teeth and getting dressed, smiling, distinguishing parents from strangers, waving "bye-bye," and imitating others.

Your child's doctor will observe your child and ask you specific questions about his skills and behaviors to determine your child's developmental progress. If at any point you have concerns about your child's development or behavior, be sure to bring them to the doctor's attention. In this situation, it may be helpful to make a videotape of your child's behavior at home for the doctor to review.

The lists at the end of this chapter contain some of the specific developmental milestones that may be used at different ages for screening.

What Do the Results of Developmental Screening Tests Mean?

Your child's pattern of development over time is a much more important indicator than the results of screening at a single visit. If your child is ill, tired, hungry, or otherwise distracted when the assessment is performed, the screening results may be inaccurate. That's why doctors usually don't get concerned about a delay unless it is present when tested at more than one visit, it is severe, or delays are present in several areas of development. Also keep the following in mind:

- Delay in reaching one or more milestones often doesn't mean that your child has a problem. Many children don't progress at the same rate in each of the major developmental categories. For example, a typical child who sits up and walks early might show slower language development than most of her peers. Also, sometimes children seem to focus on a particular aspect of development and let others lag for a while. For instance, a child who is intent on continuing to explore the world at floor level might show little interest in walking.
- Developmental screening test results do not reliably predict a child's future talents or whether a child is "gifted." They are most useful for identifying children whose development should be watched more carefully or who should be referred to a specialist for further evaluation.

Take comfort in your child's developmental progress if he reaches expected milestones, seek help if he seems to be lagging behind, celebrate advancements as they occur—and keep the love, affection, and stimulation flowing!

Why Is It Helpful to Track a Child's Developmental Progress?

Despite their limitations, developmental screening tests can provide useful information. Early recognition of a problem can help prevent or reduce disabilities that some children with developmental difficulties might otherwise face.

A child is thought to have what's called developmental delay if she shows a consistent pattern of slow progress in one or more areas. This assessment should not be based solely on the results of developmental screening tests. In most cases, the child will be referred to a pediatric developmentalist, neurologist, audiologist, or other specialist for more detailed testing and evaluation.

In some cases, an underlying health problem is the cause of a child's developmental delay. If such a problem exists, it's important to identify it promptly because early treatment of some of these conditions may prevent or lessen the likelihood of long-term disability for the child. However, in most children with developmental delay, no specific underlying medical condition or cause can be found. But these children and their families can also benefit significantly from early identification of the delay. Specially designed infant-stimulation programs, assistive devices and equipment, and other therapies have a good chance of improving a child's developmental outlook if they're started in the early years when the child's brain is still growing rapidly and before potential complications of the condition occur. Early identification of the delay can also help parents adjust their expectations for the child appropriately and be more effective in helping the child reach his potential.

What Can Parents Do to Promote a Child's Development?

How quickly or how slowly your child develops is largely dependent on preprogrammed genes. As long as he is otherwise healthy and receives adequate environmental stimulation, proper nutrition, and lots of love and affection, there is probably little else you can (or should) do in an attempt to "speed up" or enhance his development. In fact, trying to prod a young child into doing something he is not developmentally capable of can be a frustrating experience for both child and parent, and it can even undermine a child's motivation and self-esteem.

However, a basic understanding of your child's developmental progress can still be helpful. First, it can be reassuring to know that your child is on track developmentally because this serves as a key measure of your child's overall health. Second, understanding where your child is developmentally can help you decide which toys, games, and types of play would be most appropriate and enjoyable for your child.

Speech and Language Development

As you're trying to assess your child's language development, it's important to recognize the difference between speech and language. Speech is pronunciation; it refers to how clearly a child talks. Language means expressing and receiving information in a way that is meaningful; in other words, it's understanding and being understood through communication. A child with a language problem may be able to pronounce words well but be unable to put more than two words together meaningfully. Conversely, another child's speech may be difficult to understand, but he may use words and phrases to express his ideas well. Problems in speech and language differ but frequently overlap.

What Causes Speech and Language Delays?

There are many reasons for delays in speech and language development. Speech delays in an otherwise normally developing child are rarely caused by physical oral problems, such as abnormalities of the tongue or palate. They are more commonly caused by hearing problems. If a child has trouble hearing, he may have trouble understanding, imitating, and using language. Ear infections, especially recurrent infections or chronic collections of fluid behind the eardrum, can affect hearing ability temporarily or, less often, permanently. Simple ear infections that have been adequately treated, though, should have no significant effect on a child's speech and language development. (For more information about hearing, see Chapter 15,

"Hearing and Vision," and for more about ear infections, see Chapter 32, "Health Problems in Early Childhood.")

Some children with speech delays have oral-motor problems, which means that there are problems in the way the brain communicates with the physical structures involved in speech. These children may have difficulty using the lips, tongue, and jaw to produce speech sounds. A speech or language delay may also be a sign of a more generalized developmental delay in a child.

Speech development is a mixture of nature and nurture. A child's genetic makeup will in part determine his intellect and capacity for speech and language. Certain medical conditions, such as chronic ear problems, can also have a major impact. However, much depends on his environment. Is the child adequately stimulated at home or in child care? Does he have the opportunity for communication exchange and participation? What kind of feedback does he get? These factors can have an important influence on a child's speech and language development.

How to Encourage Language Development

To encourage language development, you should begin communicating with your child from birth. One of the ways to do this is to read to her! You don't have to finish a whole book; in fact, an 18- to 24-month-old probably won't sit still for it. Start with a short book such as Dorothy Kunhardt's *Pat the Bunny*, where your child imitates the patting motion. Use high-pitched sounds as you read—babies are known to respond to these. Then go on to nursery rhymes, which have rhythmic appeal. Progress to predictable books where your child can anticipate what happens and understand why it happens, such as in Margaret Wise Brown's *Goodnight Moon*.

A Speech/Language Evaluation

If you find that your child is not meeting developmental milestones for language, you should talk with your child's doctor about the need for evaluation by a specialist. If speech, language, hearing, or developmental deficits do exist, early intervention can help your child get the help he needs to avoid or lessen the severity of future learning problems. We recommend that you speak with your child's doctor if any of these conditions exist:

- Your two- to three-year-old can only imitate speech and does not produce words or phrases spontaneously.
- He says only certain sounds or words repeatedly.

- His voice quality seems unusual, or it is very difficult for others to understand his speech.
- He cannot use oral language to communicate more than his immediate needs.
- He cannot follow simple directions.

If your child's doctor thinks there is reason for concern, he or she may refer your child to a speech-language pathologist. If speech therapy is recommended for your child, you should be involved in the process. By observing the professional therapy sessions, you can learn what your child is being taught and reinforce those concepts at home. It's important for you to learn what you can do to encourage development of language skills.

Stuttering

Children between the ages of two and five commonly repeat whole words and phrases and may interject fillers such as "uh" or "um" into their speech—this is normal dysfluency and nothing to worry about. But in some cases, stuttering causes the interrupted flow of speech.

Signs of stuttering include the following:

- Excessive repetition of whole words or phrases
- Frequent sound or syllable repetitions
- Effortful or strained speech or dysfluencies (interruptions in flow of speech)
- Increased facial tension or tightness in the speech muscles

KidsHealth Tip

Start a Toddler's Library

Introduce your toddler to the fun of reading—while encouraging language development—by trying out books that are engaging to look at and play with. Cloth books with fabric pages, books with stuffed animals or toys attached to the cover, and books with squeakers are all great bets. Books with unusual shapes or lots of textures are also good for getting your child on the reading track.

KidsHealth Tip
Getting Those Words Out

As many as 25 percent of children 18 months to seven years old go through a stuttering phase. Getting your child to relax is the best way to help break the habit. Maintain eye contact, listen quietly, and speak in calm, simple sentences.

- Vocal tension resulting in rising pitch or loudness
- Avoidance of situations requiring speech

If these signs of stuttering continue for six months or more, consult your child's doctor, who may refer you to a speech and language pathologist for further evaluation.

In addition to professional therapy, you can help your child by doing the following:

- Not insisting that she speak correctly at all times
- Using family mealtimes as conversation times, keeping the TV and radio turned off
- Avoiding the impulse to correct your child's speech or finish sentences for her
- Not forcing your child to speak or read aloud when she doesn't want to
- Not telling your child to start a sentence over or to think before she talks
- Talking slowly and clearly to your child to provide a model of slow speech
- Encouraging activities that do not require speech at times when your child is having more difficulty speaking fluently

Developmental Milestones

The following lists describe some of the characteristics and skills young children will display at different ages. For each age level, the milestones are grouped by specific area of development. In general, most children will have reached each of these milestones by the end of the age range indicated. For each age level, there is also a "talk with your child's doctor if . . ." section intended to give you some guidance when you have possible concerns about your child's development.

In using this information, remember these things:

- Many normal children will show a delay in reaching one or more milestones over the course of their development.
- This information should not take the place of the developmental assessments that will be performed at the doctor's office at your child's regular checkups.
- You should not hesitate to seek advice from your child's doctor if you think that your child may have a problem. Trust your instincts.

DEVELOPMENTAL MILESTONES—FIRST MONTH

Gross Motor and Fine Motor	• Makes jerky arm movements; moves both sides of body • Follows moving objects briefly with eyes • Moves head from side to side while lying on stomach • Has head flop backward if it is unsupported • Has strong reflex movements (sucking, grasping, Moro or startle reflex) • Brings hands within range of eyes and mouth • Is able to keep hands in tight fists
Language	• Makes sounds
Personal and Social	• Prefers to look at human faces more than at other objects
Other Characteristics and Behaviors to Expect	• Focuses on things 8 to 12 inches away • Has eyes that tend to wander and occasionally cross • Is startled by loud noises • Prefers black-and-white or high-contrast patterns
Talk with Your Child's Doctor if Your Child	• Sucks poorly and feeds slowly • Doesn't blink when shown a bright light • Doesn't focus on and follow a nearby moving object at all • Rarely moves arms and legs; seems stiff or floppy • Doesn't respond to loud sounds

DEVELOPMENTAL MILESTONES—ONE TO THREE MONTHS

Gross Motor and Fine Motor	• Raises head and chest when lying on stomach • Supports upper body with arms when lying on stomach • Waves, kicks, and squirms when lying on stomach or back • Opens and shuts hands • Pushes down on legs when feet are placed on a firm surface • Brings hands to mouth • Swipes at dangling objects with hands • Grasps toys or other objects when put in hand; shakes them
Language	• Smiles at the sound of familiar voices or sight of familiar faces • Begins to babble • Says "ooh" and "ahh" • Laughs and possibly squeals
Personal and Social	• Begins to smile in response to someone else's smile • Enjoys playing with others and may cry when people stop or leave • Becomes more communicative and expressive with face and body • Imitates some movements and facial expressions • Appears fussy at times, often at the end of the day
Other Characteristics and Behaviors to Expect	• Watches faces intently • Responds to loud sounds by becoming quiet and still, or with general body movements • Follows moving objects • Recognizes familiar objects and people at a distance • Looks at own hands and starts using hands and eyes in coordination • Stares at things a lot
Talk with Your Child's Doctor if Your Child	• Doesn't seem to respond to loud sounds • Doesn't smile at the sound of your voice by two months • Doesn't follow moving objects with eyes by two to three months • Doesn't grasp and hold objects by three months • Doesn't smile back at people by three months • Can't support head well at three months • Doesn't babble by three to four months • Has trouble moving one or both eyes in all directions • Has eyes that are crossed or don't move together most of the time • Doesn't notice new faces

DEVELOPMENTAL MILESTONES—FOUR TO SEVEN MONTHS

Gross Motor and Fine Motor	• Rolls from stomach to back and back to stomach • Sits with, and then without, support of hands • Props self up on arms when on stomach • Can support whole body weight on legs • Reaches for objects with hand • Transfers objects from hand to hand • "Rakes" at small objects (reaches for object using hand with fingers bent)
Language	• Turns to sounds and voices • Responds to own name • Begins to respond to "no" • Distinguishes emotions by tone of voice • Responds to sound by making sounds and may imitate speech sounds • Uses voice to express joy and displeasure • Babbles chains of consonants ("ba-ba-ba-ba")
Personal and Social	• Finds partially hidden object • Explores things with hands and by putting items in mouth • Works to get objects that are out of reach • Enjoys social play • Notices small things like pieces of cereal in front of him • Responds to other people's expressions of emotion • Squeals and makes other high-pitched sounds when happy • Smiles when looking at self in mirror • Shows frustration when trying new skills such as turning over
Other Characteristics and Behaviors to Expect	• Gets excited at sight of familiar people or at sight of bottle or breast • Has improved distance vision • Has improved ability to track moving objects
Talk with Your Child's Doctor if Your Child	• Seems stiff, with tight muscles, or seems weak or floppy • Has head that still lags back when body is pulled up to a sitting position • Uses only one hand for reaching, or one leg seems stronger • Doesn't cuddle or show affection for primary caregiver • Has eyes that are consistently crossed or don't move together • Doesn't respond to sounds • Has difficulty getting objects to mouth

- Doesn't reach for and grasp toys by four months
- Doesn't babble by four months
- Still has Moro (startle) reflex at four months
- Has head that isn't steady when in sitting position by four months
- Doesn't try to imitate speech sounds by seven months
- Doesn't push down when feet are placed on firm surface by four months
- Doesn't turn head to locate sounds by five months
- Doesn't roll over in either direction by five months
- Can't sit (with some support from hands) by six months
- Doesn't laugh or make squealing sounds by six months
- Doesn't actively reach for objects by six to seven months
- Doesn't follow objects with eyes at near and far ranges by seven months
- Doesn't bear some weight on legs by seven months
- Doesn't try to attract attention through actions by seven months

DEVELOPMENTAL MILESTONES—EIGHT TO TWELVE MONTHS

Gross Motor
- Gets to sitting position without assistance
- Gets to hands-and-knees position independently
- Crawls
- Stands holding on
- Pulls self up to stand
- Walks holding on to furniture
- Stands momentarily without support
- Possibly walks two or three steps without support

Fine Motor
- Uses pincer grasp (grasps objects between thumb and index finger)
- Bangs two objects together
- Puts objects into container
- Takes objects out of container
- Lets go of objects voluntarily
- Pokes at things with index finger

Language
- Pays increasing attention to spoken words of others
- Talks or "jabbers" all the time, usually with nonsensical sounds
- Responds to simple verbal requests
- Stops doing something if told "no," but only momentarily
- Uses simple gestures, such as shaking head for "no"
- Says "dada" and "mama"
- Uses exclamations such as "uh-oh!"

	• Tries to imitate words • Indicates wants
Personal and Social	• Explores objects in different ways (shaking, banging, throwing, dropping) • Finds hidden objects easily • Looks at correct picture when the image is named • Begins to use objects correctly (drinking from cup, brushing hair, listening to phone receiver) • Imitates gestures • Is shy or anxious with strangers • Cries when Mom or Dad leaves • Enjoys imitating people • Shows specific preferences for certain people and toys • Tests parental responses to behaviors • May be fearful in some situations • Prefers primary caregiver over others • Repeats sounds or gestures for attention • Feeds self with fingers • Extends arm or leg to help when being dressed
Talk with Your Child's Doctor if Your Child	• Doesn't crawl • Drags one side of body while crawling • Can't stand when supported • Doesn't search for objects known to be hidden • Doesn't imitate speech sounds • Doesn't use gestures such as waving or shaking head • Doesn't point to objects or pictures • Doesn't babble by eight months • Shows no interest in games of "peekaboo" by eight months

DEVELOPMENTAL MILESTONES—ONE TO TWO YEARS

Gross Motor	• Walks independently • Pulls toys while walking • Carries large toy or several toys while walking • Stoops to pick item up and stands again without holding on to anything • Can walk backward • Begins to run • Stands on tiptoes • Kicks a ball • Walks up and down stairs while holding on to railing

Fine Motor	• Scribbles spontaneously • Turns over containers to pour out contents • Builds tower of four blocks or more • Possibly uses one hand more frequently than the other
Language	• Turns and looks when called • Points to object or picture when it's named • Waves "bye-bye" when someone is leaving, and says "bye-bye" • Recognizes names of familiar people, objects, and body parts • Says several single words like *cup* and *out* • Uses two-word phrases such as *want drink* • Follows simple instructions • Repeats words overheard in conversation • Uses objects, body gestures, and simple words to communicate
Personal and Social	• Finds objects even when hidden under two or three covers • Can perform simple tasks or chores around the house • Can pull off some of own clothing • Begins to play make-believe • Imitates behavior of others, especially adults and older children • Is more aware of self as separate from others; recognizes self in photos • Is increasingly enthusiastic about the company of other children
Other Characteristics and Behaviors to Expect	• Demonstrates increasing independence • Strives to leave caretakers to explore things but fears separation • Begins to show defiant behavior • Displays separation anxiety, which increases toward midyear then fades as second birthday approaches • Tries to imitate adult speech and shows frustration when he cannot
Talk with Your Child's Doctor if Your Child	• Is unable to walk unassisted by 18 months • Has not developed a mature heel-toe walking pattern after several months of walking, or walks exclusively on toes • Doesn't speak at least two to three words by 18 months • Does not seem to know the function of common household objects by 15 months • Doesn't imitate actions or words by age two • Is unable to follow simple instructions by age two • Can't push a wheeled toy by age two

DEVELOPMENTAL MILESTONES—TWO TO THREE YEARS

Gross Motor
- Climbs well
- Runs and jumps well
- Walks up and down stairs, alternating feet
- Kicks ball forward
- Throws ball overhand
- Can balance on one foot for one to two seconds
- Pedals tricycle or Big Wheel
- Bends over easily without falling

Fine Motor
- Makes vertical, horizontal, and circular strokes with pencil or crayon
- Turns book pages one at a time
- Builds a tower of more than six blocks
- Holds a pencil in writing position
- Screws and unscrews jar lids
- Turns rotating handles
- Sorts objects by shape and color
- Completes puzzles with three or four pieces
- Makes mechanical toys work

Language
- Follows a two- or three-part command ("Get the doll, and bring it to me.")
- Asks questions
- Recognizes and identifies many common objects and pictures
- Matches an object in hand or room to picture in book
- Knows major body parts
- Uses four- and five-word sentences
- Can say name, age, and sex
- Uses pronouns (*me*, *you*, and so on) and some plurals
- Speaks well enough that strangers can understand most words

Personal and Social
- Plays make-believe with dolls, animals, and people
- Understands concept of "two"
- Can wash and dry hands
- Imitates adults and playmates
- Spontaneously shows affection for familiar playmates
- Can take turns in games
- Understands concept of "mine" and "his" or "hers"

Other Characteristics and Behaviors to Expect	• Expresses affection openly • Possibly puts on some clothes that are easy to get on • Expresses a wide range of emotions • Separates easily from parents by age three • Objects to major changes in routine
Talk with Your Child's Doctor if Your Child	• Frequently falls or has difficulty with stairs • Persistently drools or speaks unclearly • Is unable to build a tower of more than four blocks • Has difficulty manipulating small objects • Is unable to communicate in short phrases • Doesn't pretend play • Fails to understand simple instructions • Shows little interest in other children • Has extreme difficulty separating from primary caregiver

DEVELOPMENTAL MILESTONES—THREE TO FOUR YEARS

Gross Motor	• Hops on one foot and can balance on one foot for three to four seconds • Goes upstairs and downstairs without holding on • Catches bounced ball most of the time • Moves forward and backward with agility
Fine Motor	• Copies a circle • Draws a person with two to four body parts • Uses scissors (with supervision) • Begins to copy some capital letters
Language	• Understands the concepts of "same" and "different" • Correctly names some colors • Understands the concept of counting and possibly knows a few numbers • Follows three-part commands • Recalls some details from a story • Speaks in sentences of five words • Speaks clearly enough for strangers to understand • Tells stories
Personal and Social	• Begins to have a clearer sense of time • Engages in imaginative play • Is interested in new experiences • Cooperates with other children • Plays Mom or Dad (acts out family roles in play) • Dresses and undresses self

	• Negotiates solutions to conflicts • Becomes more independent
Other Characteristics and Behaviors to Expect	• Imagines that many unfamiliar images may be "monsters" • Views self as whole person involving body, mind, and feelings • Possibly has trouble distinguishing between fantasy and reality
Talk with Your Child's Doctor if Your Child	• Can't jump in place • Can't ride a tricycle • Can't grasp a crayon between thumb and fingers • Has difficulty scribbling • Can't stack six blocks • Still clings or cries whenever parents leave • Shows no interest in interactive games • Ignores other children • Doesn't respond to people outside the family • Doesn't engage in fantasy play • Resists dressing, sleeping, or using toilet • Lashes out without self-control when angry or upset • Doesn't use sentences of more than three words • Doesn't use the words *me* and *you* appropriately

DEVELOPMENTAL MILESTONES—FOUR TO FIVE YEARS

Gross Motor	• Balances on one foot for five seconds or longer • Jumps forward with feet together • Performs a somersault (forward roll) • Swings and climbs • Possibly skips
Fine Motor	• Copies a cross (+) and may be able to copy a square • Draws person with body • Prints some letters • Dresses and undresses without assistance • Uses a fork, a spoon, and sometimes a table knife • Usually cares for own toilet needs
Language	• Speaks sentences of more than five words • Uses future tense • Tells longer stories • Says address

	• Names at least four colors • Says what to do when a person is tired, hungry, or cold
Personal and Social	• Asks lots of questions • Can count five or more objects • Better understands the concept of time • Knows about things used every day in the home • Plays board and card games • Wants to please friends and be similar to friends • Is more likely to agree to rules • Likes to sing, dance, and act • Shows more independence
Other Characteristics and Behaviors to Expect	• Is aware of gender differences—knows boy from girl • Is able to distinguish fantasy from reality • Is sometimes stubborn and demanding, sometimes very cooperative
Talk with Your Child's Doctor if Your Child	• Exhibits extremely fearful or aggressive behavior • Is unable to separate from parents without major protest • Is easily distracted and unable to concentrate on any single activity for more than five minutes • Refuses to respond to people in general • Rarely uses fantasy or imitation in play • Usually seems unhappy or sad • Doesn't engage in variety of activities • Avoids or seems detached from other children and adults • Doesn't express a wide range of emotions • Has trouble eating, sleeping, or using the toilet • Can't differentiate between fantasy and reality • Can't understand and follow two-part commands using prepositions ("Pick up the book, and put it on the table.") • Can't correctly give first and last name • Doesn't use plurals or past tense properly when speaking • Doesn't talk about daily activities and experiences • Can't copy a circle • Can't build a tower of six to eight blocks • Seems uncomfortable holding a crayon • Has trouble taking off clothing

Need More Information?

Check the Index and Appendix C, "Resource Guide." And of course, consult your child's doctor.

chapter eighteen

Play Time

Growing up by having fun

Defined as "the spontaneous activity of children," play is invaluable; it allows kids to expand their understanding of themselves and others, and it fosters their ability to communicate.

Play is more than just fun. It's activity that builds self-esteem and confidence—especially when parents take an active role. As your child's favorite playmate, the value of the time you spend playing with him can't be overstated. Children who are "answered" by a smile when they coo or are praised for building a tower of blocks learn that they have something valuable to offer to the larger world. In addition, play provides important opportunities for physical exercise, which promotes fitness as your child grows into adulthood.

> ### *The Voice of Experience*
>
> *"Spend quality time with your kids if you cannot spend quantity time. Laundry, dishes, and cleaning can wait. Snuggling, watching Barney, finger painting, and making snow angels are more important."*
> —FROM THE KIDSHEALTH PARENT SURVEY

Play and Your Child's Development

When a baby shakes a rattle and it makes a noise, he learns about both cause and effect and coordination. He learns balance and spatial relationships when he reaches up toward a mobile hanging in his room. (For detailed information about development, see Chapter 17, "Growth and Development.")

At each well-child visit (as described in Chapter 13, "Routine Medical Care"), your child's doctor might ask you questions to determine whether your baby's play is developmentally appropriate for his age. These questions may include whether he's playing peekaboo, pulling himself up in the crib, reaching for objects, covering things and then uncovering them, and so forth. Remember that children develop at different rates, but if your child hasn't reached a certain expected milestone, you can create developmental opportunities for him—by showing him how to play peekaboo, or roll over on the floor, or shake a rattle.

Stages of Play

As your child grows, you'll probably see these common stages of play:

- Infant play involves experimenting with body sensation and movements. A 6-month-old pushes a ball and learns that he has caused the movement. He knows that if he wants the ball to move again, he has to push it. A 12-month-old shakes a rattle to hear the noise it makes and feel the shaking sensation.
- Between 12 and 18 months, children begin to explore imaginative play. You may see your child feed his teddy bear with a spoon and cup or use a banana as a telephone. Also, every game of peekaboo and patty-cake teaches your child how to interact with others and to take turns.
- Between 18 and 36 months, it's time for pretend games that mimic the world around him—raking leaves, feeding baby doll, and having a tea party are all fun ways to be "like you." This is also when you'll see a cardboard paper towel roll become a trumpet and your bathroom towels transformed into superhero capes. Children this age like to be with other children, but they don't really play *with* others; they do what's called "parallel play," in which they play independently alongside another child without actually interacting.

- Four- and five-year-olds are experts at having fun. Through imaginative play they'll build skyscrapers with blocks and action figures with clay. And they love formal games that have rules and "right" and "wrong" ways of doing things. Board games like Chutes and Ladders become favorites. These kids are ready for group play and enjoy games like ring-around-the-rosy and hide-and-seek.

Helping Your Child Play

Promote your child's development through play by following these tips:

- Think like a child, be imaginative, and play with your child.
- Choose toys according to age and ability.
- Create childproof, safe, and unrestricted play space.
- Provide playthings that promote exploration and adaptability.
- Keep toys at your child's eye level, and rotate them to avoid boredom.
- Say, "You're playing so nicely" and "I like the way you're sharing."

It's also important to give your child a chance to play with other kids while reaping the benefits of physical exercise. Playgrounds are designed specifically for this purpose.

Baby exercise classes, playgroups, and preschool classes are also perfect settings for your child's first experiences with socialization. A side benefit of these organized venues is that through your child, you get to meet other parents who have similar interests and concerns.

KidsHealth Tip
Take a Breather

Although parents may believe that more activities mean smarter, more well-rounded children, this isn't always the case. Too many new activities and new kids in each group can prove to be stressful, especially for younger children. Try to plan some unstructured play time, which allows your child to think and dream independently.

Choosing the Right Games, Activities, and Toys

Here are some suggested toys for kids of various ages:

- For the three- to six-month-old: Handheld toys, mobiles, unbreakable mirrors (attached to the side of the crib or next to the changing table), sensory toys that make noises, and rattles (Music boxes and tape players entertain even the youngest children. It's never too early to turn your child on to music.)
- For the six- to nine-month-old: Busy boards (attached to the side of the crib); soft dolls and stuffed animals; balls for rolling back and forth or crawling after; household items such as pots and pans, plastic measuring cups, and wooden spoons; wooden or soft blocks; toys that move (cars or toys that pop up when the right spot is touched); and books (with cardboard pages and bright pictures)
- For the nine- to twelve-month-old: Push toys for exercising recently acquired walking skills, balls for throwing (while standing!), textured and flap books such as *Pat the Bunny*, blocks for stacking, and a pail and shovel for the playground sandbox
- For toddlers: Large cardboard building blocks for building walls and forts, wagons and other push-and-pull toys, sorting and nesting toys, climbing gyms, washable crayons and markers, ride-on vehicles, tool bench and/or toy kitchen, and picture books
- For preschoolers: Ride-on toys like tricycles and wagons, balls for playing catch or basketball, art supplies such as washable paint and big brushes (set up where it's OK to make a mess!), percussive instruments, dress-up clothes, play dishes and food, construction toys, and puzzles and other manipulative toys

> ### The Voice of Experience
> —☙—
> *"Don't always 'teach' your child whenever you interact with him. Remember to seriously play instead of being serious."*
> —FROM THE KIDSHEALTH PARENT SURVEY

When choosing toys for your child, don't drive yourself crazy over the gender issue. Should girls play with stuffed animals or trucks? Should boys cuddle a baby doll or a superhero? Some people believe that stereotypes of gender roles are communicated to children through the toys they play with, but this is not really a right or wrong issue. Why not give your children both dolls and trucks and both stuffed animals and superheroes—let them decide which ones they like best. The important thing is to choose toys that are educational, safe, and, most of all, fun.

Toys should always be chosen carefully, and safety must be the first priority. Any home that houses a baby or toddler should be childproofed, meaning that anything that could hurt a child should be removed or blocked (as explained in Chapter 2, "Preparing Your Home and Family"). To avoid choking hazards, toy parts should be no smaller than the hole at the end of a cardboard toilet tissue roll until your child is three years old. They should be well made and in good condition. Cords can be dangerous to babies and toddlers because they can get wrapped around their necks, as can soft toys in cribs where they can pose breathing hazards for young infants. (For more on safety issues, see Chapter 24, "Child Safety.")

> ## *The Voice of Experience*
>
> *"A friend once told me to color outside the lines when I'm coloring with my kids. This way, they won't have a 'perfect' picture to compare themselves to."*
>
> —FROM THE KIDSHEALTH PARENT SURVEY

Toys, Play, and Social Skills

If you watch your child play with other children on the playground or in playgroups, you'll see social-skills training in action. They learn through trial and error (and a few experiences with pushing and hitting) how to share, how to be considerate of others, how to show good manners, and how the way you act influences how others act toward you. You alone can't teach your child all these things—they

KidsHealth Tip

Low-Tech Toys for the Tiny Ones

Even though elaborate toys look enticing and may promise to promote all types of development, simpler toys are often better for those first learning to play. Often the more features a toy contains, the less creative and imaginary play is actually involved. A plain train set can inspire your diaper-clad conductor to greatness, a simple doll without features can encourage care and nurturing, and the old favorite banging of pots and pans reinforces the concept of cause and effect.

KidsHealth Tip

Toy Washing Time

To avoid passing on germs, wash plastic toys regularly with hot soapy water, then rinse and dry them thoroughly.

have to be experienced. (For more information about dealing with common behavior problems as your child learns to socialize, see Chapter 19, "Temperament, Behavior, and Discipline.")

If your child seems to be lagging behind other children in social skills, you may be able to help by encouraging basic social activities. Even a young child can practice introducing himself to new people, starting a conversation, showing others he is interested in them, and learning how to join a group activity. Parents can play-act social situations and model appropriate social skills. Beyond this, you should consult your child's doctor if you feel that your child needs more help than you are able to give.

Fitness, Exercise, and Sports

Throughout the ages of childhood, your child can be physically active in many different ways. In infancy, the pastimes of stretching out arms and legs, of rolling over, and of learning to crawl and walk are all physically demanding and part of an infant's physical fitness regimen.

Two- and three-year-olds thrive on unstructured physical play such as running, swinging, climbing, playing in a sandbox, and participating in carefully supervised water play. By age two, your child should be able to jump with both feet, skip, and run. By age three, when in motion, your child should be able to change directions (from left to right, from forward to backward) comfortably.

Fun Games to Play with Your Children

One of our readers wrote in to remind parents that "children don't always need the big things. They tend to remember the little things like books you read together, games you play, and trips to the zoo." We think this is excellent advice! Here are some ideas for "little things" that you can do with your child, one on one:

One to Three Months

Fly, baby, fly: Sit on the floor with your baby facing you. Support her body and head with your hands. Say, "Are you ready to fly? Wheee!!" Lift your baby as you gently roll onto your back. As you lie down, hold your baby in the air.

Follow the bee: Hold your baby comfortably. Place your finger in front of her eyes while making a buzzing sound. Move your finger around in the air. Your baby's eyes should follow your "bee." Next, take your baby's finger and move it around with a buzzing sound; land the "bee" on your cheek or nose.

Elevator: Lie on your back and lift your baby up over you. Say, "I'm going to kiss you!" while you lower her down and give her a kiss.

Bouncing rides: Place your baby on your lap and hold her under her arms. Move forward until you're at the edge of the seat, then raise and lower your heels to give her a gentle bounce. Reciting rhymes while you do this will add to the fun and encourage language development.

Four to Seven Months

Balance game: Stand your baby on a bed while supporting her trunk, and gently bounce her on the mattress.

One, two, three!: Babies love to anticipate movement, so this is a favorite. Hold your baby's hands while she's lying down and say, "Are you ready to stand up? Here we go . . . one, two, three!" while pulling her up gently.

Balls and push toys: As your baby becomes more mobile, she'll be more interested in objects that move, such as balls and toys with wheels.

(continued)

Remember to remove these once she's trying to pull herself up to a sitting or standing position.

Food painting: Place some pureed food or pudding on your baby's highchair tray, and let her "finger paint" with it. It's messy, but it's a lot of fun for your baby.

Peekaboo: This old standby will delight your baby, with her budding understanding that even when an object or person is covered, it still exists (a concept called object permanence). Cover your face with your hands, then remove your hands and say, "Peekaboo, I see you!"

Eight to Twelve Months

This little piggy, itsy-bitsy spider, and pop goes the weasel: Babies love to learn these nursery rhymes and anticipate the accompanying movements.

One, two, buckle my shoe: This counting rhyme is ideally suited for climbing up and down stairs.

Hide-and-seek: This game exploits your baby's understanding of object and person permanence. Hide your baby's toys—or yourself—and encourage her to seek.

One to Two Years

Shadow game: Go outside on a sunny day and look for your shadows. Help your baby find hers, then move around and show her how your shadow moves with you.

Paint with feet: Spread out a large piece of paper. Pour nontoxic paint into a large shallow tray. Hold your child's hand and let her step into the paint—then walk across the paper. You can also make handprints this way.

Kickball: Roll a large ball toward your child's feet as she stands still, and have her kick it back to you. This helps develop good reaction skills and encourages her to stand on one foot.

Pasta art: Help your child string ziti or other fun-shaped pasta onto a shoelace, paint them with finger paint, and glue them onto paper.

Three to Five Years

Puppet show: Provide your child with puppets and a minitheater stage made out of a cardboard box. Together, you can act out a scene from a favorite and familiar nursery rhyme.

House: Offer your child a doll to represent every member of your household, and encourage her to act out a scene from your daily life, such as having a family dinner, putting a child to bed at night, or walking the family dog.

Ring-around-the-rosy: This rough-and-tumble game encourages movement and group activity.

Simon says: Encourage your child and a few playmates to listen and follow directions by playing this popular game.

Four- and five-year-olds are learning to play in an increasingly coordinated manner and can begin to participate in some organized games. Children in this age group can roll large balls, play catch, and may be able to navigate a bike with training wheels. (However, kids this age cannot safely maneuver a bicycle in traffic because they lack judgment and safety awareness as well as adequate coordination.) They may also enjoy swimming, dance, gymnastics, or ice-skating.

Most experts believe that children should be at least seven or eight before they engage in organized team sports. It depends on the child, but many team sports are contact sports, and most children under age seven aren't ready for rough contact. For them, the risk of physical injury is not the only concern. There's also the issue of winning and losing. Emotionally, losing at sports can be difficult, even for adults. At this age, it's more important that children have the chance to play without having to worry about who won or lost.

No matter what your child's age, and no matter what the sport or activity, remember that fitness should be fun. If your child isn't having fun, ask why, and try to fix the problem. Try to find out if your child has any fears or reasons to be reluctant to join in the play. If necessary, postpone the activity and try it again in a few months or years; in the meantime, find another activity your child does enjoy.

Keep these dos and don'ts in mind when your child is involved in any physical activity:

KidsHealth Tip

Share and Share Alike

Sharing can be difficult for many toddlers, who aren't able to see things from another perspective and need time to learn. If your child is reluctant to share, help her understand the concept of sharing by doing the following:

- Invent simple activities that encourage taking turns and working together, like throwing a ball back and forth or playing on a seesaw.
- Set an example by sharing with other adults (hosting a carpool ride or giving your neighbor a cup of sugar, for example), and explain to your child how happy it made you and the other adult feel when you shared.
- Offer your child choices about what she can share: It's OK for some items to be off-limits for sharing (like her favorite blanket) and other toys and objects to be available for sharing with other kids.

For more information about teaching your child to share, see Chapter 19, "Temperament, Behavior, and Discipline."

- Don't pressure young kids to compete. They may develop a negative attitude toward fitness or injure themselves while trying to perform beyond their capabilities.
- Concentrate on your child's successes rather than her failures. Praise what your child does well, and provide plenty of opportunities for her to succeed.
- Introduce new activities, especially if she shows interest. There's no need to specialize in any one sport or activity during early childhood.
- Try not to draw too many comparisons between your child and other children. As long as she is developmentally on target, let her master skills at her own pace.

Sometimes, if a child refuses to play or interact with peers, it can be an indication of a physical or psychological problem. If your child complains of pain, shortness of breath, or inability to keep up with the other children, or if she consistently refuses to join other children in play, contact your child's doctor.

Family Fitness

Whenever possible, participate in fitness activities with your children. When a family rides bicycles or hikes together, parents act as role models, and everyone has fun and gets some exercise. Walking, playing, and running in the backyard or using playground equipment at a local park can be fun for the entire family.

How to Keep Family Fitness Safe

Always keep safety and injury prevention in mind when your child is involved in any physical activity. Remember these tips for family fitness:

- All children and adults should always wear helmets when on tricycles, bicycles, and other wheeled toys; wearing a helmet will become a lifelong safety habit if started early.
- Never let your toddler be around a pool without constant supervision. It takes only a second for a toddler to slip beneath the water. A good rule to follow is to keep your toddler within arm's length of you when in or near the water.
- Put sunscreen on your child whenever she is playing outdoors, even on overcast days, to prevent sunburn and decrease the risk of developing skin cancer in adulthood.

KidsHealth Tip

Fitness for Everyone

A child with a chronic health condition or disability should not be excluded from fitness activities. Some activities may need to be modified or adapted, and some may be too risky depending on your child's condition. Talk with your child's doctor about which activities are safe.

- Do **not** allow your child to play on trampolines. The American Academy of Pediatrics (AAP) recommends that children not use trampolines due to the high number of injuries reported at all ages.

For more information about keeping your child safe, see Chapter 24, "Child Safety."

TV, Computers, and Other Media

The average American child spends three to five hours in front of a TV per day. In fact, 70 percent of child-care centers use TV during a typical day! This is not necessarily a bad thing—TV can be a great educator and entertainer. But there's also no doubt that there's a negative side to TV viewing.

Research has shown that children who consistently spend more than 10 hours per week watching TV are more likely to be overweight, aggressive, and slower to learn in school. Children who view violence on television, such as a kidnapping or murder on the news, are more likely to believe that the world is scary and that something bad will happen to them. Studies have also indicated that TV consistently reinforces gender-role and racial stereotypes.

To limit the negative effects of TV viewing, children should watch no more than one or two hours a day of all entertainment media combined (TV, computer, and video games), according to guidelines from the AAP. The AAP has also strongly urged parents to avoid TV viewing entirely for children under the age of two years because, "research on early brain development shows that babies and toddlers have a critical need for direct interactions with parents and other significant caregivers . . . for healthy brain growth and the development of appropriate social, emotional, and cognitive skills." The time spent in front of the TV is time lost to this kind of important social interaction.

Potential Negative Effects of TV on Your Child

The two negative effects of TV on young children that are most commonly discussed and studied are violence and obesity.

Violence

On TV, violence is demonstrated and promoted as a fun and effective way to get what you want. Children are taught by their parents that it's not right to hit, but

TV says it's OK to bite, hit, or kick if you're the good guy. And even the "bad guys" on TV are rarely held responsible or punished for their actions.

The images children absorb also can scare them. According to a recent study, children ages two to seven are particularly frightened by fantastic, scary-looking things like grotesque monsters. Simply telling children that those images aren't real won't console them because they can't yet distinguish between fantasy and reality.

Obesity

Research studies show a link between excessive TV watching and obesity—a significant health problem today (as described in Chapter 32, "Health Problems in Early Childhood"). TV watching is a passive activity, and when children are inactive, they tend to snack excessively. TV also bombards children with advertising messages that encourage them to eat unhealthy foods, such as potato chips and cookies, which often become preferred snack foods.

Even quality, educational TV can indirectly have the same negative effect on children's health. While children are watching four hours of *Sesame Street*, they're not exercising, socializing, or spending time outside.

What Can Parents Do?

Children's advocates are divided: Many want more hours per week of educational programming; others assert that no TV is the best solution. And some say it's better for parents to control the use of TV and to teach children that TV is for occasional entertainment, not for constant escapism or "babysitting."

To help you teach your children good TV viewing habits, observe the following guidelines suggested by the AAP and other experts:

- Set limits. You can limit the number of hours your child spends watching TV by moving the set from the most prominent room in the house to a side room and by keeping TVs out of bedrooms and turned off during meals. Again, the

AAP recommends that parents limit their children's viewing of TV and other entertainment media to one or two hours a day.

- Plan viewing in advance. Approach TV as you would a movie. An age-group rating system modeled after the familiar movie rating system has been developed for TV programs. Consult TV listings to determine which shows are appropriate for family viewing. Turn the set on for these programs only, and turn the set off and discuss programs when they're over. Use the VCR to tape shows of special importance and to eliminate commercials.

  The V-chip (V is for "violence") is designed to block TV programs you don't want your child to see. All new TV sets have internal V-chips, and set-top boxes are available for TVs made before 2000. The Federal Communications Commission requires that V-chips in new TVs recognize the TV Parental Guidelines and the age-group rating system and block programs that do not adhere to these standards. News, sports, and commercials—which aren't rated—were not addressed, even though they often present depictions of violence.

- Don't use TV to reward or punish your child. Practices like this make TV seem even more important to children.

- Watch with your child. It's important to talk to your child about TV shows to help him interpret what he sees and to share your own beliefs and values. If something objectionable appears on the screen you can ask your child, "Do you think it was OK when they hit that guy? What else could they have done? What would you have done?"

- Provide alternatives. Parents are responsible for how much TV their children watch. Encourage both indoor and outdoor activities for your child. Encourage reading time, and designate certain evenings for special family activities.

- For more suggestions on taming TV, check out the Web site of the TV Turnoff Network, www.tvturnoff.org.

- Resist advertising pressure. Don't expect your child to ignore commercials for snack foods, candy, and toys. Help him develop healthy eating habits and become a smart consumer by teaching him to recognize a sales pitch.

- Practice what you preach. Don't expect your child to have self-discipline when it comes to TV viewing if you don't. Set a good example for your child by spending your free time reading, exercising, talking, cooking, or participating in other endeavors instead of watching TV.

Parents can control what their children watch on TV. By using both the channel selector and the on/off button, and by teaching children to use TV positively, parents can overcome potentially negative influences and help their children get the most from TV.

Children and the Electronic Media Explosion

Until a few years ago, if parents decided that their young children had watched enough TV, they could turn the set off and feel fairly confident that their kids would soon find more imaginative, physically active ways to amuse themselves, like playing house, building a fort with other kids, or kicking a ball in the yard.

If the TV is shut off today, many young children will pick up a handheld electronic game device or make a beeline for the computer.

As with TV viewing, these forms of entertainment often involve frightening scenarios and should not be permitted to crowd out opportunities for children to socialize with adults and other children. Rather than just saying no, suggest fun alternatives.

Reading to Your Child: Do It!

Early childhood developmental experts agree that reading to infants, toddlers, and young children is a highly recommended activity for fun and cognitive development. Here are some of the benefits of reading to your child:

- Helps lay the foundation for speech and language skills
- Connects you with your child intellectually, emotionally, and physically
- Promotes a positive attitude toward learning to read when your child is developmentally ready to do so (This will be positively reinforced if your child also sees that you enjoy reading yourself.)
- Encourages your child to use her imagination

> ## The Voice of Experience
>
> *"It's easy to groan inwardly at the thought of reading the same book to your child for the hundredth time. But children love the comfort and familiarity that the same story provides night after night. And when kids know the story so well that they can recite the words along with you, it gives them great confidence—as if they are actually doing the 'reading.' So grin and bear it; before long, your child will be reading to himself."*
>
> —FROM THE KIDSHEALTH PARENT SURVEY

Tips for Reading to Your Child

- Think of reading to an infant as a total sensory experience. Even though your baby may comprehend nothing of what is being read, she loves the sound of your voice, the smell and feel of your body as you hold her, the feel and taste of the book, the sight of the colors and shapes on the pages, and the sight of facial expressions you make as you read. Infants particularly enjoy books with lots of textures to feel like *Pat the Bunny*. Books for infants should be sturdy (usually with thick cardboard pages) to resist the gnawing and sucking on them that will occur. And they should not have pointed or sharp edges.

- You and your child should both feel comfortable during reading sessions. A rocking chair is ideal for this activity.

- Read slowly and with lots of expression and emotion. Vary the volume of your voice, don't hesitate to exaggerate or repeat interesting sounds, and add your own comments along the way. Young children love rhymes—before you know it, your child will be chiming in with the rhyming word at the end of the sentence.

- Encourage your infant to look at the pictures. Say the names of objects, people, and animals as you point them out on the pages. Make the sounds of the animals and objects in the book.

- Take cues for reading strategies from your child. Give her a chance to imitate sounds or words as you read. Encourage her to point out or name colors, shapes, sizes, and so on. Let her make the sounds of the animals and talk about the emotions of the characters (is the boy happy or sad?). As your child's comprehension increases, discuss the story with her after you have finished reading.

- Don't approach reading sessions as an attempt to push your child to learn to read earlier. With reading, as with many other aspects of development, individual children proceed at their own pace. Attempts to drill your preschool child on reading skills before she is developmentally ready and interested will usually result in frustration for both of you. This can undermine your child's self-esteem and may cause her to resist learning to read later on. In addition, studies have shown that early readers don't tend to maintain their advantage when they enter school, anyway. Those children who haven't started to read before school entry typically catch up with the early readers by the end of first grade.

- Check out the children's section of your local library. Many offer story times as well as good advice on books for all ages.

KidsHealth Tip

Time for Dramatic Readings

When reading to your toddler or young child, don't be afraid to let the actor in you come out! You'll have an easier time keeping kids interested if you use lots of facial expressions, animated voices, gestures, and even sound effects when reading. Slow down or quicken the pace during exciting parts of the story, and involve your child in the tale by asking him to guess what might happen next.

Need More Information?

Check the Index and Appendix C, "Resource Guide." And of course, consult your child's doctor.

chapter nineteen

Temperament, Behavior, and Discipline

Learning the rules

In every family, there are moments of peace, joy, and laughter—and of course, kid chaos. Who hasn't watched a mother grapple with her screaming child at the grocery checkout, battling over a toy or candy purchase? Or known a father who was up until midnight, scooping up a runaway toddler who thinks it's great fun to climb out of his crib, over and over?

As a parent, expect to have your share of trying moments like these—they are a normal part of growth, development, and the long process of teaching children how to behave. Remember that your child is undergoing tremendous changes during his first five years, from a totally dependent infant to an autonomous, independent individual with specific wants and needs. It's natural to expect him to push limits (how else will he discover them?), test you (how else will he learn what's OK and what's not?), and assert himself as he discovers he is a person separate from you. But along with these natural explorations come problem behaviors that you need to correct with a consistent method of discipline so your child can learn what is and what is not acceptable in this world he lives in.

Without discipline, children can develop problematic behavior even by age two, and in their quest to understand and feel safe in the world, they can aggressively push you beyond all limits to "force" you to define them; they can't do it themselves.

The ultimate goal, however, is not for you to control your child's every action, but rather to teach your child to control himself in ways that are socially desirable.

The day will come all too soon when he will grow up and be forced to make decisions and actions on his own—without you there to guide him. Discipline—another word for teaching—is the tool you have at your disposal to help your child learn how to make these independent decisions. And it is without a doubt one of the most important ways you demonstrate your love for him.

But in the heat of the moment, when you just can't believe that your three-year-old colored on the walls *again*, it's easy to react and punish rather than thoughtfully discipline and teach. Prepare yourself in advance by defining your own core beliefs about discipline and behavior—they will help guide your actions when you need to act quickly and decisively:

- Develop a general philosophy of discipline to help guide you.
- Establish general principles of behavior that you want your child to learn.
- Understand what's normal for children at different ages. (Remember, you can't expect more from your child than he is able to control or understand at the time.)
- Recognize your child's unique temperament, and tailor your discipline to work with it, rather than against it.
- Agree with your partner on disciplinary tactics so that you can both be as fair and consistent as possible.

Developing a Philosophy of Discipline

Close your eyes and imagine this scenario: Several times you've told your three-year-old daughter not to pick flowers from your neighbor's garden. Yet she's done it *again*, and this time your once-patient neighbor has come over in a huff and demanded that you get your child "under control." What would you do?

How you answer may help you understand your own natural tendency as a disciplinarian—and how you may need to adapt to provide the best home environment for your child. Parenting styles vary widely and can have dramatically different effects on children. Chances are, you'll tend to fall into one of three primary parenting styles defined by Diana Baumrind, a leading specialist in this area.

Authoritarian

If you expect unquestioning and immediate obedience according to strict, unwavering codes of conduct, then you probably lean toward the authoritarian style of discipline. In these homes, parents communicate hard-and-fast rules and regulations (no exceptions) and then enforce them through stern yelling or spanking. Children learn to obey out of fear of consequences, and they usually have little or no opportunity to question rules or decisions or to share their own thoughts, needs, or explanations with their parents. In the case of the flower-picking daughter, you would yell at her without asking her side of the story, send her to her room, and consider some further form of punishment.

> ## The Voice of Experience
>
> *"Kids are great parrots. Everything I have ever said has come right back out of my children's mouth, in exactly the same tone of voice. If you want them to control their anger, you must control yours."*
>
> —FROM THE KIDSHEALTH PARENT SURVEY

Although this style of discipline may achieve immediate results, research shows that children raised in authoritarian households behave out of fear, not a learned sense of right and wrong. Not only are they less likely to learn how to control their own behavior, but they also show less independence, self-confidence, and awareness of their ability to influence their world.

Permissive

If you primarily value your child's freedom and self-expression, even if it means a few more picked flowers from your neighbor's garden, then you probably tend toward a more permissive philosophy of discipline. To discipline, you may tend to take your daughter aside and reason with her, focusing more on expressing your unconditional love for her than on setting limits, saying no, and guiding behavior. In some ways, her needs, wants, and desires are the "boss" for both child and parent because clear limits and consequences are not established.

Permissive parenting, however, has its own set of problems. Studies show that children raised in permissive homes tend to lack structure, healthy social limits, and clear expectations of what proper behavior should be. Because "anything goes," they tend to be more impulsive, self-indulgent, aggressive, and even inconsiderate when they grow up because their desires and self-expression have always come first—often at the expense of others (including the parents!). In other words, children are never taught self-control, which puts them at the mercy of their immediate needs and wants. In a world where future success is largely a function of one's sense of teamwork, reliability, and societal expectations, a permissive home may inspire a child's creativity, but it will not necessarily give her the self-discipline to put that creativity to good use.

Authoritative

If you establish clear limits for your child and set high expectations for her behavior but apply rules with some degree of flexibility and two-way communication, then you probably tend to use an authoritative approach to discipline. In the case of our imaginary scenario, you may put your child in time-out for 10 minutes, talk with her about her behavior, and explain how picking flowers makes her neighbor feel. You would also tell her what will happen if she chooses to pick the neighbor's flowers again.

Authoritative parents are firm and viewed by their children as "the boss" (especially about the big stuff!). But these children also know that their parents will always explain the rules, be fair and consistent, provide feedback, and discuss issues and rules. In these homes, there are clear, consistent consequences for breaking "rules," so children learn to internalize the rules as a guide for future behavior choices. These parents allow their children to exercise power within limits, so children learn to control their own behavior according to values learned within the family.

Children raised in an authoritative home tend to be the most well adjusted and socially competent. Growing up in a world with both order and flexibility, they learn self-respect, self-control, and independence within socially acceptable limits. Children raised in authoritative homes tend to avoid common adolescent problems like drug abuse and academic failure, and they tend to grow up to be more achievement oriented.

Which philosophy of discipline comes most naturally to you? Which comes most naturally to your partner? How can you make your approach to discipline more authoritative? Take time to think about these issues. Talk with your partner about various scenarios you may experience as parents, and think through how you would handle them. Understand that you may tend to approach discipline from opposite ends of the spectrum, and negotiate a middle ground that you both feel comfortable with.

Establishing General Principles of Behavior

What is considered "good" behavior? What is considered "bad" behavior? The answers to these questions can vary across time, culture, religion, place, and family.

Consider your own values. Are honesty and respect for authority important to you? What about generosity and sharing? Respecting others' differences and belongings? Showing understanding for others? How about follow-through? Hard work? Assertiveness? Equality of the sexes? And a willingness to admit when you are wrong? Knowing your priorities can help you stay focused on teaching (rather than reacting) during the heat of the moment. It also helps you to save your discipline strategies for what really matters.

> ## The Voice of Experience
>
> *"The best advice I ever received would be pick your battles."*
>
> —FROM THE KIDSHEALTH PARENT SURVEY

Certainly you will make mistakes—we all do. And luckily, young children are incredibly forgiving and forgetful. But even at ages three, four, and five, it's important to remember that you are laying the foundation for your child's future behavior as an adult.

What to Expect as Your Child Grows Up

Just as you can't force a newborn to walk, you can't expect a two-year-old to stop himself from running in front of a car. At this age, he is unable to understand the consequences of his actions—all he knows is that there's a puppy on the other side of the street that he absolutely *must* play with.

As children get older, they are increasingly capable of understanding rules and requests, other people's feelings, consequences, and reasoning. Most important, they can gradually learn for themselves how to behave and therefore assume more responsibility for their actions.

You can guide your child best if you understand what kinds of misbehaviors are normal for children at different ages, as well as what kinds of discipline they are mentally and emotionally capable of learning from. Our approach in the following examples presumes an authoritative parenting style, which we encourage you to try with your child.

Birth to 12 Months

Infants can have a hard time sleeping through the night, never mind exercising self-control. Their behaviors are involuntary for the most part, even when they cry to express their need for food, warmth, sleep, and comfort. Although you may be able to condition your infant to do things you prefer, such as sleep through the night, his changed behaviors are not the result of self-reflective learning or self-control.

As your baby grows, he will invariably want to do dangerous or disruptive things, such as pulling on curtains and electrical cords. Your best approach with very young children is to distract them from frustrating behaviors with fun activities, music, or a favorite toy.

As he gets older, your child will test how you react to new behaviors, such as pulling your hair, biting, poking, and high-pitched screaming. If you overreact, you can inadvertently encourage your child to repeat the behavior—strong reactions are exciting to babies and experienced as positive reinforcement rather than punishment. Instead, if your child is screaming just to get attention, ignore him until the screaming stops, and then reward him with hugs and kisses; rewarding good behavior can be a powerful tool for discipline. If your baby is biting or poking, stay calm, firmly let him know, "No, that hurts," and restrain him gently but firmly by holding him in your arms for a few moments. If he persists, then put him down for a few moments and explain your actions in simple words.

You can also start using this time to set good examples for your child by controlling your own behavior—if you tend to throw temper tantrums, your child will do the same. In addition, you can lay the foundation for later discipline by showering your child with love and attention. Have no fear—you can't spoil a child this young. Use this special time of total dependence to make your child feel loved and important, which will in turn teach him about feelings of love for you. By the time your child is a toddler, he will want to please you more than anything else.

12 to 24 Months

As your child becomes a toddler, don't be surprised if it seems her behavior is exasperating more often than not; it's quite normal for her to seek out every conceivable danger and do exactly what you told her *not* to do. Patience, humor, consistency, and ingenuity can carry you through to age two and a half or three, when your child will be more willing and able to learn how to control herself.

In the meantime, your child will need you to closely guide her as she explores her world. The best way to discipline a young child is to eliminate temptations. Keep items such as VCRs, stereos, jewelry, and cleaning supplies out of her reach. (For more information about keeping your toddler safe, see Chapter 24, "Child Safety.")

Deep down, your child desperately wants your love and approval. Especially as your child reaches age two and older, help her "be good" by giving her opportunities for her to please you and feel good about herself. For example, instead of asking your three-year-old to pick up the newspaper she scattered all over the floor, you could turn it into a contest by saying, "I wonder if you can gather up all that paper before I finish cooking dinner."

Despite your efforts, toddlers will still misbehave—a lot, sometimes. When this happens, don't spank, hit, or slap your child. Babies and toddlers are especially unlikely to be able to make any connection between their behavior and physical punishment. They will only feel the pain of the hit. Instead, when your toddler heads toward an unacceptable play object, calmly say, "No," and either remove her from the area or engage her attention with an appropriate activity. Explain in simple words exactly what she did that was wrong. If necessary, remove her from an environment so that she can calm down.

What makes these years so difficult for both parent and child is that she cannot accept responsibility for herself, and yet she must reject complete control by you

Time for Time-Out?

By age two, you can also use a brief time-out (not more than a couple of minutes) to show that there are consequences for outbursts and to help her regain self-control when she is frustrated or upset. Establish a suitable time-out place that is free of distractions so your child can focus on her behavior and the consequence. Remember that getting sent to your room may not mean much if computers, TVs, and video games are stored there.

Consider the length of time that will best suit your child. Experts say one minute for each year of age is a good rule of thumb to follow; others recommend using the time-out until the child is calmed down (to teach self-regulation). Choose what you think will work best with your child. Time-outs work well with most children, but if you find that your child gets extremely upset, talk with your child's doctor about other ways you can create consequences for your child.

(something she's terrified to do) in order to grow up. She is stuck in between being a baby and being a "big girl"—a very uncomfortable place to be, indeed.

24 to 36 Months

Around age two, your child's behavior will be naturally self-centered. Don't expect her to consider other people's feelings before she acts. Given her cognitive development, she'll be unable to understand if you try to reason with her about why she shouldn't misbehave. And because she's still unable to control her emotions, be prepared for her to lash back with sudden anger, screaming, and temper tantrums when you discipline her. You still need to continually communicate reasonable limits and consistently deliver consequences when she misbehaves.

Equally important is the need to praise your child when she behaves well. Whenever your child plays well with a friend, picks up her toys, or feeds or dresses herself, give her extra attention and specifically compliment her. Remember, your child desperately wants your approval, and the more you let her know how to get it, the more she'll want to repeat good behavior.

Children this age also begin to socialize more in playgroups where they need to learn how to get along with other children. Your child may begin testing out misbehaviors such as hair pulling, pinching, biting, and scratching on other kids, and if she's an aggressive type, she may even try pushing and shoving. These kinds of behaviors can be quite upsetting for you and other parents, but they're also quite normal. The best approach is to draw the line quickly, pick your child up, calm her down, and explain that what she did hurt the other child. If she's overly excited, you may need to hold her and restrain her until she calms down. If the behavior persists, remove her from the situation entirely and explain that she can't play with others if she can't control herself, and then try again with smaller playgroups.

The Voice of Experience

"The greatest gift we can give our children is the same thing they offer you—unconditional love. I tell my children I love them regularly, and I tell them how proud of them I am. Kisses and praise are the food of love."
—FROM THE KIDSHEALTH PARENT SURVEY

Three to Five Years

By age three, your child is mentally and emotionally ready to begin to learn how to control his behavior. Not only can he begin to understand the connection between actions and consequences, he can start to understand other people's feelings and remember your instructions. It's exciting to watch your child learn to play with other

Temper Tantrums

Tantrums are a normal part of development, especially between the ages of one and three.

Before age two, a child begins to develop a strong sense of self and wants more control over her environment. The conditions are right for power struggles: "I do it myself" or "Give me." When a toddler discovers that she can't do it herself and that she can't have everything she wants, the stage is set for a tantrum.

The best way to handle tantrums is to avoid them. Being tired, hungry, uncomfortable, frustrated, or in need of attention can all prompt a child to have a tantrum. Anticipate frustrating scenarios, such as being at the grocery store checkout line right before a much-needed naptime. A toddler in need of sleep is likely to whine and cry or demand a candy bar by the cash register. Going to the store *after* the nap can help you avoid the tantrum.

You can also avoid some tantrums by giving your child control over some things, such as which vegetable to have with dinner, which socks to wear, or whether to brush her teeth before or after she changes into her pajamas. The key is to give your child choices that will make her feel empowered without compromising your role as the parent.

But what should you do if you find yourself in the middle of a tantrum? Keep your cool. If you react strongly (or give in to your child's demands), she may learn that tantrums are an effective way of getting attention, even if it's negative attention. If the tantrum poses no danger to anyone, you might choose to ignore it; if your child may hurt herself or someone else, gently remove her from the area and let her calm down.

children and develop friendships—you will notice that he's not only less self-centered and aggressive but also more likely to share, take turns, and be sensitive to his friends' feelings. (For more information about important developmental changes during this time, see Chapter 17, "Growth and Development.")

Of course, he's still learning to get along with others, so be prepared for the occasional fight or out-of-control outburst. He may even hit another child. Your best approach if this happens is to separate him from other children quickly to calm him down, holding him tightly if you need to. Once he calms down, try to get

KidsHealth Tip

Temper, Temper!

If your child is prone to temper tantrums, try keeping a tantrum "chart." Write down the time and place of each tantrum, the persons present, and the child's activity when the tantrum started. After a week or so you may see a pattern—your child may tend to have tantrums only when he is hungry or when he feels left out because you are busy doing the laundry. Learning the "trigger" can help you prevent the tantrum rather than trying to control it once it's started.

him to talk about and understand his own feelings. It's important that you recognize his feelings (and how bad he may feel about his behavior) but also explain that hitting is not a good way to express those feelings. You can reason with him about how he would feel if his friend hit him; he needs this kind of coaching to further develop his ability to empathize with others.

In addition, now more than ever, you need to make sure that you clearly establish and communicate the rules of your house. It's important to explain to your child exactly what you expect of him before you punish him for a certain behavior. For instance, the first time your three-year-old colors on the living room wall, you should discuss why that is not allowed and what will happen if it's done again. Explain to him that he will have to help clean the wall and will not be able to use his crayons for the rest of the afternoon. If he colors on the walls again a few days later, you should remind him that crayons are for paper only and then enforce the consequences.

Although it's sometimes easier to ignore bad behavior or fail to follow through on some threatened punishment, this risks setting a bad precedent. Consistency is key to effective discipline. It's important for you to decide what the rules are, and you (and your partner) must be consistent in upholding them.

If your child is misbehaving and all discipline efforts have failed, consider setting up a chart system. Put up a calendar chart with a box for each day of the week on the refrigerator. Pick one behavior you want to "work on," let's say hitting, and then say to your child, "You know it is not nice to hit other children. To help you learn how to stop hitting, I am going to put a gold star on this chart whenever you get through the whole day without hitting anyone. Every time you earn a gold star, I will give you a treat." Have a collection of special small prizes on hand (small birthday party favors sold in party stores are numerous and inexpensive). In the beginning, you will need to reward the new behavior every time it is accomplished. Then you can offer a reward after two successful days, then three, and so on, until your child has control over his behavior. Then you can move on to another behavioral problem if you need to. As in the previous example, be specific about the behavior you want to see. Saying, "You'll get this reward when you're good," is too vague. This system will give you opportunities to praise his effort to overcome a stubborn problem.

Time-outs can also be particularly useful for children of this age because they can help teach self-control. Choose a suitable place for time-outs, and keep it free from distractions such as TV.

A final word: Don't forget that your child learns by watching you. You will make a much stronger impact on your child if he sees you putting your belongings away, too, rather than if you tell him to pick up his toys while you leave your stuff strewn across the kitchen counter.

Tailoring Your Approach to Your Child's Temperament

Children seem to come into the world with a constitutional makeup, or temperament. They may be hardwired to have certain tendencies, to be gentle or rambunctious, calm or easily irritated, shy or outgoing, lighthearted or intense. Generally, these kinds of traits are difficult, if not impossible, to change, so it's best for everyone if you try to work with your child's natural temperament.

As a result of different temperaments, even children in the same family may need to be raised differently. Your discipline style, in particular, needs to be compatible with your child's unique personality.

Equally important, understanding your child's temperament gives you an opportunity to reflect on how his tendencies may affect you and your perception of him. For example, if a father with an aggressive, physical personality has a son who is naturally more passive, shy, and gentle, the father may be embarrassed by his son and try to force him to change. Such temperament conflicts can seriously affect the parent-child relationship and how the child is raised.

Here are some general strategies to help you tailor your discipline style to your child's temperament:

- Take time to learn about your child's temperament and behavioral style. In infancy, your child may handle changes in schedule or environment extremely well or get easily upset. Look for these kinds of patterns, and by age two you'll start to see them stand out.
- Once you have a better understanding of your child's temperament, you can begin to change the way you react to him and his behavior. For example, if your shy toddler is in a large group of new people and is clinging to you, you'll want to be more sensitive to his need to feel safe and close—he's not trying to be annoying with his behavior.
- Just because your first child was headstrong and demanding does not mean that your other children will be that way. You'll need to adjust your approach to discipline accordingly. For example, a more aggressive three-year-old may need more physical restraining, time-outs, and serious consequences. A very sensitive child may need only a gentle scolding in order to feel bad about his behavior and change it.
- If you are finding that your child's temperament is very stressful for you to handle, be sure to talk with your child's doctor about other parenting techniques to help you both cope.
- Talk with other parents and friends about your own struggles understanding and parenting your child. Raising an anxious or high-spirited child can be exhausting, but it's encouraging to find you're not alone.

Dealing with Common Behaviors and Misbehaviors

As your child grows, he will do things that may worry or confuse you. In this section, we take a look at behaviors that are often of concern to parents.

Sibling Rivalry

It's normal for children in the same family to fight and even dislike each other at times—they're different people with distinct personalities, desires, and needs. For young children, who are naturally self-centered, the jealousy over the attention paid to a new baby, for example, can be excruciatingly intense. The problems can escalate as the baby grows up; perhaps your youngest may resent wearing hand-me-downs from her older sister, who gets new clothes to accommodate her growth.

At the core of sibling rivalry is jealousy, and this jealousy is never about the things that your children may fight over—ultimately, the clothes issue is about the need to feel as loved and important to parents as a brother or sister. In many ways, your children are fighting for your love—and they may purposely drag you into their fights just for the attention and support.

Here are some guidelines for dealing with sibling rivalry:

- If your preschooler is adjusting to a new baby, allow him to be the "baby" sometimes too—otherwise, he may start acting out by throwing food or even urinating in inappropriate places. If he demands to suck on a bottle or carry a blanket, be patient. Ignore the "babyish" behavior, and give him lots of time and attention. He's seeking comfort and reassurance that you love him just as much as you love the new baby.
- Schedule uninterrupted one-on-one time with each child every week. Make each one feel like the most important person in the world.
- If your older child is three years or older, create a special, safe place for his favorite things. It will not only reduce fighting but also show that you respect his individuality and needs.
- Don't overreact to their fighting—they'll read your involvement as encouragement to continue and even escalate their behavior.
- Stay out of sibling fights as much as possible. Otherwise, they will drag you in and manipulate you and force you to take sides. If the fight becomes violent, step in immediately and put each child in a separate room for a while. Make it absolutely clear that abusive behavior is never acceptable.

KidsHealth Tip

Good Behavior, Bad Behavior

When disciplining your child, remember that praise or rewards for good behavior are important than punishment of bad behavior. Giving this recognition provides the groundwork for happier children with higher self-esteem.

- Tell your children that you don't expect them to be best friends all the time—you understand that they are different people. But you do expect them to learn how to share, respect one another, and talk things out.
- Whenever possible, explain to a child in a loving way why you may need to treat a sibling in a slightly different way—because they are both special and need different things and you love them individually.
- Never compare your children or hold one of them up as an example to the other; questions like, "Why can't you be more quiet like your sister?" can be devastating and hard to forget.

Separation Anxiety

At some point between 12 and 18 months children learn the concept of object permanence. That means they know that just because they can't see something doesn't mean it doesn't exist. Until that concept is understood, however, your child has no idea that you still exist when you walk out of the room. No wonder he screams when you try to leave him! This fear of losing you is called separation anxiety, and it causes most children around the age of 10 months to become very clingy. Your child may scream, cry, throw temper tantrums, and refuse to go to sleep without you.

Your child needs to learn how to be apart from you. He needs to know that you leave him—and you return. You can teach this lesson by playing separation games. When your baby is awake, say "bye-bye," leave the room for a brief period of time, and then return with a smile and offer a cuddle. Do this often throughout the day, extending the amount of time you're out of sight each time. If your baby immediately cries when you leave the room, try maintaining voice contact while you're out of sight. Games of peekaboo and hide-and-seek are also playful ways to teach the reassuring reality of object permanence.

When you do leave your child, say good-bye with a smile, and leave quickly (no running back to dry those tears and offer yet more reassurances). When you return, enter the room

> ### The Voice of Experience
>
> "Never forget to say you're sorry when you're wrong or have been unjust. Kids have a right to be treated with respect—and they'll work to keep your respect the more you give it. Equally important, it's best to teach by example how they should handle mistakes, as well as how they should treat others."
>
> —FROM THE KidsHealth PARENT SURVEY

calmly with a happy face, and offer a warm greeting without getting carried away with hugs and tears and a litany of how much you missed your child. Tearful, drawn-out separations and returns tell your child that separation is a big deal and something to be worried about.

Bullying

There are many reasons why children become bullies. They may naturally be more aggressive children who need to learn how to control this aspect of their personality. They may use bullying as a way of dealing with stress or a difficult situation at home, such as a divorce. Some bullies have been victims of abuse themselves. And just like their victims, bullies often have low self-esteem. Whatever the cause, bullies usually pick on others as a way of dealing with their own problems, feeling powerful, and impressing other children.

Bullies will often target someone who is different from others and focus on that attribute. Wearing glasses, having big ears, or being in a wheelchair are all differences that can be fodder for a bully's ridicule. Being anxious, insecure, or smarter or slower than their peers can also make some kids the target of bullying. The bully realizes that these children are unlikely to retaliate.

If you learn that your child is a bully, try to stay calm. At first you may feel a sense of disbelief—not my child! Try not to become angry or defensive because this can make a bad situation even worse. Although it's unlikely that a child who bullies will confess her behaviors, ask your child three questions: (1) "What exactly did you say (or do) to Johnny?" (2) "Why did you do that?" and (3) "How can we make sure this doesn't happen again?" Because bullying often stems from unhappiness or insecurity, try to find out if something is troubling your child. If the behavior persists, talk with your child's doctor.

If you suspect that your child is being bullied, remember that the effects of bullying aren't as obvious as a black eye. Signs to look for include bruises, missing belongings, or the invention of mysterious illnesses or stomachaches to avoid going out. Often a child will unexpectedly change behaviors to avoid a bully. Your child may be embarrassed to admit he's the victim of a bully. To make it easier for your child to talk about it, consider asking some thoughtful questions. For example, you could ask your child what it's like on the playground.

If you learn that your child is the victim of a bully, don't overreact. You do not want to add to your child's burden with an angry or disappointed response.

What can you do? First, listen to your child. Just talking about the problem and knowing that you care can be helpful and comforting. Your child is likely to feel vulnerable at this point, so it's important that you let him know you're on his side and that you love him.

Second, explain that getting angry or violent won't solve the problem; in fact, it's giving the bully exactly what he wants. And responding with physical aggression can put your child at risk. On the other hand, going along with everything the bully says is not a good way to handle the situation. Your child needs to regain his sense of dignity and recover his damaged self-esteem.

Third, empower your child to act first. For example, suggest that your child look the bully in the eye and firmly say, "I don't like your teasing and I want you to stop right now." Your child should then walk away and ignore any further taunts from the bully. If your child fears physical harm, he should try to find a teacher or move toward friends who can provide comfort and support. Because bullies often target socially awkward children, encourage your child to develop more friendships by arranging play times with children he knows or enrolling him in group activities.

In most cases, bullying won't require your direct intervention, but if you fear that your child may be seriously harmed, it's important that you step in. That may mean staying in the room while your preschooler plays with a friend or talking to your child's teacher about the problem. It may embarrass your child, but his safety should be your primary concern.

Not Sharing

As your child moves into the preschool years, it's increasingly important that he learn the value of sharing—it's by far one of the most important social skills your child can learn at this age. If your child is having a problem with sharing, consider allowing him to choose one or two favorite toys that he doesn't have to share, and then encourage him to share the rest; this balance may make it easier for him. Usually, other children will give your child positive feedback—and much-desired friendship—when he shares well, which will naturally reinforce the behaviors you want. And when he doesn't share well and other children don't want to play with him, talk with him about how he would feel if his friends didn't share their toys with him.

Imaginary Friends

Preschoolers (ages three to five) often create imaginary friends or companions. This creation is a natural, normal extension of the vivid make-believe play that children this age engage in. In fact, imaginary friends can help children experiment and grow emotionally and socially. Sometimes this fantasy world becomes so real to a child that it can be hard for him to separate it from reality; don't be surprised if your child introduces you to his imaginary friend. Play along with your child in a low-key way, and let him guide you in his imaginary world. When the game is over, praise him for being so creative and for playing independently. It's important that you respect him and not let other siblings make fun of him.

Thumb and Finger Sucking

Babies suck on their thumbs and other fingers because it calms them down and soothes them; it's quite normal, and most babies do it. If your baby takes up this habit, don't interfere. If you allow your child the comfort of thumb or finger sucking, you'll both be much happier and less stressed. Most kids will naturally give up the habit by the time they are two anyway.

However, some children persist into their preschool years, which can result in improper teeth alignment and mouth problems as early as age five. In addition, your child may be teased by other children. If you are concerned, talk with your child's doctor and dentist about treatment. Your child's doctor will want to rule out possible emotional problems or other causes first and then engage your child's cooperation in breaking the habit (and at that point, she'll probably want to). You should start with kind reminders that make your child conscious of the habit. If the behavior persists, more aggressive treatments can make thumb sucking less pleasant for your child; the thumb can be coated with hot or bitter substances, for example, or wrapped in a bandage to serve as a reminder. You can also try a thumb guard that makes it impossible for your child to persist. In severe cases where teeth and palate are becoming misaligned, your child's dentist can install a palate guard that makes thumb sucking impossible.

Some doctors—and parents—find that these measures aren't effective either. They recommend giving children something to do with their hands while they break the habit, such as working Silly Putty. See what works for your child.

If you use guards or restraints, it's important that you explain to your child why you are subjecting her to things that may seem like torture. She should understand that they are to help avoid damage to her teeth and mouth and that you are helping her stop a behavior that you know is difficult for her to give up by herself.

Sexual Curiosity and Masturbation

When your child begins toilet training, expect him to become curious about his anatomy. Both boys and girls will naturally explore their bodies and the bodies' various openings. They may masturbate or even try to insert fingers or objects into their vaginas and anuses, and little boys may become fascinated by their occasional erections. Don't be surprised or upset with them—they are learning about themselves and new sensations. Don't try to inhibit their actions or make them feel dirty. Although you don't need to encourage this behavior, you should allow them to feel free to explore their bodies in private.

If a child starts to masturbate in public, it may be a sign that he is feeling overstimulated and stressed. Stop the behavior in a calm, gentle way and let him know that it's OK to do that in private but that other people don't want to see it. If the behavior persists or if your child spends a lot of time alone masturbating when there are other fun things to do, talk with your child's doctor about it. Your child may be feeling excessive stress for some reason or might have a medical problem like a urinary tract infection that needs treatment.

Anger and Aggression

Although aggressive behavior is quite normal, there's no doubt that it is also upsetting for you, other parents, and their children. The best approach is to draw the line quickly, pick up your child, calm him down, and explain that what he did hurt the other child. If you remove him from the fun every time he acts aggressively, he'll soon learn to "be nice."

If your child frequently goes into a rage and attacks others or if the behavior lasts for more than a few weeks, then call your child's doctor. If this kind of extremely aggressive behavior continues for more than three months, it should be viewed as a serious problem, and you should seek the help of an experienced mental health professional. It's not uncommon for this kind of extreme behavior to continue if it is not addressed. As your child grows, aggressive behavior can cause him to become an isolated, lonely child with serious self-esteem problems.

Biting

Almost all children bite at some point in their early years. Biting usually begins accidentally during the teething phase. A baby uses her mouth to get what she needs—comfort for her sore gums. Also, biting is normally one of the ways babies explore their environment. Some infants also may bite when they are excited or while playing. This, too, is part of normal development—what Sigmund Freud would describe as the "oral phase." Even though infant biting is not a concern, it's still a good idea to redirect the behavior early on. Instead of allowing your infant to bite you, give her a teething ring or soft toy to chew.

Biting to express anger or frustration may continue or escalate between the ages of two and three years, especially in the child-care setting. If another child bites your child, try to be understanding, but also find out what the child-care director is doing to make sure that it doesn't happen again. If your child is the one doing the biting, there's no need to overreact because this is normal behavior, but your child must learn that it is unacceptable. Here are some steps to help you curb biting:

- Establish the idea that all biting is forbidden. Whenever your child bites, even playfully, look her firmly in the eye and, in an unfriendly voice, say something like, "No biting," or "Stop biting. That hurts." Avoid lengthy explanations; extra attention may actually reinforce the behavior, making it more likely that your child will bite again.
- Never laugh when your child bites, even if it is done playfully. Avoid giving playful "love" bites to your child because she is unable to understand why these bites are OK but hers are not.
- Deal with biting as you would any other aggressive behavior. Quickly pull the biter away from the "bitee." After saying, "No biting," immediately give the child a brief time-out. If that does not work, take away a favorite toy or activity. Make sure the biting does not get rewarded. Do not punish biting with other aggressive behavior, such as hitting the child. Most important, don't bite the child back. This says that biting is OK if you are an adult.

KidsHealth Tip

Mental Health Help

Mental health problems affect one out of five American children, but two-thirds of these children never receive any help for their problem. The result can be school problems, substance abuse, and trouble in relationships with family and friends. Federal health experts have started a campaign called "Caring for Every Child's Mental Health." For more information, call the Center for Mental Health Services toll free at (800) 789-2647.

- Often biting continues because it allows a child to get what she wants. Offer your child alternative ways of making her desires known. If she wants the blocks another child has, tell her to point to them and ask for them nicely or to ask you to help her ask for them.

Dealing with Annoying Habits

For years, hair twirling, nose picking, nail biting, and thumb sucking have been termed "nervous" habits. A better term might be "comfort" habits because these repetitive actions may calm the child. When children are stressed, the behavior becomes so automatic that they are often unaware that they are doing it.

Although most habits seem fairly benign, they can cause social problems; other kids may tease a child about sucking her thumb or picking her nose, and she'll naturally feel embarrassed. Here's where you need to step in.

Help your child to become aware of her habit, the reasons behind it, and how others perceive it. The next time you see your child biting her nails or twirling her hair, try to recall if she has recently had a stressful experience. Your child may be trying to relieve her tension just as you would by working out at the gym.

Try these suggestions to help your child kick her habit:

- Explain what you don't like about the behavior and how others see it. This can be effective for a child as young as three years old.
- Ask your child what she thinks she could do instead of picking her nose or biting her nails, for example. If your child comes up with a solution, she's more likely to feel empowered to try it.
- Praise your child when you observe her engaging in behaviors other than the habit in times of stress or boredom.
- Be patient, and encourage your child to be patient. Just as the habit did not develop overnight, it won't disappear overnight. It may take several weeks or longer for the habit to disappear.

Most habits are harmless, but if your child's persists or is causing harm to your child, talk to your child's doctor.

- Make sure you do not display aggressive behavior toward your spouse, your children, or others. Your child may be picking up her aggressive behavior from you.
- Praise your child when she behaves well, such as asking for a toy instead of biting the child holding it.

Most biting occurs between the ages of 13 and 30 months. If the biting continues after age three, you may have a more serious situation that requires professional help. Discuss the behavior with your child's doctor.

Hyperactivity

All children have difficulty paying attention, following directions, or being quiet from time to time, but for the approximately 1 in 20 children with significant hyperactivity associated with attention deficit/hyperactivity disorder (AD/HD), this behavior can present major difficulties for the child and those around him.

Here are some strategies and tips that may help if your child has AD/HD or hyperactivity:

- Talk with your child's doctor about special parenting skills that may help you to deal with his behavior or about whether you should have your child evaluated for AD/HD.
- As your child's most important advocate, you should become familiar with his medical, legal, and educational rights. Federal laws mandate education interventions for many children with AD/HD.
- Establish a praise-and-reward system that will emphasize your child's strengths to help build his self-esteem.
- Modify the environment. Ask your child's teacher to limit open spaces in the classroom, which may encourage hyperactive behaviors.
- Provide very clear instructions.
- Help your child control impulses. Urge him to slow down when answering questions and doing tasks.
- Foster your child's self-esteem. Encourage performance in your child's areas of strength, and provide feedback to him in private. Do not ask your child to perform a task in public that is too difficult.
- Help your child organize. For example, when he goes to preschool, make a picture chart of all the things he needs to remember to bring with him each day.

For more information about AD/HD, see Chapter 32, "Health Problems in Early Childhood."

Need More Information?

Check the Index and Appendix C, "Resource Guide." And of course, consult your child's doctor.

chapter twenty

Toilet Teaching

A how-to guide for parents

Just like other parenting issues you've tackled in the past, teaching your child to use the toilet is a process that takes lots of patience, understanding, and love—and a little prep work. This chapter will help you through all the stages of toilet teaching (also called toilet training).

Get Ready!

Toilet teaching is easiest when your child is ready to take this step and to give you his cooperation. Starting before your child is ready is asking for trouble—and frequent toileting accidents. Wet and soiled underpants are usually the result of a child's inability to recognize the need to go or to regulate the muscles in charge—not a power struggle or sign of disobedience. Also, your child is likely to become frustrated if he's unable to perform as expected. At the least, by pushing your child into toilet teaching early, you're probably going to spend more time cleaning up puddles and doing laundry than you did changing diapers. And research shows that, regardless of when toilet teaching starts, most kids aren't fully bathroom-friendly until somewhere around age three and a half years, when they can independently wipe themselves clean after a bowel movement. So starting the toilet-teaching process earlier doesn't necessarily mean that you'll be finished earlier.

As tempting as it may be to rid yourself of the diaper-changing chore, the bottom line is, keep that bottom in diapers until your child is ready.

You'll know it's time when your child shows the following signs of readiness:

- Can follow simple directions
- Uses words to describe urine and bowel movements
- Can control the muscles that regulate the flow of urine and the elimination of bowel movements
- Is curious when other people use the toilet
- Can stay dry for at least two hours
- Can pull down and pull up underwear and pants
- Grabs the crotch area, grunts, or momentarily stops an activity immediately before urinating or having a bowel movement
- Knows what's going on when urinating and having a bowel movement
- Asks for a diaper change after urinating or having a bowel movement

When your child exhibits most or all of these signs, it's potty time! Most kids are ready around age 24 months—some may be ready a little earlier, some later.

Get Set!

When you decide to begin toilet teaching, pick a week when you and your child can stay close to home—a week that's free of doctor appointments, errands, and the like. The more time you can spend at home—and close to the bathroom—during the initial stages, the more likely it is that your child will have a successful bathroom experience instead of an accident on the road. You should also try not to schedule toilet teaching near other events that can complicate or add stress to your child's life, such as the switch from a crib to a big-kid bed, the move to a new home, or the birth of a sibling.

Once you've blocked out some time on the family calendar, keep that pen out—it's time to make a shopping list! When you head out to the store, consider picking up these items:

- Potty chairs (see Figure 20.1) or toddler-sized seats that fit over a regular toilet (Buy whichever style appeals to you, but be sure that your child's feet can either reach the floor or have a footstool to push against.)
- Big-kid underwear (Invest in just a few pairs now so that your toddler can pick out his own once some level of success has been achieved.)

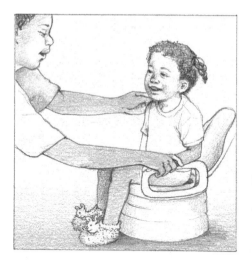

Figure 20.1. Potty chairs. Choose a potty chair that allows your child's feet to rest flat on the floor.

- Light switch extensions so that your child can turn on the bathroom lights without your help
- Nightlights for your child's solo trips down the hall at night
- Clothes with elastic waistbands so that your child will be able to undress quickly
- Books such as *Once Upon a Potty* (Alona Frankel, HarperCollins, 1999) or *What to Expect When You Use the Potty* (Heidi Murkoff, HarperCollins, 2000) to read with your child (There are a few good videos about toilet teaching also; try *It's Potty Time.*)

The toilet-teaching process usually runs more smoothly if you don't buy plastic training pants or "pull-ups." These mask wetness and make it hard for children to relate the feeling of needing to urinate with the resulting liquid that needs to be put in the toilet. If they don't feel wet and uncomfortable, why go to all the trouble of running to the bathroom?

Go!

You can introduce the idea of toileting to your child by letting her tag along into the bathroom and observe you and other family members in action. Talk about what's going on in language that your toddler can understand. It's best to use words that you and your child are comfortable with. Either *urine* or *pee*, *BM* or *poop* will do, as long as you both can say the words without embarrassment. But do avoid negative words such as *dirty diaper* that may cause your child to feel shame or disgust toward her body.

When your child has the idea of how toileting works, there are a few ways you can start your child on the road to toilet teaching:

- Let your child sit on the potty with his clothes on for a few weeks, just to get a feel for it.
- Have your child sit on the potty after waking up dry in the morning or after a nap—this can increase the odds of success.
- Remove your child's bowel movement from the diaper and show your child where it goes. Allow your child to flush the toilet if he's interested; otherwise, flush the toilet after your child has left the bathroom.
- Catch your child in the act: If you hear your child grunt or see him stop playing for a moment, suggest a trip to the bathroom. While there, talk to your child about making a connection between those cues and the need to go.
- Have an older sibling or friend demonstrate using the potty for your child. Seeing a peer in action can motivate some children to do the same.

Toileting should follow a consistent pattern. The words, timing, and attitudes you use should also be used by all your child's caregivers. That means babysitters, grandparents, child-care teachers, and whoever else might have an opportunity to help your child learn to use the potty should all be following the routine you've established. Let these people know how you're handling toilet teaching so as not to confuse your child.

KidsHealth Tip

Training the Toilet Timid

Kids in the midst of learning to use the potty may have accidents in unfamiliar surroundings because they are too shy to ask where the bathroom is. To help prevent accidents, always point out bathrooms in a new school, child-care center, or after-school program, and even in friends' and relatives' homes.

Tips for Success

- Start toilet teaching in the summer, if possible. Your child will wear fewer clothes in hotter weather and will be better able to undress quickly.
- Allow your child to have some diaper-free time. Being naked from the waist down can help your child make a connection between needing to urinate and the sensation of urine on his skin.
- If your child has an accident on the way to the bathroom, try not to show any disappointment you may feel. Instead, applaud your child's efforts for trying to get there on time and talk about ways to recognize his body's cues earlier.
- In the weeks before you start toilet teaching, keep a log with the times of day your child has a bowel movement. Most kids have regular bowel movements, and knowing your child's patterns can help you pick the best times of day to suggest a trip to the bathroom.
- Teach your child basic hygiene skills, such as how to wipe after using the toilet (girls should always wipe from front to back to avoid spreading fecal matter and germs to the urinary tract, where they could cause an infection) and how to wash hands with soap and water.
- Don't offer rewards such as food or toys for going to the bathroom. Although it's natural to want to praise your child (and you should verbally praise his attempts, regardless of outcomes), overly emphasizing his successes might make your child think that an accident would warrant punishment or disappoint you. Once your child has had somewhat regular success in the bathroom, allow him to pick out a few pairs of big-kid underwear as recognition.

KidsHealth Tip

Potty Pressures

A study published in the journal *Pediatrics* reported that most of the toilet-shy children in the study who were temporarily allowed to return to diapers had bathroom bowel movements within three months. If your toddler suffers from toilet terrors, a brief return to diapers might be the answer.

- Keep your comments positive and your tone of voice even. Don't show anger, ridicule, or disappointment when your child has an accident.
- Be prepared. Always have a spare pair of pants, underwear, socks, and shoes when away from home—just in case.

Be Patient

Toilet teaching is generally not a rapid process. How long toilet teaching takes depends on several factors, including whether your child is physically mature enough to control the muscles that regulate the release of urine and bowel movements, how interested your child is in moving beyond diapers, and your approach and attitude toward toilet teaching. Some parents try a crash-course style of toilet teaching, which means camping out at home for a few days and working intensively toward having their child learn to use the bathroom. Although this may work for some toddlers, most will need a few weeks or up to six months to really get the hang of it. Ultimately, most kids are out of diapers by age three or four years (nighttime dryness can take an additional six months or longer).

> ### The Voice of Experience
> ———— ✍ ————
> "Buy dark-colored sheets. I know it sounds silly, but when you have cleaned them for the hundredth time of vomit, pee, and other spilled items, you will thank me."
> —FROM THE KIDSHEALTH PARENT SURVEY

Common Problems

The road to independent toileting isn't always a smooth one. Along the way you may hit a few bumps—but nothing you can't get past with a patient and understanding attitude.

Accidents

Accidents will happen, no matter how ready your child is to learn how to use the toilet. So be prepared for them, and don't show your own feelings of disappointment when they happen—this can cause further accidents or setbacks, and it can also make him feel guilty for letting you down. Remember: In most cases, accidents are the result of immature muscles and poor timing.

Diarrhea

Reassure your child that it's OK to put toilet teaching on hold for a while, and allow her to use diapers for a few days if she prefers. Diarrhea in a child can be caused by infections, certain food sensitivities, and excessive intake of fruit juice. Call your child's doctor if the diarrhea persists for more than a few days, if your child has other symptoms of illness, or if there's blood in the stool.

Constipation

Some children have bowel movements each day, whereas others have them every few days without difficulty. But hard, painful bowel movements can interfere with your child's learning to use the potty. The child would rather "hold it in" to avoid pain, which creates a cycle of constipation that worsens over time.

Changing eating habits is the best way to prevent hard stools. Include fiber-rich foods in your child's daily diet, especially vegetables (broccoli, spinach, peas, or beans) and bran (in cereal, breads, or cookies). Also, make sure your child is drinking enough fluids, especially during warm weather, and eating water- and fiber-rich fruits (citrus, peaches, melons, apricots, prunes, plums, raisins, or pears) daily. Limit more constipating foods such as rice, pasta, bananas, non–whole grain bread, and other carbohydrate-rich foods low in fiber. Explain to your child that these changes in his diet will make it easier for him to use the potty.

It's also a good idea to help your child establish a regular bowel routine. Encourage him to sit on the toilet after breakfast (the meal often triggers the urge to have a bowel movement). Praise him if he has a bowel movement. If he doesn't after sitting for 15 minutes, he can get up from the potty, but be sure to commend him for his effort anyway.

If your child's bowel movements do not improve after changing his diet and establishing a regular toilet routine, or if he has abdominal pain or increasing fear of using the potty, he is probably withholding stool and may need other treatment for constipation to allow him to develop more regular bowel habits. For severe constipation, your child's doctor may initially recommend enemas or suppositories to make sure that any large masses of obstructing, hard stool are cleared from your child's bowel. Once this has been accomplished, a routine of daily stool softeners or laxatives is usually prescribed to prevent your child from having painful bowel movements and withholding stool again. Your child may need to stay on this regimen for weeks to months, in addition to maintaining a high-fiber diet and a regular toileting routine, in order to establish a pattern of regular and pain-free bowel movements.

Soiling (Encopresis)

If your child feels pressure to learn to use the potty and isn't ready yet, soiling (also called encopresis) may result. Soiling means involuntarily passing bowel movement into the diaper or underpants. If this happens, assure your child that it's not his fault, and back off toilet teaching for a while. Soiling is frequently a symptom of chronic constipation (see the section on constipation earlier in this chapter), with uncontrollable leakage of looser stool occurring around a large mass of hard stool that has collected in your child's lower intestine. If soiling persists, consult your child's doctor.

Bedwetting (Nocturnal Enuresis) and Daytime Wetting (Incontinence)

Even after daytime toileting is mastered, it often takes six months or longer for children to be able to stay dry through the night. Bedwetting (nocturnal enuresis) in a toddler usually isn't a cause for concern. Nighttime wetting is best handled by letting him wear diapers until he begins to wake up dry with some regularity.

For unknown reasons, boys are more likely to continue to wet the bed than girls are. About 10 to 15 percent of five-year-olds with no medical problems still wet the bed several times a week, and a small number may not stop until early adolescence. Most children outgrow bedwetting with time and patience. Different theories exist about why children wet the bed. In some cases, it may be due to an immature arousal mechanism that does not signal the child to wake up in time to get to the bathroom. Bedwetting is not intentional and is not your child's fault. Punishing your child for wetting the bed won't solve the problem and will only upset your child.

> ### The Voice of Experience
>
> *"When your child is 'potty-training,' let him or her stay undressed for the first couple of days. It makes trips to the bathroom quicker and less frustrating for children if they do not have to try to undress at the last minute. And let boys sit backwards on the toilet at first—they won't have as many spills onto the floor."*
>
> —FROM THE KidsHealth PARENT SURVEY

If your child is dry during the day but has never been dry for more than a few nights in a row, don't worry—your child will probably become dry soon. However, if your child has previously been dry at night and starts to wet again, it could be due to stress or a medical problem such as a urinary tract infection or diabetes.

Occasional daytime wetting accidents (incontinence) are also fairly common in children of early school age, but if a child is unable to hold his urine both day and night, he probably has a problem with his urinary tract. Speak with your child's doctor if your previously dry child begins to wet the bed again or has day- and nighttime incontinence.

If bedwetting persists in your child beyond the age of five and it is causing a problem for your child or family, consult your child's doctor about treatment options. Bedwetting alarm devices that awaken the child as he begins to pee eliminate the problem in most children. Medications can also be helpful in some cases; however, these drugs may have side effects, and bedwetting may resume when the medication is stopped.

Need More Information?

Check the Index and Appendix C, "Resource Guide." And of course, consult your child's doctor.

chapter twenty-one

Sleep

Patterns, problems, and needs

"Sleep—or lack of it—is probably the most-discussed aspect of baby care. New parents discover its importance those first few weeks, when babies routinely wake and sleep round-the-clock. But long after a child can tell day from night, the quality and quantity of the little one's sleep can make the difference between a cheerful, alert family and a cranky clan of the walking dead.

In this chapter, we'll look at how to help your child get the sleep he needs, how to avoid problems, and how to deal with problems if they arise.

Getting to Sleep and Staying Asleep

Many kids are tough to get to sleep, and they wake several times during the night. This is not a plot to rob you of your senses; it's just that children and adults have different sleep patterns, needs, and feelings about sleep.

Why Babies Wake Up So Much

Adult sleep is divided into REM (rapid eye movement) and non-REM sleep. REM sleep is the stage of dreaming. Non-REM sleep is deeper and more refreshing. Adults cycle between the two kinds of sleep every 90 minutes or so, with 20 to 25 percent of their sleep spent in REM periods.

Infants also have REM and non-REM sleep (usually called "active sleep" and "quiet sleep" in babies). But compared to adults, babies spend a greater proportion of their sleep time in REM sleep—anywhere from 50 percent for full-term newborns to 80 percent for premature newborns. In fact, some researchers think that REM sleep may play its most important role before the baby is born, perhaps helping the visual centers of the brain develop in the last two or three months of gestation.

Most important (from many parents' point of view) is that babies and young children cycle between REM and non-REM sleep more frequently than adults—about every hour. These transitions are the times children are more likely to wake up—to call for you or climb into your bed. By contrast, when children are aroused in the middle of non-REM sleep, they usually just move or whimper and fall back to sleep. So more periods of REM sleep mean more chances for them to wake up in the middle of the night.

A Note on Premature Babies

In general, you can expect premature newborns to wake more frequently, sleep more lightly, and take longer to hit sleep milestones. When we discuss patterns of sleep typical at certain ages, we're counting from the baby's due date. If your baby was born a month early, chances are he will develop those sleep patterns at least a month later than the ages listed in this chapter.

Waking and Feeding

Babies generally don't need nighttime feedings by the middle of their first year (as early as two to three months for some bottle-fed babies). Check with your baby's doctor if you're not sure of your baby's needs. Some breast-feeding mothers prefer to nurse on demand at night. If you don't, you can gradually reduce the number of minutes at each night feeding until you're down to two minutes. Then stop the feedings, offering a back rub and soft words instead. (Once feedings stop, let Dad do all the middle-of-the-night comforting, at least for a while, because the baby expects milk from Mom.) If the baby has been taking a bottle at night, you can gradually reduce the amount of formula or gradually water it down until your baby is getting a bottle of plain water. Most babies find that it's not worth waking up just for water. (A reminder: You should not water down formula except as a temporary measure to stop a nighttime feeding that your baby no longer needs. Your baby should still be getting regular full-strength formula at all other feedings.)

As a rule of thumb, if a baby is two to three months old, is eating well during the day, and weighs at least 12 pounds, she no longer needs nighttime feedings for nutrition. But if your baby is younger than four months, don't begin this night-time weaning without first talking to your baby's doctor.

Hold the Cereal

Parents sometimes are told—often by older relatives—that adding cereal to a bottle of formula or breast milk will help their baby sleep through the night. Studies have not found this to be true. So if cereal "worked" for your mother or your friend, chances are it was a coincidence. Most likely the baby happened to mature enough to sleep through the night around the same time that the parents decided to try solids. Doctors generally advise against adding solids to a bottle for several reasons:

- Sucking this thickened mixture out of a bottle can be difficult and cause babies to swallow more air.
- If an infant does eat cereal with ease, the baby may take in more calories than needed and gain too much weight.
- Breast milk and formula are nutritionally superior to cereal, so you wouldn't want either of them to be replaced by cereal.
- Feeding anything other than breast milk or formula to an infant who is younger than four months may increase the likelihood of the child developing allergies.

If your baby is four to six months old and you suspect she is not getting enough calories from liquid feedings, you can try feeding her some rice cereal with a spoon, not a bottle, as described in Chapter 22, "Healthy Eating." But don't expect cereal to change her sleeping pattern.

Helping Your Baby Go Back to Sleep

Everyone—both children and adults—wakes in the night even if they don't remember it later. You can reduce the number of times your child wakes, however, by making sure that he's comfortable—not too hot or cold, not subjected to bright lights or loud sudden noises, not sick or in pain, not wet or hungry.

But even if nothing is wrong, babies and young children will wake. Many will go back to sleep on their own without any help. For the rest, you must decide whether to keep responding to every cry or help the baby learn to go back to sleep on his own once he is about six months or older. This can involve some crying, but it usually doesn't take long for a baby to learn that he doesn't need your help to fall asleep.

Starting around six months, most babies can learn to calm themselves and go back to sleep when they wake in the middle of the night. You can help if you try the following:

- From an early age, put your baby down to sleep when she is awake, at least some of the time, so she can learn to go to sleep on her own and to associate her crib or bed with going to sleep. Then if she wakes in the night, she may be more likely to go back to sleep on her own. If you always nurse her to sleep, she is likely to need nursing to fall back to sleep in the middle of the night, even when she no longer needs night feedings for nutrition.

- After your good-night ritual, give your baby one last pat or kiss and leave the room. If your baby cries—or if she awakens and cries during the night—give her a few minutes to settle down on her own and go to sleep. You might want to start with two or three minutes. If she's still crying, check to make sure there's no problem. If she seems sick, of course, pick her up and comfort her. If it's the middle of the night and she's soaking wet, change her with as little ado as possible, preferably without taking her from the crib. If she's dry, comfort her without picking her up (talk softly, rub her back), then leave. Keep the lights low and your contact warm but brief. Don't play with her or make your visit so entertaining that she'll hanker for more. If she continues to cry, wait a little longer than before, then repeat the short cribside visit. Keep doing this, lengthening the time you wait to respond up to 10 minutes, until she stops crying. Each time you go in, try to do less. Time yourself with a clock because 5 minutes can seem like an eternity when a baby is crying. After several days, your baby should find it easier to get back to sleep on her own.

- If you're dealing with a toddler or preschooler who is fearful at night, try this: First, sit by your child's bed for a couple of nights until she falls asleep (or back to sleep). Then gradually sit farther and farther away each night until you are out the door. For a few nights, sit outside her room until she is asleep. If she calls, you can stick your head in the door and reassure her verbally. Depending on how fearful your child is, this process may take anywhere from a couple of days to a few weeks.

The alternative to teaching your child how to fall asleep by himself is to continue nursing, rocking, walking, or sitting by his side until he falls asleep. Although this may sound like a more warm, nurturing response, it can be counterproductive if you get so sleep-deprived and resentful that you're irritable and exhausted during the day. Besides, many doctors think that learning to calm himself can be a step in a child's long path to independence, fostering a sense of competence and self-confidence. As long as it occurs in the context of a close, loving relationship, it is worlds away from being abandoned, and there is no evidence that it causes emotional damage.

Either approach—responding to every cry or letting a child learn to soothe himself—is better than random inconsistency. If you usually respond to your child's calls but don't on some nights because you just feel too tired or resentful, or usually don't respond but occasionally give in, your child's world may seem capricious and untrustworthy. Pick a plan and stick to it.

Establishing Good Sleeping Patterns

We all have a biological clock that governs our sleep-wake cycles, making us sleepy at certain times and wakeful at others. Our sleep-wake clock is "set" by darkness and light, especially exposure to bright morning light. In infants, the sleep-wake clock usually develops by three months—before that time they may wake and sleep round-the-clock without regard to daylight.

You can help your baby set her internal clock to better match your own simply by putting her to bed at night and waking her in the morning at the same time every day. A consistent waking time seems to be especially important to setting this clock. This is how good sleep patterns begin.

Bedtime Rituals

As your baby grows, a bedtime ritual will help you get him into bed at the same time every night. Predictable and soothing for both baby and parent, a bedtime ritual tells your child that it's time to sleep.

A bedtime ritual consists of anything you'd like to do as you put your child to bed for the night. Parents often include things such as bathing or washing, putting on pajamas, brushing teeth, singing, rocking, feeding, reading, playing soft music, and telling a story. You might want to include prayer, massage, or relaxation techniques. You might talk about what your child did today and what is planned for tomorrow. Sometimes a consistent exit line from you—something as simple as "Sweet dreams" or "I love you"—can be a comfort, along with a promise to check on your child in 10 minutes. (Be sure you keep the promise.)

Parents should take turns putting their child to bed or share the ritual. If one parent always does it, the child may find it hard to sleep if that parent is absent. Besides, bedtime is often when children are most affectionate and more likely to share feelings, fears, and questions—an intimacy no parent should miss.

Sleep Without Tears

In studies of toddlers and preschoolers, typically 30 to 40 percent or more either resisted going to sleep, woke at night, or both. Here are some techniques parents can use to (usually) help children sleep without tears:

- Wind down to sleep with calm, quiet activities in the hour or two before bedtime. Avoid roughhousing and anything that's scary or loud. Give your child a few minutes' warning before bedtime.
- Prepare for sleep with a regular ritual of pleasurable activities, such as singing, rocking, or reading a story.
- Make sure your child's sleeping environment is safe and pleasant. Do not use time in the crib or bed as a punishment.
- Be as consistent as possible about when your child goes to bed and wakes (once your baby is sleeping mostly at night, usually by three months). This reduces nightly squabbles over when it's time for bed.
- Be persistent. If your toddler is getting out of bed to check out the family's late-evening activities, you will have to get up and put her back in however

many times it takes until she learns you mean it. That may mean 20 times in a night. If you give in on the 19th try, you'll just be teaching her how long it takes to wear you down.

• When in doubt, try more sleep. It's hard for children to fall asleep if they're overtired. A slightly earlier bedtime may help (and make your child less irritable during the day).

Six Ways in Which Sleep Is a Classic Child-Raising Issue

1. People (including grandparents, friends, and doctors) tend to have strong opinions that they don't hesitate to offer.

2. These strong opinions often are completely contradictory. For instance, in our surveys of parents, many reported that the best advice they ever received was "don't let your baby sleep in your bed." Many others said the best advice they ever got was—you guessed it—"sleep with your child." (See Where Should Your Baby Sleep? in this chapter for the full scoop.)

3. Only you can decide what is right for you, your family, and your baby. One family may decide it's fine for the baby to stay up late to play with a parent after work each evening. Another may decide the baby does better going to bed at 7:00 P.M. without fail. If you're all happy, healthy, and (reasonably) well rested, whatever you're doing is working. If not, try something else.

4. As your child grows, what works is likely to change. Just when you thought you had sleep aced, your child will start waking again or having nightmares, and you'll want to try a different approach.

5. Just as no standard growth chart can tell you how much your child should weigh, no list of average sleep times can tell you how much your child should sleep. These numbers are simply averages reported for groups of children.

6. There's no substitute for knowing your child. Is that a cry of distress, or is she just letting off steam? Is she running around because she's full of energy or because she's overtired? You'll have to make these kinds of judgments all the time.

Where Should Your Baby Sleep?

Babies should sleep in a safe place where parents can hear them (if necessary, with a baby monitor). The safest bed seems to be a well-maintained crib that meets federal safety standards (as described in Chapter 2, "Preparing Your Home and Family"). One study found that babies who slept in their parents' room, but not in their parents' bed, had a reduced risk of SIDS. During the first three or four months especially, when babies wake frequently and seem especially fragile, many parents like to have them sleep next to the parents' bed, usually in a crib, bassinet, or cradle.

Whether you'll share your room with your baby is largely a matter of personal preference. Studies indicate that babies and mothers who sleep in the same room are aroused from sleep more often, so their sleep is broken. If babies are breast-feeding, they have more frequent and larger night feedings until a later age.

As your baby grows, you may want to let her share a room with another child or move her to a room of her own. Your decision will depend on practical questions and the space in your home. Unless you are planning to continue sharing your room with the baby, it's usually easier to move her to her permanent room if you do it during the first six to nine months. After that, separation anxiety may make it harder for your baby to sleep alone until she is about two years old.

The Family Bed Debate

In the United States, it is common for older babies and children to sleep separate from their parents. Most U.S. child-care experts say this promotes better sleep for parents and children, builds independence and a sense of confidence for children, makes intimacy easier for parents, and, in the preschool years, avoids heightening the normal Oedipal conflicts (the conflicts that children feel over their love for the parent of the opposite sex and their rivalry with the parent of the same sex).

Others argue that it is natural for parents and children to sleep together, as people in many parts of the world do. Even in the United States, these advocates note, surveys show more than a third of parents often share a bed with a child, and far higher numbers do it occasionally. Advocates say that with infants, bed sharing or "the family bed," as it is sometimes called, can promote breast-feeding, bonding, and a sense of security among children.

Bed-Sharing Safety

When infants sleep in an adult bed, there is a small but apparently real danger of suffocation. (The risk increases if the sleeping is done on a water bed, daybed, or sofa; these should never be used with an infant.) Because of the risk, the AAP discourages routine bed sharing, and the Consumer Product Safety Commission says flatly that children younger than age two should not sleep in an adult bed.

The commission's position is based on a study that showed 64 deaths a year associated with bed sharing, compared to 50 deaths a year attributed to cribs—mostly old, substandard cribs. (Because we don't know how many babies sleep in each setting, we can't be sure how the risks compare. But because fewer babies are believed to share beds than sleep in cribs, bed sharing probably increases the risk more than these figures might suggest.)

The main risks of bed sharing were that the baby would get caught between the bed frame and the wall, furniture, or mattress. "Overlying," in which the parent accidentally smothers the baby, also occurred but was more rare. Almost all the deaths occurred in babies younger than 12 months. So if you do want to share a bed with your child, waiting until he's one year old can virtually eliminate the risk.

Advocates of bed sharing say the study did not take into account whether the adults drank, smoked, or had other characteristics known to raise the risks of bed sharing.

For those in the middle of the debate, an alternative is a side-sleeper or co-sleeper; this is a three-sided crib that attaches to an adult bed on its open side. If installed safely, this puts your baby within easy reach for breast-feeding but gives him space of his own that can be kept free of blankets, pillows, and the heavy bodies of adults.

Family Bed Safety Tips

If you do want to share your bed with your baby, follow these tips:

- Make sure the adult mattress is firm and tight fitting, with no gap between the frame and the mattress that could trap your child. The bed must have no loose bedding, soft surfaces, or decorative features that could trap your baby. The bed should be moved away from the wall or furniture so your baby cannot get trapped between the bed and those objects.
- Don't drink alcohol or take any drug or medication that might make you less alert or harder to wake. For the same reason, you should not share a bed with your baby if you are overtired. If you want to have a couple of drinks or were up late the night before, don't sleep with your baby that night.
- Don't smoke. In studies of babies who slept with their mothers, the risk of SIDS was much higher if the mother smoked.
- Older children or adults other than a baby's parents, should not share a bed with an infant.

"Back to Sleep" to Reduce the Risk of SIDS

By definition, sudden infant death syndrome (SIDS) is the sudden death of an infant under one year old that is unexplained even after a thorough investigation. Most cases occur in babies age two to four months; very few occur after age six months.

The good news is that SIDS is relatively rare, striking about 1 in 1,400 infants, and getting rarer. Rates declined almost 50 percent from 1988 to 1998 (the most recent year for which we have data). Most of the improvement came since 1992, when the AAP began to recommend that healthy babies be put to sleep on their backs.

Why should that make such a difference? Some speculate that when babies sleep on their stomachs the air they exhale may get trapped in folds of bedding. The babies then may rebreathe this air, which is high in carbon dioxide. Rising levels of carbon dioxide should wake a baby, so she can move her head to get fresh air. But some babies fail to wake, the theory goes, perhaps because their brain function is immature or abnormal.

The AAP and other authorities suggest the following to reduce the risk of SIDS:

- Healthy newborns, including most premature newborns, should be put to sleep on their backs (see Figures 21.1a–b). This greatly lowers the risk of SIDS. Sleeping on the side is safer than sleeping on the stomach, but it is not as safe as the back because your baby may roll onto his stomach.
- Make sure that caregivers, including grandparents, babysitters, and child-care workers, understand that your baby should sleep on his back.
- If your baby usually sleeps on his back but then is placed on his stomach to sleep or rolls onto it, he may be at particularly high risk for SIDS.
- When babies are awake, they should spend time on their stomachs so they can work on controlling their heads, pushing themselves up, and other feats of

The Mystery of SIDS

Researchers have identified other factors, besides stomach sleeping, that seem to increase the risk of SIDS. These include sleeping on a soft surface, overheating, mother's smoking during pregnancy, exposure to smoke after birth, late or no prenatal care, premature birth or low birthweight, and male sex of the baby.

infant strength and coordination. This waking "tummy time" also may help prevent flat spots from developing on the back of your baby's head. (Another way to prevent flattening is to make sure your infant's head is in different positions when he lies in the crib. If your baby usually turns his head to the right to see the doorway or a mobile, change his orientation so he has to look left to see it. Or move the mobile.)

- If your baby can roll from his back to his stomach but can't roll back, you should roll him back. Once he can roll from his stomach to his back, he can sleep in whatever position he assumes after you put him down on his back.
- The recommendation that babies sleep on their backs may not apply to some babies who have certain medical conditions. Your child's doctor can advise you on which position is best for your baby.

Safer Sleeping Quarters

Plan ahead to make your baby's sleeping environment as safe as possible.

- Make sure your baby sleeps on a firm mattress, never on a pillow, water bed, daybed, couch, sheepskin, comforter, or other soft surface.
- Make sure your baby's crib meets federal safety standards (see Chapter 2, "Preparing Your Home and Family"), is well maintained, and has a tight-fitting mattress. A toddler or adult bed may not be as safe.

Figure 21.1a **Figure 21.1b**

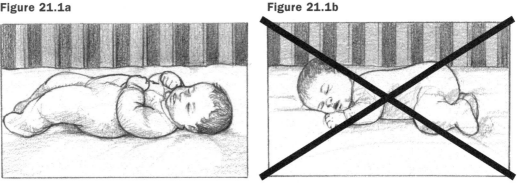

Figures 21.1a–b. Sleeping positions: (a) on back, (b) on belly. Unless a doctor instructs otherwise, babies should always be put to sleep on their back, as illustrated here. Belly sleeping and side sleeping are associated with a higher risk of sudden infant death syndrome (SIDS).

- Do not put fluffy blankets, comforters, stuffed toys, or pillows in your baby's crib or other sleeping place. If you use a blanket, tuck it in firmly so it can reach only to your infant's chest; that way there is less risk of covering the face. The AAP suggests placing your baby with her feet at the foot of the crib, then tucking the blanket in at the foot and sides of the crib. Or use a footed sleeper with no blanket at all.
- Make sure your baby does not get too warm while sleeping. Keep the room at a temperature that feels comfortable for an adult in a short-sleeve shirt. Clothe your baby lightly. She should not feel hot to the touch.

Safety Tips When You're Seriously Sleepy

Despite all the kidding, long-term sleep deprivation for parents or other caretakers can be dangerous, leading to accidents, marital tension, and even child abuse.

Depending on your circumstances, you may need someone to watch the baby so you can nap occasionally, or you may need to take a few vacation days from work. If your child has a persistent sleep problem, you may need professional advice on dealing with it.

Meanwhile, take care:

- Don't drive at times when you're sleepy, such as late afternoon.
- If you're dozing off with your newborn in your lap, put your baby down in a safe place so there's no chance she'll fall.
- Don't nap with a baby on a couch. There's a risk the baby could get trapped between your body and the sofa cushions or back and suffocate.
- Don't sleep with your baby at all if you're overtired.

Especially in those first few weeks, remember the number-one rule of parent preservation: Sleep when the baby sleeps.

Sleep Patterns Through the Ages

Sleep patterns change as children grow.

The First Three Months

Newborns generally sleep or drowse for sixteen or more hours a day, divided about equally between night and day. Their longest sleep period is generally four or five

Head Shape and "Tummy Time"

The campaign to make sure babies sleep on their backs has lowered the rate of sudden infant death syndrome (SIDS) since 1992. But several research studies since then have shown an increase in the number of infants referred to specialists for a condition called positional plagiocephaly, or flattening of the back of the skull, apparently resulting from infants spending more time lying on their backs. These infants may also develop asymmetrical facial features including flattening of one side of the forehead, lowering of one eyebrow, and changes in positioning of one ear.

These changes will disappear in most (about three-fourths) of these babies by one to two years of age with no other treatment than rotating the infant's head position frequently. It may be helpful to alternate an infant's head position in the crib (from one end to the other) in case a window scene or other distraction encourages the infant to turn in one direction. In about one of five infants with the condition, the use of a helmet or other device for a few months is recommended to treat the head deformity. Surgery is rarely required. In some cases, physical therapy exercises involving the neck muscles may be recommended. Speak with your child's doctor if you have any concerns about this issue.

As noted earlier, you should also make sure that your young infant gets plenty of chance to be in the prone (belly-down) position while awake. In addition to changing head position, "tummy time" is important for fostering an infant's development of head control and upper-body strength and coordination.

hours, but some may sleep no more than two hours at a time, and others may occasionally sleep for ten hours straight. (In the beginning, it's recommended that you wake the baby for feeding after four or five hours if he's still sleeping.) There is no sleep formula for newborns because the complex processes that control sleep aren't fully developed.

Some newborns are awake only while eating, then begin to have stretches of quiet alertness, often starting in the late afternoon. Others have alert periods before or after feeding right from the start, when you can talk or gently play with them. During the first three months, babies may get tired and fussy if they stay awake more than two hours at a stretch.

You can emphasize the differences between night and day by keeping your baby's sleeping room dark at night and doing the necessary feeding and changing in a quick, quiet way. During the day, let the sunshine in, let the noise and bustle level stay higher, and play and talk with your baby whenever she is awake. Unless your newborn is particularly sensitive to noise, it pays to keep daytime noise levels normal even when the baby is napping. That way she'll get used to snoozing through ringing phones and normal conversation.

By six weeks, babies tend to be sleeping longest in the evening, usually for three to five hours, and this trend becomes stronger as the months pass. If you feed her at 10:00 or 11:00 P.M., you may even be able to sleep until dawn. At about three months, most bottle-fed babies no longer need feedings at night, even if they may enjoy them. Breast-fed babies usually reach that point a little later, perhaps at five or six months.

> ## I Wish Someone Had Told Me . . .
> —❧—
> "... to try to make naptime a fun time. I made the mistake of using it a few times as a punishment. **Bad move. He has never forgotten that.**"

Newborns commonly fall asleep while they are feeding, especially at the breast, a sweetly peaceful transition. Or you may want to rock, cuddle, or sing to your baby as he is settling down, putting him down to sleep when he is drowsy but still awake. For the first months of your baby's life, "spoiling" is not a possibility. In fact, studies have shown that babies who are carried around during the day have less fussiness.

If your baby seems overly irritable and cannot be soothed, or is difficult to rouse from sleep and seems uninterested in feeding, speak to your child's doctor. Chances are everything is fine, but it's worth getting medical guidance.

Four to Seven Months

Some babies develop regular sleep/wake patterns as early as six or eight weeks, but usually these patterns emerge around three or four months. At that age, most babies average three to five hours of sleep during the day, usually grouped into two or three naps, and ten to twelve hours at night, usually with an interruption or two for feeding. Most babies at this age are said to sleep through the night, but often that is defined as sleeping five hours in a row, from midnight to 5:00 A.M.

At this age, babies are far more involved and interested in the world than before and may stay awake to the point of being cranky and overtired. Watch your baby closely for moments when she is drowsy, before crankiness sets in. Then try soothing her with rocking or quiet music and putting her down for a nap. Motion—rocking, strolling, riding in a car—will often put babies to sleep, but once they're out, stationary sleep may be more restful.

If you feel your baby's afternoon nap is making it hard for him to sleep at night, you can try moving the nap a bit earlier: Wake him a little earlier each morning, then start putting him down for his nap a little earlier, too. After he wakes from the nap, keep him stimulated until bedtime.

During these months, your baby will learn to roll over and position himself for sleep in his own way. Toward the end of this period, he may be able to keep himself awake or be kept awake by his surroundings, so this is the time to instill good sleep habits by sticking to a bedtime routine. Putting him in his crib when he is awake, at least some of the time, can help him learn to go to sleep on his own.

When your baby is six months old you can begin to change your response when she awakens and cries during the night. Instead of responding right away, you can wait a few minutes, and then a few minutes more.

If your six-month-old baby continues to wake up five or six times each night, talk to her doctor about it.

Eight to Twelve Months

At this age, babies average 13 hours of sleep, including two naps a day, but the range of "normal" is still quite wide.

By now most babies have no need to be fed at night, and many, especially bottle-fed babies, can sleep seven or eight hours at a stretch. But as your baby develops

A Breathless Pause

During the first few months of life, a baby's breathing may be somewhat irregular. Babies also commonly stop breathing for a few seconds. This phenomenon, called periodic breathing, is normal and usually harmless, but it can be terrifying to a parent who doesn't expect it. It is most common during REM or "active" sleep and is usually outgrown by six months. But if your baby's breathing pauses for more than 15 seconds before resuming or if his skin looks bluish or darker than usual, call your child's doctor immediately.

emotionally, some new sleep problems may crop up as she becomes more aware of her separateness from you. Separation anxiety may mean tears and tantrums when you try to leave her in her crib—and more later at night when she wakes up and looks around for some sign that you are near.

It can be difficult to respond to your child's nighttime needs with the right balance of concern and consistency, but this is the time to set the stage for future restful nights for the whole family. In many cases, you can handle the moment of separation the same way you do when separation anxiety is an issue during the day (for example, if you leave your baby with a babysitter). Follow your usual bedtime routine with an extra hug and kiss, let her know that you will see her soon, and make a quick exit. Don't delay bedtime in hope that she'll conk out; an overtired baby may find it even harder to fall asleep. In fact, if she's waking frequently during the night, you might try a slightly earlier bedtime.

At this age, make sure your baby has some favorite toys in the crib to keep her company. A beloved comfort object—a stuffed animal, a scrap of blanket, or other "lovey"—can help. Playing a tape of Mom and Dad singing lullabies may help settle her. Some parents even leave an article of their clothing in the crib so their scent stays with the baby. (Whatever toys you leave, keep safety in mind: Make sure stuffed animals are too small to smother in and that toys contain nothing she could choke on or get tangled in.)

> ## The Worst Advice I Got Was . . .
>
> "... that all babies are supposed to sleep through the night by a certain age. I spent way too many frustrating nights trying to get my daughter to sleep. Later I learned that breastfed babies often don't sleep through the night until later."

Try leaving her door open so she can hear your activity nearby. If she keeps crying and calling for you, a few words of reassurance from the bedroom door ("Mommy's right here, but it's time for you to go to sleep now") and another quick exit may do the trick. Try to lengthen the time between these personal appearances until your baby is asleep.

When your baby wakes up in the night and cries for you, reassure her quietly that you are there, but then give her the message that she needs to go back to sleep. The best bet may be a soothing pat on the back, a repositioning of the blanket, and another quick exit. If your visits are too interesting, she'll call for more of them. But if you are friendly, firm, and consistent about requiring your baby to put herself back to sleep, this stage should pass quickly.

Playing peekaboo games during the day may help her calm her fear of separation as well. Hiding and then revealing your face or a toy helps your baby learn that you—and other things in her world—still exist even when she can't see them.

Of course, if your baby keeps demanding your presence at night, you'll want to make sure she's not ill or sitting in a soiled diaper. If you need to change her, remember to keep the lights down and to keep interaction to a minimum.

Working to master big new skills, such as standing up or walking, can engage babies so much that they wake more frequently. If your baby can stand up in his crib but doesn't know how to get down again, he'll scream for help. You can help by showing him how to get down and helping him practice, but do it during the day, not in the middle of the night.

Sometimes parents grab for the quick fix to incessant crying in the middle of the night. They may camp out on the floor of the baby's room or take her into their bed so everyone can get some sleep. Almost every parent has done this at some time. But be cautious about doing it frequently unless you are open to making it your usual way of sleeping for weeks to come.

One to Three Years

Of course your toddler doesn't want to sleep. While Mom, Dad, and possibly older siblings are still up and active, the world is an exciting place of endless discovery. In addition, he may still be feeling separation anxiety. And as he learns to walk and run, he also is struggling for more independence. That leads to the famed toddler contrariness—the "No!" period—which can make bedtime a drag (sometimes literally). And as your toddler becomes more aware of his world, outside stimuli may disturb him more at night, and dreams and nightmares may begin to interrupt his sleep as well.

Although there's a wide range of normal, one-year-olds typically need around thirteen hours sleep, with two naps a day. Most two-year-olds nap only once a day, usually for one to three hours in the afternoon. By the time they turn three, children typically are sleeping ten to twelve hours, with a short and sporadic afternoon nap. If they don't nap, most seem to benefit from a rest in the crib or bed or a quiet period of reading after lunch. If your child seems to need an afternoon nap but finds it hard to fall asleep at night, it may help to move the nap earlier so it ends by 2:00 or 2:30 P.M. Then as naps fall away, you may need to try an earlier bedtime to have a well-rested child.

When sleep patterns start to change, it may take several weeks of experimenting to get the right mix of rest and sleep. Note the time in the evening when your toddler begins to show the first signs of sleepiness, and try making this his regular bedtime.

Dealing with Crib Climbing

Your toddler may be looking for ways to hoist herself over her crib railing. Don't leave toys in the crib that she can use as stairs to climb on. If you haven't taken off those bumper pads, do it now before she uses them to launch herself over the side.

If you have an active climber who is determined to scale the high crib rails, you might want to move her to a lower bed to prevent long falls. Or, as an intermediate step, take the crib railing off or put the mattress on the floor. If you worry that your baby may roam the house at night, act to prevent possible injury. Options include putting a child gate across the doorway of her room, closing her door and hanging a bell on it, or getting an inexpensive alarm that sounds when the door moves. (These alarms are often sold to travelers for use in hotel rooms.)

Moving to a Bed

You can move your child to a bed whenever she seems ready, usually before age three and a half. Many children move calmly or joyously to a bed; others miss their crib. To prevent too much nostalgia, you might make a big event of getting the "big-girl" or "big-boy" bed. Let your child help pick out special sheets and maybe have a special celebration. In the beginning, you might want to use guardrails. Make sure there are no sharp edges nearby that the child could hit if she fell out of bed. If the floor by the bed is bare, you may want to cushion it with pillows or a comforter. (Bunk beds are not recommended at this age for safety reasons.)

Three to Five Years

Three- to five-year-olds typically sleep 10 to 12 hours a night. By age four, about half have stopped routine napping, and the rest give it up by age six.

It's common for preschoolers to resist going to sleep and to seek company at night—but it's best for their overall health if you teach them to stay put and sleep during the night. Consistently insist on a regular bedtime, and return your child to the bed without fail every time he "escapes." If nighttime wandering is a problem, you can offer reward incentives to keep your child in bed. For instance, together you can make a sleep calendar and mark off each day your child stays in bed all night. Ten days in a row earns your child a predetermined treat, perhaps a special outing. Or you and your child can figure out some sleep rules—maybe even rules in rhyme—and turn them into a homemade book to read each night before bed.

Sleep Problems

Some children have more trouble than others do in getting a good night's sleep. Common problems are sleep apnea, nightmares, night terrors, and sleepwalking.

Sleep Apnea

Unlike periodic breathing (explained earlier in this chapter), sleep apnea is an abnormal condition in which children (or adults, for that matter) stop breathing for a few moments. Then they rouse from sleep long enough to choke, cough, shift position, and start breathing again before returning to sleep. This process may happen many times—even hundreds of times—each night. The child generally will not realize it is happening and cannot tell you about it. Apnea means absence of breathing. One form of this condition is called obstructive sleep apnea because the airways are partially obstructed or blocked during sleep. In children, it is most common between ages two and five.

The nighttime symptoms include snoring or noisy breathing, choking, sweating, and waking during the night. During the day, children may be sleepy, falling asleep at meals or during play. Or they may seem hyper, wired, unable to sit still or calm down, cranky, and irritable. In the long run, sleep apnea can impair children's growth and development, harm their performance in school, and, in severe cases, cause heart problems.

Sleep apnea often goes undiagnosed for a while. Although any child may snore temporarily if he has a cold, regular nightly snoring should be discussed with your child's doctor.

The most common cause of sleep apnea in children is enlarged tonsils or adenoids that partially block the throat when the throat muscles relax during sleep. The usual treatment is removal of the tonsils, adenoids, or both, through surgery.

Other causes or contributing factors may be abnormalities of the jaw or throat, allergies, frequent respiratory infections, obesity, and some neurologic problems such as cerebral palsy. Children with Down syndrome are at high risk for obstructive sleep apnea. If doctors can't eliminate or treat the underlying conditions, they may recommend CPAP (continuous positive airway pressure), in which the child sleeps with a mask over his nose that is attached to an air compressor. The air he inhales is under pressure, which forces the airways to stay open.

Nightmares: Monsters in the Night

Nightmares are as inevitable a part of childhood as skinned knees. How early they start is unknown, but children describe dreams as soon as they can talk. In young children, they generally are thought to reflect psychological tasks or conflicts that are a normal part of growing up, such as separation anxiety or competing desires to be in control and to please parents. Preschoolers typically have nightmares about monsters or wild animals, which are thought to represent the child's aggressive urges.

Preschoolers generally can understand that nightmares are not "real" and cannot hurt them but may still feel deeply frightened. If your child calls out in the night, comfort her with hugs and reassurance, reminding her that nightmares are not real and that you are there to protect and love her. Don't belittle her fear; let her know that everyone gets scared by nightmares sometimes. You will probably need to sit with your child for a while, perhaps until she falls back to sleep.

If nightmares occasionally occur, they are nothing to worry about. A nightlight, hall light, or flashlight kept by the bed "just in case" may help. It also makes sense to avoid scary movies, books, TV shows, and video games, especially right before bed.

Nightmares often peak in the preschool years, along with fear of the dark. Sometimes nightmares mirror upsetting events that happen during the day. If some task, such as learning to use the toilet, seems to be causing heavy stress, you might ease up or delay it a while. You can also encourage your child to talk about feelings he finds frightening, reassuring him that everyone has such feelings and helping him distinguish between feelings and behavior.

If your child's nightmares or daytime fears seem excessive to you, talk to your child's doctor, who may refer you to a specialist in child development issues. In some cases, nightmares or fear of sleep can be a symptom of physical or sexual abuse. If you suspect this, talk to your child's doctor immediately.

Night Terrors: Asleep at the Switch

Your sleeping child lets out a heart-stopping scream. When you run to her, her eyes are wide open, her face contorted in an unnatural way, her hair wet with sweat. She may be sitting up, or out of bed, or thrashing around in such an odd way that you wonder if she is having a seizure. Even though she may be calling for you, she may not recognize you. Trying to touch or calm her makes things worse. What's going on?

This is a night terror, one of the most dramatic—and generally harmless—sleep events of childhood. Unlike nightmares, night terrors are not dreams and do not occur during REM sleep, when dreams occur. Instead, they occur when a child in deep non-REM sleep is switching to another stage and somehow gets "stuck" between stages. This "between" state—which combines features of waking and sleeping—is called "partial arousal." Walking and talking during your sleep can also occur during partial arousals. A tendency toward partial arousals seems to run in families.

Night terrors (or sleep terrors, as they are also called) generally occur in children ages two to six. In this age group, they do not indicate any underlying problem and are usually outgrown. They may occur only once, or every once in a while, or much more frequently. They last 5 to 30 minutes and usually end as the child falls back into peaceful sleep without ever having wakened. Children generally will not recall the episode the next day, although some may remember feeling frightened.

Less is more when it comes to helping a child with night terrors. Don't try to wake or question her before or after the episode. If she'll accept it, you can touch or speak to her softly, but many children reject such contact. Keep the lights low and simply watch her to make sure she doesn't hurt herself while moving around. If your child has frequent night terrors, make sure the room she sleeps in is as free of hazards as possible.

Can night terrors be prevented? Usually not. But children who are overtired may be more likely to have them, so you can try an earlier bedtime or longer naps to see if that helps. In some cases, partial arousals also increase at times of emotional stress.

Sleepwalking

Like night terrors, sleepwalking occurs when a child gets stuck between deep sleep and waking and usually does not indicate an underlying problem in a young child. There's no need to wake a sleepwalker; you can usually gently lead her back to bed. The parent's main job is to protect a sleepwalker from injury. The area around the child's bed should be clear of rugs she can slip on or furniture she can trip over. You may need to install gates at the top and bottom of stairs, block off the kitchen, or put a bell or alarm on the child's door to alert you when she's walking about.

Other Sleep-Related Problems

Some children develop rhythmic disorders associated with sleep, such as head banging, head rocking, and body rocking, which involve movements that range from mild to seizurelike thrashing. Other rhythmic disorders include shuttling (rocking back and forth on hands and knees) and folding (raising the torso and knees simultaneously).

During the rhythmic movements, your child may moan or hum. These movements seem to occur during the transition between wakefulness and sleep or between one stage of sleep and another. There is no known cause for this type of disorder, but medical or psychological problems are rarely associated with it.

Other common sleep-related problems include bedwetting and tooth grinding (bruxism). (See Chapter 20, "Toilet Teaching," and Chapter 29, "Signs and Symptoms," for information about bedwetting and Chapter 23, "Dental Care," for information about bruxism.)

Other Opinions

As we mentioned earlier, sleep issues seem to inspire passionate advocates. The approaches discussed in this chapter for helping children go to sleep on their own are similar to those backed by the AAP, representing the consensus of many U.S. pediatricians. The AAP's *Guide to Your Child's Sleep* (Villard Books, 1999) discusses a wide range of sleep issues from birth to adolescence.

Other approaches range from the "let them cry it out" school to the "you'll never sleep alone" school, with many variations in between.

The chief proponents of what could be called "tough love" approaches to sleep are Richard Ferber, M.D., author of *Solve Your Child's Sleep Problems* (Simon & Schuster, 1985) and Marc Weissbluth, M.D., author of *Healthy Sleep Habits, Happy Child* (Fawcett Books, 1999). Dr. Ferber, the dean of the "sleep training" gurus, advises checking on a crying baby at progressively longer intervals, up to 45 minutes, letting your baby see you are there but not touching or talking to him (a process parents sometimes refer to as "Ferberizing" their child). Dr. Weissbluth takes an even harder line. Once babies are four months old, he advocates letting them cry without limit until they fall asleep at night.

At the other end of the spectrum is William Sears, M.D., author of *Nighttime Parenting* (Plume, 1999). His theory of "attachment parenting," advocated in a series of books, calls for mothers to carry babies all day and sleep with them and breast-feed them all night.

If you have questions, talk with your child's doctor about the different opinions on encouraging your child to sleep. And trust your instincts—you know your child better than anyone else does.

Need More Information?

Check the Index and Appendix C, "Resource Guide." And of course, consult your child's doctor.

chapter twenty-two

Healthy Eating

Open wide!

Eating, of course, fuels children's physical growth. But it also helps them grow in other ways. Through food, your child will encounter the larger world: She'll get more skilled at using her hands, mouth, and senses; learn to make choices; start to assert her independence; and learn to enjoy herself.

This chapter will guide you through your baby's transition from bottle or breast milk to solid foods and then give you easy-to-use nutrition tips that will help keep your child healthy throughout the following years of rapid growth.

Food Attitudes

You may find yourself worrying in the beginning that your baby is eating too much or too little, then you may graduate to frustration when your picky toddler shuns your lovingly prepared meals. Before mealtime turns into a power struggle, sit back and relax. Put food in perspective—it's simply food, not a symbol of love or resistance. Share it and enjoy it. These suggestions may help.

Make Eating a Pleasant Social Experience

Turn off the TV, put down the paper, sit, and chat. But don't expect too much; eating a meal with a young child naturally has its limitations:

- Don't expect a young child to sit still for long meals, especially at restaurants.
- Offer a reasonable choice of food, but never nag, guilt-trip, scream, bribe, or force your child to eat. Such coercion is counterproductive—kids end up eat-

ing less, not more. It's your job to decide what foods are offered; it's your child's job to decide whether and how much to eat.

- If your child is not eating your nutritious offerings, resist the temptation to offer him cookies, ice cream—anything—just to get food through his lips. Obesity—caused by a combination of genetic factors, bad eating habits, and lack of activity—is a much bigger problem for American children than calorie or vitamin shortfalls.

If you are concerned about your child's eating habits, consult his doctor first.

Healthy Eating Patterns

Help your child embrace healthy eating patterns to last a lifetime:

- Offer a diverse diet rich in whole grains, fruits, and vegetables, and avoid sweetened, highly processed foods, fatty snacks, and other foods that are nutritionally empty.
- Encourage your child to develop a taste for water, not soda, and for whole, not processed foods—apples rather than apple-flavored breakfast toaster pastries. It may mean contradicting the models set by grandparents or friends—and changing the way you shop, cook, and eat so that you are a better model yourself.
- If your child is in day care, check out the menus and try to get them changed if they are not to your liking.
- If your child is home with a caregiver, make sure that person understands and follows your approach to feeding your child.

Moving from Milk to Solid Foods

Most babies need nothing but breast milk or formula until they are six months old, according to the American Academy of Pediatrics (AAP). In some cases—if food allergies are common in your family, for instance—your child's doctor may recommend feeding your baby breast milk alone for months longer, which may help protect against allergies. But most babies take their first food at four to six months, when their bodies become ready for it.

Some signs that your baby is ready to eat solid foods include these:

- Your baby holds her head up well when she's propped to sit, or she can sit alone.
- Your baby turns her head to avoid something unpleasant.
- Your baby shows interest in food. She may try to grab your lunch or track each forkful with her eyes as it moves toward your lips.
- Your baby has lost the tongue-thrust reflex. This reflex leads newborns to push out foreign matter that enters their mouth. If your baby still has it, you'll know it after a few tries at feeding because the food that goes in will come right back out. If that happens, you can wait a few weeks and try again.

When you think your baby is ready for solid foods, don't make an abrupt switch from bottle or breast milk to food. At first, continue to nurse or bottle-feed your baby while you offer solid food only once or twice a day. When babies first start eating solids, they will often eat only a teaspoon or two at a meal. Even after a month or two they may be taking in only three to four tablespoons a day of food, with the rest of their calories coming from breast milk or formula. The food will provide extra calories your baby needs as he grows, rather than taking the place of breast milk or formula.

As the baby eats more food and nears his first birthday, you can start cutting back on nursing over a few weeks. For information on weaning, see Chapter 9, "Breast-Feeding," and Chapter 10, "Bottle-Feeding."

In the Beginning: First Foods

It's recommended that you start with a single food and offer only that food for several days. Then add new foods one at a time, serving each one a few times before adding the next. That way, if your baby gets a rash, diarrhea, or some other possible reaction to food, it will be easy to tell which food is likely to have caused it. Once foods have been introduced with no problem, you can begin mixing them.

Typically, the first food is a single-grain, iron-fortified baby cereal, usually rice cereal, followed by baby oatmeal or barley cereal. Baby cereal is fortified with iron, which a breast-fed baby will need, starting at about six months, when her inborn stores of iron will become depleted. Baby cereals come ready to eat or as dry flakes to be mixed with breast milk, formula, or water. (Don't mix them with cow's milk until your baby is one year old.) In either case, you can thin the cereal a lot at first—in the beginning it should be more like thickened milk than like a solid.

Cereal is generally followed by pureed fruit (but **not** citrus fruit) or pureed vegetables (especially carrots, peas, squash, sweet potatoes, or green beans). Then you may introduce pureed meats or chicken.

There is nothing sacred about the cereal-fruit-vegetable order. Some parents offer fruit first because it is sweet and babies seem to like it. But other parents think it's better to introduce vegetables before fruit so babies learn from the start to enjoy less-sweet foods.

Whatever you decide, never try to force your baby to eat something she doesn't like. On the other hand, don't sweeten cereal or vegetables by mixing them with fruit (and certainly don't mix them with sugar or honey).

Baby Food: Store-Bought vs. Homemade

A lot of passionate debate focuses on the question of whether babies should be fed store-bought or homemade baby food. The truth is, babies do fine with either kind of food. Do whatever makes mealtimes more pleasant for your baby and you.

Commercial Baby Foods

Commercial baby food is convenient and consistent in taste and nutritional value. It's safe—in terms of being canned without bacterial contamination—and doesn't need refrigeration unless jars have been opened. Like other processed foods, baby food tends to be lower in pesticide residues than some fresh produce. These days, most baby foods for the youngest children (labeled "Stage 1" foods) are single foods without added salt, sugar, or fillers. Some baby foods even taste good to adults!

If you buy baby food, follow these guidelines:

- Read the labels. Foods for older babies (labeled "Stage 2," "Stage 3," or "Toddler") often have sugar or fillers. You may get more veggies for your money if you buy a jar of carrots and a jar of peas and combine them yourself than if you buy a combination with filler added.
- Avoid the baby-food desserts. Your baby is better off without a lot of added sugar and without coming to expect a sweet finish to every meal. For those meals when you do want to serve a dessert, serve pureed or mashed fruit, either straight or mixed with a bit of plain yogurt.
- Avoid giving your baby too much juice—most children don't need it. If you do buy juice, be aware that juices marketed for babies cost more but aren't

necessary; any 100 percent juice that has been pasteurized is OK. The same goes for many of the so-called toddler foods. Compare the label with the label of the adult equivalent.

- When you open a jar of baby food for the first time, you should see the center of the lid pop up as the airtight seal is broken. If it doesn't, don't use the jar.

Homemade Baby Food

Homemade baby food is much less costly than commercial baby food. Serving your own food from the start gets your baby used to eating what the rest of the family eats.

If you make your own baby food, follow these guidelines:

- Follow the food safety recommendations given later in this chapter. If you want to prepare more than one day's worth of food at a time, freeze the extra portions rather than trying to can baby food yourself. (If you freeze it in an ice-cube tray, you can easily pop out one cube at a time.)
- Choose raw ingredients carefully, and peel or wash them well.
- If you plan to puree or chop processed adult foods, such as canned fruit or frozen vegetables, read the labels first to be sure they are not high in salt (sodium), sugar, or other ingredients that you don't want to have in baby food. Canned soups and canned pasta with sauce often contain large amounts of salt. Although salt won't hurt your baby, he doesn't need large amounts of it.
- Use a blender, food processor, or food mill to chop food to the proper consistency for your baby. Many parents swear by small, plastic food mills that are easy to take with you for grinding on the go.

Special Cases

Commercial baby-food versions of some vegetables—beets, spinach, turnips, and collard greens—may be safer than home-cooked renditions. These foods can contain high levels of nitrates, which can cause anemia (low blood count) in some infants. The baby-food companies screen for nitrate levels, which you cannot do at home.

How to Feed Your Baby

When you first introduce solid foods, choose a time when you are not rushed and the baby is hungry but not famished. Lunchtime works well for many babies.

Your baby should be sitting, not lying down. You can hold him on your lap, but an infant seat or highchair frees both your hands. In the beginning, nurse or bottle-feed your baby a little bit before putting him in the seat so he is not overly hungry. Show him the food and let him touch it, even smear it around if he wants to. (Make sure he wears a bib, and expect a mess—it's all part of the process.) Then take a small infant spoon (the rubber-coated kind is gentle in the mouth), a demitasse spoon, or a half-teaspoon from a measuring-spoon set. Put a tiny bit of food on the spoon and place the spoon between his lips. Do not put it far back on his tongue, or he may gag.

Once your baby tastes the food, he may suck it off the spoon and open his mouth for more. He may spit it out but seem interested. He may gag, cry, or become upset. He may reach for the spoon himself. (Let him play with it. After a while, you can try to guide it to his mouth, or you can feed him with another spoon while he hangs on to the first.)

Once your baby has had a few spoonfuls or seems tired of the process, finish up the feeding by offering more breast milk or formula. In the beginning, very little food will actually be swallowed, but the goal at this point is to teach your baby to eat, not to meet his nutritional needs with solid food.

Foods to Avoid at First

Some foods are more likely than others to cause allergic or other adverse reactions in babies. Among these foods are cow's milk, eggs, soy, peanuts, and wheat, as well as shellfish, other nuts, and corn. It is best not to give these to your baby until she is older than one year and is eating the cereals, fruits, and vegetables mentioned earlier as good first foods. If food allergies run in your family, talk to your child's doctor before giving any of the allergy-prone foods. Delaying them may reduce the chance of developing allergies. Here are tips on some potential problem foods:

- Cow's milk. Because its concentrations of protein and minerals are too high for young infants, cow's milk should not be given until your baby is one year old. Even after that age, your child may be better off drinking iron-fortified formula rather than cow's milk if she is not eating enough iron-rich food, such as meat or iron-fortified cereal. Talk to your child's doctor about this. If you do give cow's milk once your baby turns one, use whole milk, not skim, low-fat, or reduced-fat (1 percent or 2 percent) milk. After her second birthday, you can usually switch gradually to lower-fat milk. But contrary to what many people think, cow's milk is not essential for a child as long as she gets enough calcium and protein from other sources. Yogurt is a good source of both. We discuss nondairy sources of protein and calcium later in this chapter.

By age five, some children—especially those of African, Asian, or Native American descent—may start to have trouble digesting lactose, a milk sugar. Special milk and pills can help with this lactose intolerance, which often continues into adulthood.

- Peanuts and peanut butter. These products can pose a double risk, as a possible cause of allergies and as a choking hazard. (Toddlers and babies can choke on sticky globs of peanut butter, as well as on the nuts themselves.) To be safest on both counts, wait until age three before giving peanut butter, and then spread it on bread or crackers rather than serving it plain. Wait until age four to serve nuts.

- Honey and corn syrup. Do not give these sweeteners to children who are less than a year old. They can contain bacterial spores that can cause botulism (a serious illness) in babies, but they are safe for older children or adults.

A Totally Solid Food Plan

Once your baby is eating a variety of single foods, you can start to mix it up, serving mixed fruits, mixed cereals, and mixed vegetables, still thoroughly pureed. When your baby can sit on her own and is handling the purees well, you can start offering coarser textures. You can also start offering finger foods. Be sure these are soft and cut into small pieces—she will either swallow them whole or let them dissolve in her mouth. Favorite finger foods include bits of cooked carrots, potatoes, or peas; bits of whole wheat bread or crackers; and Cheerios or a similar cereal.

Many children are prone to gagging and even throwing up when they are learning to eat. This may happen if your child has too much food in her mouth or if she encounters a new taste or surprising texture, like a lump hidden in a smooth pudding.

Drinking from a Cup

Around the same time babies start eating solid foods, they can begin to try drinking from a cup. Expect your baby—in fact, encourage him—to explore and play with the cup first, empty or half filled with water. Then offer breast milk, formula, or water to drink from the cup.

Once your child is eating fruit, you can try fruit juice, but don't overdo it—kids don't need juice, and it's better for your child to learn to eat fruit (which has more fiber) and drink water (which has no sugar) than to get him bonded to juice (which has a lot of sugar and sometimes causes diarrhea). The sweet taste of fruit juice can turn some children into habitual juice guzzlers, crowding more nutrition-rich foods out of their diets. A baby of one year, for instance, shouldn't drink more than about four ounces of juice a day. Although it may sound like heresy, it's fine for a baby to drink no juice at all, as long as she eats fruit.

For ease of use, try giving your baby a two-handled cup, either open on top or with a top that has a spout. Some baby cups have a valve in the spout that prevents spills, allowing the liquid to come out only when the baby sucks it. These are neater, but you must make sure you clean the spout thoroughly. And switch off with other cups so the baby also gets to sip, rather than only suck.

Baby Vitamin Supplements

If your baby has been breast-fed, her doctor may have already suggested that you give her drops that contain iron, vitamin C, and vitamin D. If your child has dark skin or does not get out in the sun every day, her body may not produce enough vitamin D. Because most infant formulas are fortified with vitamins, formula-fed babies generally do not need supplements.

After children graduate to solid foods, eating a varied diet (as described later) should make supplements unnecessary. Even less-than-perfect diets or small servings of foods are usually good enough to give children what they need to grow. Still, toddlers are notorious for picky eating and food fads. So, as an insurance policy, many doctors will recommend multivitamin drops that contain vitamins A, D, and C; the B vitamins; and possibly iron or fluoride as well. Other doctors think vitamin supplements are mostly a waste of money.

If you do use supplements, never give more than the proper dose—overdoses can be harmful. If your toddler or preschooler takes chewable tablets, treat them like medicine—keep them out of reach, and never pretend they are candy. And don't think supplements can take the place of a good diet. Supplements do not help your child get healthy amounts of many key nutrients, including fat, protein, carbohydrates, and fiber.

Food Safety

Choking on food is a real possibility when children are learning to eat, and it remains a hazard through the toddler years, usually lessening after age four. So for the sake of safety—as well as sociability—never put food down in front of your baby and go off to do something else.

How to Guard Against Choking

Even after children have teeth, certain solid foods pose a choking hazard. Until your child is four or older, depending on how well he eats, take these precautions:

- Avoid small, hard foods. These include jelly beans; hard candies; nuts; chunks of raw carrot, celery, or other hard vegetables; popcorn; and sunflower or other snack seeds. Remove seeds from fruit if the seeds might be eaten or inhaled, as with cherries or watermelon.
- Avoid or cut into halves or quarters other small, round foods. These include raisins, grapes, tiny tomatoes, and pitted olives.
- Before serving hot dogs, cooked carrots, or sausages marketed for toddlers, slice them into strips, then into pieces. If you slice them into rounds, the pieces may be just the right size to block your child's windpipe.
- Avoid thick, sticky foods such as caramels, gum, marshmallows, and peanut butter.
- Make sure your child is sitting still rather than lying down, walking, running, or playing when he is eating or drinking. It's best if, right from the start, your child gets used to eating only at the table rather than all over the house. This will help with controlling snacks later.
- Don't let your child lie down or fall asleep with food in his mouth. This can happen if children store food in their cheek. (Children sometimes do this if they find it hard to swallow a piece of meat or other food. Or they may do it if adults insist that they eat when they don't want to.) Either get your child to spit out the food, or clear it from his mouth with your finger.

Preparing Foods Safely

When it comes to preparing baby's meals, the standard safety rules apply. But you need to follow them with special care because babies are more likely than adults to become seriously ill if their food is contaminated with certain bacteria.

- Wash your hands with soap and water before preparing food. (Try waterless antibacterial soaps if you are without water, as on a picnic.) Wash your baby's hands before she eats.
- Keep countertops, utensils, and the like clean. Wash dishtowels, get new sponges frequently (or wash them in the dishwasher), or use paper towels for cleaning.
- Never give your baby unpasteurized juice or milk or raw eggs, meat, or poultry. That means children should not eat cookie dough or eggnog if these foods contain uncooked eggs. Children should not be given cheese made from raw (unpasteurized) milk.
- Cook ground meat to an internal temperature of at least 160 degrees Fahrenheit and chicken breasts to 170 degrees Fahrenheit. (If you're not sure, use a meat thermometer.) Meat should be brown, not pink, all the way through. Chicken should be white, not pink, with clear juices.
- After preparing raw meat, poultry, or eggs, immediately wash all utensils, cutting boards, hands, and so on that touched the raw food before you use them to prepare any other foods.
- Do not let milk, eggs, meat, cheese, or cooked leftovers sit at room temperature. Refrigerate them.
- Use leftover baby food within two days or discard it, even when it has been refrigerated.
- Check freshness or expiration dates on milk, eggs, yogurt, formula, and other foods before buying or using.
- Do not buy or use cracked or dirty eggs or food in damaged cans or containers with broken seals.
- Don't feed your baby directly from a jar or big bowl of food unless you are prepared to throw all the uneaten food out when the meal is done. Instead, remove a little food with a clean spoon, place it on a plate or bowl, and feed your baby from this portion. If you need more food, dish it out again with a clean spoon. Once a utensil has been in your baby's mouth (or your own mouth) it should not touch food that you plan to keep for later.

Food Allergies and Intolerances

As mentioned earlier in this chapter, cow's milk, soy, egg whites, peanuts, wheat, citrus fruits, fish, and shellfish are among the foods that should not be given to a baby just beginning to eat solid foods. Some babies have bad reactions to these foods—they may develop diarrhea and vomiting, rashes and itching, runny or stuffed-up noses, wheezing, or puffiness around the face.

Some of these reactions are true allergies, meaning they involve a response by the immune system. But most are nonallergic reactions called intolerances.

Whether they are allergies or intolerances, most reactions to food in babies disappear by age three or four. One exception is celiac disease (to learn more about this disease, see Chapter 32, "Health Problems in Early Childhood"), or gluten intolerance. This inability to digest gluten, a protein found in many grains, requires lifelong adherence to a gluten-free diet.

If you introduce new foods one by one, as recommended earlier, it becomes easier to notice if one seems to cause diarrhea or a rash. Stop the food and check with your child's doctor. He or she is likely to suggest that you wait a week or two and try the food again to see if it was at fault. If you find that the suspect food causes the same reaction, avoid that food.

Allergies may cause more serious problems than intolerances. If an allergy is known to exist or is strongly suspected, special care should be taken to avoid the substance that causes the response, which is called an allergen. Allergens may be hidden in a wide variety of packaged foods, so read the labels carefully and take care in restaurants. All caregivers, siblings, and family friends—as well as your child himself—need to know which foods must be avoided.

If your child has asthma as well as a food allergy, the potential for a serious problem is higher. The worst-case scenario is an anaphylactic reaction: The mouth and throat swell, breathing becomes difficult, and the person may collapse. Such a reaction may be fatal. If you see anything resembling this reaction, get immediate medical help. (For more on allergies, see Chapter 32, "Health Problems in Early Childhood.")

Nutrition for Ages Two to Five

How much should your child eat? As much as it takes to keep him growing at a healthy rate. The growth charts in Appendix B of this book provide some guidance, but because healthy children can veer from these curves, parents should speak to their child's doctor about this issue. Monitoring a child's growth is one of the main tasks of routine checkups in the early years.

Children six months to one year old typically need 700 to 900 calories a day total, from food and nursing combined. A two-year-old should consume 1,300 or 1,400 calories; add 100 calories with each year. At five and a half years, he may be eating 1,700 calories a day, as much as some smaller, less-active adults. But a child's needs vary widely with size and activity level. In almost all cases, there's no need to count calories if your child is eating regular meals and snacks.

Most toddlers and preschoolers do well with three meals and a midmorning and midafternoon snack. A predictable schedule, with meals and snacks at the same time each day, seems to promote good eating. A young child may need to take a break in the middle of the meal and then come back for more. A child who eats only small amounts at a sitting may like a bedtime snack, as well (just be sure to brush his teeth afterward!).

Dealing with the Picky Eater

Parents often worry that their child isn't eating enough when he shows a toddler's normally slower growth rate and his appetite drops off. "He lives on air," they say. If you're concerned about this, watch to see if your child is filling up on juice or milk. If so, try switching him gradually from juice to water for most of that sipping. If he's drinking whole milk, try moving to a lower-fat version. That may leave him with more of an appetite for solid food.

Also, check if your child is eating too many chips, candy, cookies, ice cream, or other sweets. These foods are low in nutritional value but so high in calories that relatively small amounts can fill up a child. A couple of desserts and a fatty snack can contain half a day's worth of calories. An occasional ice cream or cookie is no problem, but such foods should not be built into the everyday routine. At least in the beginning, kids won't expect dessert unless someone continually offers it.

The Voice of Experience

"Cook one completely new dish for dinner each week. This will help your child to be more open to different kinds of food. Over the long run, it will help to ensure that your child eats a wide variety of foods (the best way to ensure a balanced diet)."

—FROM THE KidsHealth PARENT SURVEY

It sometimes helps to offer the less-favored or newer foods first—a hungry child may be more likely to bite. Who says peas and carrots can't be an appetizer? Just don't make a point of it—no "eat your vegetables first and then you can have grilled cheese." Instead, be casual: "Your sandwich isn't quite ready yet, but you can snack on this while you're waiting." (Why does everything taste better if you call it a snack?)

These other strategies may help:

- Think small. Offer small amounts, so eating doesn't seem like a big task. With new foods, try just a teaspoon or two.
- Be patient. Children may need to encounter a food 10 or 15 times before they're willing to eat it. So offer a new food again and again, without pressure or comment. In this case, familiarity breeds acceptance.
- Avoid conflict. If trips to the supermarket turn into tussles over candy, try to shop without your child.
- Let her help. Even at age two, a child can tear lettuce or rinse fruit. Older children can stir and pour, snap green beans, even crack eggs and beat them. And by three or four many children are interested in cooking and baking. Young children can also help set the table.
- Be playful. Cutting foods into special shapes or coloring them with food colors or vegetable juice makes some kids more likely to eat. For more about this, see Vegetable Strategies later in this chapter.

You should never try to force, bribe, or badger your child into eating certain foods—or into eating, period. But you don't need to cook special meals either. Accommodate your child's tastes by offering meals that include one or two healthy items she is likely to eat—bread, for instance, or applesauce. If peanut butter sandwiches are a current passion, include a half or even a quarter of a sandwich along with other foods. If your child has unconventional tastes, be flexible.

Pickiness is common, so try not to worry. If the foods you offer your child are all fairly healthy, any combination of them that she chooses can't be too bad. (And studies show that, given free rein to choose among healthy foods, children come up with a diet that is quite well-balanced over time.) Another reason not to worry: Most U.S. children do not eat as much fruits and vegetables as nutritionists recommend, but most still get the recommended doses of most nutrients. Calcium and iron may fall short, however, and, after age two, fat consumption may be a little higher than recommended. So pay more attention to those items and relax about the rest.

What if Your Child Is Overweight?

Many healthy infants and toddlers alternate between looking pudgy and looking thin as they grow. But even if your child seems to be consistently overweight, don't restrict his food intake without first consulting his doctor. You may be advised to control his food consumption enough to slow or stop weight gain as he grows and let his height catch up with his weight. Like the child who seems to never eat meals, an overweight child may be overdoing consumption of juice, milk, and nutritionally empty high-calorie foods. Another common factor: Your child may not be getting enough physically active play. Recent research indicates that genetic factors play an important role in a child's tendency to gain weight excessively. For more information on obesity in children, see Chapter 32, "Health Problems in Early Childhood."

What Should Your Child Eat?

By the time your child is two years old, he should be getting almost all of his nutrition from solid foods. Like an adult, a child should eat a variety of foods, with balanced amounts of grains, vegetables, fruits, and protein-rich foods such as cheese, meat, dried beans, nuts, and tofu.

One useful guide to choosing foods for the whole family is the Food Guide Pyramid, prepared by the U.S. Department of Agriculture. Keeping the Pyramid in mind can help you make healthy choices, even if you don't follow it exactly. (An illustration of the Food Guide Pyramid is provided in Chapter 1, "Prenatal Care.")

The serving sizes listed here are supposed to apply to children ages four or older, as well as to adults. For children ages two and three, a serving should be smaller—about one-half of the amounts listed here. The only exception is in the milk group, where children from ages two to six should all get full-size servings. (For adults, increase the number of servings of grains, fruits, and vegetables.) As long as your child is growing normally and seems healthy, don't worry about exact amounts.

Here's a brief tour of the Pyramid, starting at the bottom:

Grains

Grains include cereal, bread, pasta, and rice. These make up the broad base of the Pyramid, meaning the majority of your calories should come from these foods. They are good sources of carbohydrates (the nutrients that provide most of our energy) as well as fiber, iron, and B vitamins. In recent years, many markets and mail-order suppliers have started stocking a far wider array of grains than many of us grew up with—from couscous and millet to quinoa and spelt. Rice alone comes in a fragrant rainbow, from purple Thai rice to brown basmati. Experimenting with foods of this group can make meals more interesting. Whenever possible, choose whole grains, such as brown rice and whole wheat bread, rather than white rice and refined white bread.

Recommended daily servings of grain are 6 servings for children ages two to six and 6 to 11 servings after age six. One serving equals the following:

- 1 slice bread, preferably whole wheat, rye, or pumpernickel
- ½ cup pasta or cooked oatmeal or cornmeal
- ⅓ cup rice
- 3 graham cracker squares
- 5–6 whole grain crackers
- 3 cups popped popcorn (for children four or over)
- 9 three-ring pretzels, preferably whole wheat
- 1 ounce ready-to-eat breakfast cereal, not sugarcoated

Vegetables

Along with fruit, vegetables are the next level up the Pyramid, meaning they too should be eaten in abundance. They provide rich sources of vitamins and minerals, as well as fiber and carbohydrates. People who eat lots of fruits and vegetables appear to be healthier in many ways, including having lower risks of several kinds of cancer later in life. Eating a variety of fruits and vegetables ensures a good mix of nutrients. Within vegetables, for instance, your child should eat dark leafy greens, such as spinach and collard greens; deep yellow vegetables, such as carrots and sweet potatoes; starchy vegetables, such as peas, potatoes, and corn; and dried peas or beans. If vegetables are not on your child's short list of things he'll eat (except for French fries), check Vegetable Strategies later in this chapter for some serving suggestions.

Be careful, however, when you introduce hard raw vegetables, such as carrots or celery, which can pose a choking hazard to young children. If your child is younger than four or seems to have a problem chewing and swallowing hard foods, cook vegetables lightly, even if you are serving them as finger-food snacks.

Recommended daily servings of vegetables are three servings for children ages two to six and three to five servings after age six. One serving equals the following:

- ½ cup cooked greens (such as kale, spinach, chard, or collard greens) or other cooked vegetables (such as peas, green beans, lima beans, split peas, lentils, or dried beans)
- ½ cup tomato or spaghetti sauce
- 1 cup vegetable or bean soup
- 2 cooked broccoli spears
- 4 medium brussels sprouts
- 1½ cups cooked carrots
- 1 medium baked potato
- 10 French fries
- 1 cup leafy raw vegetables, such as lettuce, spinach, or mixed green salad
- ⅓ medium cucumber
- 1 medium tomato

Vegetable Strategies

Lots of children don't want to eat their vegetables. Here are some serving ideas for vegetable-phobic toddlers:

- Make soup by steaming vegetables, then pureeing them with low-salt broth. Adding pasta in fancy shapes may help. If the soup is a hit, you can try pureeing only some of the veggies and dicing the rest into the soup so your child actually has to chew a recognizable vegetable. Dried lentils, beans, or split peas also make simple soups many children like.
- Try spaghetti squash. After you cook it, the pulp pulls out in strands like spaghetti, which you can serve with tomato sauce.
- Cut raw or lightly cooked vegetables into sticks and serve with a dipping sauce of tomato sauce, yogurt, or cheese sauce. Some kids favor ketchup or a mild salsa.
- If your child will eat only French fries, try making oven-baked "French fries" out of sweet potatoes, or even turnips or carrots. Cut them into sticks or thin wedges, coat with a little olive oil, arrange on a baking dish, and roast at 400 degrees Fahrenheit until done. This technique works fine on white potatoes as well, producing a pseudo–French fry that is lower in fat than the real thing.
- Have fun. Some kids who shun most vegetables will eat "cute" ones, like baby corn (found in cans in the Asian-food section of supermarkets), baby carrots, tiny bananas, or tiny grape tomatoes (cut these in half before serving). Some kids will warm up to vegetables arranged into pictures on the plate—flowers with carrot-slice petals and green-bean stems, or peas that form a spiral. Some

may like to pretend they are giants eating trees (broccoli stalks) or parking meters consuming coins (zucchini rounds). The idea is that once your child gets to like the taste, the gimmicks fall by the wayside.

- Try adding vegetables to other foods. Grated zucchini or carrot can be added to pancakes or muffins; canned chickpeas or black beans can be mashed and added to hamburger meat. Although this approach may get some disguised vegetables into your child, it will not help him learn to like eating vegetables for their own taste and texture. And be wary of "hide the vegetable" recipes—zucchini muffins that contain as much sugar as they do zucchini are not a good nutritional deal.

Fruit

Like vegetables, fruit is toward the base of the Pyramid, meaning your child should eat plenty. It's always preferable for children to eat fresh fruit rather than fruit juice. In general, children tend to like the sweet taste of many fresh fruits. If yours doesn't, you can try blending mashed bananas or strawberries with milk for a shake and adding pureed fruit to plain yogurt.

Recommended daily servings of fruit are two servings for children ages two to six and two to four servings after age six. One serving equals the following:

- ½ cup cut-up melon or fresh, canned, or cooked fruit
- ½ cup applesauce
- ¾ cup orange juice
- 1 small pear
- 1 medium orange, apple, banana, peach, nectarine, or tangerine
- 1 large kiwifruit
- ½ medium mango
- ¼ medium cantaloupe
- 7 medium berries (strawberries, raspberries, etc.)
- ¼ cup dried fruit (only for children four and up, to avoid choking risk)
- 12 grapes (cut up for toddlers to avoid choking risk)

Milk and Other Dairy Products

"Calcium-rich foods" might be a better name for this group, because calcium is the crucial nutrient these foods bring to the table. (They also supply protein, but so do many other foods. Calcium, in contrast, is much less abundant in other foods.) Children who do not eat dairy products may need a supplement to get adequate calcium, which is essential for strong bones now and later in life; consult your child's doctor. On the other hand, dairy products tend to be high in fat; some children do not tolerate them well, and some vegetarians shun them. So we have included in this group some nondairy sources of calcium.

If portions seem too large, serve partial portions, but try to make sure they add up to four servings a day for all children, starting at age two.

The recommended daily servings of dairy are two servings for children ages two to six and two to three servings for children older than age six. One serving equals the following:

- 1 cup fat-free, low-fat, or whole milk
- 1 cup flavored milk
- 1 cup yogurt
- 2 ounces cheese

Servings from the dairy group are so important to children because they are good sources of calcium. Nondairy sources of calcium include calcium-fortified breakfast cereals, tofu, canned salmon mashed with edible bones, and cooked, chopped kale.

Meat, Poultry, Fish, Beans, Eggs, and Nuts

Just as "milk" could be considered the calcium group, "meat" could be regarded as the protein and iron group. Most U.S. children get more than enough protein, but many have trouble getting as much iron as recommended. Beef is the source of the most available form of iron.

Recommended servings of protein are two servings a day—the equivalent of about three and a half ounces a day for children ages two and three and four to six ounces a day for children ages four to six. One ounce of protein equals the following:

- 1 ounce cooked lean meat, poultry, or fish
- 2 tablespoons peanut butter (for children three and up only)
- ½ cup cooked lentils; chickpeas; or kidney, pinto, or white beans
- 1 egg (yolk and white)
- ¼ cup drained canned salmon or tuna
- ½ cup tofu
- 1 soy burger patty

- 1½ frankfurters (cut into pieces for children younger than four)
- 2 slices bologna or other luncheon meats

Fats, Oils, and Sweets

This entry, at the tip of the Pyramid, is not really a food group. It just serves as a reminder that fats, oils, and sweets should be consumed "sparingly"—in small amounts and not very often—but not eliminated. Foods that fall into this category include mayonnaise, most salad dressings and fast-food sauces, as well as fried chips, deep-fried foods, candy, cookies, and doughnuts.

Facts on Fat

Young children need fat to grow properly. In fact, before age two, 50 percent of a child's calories should come from fat. You should not restrict fat until your child is at least two. After that, you usually can switch gradually to lower-fat choices, such as 1 percent milk, part-skim cheese, and low-fat turkey bologna. Naturally low-fat sources of protein include water-packed tuna (without mayonnaise), many kinds of fresh fish, lentils, black beans, and chickpeas.

How Much Fat Is That?

A child two years old or older should get 20 to 30 percent of his daily calories from fat, nutrition experts say. What does that mean in real life? Say your child consumes 1,500 calories a day. Each gram of fat provides 9 calories. So it would take 33 to 55 grams of fat to provide 300 to 500 calories, roughly 20 to 30 percent of your child's daily total. How much fat is 33 to 55 grams? One example: Your child would get almost 40 grams of fat from one regular hot dog (13 grams), a peanut butter sandwich (17 grams), a cup of low-fat yogurt (4 grams), a slice of "light" American processed cheese (3 grams), and a cup of low-fat milk (2.5 grams). By checking labels on food, you can learn enough about the fat content of various foods to keep your child's diet at a healthy level.

By the time children are age five, they should get no more than 30 percent of their calories from fat. Although limiting fat is believed to reduce the long-term risk of heart disease, cutting fat levels too low may harm children's development. For that reason, the AAP's Committee on Nutrition has recommended that children's fat intake not be cut below 20 percent of calories. If you read food labels, which list grams of fat, you can begin to get a rough sense of how much fat your child is consuming.

Not all fat, of course, is created equal. Unsaturated vegetable oils are better for the heart than saturated animal fats, such as butter or lard. The best choices include olive and canola oil (which are monounsaturated), followed by safflower, soy, corn, and other polyunsaturated oils. Avoid plant oils, such as coconut and palm oils, that are high in saturated fats.

Saturated fat should account for no more than one-third of your child's fat intake—or 10 percent of your child's total calories. That means restricting fat in particular from red meat and dairy products. The fat in these foods is more highly saturated than fat in chicken, fish, or peanut butter. The amount of saturated fat is also noted on food labels.

Healthier than Thou

Toddlers tend to be naysayers, but in many cases your preschooler will wholeheartedly believe you if you tell her the truth: Some foods are better than others for children, and you offer a healthy mix of foods because you love her so much. Of course, preschoolers may find this easier to accept if they have not already become attached to junk food and don't see others in the family eating it. Rather than dividing foods into "good" and "bad," it may be better—and more accurate—to explain that it's good to eat large amounts of some foods but only small amounts of others. Even so, some preschoolers will become "healthier than thou" when it comes to food. One mother, who had previously told her son that candy was not so good for children, had her words come back to haunt her after she said he could have some at a birthday party. "What's the matter?" the five-year-old demanded. "Do you want me to die?"

Children should never be put on the kind of fat-free regimen that weight-conscious adults sometimes attempt. And they should not be given potato chips or other foods made with Olestra, the so-called fat-free fat. This substance can cause digestive upset and diarrhea.

Five on Fiber

Fiber-rich foods such as most fruits, vegetables, and whole grains may play a role in reducing the chances of heart disease and some cancers later in life, and fiber helps promote bowel regularity. How many grams of fiber a day should your child get? Add five to your child's age, and you have a rough estimate—a three-year-old, in other words, should get eight grams. If you follow the suggestions for five servings of fruit and vegetables each day and if you encourage your child to eat whole grain breads, your child will almost certainly get enough fiber. Too much fiber can cause bloating and gas.

Vegetarian Diets

Many babies seem to be natural vegetarians, shunning meat for at least their first few years. All vegetarian diets, of course, are not alike. Major types of vegetarian diets include these:

- Lacto-ovo vegetarian—eats dairy and egg products; no meat
- Lacto vegetarian—eats dairy products; no eggs or meat
- Ovo vegetarian—eats eggs; no meat or dairy products
- Vegan—eats only food from plant sources; no meat, eggs, or dairy products

Although all these types of vegetarian eating can be healthy for babies and children, the more restrictive the diet, the more planning and care it will take to see that your child gets adequate nutrition.

If your child does not eat dairy products, for example, it may be difficult for him to get adequate calcium from food. Strict vegan diets may not offer toddlers enough of several other essential nutrients, such as vitamin D, vitamin B_{12}, iron, and zinc. To get these nutrients from plant foods, your child might have to eat too much bulk for his tiny stomach. Vitamin and mineral supplements may be necessary.

Champion Fruits

Which fruits pack the most nutritional punch? The *Nutrition Action Healthletter* rated 47 kinds of fruit for some important nutrients: vitamin C, carotenoids, folate (a B vitamin), potassium, and fiber. The top-10 nutritional champs were guava, watermelon, pink or red grapefruit, kiwi, papaya, cantaloupe, dried apricots, oranges, strawberries, and fresh apricots. Bananas, apples, and pears were in the respectable middle of the pack. Bringing up the rear was that childhood staple applesauce. But, as the newsletter noted, "Even the lowest-scoring fruit beats a low-fat Twinkie hands down." For the full list, see www.cspinet.org/nah/fantfruit.htm.

In addition, as toddlers grow, they often become pickier about what they eat. With a vegan diet, which is naturally lower in calories, make sure your child is getting enough fat and calories to thrive. Discuss this with your child's doctor. As with other children, an important guide is whether your child is growing well.

Here are some other tips for vegetarian parents:

- If you use formula, milk-based formula is considered superior to soy-based formula. But if you don't want your baby to have dairy products, give her soy-based infant formula, not regular soy milk. According to the American Dietetic Association, soy milk does not contain the proper mix of nutrients to be used as the sole source of nourishment for an infant. After your baby is one year old and eating solid foods, you can switch to regular milk or soy milk.

- Start your baby on iron-fortified cereal, fruits, and vegetables. Offer other grains, such as soft pasta and soft breads. But don't overdo high-fiber cereals or bulky vegetables that can fill your child's stomach without providing many calories.

- When your baby is seven to eight months old, give her protein-rich foods such as yogurt; cottage cheese; tofu; and cooked, pureed dried beans, lentils, and split peas. After the baby is three years old, give smooth peanut butter (unless you suspect an allergy) or other nut butters, spread thinly on bread.

- If you want your child to eat a vegetarian diet, the rest of the family should do so as well. If you are not knowledgeable about nutrition and healthy vegetarian lifestyles or are a newcomer to meatless eating, take the time to read up on it. You may need to learn about new ways of preparing grains and planning meals. It is not a good idea to drop meat in favor of a vegetarian diet of French fries, pastries, and sugarcoated breakfast cereal.

Things Worth Limiting in Your Child's Diet

While you're planning a healthy diet for your child, watch out for sugar, caffeine, salt, pesticides, food additives—and TV. These are all components of our daily diets that should be minimized.

Sugar

First, the good news. Contrary to what many parents believe, sugar does not appear to make kids wild, jumpy, uncontrollable, or hyperactive. Repeated studies have failed to show any such link.

That's about the best you can say for sugar. Sugar in food and drink promotes tooth decay and fills children up so they don't feel like eating more nutritious food. It gets children used to extremely sweet tastes, making them less likely to enjoy healthier foods like vegetables or grains. Sugar often comes packaged with fat—think of cake, cookies, doughnuts, and ice cream. These sweets are usually high in the kind of artery-clogging saturated fat that raises the risk of heart disease.

The strategy to cut down on sugar is simple (but not easy if you have a sweet tooth yourself): Keep sugary foods out of your house and out of your child's mouth as much as possible.

Some tips: Don't make dessert a daily ritual, or, if you must have it, try fruit or plain yogurt. Keep soda and fruit punch away from your child as long as possible. Don't use sweets as bribes, rewards, treats, signs of love, or threats ("no vegetables, no ice cream"). For after-dinner bonding, try a game of tag or catch rather than a stroll to the ice-cream shop. For a special lunch-bag treat, pack a sticker, a small toy, or a funny drawing or note rather than a cupcake. To express love, give a real kiss, not a candy kiss.

A Day's Menu for a Preschooler

Here is one day's menu that follows the Food Guide Pyramid. Portions are ample for children ages four or five. For two- or three-year-olds, cut portions by about one-third except for dairy items.

- Breakfast: ½ banana, 1 slice whole wheat toast with 1 tablespoon peanut butter, 1 ounce iron-fortified cereal, ½ to 1 cup milk
- Midmorning snack: 2 graham crackers, ½ cup low-fat yogurt, water
- Lunch: 1 peanut butter sandwich (2 tablespoons peanut butter and two slices whole wheat bread), ½ cup cooked carrot sticks, 1 wedge cantaloupe cut into chunks, water
- Midafternoon snack: 6 saltines, 1 string cheese stick, water
- Dinner: 1 cup vegetable soup, 3 ounces skinless chicken, ½ cup brown rice, ½ cup broccoli, ½ to 1 cup milk

Caffeine

Some children, health experts say, get so much caffeine from soda, chocolate, and iced tea that they may be jittery and have trouble concentrating. It has even been suggested that some children who seem to have attention deficit/hyperactivity disorder (AD/HD) may instead be overcaffeinated. Many sodas besides cola contain caffeine; some of these sodas, such as Mountain Dew, have ads that seem to be aimed specifically at children. Because of their small body weight, children who drink a can of caffeinated soda may get proportionally as much caffeine as adults who drink a couple cups of coffee.

If you give your child iced tea, make sure it is caffeine-free. If your child likes the fizz of soda, mix juice and seltzer for a light refreshing drink.

Salt

Excess salt seems to do no harm in most people. But in some salt-sensitive adults it can make high blood pressure worse, which is dangerous. Because you don't know if your child will be one of those salt-sensitive adults, it's better not to promote a love of salt. Don't routinely salt your child's food. Avoid highly processed salted snacks and processed deli meats (which also tend to be high in fat). Check food labels; many processed foods are high in salt even if they don't taste salty. Set a good example by not putting a salt shaker on the table. But don't completely do without. A little salt, added while cooking or afterward, can make some bland foods come alive, without doing any harm. But remember before you shake on the salt: A normal diet provides more than enough salt to meet the body's needs.

Pesticides

Many of the foods that young children eat, especially various kinds of fruit, commonly contain minute traces of pesticides, usually in amounts so small they do not violate federal standards. We do not really know whether eating tiny traces of pesticides every day for years will cause health problems. But we do know that eating lots of fruits and vegetables has important health benefits. So you should not cut back on fruits and vegetables out of fear of pesticides.

At the same time, it makes sense to reduce the pesticide residues your child consumes. In 1993, a panel of experts from the National Academy of Sciences recommended that U.S. pesticide standards be changed to give greater protection to children. They pointed out that children might get a relatively heavier dose of pesticides because children eat more produce per pound of body weight than grown-ups do. Data suggest that low-level consumption of some kinds of pesticides "may have subtle, but measurable effects on neurologic function" in children.

In part as a result of that report, the federal Environmental Protection Agency has been reviewing standards for pesticides. Although the review is supposed to be complete by 2006, it certainly will not end debate over this issue.

In the meantime, here are some ways you can reduce pesticide residues:

- Peel fruits and vegetables, if possible.
- Buy organic foods, especially produce, if you can. It is more likely to be pesticide-free than conventionally grown food. Guidelines for labeling foods "organic" have varied from state to state, but federal standards were recently established and are now being implemented. Check the Web site of the U.S. Department of Agriculture (www.usda.gov) for details.
- If you can afford to buy only a few foods in their organic form, choose those that can't be peeled (such as strawberries and leafy greens) or that are more likely to contain pesticide residues when grown conventionally (such as fresh peaches and apples).
- Wash fruits and vegetables well under running water. For produce that can stand such treatment, scrub with a brush. In experiments, researchers got

good results by washing produce with extremely diluted dishwashing liquid, then rinsing. (Do **not** use dishwashing machine detergents; they are toxic.)
- Discard the outer leaves of leafy vegetables, such as lettuce.
- Discard all skin and visible fat on poultry, fish, or meat. If pesticide residues are present, they are likely to be more concentrated in fat.

Food Additives

Hundreds of additives are used in American foods, including many that add nutritional value or make food safer to eat. But concerns have been raised about some:

- Sulfites, chemicals that are added to many foods to delay spoiling, can cause serious allergic reactions in a small percentage of people, especially in some with asthma. They have been barred from most common fruits and vegetables that are to be eaten raw, but they may be found in dried fruit and precut potatoes, as well as in some baked goods, jams, juices, and soup mixes. They must be listed on the label if they are present above a certain concentration.
- Monosodium glutamate (MSG—a flavor enhancer) and some food colorings may cause headaches or other physical reactions in some individuals. Some parents believe food colorings and other additives cause behavior problems or hyperactivity in their children, but scientific studies have not found such a link.
- Nitrites and nitrates, used to kill the botulism bacteria in cured meats such as most bacon, ham, and hot dogs, can be converted in the body to nitrosamines, which promote cancer. But cured meats also have vitamins added that block formation of nitrosamines. Still, it makes sense to limit cured meats, which tend to be high in fat and salt, or to seek out nitrite-free versions. (Nitrosamines also form in any meat that is broiled, grilled, or barbecued at high temperatures. Although an occasional barbecue should do no harm, a steady diet of grilled meat is not advisable.)
- Artificial sweeteners don't belong in young children's diets unless there is a medical reason to use them. Aspartame should not be consumed by anyone with phenylketonuria (PKU). This condition prevents the body from metabolizing phenylalanine, one of the amino acids in aspartame.
- Olestra (or Olean), the "fat-free fat" found in fat-free potato chips and other snacks, can cause diarrhea and stomach upset when eaten in large amounts.

TV

OK, TV is not a food. But studies have shown that children who are on a steady diet of TV are more likely to be obese. Why? Several theories have been proposed: If they're not watching TV, kids naturally get more exercise, without even trying. While they watch TV, many kids snack on high-calorie junk foods. And kids' shows tend to be loaded with commercials for sugary foods and fast-food meals packed with fat. For all these reasons, a no-TV or low-TV diet can be regarded as part of good nutrition. Here are some tips to make TV healthier:

- Tape favorite shows and zap the commercials when you play them back.
- Explain in simple terms what commercials are.
- Don't let your child eat while watching TV (and don't do it yourself).

The Voice of Experience

"Set aside mealtimes and eat together as a family. Encourage dinner conversation and have a no-TV rule."
—FROM THE KIDSHEALTH PARENT SURVEY

Need More Information?

Check the Index and Appendix C, "Resource Guide." And of course, consult your child's doctor.

chapter twenty-three

Dental Care

Open wider!

You may think that it isn't necessary to spend much time taking care of baby teeth because—after all—they're going to fall out soon anyway. But keeping baby teeth healthy is important for many reasons:

- Nutrition. If your child can't chew or swallow properly, she may not get the nutrients she needs.
- Speech. Problems with the alignment of teeth can affect pronunciation, slowing the development of speech and making your child self-conscious.
- Permanent teeth. Primary teeth (baby teeth) hold space for the permanent teeth and guide them into proper position. If baby teeth are lost, the dentist sometimes needs to install a "space maintainer" for the teeth to come. In addition, if baby teeth have unrepaired decay, the permanent teeth coming in are more likely to suffer decay as well.
- Looks. Having a nice smile and looking like other children make life easier for a child.
- Comfort. No one wants a child to have pain or to undergo dental treatments that could have been avoided.

Teething

By the time babies are born, they have a full set of primary teeth (commonly called baby teeth) hidden below the gum line, as well as the beginnings of the permanent teeth that will come later.

The first baby tooth usually breaks through—*erupts* is the medical term—between four and seven months, although the big event may occur as early as three months or as late as twelve months.

The two bottom front teeth (central incisors) usually appear first, followed within a couple of months by the four upper front teeth (central and lateral incisors) and the bottom lateral incisors (the two teeth flanking the bottom front teeth). Then there's usually a breather before the next wave: the first molars (the molars closest to the front of the mouth); then the eyeteeth, or canines (the pointy teeth next to the lateral incisors); then the second molars, behind the first molars. All 20 primary teeth—10 on top, 10 on the bottom—are usually in place by age three (see Figures 23.1a–d).

In rare cases, delays in teeth coming in can reflect a medical problem, but usually they are just normal variations that tend to run in families. Also rare: One or two teeth may already have emerged before your baby is born or may break through during the first few weeks. If they interfere with feeding or are loose enough to pose a choking risk, your child's doctor may recommend removing them.

Symptoms of Teething

Drooling and wanting to chew on almost anything are the hallmarks of teething. For most babies, the process seems to be almost completely painless. Others have short bursts of irritability, and a few may seem cranky for weeks, crying frequently, waking more often, and eating fretfully. If their gums grow tender and swollen, their temperature may be a little higher than normal, but teething does not cause high fever, diarrhea, earaches, runny noses, or coughing.

A rule of thumb: If your child seems sick, don't chalk it up to teething. Instead, handle it the same way you would if your child weren't teething. (For information on dealing with such symptoms, see Chapter 29, "Signs and Symptoms.")

Soothing the Discomfort of Teething

To make teething less unpleasant for your baby, take these actions:

- Wipe your baby's face often with a soft cloth to remove the drool and prevent rashes or irritation.
- Place a clean flat cloth under her head when you lay her down to sleep. If she drools, you can replace it with a dry cloth without having to change the whole sheet.

23.1a

23.1b

23.1c

23.1d

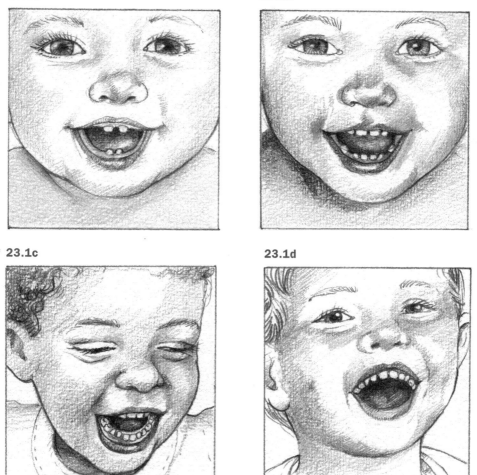

Figures 23.1a–d. Primary ("baby") teeth gradually erupt between the ages of about 6 months and two and one-half years. (a) 6 to 12 months, (b) 12 to 18 months, (c) two years to two and one-half years—bottom teeth, (d) two years to two and one-half years—top teeth.

- Try rubbing your baby's gums with a clean finger.
- Give your baby something firm to chew on, but be sure it's not small enough to swallow and can't break into pieces that might pose a choking risk. Hard rubber teething rings work well; look for one-piece models.

KidsHealth Tip

Look Out

Never tie a teething ring—or anything else—around your child's neck. It could catch on something and strangle your baby.

- Make it cold. Many babies seem to enjoy teething on objects that have been chilled but aren't rock-hard. Try freezing a clean wet washcloth for 30 minutes, then let your baby chew on it. Or try a cool spoon.
- If your baby seems to be in a lot of pain, it may be worth giving her acetaminophen drops, but consult your baby's doctor first. Painkillers that are applied to the gums (such as Baby Orajel or Baby Anbesol) are probably no more effective than rubbing without painkillers. Never place an aspirin against the tooth, and don't rub whiskey on your child's gums.

Tooth Decay

Over the past 25 years, tooth decay has been reduced among American children, but it's still common—by age three, about 25 percent of U.S. children have some decay. That's a big decrease since you were a kid, but that's still one out of four kids.

How Tooth Decay Happens

Decay occurs when bacteria in the mouth break down sugars in food we've eaten and produce acid. The acid eats away at the hard enamel covering the tooth, causing cavities (or caries, as dentists call them). The germ that causes most decay is called *Streptococcus mutans*. Although any carbohydrate can provide fuel for the bacteria, more damage is done by simple sugars such as sucrose (table sugar), lactose (found in milk), and fructose (found in fruit).

What matters most is how long the sugar remains on the teeth. A bottle of milk that is sipped gradually for an hour will lead to the production of far more acid than a bottle of milk that is downed in 10 minutes. A less sugary food munched on throughout the day may do more damage than a high-sugar candy bar that is eaten quickly and washed down with water. So a child who snacks or sips through-out the day is at higher risk for cavities than a child who eats only at meals or set snack times. As described later, the child most at risk for tooth decay is one who goes to sleep with a bottle of formula, juice, or milk.

These are other important factors in tooth decay:

- The virulence of the bacteria. If there is a lot of tooth decay in your family, it may indicate that your family members have a particularly damaging strain of bacteria. Because your child is likely to catch this bacteria, he may be at risk for decay, too. So if tooth decay is a problem for members of your fam-ily, be extra careful about cleaning the teeth and seeing the dentist.
- The health of the teeth. Getting adequate fluoride can strengthen the teeth and make them better able to resist acid. In some cases, babies are born with inadequate enamel on their teeth, which makes them more likely to get cav-ities. This sometimes happens if the baby was premature or if the mother had problems with her health or nutrition during pregnancy.

How to Prevent Tooth Decay

From the moment your baby's teeth first show themselves as little white dots on the gums, you can begin to keep them strong and healthy.

KidsHealth Tip

A Mother's Kisses and Tooth Decay

Can you prevent your child from becoming infected with the *Strep mutans* bacteria that causes decay? In theory, this should be possi-ble. Children generally get the bacteria from family members—most com-monly, Mom—or caregivers. To prevent transmission, some dentists advise against sharing spoons, toothbrushes, or other utensils with a child or kissing children on the mouth. But others think this is unlikely to pre-vent transmission because it appears that by age seven virtually all Amer-icans have been infected with *Strep mutans*. It will take a vaccine, they say, to block the bacteria—and researchers are working to develop one.

Beware the Bottle

To protect your child's teeth from early decay, take these actions:

- Never put your baby to bed with a bottle of formula, milk, juice, or anything but water. These liquids can pool in your child's mouth, bathing the front teeth (especially the upper set) for hours in decay-promoting sugars. The results can be dramatic: The front teeth can decay so badly that they have to be removed, which may require the use of general anesthesia. This kind of decay is sometimes called "nursing caries" or "baby-bottle tooth decay."
- For the same reason, don't use a bottle as a pacifier, letting your baby hold it and sip throughout the day. Reserve the bottle for mealtime or snack time, and remove it when the meal is done.
- Once your baby can handle a cup, minimize use of a bottle; use it only for water, or wean your baby completely.

What About Breast-Feeding?

Some say that breast-feeding also may have a role in tooth decay, but the case isn't clear-cut. Prolonged breast-feeding, especially at night, has been reported to make babies more likely to get tooth decay. As a result, the American Academy of Pediatric Dentistry advises mothers not to let their baby fall asleep with a breast in his mouth, not to nurse for long periods at night, and not to continue nursing past age one. But other experts say that studies of large groups of breast-fed children have not provided strong evidence of a link to tooth decay. A Swedish study of children breast-fed past 18 months found they were more likely to have cavities but also that they ate more cavity-promoting foods than children who were no longer nursing.

What should you do? Breast-feeding has many well-established benefits, but any risk it may pose for tooth decay is not well established. So you shouldn't hesitate to breast-feed for fear of promoting tooth decay. But if you do nurse your baby to sleep or if you decide to nurse past age one, be particularly careful about taking care of your child's teeth: Avoid sugary snacks, thoroughly brush your child's teeth, and take your child for checkups starting with her first tooth or first birthday.

Eat Well, Drink Well, and Avoid Decay

When your baby begins to eat solid food, aim for well-balanced variety, as described in Chapter 22, "Healthy Eating." Choose healthy foods right from the start to set a pattern for your child's tastes: If your child doesn't develop a "sweet tooth" when he's young, he's less likely to struggle with controlling one later on. Some feeding strategies are particularly important for dental health:

- Discourage your child from snacking on and off all day long. Instead, try to set a pattern of meals and snacks that are consumed in brief periods of time.
- Candy, cookies, cake, chips, and crackers are high in sugar and simple carbohydrates that tend to promote tooth decay. Give them

> ### I Wish Someone Had Told Me . . .
> ───────── ❧ ─────────
> ". . . how important baby dental care is before they had to pull out my son's two front teeth because of no enamel."

  to your child rarely, and don't keep them around the house. As a snack, offer cheese, fruit, or plain yogurt; or, when your child is old enough, offer cut-up cucumber, celery, carrots, or other raw vegetables. Read the labels: Many processed foods—from breakfast cereal to peanut butter—may contain more sugar than you expect.
- Sugary and sticky foods (including raisins and other dried fruit) are less damaging if they are eaten as part of a meal rather than if they are eaten alone.
- Don't be seduced by fruit juice. Even 100 percent juice can keep your child's teeth bathed in sugar. It also can train children to expect sweet drinks, a taste that will lead them straight to soda when they are older. And fruit juices can crowd out milk, which children need to get enough calcium for the strongest possible bones and teeth. For all these reasons, keep juice drinking within limits, perhaps a cup a day or less.

Decay-Fighting Fluoride

Fluoride is a mineral that, used in the right dose, helps prevent cavities. In most large cities, fluoride is added to the tap water; in some other communities it occurs naturally in the water. In these cases, your baby will get enough in breast milk or in formula made with tap water. (Premixed formula generally contains adequate fluoride as well.) A local pediatrician, family physician, or dentist should be able to tell you whether your water supply contains enough fluoride (at least 0.3 part per million); if not, he or she may prescribe fluoride drops for your baby or vitamin drops that include fluoride. The American Academy of Pediatrics (AAP) recommends that such fluoride supplements should not be given to babies younger than six months.

If your child's doctor or dentist doesn't know the local fluoride level, the public health department or water authority should. If you use well water or another private source, you should have the fluoride level checked by a lab. Most bottled water lacks fluoride. But you often can find fluoridated bottled water, usually sold as "baby water" or "nursery water" alongside baby food in supermarkets.

Knowing the fluoride level of your water is important because you don't want to give too much of a good thing. If your water contains adequate fluoride and your baby takes a supplement as well, the combination could cause a discoloration or mottling of the permanent teeth called fluorosis. This condition, harmless but unsightly, has become more common in recent years.

Fluoride that is applied to the teeth but not swallowed—such as fluoride toothpaste or fluoride rinse—does not contribute to fluorosis and appears to be particularly important in preventing decay.

Cleaning Your Child's Teeth

Even before your child's first tooth emerges, you should wipe her gums daily with a clean, damp washcloth or brush them gently with a soft, infant-sized toothbrush and water. As soon as the teeth emerge, brush them with water. This early cleaning routine not only may help prevent decay, it also will get your child used to the idea that cleaning the mouth and teeth is a routine part of the day.

Start using toothpaste on your child's teeth when she gets old enough to spit it out, usually around age three. Use toothpaste that contains fluoride, which is absorbed into the tooth enamel. Use only a pea-sized amount, and teach your child to spit it all out. Some children seem to regard toothpaste as pudding in a tube; if yours is among them, keep it out of reach to avoid extra doses.

By the time all your baby's teeth are in, you should be brushing them at least twice a day—after breakfast and before bed. While you do it, look for brown or white spots on the teeth, which can be signs of decay.

Early flossing is also a good idea. If you have difficulty doing it in that little mouth, ask your child's dentist for advice. Later, you can give your toddler a small piece of flavored floss and encourage him to imitate you as you floss your teeth. Even if he misses some teeth, he will get used to flossing. Be sure to discard the floss afterward.

According to studies, most children under eight do not have the coordination to brush their teeth as well as needed, getting at every surface—the outside, inside, and chewing edges—of every tooth. So it's better if a grown-up does the job or at least helps with the bedtime brushing. If your child insists on brushing her own teeth or resists brushing entirely, try to make the job more fun:

- Brush your teeth with your child.
- Let the child choose a toothbrush with a favorite cartoon character or color.
- Sing while she brushes. You can adapt "Row, Row, Row Your Boat," for instance. ("Brush, brush, brush your teeth/get them nice and clean/brush them up and brush them down/brush them in between.")

> ## The Voice of Experience
>
> *"Insist on things like bike helmets, seat belts, and flossing from the very beginning. It will become second nature and will never be questioned. If you try to get a 10-year-old to start flossing, it's like pulling teeth (pun intended!)."*
>
> —FROM THE KidsHealth PARENT SURVEY

- Ask your child's dentist or doctor to talk to your child about brushing. Children who resist a parent often accept the word of an outside authority.
- Use a timer or stopwatch to encourage your child to brush thoroughly (for two minutes, for instance).
- If your child likes machines or gadgets, get a child-sized electric toothbrush. (There's some evidence these do a better job of removing plaque than brushing by hand, although the studies were done on older children brushing their own teeth.)
- Have your child shine a flashlight in her mouth while you use the toothbrush. She may sit still, occupied by her important job. An added bonus: The light will allow you to see inside her mouth more clearly.
- Compromise. She brushes her teeth in the morning; you do it at night, which is the most important session. Or she brushes but you supervise.

Visiting the Dentist

Until recently, it was standard to take a child to the dentist for the first time at age three or when all 20 primary teeth had come in. The AAP recommends that before age three, the child's doctor should check for dental problems at the regular medical checkups and refer the child to a dentist if necessary.

But the American Dental Association and the American Academy of Pediatric Dentists now recommend that children see a dentist by age one, when they generally have about six to eight teeth. Dental problems in young children may be difficult to spot, dentists say. In addition, a dentist experienced in treating young children can give parents extra guidance on how to prevent problems.

There really isn't proof which piece of advice is better. You can decide based on your own feelings and the health of your baby's teeth.

Pediatric dentists have had special training in dealing with children, and some family dentists have lots of experience with kids. An office that caters to children generally will have interesting toys and books in the waiting room, hygienists who know how to talk to young children, and cheerful props such as cool-looking sunglasses (to protect kids' eyes from the bright light) and take-home toothbrushes.

Your child's first visit should be for a checkup only. This can be a pleasant visit without discomfort or fear that can help your child avoid dentist-phobia.

You can also make a visit to the dentist less threatening by describing in advance what will happen. Explain how the dentist will shine a light in your child's mouth, look in his mouth with a special mirror, count his teeth, and use a machine that's like an electric toothbrush to make his teeth shiny. Go over this before each visit—knowing what to expect will help give your child a sense of control and make for an easier examination. If you're not sure what the dentist will do, find out ahead of time so you can be accurate.

Thumb Sucking and Pacifiers

For information about thumb sucking, see Chapter 19, "Temperament, Behavior, and Discipline."

Paging the Tooth Fairy

Permanent teeth usually begin to appear around age six, but it can happen as early as four and a half or as late as eight. The bottom center teeth (incisors) usually fall out first, although it's not unusual for the permanent lower incisors to start pushing through even before the primary ones fall out. Once a tooth starts to loosen, it can take several months for the roots to dissolve and the tooth to fall out. In a healthy child, there's usually no need to hurry the process. If you have any doubt about whether a primary tooth is loosening normally or is wobbling because of a possible injury, consult your child's dentist.

Tooth Grinding

What are those creaking, grating sounds coming from the bed of your sleeping angel? It might be the noise of your child's teeth gnashing and grinding together as she sleeps. Bruxism, as this condition is called, is common especially during deep sleep or when a young child is under stress. About 3 out of 10 kids grind or clench their teeth, with the highest incidence in children younger than five.

Bruxism can have many causes, including top and bottom teeth that are not aligned properly, pain from an earache or teething, nervous tension, or anxiety. Often the cause is not clear. Usually the grinding does no harm and stops when the permanent teeth come in. In some cases, however, the grinding may be so extreme that it damages the teeth and causes jaw problems. In such cases, your child's dentist may prescribe a special mouth guard to be worn at night.

If you think your child is grinding her teeth, take her to the dentist. He or she will check for damage and try to determine if the cause is physical, such as misaligned teeth, or emotional, such as stress. In either case, it sometimes helps if your child can relax before bedtime, perhaps by taking a warm bath, listening to soothing music, or reading a favorite book. Find a relaxing activity that she likes, and make that part of her nightly bedtime routine.

Need More Information?

Check the Index and Appendix C, "Resource Guide." And of course, consult your child's doctor.

chapter twenty-four

Child Safety

The job that's never done

"What do you wish you had known that no one told you about keeping a baby or young child healthy and safe?"

When we asked parents that question, we got back a bookload of stories about the athletic feats of toddlers and preschoolers—how fast they move, how high they climb, and how relentless they are in finding the one thing you never thought they'd find:

- The one-and-a-half-year-old who stacked items on a chair, climbed to the top of the refrigerator, found a bottle of prescription cough syrup stored there, opened the childproof cap, and drank half of it
- The baby who flipped himself and his booster seat off the kitchen counter
- The child who put venetian blind cords in his mouth and jumped off the furniture, losing a few teeth in the process
- The baby just learning to "cruise" (walking while holding on to furniture) who, while his mother took a quick shower, opened a sliding closet door and ate mothballs from a box on the shelf

After describing these feats of daring, parents often said, "I never would have thought he was capable of doing such a thing!"—with lots of exclamation points. Parents were surprised! shocked!! amazed!!! at their children's behavior.

Those exclamation points seemed to mix horror with delight. After all, kids may get into danger for joyful reasons—they are strong, fast, curious, often fearless, growing more independent every day. But you can make your child's risk-taking safer without robbing life of adventure or fun. Although this process is a difficult balancing act, it can be done if you know the predictable ways kids get hurt and the reliable ways you can prevent many injuries. Prevention does work—accidental childhood deaths have become rarer over the past decade, thanks to car seats, child-resistant packaging, safer play equipment, public-education campaigns, and other advances in safety.

Safety in Perspective

Once children are past the hazards of birth and inborn illnesses, injuries are the biggest threat they face. Of these injuries, car crashes and child abuse are by far the biggest killers, with parents—careless or violent—causing most of these deaths. Alcohol and drugs play a role in many of these sad cases. One of the most important things you can do to keep your child safe is to get help if you or anyone in your household has a drinking problem, uses drugs, or can't cope with the frustrations of caring for a young child.

> ### The Voice of Experience
> *"You'll never be prepared for what your child can put up her nose."*
> —FROM THE KidsHealth PARENT SURVEY

The other main types of fatal injuries to children are listed in the box on page 417. Scary as this list may seem, when you consider that there are almost 19 million children younger than five in the United States, the numbers show most kinds of fatal accidents are extremely rare.

Yet less-serious injuries are as common as falling off a swing set. It's estimated that each year one out of every four or five children gets an injury that sends him to a hospital emergency room. Falls are the number-one culprit. In all but about 3 percent of the cases, the child is sent home without needing to be hospitalized. Yet such injuries can be painful and scary, even when they do no lasting damage.

A General Approach to Keeping Your Child Safe

To prevent childhood injuries, all young children need to be closely supervised by an adult, experts say. In our survey, parents put it this way: You have to watch them every minute. Here are two other pointers to keep in mind:

Major Causes of Fatal Injuries in U.S. Children, Birth to Age Four, 1998

Here is a list of major causes of fatal injuries to children birth to age four in the United States:

- Motor vehicles—785 (including 8 involving bike or trike riders)
- Homicide (child abuse)—721
- Drowning—559
- Suffocation—528
- Fires and burns—307
- Other pedestrian accidents—108
- Falls—65
- Natural/environmental causes—47
- Poisonings—36
- Other transportation accidents—34
- Struck by or against something—31
- Gun accidents (unintentional injuries)—19

(Source: National Center for Health Statistics, *National Vital Statistics Reports*, Vol. 48, No. 11, July 24, 2000.)

- Don't underestimate your child's physical abilities. Even the most attentive parents can be caught by surprise when their baby develops a wonderful new skill—such as rolling (off the changing table, perhaps) or climbing (onto the kitchen counter). To work, childproofing must stay several steps ahead of your child's development.
- Don't overestimate your child's mental abilities. Teaching your children safe behavior is important, but it's not enough to keep them safe because they may not be able to understand, remember, or control themselves as much as you'd like. "Stay near Mommy" won't work if you don't know what "near" means.

This chapter is divided into three sections: "On the Road," which discusses auto safety and car seat use; "At-Home Safety," which will help you protect your child from falls, burns, choking, and poisoning; and "Safe Fun," which deals with water safety, sun protection, pets, trikes, bikes, and other playthings.

On the Road

As passengers and as pedestrians, children are at greater risk for injuries from cars than from any other cause of unintentional injury. This is an area where you need to be especially vigilant and safety conscious.

Auto safety starts with the basics of careful, safe driving. That means absolutely no drinking and driving, of course. It also means no driving when you're overtired or seriously sleep-deprived, as new parents tend to be. Reaching back to mop a spill or retrieve a dropped toy can dangerously distract you on the road, so pull over for such chores. Making cell phone calls can be distracting, too, as can free-ranging pets. And make sure that others who drive your child, such as babysitters or grandparents, are safe drivers.

Securing Little Passengers

You must have a car seat that's right for your child's age and weight, install it properly in the backseat, and use it always. For details about choosing and installing a car seat, see Chapter 2, "Preparing Your Home and Family." Many parents find it helpful to have a trained person check that their seat is properly installed. Some hospitals and organizations such as the National SAFE KIDS Campaign (www.safekids.org) and the Child Passenger Safety Web (www.childsafety.org) offer "car seat checkups."

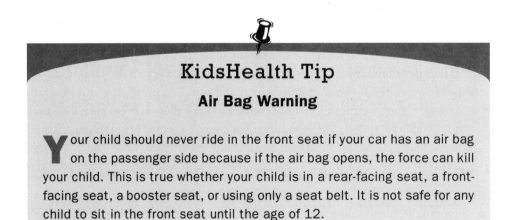

KidsHealth Tip

Air Bag Warning

Your child should never ride in the front seat if your car has an air bag on the passenger side because if the air bag opens, the force can kill your child. This is true whether your child is in a rear-facing seat, a front-facing seat, a booster seat, or using only a seat belt. It is not safe for any child to sit in the front seat until the age of 12.

Check that the car seat is tightly buckled each time you use it. It can gradually grow loose. Or sometimes a backseat passenger may mistakenly unbuckle it while fumbling for his own seat belt.

Staying Buckled

Using the car seat during every car ride may not be as simple as it sounds. Some babies scream every time they're put in a car seat, and many toddlers find ways to escape their seats soon after. What can you do? First, resolve that you will always use the car seat, no matter what. And be sure you serve as an example by always using your own seat belt. Then try these ideas for your child's maximum comfort.

For infants:

- Drive as little as possible.
- Station an adult in the backseat to reassure and distract your infant.
- Be sure your baby is shielded from bright sun.
- Experiment with the angle of the rear-facing seat (within the recommended limits).
- Try to drive when your baby is likely to nap.

For toddlers:

- Entertain your child with singing, stories, tapes, soft toys, or cloth books (hard objects could do damage if there's a crash or even a sudden stop).
- Encourage your child to pretend that the car seat is a space capsule, cockpit, saddle, canoe, or whatever will distract him.
- Take the car seat inside and let your child play at strapping in a doll or stuffed animal. Ask your child to explain to the "baby" why car seats are needed.
- If your child is in child care, suggest the group do a project on car seat safety. The Bucklebear Program (www.cipsafe.org), for instance, features coloring books, dolls, and decals sold in bulk.
- If your child unbuckles himself or the seat while you're driving, pull over and reattach it before going on, even if you have to do it repeatedly or it makes you late. If you're late for a fun activity, like a birthday party, it may make a lasting impression on your child.
- Slipping a soft tube—such as the sleeve of an old sweater—over the buckles can make them harder to open. It can also prevent other backseat passengers from inadvertently unbuckling the car seat.

The (Almost Magic) School Bus

If you're looking for a safe method of transportation, consider the school bus. Each day, school buses move 23 million passengers; each year about 9 of those passengers are killed in accidents, and a similar number of children are fatally hit by buses as they walk near them. Compared to the overall U.S. highway toll of 41,000 dead, this is a reassuring statistic.

But safety advocates are trying to improve that record. The National Highway Transportation Safety Administration (NHTSA) recommends that preschoolers who ride big school buses should ride in child safety seats, just as they do in cars. The National Transportation Safety Board (NTSB) is urging an overhaul of school bus design, which has been frozen since 1977. For now, advocates differ on whether wearing seat belts on a school bus (if they were available) would reduce the risk of injury. The NTSB says the answer is unknown. Some auto safety advocates argue that kids should wear seat belts on school buses just to get them in the seat belt habit because it's so important in other vehicles.

Hand in Hand

Young children should always hold hands with an adult when they are in parking lots, crossing streets, or crossing driveways. Children should be taught not to get out of the car until an adult is outside the car; if this is a problem, most cars have child safety locks that can make it impossible for a child to open the door from the inside.

Teach your child the "hand on the car" routine: She has to keep one hand on the car until you're ready to go. This specific instruction is grasped more easily by kids than a rule like "stay nearby."

Garage Safety

Garages tend to have dangerous objects in them, including the most dangerous, cars or trucks. Even though garages should be childproofed as much as possible, with chemicals and tools placed out of reach, they usually cannot be made safe enough to play in. It's better to keep little ones out except for the escorted walk to and from the car.

To prevent accidents, electric garage doors should automatically reverse if they hit something or should stop automatically before they hit something. At least one test has found many garage doors fail to perform well at these safety tasks. Experts recommend you test your doors by trying to close them on a roll of paper towels. If they touch the towels and do not reverse, get them repaired or replaced.

If your doors are too old to have these safety features, replacing them is a wise investment. When your child and his friends get old enough to be in and out of the garage with little supervision, they will still be young enough to be severely injured by a runaway door.

Riding a Shopping Cart

Shopping cart injuries send about 21,000 children a year to emergency rooms, many with head injuries from falls. Whether you're using the built-in infant or child seat on a cart or have a car seat that snaps onto a cart, always strap your child in. If you can't find a cart with a working seat belt, don't shop in that store with a child—and complain to the management. Because broken belts are so common, some parents bring along their own child safety harness to use with the cart.

Kids should not ride in the main part of the cart or stand in the cart or push the cart alone. But even belted into a seat, your child should never be left alone in a shopping cart—not even for a moment while you run back for one last-minute item. Instead, take the cart (or just your child) with you. Other techniques: Carry your baby in a sling or cloth carrier while you push the cart. Trade off shopping/babysitting with another parent so each of you can shop childfree. Shop with your partner so one of you can push your toddler in a stroller while the other

KidsHealth Tip

Where Is Your Child?

If you're taking the car but not the child, always make sure you know where she is before you get into the car and pull out of the garage or driveway. Once you're in the car, you may not be able to see your child if she's near the car.

wheels the cart. Or if you're alone, use the stroller and carry purchases in a basket, even if it means buying only a few things at a time.

At-Home Safety

Many childhood accidents occur in the safety of the child's own home, under the nose of conscientious parents. General childproofing and close supervision by an adult are key to preventing these injuries.

General Childproofing

In Chapter 2, "Preparing Your Home and Family," we outlined the basics of babyproofing, such as removing or locking up things that could fall on, choke, poison, cut, or burn your child and blocking off stairs and windows. But even after you babyproof your house when your child is an infant, you need to routinely scan your home for dangers that emerge as your child gets bigger and stronger. Before your child can open doors, for instance, you may need to get doorknob covers or install a latch high on the doors.

Preventing Falls at Home

Falls are the number-one reason children visit hospital emergency rooms, even though most falls aren't serious. Kids are especially prone to fall down stairs, off changing tables, and out of cribs. A few precautions can help:

- Never leave your baby, even for a moment, in a place from which she could fall. If she's on the changing table when the doorbell rings, take her with you to answer it. If you must leave her, put her in a crib or a playpen. For the first few months, the floor also can be a safe spot.
- Before you put your baby on the changing table, make sure everything you need is within reach. If you find you've forgotten something, take your baby with you when you go to get it. Follow the one-hand rule—if you have to reach for something, make sure you can always keep one hand on your baby.
- Keep the side rails of the crib up and the mattress in its lowest position. Once your child shows an interest in climbing out, it may be safest to move her into a bed. A gate or a screen door can be used to keep her in the room at night.
- Strap your child in. This goes for changing tables, highchairs, strollers, infant seats, and swings. The most secure seat belts include a strap between the legs.

Do not rely on a highchair tray to keep your baby safe; often babies slip out below them or stand and fall from a higher height.

- Move your child out. If your child struggles constantly to get off the changing table or out of the highchair, it may be best to do things differently. Let her picnic on a towel on the floor or eat sitting in a kiddie chair. Change her on the floor instead of on the changing table.
- Keep your child low. Don't put your baby, on her own or in seats or bouncers, on top of tables, railings, or cars. Your child may seem immobile, but by shifting her weight, she can go sliding. Don't put your child on washers, dryers, or other machines that vibrate.
- Don't hang bags or packages from the handles of strollers. If you let go of the handle, the stroller may tip backward or your child could get tangled in the straps of the bags.
- Block off stairs at the top and the bottom using either doors or hardware-mounted gates. Gates held in by tension can fall over too easily to be used on stairs. An adult must still watch your child in case she tries to climb the gate, but at least it'll slow her down long enough to be caught.
- Don't let your baby use a walker. These seats on wheels are falls waiting to happen when babies too young to walk on their own plummet down stairs. Safer substitutes (called "baby exercisers," "baby entertainers," or "Exer-saucers," a trade name) bounce or swivel in place.
- Get window guards. (In some places, including New York City, landlords are required to install guards for tenants who have young children.) Otherwise, open windows only from the top and keep windows locked when closed. Do not rely on screens as window guards. Do not place a crib next to a window. Discourage your child from climbing onto windowsills by moving away furniture, toy boxes, and any other objects that could serve as steps.

Home Office Alert

If you have a home office, don't forget it when you're childproofing—it's probably full of sharp edges, electrical cords, and small, attractive objects that should be put out of reach.

- Make sure electric cords don't dangle where your child could tug at them.
- Cover exposed electrical outlets with special covers, and use safety plugs on equipment that's plugged in.
- Keep office supplies—like scissors, markers, paper clips, staplers, and fasteners—locked up or far from your child's reach.

- Put tiny file cabinet or desk keys on a key ring and hang them high, so they can't be swallowed.
- Lock file cabinets, if possible. They could tip over if your child pulls out a heavy upper drawer.
- Close and lock your office, if possible, when you're not using it.

Cutting the Cords

Anything with a string or cord has the potential to strangle a child.

- For safety's sake, most children's clothing no longer comes with drawstrings around hoods or necklines. But if you have clothing with cords, remove them.
- Cut the strings on mittens.
- While he is playing or sleeping, your child should not wear necklaces, scarves, headbands, tie-on hats, whistles, stopwatches, keys strung on cords around the neck, or anything else with ribbon or string.
- Never tie a pacifier on a string around your baby's neck or to his clothing or wrist.
- Always tie up window blind cords so they are out of your child's reach. Cut the cords so there is no loop at the bottom, then tie or clip them up with clothespins or specially designed cord clips.
- Strings on crib bumpers should be no longer than six inches.
- If you want to tie a toy to a car seat or stroller, make sure the string is no more than six inches long.

Don't Bank on Bunk Beds

Bunk beds cause the deaths of about 10 U.S. children a year, when children's heads or chests get trapped in the railings or other parts of the structure. In the late 1990s, the Consumer Product Safety Commission (CPSC) recalled more than 630,000 bunk beds for not complying with rules designed to prevent those deaths. Stricter standards now state that any openings in the upper-bunk structure must be less than three and one-half inches wide, and openings in the lower-end structures must be either too small for a child's chest to slip through or large enough for the chest and head to pass freely. Even with these precautions, children younger than six years old are not supposed to use the upper bunk.

Poison Prevention

The good news is that most of the yucky things kids eat will not harm them. The other good news is that fatal poisonings of children younger than five are way down in the United States—from 226 in 1970 to 36 in 1998. Experts attribute that to child-resistant packaging, dose restrictions on medications, and greater awareness by parents about safety measures like those described here.

10 Common Items That *Aren't* Poisonous

These substances are certainly not part of a healthy diet, but if your child does down a bit of the following items, don't panic. They should do no harm unless eaten in large amounts.

1. Antibiotics, antacids, and contraceptive pills
2. Bubble bath and bath oil
3. Calamine lotion
4. Chalk, crayons, markers, and ballpoint pen ink
5. Glue and paste
6. Lipstick, foundation, hand lotion, and most other cosmetics (except hair dye and nail polish remover)
7. Pencil lead (it's really graphite, not lead)
8. Petroleum jelly, such as Vaseline
9. Soap and shampoo
10. Sun protection lotion

10 Common Items That *Are* Poisonous

If you suspect that your child has eaten any of these items, get in touch with your child's doctor or the local poison control center immediately. You should have their phone numbers posted near the phone.

1. Alcohol—both rubbing alcohol and alcoholic beverages (A few ounces of a high-proof liquor may be enough to kill a two-year-old.)
2. Aspirin, acetaminophen, ibuprofen, antidepressants, nico-

I Wish Someone Had Told Me . . .

"*. . . to install a door chain up high on your front door because your toddler will unlock the door and try to leave on her tricycle to visit Grandma in the middle of the night.*"

tine patches, and most other medications, both over-the-counter and prescription
3. Automatic-dishwasher detergent
4. Automotive windshield-washer fluid, fuel additives, radiator fluid, and anything else containing methanol or ethylene glycol
5. Drain cleaners, toilet bowl cleaners, and other caustic substances
6. Gasoline, kerosene, benzene, naphtha, mineral spirits, and other hydrocar-
bons (including certain types of furniture polish)
7. Hair coloring and nail polish remover
8. Iron supplements and vitamins containing iron
9. Lead (chiefly from old, peeling house paint)
10. Pesticides, insecticides, and mothballs

Medications

Store all medications—prescription or not—in a locked cabinet out of your child's
reach. Child-resistant packaging is not childproof. Don't rely on packaging to protect your child. Here are some more tips:

- Be especially careful with iron or vitamins that contain iron—even a nonfa-
tal iron overdose can permanently damage your child's digestive system. Iron
supplements, surprisingly enough, are the number-one cause of poisoning
deaths in young U.S. children.
- Never leave bottles of vitamins, aspirin, or other pills in a pocketbook, where
your child may find them while searching for a toy.
- If you have houseguests, be sure their medicines are far from reach, preferably locked in their luggage. Put visitors' purses or knapsacks out of reach.

KidsHealth Tip
Avoiding Medication Mishaps

If you must give your child medicine in the middle of the night, don't do
it in the dark—it's too easy to make a dosage mistake. Turn on the light
to measure the medicine, and don't forget to put on your glasses if you
need them. Day or night, always read the medicine's label before giving a
dose, just to make sure you picked up the right bottle.

- Always keep medicines, cleansers, and chemicals in their original containers, with labels intact, so if your child does swallow some, you know what it is.
- Don't ever tell your child that medicine or vitamins are candy.

Cleansers and Household Chemicals

If you have a baby and a household to run, there's no doubt you have lots of cleaning supplies and household chemicals. When you're childproofing your house, make sure these items are all out of reach.

Store household cleaning products and aerosol sprays in high cabinets far from reach. Don't keep any cleaning supplies, including dishwasher detergent, under the sink or leave them unattended during cleaning. Never put roach powder or rat poison on the floors of your home. Avoid using chemical insecticides, herbicides, and other toxic gardening or lawn chemicals. Choose nontoxic solutions instead.

Household Plants

Contrary to popular belief, poinsettias, the leafy red heralds of Christmas, are not poisonous. But some other plants associated with the holidays are. These include amaryllis, the showy bulb often timed to bloom on Christmas Day; yew, which grows as a shrub; and the berries of mistletoe. If these plants are eaten, symptoms include vomiting, upset stomach, and diarrhea.

Some other common house and garden plants also are considered toxic if eaten, although kids rarely get seriously ill. Toxic plants you might have around your home include philodendron, pothos, skunk cabbage, daffodils, tomato-plant foliage, and jimsonweed. You should know the names of your plants, so in case your child does eat one, you can check with her doctor or local poison control center.

Choking Hazards

What do hot dogs, popcorn, and balloons have in common? They're festive favorites for many kids, and they're also among the choking hazards young children encounter. Anything small enough to fit through a toilet paper roll (smaller than one and one-fourth inches) can be dangerous to a child younger than three or four years. The list of household objects that can cause choking includes coins, small parts of toys, marbles, sewing supplies, sequins, nails, and other small hardware items. To keep your child breathing freely, here are some pointers:

KidsHealth Tip

The Party's Over

Grown-up parties call for special precautions. If your child is present, make sure he can't get to alcoholic drinks—guests may not be conscious of where they've put down a glass. And watch out for guests' purses that may be left where your child can reach them—they may contain risky objects, including medications. Because you, as host, are going to be distracted, it may be wise to assign another adult to chaperone the young partygoers. Tired as you may be when the party's over, you need to clean up right away. The remains—including half-full glasses, cigarette butts, and hors d'oeuvres that may be choking hazards—can be dangerous to a child who wakes up before you do and decides to explore.

- Do **not** give small, hard, or round foods that, if inhaled, could block the windpipe of a child younger than four. Caution older siblings to avoid sharing such foods with your infant or toddler. These hard-to-swallow foods include popcorn, grapes, raisins, caramels, cherries, watermelon and other fruit with seeds or pits, tiny tomatoes, olives, nuts, hard candy, gum, and hard vegetables such as raw carrots or celery. When hot dogs, sausage, or cooked carrots are sliced into round pieces, the pieces are just the right size to block the airway. Slice these foods into short strips, or cut each round into quarters. Grapes can also be cut into smaller pieces for safer eating. For some children, a glob of peanut butter may also be a choking hazard.
- Encourage your child to eat while sitting still, not while lying down, running, or playing, especially if she is eating food on a stick. If your child becomes drowsy during dinner, wake her up long enough to make sure anything in her mouth has been safely swallowed.
- If you have a hobby that involves small objects, such as sewing or carpentry, keep your supplies out of your child's reach. After you've finished, vacuum the area for things that may have fallen.
- Discard used button-cell batteries safely, and store any unused ones far from your child's reach. They are not only a choking risk but poisonous, too.

- If a toy is labeled for age three and up, don't give it to a younger child, even if she seems advanced for her age. The label means the toy has small parts that could pose a choking risk. In fact, many children older than three are still prone to chewing on small objects and shouldn't play with toys that include them. You'll need to look at the toy as it relates to your own child.

Despite the endless warnings about toy parts that a child might choke on, it is reassuring to know that toy-related deaths are extremely unlikely. In 1998, for instance, 14 were reported to the Consumer Product Safety Commission, so the risk was less than one in a million. The largest single cause of these deaths was latex balloons, which caused four choking deaths that year. For this reason, many children's hospitals have banned latex balloons on their premises. To prevent such tragedies, rare as they are, keep uninflated balloons out of your child's reach, pop and discard balloons before they deflate, and don't leave balloons overnight in your child's room. If you want to give your child a balloon, shiny Mylar balloons are a safer alternative.

Watch the Pet Food

Make sure your baby or young child doesn't have access to pet food in a bowl on the floor (or remove food as soon as your cat or dog eats). Moist food that's left to stand is fertile

I Wish Someone Had Told Me . . .

"*. . . to look out for those doorstops that screw into a door near the floor. They have little rubber tips that can come off in kids' hands (or mouths).*"

KidsHealth Tip

For Infants Only

Don't give infant drops of acetaminophen to older children. Infant drops are concentrated to allow for smaller doses in babies' mouths. In some cases, the infant version is far more potent than older kids' formulas. Rather than trying to figure out the right dose for an older sibling, get the version of the drug designed for older kids.

The Sibling Menace

"My one-year-old daughter's biggest safety hazard is her brothers (ages six, seven, and eight)," one mother told us. "They leave small Lego pieces, coins, and crayons around for her to put in her mouth." This is a common problem with no easy answer. You can try enlisting the older kids to help keep the younger ones safe; you can try setting aside one "clean room" in the house, where small items aren't allowed, or a smaller safe area, like a playpen; you can pay special attention to after-play cleanup. But in the end, you'll probably need to be extra vigilant.

ground for bacteria; dry food, with its hard little pellets, can pose a choking risk. And you don't want your baby and Bowser tussling over the Alpo.

Preventing Burns and Scalding

Fires are a hazard to people of all ages. For children younger than five years, they are the most common cause of death at home. In Chapter 2, "Preparing Your Home and Family," we discussed the basics of household fire protection and recommended getting smoke alarms, fire extinguishers, and an escape ladder, if necessary, as part of making your home ready for a baby. You should also take these additional precautions to prevent burns and scalding:

- Never leave matches or lighters within reach of your child (if you keep these in a purse, for instance, be sure it's out of reach).
- Make sure lit candles are far from your child's reach.
- Choose sleepwear for your child that is labeled flame-retardant (either polyester or treated cotton). Cotton sweatshirts or pants that are not labeled as sleepwear generally are not made of fire-retardant material.
- Teach your young child about "hot." Act out pulling your hand away as you say the word *hot*! It may help to let your child feel something that's hot, but not too hot, such as the outside of a coffee mug.
- Using your "hot!" routine, teach your child to stay away from the stove, fireplace, coffeemaker, and other small, hot appliances. Watch your child closely when she is near these items.
- Turn pot handles toward the center of the stove to prevent pots from being grabbed by your child or accidentally brushed off the stove.

- Set your water heater temperature gauge at no more than 120 degrees Fahrenheit.
- Test bath water or heated formula by putting some on the inside of your wrist.
- When running water in a bathtub or sink, always turn the cold water on first and turn it off last.
- Never heat bottles for your baby in the microwave. The bottle can feel cool enough on the outside and still contain pockets of liquid that are too hot.
- Don't carry coffee, tea, or other hot liquids around your child.

Fire Drill

Even preschoolers can learn simple rules for how to behave during a fire. It helps to repeat the rules periodically and have your child practice them.

Start by creating an escape plan. Walk your child through the house or apartment and show him possible exits in every room—including windows, doors, balconies, and porches. In an apartment building, show your child the nearest stairway marked fire exit. Stress that in a fire, people should use only fire exits—never the elevator. Then choose a safe spot away from the house where family members can meet after they've left the house. Emphasize these rules:

- Stay low. Explain that the smoke from a fire is often more dangerous than the fire itself. To avoid the smoke, your child must crawl on the ground ("walk like a dog or cat on all fours") until he reaches the nearest exit.
- Check doors before opening them. If your child is in a room with the door closed, he should first look around the edge of the door. If he sees smoke, he must leave the door closed and go to a window to wait for help. If he doesn't see smoke, he should touch the doorknob. If it feels warm, he must leave the door closed and wait for help at the window. If the doorknob feels cool, he can slowly open the door.
- Never hide. As frightening as a fire may be, your child should not hide under beds or in closets where a rescuer may not see him.
- Don't go back. Stress that your child should never go into a burning building to get anything or anyone, including toys, pets, or parents.
- Stop, drop, and roll. Explain that if a piece of your child's clothing catches on fire, he should not run, which fans the flames. Instead, he should drop to the floor and roll around, which will smother the flames.

For a child four or five years old, have a fire drill twice a year. With your finger, set off the smoke alarm. Have everyone freeze in place. Then family members should explain how they would escape from wherever they are. You can ask your child how she would handle various obstacles—for instance, a doorway filled with smoke. Then the whole family can go to the planned meeting spot.

Gun Control

Recently, a TV news magazine showed a chilling experiment. Young children in a playroom were warned never to touch guns, and they promised they never would. Moments later, as hidden cameras rolled, the children uncovered an unloaded gun hidden there on purpose. Many of the children didn't even hesitate before picking it up to play with—some pointed it at a playmate and pulled the trigger. Their parents were shocked. Some were more shocked later when several older children confessed they knew the "secret" places where their parents' guns were hidden at home.

Firearms kill almost 100 children younger than five each year. Most of these deaths are homicides, but about 20 a year are unintentional injuries, sometimes occurring when a young child shoots another in play. A three-year-old child can be strong enough to fire a handgun. For this reason, child safety experts advise parents to get rid of guns in their homes or vehicles. If you do keep a gun, it needs to be locked away, unloaded, with the ammunition locked in a separate place. Leaving a gun in a dresser drawer, a night table, or even high on a closet shelf is risky if a young child spends time in your house.

Even if you rid your home of guns, your child may be exposed to them at a neighbor or friend's home. Check with the parents of your child's friends to ensure gun safety when your child is away from your home.

Safe Fun

The possibility of danger is with us every time we cross a street—but that doesn't mean we should keep our children locked up safe inside a bare room. Let your child explore the world and enjoy childhood—after you take a few precautions.

Water Safety

If you live in an area where backyard pools are common, you know that every summer brings the same frightening news stories about toddlers who fall into the water. But young children can drown in even an inch or two of water in a bathtub or cleaning bucket. Because drowning can occur in roughly four minutes (and brain damage from lack of oxygen can occur even sooner) this is one area where you need to be extremely watchful. Here are the basics:

- Never leave your baby or young child alone or in the care of an older child for even a minute near water—not in or near a bathtub, bucket of water, toy pool, open toilet, or deep puddle. An adult must always be watching.
- If you are supervising your child in or near the water, you cannot do anything else like read or nap. You need to pay full attention to your child.
- Do **not** drink alcohol while supervising your child near the water or using a boat. Many boating and other water accidents involve drinking.
- Even a child wearing a ring, water wings, or other flotation devices should never be left alone in or near the water, even for a minute. Such devices cannot be relied on to hold your child's head above water, especially if your child falls in from the side.
- For safety's sake, as well as for fun, it's good for your child to learn to swim, usually at age four to six. But even a child who can swim should never be left alone in the water. Despite what some swim programs may say, there is no such thing as "drown-proofing" a child.
- In public pools, lakes, or beaches, always supervise your own child. Don't rely on lifeguards to do it. But at the ocean, in particular, do not take your child swimming unless a lifeguard is also watching, and swim only in designated areas.
- No dunking others underwater, no running around the pool, no pushing or throwing anyone into the pool or lake, and no eating in the water.

The Well-Dressed Pool

If you have an in-ground pool, it should be surrounded by a five-foot, self-locking fence (check local regulations before installing) that is kept locked even when the pool is covered. With aboveground pools, ladders should be removed when the pool is not in use. In either case, remove rocks or trees that your child could use to climb into the pool.

Keep certified life preservers at hand (the white, solid kind—not inflatable rings). The pool should be fully uncovered before use. Your child should not be allowed to walk on a pool cover, even the rigid kind.

After swimming, remove all toys from the pool and the fenced-in area so your child isn't tempted to go in to get them.

Staying Afloat

In boats or on docks your child should wear Coast Guard–approved life jackets (called personal flotation devices, or PFDs) in the proper size. These are designed to keep your child's head above water. Toy life rings, water wings, "swim sweaters," and similar inflatables cannot be relied upon to hold your child's head out of the water, particularly if your child falls in or loses consciousness.

Speed Counts

If your child does slip underwater, every second counts in preventing death or brain damage. Here are three tips that can help save your child's life:

1. Take training in cardiopulmonary resuscitation (CPR). Make sure anyone who regularly watches your child takes it, too. Repeat the training each spring before swimming season begins; unless you practice, you will forget.
2. If you can't find your child, check the pool first. Do this even if it's a shallow inflatable kiddie pool or a pool that's covered for the winter.
3. Always have a phone with you near the pool to call 911.

Sanitary Swimming

Parents make a lot of jokes about the suspiciously warm water in public kiddie pools. But urine is generally sterile and doesn't spread illness. It's the bowel movements you have to worry about. Even in chlorinated pools, children in diapers can spread infection, especially if they have diarrhea. So think twice before you allow your child in a kiddie pool with a diaper-wearing tot. If your own child is in diapers, consider keeping him out of pools used by other people. Certainly he shouldn't be in the pool if he has diarrhea, if he recently had it, or if he's due to have a bowel movement soon. And don't believe the ads for bathing suits that claim to contain "accidents."

Sun Safety

All of us, no matter what our age, need protection from the sun's ultraviolet rays. But children need it more, in part because their skin and eyes are more vulnerable to sun damage. They also get more sun—50 to 80 percent of a person's lifetime sun exposure occurs by age 18. Severe sunburns during childhood can increase the risk that a person will get melanoma, an often deadly skin cancer, later in life. But simple exposure to sun over the years can wrinkle and toughen the skin and increase the chances a person will get other, less deadly forms of skin cancer. It can also damage vision and promote cataracts, and evidence is emerging that it suppresses the immune system. There's no such thing as "a healthy tan"—a tan is a sign of skin damage.

Skin cancer has been on the rise in recent years. Kids who have fair skin and hair, moles on their skin, and a family history of skin cancer are at increased risk and need to be extra careful about sun protection. But skin cancer is a risk for dark-skinned people as well, and all children should be protected. Damage to the ozone layer, which blocks ultraviolet rays from reaching Earth, may increase these risks by the time your child is an adult. Habits she learns now can let her enjoy the sun safely all her life.

The Big Four of Sun Protection

1. Stay out of the sun as the surest means of protection. Your child should not spend long periods in the sun when it is strongest (from 10:00 A.M. to 4:00 P.M. in the northern hemisphere). Even on cloudy days the sun's ultraviolet rays can do damage, especially if reflected off sand, water, snow, or even concrete. Rays are strongest near the equator and at high altitudes. You needn't stay indoors, but seek out shade—or bring it with you—when you're out.

2. Cover your child. Long-sleeved shirts and long pants in lightweight cotton can provide skin protection. The cloth should be woven tightly enough so you can't see your hand through it. Clothing that gets wet does not block UV rays as well. "Sun protective" summer shirts, jackets, and pants made of special fabrics are available through many children's clothing catalogs. Some of them claim to have a sun protection factor (SPF) of 30 or more, as high as most sunscreen lotions.

3. Protect your child's eyes. Hats with wide brims or caps with bills help shield the eyes. Even so, the American Academy of Pediatrics (AAP) recommends UV-blocking sunglasses for all children, even infants. The label should say that the sunglasses absorb "99 percent of UV" or more, have "UV absorption up to 400 nm," or meet American National Standards Institute (ANSI) standards. UV protection is provided by an invisible chemical on the lenses, not by the darkness of the lens.

4. Use sunscreen if your child will be in the sun for more than 30 minutes; that's the advice of the AAP. Most light-skinned people should use a sunscreen with an SPF of 15. Although dark-skinned people burn less easily and tan less visibly, they also need sun protection. Children with very dark skin should still use an SPF of at least 8.

Sun When Baby Is Younger than Six Months

Babies younger than six months should be kept out of direct sun entirely. Keep your baby in the shade of a tree, umbrella, or stroller canopy. Babies are prone to sunburn and heatstroke, both of which can be dangerous at this age. For years, the American Academy of Pediatrics (AAP) recommended against putting sunblock on babies younger than six months because of concerns about the way their skin might absorb the chemicals. But in 1999, the AAP changed its position, saying that if clothing and shade to block the sun are not available, "it may be reasonable to apply sunscreen to small areas, such as the face and back of the hands." Still, it's better to protect your baby by keeping her out of the sun.

Using a Sunscreen Correctly

The SPF number on a sunscreen tells you how much longer a person can stay in the sun without burning. For instance, if your child would burn after 20 minutes in the sun, using a sunscreen with an SPF of 15 would prevent him from burning for 15 times 20 minutes, or five hours.

For most sunscreens to live up to their SPF billing, they should be applied in generous amounts 30 minutes before your child goes into the sun (one ounce is considered the right amount for an adult). Cover any exposed areas, including the face, ears, nose, feet, and hands. Use a water-resistant or waterproof sunscreen, and reapply it every three or four hours if your child is sweating, every two hours if he is swimming.

The SPF number isn't the only thing to look for when choosing a sunscreen. SPF measures the extent to which the lotion blocks one form of ultraviolet rays— UVB light. (An SPF of 15 blocks about 92 percent of UVB light.) UVB has long been known to damage skin and promote skin cancer. But now another form of UV light, UVA, is believed to be harmful as well. Sunscreens aren't rated for UVA protection, but look for one that promises "broad spectrum" protection or that contains ingredients that block UVA, too.

Titanium dioxide and zinc oxide physically block both UVA and UVB. They used to come in a white cream often seen on lifeguards' noses. But now micronized versions are available in transparent sunblocks. In addition, a variety

KidsHealth Tip

Five Safety Devices That Are Fun for Kids

1. Color-changing sunblock (goes on purple or green and turns clear)
2. Jazzy bike helmets (or plain ones decorated with stickers)
3. Anything that glows in the dark (sneaker laces, jackets, etc.)
4. Flashlights (especially the kinds with compasses or sirens)
5. "Tap lights" (battery-operated lights that stick to walls or windowsills and turn on when you press them; an easy way to provide a light for children too short to reach the light switch)

of substances can chemically absorb UVA. Some of the most common are benzophenone and avobenzone (Parsol 1789).

Most sunscreens work chemically. If one irritates your child's skin, try switching to one with different ingredients or to a physical blocker like zinc oxide.

The Voice of Experience

"Let your child put sunscreen on you and rub it in while you do the same to him. It'll make it fun for him, and he won't fight it so much."
—FROM THE KIDSHEALTH PARENT SURVEY

Fun at the Playground

Here are some tips on preventing falls and other injuries:

- Children, especially toddlers, should use playground equipment designed for their age. Parents, eager to show how advanced their toddlers are, often encourage them to try the "big kids'" equipment before they are ready. One hazard is the big kids themselves; it's easy for them to knock over your little one without even noticing.
- Whether in a backyard or a park, playgrounds should have a forgiving surface—such as rubber mats, fine sand, or wood chips—rather than asphalt, concrete, grass, or dirt.

KidsHealth Tip
No Trampolines, Please

Because trampolines cause injuries, including many fractures to arms and legs, the AAP recommends that they never be used in homes or public playgrounds. Even in schools, the AAP says, they should be limited to supervised athletic training programs.

- Teach your child some simple rules such as "feet first" (down a slide or ladder) and "hold on" (on a slide or swing). He should be warned to stay far from a swing in motion.
- On hot days, slides can be hot enough to burn, so check them first.
- Keep food and drinks off the playground. When melted, they can be slippery underfoot. And a child who runs or plays with an ice pop in his mouth can be hurt if he falls or gets jolted.

Trikes and Bikes

Most children start riding a tricycle at age two and a half or three and move on to a bicycle (often with training wheels, initially) around age five. Children should ride only on the sidewalk or in other car-free places until they are at least six or seven. Because a bicycle is the most dangerous plaything your child will have, don't rush the transition from trike to bike. You want your child to have not only the physical skills to balance and pedal but the emotional maturity to follow safety rules and use good judgment.

Choosing a Trike

- Look for a trike that's low to the ground with widely spaced rear wheels so it is difficult to tip over.
- Make sure your child can reach the pedals even when they are farthest from him. If he can't, you can buy blocks that attach to the pedals to make them bigger. But these don't always work well and can be frustrating.
- Make sure the trike has a bell or horn and a trunk or basket so your child can carry items and still keep both hands on the handlebars.

Figure 24.1. Helmet safety. A properly fitted bike helmet is a must for helping to prevent head injuries. It's a good idea to get your child into the habit of wearing one early by starting when she first gets on a tricycle.

Choosing a Bike

- Get a bike that fits now, not one your child will grow into. Your child should be able to sit on the seat with feet flat on the ground and handlebars no higher than her shoulder. Most children start out with either a 12-inch or a 16-inch bike.
- The bike should have foot (coaster) brakes, rather than hand brakes.
- The bike should be well maintained, with bolts tightened. Brake pads should not be worn out, the chain should be clean and oiled, and tires should be kept at the recommended pressure.

Choosing and Using a Bike Helmet

Remember the number-one safety rule of bike riding: Your child should always wear a helmet. This is the law in at least 17 states and some additional cities and towns, but it's good advice everywhere. Head injuries are the chief risk in bicycle riding, and it's estimated that use of helmets reduces the risk of head injuries by 85 percent.

It is important to make a strict rule that your child must always wear a bike helmet. One study found that when parents had such a rule, 88 percent of children followed it. When parents did not enforce this rule, only 19 percent of children wore helmets consistently. (Of course, parents who bike should wear helmets as well, for their own safety and to be a role model for their children.)

Even though tricycles are safer than bikes, your child should wear a helmet on a trike as well. Besides possibly preventing some injuries, it will get him used to wearing a helmet whenever he pedals—and that will help keep him safe when he starts riding a two-wheeler.

When you choose a bike helmet, follow these guidelines:

- The helmet should have a label saying it meets the Consumer Product Safety Commission (CPSC) standard, which applies to helmets manufactured after March 10, 1999. The new standard requires, among other things, that helmets cover more of the head in children ages one to five. The label may also say it meets Snell, ANSI, or ATSM standards.
- The helmet should fit snugly in a level position on top of the head without rocking front to back or side to side. It should cover the forehead, the area most likely to be injured.
- The chinstrap should fit well around the ears, and you should be able to insert only the width of one finger between chin and strap.
- Because a helmet that has been in a crash may lose its capacity to absorb shock, either buy the helmet new or be sure it has never taken a serious hit. If your child's helmet ever takes a serious impact, it's best to get a new one.
- For comfort (which will make your child more willing to wear it), it should be lightweight and ventilated.

The Child as Passenger

If safety is your main concern, it's better not to bike with your child as passenger. That's especially true if you'll be riding in traffic or on rough roads or if you are not an experienced and strong cyclist. The added weight can throw off your balance and steering. If you haven't ridden in a while, practice first.

If you do choose to bike with your child on board, here are some safety tips:

- Your child should be at least one year old. The jostling of the head can be too rough for younger babies.
- Your child should always wear a helmet.
- Your child should have her own seat—either a frame-mounted seat that goes over your rear wheel or a low trailer that rolls on two wheels behind your bike. In either case, the seat should have a lap and shoulder harness, which should always be used.
- A rear seat should have a back high enough to support your child's neck and guards that prevent her feet from touching your rear wheel.

- A trailer should have a sturdy frame to provide accident protection, a tall red warning flag for visibility, and a flexible joint in its hitch so that it can stay upright if your bike falls. (A trailer may be safer in an accident, but it is wider than your bike, so its wheel could slip off the road or hit a curb if you're not careful.)
- Before you take your child out, bike the same route at the same time of day by yourself, so you see road conditions up close.

Scooters

You might think that the repopularized scooter is something enjoyed by only older children (as well as the occasional adult!). But scooters come in all shapes and sizes, and even four- to five-year-olds are using them—and at breakneck speeds. Helmet and road safety rules apply here, too. We've seen a rash of scooter injuries lately, including fractures of the arms and wrists, as well as traumatic head injuries.

Animal Safety

If your family already has a dog or cat when your baby arrives, try to prepare the animal as described in Chapter 2, "Preparing Your Home and Family," and be particularly careful in the early weeks. Even after the animal and the baby are used to each other, babies and toddlers should not be left alone with uncaged pets. At night, even a kindly old pooch should not have access to your baby's crib or cradle. Preschoolers, too, need to be supervised around pets.

If you have an animal that has bitten someone in the past or that seems aggressive or extremely defensive, the wisest course may be to find someone without

Dogs and Cats

Most serious pet injuries are dog bites, which unfortunately kill several children a year. Children are more likely than adults to be bitten and to be bitten on the face or head at mouth-level to the dog. Cats generally ignore—or flee from—children, but they can bite or claw a child accidentally during play.

children who can take it. Difficult as that may be for you emotionally, it pales beside the possibility of seeing your child injured.

Choosing a Safer Pet

If you do not have a dog or cat, it is best to wait until children are older—at least five or six—before bringing one into the house so your children can understand the responsibilities that come with having an animal. Until then, try an easily managed pet, such as fish or a bird.

- Avoid reptiles, such as snakes, lizards, iguanas, or turtles, which can transmit salmonella, a kind of bacteria that can be dangerous. (For more information, see Chapter 2, "Preparing Your Home and Family.")
- Avoid wild animals, including ferrets, monkeys, hedgehogs, and prairie dogs, even if they were born or raised in captivity.
- Domesticated rabbits, guinea pigs, hamsters, gerbils, birds, and fish make relatively safe pets in the proper environment.
- If you want to get a dog or cat, consider getting an adult animal that already has lived safely with children. Puppies and kittens are more likely to play roughly.
- Get obedience training for your dog to make it safer for a young child.
- Avoid dogs that grow to more than 50 pounds, such as German shepherds, Dalmatians, and Labrador retrievers. A large dog's bite can do more damage than a small dog's.
- Avoid dogs that may have been bred to be aggressive or that are described by dog fanciers as not recommended for first-time owners. These include rottweilers, Doberman pinschers, and pit bulls.
- Do not rely on a breed to ensure safety. Just because your family has always had—and loved—golden retrievers or dachshunds does not mean that an individual animal will be safe with your child. Training and supervising both dog and child are necessary for safety.

Teaching Your Child Animal Safety

Children need to be taught to move calmly, speak softly, and touch gently when they are dealing with pets. They should not bother animals when the animals are eating, sleeping, or tending to their young. They should not grab animals suddenly, pull their ears or tail, drop them, fall on them, hit them, or yell at them. They should pat animals from the head to the rear, rather than rumpling the fur against the grain. And they should wash their hands with soap and water after handling their pets. Although it's good to keep repeating such advice, most young children cannot be depended on to follow it every time, so adult supervision is needed.

Also teach your child how to handle strange dogs:

- Your child should never approach a dog unless the owner says it's friendly. Then your child should stand still and let the dog sniff her, then put out her hand to be sniffed. After that, she may gently pat the animal.
- Your child should not run from a strange dog, even if it barks at her. She should stand still, face the dog without making eye contact, and slowly back away. Your child should never be alone in a setting where a dog might attack her.
- Your child should not go near any wild animals, including squirrels, chipmunks, raccoons, and geese.

Need More Information?

Check the Index and Appendix C, "Resource Guide." And of course, consult your child's doctor.

chapter twenty-five

Choosing Child Care

References, please?

For working parents, child care is an essential link that helps them balance the responsibilities of jobs and family. But that doesn't stop parents from worrying about their young children when they leave the children behind.

Choosing a Caregiver

The idea of leaving your child with someone else—who may be a stranger at first—seems to go against everything you feel about good parenting. But if you take time to choose the right place and the right person, the experience for both you and your child can be a very positive one.

Types of Child Care

There are many types of child care today, including family members who will babysit, child-care centers, corporate day care, family- or home-based day care, nannies and au pairs, and parenting co-ops. Some parents use a combination of several types; they may leave their child with Grandma a few days each week and in their company-sponsored day-care center the other days of the week.

In-Home Care

In-home care means a family member or a nanny or au pair will take care of your child at your home. Many parents prefer this arrangement. Your child will stay in a familiar, comfortable environment with his own toys, his own bed, and his own food. It also may give you greater flexibility; you can accept overtime or attend late meetings at work because your caregiver is at home until you arrive, usually working 40 to 60 hours a week. If your child is sick, he can stay in his own home and recuperate without disrupting your work schedule. (Sick children are generally not allowed at day-care facilities, so parents must stay home from work to care for them.) And your child may not be sick quite as often if he is not exposed to the germs of other children.

What's the downside of in-home care? It's usually the most expensive type of child care—unless you're fortunate enough to have a family member who is willing to take on the job. In-home care is also a problem if your caregiver becomes ill and cannot take care of your child. Also, some toddlers and preschoolers enjoy the company of (and learn socialization skills from) other children, which they may not experience at home. Finally, if you opt for a live-in nanny or an au pair, you face two concerns you need to think about carefully: You and your family will lose some privacy when you bring someone into your home 24 hours a day. And you also must be able to trust this person not only with the valuables in your home but also with your child—there is no one supervising this person all day long (which is why the hidden camera industry has seen a recent boom).

Family- or Home-Based Child Care

Family- or home-based child care provides care for children in the caregiver's home, often with one adult supervising several children. The benefits of this type of care include small group size and a homelike setting for kids. Often, too, family day care is less expensive than other options, and some parents find they can work out parenting co-ops, where parents each take responsibility for providing child care to a group of children on a rotating schedule.

What are the cons? Family child care is not as strictly regulated as day-care centers are, and the laws on licensing are different from state to state. In many places, there is little or no oversight. Also, many of the caregivers are not trained, although often they have young children of their own. And, if the caregiver is ill, parents are left without backup arrangements for their children.

Day-Care Center

Day care in a center, preschool, nursery school, or your workplace offers certain advantages: It is probably run in accordance with state regulations that set minimum standards for staff-to-child ratios, group size, staff training, and building safety. Day-care centers usually take children from six-week-old infants to school-age children. The caregivers usually have training in early childhood development, and a staff illness doesn't affect access to reliable care for your child.

KidsHealth Tip

Calming Down After Day Care

To help head off tantrums and make a calm transition from day care to the outside world, don't rush your child off when you pick him up at the end of the day. Having him change gears so abruptly when he's tired can cause anxiety, so it's best to leave a few extra transition moments. Sit down and become involved in what he's doing, and after a few minutes, suggest that you'll both leave after he says good-bye to his pals.

The disadvantages of day care include waiting lists because of a limited number of licensed centers, a more structured environment for your child because of the focus on regulations, frequent turnover of staff, and usually inflexible pickup and drop-off times.

Age Considerations

The setting that is best for your child often depends on his age. A priority for infants is to make sure they are held and nurtured and that all their needs are met. Finding a completely trustworthy caretaker is crucial because the child has no way of telling you if there is neglect or abusive behavior.

For toddlers ages 12 months to three years, the key is to find a safe and supervised situation. Toddlers need to explore, but they must always be watched closely because they are so vulnerable to accidents and injuries. Having lots of toys for learning to share is important, as is a caregiver who will spend time talking with toddlers and helping them learn to talk.

Preschool children between ages three and five start making friends, so look for child care where there are other children their age. Also, there should be fun opportunities for preschoolers to learn about colors, shapes, and numbers, as well as time for reading stories.

Think Safety

With any type of child care, safety is a primary consideration. When you're looking for care for your child, consider the answers to these questions:

- How does the caregiver supervise the children on the playground? How old is the equipment, and has it been inspected recently? Is there soft sand, wood chips, or rubber mats under the equipment?
- Are the children grouped by age? If not, younger children could be hurt by older youngsters.
- Is the facility childproofed?
- Do staff-to-child ratios meet or exceed the recommended levels?
- Are infants always fed in the upright position, with no bottles ever propped or placed in bed with the baby?
- Are babies always put to sleep on their backs?
- Is the day-care center or home licensed or registered with the local government? Ask to see current inspection documents. Also, is the center accredited by the National Association for the Education of Young Children or the National Child Care Association?
- Are staff members or your in-home caregiver trained in first aid and CPR, and do they know how to respond if your child is choking? Do they know and follow the basics of sanitation, including frequent hand washing and changing diapers with disposable gloves to prevent the spread of infections?
- Does the day-care center perform monthly evacuation and emergency drills?

A child-care facility should be as safe as your home. If you feel there are dangers, including open stairways, doors that can slam, uncovered electrical outlets, or hot radiators, look for another facility. If all looks fine but you want additional peace of mind, call the local health department to make sure there aren't any outstanding complaints about the center.

Conduct an Interview

While touring a day-care or home-based center, spend some time observing the children and the staff. You may want to ask the following questions:

- Do you have an open-door policy on visits from parents?
- What is the policy on caring for sick children?
- What is your discipline policy?
- What are the educational backgrounds of the teachers or caregivers? Do they have basic training and experience in early childhood development?
- Does the center conduct reference and background checks?
- If your child has special needs, is the center or home accessible and able to meet your child's needs?

If you've opted to hire an in-home caregiver, such as a nanny, you should interview the applicants at least twice. Ask about their child-rearing philosophy, methods of discipline, and previous experience. Present specific situations and ask how they would handle the situations. If you are using a placement agency, ask if they have conducted a criminal background check. Also, ask for several references and check them all. If the caregiver will be driving your child, it's important to check her driving record.

Besides inquiring about training in early childhood development, you should also ask a potential nanny or au pair these questions:

- Why are you interested in working with young children?
- Why did you leave your last job? (Check references; ask that family why the relationship ended and whether they would recommend that caregiver.)
- What is your discipline policy? (Offer "what if" scenarios to elicit responses to situations that could arise. For example, if a child throws a tantrum over a toy someone else is playing with, what should the consequences be?)
- How will you provide new experiences to enhance my child's mental and physical development? What are the opportunities you can offer to experience art, music, group and individual play, and indoor and outdoor play?
- How would you handle toilet teaching?
- How would you handle separation anxiety?

During the interview for an in-home caregiver, put all the details on the table. Outline the duties, expectations, hours, salary, and paid-vacation and sick-leave policies. Talk about your own obligations as well. If the caregiver will be living with you, discuss living arrangements; personal, off-duty time; visitors; and holiday arrangements.

Getting to Know the Caregiver

Once you have chosen a caregiver, ease your child into the day-care experience. Visit the chosen day-care center or home-based program before the day you will be leaving your child behind. Invite your new nanny or au pair over for lunch; let her work a few days while you are still at home. Make sure your child knows that you like and trust the caregiver.

Once your child has begun child care, give him and the caregiver a little time to adjust to each other before you make any judgments. Some days, your child

KidsHealth Tip

Emergency Plans for Caregivers

Safety is all about planning ahead—so what should you do? Give your child's caregiver work phone numbers, beeper numbers, cell phone numbers, and email addresses. Make sure your caregiver knows what to do in an emergency and where first-aid supplies are, and provide the phone numbers of friends, relatives, and your child's physician. Make sure in-home caregivers know the exact address and phone number of your home and can give clear directions to your home. Clearly post the phone number of the poison control center. And finally, your caregiver should have a set of door keys in case she needs to lock up the house and take your child to a medical care facility.

might say he doesn't like his teacher or he doesn't want to go to day care. If you are concerned about your child's feelings, talk with the caregiver and plan to sit in on the child-care program to help you understand why your child is having difficulty. If you find that there's nothing wrong otherwise, it could be that your child is anxious about leaving you—sometimes called separation anxiety.

For babies up to seven months, separation anxiety isn't usually an issue. Older infants, however, may get upset when their parents leave them. Toddlers may cry or act angry, and preschoolers sometimes regress and take on behaviors of younger children when they see their parents leave. If your child is usually happy, these moments may be normal separation anxiety. (See Chapter 19, "Temperament, Behavior, and Discipline," for more information about separation anxiety.)

If, after several weeks, your child is still upset when you leave, it could indicate a more serious problem. Talk with your child, your child's doctor, and the staff to get to the root of the problem.

Keeping Your Child Healthy in Child Care

It's going to happen. Your child is going to get sick, and it's more likely to happen if she is in a day-care center or home-based center. In these environments, she'll be around more children, and that means more germs.

Common Illnesses in Child-Care Settings

Children in day care are more prone to ear infections. If your child shows symptoms such as ear pulling, fussiness, or fever, contact her doctor.

Conjunctivitis, otherwise known as pinkeye, is an infection of the lining of the eye, and it spreads among young children easily because they are often touching each other and sharing toys. Again, call your child's doctor if she develops eye redness or discharge.

Rash-producing illnesses, usually caused by viruses such as chicken pox, spread easily in a child-care setting. Because increasing numbers of children now receive the vaccination for chicken pox, this disease is becoming less of a concern for children in child care and for their parents. But if your child has not been immunized and develops chicken pox, expect to keep your child home from day care for about 10 days, until the blisters are scabbed over.

For more information on these and other common infections encountered by children in child care such as head lice, pinworms, scabies, and ringworm, see Chapter 30, "Childhood Infections."

More Serious Concerns

Some diseases of greater concern can spread in a child-care environment, especially if strict health and sanitation rules are not followed. Hand washing is a must, and diapering and food preparation areas must be entirely separate from each other. Each should be cleaned immediately after each use. Proper handling of dirty diapers and human waste must be observed to help prevent the spread of infections such as hepatitis and the diarrhea-producing parasitic infection giardiasis.

Caregivers should have a written policy on how they handle bloody noses, dirty diapers, and other situations where illnesses might spread. Hepatitis A, a viral infection, and many bacterial diseases can be spread through human feces. HIV can be spread through contaminated blood, although the virus is extremely rare among U.S. children. Hepatitis B can also spread through blood, but the vaccinations children now routinely get during their first year protect them from this disease.

Child abuse in day care is every parent's nightmare. While reports of child abuse by nannies or day-care workers get a lot of attention, the U.S. Department of Health and Human Services found that 75 percent of child abuse is committed by parents, while another 10 percent is committed by other relatives. Less than 1 percent of child abusers are child-care providers.

Still, it's important to keep a close eye on how your child is being cared for. Watch for bite marks, unusual bruises, cuts or burns, a high incidence of injuries or accidents, and injuries to the face. For more information about signs of abuse and what to do if you suspect abuse of your child, see Chapter 32, "Health Problems in Early Childhood."

If the caregiver and your child give inconsistent stories about how the injuries occurred or your child seems frightened of the caregiver, see your child's doctor about the injuries. If you believe your child has been abused, remove her from the situation immediately. If your child tells you she was abused, make sure you tell her she did the right thing by informing you. Also, make sure you report suspected abuse to the police.

Need More Information?

Check the Index and Appendix C, "Resource Guide." And of course, consult your child's doctor.

chapter twenty-six

Medical Issues in Adoption

The more you know, the better parent you'll be

All parents have concerns about their child's health—and adoptive parents have some special ones particular to their situation. This chapter is certainly not meant to frighten adoptive parents—just the opposite. The more you know, the more prepared and confident you'll be.

Gathering Information Before You Adopt

If you have an open or semi-open adoption—one where you meet the birth mother and sometimes the father as well—you should be able to get a lot of health information. In an open independent adoption, you may help arrange the birth mother's prenatal care, go along on her doctor visits, and be present for the birth. You can also ask for health records through the agency or attorney who is helping to arrange the adoption.

With an older child living in this country, you may be able to evaluate health issues by spending time with him over weeks or months or perhaps even serving as a foster parent before adopting him.

With international adoptions, you are likely to get a photograph and perhaps a short video of the child, but health and family information may be scanty or unreliable. If you can afford it, it may be worth making a trip to meet the child before deciding to adopt, especially if the child is older.

Some health information may be available as part of a child's health record and can be the kind of information doctors would want to know about any child they were treating, adopted or not:

Sources for Exploring Adoption

If you are just starting to consider adoption, you need more information than this chapter can provide. A good start is *The Complete Adoption Book*, second edition, by Laura Beauvais-Godwin and Raymond Godwin, Esq. (Adams Media Corporation, 2000). The Web is also filled with information on this subject.

- Age, ethnic background, education, occupation, height, weight, and medical condition of the birth parents (although often little is known about the father)
- Diseases or medical conditions that run in the biological family, from allergies and nearsightedness to cancer and mental illness
- Whether the birth mother has other biological children and, if so, how they are doing
- Whether the birth mother drank alcohol, smoked cigarettes, or used illegal drugs during pregnancy; if so, what and how much (The potential impact of alcohol abuse is discussed later in this chapter.)
- Whether the birth mother used any prescription or over-the-counter medications during pregnancy; if so, what and how much
- Whether the birth mother engaged in sexual conduct that would raise the risk of sexually transmitted diseases
- Whether the birth mother received prenatal care
- The results of any tests done during pregnancy
- Any problems during pregnancy, labor, or delivery
- The child's weight, length, and head circumference measurements since birth (her growth records)
- Any medical problems the child has had since birth
- The results of any tests the child may have had, such as tests for hepatitis B, HIV, syphilis, or tuberculosis
- How the child is developing in relation to standard milestones for her age such as sitting up, walking, talking, or fine motor skills
- A description of the child's personality (outgoing, reserved, fearful, confident) and her relationships with others
- As much as possible about the child's living situation
- Whether the child has suffered physical, sexual, or emotional abuse

Interpreting Information

Once you have gathered all available information, you need to understand it as thoroughly as possible. Ideally, your adoption agency, if you have one, should help you evaluate the information without glossing over potential problems. It's also wise to consult a doctor to help you interpret the medical record. In many cases, for example, a family history of an illness does not mean the child definitely will get the illness or is even likely to get it.

In some cases, it may be a good idea to consult a pediatrician who has experience with adopted children from the same background as the one you may adopt. This is especially true if you are adopting internationally. Russian medical records, for instance, often contain terms that are unfamiliar to most U.S. doctors but that are known to doctors who have many patients from that area of the world. And healthy children from Central America routinely are lighter and smaller than children of the same age from other areas.

A number of medical centers around the country specialize in evaluating medical records and videos for would-be adoptive parents. This can be done by mail and phone. Many of these specialists are listed at adoption group Web sites such as the site of the Eastern European Adoption Coalition, www.eeadopt.org. Adoption agency social workers and support groups also can refer you to these medical centers. Such centers include the International Adoption Clinic at the University of Minnesota Hospital in Minneapolis [Dr. Dana Johnson, (800) 688-5252], the New England Medical Center International Adoption Clinic at the Floating Hospital for Children in Boston [Dr. Laurie C. Miller, (617) 636-8121], and the Adoption

No Guarantees

Whether you adopt, give birth to, or foster parent a child, no amount of information or planning can guarantee that your child will be healthy or develop as you would wish. Adoptive parents may not know their child's full genetic history—all the medical conditions that run in the child's birth family—but neither do most biological parents. That's because branches of the family may have lost touch with each other, and illnesses may have gone undiagnosed or been kept secret (especially in generations past).

Consultation Service at the duPont Hospital for Children in Wilmington, Delaware [Dr. Kate Cronan and Dr. Steven Bachrach, (302) 651-5956].

Once You've Decided, Get More Information

Once you've decided to adopt or provide foster care for a specific child, try to gather more information, especially concerning her daily schedule, her abilities, and her likes and dislikes.

Consider asking these questions about the child:

- What foods does she like or dislike? How are they prepared? Is she allergic to anything? How is she fed, or how does she feed herself?
- When does she sleep (at naptime and bedtime) and for how long? Does she have a bedtime routine? What is her bed like?
- What kind of diapers does she wear?
- What are her favorite songs? (Try to get a tape.)
- What does she usually wear? What does she usually play with? Does she have a favorite toy or "blankie"?
- How is she best comforted?
- How does she get along with other children? With adults? (Some children raised in orphanages staffed solely by women may be frightened by men, including their adoptive father, until they get used to them.)
- Can you take pictures of the child's surroundings and friends or caretakers? Can you make arrangements to keep in touch?
- Can you get the names, addresses, and phone numbers of everyone you meet who knows your child (such as a neighbor, a child-care worker, or a doctor) in case you need more information later?
- What vaccinations has your child received, and when?
- Can you get a copy of your child's medical record or photograph it?
- If you are not in touch with the birth mother, can you arrange some way to contact her if a medical crisis makes that important?

Health Care When Your Child Comes Home

Soon after your child comes home, she should have a thorough evaluation by a doctor. If you consulted an adoption-medicine specialist before the adoption, you

Talk About It

Although most children are too young to understand adoption until about age seven, parents should bring up the subject while their child is still preschool aged. There is evidence that adopted children who know more about their birth parents have an easier time with identity issues when they become teens.

may want to have the same person do your child's initial evaluation. Or you may prefer to use the doctor who will be your child's regular health care provider. With a foster child, the agency may be able to tell you where the child has been getting health care so you can either use the same providers or have the records sent to a doctor you choose.

If your child is an infant, the examination may consist mostly of taking a history from you and performing a first checkup.

If your child was born in another country and there is any doubt about her vaccinations, she probably should be revaccinated. If your child is past infancy, the doctor may refer her to specialists for further evaluation, possibly including eye and ear doctors, a neurologist, a psychologist or speech therapist, and a dentist. These visits can be spread over weeks or months to avoid bombarding your child with many (and possibly unpleasant) medical experiences right away. It is important, however, to complete these evaluations, experts say, because they are a prelude to getting help for possible psychological problems or developmental delays.

Screening Tests

It is often recommended that children adopted from other countries be screened for the following conditions, as appropriate for their age. With U.S.-born children, doctors may check for some or all of these, depending on the child's risk factors and the completeness of her medical records:

- Anemia
- Speech, language, and other developmental delays
- Hepatitis B and C (If hepatitis B testing is negative initially, it should be repeated six months later.)
- HIV

- Impaired hearing
- Impaired vision
- Intestinal parasites
- Lead poisoning
- Metabolic disorders (such as PKU)
- Psychological problems
- Rickets
- Syphilis
- Thyroid conditions
- Tuberculosis

Problems of Special Concern

Some adopted children need long-term care for a variety of problems. Your child's doctor will check for hepatitis B, fetal alcohol syndrome (FAS), and attachment difficulties. (For information on hepatitis B, see Chapter 32, "Health Problems in Early Childhood.")

Fetal Alcohol Syndrome and Related Problems

Alcohol use during pregnancy is the leading known cause of mental retardation in the world. The heavier the drinking, the higher the risk. But even moderate drink-

KidsHealth Tip

Applying for Financial Aid

The American Academy of Pediatrics encourages families to apply for all existing federal and state adoption-subsidy programs even if they don't think they will need financial aid. That's because applications for subsidy programs may be accepted only at the time of adoption, but problems that could require long-term therapy may not be apparent until later. These programs generally apply only to domestic adoptions, not to international ones.

ing can do damage, especially early in pregnancy, when the woman may not even know she is pregnant. For this reason, adoptive parents often wonder and worry, "Did the birth mother drink enough alcohol during her pregnancy to cause serious mental and physical problems?" This possibility is one of the chief risks of adoption.

About 1 in 750 babies born in the United States has fetal alcohol syndrome (FAS), the most severe form of damage. These children generally are small and may have small heads, delayed development, specific birth defects, poor motor skills, poor memory and language comprehension skills, an inability to understand concepts such as time or money, and behavioral problems such as impulsiveness and anxiety.

Children with FAS often have a typical set of facial abnormalities: small eye openings, flat cheekbones, a thin upper lip, and a flattened philtrum (the groove between the nose and lips). In some cases, a doctor can diagnose FAS with confidence in infancy. But often it is difficult: The facial features may not become obvious until later, and other early symptoms may be caused instead by malnutrition or neglect, which are reversible. To help with the diagnosis, it is important to get as much reliable information as possible about the birth mother's drinking habits.

If there is any doubt whether a child has FAS, it is worth consulting an expert. If you adopt or become a foster parent for a baby with FAS, you should take on this challenge with your eyes open.

Many more children have more limited, but still serious, problems caused by alcohol use during pregnancy. Children with fetal alcohol effects (FAE) have symptoms similar to those of FAS but to a lesser degree and without obvious physical abnormalities. Also, alcohol-related neurodevelopmental disorder (ARND) involves similar emotional and behavioral symptoms but without delays in development or growth problems. Children with FAE and ARND often grow up with these problems remaining undiagnosed. Their learning and behavioral problems may be mistakenly attributed to obstinacy, belligerence, or—if they were adopted—to adoption itself, and they often get into trouble with the law. These children may also have a range of physical problems, including heart defects and impaired vision or hearing.

Although the effects of alcohol cannot be reversed, early intervention may help children reach their potential and live more satisfying lives. Parents often find it much easier to cope when they know a child's difficult behavior is caused by a medical condition, not an attitude problem.

Information about fetal alcohol problems can be found online. For a start, try the FAS Community Resource Center (www.azstarnet.com/~tjk/fashome.htm) or FASlink (www.acbr.com/fas/faslink.htm).

Attachment Problems

When children have been abused or neglected in infancy, or have had a series of temporary homes and caregivers, they may have difficulty becoming attached to their adoptive parents (or to any adult). These problems range in severity. Not all children who suffered abuse or neglect have serious attachment problems, especially if they were cared for by nurturing adults after leaving the abusive setting.

Children with severe attachment disorders may seem charming on the surface and affectionate with strangers. With their parents, they may be very clingy and whiny but resist being hugged or cuddled and refuse to make eye contact. They may reject attempts to help them with tasks like getting dressed and may engage in continual battles with caregivers over control of the activities of daily life. They may also act out in ways that can be hurtful to others, or they may tell obvious lies.

Attachment problems may be difficult to diagnose. After children come home, their problems may be wrongly labeled attention deficit disorder or depression. Once the condition is diagnosed correctly, the family may require special therapy to begin building bonds of trust. These children can present a big challenge, but attachment problems often can be overcome with effort, patience, and help.

Need More Information?

Check the Index and Appendix C, "Resource Guide." And of course, consult your child's doctor.

PART FOUR

Using the Health Care System

chapter twenty-seven

The Health Care System for Children

People, places, and costs

I f you're unusually lucky, your child will never need referral to a specialist, a surgical procedure, a visit to the emergency room, or admission to the hospital; and your insurance plan will cover nearly all of the costs for your child's health care with a minimum of paperwork or hassle. However, the odds are overwhelming that at some point your child will need to encounter the health care system outside the walls of her primary care doctor's office. In this chapter we'll discuss some of the insurance and financial issues you may face in getting health care for your child, some basic information about specialists who treat children, and a tour of the emergency room and hospital from a pediatric patient's perspective.

Health Insurance and Managed Care: Is Your Child Covered?

Today, nearly 14 percent of U.S. economic production is spent on health care. This makes ours the most expensive health care system in the world and makes it imperative that you have health insurance coverage for your children. About one in six children will be born with or develop one or more chronic (and potentially costly) health problems. And although most kids make it through childhood with just the usual assortment of minor illnesses and injuries, even the cost of the recommended routine health care for children in the first years of life (frequent checkups, immunizations, screening tests) can be a major burden for many families if paid for out-of-pocket.

In what follows, we'll discuss the various forms of health insurance that may provide coverage for your child and family and the advantages and disadvantages of these plans. We'll also offer tips to help you navigate the health care system to obtain the care your child needs, regardless of your insurance coverage. (See Chapter 33, "Caring for Your Child with Special Health Care Needs," for additional information on the financial aspects of caring for a child with special or complex health problems.)

Types of Health Insurance

Two major forms of health insurance are available in the United States today: fee-for-service (or indemnity) insurance and managed care.

Fee-for-Service (Indemnity) Insurance

Fee-for-service (indemnity) insurance is the traditional type of health coverage that most Americans had until a few years ago. In this kind of insurance plan, patients could usually choose any primary care doctor or specialist they wished to see, and the insurance company would pay the fees for doctor visits, tests, hospital care, surgery, and supplies and equipment without questioning the need for the service or attempting to limit the number or kinds of services that patients could

KidsHealth Tip

Heading Off Insurance Inquiries

When leaving all pertinent information for babysitters, such as the telephone numbers for poison control centers and your child's doctor, consider writing down your family's health insurance information as well. If the sitter needs to bring your child to the hospital, this information will help things progress more quickly and smoothly. Include the name of the insurance provider, the group number, the ID number, and which parent's employer provides the coverage.

receive. Because this form of insurance did little or nothing to contain costs and therefore presented employers and patients with escalating premium payments, it's rapidly being replaced by managed care coverage as described later.

Although doctors, hospitals, and patients tended to like the unregulated aspects of fee-for-service health coverage, many of these plans had other limitations and disadvantages. Typically, these policies focused on providing coverage for people when they got sick—hospital care, surgery, and procedures performed related to acute or chronic illness. Preventive care visits, such as routine checkups and childhood immunizations, were often covered poorly or not at all. Also, high deductibles often had to be met before these policies kicked in for reimbursement of lab tests, medications, and other services.

Managed Care Insurance

Managed care is a general term that refers to a health plan's attempt to control the costs and quality of care by "managing" the amount, type, and manner by which services are delivered to patients or "members" in the plan. At the time of this writing, more than three-quarters of privately insured individuals in the United States are enrolled in managed care health plans. This shift to managed care is also sweeping through government-sponsored health insurance programs—Medicaid (for the poor and those with disabilities) and Medicare (for the elderly).

The central feature of most managed care plans is the role of the primary care physician as "gatekeeper." This means that the patient's primary care doctor is responsible for authorizing or controlling the services the patient receives, such as referrals to specialists, lab tests, X-rays, nonurgent ER visits, and medical equipment and supplies. Plans may financially reward or penalize primary care doctors based on how well they limit presumably unnecessary and costly services in caring for their patients.

The escalation of health care costs was slowed initially with the spread of managed care, but health care costs are continuing to increase. Some believe that the continuing pressure of rising costs eventually will lead to a shift to a "single payer" government-sponsored plan similar to the systems in place in Canada and most other industrialized nations around the world.

But how does managed care affect the care your child receives? By slowing the rise in health care costs, managed care has helped to increase the percentage of U.S. children who have private health insurance coverage. Also, these plans tend to cover more of the costs of preventive care services, such as well-child checkups and immunizations, than traditional indemnity insurance plans. Supporters of managed care also point to the fact that, in the attempt to control costs through reducing variations in the way doctors diagnose and treat patients, many of these plans have established guidelines and standards for physicians to follow in managing common health problems. In some cases, there is evidence that this has improved the quality of care received by patients in the plan.

In general, families with healthy children who are enrolled in managed care plans also seem to be satisfied with the care they receive. But many families—particularly those who have children with special health care needs—may encounter a variety of barriers, restrictions, and frustrations as they attempt to navigate the managed care system.

Questions to Ask About Insurance

The following are some of the issues you may face in choosing and using a health plan for your child, and some suggestions on how to deal with them:

- Do you have a choice of health plans? Most employers who offer health insurance as a benefit have at least two options for employees. However, because managed care plans usually charge a lower premium per member to the employer if a large number of employees are enrolled in the plan, employers tend not to offer employees more than a few choices.
- Are preexisting conditions excluded? If you are considering changing jobs that will involve a change in insurance, find out in advance whether the new plan will cover the care for a chronic health condition your child may have.
- Is there a limited choice of primary care providers and specialists? Most managed care plans will allow you to select a primary care doctor for your child only from the list of physicians enrolled in their provider network. If your child already has a primary care doctor you are happy with, check to see if that doctor is in the new plan's network—or if he or she is willing to enroll as a provider in that plan.

  If you must choose a new doctor for your child, make sure that the plan's network has several primary care physicians in your area on their list. Just as important, find out whether the doctors on the list are accepting new patients. And remember to verify the enrollment status of the doctors on the list you're interested in using—the lists provided by the plan are constantly changing and may not be up-to-date.

  Similar issues apply to the services of other specialists and subspecialists that your child may need to see, particularly if he has complex health problems.

Again, check to see whether specialists your child already uses are in the network. Many plans will allow you to see an out-of-network specialist but will pay for a smaller portion of the specialist's fee (such as 70 percent instead of 90 percent for an in-plan specialist). In addition, some managed care plans may include few or no pediatric subspecialists in their provider network. This may be an unacceptable situation for meeting your child's needs. In some cases, particularly if your child's primary care physician supports the request, the plan will cover the cost of an out-of-plan pediatric specialist. If your child has complex medical problems and sees a subspecialist for most of his health care, you will want to find out if the new managed care plan will allow a subspecialist to act as your child's primary care physician—some, but not all, plans will permit this.

- How are referrals for specialist care, lab tests, and ER visits handled? Does the managed care plan require authorization of specialist referrals by the primary care physician? If so, is the primary care doctor financially penalized by the plan for making these referrals? Although most doctors will still see that their patients receive any medically appropriate service, financial disincentives may cause some providers to place barriers in your path as you seek to obtain the services you believe may benefit your child.

- What about lab tests and X-rays? Do they require the primary care doctor's authorization? And if your child needs care from a hospital-based specialist or specialty service, can blood tests and X-rays be done at the hospital at the time of a visit, or will they have to be done somewhere else that is less convenient or has less pediatric expertise?

- What are the plan's rules for reimbursing for ER visits—will you be expected to pay for your child's visit if it is determined by the plan that the visit was not for an urgent problem?

- Are there any limitations on provided services? Some of your child's other medical needs may not be covered by the health plan. For example, many managed care plans may not pay for childhood immunizations and may exclude or severely limit reimbursement for mental health services or alternative therapies (such as acupuncture). Also, many plans may limit the number of reimbursable routine health care visits for your child.

If your child has complex medical problems, the plan's representatives may not acknowledge or understand the different developmental and special needs of your child and may question or deny certain services and treatments. Documentation and support from your child's doctors—primary care and specialists—may be required to resolve struggles with the health plan regarding what is appropriate and necessary care for your child.

- What is the prescription medication coverage? Although most managed care plans reimburse the costs (above your co-payment) for routine prescriptions, plans vary widely regarding their coverage of more expensive, specialized, or recently approved drugs. If your child requires treatment with such a medication, make sure that the plan will cover it. Also, some plans will cover only the generic form or only one proprietary brand of some medications. If your child needs medication for a chronic illness, check with your child's doctor as to whether this might be a problem under your current or prospective health care plan.

- Are there spending caps? Many health insurance plans limit the amount of expenses that will be reimbursed in a certain period. In most plans, these caps are set at high levels; however, for the family with a child with extensive health care needs, spending caps can result in a huge financial burden.

KidsHealth Tip
Travel Planning

If you and your children are traveling for vacation, you may be staying in hotels or homes that are unfamiliar and not childproof. Wherever you stay, ask for the telephone number for emergency help and poison control. Always carry your family's health insurance cards when you travel, and ask your insurance company beforehand about emergency coverage, especially if you're traveling out of state.

More Tips for Choosing and Using Health Plans

Here are more tips for choosing and using health plans:

- Seek the opinions of others. Ask fellow employees, other plan members, and physicians in the plan's network how satisfied they are with the health plan's services and operation.

- Consult sources of consumer information about health plans. There are a number of organizations, agencies, and news services that provide ratings or "report cards" to be used for comparing health plans. The National Committee for Quality Assurance (NCQA) (www.ncqa.org) is a nonprofit accreditation group that produces Quality Compass, a database of health plan performance indicators (such as the

percentage of children in the plan who have received the recommended immunizations) that consumers can use to evaluate plans. (Be aware that plans provide this information to the NCQA on a voluntary basis and the information may not be entirely accurate.) Consumers can also get information on plans from the government's Health Care Financing Administration (HCFA) at www.hcfa.gov. The Consumer's Union publishes ratings of health plans periodically in their magazine *Consumer Reports*. *Newsweek* produces an annual rating of health plans that can be found at www.healthgrades.com.
- Be persistent. If you are having difficulty getting the plan to authorize or provide services that you and your child's doctors believe are important for his care, don't give up. In most cases, if you keep pressuring the plan's representatives with all the supportive documentation and medical opinions you can gather, they'll eventually give in.
- Know the plan's grievance and appeals policies. If the plan continues to deny needed services for your child, use the established grievance and appeals policies.

What if Your Child Doesn't Have Health Insurance?

In the United States at the time of this writing, more than 11 million children under age 18—about one in seven—do not have health insurance. This makes them more vulnerable to certain health problems and their complications. For example, they're more likely to require hospitalization for asthma and other inadequately treated conditions. Because they often don't have a primary care doctor to visit for routine checkups, they're also less likely to receive their immunizations on schedule and be screened for developmental and vision problems.

Although most uninsured children live in low-income households, about 90 percent have one or more parents who are employed. Many low-income parents are unaware that the majority of uninsured children are now eligible for free or very-low-cost health insurance through one of two government-sponsored programs: traditional Medicaid (www.hcfa.gov/medicaid/medicaid.htm) or the new Children's Health Insurance Program (CHIP) (www.hcfa.gov/init/children.htm).

Medicaid

Medicaid, established by Congress in 1965, is a program that provides health insurance for adults and children from low-income households. In 1996, about 30 percent of U.S. children (younger than age 21) were insured through Medicaid. The program is funded by a combination of federal and state tax dollars. Although the federal government sets certain general standards for the program, each state operates its own Medicaid program; therefore, there is some variation in eligibility requirements and the health services provided from state to state.

Unfortunately, many low-income working parents are under the impression that only people on welfare are eligible for Medicaid. Even if one or both parents is employed, their children may be eligible for the program if the household's income is below certain limits based on federal poverty guidelines. Also, parents who move off welfare as part of a state welfare reform program should be aware that generally their children continue to be eligible for Medicaid.

The health benefits provided to children under Medicaid usually include the same services that commercial health insurance plans cover. In most states, this includes regular checkups, immunizations, sick visits, referrals to specialists, lab tests, X-rays, prescription medications, eyeglasses, ER visits, and inpatient hospital care. To control costs, most states are currently enrolling Medicaid-eligible children in managed care health plans that contract with the state's Medicaid program.

Children's Health Insurance Program

In 1997, Congress enacted legislation creating the Children's Health Insurance Program (CHIP). This represents the most significant funding increase for children's health coverage since Medicaid was created. CHIP provides free or very-low-cost health insurance to children up to age 18 in low- and moderate-income families who don't have commercial health insurance coverage and are not eligible for Medicaid.

In some states, CHIP is simply an expansion of the Medicaid program, covering children in families whose incomes were too high to qualify for traditional Medicaid. In other states, CHIP is a separate program from Medicaid but generally provides similar benefits. In most states, a family of four can receive CHIP services at no cost if it earns less than $25,000. Families that earn more than this may have to pay small monthly insurance premiums and visit co-pays.

If you think your child may be eligible for Medicaid or CHIP, you can find a list of telephone numbers for state offices that can provide you with further information and help you enroll your child in the insurance program he is eligible for at www.hcfa.gov/medicaid/obs5.htm. Or call (877) KIDS-NOW. You can also contact the state or local Medicaid office or health department for help. Most hospitals, clinics, and doctor's offices and many state agencies and community centers can also help connect you to the appropriate office in your state.

Medical Care Specialists

As your child grows, it is her primary care doctor who cares for her when she is ill and monitors her health and developmental progress. But what if your child develops a medical problem that can't be taken care of by her primary care physician alone? In this situation, the doctor may refer your child to a specialist for additional evaluation or treatment. A specialist is a physician who focuses on a specific system of the body, patients in a specific age group, or the use of a specific type of medical technology or technique for diagnosis or treatment. A specialist has more extensive training and more expertise in diagnosing and treating specific types of illness and is therefore better able to diagnose and manage complicated medical problems that may be beyond the expertise of a primary care physician. (For more detailed information about health problems that affect children, see Chapter 32, "Health Problems in Early Childhood.")

There's much confusion regarding the term *specialist*. Nearly every physician practicing in the United States today is a specialist, because after graduation from medical school, each one has gone on to complete three or more years of residency training in a specialty area of medicine. Even primary care physicians such as general pediatricians, internists, and family physicians have completed this type of postgraduate medical training and are considered specialists in that area of health care. This discussion mainly focuses on physicians who have completed additional training beyond a residency in one of the "general" specialty areas. These doctors are more properly called *subspecialists*; however, the term *specialist* is commonly used when doctors or lay people refer to them in conversation. This more generic use of the term *specialist* is used here.

Pediatric vs. Adult Specialists

From a medical point of view, children are not just little adults. They have specific and complex medical needs all their own. Consequently, an important distinction must be made between the adult specialist and the pediatric specialist. Some specialists treat both adults and children, although the percentage of time that they spend treating children may vary dramatically. Pediatric specialists treat children and adolescents (and sometimes young adults) exclusively. What distinguishes pediatric from adult specialists is that the pediatric specialist has had additional years of fellowship training that are almost completely focused on the care of children. In general, if your child needs specialized medical care, it's best to choose pediatric specialists because of their greater knowledge of pediatric diseases and conditions and their familiarity and experience with children.

Understanding a Specialist's Credentials

When taking your child to see a specialist, it's helpful to know about the training and experience the doctor has had. Ask your child's primary care doctor about the credentials of the physician to whom your child is being referred. Although in some specialty areas no official examination process or certifying sub-board has been established yet, board (or sub-board) certification in a specialty or subspecialty indicates that the doctor has met a specific set of standards in that field. These standards generally include completing an accredited residency (and sometimes fellowship) program, passing a certification examination in that area of medicine, and, in some cases, completing a required period of experience practicing in that specialty or subspecialty area in order to qualify to take the board examination.

To determine whether a physician is a certified specialist, you can call the American Board of Medical Specialties (ABMS) at (847) 491-9091. Indicate that you'd like to obtain unlimited searches of certified specialists. *The Official ABMS Directory of Board Certified Medical Specialists* can also be found in your community library or at your local hospital's library.

Getting Specialty Care for Your Child: Insurance and Managed Care Issues

In the current predominantly managed care environment, it's not always easy to get a referral to the specialist of your choice. Insurance companies exert significant influence on the referral process and may require that you see only those specialists who are in their network. In many cases, the network for specialists is more limited than for primary care physicians. For example, if your child has severe asthma and her primary care doctor feels that she should be seen by a specialist, you may be referred to one of the five "in-network" pulmonologists, only to find out that none of these physicians is certified in pediatric pulmonology. This may not be a major problem if you take time to collect some information on these doctors' experience. You may find that at least one works primarily with children and can competently care for your child. But if you find that none of the in-network specialists has the required expertise to treat your child, you may need to find an out-of-plan specialist. Some health plans allow you to do this but will cover a smaller portion of the fee than they would for a network specialist's care. Other plans may require that you justify (usually in writing) the need to go outside the network to get coverage for that visit or treatment. In some cases, your child's primary care physician will need to write a letter on your behalf recommending a specific referral. For example, if only adult specialists are available in your plan's network, your child's doctor can state that a pediatric subspecialist is necessary for your child. You may also provide the insurance company with a list of required credentials and qualifications to further support your case.

Getting the Information You Need from a Specialist

When you take your child to see a specialist, you are in search of more or better information about how to help your child. You can prepare for this visit by finding out ahead of time whether you need to bring, or have your child's doctor's office send ahead, specific medical records or test reports. The more information you can provide to the specialist, the more helpful the specialist's consultation can be. Also, prepare a list of questions that you would like answered. It's easy to become flustered and forget to ask all of your questions during an office or clinic visit if you do not have things written down. Like many physicians, specialists may sometimes use medical language or terms that can be confusing. Do not hesitate to ask for clarification if the doctor says something that you do not understand. You are the primary advocate and caretaker of your child's health and may need to communicate this information to other doctors in the future, so make sure you have a clear picture of what is going on.

The more complex your child's medical condition, the more important it is to coordinate the care that he receives. Have any specialists who see your child send copies of test results and reports back to your child's primary care doctor; that way there will be a comprehensive medical record of all of your child's care. When several physicians become involved in treating your child, it's vital that someone, usually your child's primary care doctor, has all of the information necessary to coordinate the communication and treatment plans that are put in place.

Pediatric Multispecialty Clinics

Many children's hospitals and some pediatric departments in general hospitals have pediatric multispecialty clinics that treat children who have a condition requiring ongoing monitoring by a variety of medical specialists. In most cases, such children will visit a multispecialty clinic every few months or yearly for ongoing follow-up. These clinics can save time and effort by allowing the child and family to see different physicians and other special health care personnel all in one place at one time. Examples of problems for which children are commonly seen in pediatric multispecialty clinics include cerebral palsy, cystic fibrosis, hemophilia, cleft palate, and arthritis. Infants being followed up for medical problems associated with prematurity may also be seen in a multispecialty clinic.

These clinics are made up of teams of specialists who together provide comprehensive medical evaluation and update treatment plans accordingly. For example, a medical team at a cerebral palsy clinic might include specialists from orthopedics, pediatrics, neurology, nutrition, physical and occupational therapy, and others. Team members generally work closely together, which simplifies the communication and coordination of care.

The Hospital

Despite the best efforts of parents and doctors, many children will require hospitalization at some point. It helps to be prepared for this possibility, whether your child is in need of emergency care or is scheduled to undergo a planned surgical procedure. In this discussion, we will explore some of the characteristics of hospitals that provide services for children. We will also take a walk through the hospital itself and provide you with the basic tools that you need to navigate the maze of specialists, medical technology, and procedures that await you and your child.

Choosing a Hospital for Your Child

Choosing the right hospital for your child depends on the type of problem and the complexity of your child's medical needs. It also depends on the types of hospitals available in your geographic area and, of course, on your health insurance plan.

Children's Hospitals and Large Pediatric Departments vs. General Hospitals

When it comes to pediatrics, all hospitals are not created equal. There are some important differences between hospitals that specialize in the care of children and those that have small pediatric departments or no dedicated units for children at all. At a children's hospital or a hospital with a large pediatric department, all or most of the medical and professional staff caring for children are pediatric specialists. The physicians generally have separate and specific training in the diagnosis and treatment of childhood medical problems. Many nurses and other professional staff also acquire additional training and experience to help them build the specific skills that are required to treat children. Children's hospitals and those with large

KidsHealth Tip

What to Do in an Emergency

In an emergency, getting your child medical assistance quickly is often the most critical issue. In that case, your first choice is the hospital that is nearest to you. After arrival, if your child's condition appears to require more specialized care, most community hospitals will transfer a child to a hospital that focuses on the care of children.

pediatric departments also have the medical equipment and supplies that are needed for children of various sizes.

Many children's hospitals and those with large pediatric departments are also teaching hospitals that are dedicated to educating future pediatricians and pediatric specialists. At a teaching hospital, physicians who are still in training, such as residents and fellows, provide much of the day-to-day care. A resident is a doctor who has graduated from medical school and is doing his or her postgraduate training under the supervision of attending staff physicians. A fellow is a doctor who has completed residency training and is pursuing additional training in a subspecialty area (such as pediatric cardiology). Both residents and fellows are generally very accessible to you as a parent so that you can ask questions and get information on the status of your child. If you wish to speak to the attending physician (the doctor who is in charge of the care of your child—your child is on his or her "service"), don't hesitate to ask. In the morning, the doctors usually make "rounds," during which the residents and fellows check in on each patient and discuss their care. So even if you miss seeing the attending physician when he or she makes rounds, you can be assured that the team is keeping an eye on how your child is doing and is reporting any important developments to the attending physician promptly.

General hospitals with no dedicated pediatrics department generally do not staff a full range of pediatric specialists, may not have residents or fellows, and do not always have the equipment needed for little patients. However, you should know that a good local community hospital is usually capable of handling many children's medical and surgical needs well, particularly those that are less complex.

Getting Your Child Ready to Go to the Hospital

The best way to prepare your child for a hospital stay is to reduce the fear of the unknown. Many hospitals now offer preadmission tours of the hospital and the operating room for children who are going to have a scheduled surgical procedure. During the tour, children have the opportunity to see the operating room's equipment as well as the way operating room personnel are dressed. Make sure that your child (depending on his age and ability to comprehend) has a clear understanding of the medical reasons why he is going to the hospital, and assure him that everything that is going to be done is to make him better.

KidsHealth Tip

A New Toy for Time Away from Home

To make going to the hospital for treatment or an overnight stay less anxiety-filled, buy a small toy and wrap it up before your day of departure. Give it to your child once you arrive; the excitement of opening a gift will be fun, and the new toy will hold her attention while registering or waiting for the doctor or nurse.

Children also fear being left alone in the strange surroundings of a hospital. Find out your hospital's policy about waiting with your child before surgery so that you can prepare him ahead of time. Let him know that you will be there when he wakes up, and show him where that will be.

In recent years, there has been a trend toward performing simpler surgical procedures on an outpatient or "day surgery" basis, which doesn't require an overnight stay. Speak with your child's doctors about this option—it's a way for your child to get home sooner to recover in more comfortable and familiar surroundings.

When packing to go to the hospital, pack some items to make your child's stay more comfortable. It's fine to bring your child's own nightgown or pajamas. Make sure they are short-sleeved so that they don't need to be rolled up for blood pressure checks, intravenous lines, or blood tests. Sometimes after surgery, your child will need to wear a hospital gown so doctors have better access to what they need to see and examine, but his own bathrobe will give him something warm and familiar to wear. For young children, it is helpful to bring a doll or stuffed animal, especially one with arms and legs like a teddy bear. When someone comes in to check vital signs, like heart rate or blood pressure, the animal can have it done first so that your child knows what to expect. (Psychologists recommend that the "patient" not be the child's favorite doll because it can create too much anxiety if the child identifies with it too closely and worries when it is being "tested" or must be left behind during procedures.) You can also bring your child's own toothbrush, toothpaste, hairbrush, and other toiletry items. Many hospitals have VCRs available, so check ahead and bring a favorite movie or two from home.

Hospital Rules and Regulations

Every hospital has its own set of rules regarding visitation, overnight accommodations for parents, and general hospital policies. These are often made available to you in writing ahead of time so that you can plan accordingly. Many hospitals have facilities that allow parents and sometimes even siblings to stay overnight during the hospital stay. In situations where your child is going to be admitted for an extended stay, ask about facilities such as a Ronald McDonald House, which provides free or low-cost accommodations to families.

Communication with the Medical Team: How to Get Answers

How do you know whom to ask about what? Generally, there is one physician "in charge." When your child is admitted to the hospital, he is placed on the "service" of one physician who coordinates the work of the medical team taking care of your child. Make sure you know which doctor is in charge, who the attending physician will be, how to contact him or her, and which other doctors will be consulted during your child's admission. Record all this information in a notebook—it's amazing how quickly you will forget who is who if you don't write this

KidsHealth Tip

A Little Sip Before Surgery

Until recently, a child waiting for scheduled surgery was not allowed to eat or drink anything for eight hours ahead of time—a long stretch for an anxious and hungry child. Now the American Academy of Pediatrics states that it's OK for kids to have liquids up to two hours before undergoing anesthesia; solid foods must still be completely avoided, but pulp-free juice, clear liquids, and even ice pops may be safe. Ask your child's doctor or anesthesiologist before the day of surgery for specific instructions.

information down. If a new doctor comes in to examine your child or consult on the case, write down his or her name and specialty, and make sure you understand his or her role on the medical team. That information helps you know which physician is the best person to answer a specific question.

Your child's nurse can also provide a wealth of information. Nurses have full access to the medical chart and are often present during physician rounds. They can give you a good picture of your child's medical status and can relay information between you and the medical team. When you need to speak to the doctor directly, your child's nurse is the best person to contact him or her. Most doctors wear pagers so that they can be contacted quickly; however, when trying to reach a surgeon, there can be a delay if he or she is in the operating room. If the medical staff uses terms or says something about your child's condition that you don't understand, do not be afraid to ask them to explain. To be the best advocate for your child, it is essential that you have a clear understanding of your child's condition and medical needs.

> ## The Voice of Experience
>
> *"When my child was in the hospital, there were so many people involved in her care that I couldn't keep them straight—which made it much harder to know whom to ask what questions! I finally got a little notebook pad and kept it in my purse, where I wrote down names, titles, a little note about what they were responsible for (one of my first questions when I first met them), and other information about my child's treatment."*
> —FROM THE KIDSHEALTH PARENT SURVEY

What to Do When Your Child Has Pain or Discomfort

Having your child in the hospital can be stressful enough by itself, but seeing him in pain can be difficult for both of you. Even small procedures, like having blood drawn or starting an IV, can be scary for a child. If something is going to hurt, say so; if you lie about it, you will undermine his trust. Instead, tell him how long it will hurt (3 seconds, 10 seconds), and count with him. Knowing that it will be over soon is often the best way for a child to cope. Ask the person who is administering the procedure about how long it will take so that you don't underestimate the time.

Pain after surgery is often an issue of concern. If you suspect that your child is in pain, let the nurse know. There are different kinds and strengths of medicines that can relieve pain, and some may work better for your child than others. In addition, you can help your child cope with pain by doing your best to keep him calm and distracting him with a favorite toy, game, book, activity, or TV show if possible. When your child tells you he is hurting, acknowledge his pain and let him know that you and everyone on the medical team will do everything possible to make it better.

Other Supports for You and Your Child

It is normal for you to feel overwhelmed when your child is hospitalized. It is not easy to hand over the care of the most precious person in your life to strangers. No wonder parents find it incredibly stressful! The hospital staff realizes that patients and their families sometimes need extra support from people who are outside of their network of family and friends, and so within the hospital, there are many professionals to support you. These include hospital clergy, social workers, patient advocates, case managers, and counselors. If the financial concerns of paying for medical care are an issue, the hospital social worker and billing office can work with you to find alternative sources of funding or make payment arrangements. Many hospitals offer support group meetings of various types where you can share your feelings and experiences with other families who are going through similar experiences. In children's hospitals and hospitals with large pediatric programs, a child-life therapist can be a valuable source of support to your child by providing him with activities and the opportunity to interact with other children. Play therapy can be a great way for your child to express how he is feeling and what he is fearing. This can give you insight into how well he is coping with his situation.

When you feel exhausted or drained by the hospital experience, remember that it is OK to leave for a while and take a break. Parents sometimes feel guilty about going out and doing something as simple as seeing a movie or going shopping when their child is ill. But you need to find healthy ways to keep up your spirits and your strength so that you can be a strong support for your child. Taking care of yourself is not selfish; it is a necessity.

> ### The Voice of Experience
>
> *"When your child's in the hospital, ask lots of questions, understand what's going on and why, and make your child's needs known. You need to be a strong advocate for your child to make sure he gets the best care possible."*
>
> —FROM THE KIDSHEALTH PARENT SURVEY

Taking care of your child when he is in the hospital is undoubtedly one of parenting's greatest challenges. By staying fully informed about your child's medical status and by being a loving and supportive presence, you play a vital part in helping your child get well. The hospital can be a scary place, but it can also help strengthen the relationships between children and their families as they work together for recovery.

The Emergency Room

How do you know when your child's illness is a real emergency? Simply stated, an emergency is anything that might be life-threatening—or if not immediately treated, might lead to serious consequences such as worsening illness or a high level of discomfort. Of course, that can apply to a wide range of conditions. Sometimes, it's obvious that something is an emergency. Often, though, it's a judgment call for parents. This discussion will give you some basics about how emergency rooms operate and help you decide whether your ill child should visit one.

What's an Emergency Room?

An emergency room (ER) is a specialized area in a hospital dedicated to evaluating and treating urgent and life-threatening conditions. Sometimes it's known as an emergency department to acknowledge that it's larger and more complex than a simple "room," often involving suites of rooms, dozens of staff members, and endless amounts of equipment.

When Should Your Child Go to an Emergency Room?

Here's a list of conditions where an urgent visit to an ER would be advisable. (For more detailed information on these conditions, see Chapter 28, "First Aid and Emergency Care.")

- Breathing troubles. Labored breathing, turning blue, inability to catch breath, or extremely painful breathing can be the result of a variety of conditions, including asthma, pneumonia, collapsed lung, uncontrolled diabetes, cracked ribs, and other illnesses that must be diagnosed and treated.

- Burns resulting in blisters or charring (a second- or third-degree burn). These could be caused by scalding liquids, direct exposure to flames, or contact with chemicals or a hot surface.
- Changed level of consciousness or alertness; lethargy. Besides head injuries, many things can affect the level of consciousness: infection, dehydration, heatstroke, poisoning, irregular heartbeat, drug or alcohol ingestion, migraine, bleeding in the brain, and other conditions. Whatever the cause, a change in your child's level of consciousness requires immediate evaluation and treatment.
- Dehydration (significant loss of fluid from the body). Infants with diarrhea or vomiting, overheated child athletes, or feverish children with poor fluid intake can all become significantly dehydrated and lethargic. Other signs of dehydration include dry mouth, sunken eyes, lack of tears, and reduced output of urine.
- Dog (or other animal) bites or human bites. The wound will need to be cleaned, perhaps stitched, and the child may need a tetanus shot and possibly antibiotics or rabies vaccination.
- Fever and irritability. Fever (rectal temperature above 100.4 degrees Fahrenheit) in an infant younger than three months of age always requires prompt attention. But in older infants and children, fever by itself may not necessarily require an ER visit, particularly if the child seems otherwise reasonably well and alert. But a child who has a high fever and appears very ill could have a serious infection, such as meningitis, that requires immediate evaluation and treatment.
- Head injury resulting in a loss (or change) of consciousness or any head injury followed by repeated episodes of vomiting. Kids get bumped on the head all the time—and to a certain extent you'll need to use your own judgment to decide if your child needs a trip to the ER. Repeated vomiting, though, may indicate significant injury to the brain or rising pressure inside the skull. If your child repeatedly vomits after a hit to the head, is complaining of severe headache, or isn't walking or talking normally, she needs immediate medical attention.
- Laceration (cut). Most kids get cut from time to time, and most small ones will heal on their own quite nicely. But a larger cut, or one that looks like it will not close on its own or will not stop bleeding, may require a few stitches.
- Poisoning (accidental ingestion). Bring the container with you so that the doctors know which chemical substance or drug is involved.
- Seizures (also called convulsions or fits). This is especially true for first seizures, otherwise unexplained seizures without fever, and seizures that are prolonged.

- Severe allergic reactions (hives spreading on the body, swelling of the face), particularly if they affect breathing.
- Stiff neck and irritability. A child who has a stiff neck and is very irritable could have a serious infection, such as meningitis, that requires immediate evaluation and treatment.
- Suspected broken bones. It can be difficult to tell the difference between a broken bone and a lesser injury, such as a sprain, even for a doctor. So if you suspect a serious problem, head for the ER.

Should You Call the Doctor First or Go Directly to the ER?

The decision whether to call your child's doctor first or go directly to the ER depends on how urgent you think the problem is. If you're not sure and you think you have time, contact your child's doctor for advice. The doctor can help you determine whether an ER visit is necessary and can suggest the appropriate ER to visit, based on how close it is, the nature of the problem, and, in some cases, whether the ER is at a hospital where your child's doctor can be the one who treats your child. On the other hand, if the condition seems life-threatening, you should call 911 first and get help. Then, while help is on the way, you or someone else can call your child's doctor.

If you speak with your child's doctor before going to the ER, he or she may call the ER to let them know you are on the way and to give any helpful medical information about your child. It's always a good idea to bring available copies of your child's health information, including medications taken, allergy history, and immunization records.

Should You Go to the Closest ER or to a "Pediatric" ER in the Area?

There are two types of emergency rooms to consider: One is the general ER found in almost all hospitals. The other is the emergency room found in children's hospitals and some larger general hospitals that is specially equipped to care for children. These emergency rooms are staffed by doctors, nurses, and other personnel trained in the emergency care of infants, children, and teenagers. Often the doctors are pediatricians with additional specialty training in the emergency care of critically ill and injured children.

Which one should you choose? If you do have a choice of hospitals in your area and the children's hospital is farther away, the question is whether the general hospital ER is capable of providing adequate care for children. Do they have personnel with pediatric training, and do they have child-sized emergency medical equipment immediately at hand? (Some do, but many don't.) Even if they don't, most of the time a well-trained general emergency doctor can evaluate and stabilize a child for transport to a more specialized children's facility if necessary.

Certainly, if the condition is immediately life-threatening (such as choking) your child needs to be taken immediately to the closest ER whether or not it's a pediatric ER. The extra minutes traveling to a pediatric ER would be much too hazardous. Based on your child's condition, the paramedics and the doctors will make the judgment call as to whether your child can afford those extra minutes. Sometimes ambulances are required to go to the nearest ER—so the choice is made for you.

Should You Wait for an Ambulance or Use Your Car?

Is the emergency serious enough for an ambulance? It might seem that the best way to get to the hospital would be to get into your own car and drive there yourself. You might (or might not) get there faster—if you can keep your attention on the road and not on your ill child. However, there are a number of good reasons you might not want to drive, particularly with a severely ill child. A child might get worse during a car ride, especially if there is a breathing problem. He might be crying, anxious, or unable to wear a seat belt.

Ambulances are often the best choice because they are specially staffed and equipped to stabilize your child for transport. That means, when necessary, giving oxygen or keeping a child's airway open to assure that he continues to breathe adequately. It may mean giving intravenous (IV) fluids or medicines or any number of other treatments providing life support. Ambulances are staffed with trained drivers fully concentrating on getting to the hospital safely and quickly while the other members of the team are giving their full attention to your child.

What Happens in an ER?

After you arrive at the ER, your sick or injured child will go through the triage process. Triage means that an ER staff member evaluates your child and categorizes the severity of his illness or injury. Why the triage? So that the sickest children will be seen first. That means, of course, that children who are less ill may need to wait longer.

A chart is then made up, and registration and insurance information is recorded. You'll be asked to sign a consent form giving the ER staff permission to treat your child. Your child will then wait until called to the patient-care area of the ER.

If your child is critically ill, he's brought directly to the patient-care area to be evaluated by a doctor as soon as possible. Once your child is in a bed, the doctor comes in to evaluate the situation, take a history, and examine your child. Remember to tell the doctor and staff about any allergies or other health problems your child has and what medications he takes. The doctor who sees your child first may be a resident doctor if the ER is in a teaching hospital. (A resident doctor is a physician still in the training phase of his or her career.) The resident presents the case to the supervising doctor (attending physician), and generally the child is examined again by the supervising doctor. In some cases, your child's own doctor (or someone covering for him or her) may see your child in the ER. The ER doctors may also contact your child's doctor to obtain additional medical information about your child and let him or her know about their evaluation and treatment plans. The doctors will explain to you their findings and treatment recommendations.

If your child has a life-threatening or serious illness, everything will move very quickly, and explanations may initially be brief. Blood tests, X-rays, and other procedures may be performed, and medications given. Depending on the situation, your child may be admitted to the hospital for further testing or treatment, or be discharged to go home. If your child is sent home, you will be given discharge instructions. Follow up with your child's primary care doctor within a few days. If your child is admitted, your child's doctor will be notified.

Can You Stay with Your Child in the ER?

You can almost always stay with your child in the ER unless your child is critically ill or is having a complex medical procedure performed. You can stay throughout the visit, and if your child is admitted to the hospital, you can usually stay with her (even overnight) on the pediatric inpatient floor.

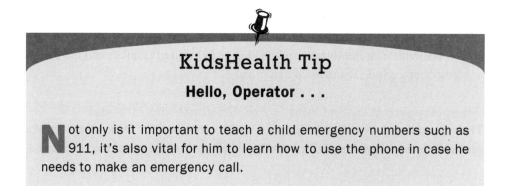

KidsHealth Tip

Hello, Operator . . .

Not only is it important to teach a child emergency numbers such as 911, it's also vital for him to learn how to use the phone in case he needs to make an emergency call.

In many situations, procedures are performed more easily and smoothly if the parents leave the room. But if you wish to stay with your child, this usually can be arranged. ER policies differ from place to place about allowing parents to be present during invasive procedures and resuscitations. You might want to leave the room if you feel emotionally overwhelmed because your child will sense this and might become more upset or fearful. If you do choose to stay with your child, you should focus on supporting her and avoid unnecessarily frightening her.

Who Are All Those People in the ER?

In the emergency room, you're likely to see many people. There might be attending doctors, nurses, clerks, volunteers, respiratory therapists, paramedics, police, clergy members, and of course families and patients. In a teaching hospital, there might also be medical students and residents. It can be quite a crowd depending on the time of day and how busy the ER is. It can be stressful seeing all those people in the ER, but remember that they're all there to help your child if needed.

What Are All Those Things in the ER?

An emergency room is full of unfamiliar equipment and supplies that need to be on hand to treat patients, and this can be intimidating if your child is very ill. These include noisy, beeping monitors; IV fluids and tubes; X-ray machines; splinting materials; wheelchairs; stretchers; bandages; catheters; metal clamps and tools; and many other types of specialized equipment.

What Tests Will Be Ordered in the ER?

The tests that will be ordered in the ER depend on your child's problem and the findings from the history and physical exam. A large array of tests and procedures are used in hospitals, including blood tests to detect infection and chemical imbalances, urine tests, spinal taps, cultures, X-rays, computerized tomography (CT) scans, magnetic resonance imaging (MRI), and others. Frequently, bone X-rays are ordered for injuries that result from a tumble. CT scans may be ordered for head injuries. Most of the time, however, the most effective way of diagnosing problems is with a careful history and physical examination. Lab tests often are used to confirm or exclude a suspected diagnosis.

What Happens if Your Child Is Admitted into the Hospital?

The emergency doctor will admit your child to the hospital if he or she thinks admission is necessary. He or she will then notify your child's primary care doctor of this decision. Together, they will decide who will care for your child during his stay—the primary care doctor or a doctor on the inpatient hospital staff.

Who Pays for the ER Visit?

Emergency room care can be expensive, so naturally insurance companies want to avoid paying for unnecessary visits. As a result, some HMOs and managed care health plans cover the ER bill only if the visit was considered a true emergency, although the rules on this vary from company to company. Some are now relaxing their policies to cover those visits that occurred because "a reasonable person" considered the problem urgent, even if it turns out not to be a true emergency. Some health plans require a co-pay at the time of the visit, and some refuse to pay if the visit isn't authorized by the child's primary care doctor beforehand or within 24 hours after the visit. (Don't forget to bring your health plan card with you to the ER.) If your child is uninsured or not covered for an ER visit, then you may need to speak with the ER staff or hospital billing office to make payment arrangements.

What About Follow-Up After You're Sent Home?

Follow-up care depends on the circumstances. Discharge instructions for you to follow at home should be given and explained by the doctors and nurses who took care of your child in the ER. In general, a follow-up phone call or visit to your child's primary care doctor a day or two after the ER visit is often recommended.

Of course, it's best to do everything you can to keep your child healthy and avoid ER visits for preventable problems such as falls and accidents. Keep your eyes open and always think "safety and injury prevention." (For more information about keeping your child safe, see Chapter 2, "Preparing Your Home and Family," and Chapter 24, "Child Safety.")

Need More Information?

Check the Index and Appendix C, "Resource Guide." And of course, consult your child's doctor.

PART FIVE

What to Do if Your Child Is Injured or Sick

chapter twenty-eight

First Aid and Emergency Care

Be prepared

Index to Chapter

Y ou are visiting your relatives' home—which is always a madhouse. You leave the room for a moment to fetch a diaper and return just in time to see your curious 15-month-old emerge from the bathroom carrying an open bottle. He begins to choke and turn blue.

Your daughter loves to climb. You watch in horror when, perched at the top of the jungle gym, she decides to jump off and falls, landing on her face and leaving her nose and lip split wide open. Blood is streaming everywhere.

You leave the kitchen to answer the doorbell and then hear an ear-splitting scream. As you rush back to the kitchen, you see your four-year-old standing next to the hot stove, and within minutes you notice a burn on his hand beginning to blister.

No matter how careful you are, accidents happen. More than five million injuries and poisonings occur each year among children ages twelve and younger. In fact, accidental injuries are the leading cause of death among children. And more than one-fourth of all reported poisonings occur among children age six years and younger.

Clearly, preventing accidents before they occur is the best way to keep your child safe. There is a lot you can do to minimize potential dangers, from seeing that your child uses a properly fitted car seat to childproofing your house to helping him understand what is safe and what is not. (For more information on safety, see Chapter 24, "Child Safety." Also, for more information on car seats, see Chapter 2, "Preparing Your Home and Family.")

The purpose of this chapter is to help you be prepared for an emergency before it arises and to give you a step-by-step guide on first aid for emergencies and common injuries you may encounter with your child.

Preparing for an Emergency—Before It Happens

Remember the motto of the Boy Scouts, "Be prepared"? It'll never be more relevant than after you have a child. Here's a list of what you should have on hand:

1. First-aid kit. Keep one at home and in your car, and take one with you when you travel. Check the contents regularly, and replace any medications that have expired. According to the American Medical Association (AMA), a kit should contain the following:
   - First-aid manual (available from the local bookstore, from the AMA, or from the American Academy of Pediatrics)

- Roll of sterile gauze and gauze pads
- Sterile gloves
- Adhesive tape
- Plastic adhesive bandages
- Elastic bandage (such as an Ace bandage)
- Sling
- Roll of cotton
- Scissors
- Tweezers
- Thermometer
- Disposable cold packs
- Antiseptic wipes
- Antibiotic cream
- Soap
- Calamine lotion
- Infant's or children's versions of acetaminophen for treating fever and pain (Do not use adult pills.)
- Diphenhydramine tablets and liquid (Benadryl) for younger children (for treating allergic reactions)
- Blanket
- Ipecac or other emetic (for inducing vomiting)

2. Emergency phone numbers. A full list of the following phone numbers should be next to every phone in the house. A cell phone (if you have one) and the main household phone should be preprogrammed with the most important numbers.

- Emergency medical services: 911 or the emergency services number in your area
- Fire
- Police
- Ambulance
- Doctors
- Poison control center
- Hospital emergency room
- Parents' phone numbers at work, including cell phone or beeper numbers if you have them
- Babysitter
- Neighborhood and 24-hour pharmacy

- Neighbors
- Local public health department

As soon as your child is old enough, teach him the following:

- How to call 911 and what it means
- To memorize his complete name and phone number (When he is old enough, he should memorize his address, too.)
- To memorize the complete names of his parents or guardians
- To memorize the phone number of a relative or neighbor in case you're not home

3. Medical information file. Prepare a medical record for each member of the household, including lists of chronic illnesses such as asthma, medications and dosages the child takes regularly, allergies to medications and foods, immunization record, the names of your child's primary doctor and specialists, and previous hospitalizations, surgeries, and significant injuries. Remember to keep this file updated. (See Appendix A for a sample medical record you can use.)

4. Health care insurance card. If your health care insurance provides you with a card for your child, carry it with you or keep it in an accessible place. Each health plan has its own requirements about when and how you should inform the insurer about a visit to the emergency room. Be aware of the requirements of your plan. (To learn more, see Chapter 27, "The Health Care System for Children.")

5. Information for the babysitter. Whether you are going to work or out for the evening, the babysitter should know how to contact you immediately. The sitter should also know where to find the first-aid kit and the medical information file and have instant access to emergency phone numbers.

Lifesaving Techniques

Cardiopulmonary Resuscitation (CPR)

Cardiopulmonary resuscitation (CPR), sometimes called "mouth-to-mouth resuscitation," is an emergency procedure used when someone is not breathing and/or her heart is not beating. It can save a person's life. The techniques can be used in critical situations such as drowning, poisoning, suffocation, head injury, choking, unconsciousness, or any situation where a child's heart and lungs are in danger of failing.

The following is a summary of the American Heart Association's guidelines for CPR taught in the Basic Life Support course. This course includes training in both CPR and emergency treatment for choking (see Choking in this chapter). However, reading about these procedures in this or any other book is not a substitute for taking a certified training course. It is supplied here to give the untrained person an idea of the scope of what's involved and to give the already trained person a reference to refresh skills.

The American Academy of Pediatrics and the American Heart Association urge parents and all those who take care of children to train in basic life support. This is especially important if you have a swimming pool or live near water. Contact your local Red Cross, the American Heart Association, or local hospital to locate a training course.

If your child is not breathing and you are with someone else, have that person call 911 for emergency help while you assess the need for CPR. If you are alone, first shout out a call for help and then assess the need for CPR.

Here are the steps for performing CPR:

Step 1: Assessment. Rapidly evaluate your child's condition. First, determine if your child is unconscious by calling him loudly, tapping him on the shoulder, or shaking him gently. Consider your child unconscious if he is unresponsive to three quick attempts to rouse him. Next, check for breathing by the "look, listen, and feel" method: Look for chest movement, then listen and feel for breaths by placing your ear directly over your child's mouth. If your child is breathing, make sure emergency help is on the way. If your child is unconscious and has stopped breathing, start CPR beginning with Step 2. If you are by yourself and no one responds to your yell for help, perform CPR for one minute, then call 911 yourself. Return immediately and continue CPR.

Step 2: Positioning. If your child is not breathing, position him on his back on a firm, flat surface. If you suspect an injury to the head or neck, be careful to position your child without bending the neck (see Head and Neck Injuries in this chapter). Carefully position your child on his back, supporting the head and neck as a single immobile unit. Kneel facing your child from the side at chest level.

Step 3: Opening your child's airway. If there is no suspected injury to the head or neck, open your child's airway by tilting the head back slightly so that the nose is lifted back slightly (in the sniffing position). If there is a suspected neck injury, open the airway by gently moving the jaw forward while taking care not to tilt or move the head. In some cases, opening the airway will allow

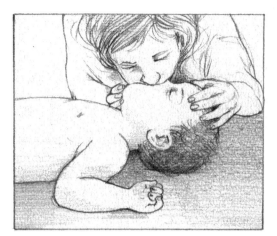

28.1a. Rescue breathing. Tilt the infant's head back slightly and seal your lips tightly around his mouth and nose. Give two slow, gentle breaths, causing the chest to rise. Take care not to blow into the infant's mouth too forcefully.

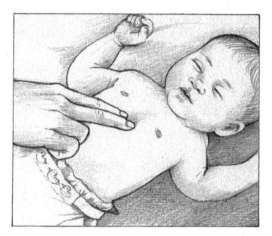

28.1b. Chest compressions. Place your index, third, and fourth fingers on the breastbone, just below an imaginary line between the nipples. Press down one-half to one inch at a rate of about 80 to 100 times per minute, taking care not to press down too forcefully.

Figures 28.1a–b. CPR for infants.

your child to breathe on his own. Look, listen, and feel for breaths again. If your child is still not breathing, look into the throat to see if an object, such as a piece of food, is blocking it. If it is blocked, follow the instructions found in Choking in this chapter.

Step 4: Breathing. If your child is still not breathing and his airway appears to be open, give mouth-to-mouth resuscitation. First, take a deep breath. If your child is an **infant**, place your mouth over his nose and mouth, making as tight a seal as possible (Figure 28.1a). For a child **one year or older**, pinch the nose closed with the thumb and index finger of the hand that is resting on the forehead (Figure 28.2a). Place your open mouth over your child's open mouth to

KidsHealth Tip

Know Your ABCs

A helpful way to recall the steps involved in assessing the need for CPR in a child is to remember your ABCs. Throughout this chapter you will see reminders to assess for CPR by following your ABCs: Maintain an open **A**irway, and check for **B**reathing and **C**irculation. Start CPR if the child stops breathing.

form an airtight seal. Give two "rescue breaths": slow, gentle breaths causing the chest to rise. Allow the lungs to deflate fully between breaths. With an infant, be careful not to exhale into the child's mouth with too much force because this can be dangerous. If no air seems to be getting into the chest, the airway is still blocked, and you should repeat Step 3.

Step 5: Circulation. Check for signs of blood circulation after the two rescue breaths. Signs of blood circulation include the presence of breathing, coughing, or movement in response to stimulation. If none of these signs is present, proceed to chest compressions (Step 6).

Step 6: Chest compressions. Assume the heart has stopped, and begin chest compressions (CPR) to keep the blood circulating to the vital organs. For chest compressions on an **infant**, place two fingers on the breastbone one finger-width below the nipple line (Figure 28.1b). Press down one-half to one inch at a rate of about 100 times per minute. Be careful not to apply too much pressure. For chest compressions on an **older child**, place the heel of one of your hands over the lower third of the breastbone (Figure 28.2b). Press down one to one and a half inches at a rate of 80 to 100 times per minute. After five compressions, give your child one rescue breath, as described in Step 4. Continue the pattern of five compressions followed by one breath until you see signs of restored blood circulation, as described in Step 5, or until emergency help arrives.

Choking

Choking is a life-threatening emergency that occurs when an object—often food—blocks the airway, preventing airflow into and out of the lungs. When the

28.2a. Rescue breathing. Tilt the child's head back and seal your lips tightly around his mouth. Pinch his nose shut. Give two slow, gentle breaths, causing the chest to rise.

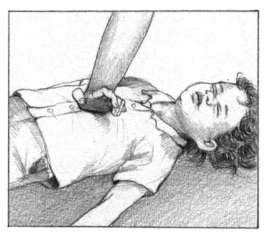

28.2b. Chest compressions. Place the heel of one hand over the lower one-third of the breastbone. Compress the child's chest about one to one and one-half inches with each thrust, at a rate of about 80 to 100 times per minute.

Figures 28.2a–b. CPR for young children.

airway is blocked, the child will not be able to breathe or talk or make normal sounds, and her face will turn from bright red to blue.

Choking calls for immediate intervention. If the situation appears critical, have someone call 911 while you or someone else trained in basic life support performs the maneuvers for choking described later.

Your child is choking and coughing but able to breathe and talk. In this situation, the airway is not fully blocked, and she will likely clear the airway by herself. Coughing is the body's natural mechanism for expelling an object blocking the airway. Instead of attempting a maneuver for choking as described later, which could make the situation worse, let your child cough to expel the object herself. Do **not** attempt to remove an object by trying to reach in and grasp it with your fingers; that could push it farther into the throat and totally block the airway.

Your child is conscious but cannot breathe and is turning blue (child younger than one year). This situation requires the modified Heimlich maneuver designed for infants younger than one year to expel the object blocking the airway (Figure 28.3). Because the infant's organs are fragile, you must be gentle. Do **not** use the Heimlich maneuver recommended for older children and adults (described later). Instead, follow the American Heart Association's guidelines for back blows and chest thrusts summarized here.

Step 1: **Positioning.** Place your infant face down on your forearm in a head-down position with head and neck stabilized. Rest your forearm firmly against your body for support. For a larger infant, you may instead lay the baby face down over your lap, with his head lower than his trunk and firmly supported.

Step 2: **Back blows.** Give four back blows in succession with the heel of the hand between the shoulder blades (see Figure 28.3). Adjust the force of your blows to your infant's size.

Step 3: **Chest thrusts.** If he still cannot breathe, turn your infant over onto his back, resting on a firm surface, and give four rapid chest thrusts over the breastbone, using only two fingers. Adjust the force of your thrusts to your infant's size.

Step 4: **Foreign body sweep.** If he is still not breathing, open the airway by using the head tilt/chin lift: Place your hand—the one closest to his head—on his forehead. Place one or two fingers—but not the thumb—of your other hand under the bony part of his chin. Gently tilt his head back to a neutral posi-

Figure 28.3. Heimlich maneuver for infants. Position the baby face down on your arm, with your hand supporting his head. Give four back blows with the heel of your hand between the baby's shoulder blades.

tion by applying gentle backward pressure on his forehead and lifting his chin. While in this position, open the mouth as wide as possible and look into the mouth and throat for a possible foreign object. Do **not** try to remove the object unless you can see it. If you see it, sweep it out with your finger rather than attempting to grasp it.

Step 5: Mouth-to-mouth resuscitation (rescue breathing). If your child doesn't start breathing on his own, either his airway is still obstructed or he needs rescue breathing. With the child still positioned as in Step 4, do the following:

A. Take a deep breath.

B. Place your mouth over his nose and mouth, making as tight a seal as possible.

C. Attempt to give a slow, gentle breath and observe if the chest rises.

D. If the chest *doesn't* rise (air is not going in), reposition your child's head (as in Step 4) and try giving a breath once again.

E. If the chest *still* doesn't rise, then immediately repeat Step 1 through Step 4.

F. If the breath *does* go in and you see your child's chest rise, then remove your mouth between breaths and look and listen for air leaving the lungs. Continue rescue breathing until help arrives.

Your child is choking, cannot breathe or talk, and is turning blue (child one year or older). This situation requires the Heimlich maneuver designed for adults and older children (Figures 28.4a–b).

Step 1: Positioning. If your child is small, place him on his back to use the Heimlich maneuver. Kneel at your child's feet if he is on the floor, or stand at his feet if he is on a table. An older, larger child can be treated while standing, sitting, or lying down.

Step 2: Locating landmarks. Place the heel of one hand in the center of your child's body between the navel and rib cage; place your second hand on top of your first.

Step 3: Abdominal thrusts. Press into the abdomen four times with a rapid inward and upward thrust. In a small child, apply the thrusts more gently (with less force).

Step 4: Foreign body sweep. If the object does not come out with the abdominal thrusts, while he is lying on his back, open your child's mouth using the tilt–chin lift: Place your hand—the one closest to his head—on his forehead.

Place one or two fingers—but not the thumb—of your other hand under the bony part of his chin. Gently tilt his head back to a neutral position by applying gentle backward pressure on his forehead and lifting his chin. In this position, open the mouth as wide as possible and attempt to see the foreign body. If you see it, sweep it out with your finger. (If you can't see the object, a finger sweep may push the object farther in.) Do **not** try to grasp and pull out the object.

Step 5: Mouth-to-mouth resuscitation (rescue breathing). If your child doesn't start breathing on his own, either his airway is still obstructed or he needs rescue breathing. With the child still positioned on his back as in Step 4, do the following:

A. Take a deep breath.

B. Place your mouth over his nose and mouth, making as tight a seal as possible.

C. Attempt to give a slow, gentle breath and observe if the chest rises.

D. If the chest *doesn't* rise (air is not going in), reposition your child's head (as in Step 4) and try giving a breath once again.

E. If the chest *still* doesn't rise, then immediately repeat Step 1 through Step 4.

F. If the breath *does* go in and you see your child's chest rise, then remove your mouth between breaths and look and listen for air leaving the lungs. Continue rescue breathing until help arrives.

Your child is choking but is unconscious and no longer breathing. If your child was choking and is now unconscious and no longer breathing, proceed immediately to cardiopulmonary resuscitation (see CPR in this chapter) without first attempting, or continuing to attempt, the Heimlich maneuvers for choking already described. According to recent changes in the American Heart Association's basic life support recommendations, the chest compressions given in CPR should be adequate to expel an object blocking the airway. During CPR, your child's mouth should be opened wide before you attempt to give breaths, to look for a foreign object, or to use the finger sweep to remove it (which whould be done only if the object is visible).

After a choking episode, if your child has a persistent cough, excessive salivation, gagging, wheezing, or difficulty swallowing or breathing, it may mean an object is still partially blocking the airway. After any significant choking episode, seek immediate medical attention at the emergency room or by calling 911 or the operator.

28.4a. Heimlich maneuver—child upright. Stand or kneel behind the child and wrap your arms around his abdomen. Place the thumbside of a fist against the middle of the child's abdomen, just above the navel. Grasp the fist with your other hand. Give four firm, rapid, upward thrusts into the child's abdomen.

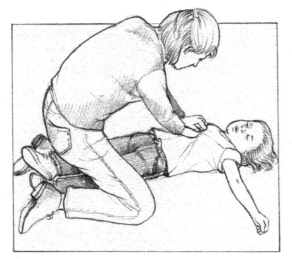

28.4b. Heimlich maneuver—child lying on back. Kneel over the child and place the heel of one hand on the middle of the child's abdomen (above the navel and below the rib cage). Place your other hand over the first. Press into the abdomen, giving four quick, firm, upward abdominal thrusts.

Figures 28.4a–b. Heimlich maneuver for conscious young children.

Common Injuries and Emergencies

Childhood injuries and emergencies are bound to happen. The following sections will give you an overview of how to handle the most common or important problems that occur during childhood that require emergency care. In each case, remember that these are guidelines and you should always seek medical help as well.

Abdominal Pain

Abdominal pain is one of the most frequent complaints of childhood and usually doesn't indicate a serious illness. It's most commonly due to conditions such as viral gastroenteritis ("stomach flu"). But there are several conditions that cause abdominal pain that require emergency attention. Distinguishing between the serious and commonplace problems can be difficult (for further information, see Abdominal Pain in Chapter 29, "Signs and Symptoms"). As a general rule: If the pain lasts less than an hour or is not severe, it is usually not serious. But if the abdominal pain is present along with some of the following situations and symptoms, you should call your child's doctor or go to the emergency room:

- Your infant seems to be having repeated episodes of severe abdominal pain marked by irritability and drawing the knees up to the chest, with lethargy between bouts of pain and red, jellylike stool or little or no stool at all. (These are signs of intussusception, an immediate surgical emergency involving the bowel, most common at 8 to 18 months.)
- The location of the pain moves from around the navel area to the right lower part of the abdomen and is accompanied by a loss of appetite, vomiting, or possibly low-grade fever. (These are signs of possible appendicitis, most common between the ages of 6 and 14 years, although it can occur at any age, including infancy.)
- There is vomiting of greenish-brown (containing bile), bloody, or "coffee-ground"-appearing material.
- Your child has had recent abdominal surgery or an endoscopy procedure.
- The abdomen appears swollen and is hard or very tender to the touch.
- There is a hard lump in the groin or lower abdomen.
- There is any of the following along with abdominal pain: difficulty breathing, pain or burning with urination, or suspected injury to the abdomen such as from a fall, bicycle handlebar, or vehicle accident (especially if bruising is noted).

Allergic Reactions and Anaphylaxis

Allergic reactions are caused by the immune system's overresponse to allergens—substances such as certain insect venoms (bees, wasps), foods (peanuts, seafood, eggs), or chemicals (medications like penicillin or sulfa-containing drugs).

Most allergic reactions in children are not life-threatening, but there are important exceptions: Severe allergic reactions that cause swelling of the upper part of the airway can make it difficult or impossible to breathe, and the whole-body allergic reaction known as anaphylaxis is a rapidly progressing, life-threatening emergency.

What to Do

Call 911 promptly if you notice the sudden onset of the following signs of anaphylaxis or severe allergic reaction:

- Difficulty swallowing (often beginning with a "tickle in the throat")
- Swelling of the tongue
- Difficulty breathing with wheezing or stridor (a high-pitched noise with each breath in)
- A change in or loss of voice
- Dizziness, fainting, or unconsciousness
- Intense itching, hives, or swelling
- Stomach cramps, nausea, or vomiting
- Anxiety or an impending sense of doom

While waiting for emergency help to arrive, do the following:

- Assess ABCs: Maintain an open Airway, and check for Breathing and Circulation. Start cardiopulmonary resuscitation (CPR) if your child stops breathing (see CPR in this chapter).
- If your child has an emergency allergy medication (such as injectable epinephrine), make sure it is given.
- Remove your child from the offending allergen. If it's a chemical or other airborne allergen, move your child to a well-ventilated area.

- Keep your child resting in a comfortable position. He may prefer to sit slightly forward with the chin held up (a "sniffing" position) if his upper airway is swollen. Do **not** force him into an uncomfortable position.

Bites and Stings

Animal and Human Bites

Animal bites, most commonly from dogs and cats, can cause lacerations (cuts) and bleeding (see Bleeding, External in this chapter) that need medical attention. These bites also carry the risk of serious infection such as cellulitis (infection of the tissue around the bite), rabies (most cases in the United States are due to bats, raccoons, skunks, and foxes), and tetanus. Human bites are even more likely to cause infection than animal bites, so any human bite that breaks the skin should receive prompt medical attention.

What to Do

- If the bleeding is not severe, first clean the wound site. Wash with soap and running water for five to ten minutes. Do **not** apply antiseptics or other creams or ointments.
- Control bleeding by applying direct pressure for five minutes with a clean cloth or sterile gauze compress and raising the wound site *above* the level of the heart (see Bleeding, External in this chapter).
- Call your child's doctor or go to the emergency room. Your child may need a more thorough cleaning of the wound site; she may also need stitches (especially if the wound is on the face), a tetanus booster,

antibiotics, or possibly treatment to prevent rabies. If the bite is on the hand or neck or if it's from a human, the risk of infection is particularly high.

- If you suspect that the animal may have rabies, call the health department or police right away. The animal may need to be confined for evaluation. Attempt to identify the dog and the owner, even if rabies is not suspected.
- Note when your child's last tetanus immunization occurred, or bring an updated record to the emergency room.

Insect Stings

Insect stings (most commonly from bees, wasps, hornets, and ants) are usually painful and distressing but not dangerous. But they can cause life-threatening emergencies in the case of severe allergic reaction or the whole-body allergic reaction called anaphylaxis (see Allergic Reactions and Anaphylaxis in this chapter).

A few insects (like mosquitoes) can transmit infection. Mosquito bites cause a small area of redness and swelling that often has a lighter or whitish center. Although they are not serious, these bites can be extremely itchy. Applying a cool compress or wet cloth to the site of the bite helps reduce the itching. Keep your child's fingernails trimmed and clean, and discourage your child from scratching the bite because this can lead to infection.

What to Do

If the reaction to the insect sting appears to be severe, call 911 promptly. Look for the sudden onset of the following signs of anaphylaxis or severe allergic reaction:

- Difficulty swallowing (often beginning with a "tickle in the throat")
- Difficulty breathing with wheezing or stridor (a high-pitched noise with each breath in)
- A change in or loss of voice
- Dizziness, fainting, or unconsciousness
- Intense itching, hives, or swelling
- Stomach cramps, nausea, or vomiting
- Anxiety or an impending sense of doom

While waiting for emergency help to arrive, do the following:

- Assess ABCs: Maintain an open Airway, and check for Breathing and Circulation. Start cardiopulmonary resuscitation (CPR) if your child stops breathing (see CPR in this chapter).
- If your child has an emergency allergy medication (such as injectable epinephrine), make sure it is given.
- Keep your child resting in a comfortable position in a well-ventilated area. He may prefer to sit slightly forward with the chin held up (a "sniffing" position) if his upper airway is swollen. Do **not** force him into an uncomfortable position, and reassure your child while keeping him calm.

If the reaction to the insect sting does not appear severe, do the following:

- Call your child's doctor or go to the emergency room if your child has a history of allergic reactions to insect stings.

- Examine the sting site. If the stinger is still in the skin, remove it while taking care not to squeeze it (this may inject more venom). Try scraping the stinger out of the skin with a fingernail, dull knife blade, or plastic card. But do **not** delay in removing it, as the amount of venom injected depends on the length of time the stinger remains in the skin.
- Wash the site with soap and water.
- Apply a compress of ice wrapped in cloth to the sting site.
- If there is swelling, give an oral antihistamine (such as the diphenhydramine in your first-aid kit). Check with your child's doctor if he is less than one year old.
- Do **not** apply a home remedy such as meat tenderizer or mud, which may do more harm than good.

Spider Bites

Two species of spider can cause life-threatening reactions in humans—the black widow and brown recluse spiders. The female black widow spider produces venom that can be lethal, particularly in small children. Black widow venom causes the sudden onset of the following symptoms soon after the bite: severe pain, nausea, vomiting, chills, cramping throughout the body, headache, numbness and tingling, and difficulty breathing. Antidote to the venom is available, so it is important to seek immediate medical attention if a black widow bite is suspected.

The bite of a brown recluse spider can cause severe tissue damage, usually over a period of hours (with redness at the site, followed by swelling, blisters, and skin ulcers), and it can cause severe illness and even kidney damage (with bloody urine) over a period of a few days.

What to Do

Seek medical attention immediately for a suspected bite from a black widow or brown recluse spider: Call 911 or take your child to the emergency room immediately.

While waiting for emergency help to arrive, do the following:

- Assess ABCs: Maintain an open Airway, and check for Breathing and Circulation. Start cardiopulmonary resuscitation (CPR) if your child stops breathing (see CPR in this chapter).
- Keep the bitten body part *below* heart level.
- Only if instructed to do so by emergency personnel, tie a constricting band a few inches above the bite to slow the circulation of the venom through the bloodstream. This band should not be a tourniquet—tie it loosely enough to allow space to insert two fingers.
- Apply a compress of ice wrapped in cloth to the bite site.
- Do **not** cut the bite site in an attempt to drain venom from the bite.
- If the spider is dead or has been captured, bring it with you to the emergency room.

Tick Bites

Certain species of ticks can transmit diseases such as Lyme disease and Rocky Mountain spotted fever. If a tick is found on your child's skin, it should be removed carefully right away, because the chance of getting a tick-borne illness increases with the length of time the tick is attached to the skin.

What to Do

- Remove the tick quickly and safely. Do **not** try to burn the tick off. Instead, use tweezers to grasp the tick's head and mouth as close to the skin as you can, and pull it straight out with steady, slow traction. Take care to remove the whole tick in one piece. If part of the tick remains, it can be tougher to remove.
- Put the tick in a jar containing rubbing alcohol for later identification.
- Clean the bite with an antiseptic wipe, rubbing alcohol, or soap and water.
- Call your child's doctor to discuss the need for examinations, tests, and treatment. Bring the tick with you if possible. The doctor may recommend blood tests to evaluate for possible Lyme disease or other tick-borne illness (often done some time after the bite occurs because these tests are usually negative just after tick exposure). In the meantime, be sure to discuss with the doctor what symptoms to watch for. (See Lyme Disease in Chapter 30, "Childhood Infections.")
- Seek medical aid immediately if over the next few days to several weeks your child develops symptoms of Rocky Mountain spotted fever (which can be life-threatening): a high fever with headache, nausea, and vomiting; a rash beginning with reddish spots on the wrists and ankles and spreading to the palms of the hands and soles of the feet and then

to the rest of the body; and swelling around the eyes, hands, and feet.

Bleeding, External (Lacerations and Abrasions)

Many accidents cause external bleeding through lacerations (cuts) or abrasions (scrapes). Minor bleeds are easy to control with the technique of direct pressure described here. But more rapid and serious bleeding can occur if an artery has been severed or if there is a deep laceration. If you suspect an arterial bleed (with spurting, bright red blood) or if the injury is otherwise severe, have someone dial 911 while you attempt to control bleeding using direct pressure or pressure on arterial points (described later).

What to Do First

- Assess ABCs: Maintain an open Airway, and check for Breathing and Circulation. Start cardiopulmonary resuscitation (CPR) if your child stops breathing (see CPR in this chapter).
- Apply direct pressure or pressure on arterial points (for severe bleeds) as described later.
- Watch for signs of developing shock (weak, rapid pulse; clammy skin; difficulty breathing; decreased alertness or responsiveness). If these are present, elevate your child's legs 8 to 12 inches and keep your child warm and reassured.

How to Apply Direct Pressure for Bleeding

1. Wash your hands with soap and water and, if possible, put on sterile gloves.

2. Place a thick, clean compress of sterile gauze or clean cloth over the wound, pressing firmly with your palm. If you can, raise the bleeding body part above the level of your child's heart. Do **not** apply a tourniquet.

3. Apply direct, constant pressure to the compress using your palm for five minutes. During that time, do **not** remove pressure to check the wound. If blood soaks through the compress, do **not** remove the gauze to replace it. Add more gauze on top while continuously applying pressure.

4. If bleeding is controlled after five minutes, secure the compress in place by tying a pressure dressing around it. Wrap the gauze compress snugly with an elastic bandage or other stretchy material (or tie it with a necktie, stockings, or gauze wrap). Be sure to check for pulses in the area below the pressure dressing to make sure that blood circulation is good.

5. Call 911 or go to the emergency room if any of the following occurs:
   - Your child shows signs of shock (pale, with weak, rapid pulse; clammy skin; difficulty breathing or staying alert).
   - You suspect arterial bleeding (blood actually spurts from wound).
   - You are unable to control the bleeding after five minutes of direct pressure.

You should also seek medical aid if any of the following is true:

- The wound involves dirt and debris.
- You suspect your child needs a tetanus booster.
- An object is sticking into the skin.

- There is a laceration on the face, head, or neck.
- The wound is deep or gaping and may require stitches

As with any skin wound, watch the site for several days following injury for any signs of infection: redness, swelling, pus drainage, pain, or fever. Contact your child's doctor if any of these occur.

How to Apply Pressure on Arterial Points

If bleeding is severe (and has not been controlled through direct pressure and after elevating the wound above the heart), you should first call 911. Then, while waiting for emergency help to arrive, attempt to control bleeding by locating and pressing the arterial pressure point (while continuing elevation and direct pressure). This technique will slow blood flow to the wound by compressing the artery against the underlying bone.

- If the wound is in the arm, the pressure point is halfway between the armpit and the elbow, on the inside of the arm (locate it now on your own arm—you should feel the artery pulsating).
- If the wound is in the leg, you can locate the pressure point in the groin area (locate the strong pulse on either side of the groin).
- If the wound is on the face, head, or trunk, apply direct pressure to the wound.

Watch for signs of developing shock (rapid, weak pulse; clammy skin; difficulty breathing). If these are present, elevate your child's legs 8 to 12 inches and keep the child warm and reassured. Call 911 for emergency help.

Bleeding, Internal

Internal bleeding is usually not obvious on the outside, but it is a serious emergency. Children can lose a large amount of blood from an injury to three areas in particular—the chest, abdomen, and thigh. It is important to watch for signs of an internal injury or bleeding if your child sustains a severe body blow, such as a punch to the abdomen, injury in a car or bike accident, or a crush injury.

You should suspect internal bleeding if you notice signs of rapid blood loss (paleness, rapid and weak pulse, cool and clammy skin, light-headedness, and tiredness), blood loss into the abdomen (swollen or tender belly, vomiting bloody or "coffee-ground"-appearing material, bloody or black stools, and bloody urine), blood loss into the lungs (difficulty breathing, coughing up of blood), or blood loss into the thigh (bruising or swelling, particularly on whatever area is lowest to the ground).

What to Do
- Have someone call 911, or go to the emergency room if your child has sustained a serious body injury and has any of the previously listed signs of internal bleeding.
- Assess ABCs: Maintain an open Airway, and check for Breathing and Circulation. Start cardiopulmonary resuscitation (CPR) if your child stops breathing (see CPR in this chapter).

- If there are signs of rapid blood loss, have your child lie down with legs elevated 8 to 12 inches, and keep your child warm and reassured while awaiting emergency help.
- Do **not** give your child any liquid or food to eat.

Breathing Problems

Breathing problems in children are fairly common and usually are not serious. But there are several causes of severe respiratory distress that require medical attention. Some of these are described here and elsewhere in this book. They include asthma and allergies, choking, croup, apnea, bronchiolitis, pneumonia, and respiratory distress due to a life-threatening injury such as bleeding (see Bleeding, Internal and Bleeding, External in this chapter) or poisoning (see Poisoning in this chapter).

Recognizing Severe Respiratory Distress
Regardless of whether the cause is known, you should call 911 or go to the emergency room if you notice symptoms of severe respiratory distress:

- Grunting noise or flaring (opening) of the nostrils with each breath
- Bluish lips or fingertips
- Rapid breathing rate
- Retractions with each breath (use of extra muscles to help when breathing becomes difficult—look for a "sucking in" above the collarbone and between the ribs, and "belly breathing" just below the rib cage, especially in infants)

- Lethargy (poor responsiveness)
- Confusion or agitation

Apnea

Apnea is defined as the stopping of breathing for 15 seconds or longer. Young infants are most at risk, particularly those who were born prematurely. Apneic spells are more likely when an infant has an ongoing respiratory infection (such as bronchiolitis), gastroesophageal reflux disease (GERD), poisoning, or an underlying nervous system injury or other illness—or sometimes the apnea may have no clear cause at all.

What to Do

- If your child has had an apneic episode but is now breathing normally again, call 911 or go to the emergency room right away. Do **not** wait for another episode to occur.
- Assess ABCs: Maintain an open Airway, and check for Breathing and Circulation. Start cardiopulmonary resuscitation (CPR) if your child has clearly stopped breathing and is not responsive to attempts to rouse him (see CPR in this chapter).

Croup

Croup is characterized by a distinctive cough that sounds like a seal's or dog's bark. It is usually caused by a viral infection of the upper airways, although it may also be due to an allergy or a bacterial infection. Croup occurs most frequently in children younger than age three in the fall and winter months and typically worsens as the child goes to bed in the evening.

What to Do

- Call 911 or go to the emergency room if you notice signs of severe respiratory distress (see page 509) or signs of obstruction of the upper airway such as drooling and stridor (a high-pitched noise with each breath in).
- Bring your child into air that is humidified by a vaporizer or into a bathroom while running a hot shower in the background to produce steam. Or, you can bring your child outside into cool air after wrapping him with a blanket to keep him warm.
- Keep your child reassured and calm.
- If the breathing difficulty lasts longer than 15 minutes or worsens, call your child's doctor or go to the emergency room.

Lower Respiratory Tract Disease: Asthma, Bronchiolitis, and Pneumonia

Asthma, bronchiolitis, and pneumonia are three examples of illnesses that affect the lower respiratory tract—the airways located below the trachea (or windpipe) and within the lungs. Bronchiolitis and pneumonia are usually caused by infection.

Asthma is a common chronic disease affecting children of all ages. When a child with asthma comes in contact with an asthma "trigger" such as cigarette smoke, an allergen, cold air, or a cold or other respiratory infection, he can have an asthma attack in which the lung's airways become inflamed and narrowed due to spasm. The result is wheezing and respiratory distress that can be life-threatening. See Chapter

32, "Health Problems in Early Childhood," for more information about asthma.

Bronchiolitis is most common in infants and young children during the winter months and is usually caused by viruses such as respiratory syncytial virus (RSV). The child typically has cold symptoms (such as mild fever, congestion, and runny nose), and the infection progresses to involve the bronchioles, the tiny airways within the lung. The result is wheezing (a high-pitched whistling or hissing noise that can be heard when the child breathes out) and respiratory distress.

Pneumonia is an infection of the lung itself, usually caused by a virus or bacteria. Children with pneumonia also have respiratory distress along with a fever, cough, and sometimes abdominal pain. If you suspect pneumonia, have your child evaluated by the doctor.

What to Do

- If you see signs of severe respiratory distress (see page 509), take your child to the emergency room or call 911.
- If your child is having difficulty breathing but it is not severe or you suspect an infection such as pneumonia or bronchiolitis, call your child's doctor or go to the emergency room.
- If your child has asthma and you suspect an asthma attack, immediately start any medications you usually give your child as part of her previously established action plan for asthma flares. If there is no improvement, call your child's doctor for further instructions or take your child to the emergency room.

Broken Bones, Dislocations, and Sprains

A broken bone (also called a fracture) requires medical care. Suspect a broken bone if you or your child heard or felt a bone snap during an injury, if your child has difficulty putting weight on the limb or moving the injured area without significant pain, if the injured area appears bent or crooked, or if the area is very swollen and painful to the touch. A more subtle break may be present if your child complains of continued pain in an area for several days after an accident or injury.

Dislocations are not broken bones. Instead, an intact bone becomes moved (dislocated) out of its usual position in a joint, usually due to being pulled or twisted out of the joint socket. A similar type of injury called a subluxation is very common in children younger than six years. This injury occurs at the elbow when a child's arm is pulled forcefully. Children with this so-called nursemaid's elbow do not seem to be in pain if the arm is not moved, but they may refuse to use the arm and keep it held at the side. These subluxations do not require splinting and can be treated in the emergency room or doctor's office.

A sprain occurs when ligaments, which hold bones together, are overstretched or partially torn. Sprains generally cause swelling and pain, and there may be bruising.

What to Do

If there is a suspected broken bone, do the following:

- If the injury is to your child's neck or back, do **not** move him unless he is in imminent danger. Movement can cause serious nerve damage. Call 911 immediately. If your child must be moved, your child's neck and back must be completely immobilized first. Move the head and neck only as a single unit, keeping his head in line with the spinal column.

- If your child has a break in which the bone protrudes through the skin and there is severe bleeding, apply pressure on the bleeding area with a gauze pad or clean piece of material. Call 911 immediately. Do **not** wash the wound or try to push back any part of the bone that may be sticking out. If your child must be moved because of imminent danger, apply splints around the injured limb to prevent further injury. Leave the limb in the position you find it. The splints should be applied in that position.
- Do **not** allow your child to eat or drink because these injuries frequently need treatment in the emergency or operating room with IV sedation or anesthesia, which requires that the child have an empty stomach for at least a few hours.

Splints can be made by using small wooden boards, a piece of a broom handle, a stack of newspapers or magazines rolled into a *U*, cardboard, or anything firm that can be padded with anything soft (like pillows or shirts). Splints must be long enough to extend beyond the joints on each side of the fracture. Place cold packs or a bag of ice wrapped in cloth on the injured area. A bag of frozen vegetables, such as peas, is a good alternative to a bag of ice. Keep your child lying down until medical help arrives.

If there is a suspected sprain, do the following:

- If the injury is to your child's neck or back, do **not** move him unless your child is in imminent danger. Movement can cause serious nerve damage. Call 911 immediately. If your child must be moved, his neck and back must be completely immobilized first. Move him as a single unit, keeping his head in line with his spinal column.
- It may be difficult to tell the difference between a sprain and a break. If there's any doubt, call your child's doctor or go to the nearest emergency room. An X-ray can determine whether a bone is broken.
- First aid for sprains includes rest, ice, compression, and elevation (known as RICE):
  - Rest. Do **not** use the injured part.
  - Ice. Apply ice packs or cold compresses for 10 to 15 minutes every few hours for the first two days to prevent swelling.
  - Compression. Wear an elastic compression bandage for at least two days to reduce swelling.
  - Elevation. Keep the injured part above the level of the heart to reduce swelling.
- Do **not** apply heat in any form for at least 24 hours. Heat increases swelling and pain. The doctor may recommend an over-the-counter pain reliever such as acetaminophen or ibuprofen.
- Notify your child's doctor or seek medical attention if the area of the arm or leg beyond the injury becomes numb or turns pale or blue, or if pain is unrelieved by acetaminophen or ibuprofen.

Burns

The most common burn injury to infants and toddlers is scalding with hot liquid, which is often caused by spilled hot foods or putting a child into bathwater that's too hot. Young children are easily burned because their skin is so thin. Other common childhood burns include sunburn, chemical burns, thermal (heat-related) burns from clothing that has caught fire, or direct contact with a hot object. Because burns are common injuries and proper first aid can minimize further injury, it's important to know how to provide first aid for different types of burns. Any child with an extensive (significant) first-degree burn or **any** second- or third-degree burn needs to be evaluated in the emergency room as soon as possible.

Burn injuries are staged according to the depth of injury:

- First degree. The burn is limited to the top layer of skin, causing redness and pain but no blistering. First-degree burns typically result from sunburn, minor scalds, or brief contact with hot objects.
- Second degree. A more serious burn, a second-degree burn involves the skin layers beneath the top layer, resulting in blisters, severe pain, and redness. These burns are commonly due to severe sunburn, severe scalds, or contact with a hot object or flame.
- Third degree. These severe burns involve all the layers of the skin and underlying tissue. The remaining surface appears waxy, leathery, or blackened and is not painful because the underlying nerves have been destroyed. Third-degree burns result from severe electrical burns and

prolonged contact with flames or hot substances.

First aid for all types and degrees of burns is aimed at quickly removing the source of the burn (such as an electrical current, chemical, or hot or burning clothing) and quickly reducing the temperature of the skin to minimize further injury.

Thermal (Heat-Related) Burns—First Degree

What to Do

- Remove clothing over burned area.
- Immediately place the area under cool (not cold) running water, immerse it in cool water, or apply a cool compress until the pain subsides. Do **not** use ice.
- Gently wash the area with soap and water, and cover it with a clean dressing.
- Do **not** apply butter or grease to the burn, as these increase the risk of infection.
- Do **not** apply medication or a home remedy to the burn without first talking to your child's doctor.
- Call your child's doctor to help determine if your child needs to go to the emergency room.
- Seek medical attention if any signs of infection develop—fever, pus, or increasing pain, redness, or swelling.

Thermal (Heat-Related) Burns—Second Degree

What to Do

- Remove clothing over the burn unless it's sticking to the skin.

- Immediately cool the burned skin by immersing it in cool (not cold) water. Do **not** apply ice.
- Gently wash the area with soap and water, and pat it dry with a clean dressing.
- Do **not** apply grease, butter, ointment, sprays, or antiseptics.
- Leave any blisters intact.
- Elevate burned legs and arms.
- Go to the emergency room or call 911.

Thermal (Heat-Related) Burns— Third Degree
What to Do

- Immediately smother any flames by wrapping your child in a blanket or jacket and performing the "stop, drop, and roll" maneuver.
- Have someone call 911 while you assess the child's ABCs: Maintain an open Airway, and check for Breathing and Circulation. Perform cardiopulmonary resuscitation (CPR) if your child is not breathing (see CPR in this chapter).
- Apply cool water or a cool compress. Cover with sterile dressing or a clean cloth. Do **not** apply ice.
- Elevate burned extremities.
- While waiting for emergency help, assess your child closely for signs of respiratory distress and a swollen upper airway (see Breathing Problems in this chapter), especially if the face has been burned. Look for signs of shock (rapid, weak pulse; difficulty breathing). If your child is in shock, keep your child lying

down, elevating the feet 8 to 12 inches. Keep your child warm with a blanket, and calmly reassure him while awaiting help.

Chemical Burns
What to Do

- Quickly flush the area with lots of cool (not cold) running water for five minutes or more. Use a garden hose or a shower or tub faucet with a generous stream.
- While flushing the burn, remove clothing from the burned area.
- Protect yourself and others from exposure to the chemical.
- Take care to avoid getting the chemical in the eyes.
- If the eyes were burned, thoroughly flush them with water (as described in Eye Injuries in this chapter) and go to the emergency room.
- Cover the burn with a clean cloth or sterile dressing.
- Call 911 or go to the emergency room.

Electrical Burns

See Electrical Injuries in this chapter.

Drowning

Parents should not only take steps to prevent a child from drowning, they should also be familiar with what to do in case a child needs to be rescued from the water.

(For water and pool safety information, see Chapter 24, "Child Safety.")

What to Do

- Rescue your child without putting yourself at risk. To avoid being pulled underwater by a panicked older child or teen, lie belly down at the water's edge or on a pier, and extend an arm, leg, board, stick, or rope toward your child. Pull your child to safety. If you have to enter the water to rescue your child, bring a flotation device or rope he can grab onto so he does not pull you under.
- If your child is not breathing on his own, first give two rescue breaths (see CPR in this chapter).
- Have someone call 911.
- Assess ABCs, being careful in case there is a neck injury (see Neck Injury under Head and Neck Injuries in this chapter): Maintain an open Airway, and check for Breathing and Circulation. Continue CPR if your child is still not breathing (see CPR in this chapter) while awaiting emergency help.
- If your child is breathing but is lethargic or at any time was unconscious or had stopped breathing, go to the emergency room.

Ear Injuries

Because of the risk of hearing loss, any injury to the ear is considered serious and requires medical attention. The ear can be damaged by a direct blow, a loud noise, a fall, or a foreign object in the ear canal.

Blow to the Ear
What to Do

- First examine your child for any sign of a head or neck injury (see Head and Neck Injuries in this chapter).
- If blood is coming only from a cut to the outside of the ear, treat it like any other laceration by applying direct pressure with gauze or a clean towel and seeking medical attention (see Bleeding, External in this chapter).
- If blood is coming out of the ear canal, cover the ear loosely with gauze, but allow blood to drain, and place your child with the injured ear facing down. Do not plug the ear canal. Call 911 or go to the emergency room.

Object in the Ear Canal
What to Do

- Do **not** try to remove the trapped object with a swab or tweezers; this usually forces the object farther back.
- Do **not** try to flush the object out with a liquid, as doing so may cause certain objects to swell, making them more difficult to remove. The only time you should put a liquid into the ear canal is in the case of a live insect.
- If the object trapped in the ear canal is a live insect, its buzzing and wiggling can be painful and traumatic for a child. Kill (suffocate) the insect by putting several drops of room-temperature mineral or cooking oil in your child's ear canal.
- Call your child's doctor or go to the emergency room. Any object trapped

in the ear canal should be removed under a doctor's care.

Electrical Injuries

Depending on the voltage of the current and the length of contact, an electric shock can cause anything from brief discomfort to serious burns and cardiopulmonary arrest (see CPR in this chapter). Brief shocks from electrical wall outlets are usually minor and rarely cause serious injury. But children can sustain dangerous electrical injuries such as burns from chewing electrical cords or from coming into contact with high-voltage wires, both of which can be life-threatening. Because the tissues and organs beneath the skin are usually damaged more than the skin (so you can't see the damage), you should seek medical attention for any electrical burn injury.

If Your Child Is Still in Contact with the Electrical Current
What to Do

- The first priority is to safely remove your child from the electrical current without getting electrocuted yourself. Never touch a live wire, and do not touch your child until the electrical source has been shut off.
- If possible, quickly shut off the electrical current if you know the location of the main power switch, circuit breaker, or fuse. If your child is outside, have someone call the electric company to have them cut the electricity.
- If it's not possible to cut the current, be very careful when attempting to

remove your child from the electrical source. Standing on a dry surface, push your child from the wire with a dry wooden object, such as a board, broom, or stick. Never use an object made of metal to push the child away, as metal will conduct the electrical current to you. Another way to remove your child from the electrical source is to attempt to pull your child from danger with a dry rope looped around a leg or arm. Wear insulated or dry gloves if possible.
- Continue care as described later if your child is no longer in contact with the electrical current. Once your child is no longer in contact with the electrical source, it is safe to touch him.

If Your Child Is No Longer in Contact with the Electrical Current
What to Do

- Assess ABCs: Maintain an open Airway, and check for Breathing and Circulation. If your child is not breathing, have someone call 911 and perform cardiopulmonary resuscitation (see CPR in this chapter).
- If the injury is severe (if, for example, there is a burn to the skin), it's important that your child be taken to the emergency room for further examination. See Burns in this chapter for further treatment, and follow the guidelines for treating thermal burns.
- If the injury is minor, resulting in no visible burn, call your child's doctor for advice.

Eye Injuries

Minor eye irritations and some small particles on the eye surface can be treated at home by flushing the eye with water. But some eye injuries can be serious, and in some cases, they can lead to eye damage, vision loss, or blindness if not treated quickly by medical professionals.

Sand, Dirt, and Other Foreign Objects on the Eye Surface

What to Do

- Wash your hands with soap and water before examining the eye or flushing it with water.
- Do **not** touch, press, or rub the eye, and do whatever is possible to keep your child from touching it. A younger child can be swaddled snugly in a towel or blanket as a preventive measure.
- Do **not** try to remove any object (except by flushing the eye with water).

Flushing the Eye

- Tilt your child's head over a basin with the affected eye down, and gently pull down the lower lid, encouraging your child to open her eyes as wide as possible. For an infant, it is helpful to have a second person hold your child's eye open while you flush.
- Gently pour a steady stream of room temperature water from a pitcher or bottle across the eye. Sterile saline or contact lens solution can also be used.
- Flush for up to 15 minutes, checking every 5 minutes to see if the foreign body has been flushed out. If your child still complains of pain or a foreign object still can be seen, seek medical attention.

Because a particle can cause a corneal abrasion or infection (which can be very serious if not treated), the eye should be watched closely for increasing redness, swelling, visual disturbances, or pain. A doctor should examine the eye if any of these occur.

Embedded Object (an Object Penetrates the Eyeball)

What to Do

- Prevent your child from rubbing the eyes. Swaddle an infant or young child if necessary.
- Do **not** attempt to remove the object; this could cause further damage to the affected eyeball.
- Gently cover both eyes to prevent eye movement and rubbing of the eyes. The unaffected eye should also be covered to prevent movement of the injured eye (because the eyes move together). If the embedded object is small, use eye patches or sterile dressings to cover both eyes. If the embedded object is large, cover the injured eye with a small cup taped in place, and cover the other eye with an eye patch or sterile dressing. Keep pressure off the injured eye.
- Seek medical attention immediately, preferably from an eye specialist (ophthalmologist) or the nearest emergency room. Call 911 for an ambulance if there is no emergency room close by. Eyeball injuries should be treated as soon as possible.

Cut Eyeball or Eyelid

What to Do

- Do **not** wash or flush the eye. If your child is wearing contact lenses, do **not** try to remove them yourself.
- Do **not** press on the eye or allow your child to rub it.
- Cover the eye with a paper cup or similar protective covering to protect the eye, while taking care to avoid putting pressure on the eye. Secure the covering with tape.
- Do **not** allow your child to eat or drink. (Children with eye injuries frequently will vomit and may also require anesthesia for eye surgery, which requires the child to have an empty stomach.)
- Seek medical attention immediately, preferably from an eye specialist (ophthalmologist) or the nearest emergency room. Call 911 if necessary.

Chemical Exposures of the Eye

Exposure of the eyes to chemical agents can be very serious. It's important to remove the chemical quickly to prevent possible blindness or other serious eye damage.

What to Do

- Before calling your child's doctor, flush the eye (see Sand, Dirt, and Other Foreign Objects on the Eye Surface in this section) with room temperature water for 15 to 30 minutes. If both eyes are affected, consider flushing both eyes in the shower.
- Cover eyes with a sterile dressing or clean cloth.
- Call the poison control center for further advice. Be prepared to give as much information about the chemical as possible.
- Take your child to the emergency room as quickly as possible. If necessary, call 911. Bring the container of the chemical with you if possible.
- Do not press on the injured eye or let your child touch it.

Black Eye (Due to Direct Blow to Eye)

Even though a blow to the eye or a black eye may not seem serious, any time the eye receives a hard blow, you should seek medical attention. Internal bleeding or other damage to the eye may not be apparent. A visit to your child's doctor may be necessary to identify serious injury, particularly if its cause is unclear.

What to Do

- Apply cold compresses to the eye intermittently: 5 to 10 minutes on, 10 to 15 minutes off. If you use ice, make sure it is covered to protect the delicate eyelid skin.
- Seek medical attention quickly, preferably from an eye specialist (ophthalmologist) or the nearest emergency room.
- Use the cold compresses three to four times a day for 24 to 48 hours, then switch to applying warm compresses intermittently.

- If your child is in pain, give acetaminophen, not aspirin or ibuprofen, which can increase bleeding.
- Prop your child's head with an extra pillow at night, and encourage her to sleep on the uninjured side.
- Call your child's doctor immediately if any of these symptoms appear: increased redness, drainage from the eye, persistent pain, distorted vision, or any visible abnormality.

Fainting

Fainting is a brief and temporary loss of consciousness due to inadequate oxygen or glucose (blood sugar) delivery to the brain. Fainting may result from a variety of causes including a sudden change in position from lying down or sitting to standing (or standing upright and still for prolonged periods), hyperventilation (overbreathing), anxiety, pain, dehydration, or underlying disease.

What to Do

- At the first indication of fainting (dizziness, light-headedness, paleness, or unsteady balance), try to keep your child from falling.
- Help him lie down or sit down with his head between his knees to keep the head below the level of the heart.
- Loosen tight clothing and make sure the room is well ventilated.
- Wipe your child's face with a cool washcloth.
- Do not let him stand or walk until recovery is complete.

If Your Child Has Already Fainted

- Assess ABCs: Maintain an open Airway, and check for Breathing and Circulation. Start cardiopulmonary resuscitation (CPR) if your child stops breathing (see CPR in this chapter).
- Lay your child down and elevate the legs 8 to 12 inches.
- If she vomits, turn her head to the side or roll her on the side to keep the airway open and prevent choking.
- If your child is unconscious but breathing, do **not** give her anything to drink.
- Do **not** try to rouse her by slapping her, shaking her, or throwing water in her face.
- Loosen tight clothing around the neck, and provide good ventilation.
- Wipe your child's face with cool water.
- If your child has fallen, check for head injury or other injuries from a fall (see Head and Neck Injuries in this chapter).
- Do **not** let her stand or walk until recovery is complete.
- If your child does not recover fully in five minutes or feels ill, seek medical attention immediately.

Finger and Toe Injuries

Injuries to the fingertips or toes due to slammed doors, heavy dropped objects, or hammer hits are common and painful. Usually the damaged area will become blue and swollen, and there may be a cut or bleeding around the cuticle. The skin, the tissue below the skin, the nail bed, as well as underlying bone, may all be affected. If bleeding occurs underneath the nail, it will turn black and blue, and the resulting pressure may cause significant pain.

What to Do

- If the fingertip or toe is bleeding, wash it with soap and water and cover it with a soft sterile dressing. Apply direct pressure to control bleeding (see Bleeding, External in this chapter).
- If the fingertip or toe is simply bruised, apply an ice pack or a cold-water soak.
- If there's a deep cut, excessive swelling, or blood under a fingernail or toenail or if the nail has become detached or it looks as if the finger or toe may be broken, call your child's doctor or go to the emergency room immediately. Do **not** attempt to straighten a deformed finger or toe.
- Be alert to any increase in pain, swelling, warmth, redness, or drainage from the injured area or a fever beginning 24 to 72 hours after the injury. These may be signs of infection.
- If blood collects under the nail it may be very painful. Call your child's doctor or go to the emergency room. The pressure under the nail may need to be relieved by a simple procedure that creates a hole in the nail, allowing the blood to escape, which relieves pain and prevents additional tissue damage to the tip of the finger.
- If the tip of a finger or toe is severed (amputation), always bring the tip to the hospital (it can sometimes be reattached). The amputated tip

should be wrapped in a paper towel moistened with cool water and placed inside a plastic bag, which should then be placed inside a larger plastic bag containing a mixture of crushed ice and water.

Frostbite

Frostbite is cold injury of body tissues (most commonly affecting the fingers, toes, and nose), and, in some cases, it requires immediate medical attention to prevent permanent injury. Children are at greater risk for frostbite than adults are because they lose heat from their skin more rapidly.

Frostbite injuries are staged according to four categories in a manner similar to burn injuries (see Burns in this chapter):

- First degree. The frostbitten area is painful with a stinging and burning sensation. The area may first appear white and then become red and swollen as it becomes warm.
- Second degree. The burning progresses to a pins-and-needles sensation and then to numbness as the nerves of the skin are further damaged by the cold. The affected area looks mottled (discolored or pale) or may be blistered.
- Third degree. The numb, frostbitten area may look "waxy" or white, blue, or gray with blisters.
- Fourth degree. The frozen area will be hard and numb, with blisters and ulceration.

What to Do for All Degrees of Frostbite

- Rapidly immerse the frostbitten areas in warm (but not hot) water (100 to

104 degrees Fahrenheit). Continually test the water temperature yourself as the numbness in the frostbitten area may prevent your child from reacting to excessively hot water. Or apply warm compresses for 30 minutes. If warm water is not available, wrap the frostbitten area in a warm blanket or hold the area against warm skin (under the armpit for example).

- Do **not** use warmth of direct heat such as a fire, heating pad, stove, or radiator.
- Do **not** rub frostbitten skin or rub snow on it.
- Do **not** break blisters.
- Rewarming may be accompanied by a burning sensation. Skin may blister and swell and may turn reddish, blue, or purple. When skin is pink and no longer numb, the area is thawed and you can stop warming techniques.
- Apply a sterile dressing to the area, placing it between fingers and toes if they are affected. Try not to disturb any blisters.
- Wrap rewarmed areas to prevent refreezing, and have your child keep thawed areas as still as possible.

What to Do for Third- and Fourth-Degree Frostbite
- Call 911 immediately Third- and fourth-degree frostbite is a serious medical emergency.
- Get your child into dry, warm clothing or under a blanket, and then take him to the emergency room. If his feet are affected, carry him.
- If you can't get your child to a hospital right away or must wait for an ambulance, give him a warm drink, keep him warm, and begin the treatment already described.

Head and Neck Injuries

Falls, vehicle accidents, and blows to the head cause most head injuries in children. Although these injuries are common, they should always be taken seriously because of their potential for damage to the brain and spinal cord.

Head Injury

Head injuries are the leading cause of injury-related death and disability in children. Any head injury that results in loss of consciousness or other signs of severe head injury described here is serious and requires immediate medical attention. With certain head injuries that appear minor at first, the child may not show signs of brain injury until after a delay of many hours. For this reason, it is important that you observe a child closely for delayed symptoms of brain injury for at least 24 hours after a head injury.

Many children will appear a little sleepy shortly after a minor head injury, and occasionally, they will vomit once or twice. By themselves, these symptoms are not a cause for major concern. Know the signs of a potentially serious head injury.

Signs of a Potentially Serious Head Injury
- Unconsciousness or unresponsiveness
- Pupils that are of unequal size
- Bloody or clear fluid draining from ears or nose
- Seizures or convulsions
- Bruising around the eyes or behind the ears
- Depression or "sinking in" of a portion of the skull
- Change in breathing or heart rate

- Lethargy, confusion, or excessive sleepiness
- Persistent or delayed (hours after the injury) vomiting
- Severe headache

What to Do

- If you note any of the signs of serious head injury listed here, have someone call 911 while you assess your child.
- Assess ABCs, being careful in case of neck injury (see Neck Injury, coming up): Maintain an open Airway, and check for Breathing and Circulation. Start cardiopulmonary resuscitation (CPR) if your child stops breathing (see CPR in this chapter).
- Control any bleeding by direct pressure using a clean towel or gauze compress (see Bleeding, External in this chapter).

It is important that your child be observed carefully for signs of serious injury for a few days after a head injury. Follow the instructions of the emergency personnel or your child's doctor.

Neck Injury

Often accompanying head injuries, neck injuries can be just as serious and call for extreme caution on the part of any caregiver. If the child is unconscious, assume there could be a neck injury. Moving the head or neck of a child who has a broken bone in the neck can damage the spinal cord, causing paralysis or even death. For this reason, you must not move a child with a suspected neck injury without the help of medical personnel, unless the child's life is in immediate danger.

Signs of a Serious Neck Injury

- Stiff or painful neck
- Inability to move any body part
- Tingling or numb sensation in the feet and/or hands

What to Do

- Call 911 and await the arrival of emergency personnel before moving your child.
- Do **not** move your child's head or neck unless his life is in immediate danger. If he must be moved, the neck must be immobilized; this is best done with assistance from other people. One person should concentrate on keeping the head and neck immobilized. Carefully wrap a rolled towel or newspaper behind the neck, tied or taped loosely in the front to allow for ease of breathing. Place a board behind the head, neck, and back extending to the buttocks, and, if possible, immobilize your child further by tying or taping your child to the board at the forehead and chest. Move your child gently as a single unit without allowing twisting or bending. Lay towels, clothing, or other soft objects on either side of the head and neck to prevent the child from moving the neck.
- Assess ABCs: Maintain an open Airway, and check for Breathing and Circulation. If your child is having trouble breathing, first try to open the airway by lifting the jaw. If this is unsuccessful, you may tilt the head slightly backward (without twisting or bending the head) to maintain an open airway. Start cardiopulmonary resuscitation (CPR) if your child stops breathing (see CPR in this chapter).

Heat Illness (Heat Cramps, Heat Exhaustion, and Heatstroke)

In unusually high temperatures or high humidity, or during vigorous exercise in hot weather, the body's natural cooling systems may begin to fail, allowing internal body heat to build up to dangerous levels. Excessive exposure to heat can cause symptoms ranging from the relatively mild to the life-threatening. The more serious forms of heat illness can be avoided with some commonsense prevention strategies such as keeping infants in light clothing on hot days, never leaving children unattended in the car, making sure children are drinking enough fluids, and recognizing and treating heat illness.

Heat Cramps

Heat cramps are a mild form of heat illness. They are brief but severe muscle cramps, typically in the leg, arm, or abdomen, that can occur during or after vigorous exercise in extreme heat. They are painful but not otherwise serious. Children are particularly susceptible when they have not been drinking enough fluids.

What to Do

- Most heat cramps do not require special emergency treatment. Have your child rest in a cool, preferably air-conditioned, place and drink fluids. Avoid very cold drinks, which can worsen stomach cramps, and caffeinated drinks such as iced tea and soda.
- Loosen or remove clothing.
- Massage the cramped muscles.

Heat Exhaustion

Heat exhaustion is a more severe form of heat illness that can occur when a child in a hot climate or environment has not been drinking enough fluids. If left untreated, heat exhaustion may escalate into heatstroke, which can be fatal.

Symptoms of heat exhaustion can include signs of dehydration such as intense thirst, fatigue, clammy skin, lightheadedness especially while standing, dry lips, sunken eyes, and rapid heart rate. There may also be headache, nausea and/or vomiting, rapid breathing, or irritability.

What to Do

- If your child is an infant, call 911 or go to the emergency room.
- Bring your child indoors or into the shade.
- Loosen or remove clothing.
- Encourage your child to drink cool fluids. Avoid caffeinated drinks such as iced tea and soda.
- Sponge or spray your child's entire body with cool water.
- Call your child's doctor for advice, especially if symptoms persist for more than one hour. If your child is too exhausted or ill to eat or drink or is vomiting with attempts to drink, intravenous fluids may be necessary.

Heatstroke

Heatstroke is a life-threatening emergency in which the body's temperature-regulating system malfunctions due to overexposure to heat. Factors that increase the risk for heatstroke include overdressing and extreme physical exertion with inadequate fluid intake in hot weather.

Symptoms can include hot, dry skin; body temperature of 105 degrees Fahrenheit or higher; headache; dizziness or weakness; sluggishness or fatigue; agitation or confusion; and loss of consciousness.

What to Do

- Assess ABCs: Maintain an open Airway, and check for Breathing and Circulation. Start cardiopulmonary resuscitation (CPR) if your child stops breathing (see CPR in this chapter).
- Call 911 immediately.
- While waiting, follow instructions for heat exhaustion, or cool your child by wrapping him in wet, cold towels or sheets; spraying the skin with cold water; placing him in front of an air conditioner or fan; or applying cold compresses to his neck, armpits, and groin until his temperature is reduced to 101 degrees Fahrenheit.
- When his temperature (best taken in the rectum) is reduced to 101 degrees Fahrenheit, dry him off.
- Repeat cooling measures if his temperature rises.

Mouth and Tooth Injuries

Traumatic injuries to the mouth and teeth call for prompt medical or dental attention in a few specific situations. For example, an avulsed (knocked-out) permanent tooth can be reimplanted if cared for correctly and promptly, and a cut to the lip often needs to be repaired with stitches. And as with any facial trauma, there is always the possibility of a more serious injury to the head or neck.

Oral and Dental Injuries
What to Do

- First check to see if there is an injury to the head or neck. (See Head and Neck Injuries in this chapter.)
- Wash your hands with soap and water and, if possible, put on sterile gloves.
- Lean your child slightly forward to prevent her from swallowing large amounts of blood.
- If there's a cut to the lip or inside of the mouth, follow the instructions in Cuts to the Lip and Inside of Mouth, coming up.
- Remove any foreign objects including broken teeth. If you see any knocked-out teeth, follow the instructions under Avulsed (Knocked-Out) Tooth in this section.

Cuts to the Lip and Inside of Mouth
What to Do

- Wash your hands thoroughly and, if possible, put on sterile gloves.
- See if there are more serious injuries to the head or neck.
- Clear the mouth of any broken teeth. If permanent teeth are knocked out of their sockets, wrap them in a cool, moist cloth and bring them immediately to your child's doctor or dentist for possible reimplanting.
- Lean your child slightly forward so she doesn't swallow blood.
- Control bleeding by pressing both sides of the wound with a sterile dressing or clean cloth, provided this does not cause the child to gag or choke.
- If a cut in the mouth or lip is deep or long, penetrating from the outside

completely through to the inside of the mouth, crosses the border between the skin and the pink part of the lip, or will not stop bleeding, go immediately to your child's doctor's office or the emergency room.

- If the cut is a relatively mild one that stops bleeding with direct pressure and there is no sign of head, neck, or dental trauma, the injury may be treated at home. Consider giving acetaminophen or ibuprofen for pain, and apply a cold compress if the area is swollen.
- Watch for signs of infection over the next week, including fever, swelling, pus, and pain at the wound site. Call your child's doctor or dentist if any of these signs are present.

Avulsed (Knocked-Out) Tooth

A dislodged baby tooth cannot be reimplanted. The baby tooth's root structure is immature, and it will be replaced soon enough anyway with a permanent tooth. But if a permanent tooth is avulsed, you should seek dental or emergency care immediately, because it can be reimplanted if handled correctly and medical attention is received quickly. The longer the tooth is out, the lower the chances it will survive reimplantation.

What to Do
- Clear the mouth of any broken or dislodged teeth.
- Briefly rinse the dislodged tooth under tap water. Do not brush the tooth with a toothbrush. If your child is old enough to cooperate, place the tooth back into its socket and have him hold it in place with

gauze until you arrive at the doctor's or dentist's office. Be sure it is facing in the correct direction and placed in the correct socket.
- If the tooth cannot be repositioned into the socket, place it in cool whole or reduced-fat (not skim) milk or sterile contact lens solution until it can be reimplanted (cow's milk is a good solution for a tooth's vital tissues until it can be reimplanted). If milk or lens solution is not available, an older child can hold the tooth between his gums and inner cheek. For a younger child, an adult can hold the avulsed tooth in her own mouth between the gums and inner cheek.
- If there is bleeding at the socket site, moisten a piece of gauze with cold water and apply pressure to the site.
- Call your child's dentist or go to the emergency room as soon as possible.

Nose Injuries

Although sometimes dramatic in appearance, most nosebleeds are not serious and are due to nose picking. But a nosebleed that occurs following a blow to the nose or is the result of a foreign object in the nose should receive medical attention.

Nosebleed
What to Do
- Wash your hands with soap and water and, if possible, put on sterile gloves.
- Sit your child upright in a chair or in your lap and have him tilt his head slightly forward. Firmly pinch shut

his nose just below the bony part using a tissue or clean washcloth. Keep his nose shut for about 5 to 10 minutes. Apply cold compresses to the nose while pinching.

- Repeat the previous step if bleeding persists.
- Keep your child quiet for several hours after the nosebleed, and discourage him from blowing, picking, or rubbing his nose.
- Call your child's doctor or go to the emergency room if your child gets a nosebleed as a result of a blow to the head or a fall (see Head and Neck Injuries in this chapter) or if you are unable to stop the bleeding. Call your child's doctor if nosebleeds are occurring frequently.

Foreign Object in the Nose

It usually is not obvious when a child has a foreign object in the nose. Signs of this fairly common problem include a foul-smelling odor or drainage from one nostril and difficulty breathing through one nostril.

What to Do

- Have your child attempt to blow the foreign object out of the nostril. Holding the unobstructed nostril closed, have her breathe in through the mouth and out through the nose. Repeat several times.
- Attempt to pull out the object only if it can be grasped with the fingers.
- Do **not** attempt to retrieve the foreign body by inserting a tool; doing so could force it farther up the nostril.

- If the object does not come out easily, go to your child's doctor or emergency room.

Blows to the Nose

A broken nose can result from a blow to the nose, and sometimes blood can collect on the nasal cartilage. Both of these conditions require medical attention and can be difficult to detect due to bleeding and swelling.

What to Do

- As with any trauma to the face, first check for serious injury to the head or neck (see Head and Neck Injuries in this chapter) or for injury to the mouth and teeth (see Mouth and Tooth Injuries in this chapter).
- Control the bleeding (see Nosebleed in this section).
- Gently place cold compresses over the nose.
- Do **not** try to straighten the nose.
- Take your child to the doctor or the emergency room.
- Because a broken nose may not be apparent for a few days due to swelling, after the swelling has gone down, call your child's doctor if the nose appears crooked or is deformed.

Poisoning

If you suspect your child has swallowed a poison (or medications, or even a household cleaner you are unsure of), it is important that *before* you attempt to treat the child's poisoning (such as making your child vomit or giving her water to drink) you first call the poison control center, emergency room, or 911. You can do more harm than good if you attempt to treat your child without medical guidance.

Even before symptoms of poisoning appear, you might suspect poisoning if, for example, your child comes to you saying she has swallowed something or shows you an empty container. Do **not** wait for symptoms to appear; instead, gather the necessary information and call the poison control center.

The following are some signs that your child may have swallowed a poison:

- Sudden change in level of alertness or change in behavior, such as unusual sleepiness, irritability, confusion, or jumpiness
- Sudden change in breathing or heart rate
- Unexplained stains on clothing
- Burns on the lips or mouth
- Unusual odors on the breath
- Sudden onset of nausea, vomiting, or abdominal cramps
- Suddenly unsteady gait or clumsiness
- Seizures
- Unconsciousness

What to Do

- Call the poison control center immediately. If the number is unavailable, call 911 or the emergency room. Again, do **not** attempt to treat your child's suspected poisoning without medical guidance.
- Be prepared to give as much of the following information as possible when calling for medical help:
    - Who: Give your child's age and weight.
    - What: Give the name of the substance swallowed if known (find the container if possible).
    - When: Estimate the time your child may have been poisoned.
    - How much: Estimate the amount of poison your child may have swallowed.
    - How: Describe how your child appears now.
- The poison control center or the emergency room may instruct you to induce vomiting, to dilute the poison by giving water or milk to drink, to take your child to the emergency room, or to await the arrival of an ambulance.
- If you are instructed to go to the emergency room, take the following with you, if possible:
    - Empty containers of suspected poisons or medications
    - Any material your child has vomited (collect in a bottle or plastic container)
- While waiting for emergency help to arrive, assess ABCs: Maintain an open Airway, and check for Breathing and Circulation. Start cardiopulmonary resuscitation (CPR) if your child stops breathing (see CPR in this chapter).
- While waiting for emergency help, position your child lying down on her side (unless there has been a head or neck injury) to prevent choking if your child vomits.

Seizures/Convulsions

A seizure occurs when normal electrical activity in the brain is temporarily interrupted. A convulsion is a common type of seizure, with shaking of the arms and legs and loss of consciousness. Seizures are common (4 to 6 percent of children will experience at least one) and are usually more frightening than dangerous. It is not uncommon for children under five years of age to have seizures because of a high fever (febrile seizures). They are usually not dangerous in themselves, except if a child hits his head in a fall (see Head Injury under Head and Neck Injuries in this chapter) or has an extended period with limited oxygen. Seizures are caused by multiple conditions including some requiring emergency care, so you should seek medical attention if your child has a seizure. (See Chapter 29, "Signs and Symptoms," and the section on epilepsy/seizures in Chapter 32, "Health Problems in Early Childhood," for more information on seizures.)

What to Do

- Try to prevent your child who is having a seizure from falling; lay her down gently on her side.
- Clear the area of hard or sharp objects that might cause injury. Loosen clothing that is tight around the neck.
- Assess ABCs: Maintain an open Airway, and check for Breathing and Circulation. Start cardiopulmonary resuscitation (CPR) if your child stops breathing (see CPR in this chapter).
- If your child vomits, turn her head to the side to prevent choking.
- Do **not** give your child anything to drink during the seizure.
- Do **not** place anything between the teeth. (A child will not swallow her tongue during a seizure.)
- Do **not** restrain your child, but allow the convulsions to occur.

- If your child has a fever or feels hot, you can apply cool compresses.
- If the seizure does not stop in five minutes or if your child has multiple seizures, have someone call 911.
- When the seizure subsides, make sure your child is on her side to prevent choking if she vomits.
- If your child doesn't have a known seizure disorder, immediately seek medical attention.

Splinters and Slivers

Most splinters or slivers can be removed at home if you're well prepared. Removing these small pieces of wood, glass, or other material lodged in the skin can be a scary event for a young child, so good preparation is important. Because you will be using sharp tools (and because children have sharp teeth and nails), make sure you have an assistant to help hold your child, and consider swaddling the child in a blanket or towel.

What to Do

Call your child's doctor or go to the emergency room if the splinter involves a fingernail or toenail, if it appears to be deeply imbedded or difficult to retrieve, or if you are concerned your child will not cooperate with the removal. The doctors in the emergency room can numb the area, if necessary, before further attempts are made.

If you attempt to remove the splinter at home, do the following:

- Wash your hands and the area around the splinter (gently) with soap and water.

- Sterilize a pair of tweezers and a sewing needle by placing in boiling water for five minutes or by exposing the tips to an open flame. Make sure they have cooled before applying them to skin.
- If the splinter is protruding from the skin, use the tweezers to gently pull out the splinter at the angle at which it entered.
- If the splinter is embedded just under the skin, gently loosen the skin around the splinter with the sewing needle until the splinter tip is exposed. Use the tweezers to gently pull out the splinter at the angle at which it entered.
- After removal of the splinter, wash the area with soap and water and cover with a bandage.
- Call your child's doctor or go to the emergency room if you are unable to remove all or part of the splinter, or if you find the splinter breaks apart easily as you attempt to retrieve it.
- Check with your child's doctor to make sure your child's tetanus shots are up-to-date.
- Over the next several days, watch for signs of infection including fever and redness, swelling, pain, or pus at the wound site. Call your child's doctor or go to the emergency room if these signs are present.

Swallowed Foreign Objects

If swallowed, a smooth object about the size of a quarter or smaller will typically pass harmlessly all the way through the gastrointestinal tract and out with the stool. But certain ingested foreign objects can be very dangerous and need to be removed promptly; sharp or long objects can get stuck easily and can perforate the intestine or esophagus; alkaline batteries (and disk batteries like those found in watches and hearing aids) can cause burns if they become stuck in the esophagus. Objects containing lead or mercury can cause poisoning.

What to Do

- If you suspect your child has swallowed a foreign object, call your child's doctor or go to the emergency room. Your child may tell you he swallowed an object, or he might have pain in the upper chest, increased drooling, or trouble swallowing.
- If it is decided not to remove the object, but rather to let it pass through the gastrointestinal system, you should watch for symptoms such as abdominal pain, swollen tender abdomen, vomiting, fever, or blood in the stool. These could point to an abdominal emergency such as a perforation of the intestinal wall. Go to the emergency room immediately if these signs are present.

Unconsciousness

Unconsciousness is a state of deep unresponsiveness. A child who is unconscious will not awaken when shaken gently and will not respond when her name is called loudly. It is important to note that a child who is unconscious has not necessarily stopped breathing. You should carefully assess an unconscious child for breathing and start cardiopulmonary resuscitation (CPR) if the child is not breathing (see CPR in this chapter).

There are multiple causes for unconsciousness, many of which are described elsewhere in this chapter (head injury, a large amount of blood loss, seizures or convulsions, anaphylaxis, poisoning, heatstroke, and others). Other causes of unconsciousness include complications of diabetes (to learn more, see Chapter 32, "Health Problems in Early Childhood"), low blood sugar (hypoglycemia), or any illness that has worsened to the point of being life-threatening. Regardless of specific cause, any child who is unconscious requires emergency medical attention.

What to Do

- If you suspect your child is unconscious, attempt to awaken her by calling her name loudly, tapping her on the shoulder, and shaking her gently. If she is unresponsive and others are with you, have someone call 911.
- If your child is unconscious, "look, listen, and feel" for your child's breaths as described in the cardiopulmonary resuscitation (CPR) guidelines (see CPR in this chapter). If your child is not breathing, start CPR. If you are alone, yell for help, perform CPR for one minute, and then go to contact 911 yourself. Return to continue CPR.

What to Do if Your Child Is Unconscious but Breathing on Her Own

- Carefully loosen tight clothing around the neck, and make sure your child is able to get plenty of air.
- Do **not** attempt to give an unconscious child anything to eat or drink.
- If the cause of the unconsciousness is not known, always suspect an injury to the head or neck, and do **not** move your child except to keep the airway open, being careful not to move the victim's neck (see Head and Neck Injuries in this chapter).
- If it is known that your child *has not* sustained an injury to the head or neck, turn your child to the side to prevent choking on vomit.
- Check for signs of bleeding (see Bleeding, External and Bleeding, Internal in this chapter), possible poisoning (see Poisoning), or heatstroke (see Heat Illness). If the child is not your own, check to see if the child has a medical alert necklace or bracelet indicating that the child has a medical condition that might affect treatment.
- Continue to monitor ABCs: Maintain an open Airway, and check for Breathing and Circulation. Start cardiopulmonary resuscitation (CPR) if your child stops breathing (see CPR in this chapter).

Need More Information?

Check the Index and Appendix C, "Resource Guide." And of course, consult your child's doctor.

chapter twenty-nine

Signs and Symptoms

What they mean and when to call your child's doctor

Index to Chapter

How to Use This Chapter

Sooner or later, every child gets sick. When your child is sick, symptoms are the clues that guide you and your child's doctor in finding out what's wrong. Technically, the word *symptom* refers to what a person says he is feeling or experiencing, such as pain. The word *sign* refers not to the person's subjective experience but to something that can be observed and measured by a health professional, such as a fever or a heart murmur. Infants and young children are often unable to communicate their specific symptoms verbally. In this book, as in much of the literature on children's health, we often use the two terms interchangeably.

This chapter takes a basic look at a number of health problems grouped by the symptoms they usually present. Of course, many symptoms (such as "cough") may occur with dozens of different medical conditions. And although most medical problems show a typical cluster of symptoms, not all of the symptoms appear in every case. For example, although children with chicken pox usually have a mild fever in the beginning of the illness, some have no fever at all.

The exact symptoms that a medical condition produces in a given child depend on many things: his age, other medical problems he might have, his body's particular response, the strain of the virus or bacteria causing an infection—and many other factors, some of which we simply don't understand completely. Still, symptoms—sometimes along with a doctor's physical examination or lab tests—are the keys to diagnosing a child's illness.

Each section of this chapter describes a common symptom and some of its causes. For each symptom, there are lists of suggestions of what you can do at home, advice on when to call the doctor, and conditions that indicate the need for immediate medical attention. For example, the section on Abdominal Pain discusses a number of childhood conditions that might have belly pain as a major symptom. Despite the large amount of information you'll find under this heading, we can only touch upon some of the possible things that such a symptom might mean. That's why this chapter is not meant to be used by parents to diagnose their child's illness on their own. No book (or Web site) can provide a shortcut to the frequently complex process that doctors are trained to go through in determining the cause and treatment of a child's problem.

Although in this chapter we discuss situations in which you definitely need to call your child's doctor or seek emergency care for your child, you'll still need to use your common sense and best judgment. If you think your child is sick and you need help deciding what to do, or if you are simply concerned, call the doctor, even if the specific symptom is not listed under When to Call Your Child's Doctor. Your doctor is there to answer your questions and expects to be called if you have a concern.

What does the instruction "Seek emergency care" mean as it appears in this chapter? The symptoms or situations listed under this instruction call for immediate attention, but once again, you'll have to use some judgment. In general, if you think there is time to call the doctor for additional advice, do so. But don't wait long for a call back if you can't get through to the doctor right away. Call 911 if you're concerned that your child may have a life-threatening condition or one where delay might seriously threaten your child's health. If your child is truly in an unstable condition and is likely to need urgent treatment or close observation while in transit, it's usually better to make the trip to the emergency room in an ambulance or other rescue vehicle with a trained staff. But in some cases, you may feel it would be safe enough and faster to take your child to the hospital in your own vehicle, especially if it will take the ambulance a long time to reach you.

You can read more about how to deal with medical emergencies in Chapter 28, "First Aid and Emergency Care."

Crying/Colic

Warning/Emergency Signs

Seek emergency care if your child shows any of the following signs:

- Continuous crying for more than two hours
- Fever and bulging fontanel (the soft spot on the infant's head looks or feels like it is pushing out and doesn't move up and down during crying) in an infant
- Unexplained, prolonged crying in an older infant or child
- Irritability and headache or stiff neck in an older child

Also get help if you are afraid you may harm or shake your baby.

When to Call Your Child's Doctor

Call your child's doctor if your child shows any of the following signs:

- Crying for longer than you feel is normal after a fall or other injury
- Crying that sounds like pain, not fussiness
- Possible ear infection (complaining of ear pain; grabbing at the ear in an older infant or toddler)
- Acting ill (includes inconsolable crying, difficulty awakening, trouble breathing, lack of interest in toys or favorite things, or refusing to eat or drink)
- Possible food intolerance or food allergy
- Indication that child may have fallen or gotten hurt

Infants and young children cry for many reasons. Infants have a limited number of ways to express their needs, and, for better or worse, crying is the primary means of communication for the first several months. An infant will cry to indicate a wide variety of basic needs or feelings. Parents become amazingly skilled at distinguishing among these different kinds of crying and knowing what their babies want or need.

Infants also cry to indicate that they are in pain or not feeling well. As babies get older, they are more likely to cry when they are separated from parents and caregivers or when they are lonely or scared. Toddlers often cry out of frustration when they do not have enough words to express how they feel or what they want. Determining the cause of crying is not always easy. Here are a few common causes:

To convey a basic need or emotion. Unfortunately, the ability to communicate clearly is not one of an infant's early skills. For the first several months, crying is the way a baby lets people know he needs something. A baby may cry because he is hungry, thirsty, wet, tired, too hot, or too cold. In addition to these rather basic needs, babies also cry when they are bored, tired, overstimulated, or just plain frustrated. Although babies often cry because they are hungry, resist the urge to feed your baby each time he cries. A newborn usually needs to eat about every two to four hours. Crying less than two hours after a feeding could be due to hunger, but it is just as likely due to boredom or a desire to be held. The good news is that parents usually quickly learn to understand the meaning of their baby's unique cries.

Colic. No one knows the exact cause of colic. Colic tends to start when an infant is about two weeks old and lasts for roughly three to four months. An infant will often cry and draw his legs upward as if in pain. The baby may cry for as long as three to five hours a day (as compared to one to three hours in an average infant without colic). These infants tend to cry at roughly the same time each day, often in the evening. For more information on colic, see Crying and Colic in Chapter 11, "Baby-Care Basics."

Food or formula intolerance. Some infants who appear to have colic actually may have a formula intolerance, so your baby's doctor may suggest that you try switching formulas if your baby is fussy. Be sure to check with the doctor before changing formulas. If you are breast-feeding, your baby may react to things you have eaten. Caffeine and certain medicines can get into the breast milk and make a baby irritable, so check with the doctor if you are taking any medicine and plan to breast-feed. If your child has a food intolerance, avoid the offending food (and check with the doctor about if and when you should try to reintroduce the food).

Fever or illness. Being sick can make anyone feel cranky, and infants and young children are no exception. A child with a cold is likely to whine more than usual. Unfortunately, there is not much you can do to help this type of fussiness aside from giving your child some extra tender loving care. Acetaminophen or ibuprofen can help if the fussiness is related to a high fever or general aches from the illness. Ear infections and urinary tract infections can cause pain that leads to crying. A simple cold in a child does not require a trip to the doctor, but if you are worried that something more serious is going on, call your child's doctor. (For more on how to tell if a fever may indicate a more serious problem, see Fever in this chapter.)

Pain. Pain can, of course, be a reason for crying. Infants can't tell us when and where they hurt, so finding the source can be a mystery for parents. Even older children are often not good at describing what is wrong. After making sure your baby has been fed and had a diaper change, where do you look? Do a quick check for elastic that has become too tight around your baby's legs and arms (they outgrow outfits quickly). While you are checking the clothes, make sure there are no zippers, buttons, or other pointy objects poking your baby. Look for toys that may have slipped into an uncomfortable place near your infant. Sometimes babies get a piece of hair or string wrapped around a finger or toe, which cuts off circulation. If you catch this quickly you can unwrap it yourself, but sometimes the finger becomes swollen and your child's doctor should assist. Consider the possibility of a fall or accident that you may not have seen (toddlers move quickly, and no one can watch them all of the time).

Intussusception. Intussusception is an uncommon cause of pain and crying. For more information about intussusception, see Abdominal Pain in this chapter.

What You Can Do at Home

- Remember that you can't spoil an infant in the first few months of life by holding him too much. If your baby wants to be held and you want to hold him, don't worry about spoiling him.
- Make sure your baby has been fed recently and is not hungry.
- Check for a wet or dirty diaper.
- Check the temperature in the room. Could your baby be hot or cold? (A rule of thumb is that to be comfortable, an infant will need one more layer of clothing than you do.)
- Check your baby's clothing to make sure nothing is too tight and that there are no zippers, buttons, or other objects poking him.
- Provide your baby with a different view or offer a new toy. Babies get bored just as we do—keep the environment interesting but not overwhelming.
- Swaddle the infant (this involves wrapping the baby snugly in a blanket with arms tucked in). Some infants like the warm, secure feeling they get when swaddled.
- Cuddle and rock your baby.
- Try an infant swing or bouncy seat.
- Walk around the house holding your baby. Sometimes adding humming or singing to this works even better. (A baby sling is often helpful—it allows you to carry your baby and still have use of your arms and hands.)
- Give your baby a gentle massage by rubbing his back.
- Take a short drive. Something about the motion and vibration of an engine puts babies to sleep. (Remember to always use a car seat for the baby and not to drive if you are too tired.)
- If all else fails and you are at your wit's end, take a break. If you have friends or family nearby, see if someone can relieve you for a while. If no one is available to physically come and take care of the baby, give yourself permission to put your baby down for a while. Make sure the baby is in a safe place where he will not get hurt (like his crib or bassinet), then go to a quiet part of your home and try to relax until you feel ready to deal with the baby again.

Ear Pain/Discharge

Warning/Emergency Signs

Seek emergency care if your child shows the following sign:

- Blood or clear fluid coming out of the ear after a fall

When to Call Your Child's Doctor

Call your child's doctor if your child shows any of the following signs:

- Indication that there may be something stuck in her ear
- Fever for more than three days or a fever that reappears after being gone for a day or two in a child with a cold
- Pain or itching in an ear or persistent grabbing at the ear in an older infant or toddler
- Drainage of pus, blood, or fluid from the ear (You do not need to call if

you are sure the drainage is just wax, which will emerge in small amounts and look light brown, dark brown, or brownish-orange.)

- Pain, redness, or swelling over the bone behind the ear
- Pain with swallowing
- Difficulty hearing
- Fever or other indication of illness in a child who is teething (Crankiness is common with teething, but excessive sleepiness or prolonged crying is not.)
- No sign of improvement after three days of antibiotic treatment in a child who was diagnosed with an ear infection

Your nine-month-old has spent the past four hours trying to put her fingers into her left ear and is tugging on her earlobe. Does the ear hurt? Could she have an ear infection? Is she teething? Did she just realize that her ear is a fun thing to play with?

If babies could talk to us, questions like these would be much easier to answer. Unfortunately, parenting often involves playing a "what could be causing him to do that?" guessing game. A baby tugging on her ear could be showing a sign of an ear infection, teething, or just taking part in the natural process of self-discovery. You need to look at other things the child is doing to get a better idea of what could be causing ear tugging. Ear tugging and fussiness that becomes worse when a child lies down are two clues that an ear infection might be the problem. Here are some common causes of ear pain or ear discharge:

Middle ear infection (otitis media). When most people say their child has an ear infection, they are talking about otitis media (middle ear infection). This is an infection in the part of the ear behind the eardrum.

The infection usually causes pain in the infected ear, and this may be associated with fever. Ear infections tend to happen when a child has a cold and may be the reason a fever reappears after a day or two without fever. Some children will have drainage that looks thick and yellow out of the infected ear. This drainage is built-up pus escaping through a small hole in the eardrum. (Don't panic if this happens—it is the first step toward healing, and the hole in the eardrum will almost always heal on its own. Relief of pain usually occurs when the ear drains. The doctor can prescribe antibiotics for your child to help the healing process.) Some children have recurrent ear infections. Children who are exposed to cigarette smoke are more likely to get ear infections. (This is yet another good reason to quit. While you're working on quitting, go outside to smoke.) To learn more about ear infections, see Chapter 30, "Childhood Infections."

Ear canal infection (otitis externa/swimmer's ear). To find information about outer ear infection, see Chapter 30, "Childhood Infections."

Injury/irritation of the ear canal. Any irritation in the ear canal will cause the ear to feel strange and may cause your child to tug on the ear or say it hurts. Cotton swabs are fine for cleaning the outside of the ear, but they should not be used inside the ear canal. Sticking anything into the ear (even something as soft as a cotton swab) can irritate the ear canal. It can also push wax farther into the ear. Children who stick pencils or other objects into their ears can scratch or irritate the ear canal.

Teething or throat pain. It may sound strange, but teething or other pain in the back of the mouth can cause your child to tug on or complain about his ears. Pain signals from the back of the mouth and throat travel right past the ear canal on their way to the brain, and they can confuse the child as to the location of the pain. For simple teething pain, acetaminophen (Tylenol) or ibuprofen (Motrin/Advil) is helpful. Numbing medicines that are put on the gums are generally less effective. Call your child's doctor if your child has a fever or is acting like he is having pain with swallowing.

Wax (cerumen). Everyone has earwax. Wax, which is yellowish-brown, is produced by the ear to help protect the ear canal. Normally, wax buildup does not cause any problems (except that a doctor can't see through it to examine an ear). If wax becomes hard and dry or gets pushed far back into the ear (usually by a cotton swab), it can sometimes cause discomfort or hearing problems. Sometimes wax will become thin enough to run out of the ear and can look like a light brown crust on the edge of the ear canal or on a pillow. However, significant light yellow drainage is probably due to an infection. If you see wax on the outside of the ear, clean it with a warm, wet washcloth or a cotton swab. Never push anything into the ear, not even a seemingly innocent cotton swab. This can push wax farther into the ear and irritate the ear canal.

Foreign body. Some toddlers will try to put almost anything they can find into their mouths, noses, and ears. You might not notice that you are missing a raisin, but you will notice your child tugging on the ear where it is hiding. Children can be creative with what they stick into their ears— hamster food, pieces of paper, and little clumps of dirt are all fair game. A child with something stuck in the ear does not act ill and will not have cold symptoms or a fever. Even if you can see the object, don't try to pull it out yourself. You may push it farther in or injure the ear canal. Your child's doctor has special tools that make it much easier to remove a foreign body.

What You Can Do at Home
For an ear infection:

- Make sure your child finishes all of the antibiotics prescribed by her doctor even if she feels better.
- Give acetaminophen or ibuprofen for pain relief.
- Have your child put the ear on a heating pad; this sometimes soothes the pain. Limit this to 10 to 15 minutes at a time on low to medium heat to prevent burning the outside of the ear.
- Call the doctor if your child is not feeling better after three days of antibiotics.

For earwax:

- Check with your child's doctor before using anything in your child's ear, and make sure that wax is really the problem. Never put anything into the ear if there may be a hole in the eardrum (except for medicines prescribed by the doctor).
- Remember that earwax rarely causes a problem and seldom needs to be removed.
- Clean the outside of the ear with a warm, moist washcloth. The humid air this creates often helps to loosen wax inside of the ear.
- You can also clean the outside of the ear with a cotton swab, but never put

anything into your child's ear. It could push the wax farther in or irritate the ear canal.

- Occasionally your child's doctor may recommend that you use an over-the-counter medicine to soften the wax (like Debrox or Cerumenex). To use these, have your child lie down with one ear facing upward. Fill the ear canal with several drops (usually three to five are needed to fill the canal). Have the child stay still for about five minutes. If this is not possible, you can gently put a cotton ball into your child's ear to keep the drops in place. After about five minutes, flush the ear with warm water using a bulb syringe. (The water should be warm, not cold. Warm water helps to keep the wax soft, whereas cold water in the ear can make your child dizzy or cause her to vomit.) You may need to repeat this process for a few days to remove all of the wax. If this doesn't work or you are unable to do this with your child, call the doctor. He or she has other techniques for removing wax.
- **Never** insert any object or device into the child's ear to remove wax.

For teething, take these actions:

- Give acetaminophen or ibuprofen for severe teething pain.
- Put teething rings into the freezer for an hour or two and then give them to your child. Chewing on a smooth, cold, hard object can help to soothe sore gums. (Avoid teething rings with gel in them because if they rip or get a hole, your baby may swallow the gel.) A wet washcloth that has been placed in the freezer for 30 minutes can also be used to chew on.

- Never tie a teething ring (or anything else) around your baby's neck. It could get caught on something and strangle the child.
- Keep in mind that teething may make your baby drool more and act cranky, but it should not cause high fevers or make your child act ill.

Eye Redness/Discharge

Warning/Emergency Signs

Seek emergency care if your child shows any of the following signs:

- A chemical or cleaning product splashed into the eye (but first flush the eye with lots of water)
- A stick or similar object stuck in the eye
- A foreign object in the eye that does not come out with tearing or flushing the eye with water
- Blurry vision with red, irritated eyes
- Swelling or redness around the eye or eyelid that makes it difficult to open the eye

When to Call Your Child's Doctor
Call your child's doctor if your child shows any of the following signs:

- Red, gooey, or irritated eyes
- Eyes that are stuck together in the morning and have watery or yellow drainage throughout the day
- A red, swollen, or painful area around the eye or eyelid
- A red, painful bump on the eyelid
- Eye pain or an eye that is very sensitive to light
- Red or sticky eyes in an infant less than three months old

Eyes can become itchy, watery, or red for many different reasons. Allergies can cause children to have itchy eyes and a stuffy nose. Conjunctivitis, commonly called "pinkeye," gives eyes a bloodshot appearance and causes discharge. A speck of dust or an eyelash in the eye can be irritating and cause tearing and eye redness. Rarely, eye inflammation can appear as a symptom of certain chronic medical conditions such as inflammatory bowel disease or juvenile rheumatoid arthritis. Other eye problems are not as dramatic but can also cause concern. Listed here are some common eye problems.

Blocked tear duct. If your newborn has watery or yellowish discharge from one eye, it could be because of a blocked tear duct. The eyes are constantly making tears to keep the eyes moist and to allow the lids to glide gently over the eyes. These tears usually drain through a duct leading from the inner corner of the eye down into the nose. If the tear duct is blocked, the tears back up and a watery discharge from the eye occurs.

Blocked tear ducts usually go away on their own by the time a baby is 6 to 12 months of age. You can wipe the eye with a clean, damp washcloth and gently massage the area between the top of the nose and the inner corner of the eye. (Ask your child's doctor to demonstrate how to massage the duct to open it. Make sure your hands are clean when you do this so you don't infect the eye.)

Conjunctivitis (pinkeye). Conjunctivitis is usually to blame when children have red, gooey, sticky eyes. Conjunctivitis is an infection in the eye caused by either a virus or bacteria. For more information on conjunctivitis, see Chapter 30, "Childhood Infections."

Seasonal and environmental allergies or irritants. Red, itchy, watery eyes may be signs of an allergy. Irritants like cigarette smoke can also irritate a child's eyes. For more information, see Seasonal or Environmental Allergies or Irritants under Cough in this chapter.

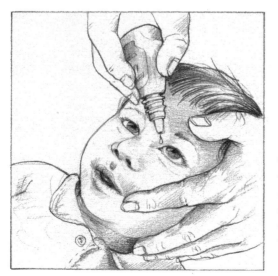

Figure 29.1. Giving eyedrops. When administering eyedrops to your infant or young child, use the following technique: Your child should lie flat on his back with your hand steadying his head as shown. Drop the prescribed number of eyedrops into the corner of his eye (next to the nose). If your child won't keep his eyes open, the drops will collect on the skin at the corner of his eye; when your child opens his eyelids, the drops will run into his eyes. Another adult may be needed to help steady a struggling child.

Foreign body. The eye gets irritated easily, and even small things, like little pieces of trapped dirt and dust, can make an eye red. This type of foreign body in the eye usually doesn't scratch the cornea or cause any lasting damage but can be annoying. Tearing alone usually does a good job getting this type of material out of the eye. If the eye continues to look red for more than an hour, it's time to call the doctor. Little particles sometimes get trapped under the eyelid. If something large gets into the eye (like a twig), do not try to remove it yourself because you could cause more damage. Call your child's doctor if the eye remains irritated or if there is something large trapped under the eyelid.

Sty (hordeolum). A sore, red bump along the eyelid is called a hordeolum, or sty. A sty is an infection of a meibomian gland (the gland that helps to keep the eye moist) located along the eyelid. A sty can appear fairly quickly or grow larger over the course of a few days. They are almost always painful but do not interfere with vision or make a child feel ill. Warm washcloth compresses often help the infection to drain and subside, but antibiotics may be needed.

Corneal abrasion. The cornea is part of the outer covering of the eye. Trauma to the eye or foreign bodies—even small particles of dirt and dust—can cause a scratch (abrasion). A scratch on the cornea is usually painful (burns or stings). The eye will look red, tear frequently, and be sensitive to light. If treated properly, most corneal abrasions heal well and do not have long-term effects on vision.

Chemical injury. Accidents happen. Cleaning products can splash as you are pouring them, or your child can cause a spill despite your best efforts to keep dangerous chemicals out of reach. If a chemical does get into your child's eye, you should immediately flush the eye with clean, lukewarm water. Flush the eye for at least 10 to 15 minutes (see Chapter 28, "First Aid and Emergency Care," for detailed instructions for emergencies). Some chemicals can damage the cornea. Your child's doctor will need to know what product got into the eye. Sometimes flushing the eye will be enough, but more may need to be done to protect your child's vision.

What You Can Do at Home

For conjunctivitis (pinkeye):

- Remove sticky or crusted discharge to make your child feel better. Wipe the outside of the eye with a clean washcloth moistened with lukewarm water. You will not be able to keep the eye completely clean, so don't overdo it. Wipe the eye a few times a day or when the discharge becomes particularly thick.
- Remember that pinkeye is contagious. Everyone in the household needs to wash their hands frequently. Remind your child to avoid touching his face or rubbing his eyes. Wash your hands before you touch your face. Do not share towels because these can spread the infection.

For allergies:

- Try to keep track of your child's symptoms if you think he has allergies. Keeping a journal or diary of when symptoms occur and what your child was doing or where he was at the time can reveal patterns that point to what is causing the allergy. Your child's doctor will probably ask you for this information.

If something gets in the eye:

- Flush it out with clean water (emergency care directions are found in Chapter 28, "First Aid and Emergency Care"). If your child gets something large like a twig in his eye, do **not** try to remove it—seek emergency care.

Fever

Fever in a Baby Younger than Three Months of Age

Warning/Emergency Signs

Seek emergency care if your infant shows any of the following signs:

- Fever (as defined below)
- Lethargy and difficulty waking
- Inconsolable crying for several hours
- Refusal to feed

- Low temperature (less than 97 degrees Fahrenheit), despite being clothed appropriately
- Skin that feels cool and clammy
- Lips, tongue, or nails that look blue
- Weakness and floppiness compared to his normal muscle tone and activity
- Soft spot on the head that seems to be bulging or pushing outward and doesn't move up and down with crying

An older child's activity level will often indicate whether she is significantly ill or just has a cold. Making this distinction is much harder in young infants. Your child's doctor might have to perform a group of tests to be sure that a serious infection is not the cause of the baby's fever. This often involves checking the baby's blood, urine, and spinal fluid. Sometimes a baby is admitted to the hospital for a few days for close observation and precautionary treatment with antibiotics until tests show that the baby is not seriously ill. Although most fevers in very young infants are caused by viral infections that result in no harm, doctors take a "better safe than sorry" approach

Definition of a Fever

- Rectal temperature higher than 100.4 degrees Fahrenheit
- Oral temperature higher than 99.5 degrees Fahrenheit
- Axillary (armpit) temperature higher than 99 degrees Fahrenheit
- Ear temperature (in rectal mode) higher than 100.4 degrees Fahrenheit
- Ear temperature (in oral mode) higher than 99.5 degrees Fahrenheit

Taking Your Child's Temperature

A gentle kiss on the forehead or a hand placed lightly on your child's skin is often enough to tell that your child has a fever. However, this method of taking a temperature (called tactile temperature) is dependent on the person doing the feeling and does not give an accurate measure of a child's temperature.

Choosing a Thermometer

Years ago the choice was simple. You either felt your child's head with your hand or you used a glass thermometer. But times have changed. Because of concerns about possible exposure to mercury (an environmental toxin), the American Academy of Pediatrics now advises that parents stop using glass mercury thermometers. Safe and accurate alternatives include home digital thermometers (which can be used orally, rectally, or in the armpit) and ear thermometers.

Forehead thermometers (the ones that resemble small plastic strips) are quick and easy to use, but they are not accurate. They tell you about as much as you knew by simply touching your child. They may be useful for a quick screen, but they do not give an exact reading. Pacifier thermometers are not always accurate. Although it is tempting to use a pacifier thermometer in a small infant, they should not be used in infants younger than three months. Digital ear thermometers are fairly accurate if used correctly, which takes some training and practice; however, they tend to be expensive. Other types of digital thermometers come in many shapes and sizes, and most give accurate readings. No matter what type of thermometer you choose, make sure you know how to use it properly and how to read the temperature.

I Couldn't Put a Thermometer There, Could I? Taking the Temperature

The three basic options for taking a temperature (unless you have an ear thermometer) are: rectal (in the bottom), oral (in the mouth), and axillary (in the armpit). The method you use should depend upon your child's age and ability to cooperate. It is best to take a temperature rectally until a child is old enough to keep the thermometer in his mouth and keep his mouth closed. Although taking a rectal temperature is safe and is the most reliable, the idea of doing this makes some parents uncomfortable and they prefer to use a different method. If this is the case, you can use the axillary method for infants. The axillary method is also good for an older child who has a stuffy nose and has difficulty breathing with his mouth closed.

Taking Your Child's Temperature with a Digital Thermometer

Note: If you're using an ear thermometer, follow the manufacturer's directions that come with the device.

Rectal Method

- Read the directions carefully so that you know which beep, or series of beeps, is the sign that the thermometer is finished reading. Make sure the screen is clear before you begin.
- If your thermometer uses disposable plastic sleeves, place a clean sleeve on the thermometer.
- Coat the tip of the thermometer with a water-soluble lubricating jelly—**not** petroleum jelly (like Vaseline).
- Place your baby across your lap with his bottom facing upward and his legs relaxed. Remember to support the baby's head. If you have an older child or a squirmy baby, lay the child down on a firm, flat surface such as a changing table or on a blanket on the floor.
- Put one hand on the baby's lower back to keep him still.
- Use your other hand to insert the lubricated thermometer into your child's rectum through the anal opening. Gently insert the thermometer one-half to one inch into the rectum. Always stop if you feel resistance.
- Steady the thermometer between your second and third fingers as you cup your hand against your baby's bottom. Soothe your baby by speaking quietly to him as you hold the thermometer in place.
- Wait for the beep (or beeps) that signals that the reading is done, and gently slide the thermometer from your baby's bottom.
- Read and record the number on the screen.
- If you used a disposable plastic sleeve, be sure to discard it.
- Clean the thermometer and replace it in its case.

(continued)

Oral Method

- If your child has just finished eating or drinking, you should wait 20 to 30 minutes before taking an oral temperature.
- Read the directions carefully so that you know which beep, or series of beeps, is the sign that the thermometer is finished reading. Make sure the screen is clear before you begin.
- If your thermometer uses disposable plastic sleeves, place a clean sleeve on the thermometer.
- Make sure your child's mouth is clear of candy, gum, or food.
- Place the thermometer under your child's tongue and ask him to close his lips around it. Remind your child not to bite the thermometer or talk with the thermometer in his mouth. Ask him to relax and breathe normally through his nose.
- Wait for the beep (or beeps) that signals that the reading is done, and remove the thermometer from your child's mouth.
- Read and record the number on the screen.
- If you used a disposable plastic sleeve, be sure to discard it.
- Clean the thermometer and replace it in its case.

Axillary (Armpit) Method

- Read the directions carefully so that you know which beep, or series of beeps, is the sign that the thermometer is finished reading. Make sure the screen is clear before you begin.
- If your thermometer uses disposable plastic sleeves, place a clean sleeve on the thermometer.
- Insert the thermometer into your child's armpit. Clothing such as undershirts should be removed so the thermometer directly touches your child's skin. Fold your child's arm across his chest and hold the thermometer in place.
- Wait for the beep (or beeps) that signals that the reading is done, and remove the thermometer from your child's armpit.
- Read and record the number on the screen.
- If you used a disposable plastic sleeve, be sure to discard it.
- Clean the thermometer and replace it in its case.

and treat young infants more aggressively than they would an older child with a fever.

Fevers in young infants are usually caused by the same things (infections with viruses or bacteria) that cause fevers in older children. Sometimes a fever is not caused by an infection but by an infant's environment. The major causes of fever in infants younger than three months old are listed here.

Colds and other virus infections. Common colds and viral infections can cause fevers in infants just as they can in older children. It's difficult to distinguish a virus from a more serious cause of fever in young infants, so your child's doctor may want to perform tests before attributing a fever to a minor viral infection.

Environment. Babies, especially newborns, can't regulate their body temperatures as well as older children can. A baby with too many layers of clothing or blankets will tend to become overheated. Babies also get cold easily because they have a relatively large skin surface area from which to lose heat. An infant's body temperature may decrease if she is not dressed appropriately in a cold environment. A general rule of thumb is that in the first few weeks, a baby will need two more layers of clothing than you do to be comfortable. After the first few months, the baby needs one additional layer. If you think your infant may have a fever, make sure the baby has been unbundled and dressed lightly for 10 to 15 minutes before taking the temperature.

Immunizations. Babies usually get their first dose of DTaP vaccine when they are two months old. This vaccine as well as some others can cause a fever (usually within the first 24 hours after a dose of DTaP). The fever is a reaction to the vaccine and does not mean that the infant will need to be evaluated for infection. If you have any questions about whether a fever following an immunization is normal, call your child's doctor.

Urinary tract infection. An infection in the bladder or kidneys can cause fever in a baby. Infants can't tell you that it hurts when they urinate, so these infections may be difficult to distinguish from other causes of fever. Urine testing is usually part of the evaluation workup that doctors do when young infants have a fever.

Meningitis. Meningitis is an infection of the covering of the brain (see Chapter 30, "Childhood Infections," for more information). Meningitis, particularly when caused by bacteria, can be a serious infection and usually needs to be treated with antibiotics. A baby with meningitis may be extremely sleepy or irritable. The baby may cry continuously and can't be calmed or comforted. Some babies become weak and refuse to suck or feed. The soft spot on the baby's head may bulge outward and doesn't move with crying as it does normally. Your child's doctor may perform a procedure called a spinal tap (lumbar puncture) to obtain a small amount of the fluid surrounding the spinal cord to check for evidence of infection. Tests can be performed to identify bacteria or viruses in the fluid.

Sepsis. *Sepsis* means "bacterial infection in the bloodstream." The infection can start either in the blood or in some other part of the body and spread to the blood. Some babies seem normal except for a fever or a tendency to develop a low body temperature despite proper clothing. Others may become irritable, have poor feeding or

FEVER AND PAIN MEDICATION DOSAGES FOR INFANTS AND YOUNG CHILDREN
Recommended Dosing of Acetaminophen

Age	Weight	Single Dose	Preparation	Single Dosage
0 to 3 months	6–11 lb 2.7–5.0 kg	40 mg	Infant Drops (Infants' Tylenol Concentrated Drops; Infants' Panadol Drops; Tempra 1; Infants' Genapap Drops)	½ dropperful or .4 ml concentrated drops
4 to 11 months	12–17 lb 5.4–7.7 kg	80 mg	Infant Drops (Infants' Tylenol Concentrated Drops; Infants' Panadol Drops; Tempra 1; Infants' Genapap Drops)	1 dropperful or .8 ml concentrated drops
			Children's Elixir/Liquid (Children's Tylenol Liquid; Children's Tempra 2 Syrup; Children's Genapap Drops)	½ tsp.
12 to 23 months	18–23 lb 8.2–10.4 kg	120 mg	Infant Drops (Infants' Tylenol Concentrated Drops; Infants' Panadol Drops; Tempra 1; Infants' Genapap Drops)	1½ dropperfuls or 1.2 ml concentrated drops
			Children's Elixir/Liquid (Children's Tylenol Liquid; Children's Panadol; Tempra 2 Syrup; Children's Genapap Drops)	¾ tsp.

(NOTE: Doses listed may be given every 4 to 6 hours but should not exceed five doses within a 24-hour period.)

FEVER AND PAIN MEDICATION DOSAGES FOR INFANTS AND YOUNG CHILDREN

Recommended Dosing of Acetaminophen

Age	Weight	Single Dose	Preparation	Single Dosage
2 to 3 years	24–35 lb 10.9–15.9 kg	160 mg	Infant Drops (Infants' Tylenol Concentrated Drops; Infants' Panadol Drops; Tempra 1; Infants' Genapap Drops)	2 dropperfuls or 1.6 ml concentrated drops
			Children's Elixir/Liquid (Children's Tylenol Liquid; Children's Panadol; Tempra 2 Syrup; Children's Genapap Drops)	1 tsp.
			Children's Chewable Tablets (Children's Tylenol Soft Chews; Children's Panadol; Tempra 3)	2 tablets
4 to 5 years	36–47 lb 16.3–21.3 kg	240 mg	Children's Elixir/Liquid (Children's Tylenol Liquid; Children's Panadol; Tempra 2 Syrup; Children's Genapap Drops)	1½ tsp.
			Children's Chewable Tablets (Children's Tylenol Soft Chews; Children's Panadol; Tempra 3)	3 tablets

(Source: Health Management Bulletin. *Proper Use of Pediatric OTC Analgesics/Antipyretics*. June 2000. American Medical Association. Used with permission.)

(NOTE: Doses listed may be given every 4 to 6 hours but should not exceed five doses within a 24-hour period.)

FEVER AND PAIN MEDICATION DOSAGES FOR INFANTS AND YOUNG CHILDREN

Recommended Dosing of Ibuprofen (for children 6 months and older)

Age	Weight	Single Dose	Preparation	Single Dosage
6 to 11 months	12–17 lb 5.4–7.7 kg	50 mg	Infant Drops (Infants' Motrin Concentrated Drops; PediaCare Fever)	1 dropperful (1.25 ml)
			Children's Oral Suspension (Children's Motrin Suspension; Children's Advil; PediaCare Fever)	½ tsp. (2.5 ml)
12 to 23 months	18–23 lb 8.2–10.4 kg	75 mg	Infant Drops (Infants' Motrin Concentrated Drops; PediaCare Fever)	1½ dropperfuls (1.875 ml)
			Children's Oral Suspension (Children's Motrin Suspension; Children's Advil; PediaCare Fever)	¾ tsp. (3.75 ml)
2 to 3 years	24–35 lb 10.9–15.9 kg	100 mg	Children's Oral Suspension (Children's Motrin Suspension; Children's Advil; PediaCare Fever)	1 tsp.
4 to 5 years	36–47 lb 16.3–21.3 kg	150 mg	Children's Oral Suspension (Children's Motrin Suspension; Children's Advil; PediaCare Fever)	1½ tsp.
			Children's Chewable Tablets (Children's Motrin Chewable Tablets; Children's Advil Chewable Tablets)	3 tablets

(Source: Health Management Bulletin. *Proper Use of Pediatric OTC Analgesics/Antipyretics.* June 2000. American Medical Association. Used with permission.)

(NOTE: Doses listed may be given every 6 to 8 hours but should not exceed three doses within a 24-hour period.)

trouble breathing, or appear weak, limp, and very ill.

What You Can Do at Home

Make rules for visitors:

- Try to keep the number of people visiting your newborn to a minimum. The first two to three months are also not a good time for trips to the mall or other areas where there are lots of people (and lots of germs).
- If people are sick (even if it is just a mild cold), do not let them hold the baby.
- If people are going to hold the baby, have them wash their hands first. Try to keep your infant in a place with a comfortable temperature, away from extremes of heat or cold.

Fever in a Child Three Months of Age or Older

Warning/Emergency Signs

Seek emergency care if your child shows any of the following signs:

- Lethargy and difficulty waking
- Limpness and refusal to move
- Extreme irritability
- Red/purple spots that look like bruises on the skin (that were not there before the child got sick)
- Inconsolable crying for several hours
- Stiff neck
- Severe headache
- Difficulty breathing that does not get better with clearing the nose
- Leaning forward and drooling
- Seizure
- Lips, tongue, and nails that look blue

- Soft spot on the head that seems to be bulging outward

When to Call Your Child's Doctor

Call your child's doctor if your child shows any of the following signs:

- Irritability even after the fever comes down
- Lack of interest in toys or favorite things
- Refusal to drink for several hours
- Fever that lasts more than three days
- Fever that reappears after being gone for one to two days
- Frequent fevers that are not associated with cold symptoms or other obvious cause

Your child wakes up in the morning with flushed cheeks and glassy eyes. You know before you put your hand on his forehead that he has a fever. By watching how your child behaves when he has a fever, you can usually tell if he has a minor illness that you can handle at home or if you need to call the doctor.

There is a surprisingly wide range for normal body temperature. It is also normal for body temperature to vary throughout the day. (For the definition of fever, see the box on page 541.) There are many causes of fever. Running around and exercising cause an increase in temperature. Young infants can't regulate their body temperature well and can get a fever if they are overdressed or in a hot environment. This can also happen to older children, but it is not as common. Leaving a child of any age in a parked car without ventilation on a hot day can cause the child to become dangerously overheated and die.

Fever usually indicates that your child has an infection. Almost every infection listed in Chapter 30, "Childhood Infec-

Fever Myths

Myth: *All fevers are harmful to children.*
Fact: Fever usually causes no harm itself and, in fact, can be helpful in "turning on" the body's immune system and fighting infection.

Myth: *Fevers cause brain damage.*
Fact: The majority of fevers do not cause brain damage or any lasting problems. Fever itself usually doesn't cause any symptoms until it reaches 102 degrees Fahrenheit or higher. Young children may experience brief seizures with a fever (see Chapter 32, "Health Problems in Early Childhood," for more about seizures) but are not harmed by them.

Myth: *The higher the fever, the more serious the illness.*
Fact: The height of a fever does not necessarily mean anything. The number on your thermometer is less important than the way your child is acting (see Warning/Emergency Signs and When to Call Your Child's Doctor, throughout Fever section). Some children will develop high fevers with virus infections that need no specific treatment.

Myth: *All fevers need to be treated.*
Fact: In most cases, a fever should be treated only if it is causing discomfort. Fever medicines may temporarily lower a fever, but they will not fix the underlying cause of a fever. If the child is acting very ill or if a fever lasts longer than two to three days, the doctor should evaluate the cause of the fever and determine whether the illness needs specific treatment.

Myth: *Temperature should return to normal when a child is treated with fever-reducing medication.*
Fact: Fever medicine will lower a temperature by one to two degrees but will not necessarily bring the temperature back to normal. The medicine does usually lower the temperature enough for your child to be more comfortable. If the temperature does not return to normal, it does not necessarily mean the child has a more serious infection.

Myth: *Ice packs, cold baths, or rubbing alcohol can be used to treat a fever.*
Fact: Rubbing alcohol can be absorbed through the skin and cause poisoning. Ice packs and cold baths can cause a child to have shaking chills. This shaking can actually raise the child's body temperature (and make your child even more uncomfortable).

Myth: *Teething causes fever.*
Fact: Teething is a normal process that may cause mild discomfort, but it does not cause significant fevers. Body temperature may be slightly higher when an infant is teething, but it does not usually go above 100 degrees Fahrenheit because of teething alone. If your child who is teething has a significant fever, you and your child's doctor should consider another source, such as an infection.

tions," can cause a fever. The height of a fever does not tell you much about how sick your child is. A simple cold or other minor viral infection can sometimes cause a rather high fever (in the 102 to 104 degrees Fahrenheit range) but doesn't usually indicate a serious problem, and serious infections may cause no fever or even an abnormally low body temperature, especially in young infants.

Sometimes fever is caused by something other than an infection. Chronic diseases like juvenile rheumatoid arthritis or lupus can cause fevers that come and go. It isn't normal for children to have recurrent fevers, even if they last only a few hours each night.

For older infants and children (but not necessarily for infants younger than three months), the way your child is acting is far more important than the reading on your thermometer. Everyone gets cranky when they have a fever. This is normal and should be expected. The illness is probably not serious if your child is still interested in playing, is eating and drinking well, is alert and smiling at you, has a normal skin color, and looks well when his temperature comes down. (Don't worry too much about a child with fever who doesn't want to eat. This is very common with infections that cause fever.)

Call your child's doctor if your child has any of the signs or symptoms listed previously or if you are concerned for any other reason.

What You Can Do at Home

- Dress your child in a lightweight outfit and use only a thin sheet or blanket on the bed. Layers of clothing and blankets will actually prevent heat from escaping and can cause body temperatures to rise.
- Not all fevers need to be treated, but if your child has symptoms from the fever (such as feeling achy, being cranky, or not wanting to eat), you can treat the fever with medicine (see Fever and Pain Medication Dosages for Infants and Young Children on pages 546–549). Acetaminophen (Tylenol) can be used in young infants, but remember, if your infant is younger than three months old, call your child's doctor for any fever and do **not** give fever medication unless instructed to. Ibuprofen (Motrin/Advil) can be used in infants six months or older. Do **not** give aspirin to a child unless your doctor tells you to. Aspirin has been associated with Reye syndrome, a dangerous disease of the liver and brain that can be fatal.
- Offer your child plenty to drink. Children can become dehydrated more easily when they have a fever. Drinking cool fluids makes them feel better and prevents dehydration.
- Do **not** force your child to eat. The old saying "feed a cold and starve a fever" is false, but many children with fevers just do not feel like eating. If your child wants food, give it to him. If your child is not particularly interested in food, offer lots of liquids. Most healthy children have enough reserve to be fine for a day or two without food, but they need adequate amounts of fluid every day.
- Have your child get plenty of rest.
- Do quiet activities together like reading books, playing board games,

or watching your child's favorite videos.

For advice on what to do to treat specific symptoms that are often accompanied by fever, see Congestion/Runny Nose, Cough, Diarrhea, and Vomiting entries in this chapter.

Limb or Joint Pain/Swelling

Warning/Emergency Signs

Seek emergency care if your child shows any of the following signs:

- An injured limb that looks crooked or deformed
- Arm or leg kept in an unusual position
- Refusal to bear weight on a leg
- Refusal to use or move a hand or arm
- Crying for much longer than you would expect from the type of injury
- Severe pain
- Multiple injuries after a fall or other accident
- Numbness or tingling in the fingers or toes following an injury
- An injured limb that feels abnormally cool or looks pale

When to Call Your Child's Doctor

Call your child's doctor if your child shows any of the following signs:

- Any pain that is still present two weeks after the injury
- Swelling or pain that is not improving or is increasing 24 to 48 hours after the injury

- Joint that looks swollen for more than a day
- Joint or limb pain that wakes him from sleep
- A limp that does not improve after one or two days
- Abdominal pain and joint pain

Minor accidents and falls are the most common reason for joint and limb complaints in young children. The shins and knees of many normal toddlers are covered with minor bumps and bruises. Leg pain or a limp can be caused by one of these bumps or by a simple sprain or strain sustained during a sudden turn or fall. Splinters, scrapes, and blisters on the child's foot can also cause a limp, but most of these injuries are not serious.

Sometimes joint and limb complaints are not caused by injuries but by infections or other diseases. Joints and muscles often feel achy and sore when a child has a fever, particularly with the flu or other virus infections. These aches usually feel better after a dose of acetaminophen (Tylenol) or ibuprofen (Motrin/Advil). Infections like Lyme disease and fifth disease (see Chapter 30, "Childhood Infections," to learn more about infections) can cause joint pain in addition to other symptoms. Untreated strep throat can sometimes lead to rheumatic fever and swollen, painful joints. Warm, red, swollen joints are never normal. Pain that lasts for more than a day or two might just be a slow-healing injury, but it could be due to a more serious problem. Some of the most common or important causes of limb and joint pain are listed below.

Sprain or strain. Muscles are attached to bones by ligaments. If your child twists or stops suddenly, the muscles or ligaments can be stretched or partially torn. These stretches and tears are called strains and sprains and are a common result of the rough and tumble play of childhood. These injuries usually hurt immediately and swelling occurs quickly. If you think your child has sustained a sprain or strain, quickly ice and elevate the limb. Minor strains usually get better with some rest and ice. Pain and swelling usually peak around 48 hours after the injury and then gradually improve. If your child is in severe pain or does not start to feel better after two days, the injury could be more serious—call the doctor.

Dislocations. Dislocations occur when a bone is pulled out of its normal position in a joint. Dislocations are common in the shoulder, thumb, and kneecap. These injuries usually happen after an injury that involves pulling on the joint. The child will be reluctant to use the injured part of the body. A mild type of dislocation is seen in a condition called "nursemaid's elbow." This injury is most common in two- to seven-year-olds because of the structure of the bones at this age. Nursemaid's elbow usually occurs after a caretaker (the "nursemaid") suddenly pulls a child's arm to prevent the child from falling or running into the street or swings a child by the arm during play (seems like fun, but not a good idea). The pulling motion causes the radius (one of the bones in the arm) to slip out of the elbow joint. The child often keeps the arm extended by his side with the palm facing his back and will refuse to use the arm or hand.

Broken bone (fracture). It's not always easy to tell whether a bone is broken by simply looking at the area. X-rays are often required to tell for sure. Injuries involving a lot of force are more likely to cause a bro-

ken bone than are minor stumbles or falls. Because the bones of small children are more flexible than the bones of older people, children often bounce back from injuries that could seriously hurt an older person. Sometimes these flexible bones can bend the way a healthy green twig will bend. A "greenstick" fracture occurs when the bone bends and little pieces splinter off of the bone without the bone breaking in two. If your child's limb looks crooked or is positioned at an unusual angle, there is probably a fracture. Marked bruising of the area after an injury or pain that prevents full movement of the injured limb are other signs suggesting a fracture is likely. A broken collarbone will often prevent your child from raising the arm on the affected side. (For first aid for injuries like these, see Chapter 28, "First Aid and Emergency Care.")

Arthritis. The word *arthritis* often makes people think of a grandparent who has stiff joints, but arthritis can also affect children. Arthritis means inflammation of a joint that is often associated with pain and swelling. Arthritis has many causes and can occur in almost any joint. It can sometimes appear after an infection with a virus. An infection in the joint itself usually causes a warm, red, swollen, and painful joint accompanied by a fever. Some infections such as Lyme disease and fifth disease can cause joint swelling in addition to other symptoms (see Chapter 30, "Childhood Infections," for a description of symptoms). Noninfectious illnesses like juvenile rheumatoid arthritis can also cause arthritis (see Chapter 32, "Health Problems in Early Childhood").

Infection. Infections can occur in joints, bones, and sometimes in muscles. A bacterial infection in a joint is called septic arthritis (the word *septic* means "infected"). Septic arthritis can occur after an injury if germs get into the joint. Joint infections can also result if an infection in the blood spreads to a joint. Infected joints are usually warm, red, and painful, and the child will usually have a fever. Osteomyelitis (bone infection) can also occur after an injury or an infection in the blood. The child usually has a fever and may complain of pain in a particular part of a limb. The child may not be able to point to one spot that hurts but may limp or not use an arm normally.

What You Can Do at Home

- After an injury, use the RICE approach for 24 to 48 hours:
  - R: Rest the injured limb. Try to keep your child from running, climbing, and doing other things that will put more stress on the injured extremity. Direct him toward quiet activities like reading or watching a favorite video.
  - I: Ice the injury with ice wrapped in a washcloth or a cold pack to reduce pain and swelling. Do not put the ice directly on the skin because this may cause frostbite. Leave the cold pack on for about 15 minutes, and then remove it for at least 15 minutes to prevent the skin from getting too cold.
  - C: Compress the injury with an elastic bandage. The wrap helps to keep swelling down and gives more support to an injured joint. It can also serve as a reminder to a child to take it easy for a while.
  - E: Elevate the injured limb. Keeping the injured area elevated helps to reduce swelling.
- Use the appropriate dose of acetaminophen or ibuprofen to help with pain control.

- If you suspect your child has broken a bone, see Chapter 28, "First Aid and Emergency Care," for instructions on how to splint or immobilize the injured area before going to the doctor's office or emergency room.

Mouth Pain/Problems

Warning/Emergency Signs

Seek emergency care if your child shows any of the following signs:

- Leaning forward
- Drooling
- Difficulty breathing

When to Call Your Child's Doctor

Call your child's doctor if your child shows any of the following signs:

- Light brown spots on the teeth that do not come off with brushing
- Refusal to eat or drink anything after several attempts
- Signs of dehydration (see box on dehydration on page 579)
- White patches (like milk) inside the cheeks that do not wipe off easily
- A fever that lasts for more than three days
- A high fever or extreme irritability with teething
- Rectal temperature over 100.4 degrees Fahrenheit in a child under three months old

Here are some common causes of mouth pain:

Teething. For information about teething, see the section on teething in Chapter 23, "Dental Care."

Thrush. White patches inside a baby's cheeks and on the tongue can be caused by an infection with a type of yeast called candida (see Chapter 30, "Childhood Infections," for more information). A candida infection in the mouth is called thrush, which may cause some discomfort and fussiness during feedings. Thrush is common in young infants and can be treated with medicine. Some infants with thrush also develop a diaper rash from the yeast. If you think your baby has thrush, call your child's doctor.

Hand, foot, and mouth disease (Coxsackie virus infection). Coxsackie virus infection is common in young children (see Chapter 30, "Childhood Infections," for more information). Infection with some types (strains) of the virus can cause small, painful ulcers on the tongue, throat, and sides of the mouth. Some children also get blisters or red bumps on the palms of their hands and on the soles of their feet, which is why this infection is sometimes called "hand, foot, and mouth disease." The worst of the mouth pain is usually gone after three to four days, and the ulcers usually disappear in about a week. A child with Coxsackie may not want to eat because eating often irritates mouth ulcers. Coxsackie itself does not cause any lasting problems for the child, but there is the risk of dehydration in children who refuse to eat or drink. Call your child's doctor if you are concerned your child is becoming dehydrated or has a fever for more than three days.

Aphthous ulcers (canker sores). Aphthous ulcers are small, shallow, grayish-white ulcers usually located on the inside of the lips. The ulcers can be quite painful and last for one to two weeks. Children tend to have only a couple of ulcers at a time. Sometimes they appear after an injury to the lining of the mouth (for example, a child biting his lip), but usually the ulcers appear for no obvious reason. No fever or other symptoms are associated with these ulcers. Call your child's doctor if your child has other symptoms of illness in addition to the ulcers.

Herpes virus (fever blisters or cold sores). Blisters in the mouth and around the lips can be caused by an infection with a virus called herpes simplex 1 (HSV-1). Herpes virus causes what are commonly known as fever blisters or cold sores around the lips. For more information, see Chapter 30, "Childhood Infections."

Bottle caries (dental cavities). Babies and toddlers can get cavities in their teeth just as adults can. Young children, particularly those who fall asleep with bottles in their mouths, are prone to developing cavities in their front teeth because small drops of milk or juice collect there and cause decay. The cavities look like small brown spots on the teeth that do not go away with brushing. For more on dental care, see Chapter 23, "Dental Care."

What You Can Do at Home
For teething:

- Give a child with sore gums a smooth, hard object to chew on. Cold objects often work well to numb the gums. Try giving your child a frozen teething ring or a wet washcloth that has been in the freezer for 30 minutes.
- Avoid giving your child hard foods that do not dissolve when wet because they are a choking hazard.
- Give a dose of acetaminophen (Tylenol) to help ease teething discomfort.

- Never tie a teething ring (or anything else) around your baby's neck. It could get caught on something, and your baby could accidentally be strangled.
- Remember that teething may make your baby cranky, but it does not cause high fevers or extreme irritability.

To prevent thrush from recurring:

- Clean all nipples and pacifiers in hot or boiling water.
- If you're breast-feeding, it is possible to get a yeast infection on your breast. If your breasts are red or sore and your baby has recurrent thrush, tell your doctor because you may need to be treated as well to keep your baby from getting reinfected.

For a sore mouth or throat due to infections or ulcers:

- Offer your child foods of different temperatures. Cold foods like ice pops (not for infants) help to numb the mouth and throat, and some children prefer bland warm things like broth when their mouth or throat hurts.
- Give a dose of acetaminophen (Tylenol) or ibuprofen (Motrin/Advil) to ease pain.
- Avoid foods that are spicy, salty, or acidic (like tomatoes and citrus fruits such as oranges and grapefruits). These foods sting when they come in contact with mouth sores or ulcers.

To prevent cavities:

- Never put your child to sleep with a bottle in his mouth or in his crib.

- Wipe your baby's teeth with a damp washcloth or soft-bristle toothbrush after eating.
- Start early with a toothbrushing routine. Let your child play an active part in toothbrushing, although you may have to help to get the teeth clean. Don't put more than a small dab of toothpaste on the brush because small children tend to swallow the toothpaste instead of spitting it out.

Respiratory and Breathing Problems

Breathing Problems

Warning/Emergency Signs

Seek emergency care if your child shows any of the following signs:

- Bluish color of the lips, tongue, nails, or skin
- Rapid breathing or having to work very hard to breathe
- Struggling for each breath or retracting (sucking in of the skin between the ribs or above the collarbone)
- Inability to speak or cry due to difficulty breathing
- Trouble breathing with stridor (high-pitched squeaking noise when breathing in) or leaning forward and drooling
- Trouble breathing and seems to be tiring out
- Trouble breathing with confusion or agitation

When to Call Your Child's Doctor

Call your child's doctor if your child shows any of the following signs:

- Noisy breathing that seems to be more than expected from a stuffy nose
- Fever for more than three days or that reappears after a day or two without fever
- Cough that is not improving after the first five days of the illness or cough that lasts for longer than ten days
- Stridor (high-pitched noise when breathing in) that does not improve with humidified or night air (See Croup section under Cough in this chapter.)

Also call your child's doctor if your child with asthma (see Chapter 32, "Health Problems in Early Childhood") has any of the following:

- A severe attack with little or no response to home treatment
- An atypical attack (an attack that is not like those your child usually has)
- A pattern of frequent attacks, ER visits, or hospitalizations

Trouble breathing can be a sign of many different problems, some more serious than others. Sometimes what looks like a problem is just a variation of normal. Infants can have what is called periodic breathing where they pause for up to 15 seconds before taking another breath. This is scary for a parent to witness, but it is normal and harmless. All children breathe more quickly when they have been running around and exercising, but their breathing should return to normal within a few minutes of

stopping vigorous activity. Stopping in the middle of play to catch their breath or huffing and puffing a lot afterward can indicate a problem. Most children also breathe somewhat faster when they have a fever, but the breathing rate becomes normal again when the fever goes down. Breathing very fast with a fever may also be a sign of pneumonia or another problem that may need treatment.

A mild degree of breathing trouble is often seen in children who have a cold and a stuffy nose. This is particularly true in infants because of their narrow nasal passages. This is why it's important to help clear the nose of an infant, especially before feeding or if the baby is having breathing difficulties (see Congestion/Runny Nose in this chapter).

More serious breathing trouble is seen in children with asthma, pneumonia, and bronchiolitis. When children have these problems, they may wheeze (a high-pitched whistling or hissing noise when the child breathes out), cough (see Cough section of Respiratory and Breathing Problems in this chapter), or breathe quickly. Bouts of coughing during or after exercise or laughter are also associated with asthma. Sudden onset of breathing trouble in a previously well child can result from an allergic reaction or choking. Children with some chronic medical problems such as immune deficiencies or cystic fibrosis (see Chapter 32, "Health Problems in Early Childhood") frequently get lung infections and have breathing difficulties.

Rapid breathing or difficult breathing can sometimes be seen in children with problems not related to their lungs or breathing passages. Infants and children with congenital heart disease (see Chapter

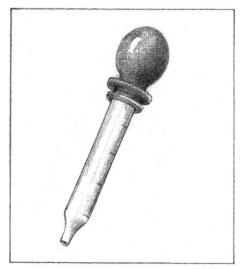

Figure 29.2. Bulb syringe. A bulb syringe is helpful for clearing mucus from your infant's nose.

32, "Health Problems in Early Childhood") or other heart problems often breathe quickly or look blue around their lips, tongue, and nails. In some infants and children, rapid breathing may be a sign of a serious infection of the blood (sepsis). Children with diabetes that is not controlled may develop very deep, fast breathing in addition to other symptoms.

Congestion/Runny Nose

Note: If your child has significant coughing, first see the Cough section of Respiratory and Breathing Problems in this chapter.

Warning/Emergency Signs

Seek emergency care if your child shows any of the following signs:

- Bluish color of the lips, tongue, nails, or skin
- Rapid breathing or having to work very hard to breathe

- Struggling for each breath or retracting (sucking in of the skin between the ribs or above the collarbone)
- Inability to speak or cry due to difficulty breathing
- Trouble breathing with stridor (high-pitched squeaking noise when breathing in) or leaning forward and drooling
- Trouble breathing and seems to be tiring out
- Trouble breathing with confusion or agitation

When to Call Your Child's Doctor

Call your child's doctor if your child shows any of the following signs:

- Fever for more than three days
- Fever that reappears after a day or two without fever
- A cold that does not gradually improve after the first three to five days

- Thick yellow mucus from only one nostril
- Thick yellow or green mucus from the nose that lasts more than 10 days
- Cough that lasts longer than two weeks
- Stridor (high-pitched noise heard when breathing in) that does not improve quickly (within 10 to 15 minutes) with humidified or night air (see Croup in the Cough section of Respiratory and Breathing Problems in this chapter).

If you look around a child-care center or playgroup during the winter months, you will probably notice that most of the children have runny noses. Colds are extremely common in this age group and are usually the cause of stuffy noses. Unfortunately, children often start to share germs before they learn to share toys. The good news is that a runny nose is usually not serious and your child will outgrow the period of having "a new cold every week." Here are some causes of congestion and runny nose:

Colds. Colds can be caused by a large number of different viruses (see Chapter 30, "Childhood Infections"). Although colds may cause discomfort, they are not usually serious. A child with a cold may have a runny nose with clear or yellow mucus. Nasal mucus usually looks more yellow in the morning because it has dried out and thickened overnight. A child with a cold may also have a fever for the first two to three days of the illness. But a fever that starts a few days or more after the cold began might indicate a complication such as an ear infection or pneumonia. Most colds last for one to two weeks (the first three to five days are usually the worst). After ten to fourteen days the runny nose and other

symptoms should be resolved. There's nothing a doctor (or parent) can do to make a cold go away faster. Antibiotics do not cure or relieve the symptoms of a viral infection. Over-the-counter cold medicines do not make a cold go away faster either. Colds can be more troublesome in young infants because they breathe almost exclusively through their noses. It's difficult or impossible to simultaneously suck from a breast or a bottle and breathe through a clogged nose. This is why it's often helpful to clear an infant's nose (using a rubber suction bulb), especially before feeding or if the baby is having breathing difficulties.

Seasonal and environmental allergies and irritants. A continuous runny nose in a child who is otherwise feeling well may be the result of allergies or exposure to irritants such as cigarette smoke. For more information, see Seasonal or Environmental Allergies or Irritants under Cough in this chapter.

Enlarged tonsils and adenoids. Children who sound "nasal" or stuffy all of the time may have enlarged tonsils and/or adenoids. Tonsils are lymph "glands" located in the back of the throat, and adenoids are above them, behind the nose. When adenoids get too large, they can partially block drainage of the nose, resulting in stuffiness and causing the child to keep her mouth open to breathe. Children with large tonsils and adenoids often snore loudly and may have more frequent sore throats and ear infections than other children. Surgery to remove the tonsils and/or adenoids is performed much less often than in the past, but it may be helpful in some situations. (For more information on surgery, refer to Chapter 32, "Health Problems in Early Childhood.")

Sinusitis. Sinusitis is an infection of the sinuses (air-filled areas in the facial bones behind the cheeks, nose, and forehead). It can cause a runny nose, persistent sniffling, facial swelling, cough, and sometimes a fever, headache, or bad breath. Sinus infections usually appear following a cold (or sometimes a flare-up of allergy symptoms) and are caused by the growth of bacteria trapped in the sinuses (further explanation of infections can be seen in Chapter 30, "Childhood Infections").

Foreign body. Children and toddlers have a tendency to put things into their mouths, noses, and ears that were never intended to go there. A foreign body (like a small Lego piece or a bead) stuck in the nose can cause a lot of irritation and thick yellow or green mucus. The mucus usually comes from only one nostril (because the object is stuck in one side of the nose), and the nasal discharge often has a foul odor. If you suspect this problem in your child, call your child's doctor who can look into the nose and remove anything that is stuck. (Don't try to remove a foreign body yourself—you may cause further harm.)

What You Can Do at Home

- Encourage your child to drink plenty of clear fluids (things you can see through like water, broth, and apple juice), which will help to thin her mucus and keep her well hydrated.
- Give your child warm liquids to soothe a sore, irritated throat.
- Give your child ice pops; they are a great "treat" and provide some extra fluid.
- Use a cool-mist vaporizer to keep mucus thin and moisten the airway. (Hot- or warm-mist vaporizers are not recommended because the hot water can burn a child, and bacteria are more likely to grow in a warm environment.) Make sure to carefully clean your vaporizer daily to prevent mold and bacterial growth. Do not add any medications to the water in the vaporizer—this can actually cause more airway irritation and make a cough worse. Note: Allergies (and asthma) may be aggravated by extra moisture in the child's environment (because moisture promotes the growth of molds and dust mites), so don't use a vaporizer in the case of allergy or asthma problems.
- Keep the nose as clear as possible.

For an infant or child who is too young to blow his nose:

- Use warm water or saltwater (saline) nose drops. Place three or four drops into one nostril. Wait about one minute and then gently insert the tip of a rubber suction bulb into the nostril. Keep the other nostril "closed" with your other hand. Suck out the mucus with the bulb. (Be sure to squeeze the bulb before you put it in the baby's nose, then release the pressure on the bulb once it is inside the nose.) Be careful not to push the tip in too far. Stop if you feel resistance. You can repeat this procedure several times until each nostril is clear. Using drops without suction is not very helpful in clearing mucus. Remember to clean the bulb syringe with hot, soapy water between uses.

For a child who can blow his nose:

- Encourage or remind your child to blow his nose. If mucus is thick and dried, you can use drops with an older child as you would with an infant. Have your child lie down on a bed with his head leaning back off of one side of the bed. Place three or four drops into each nostril and wait for the drops to loosen the mucus. After roughly one minute, have the child blow his nose.

Avoid using over-the-counter medications unless your doctor instructs you to use them. At best, cold medicines may have a mild effect on symptoms and they may cause troublesome side effects (excessive sleepiness or "hyperness"). In young infants, excessive sleepiness or irritability might signal a serious illness or might simply be a side effect, so it is best to avoid both the cold medicine and the confusion. Also, a cold will last the same number of days whether you treat it or not. Combination cold and cough medications often contain extra medications that can have additional side effects. Parents should read labels carefully to avoid accidental overdose of any of the components of a combination medicine. After some nose sprays designed to stop a runny nose wear off, they can cause the nose to run even more than it did before the child took the medicine. Cough medicines may be useful at night for a dry cough that is keeping your child awake, but check with your child's doctor prior to giving your child any medication.

Cough

Warning/Emergency Signs

Seek emergency care if your child shows any of the following signs:

- Bluish color of the lips, tongue, nails, or skin
- Very fast breathing or working very hard to breathe
- Struggling for each breath or retracting (sucking in of the skin between the ribs or above the collarbone)
- Inability to speak or cry due to difficulty breathing
- Trouble breathing with stridor (high-pitched noise when breathing in) or leaning forward and drooling
- Trouble breathing and seems to be tiring out
- Trouble breathing with confusion or agitation

When to Call Your Child's Doctor

Call your child's doctor if your child shows any of the following signs:

- Fever for more than three days
- Fever that reappears after a day or two without fever
- Cough that is not beginning to improve after the first three to five days
- Any cough that lasts longer than two weeks
- Stridor (high-pitched noise heard when breathing in) that does not improve quickly (within 10 to 15 minutes) with humidified or night air

Also call if your child with asthma has any of the following:

- A severe cough
- An attack that doesn't respond to home treatment
- An atypical attack (an attack that is not like the ones your child usually has)

It's 3:00 A.M. and you wake up to what sounds like an invasion of seals barking in your toddler's bedroom. A cough that keeps the child and the rest of the family awake is a common reason for a call to your child's doctor. Children cough for a variety of reasons. Coughing is the body's normal response to irritation in the breathing passageways. A cough forces air through the breathing passageways and helps to clear foreign particles, bacteria, and mucus from the lungs. It is a protective reflex and helps to prevent damage to and infection in the lungs. The sound made by a cough varies from a dry hacking or barking cough to a loose, wet, "junky" sounding one. The sound depends on what is causing the child to cough and what part of the airway is involved. Here are some causes of cough:

Colds and other upper respiratory infections. In addition to being the most common cause of runny noses in children, colds are also to blame for most of the coughing that children do. For more information, see Colds under Congestion/Runny Nose in this chapter, and see Common Cold in Chapter 30, "Childhood Infections."

Sinusitis. The mucous drip in the throat associated with sinusitis can cause a cough, which may be chronic. For more information, see Sinusitis under Congestion/Runny Nose in this chapter.

Bronchiolitis. Cough and cold symptoms are sometimes caused by bronchiolitis. Bronchiolitis is an infection in the small airways in the lungs that is usually caused by a virus—respiratory syncytial virus (RSV) is the most common. (For more information, see Chapter 30, "Childhood Infections.")

Croup. The child barking like a seal in the middle of the night probably has croup. Croup is caused by an infection around the vocal cords that causes a characteristic barking cough (often called a "croupy" cough). To learn more about this infection, see Chapter 30, "Childhood Infections."

Seasonal or environmental allergies or irritants. Seasonal allergies can cause coughing in a child who is otherwise feeling and acting well. The child will often have a continuous runny nose with clear mucus, frequent sneezing, and a daytime cough with no fever. Sometimes the child complains of itchy eyes or nose (in a young child you may notice frequent eye or nose rubbing). You may notice symptoms at a particular time of year or whenever your child visits a house with a cat or other furry pet. Irritants in the environment like car exhaust and cigarette smoke can also cause coughing. Minimizing the child's exposure to cigarette smoke is a good idea (and better for your health as well). If the symptoms are bothering your child, discuss with the doctor what might be triggering the cough and what you can do to treat it. Children with allergy symptoms who cough may also have asthma.

Asthma. Asthma is a common cause of cough, particularly chronic cough, in children. See Chapter 32, "Health Problems in Early Childhood," for more information on asthma.

Choking. Choking occurs when solid food or a piece of a toy or other object is sucked into the airway and interferes with breathing. This is particularly common in small children who have not yet learned to completely chew their food and who like to explore the environment by putting things in their mouths. Coughing caused by choking usually starts suddenly in a child who has been healthy and acting normally. See Chapter 28, "First Aid and Emergency Care," for information about first aid for a choking child. (See also Chapter 24, "Child Safety," for information about prevention of choking.)

Pneumonia. If your child has a cough and persistent fever for more than three days (or fever reappears after a day or two without fever), is having trouble breathing, is breathing rapidly, or develops a worsening cough several days into an illness, he may have pneumonia. For more information, see Chapter 30, "Childhood Infections."

Whooping cough (pertussis). Whooping cough is not common today because most children get the vaccine that protects them from the illness (*pertussis* is the *P* in the DTaP vaccine). For more information, see Chapter 30, "Childhood Infections."

What You Can Do at Home
In general:

- Encourage your child to drink plenty of clear fluids (things you can see through like water, broth, and apple juice), which will help to thin his mucus and keep him well hydrated.
- Give your child warm liquids to help soothe a sore, irritated throat and to help stop coughing bouts by relaxing the airway and loosening thick, sticky mucus.
- Use a cool-mist vaporizer to keep mucus thin and moisten the airway. (Hot- or warm-mist vaporizers are not recommended because the hot water can burn a child, and bacteria are more likely to grow in a warm environment.) Be sure to carefully clean your vaporizer daily to prevent mold and bacterial growth. Do **not** add any medications to the water in the vaporizer—this can actually cause more airway irritation and make a cough worse. Note: Allergies (and asthma) may be aggravated by extra moisture in the child's

environment (because moisture promotes the growth of molds and dust mites), so don't use a vaporizer in the case of allergy or asthma problems.
- Avoid the use of over-the-counter cough medications unless told to use them by the doctor. Coughing helps to clear the airway of excess mucus and germs. Note: Over-the-counter medications can cause troublesome side effects, particularly in infants younger than six months. Combination cold and cough medications often contain "extra" medications that can have additional side effects. Read labels carefully to avoid accidental overdosing of any of the components of the combination medicine. Cough medications may be useful at night for a dry cough that is keeping your child awake. Check with your child's doctor prior to giving your child any medication.

For croup:

- Humidified air is particularly important for children with croup because it helps to reduce irritation, swelling, and spasms of the vocal cords and upper airway. There are several methods you can use to create moist air if you do not have a vaporizer. The simplest way is to turn on your shower with hot water and close the bathroom door to allow the room to fill with mist. After a few minutes bring your child into the bathroom and sit with him in the warm fog (don't take your child into the shower itself).
- Try taking your child for a walk in the cool night air or having him breathe next to an open window to

help relieve croup symptoms. The cool air decreases swelling in the linings of the child's upper airways.

- Try to keep your child calm—crying and agitation often make croup symptoms worse. Encourage quiet activities that your child enjoys like reading or playing with a puzzle.

For asthma:

- Follow the treatment plan from your child's doctor. Cough medicines are not recommended for asthma. They can interfere or interact with asthma medications.
- Try to reduce the number of asthma "triggers" your child is exposed to. Keep pets out of your child's bedroom. Limit the number of stuffed animals in your child's room because they collect dust that can trigger an attack. Hardwood floors or tile are often better than carpet because this cuts down on trapped dust or fur. Avoid exposing your child to cigarette smoke and other irritants (such as incense, perfumes, and household sprays).
- Plan ahead. Make sure you have enough medicine in the house to treat an asthma attack in the middle of the night. Before going on vacation make sure you have enough medicine to last through the entire trip (and to replace an inhaler that accidentally is left on the beach).

Seizures/Convulsions

Warning/Emergency Signs

Seek emergency care if your child shows any of the following signs:

- Bluish color of the lips, tongue, nails, or skin
- Seizures in a child who has never had a seizure before
- Any seizure lasting longer than five minutes
- Seizure after a recent fall or head injury
- Indication that your child may have swallowed alcohol, medicine, a household product, or a poisonous or unknown substance

When to Call Your Child's Doctor
Call your child's doctor if your child shows any of the following signs:

- Your child with epilepsy is having seizures that are not typical for him or are more frequent than usual
- Note: Even if your child has epilepsy or is having a febrile seizure (see upcoming information) and has had one before, you should call the doctor. The doctor may not feel it is necessary to see your child, but it is good to check in and let the doctor know what is happening.

Despite the fact that they look scary, most seizures in children are not serious. The child may suddenly fall to the ground, become very stiff, or have rhythmic jerking movement of the arms and legs. A child's eyes may seem to roll back into his head, or he may pass urine or stool while having a seizure. The most important thing to remember if your child is having a seizure is to stay calm. (For details on what to do if your child has a seizure, see Chapter 28, "First Aid and Emergency Care.")

Seizures are caused by a kind of "short circuit" in the brain. The brain sends abnormal messages to the body that lead to the strange movements and behaviors you see with seizures. The child has no control over the seizure and is usually not aware of what is happening. Children are usually very tired after having a seizure and may not remember the seizure at all. Some children have a different type of seizure in which they stare blankly but have no unusual movements. Most children who have seizures recover completely after the seizure is over and do not have any resulting brain damage or learning problems. Here are some causes of seizures:

Febrile seizures. Febrile seizures are the most common type of seizures in children. They occur in children younger than six years. About 5 percent of children will have at least one febrile seizure. This type of seizure usually happens when a child's temperature rises quickly. The exact temperature is probably not as important as the speed at which it rises. Most children get fevers of up to 105 degrees Fahrenheit without ever having a seizure. The seizure usually causes stiffening and jerking movements of the arms and legs that last for a few seconds or minutes. Children who do have a febrile seizure recover with no long-term side effects. About one-half of children who have one febrile seizure will have another one at some point, but this usually does not mean the child has a serious problem or epilepsy.

Epilepsy. A small percentage (less than 1 percent) of children will have recurrent seizures that may not be associated with a fever. Epilepsy is a general term for recurrent seizures. There are many different types of epilepsy (for further explanation, see Chapter 32, "Health Problems in Early Childhood").

Infection. Seizures can sometimes be triggered by infections in and around the brain. An infection of the covering of the brain is

called meningitis. An infection of the brain itself is called encephalitis (to learn more about infections, see Chapter 30, "Childhood Infections"). Children with these types of infections often look quite sick and usually have a fever, severe headache, and stiff neck. Call your child's doctor immediately if your child has these symptoms. Younger infants with these infections usually don't have a stiff neck. The doctor may do a test called a spinal tap (where a small needle is inserted into the back to collect a small sample of the fluid surrounding the brain and spinal cord) to look for infection. A child with meningitis or encephalitis needs to be observed and treated in a hospital. Other infections that may also require treatment can trigger a febrile seizure even though the infection is not in the brain.

Head injury. Many toddlers will trip, fall, and bump their heads while learning to walk and explore the world. Most of these injuries involve minor bruises and bumps but do no serious harm. Occasionally, an injury to the head can be more severe and cause a seizure. A seizure that occurs immediately after an injury may be caused by the brain being "bounced around" in the skull. This may not necessarily indicate a serious problem, but the child should be seen immediately by a doctor for a complete exam. Rarely, seizures occur a few days after an accident. If this happens, seek emergency care. The seizure could be due to bleeding in or around the brain or other type of serious brain injury (see Chapter 28, "First Aid and Emergency Care," for information about head injuries).

Poisoning or ingestions. Poisoning can cause many problems in infants and children—seizures are among them. If your child is having a seizure and you think he has swallowed alcohol, a medication, a plant, a cleaning product, or other dangerous substance, seek emergency care. For more information, see Chapter 28, "First Aid and Emergency Care."

Brain tumor. A tumor is actually a very rare cause of seizures in young children. Brain tumors occur in fewer than 1 in 10,000 children. It's true that a brain tumor can cause seizures, but there are usually other signs first. A child with a brain tumor may become clumsier (toddlers haven't developed much coordination yet, so don't panic if your toddler occasionally tumbles or falls), have headaches, vomit without any other signs of illness, and have a number of other symptoms. If your child has any of these symptoms, call your child's doctor, who will do a thorough exam.

What You Can Do at Home
- Try to stay calm; panicking will not help your child.
- Stay with your child and have someone call for help. Most seizures stop after a few minutes without any treatment. Do **not** try to stop the seizure or restrain your child.
- The biggest risk of injury comes from falling on something hard or hitting something hard while having a seizure. Prevent this by doing the following:
  - Gently place your child on the floor or other flat surface (to prevent him from falling there from a couch or a bed).
  - Move hard or sharp objects like coffee tables out of the way so your child does not hit them.
  - Do **not** try to put anything in the child's mouth—your child will not "swallow his tongue."

- If your child has trouble breathing, gently extend his neck (pulling the chin away from the chest) and try to pull the jaw forward, which usually helps to open the child's airway. Do **not** try to put anything into the child's mouth. It will not help his breathing and may make the child more likely to choke or vomit.

If your child has epilepsy:

- Follow the plan given to you by your child's doctor for what to do when your child has a seizure.
- Make sure your child takes all of the medicines prescribed by the doctor to control seizures. Children can have seizures if the level of medicine in their blood gets too low. Some children who are growing rapidly may have low levels of medicine because they have outgrown the dose. (Always check with your child's doctor before changing the dose of medicine your child is taking.)
- Plan ahead for vacations and travel. Make sure you have enough medicine to last through the entire trip (and some extra in case you lose some). Keep track of when the medicine will run out so that you are not on your last dose on a Sunday night when no local pharmacy is open.

Skin Problems

Diaper Rash

When to Call Your Child's Doctor
Call your child's doctor if your child shows any of the following signs:

- A diaper rash that does not improve after three days despite frequent diaper changes and use of barrier ointments with zinc oxide (such as Desitin)
- Pimples, blisters, or open sores in the diaper area
- A rash that looks infected or has areas of crusted skin
- A whitish coating in the mouth along with a diaper rash

Few babies get through infancy without having diaper rash at some point. The good news is that most diaper rashes are not serious, and the red, irritated, and sore skin quickly heals. Here are two common types of diaper rash.

Irritant rash. Most diaper rashes are caused by prolonged contact with urine, feces, and sweat. The plastic that so effectively serves to prevent diapers from leaking also prevents air from circulating and creates a warm, moist environment where rashes tend to develop.

Candida rash. Sometimes diaper rashes are due to more than just simple irritation. Candida (a type of yeast) causes a solid red rash with small circular "satellite" red patches around it. The rash is usually moist and typically involves the skin surfaces on the front of the child. (The type of candida that causes diaper rash also causes the white patches called thrush in a baby's mouth. An infant with thrush is more likely to develop a candida diaper rash.) A candida rash often starts in the folds of the baby's skin and spreads to other nearby skin. Some of these rashes clear up on their own, but others need treatment with antifungal creams to kill the yeast.

What You Can Do at Home

- The key to preventing diaper rash is keeping the skin as dry and free of contact with irritants as possible. Change your child's diaper frequently to help prevent feces and urine from irritating the skin. This is particularly important if your child has diarrhea.
- If possible, increase the amount of time your child spends without a diaper. If this poses too much of a risk to your carpet or furniture, keep the waistband of your child's diaper loose to increase air circulation.
- With each diaper change, wash your child's diaper region with warm water alone. Soaps and baby wipes can be irritating to some children's skin.
- If your child is prone to rashes, use a barrier ointment with zinc oxide (such as Desitin) with each diaper change. Petroleum jelly (Vaseline) is also effective.
- Use a barrier ointment with each diaper change if your child has diarrhea. When a child has diarrhea, the stool is more acidic and is more likely to irritate the skin.

Jaundice (Yellow Skin)

Warning/Emergency Signs

Seek emergency care if your newborn with jaundice shows any of the following signs:

- Lethargy, poor feeding, or other indications of illness
- Fever (rectal temperature) over 100.4 degrees Fahrenheit

Seek emergency care if your child with jaundice shows any of the following signs:

- Confusion or extreme lethargy
- Unusual bruising or bleeding

When to Call Your Child's Doctor
Call your child's doctor if your newborn shows any of the following signs:

- Jaundice develops during the first 24 hours of life
- The yellow color of the skin deepens after infant has reached seven days of age
- Jaundice lasts longer than 10 days
- Jaundice involves the arms or legs
- Jaundice is accompanied by no wet diapers for more than six hours
- Jaundice appears in a child who is older than 10 days
- Bowel movements repeatedly look white or clay colored

Jaundice is caused by high levels of a pigment called bilirubin in the blood and can cause a newborn's eyes and skin to appear yellow. Bilirubin is cleared from the blood by the liver and leaves the body in bowel movements. (Bilirubin is partly responsible for the color of stool.) Many normal newborns develop jaundice when they are two to three days old. Jaundice can also be caused by an infection of the liver that prevents the liver from handling bilirubin properly. A blockage of the bile ducts (the drainage system in the liver) will also cause jaundice. Other people develop jaundice because of a genetic liver problem. Some medicines can cause jaundice as a side effect.

Some infants and toddlers who look yellow do not actually have jaundice. Eating lots of carrots or yellow vegetables can sometimes make the skin appear yellow. Jaundice in the first week of life is usually normal and should not concern you, but if the jaundice develops after leaving the hospital it is best to call your child's doctor. Here are some causes of jaundice (or yellow skin):

Newborn jaundice. For information about newborn jaundice, see Chapter 5, "Common Newborn Medical Conditions."

Carotenemia. Yellowish coloring of the skin caused by eating orange and yellow vegetables is called carotenemia. Carotene, the substance that makes vegetables yellow, can also make your child look yellow when the pigment accumulates in her skin. A child with carotenemia will have yellow skin, but the whites of the eyes will remain white. This is a harmless condition that goes away on its own and is not a reason to stop giving your child vegetables.

Medications. Some medicines can affect the liver. If your child's skin looks yellow after starting a new medicine or if your child has been taking a medicine and starts to look yellow, call your child's doctor.

Hepatitis. Hepatitis is usually caused by a viral infection of the liver. There are several viruses that cause hepatitis (see Chapter 30, "Childhood Infections," for more information). Infants now routinely receive a vaccine to protect them from hepatitis B. Hepatitis A is found in contaminated water (and in seafood or in things washed in contaminated water). In children, hepatitis A causes nausea, vomiting, diarrhea, and jaundice. A vaccine is available to protect against hepatitis A, but it is usually given only to children who are in certain high-risk groups, who live in high-risk areas, or who will be traveling to areas where contracting the virus is likely.

What You Can Do at Home

- Feed your baby frequently. Babies get rid of extra bilirubin through their bowel movements. If you are breast-feeding, your milk may not come in until the baby is a few days old. Breast-fed babies may become more jaundiced because of this. This should not mean you have to stop breast-feeding, but your child's doctor may recommend giving a supplemental formula with each feeding after the baby comes off the breast. This helps the baby clear the extra bilirubin. Always put the baby to the breast first to stimulate your milk production and have the baby get as much colostrum (the early breast milk) as possible. You will be able to stop giving supplements once your milk comes in.
- Keep your baby in a bright, sunny room. Sunlight helps to reduce jaundice. Keeping the crib or bassinet on the sunny half of the baby's room may help the jaundice to clear up faster. Make sure the baby does not become too warm sitting in the sun, though.

Rash (See Also Diaper Rash)

Warning/Emergency Signs

Seek emergency care if your child shows any of the following signs:

- A rash that looks like multiple bruises or tiny spots of blood beneath the skin with no injury that explains the bruising

- Difficulty waking or confusion or lethargy
- Trouble breathing
- Wheezing (a whistling or hissing noise when breathing out)
- A rash with a headache, stiff neck, and fever
- Difficulty swallowing or slurred speech
- Fever in an infant under three months old (100.4 degrees Fahrenheit rectally)

When to Call Your Child's Doctor

Call your child's doctor if your child shows any of the following signs:

- Poison ivy or other contact-type rash that covers a large part of the body, involves the eyes or genitals, looks infected, or is not responding to over-the-counter medication
- A rash or insect bite that shows increasing redness, swelling, or pain; is draining pus or yellow fluid; or looks infected
- A rash that occurs while taking a new medication
- A rash that looks like a bull's-eye target (red outer ring with a clear center)
- Fever, rash, joint pain, or headache that develops within three weeks of a tick bite
- Chicken pox with a fever that reappears after being gone for a day or two
- Ringworm (fungal infection of the skin) that does not respond to home treatment or involves the scalp
- Dry, irritated skin that worsens despite home treatment
- Itching or pain that interferes with sleeping

Rashes can be caused by irritation, infection, or allergic reactions. Some children have dry skin that gets irritated easily. Other children seem to have built-in radar for finding poison ivy or other irritating plants. Insect bites are also a common cause of itchy rashes. Many infections can also cause a rash. Viruses frequently cause red, blotchy rashes and mild fever. Lyme disease causes a characteristic bull's-eye rash, which looks like a round red ring with a clear center. Round, red patches with clear centers can also be caused by a fungal skin infection (ringworm). Allergic reactions to bee stings or to foods and medicines can cause mild rashes or more serious reactions, such as hives. Here are some causes of rashes in young children:

Contact dermatitis (poison ivy and poison oak). Contact dermatitis is a general term describing skin irritation that results from contact with something in the environment. In a child with skin hypersensitivity, a rash can develop after certain soaps or metals touch the skin. Plants like poison ivy and poison oak cause contact dermatitis. The rash from poison ivy is caused by the body's reaction to oils on the leaves of the plant. Once the oil is washed off, the rash can't be spread to others. A rash from poison ivy breaks out first in the area that had the most contact with the oil. The parts of the rash that appear to be spreading are actually areas of skin that had less oil on them and as a result have taken longer to appear. The rash itself often looks like small blisters on a red base in large patches or in thin streaks or lines. It's usually quite itchy. Call your child's doctor if the rash covers a large part of the body, involves the eyes or genitals, or looks infected or if your child is uncomfortable despite using over-the-counter medicines.

Eczema (atopic dermatitis). Children with eczema tend to have sensitive skin that reacts to changes in the environment such as exposure to cold, soaps, or certain foods. For more information, see Eczema/Atopic Dermatitis in Chapter 32, "Health Problems in Early Childhood."

Viral rashes. The most common type of viral rash is a flat, pink or red, blotchy rash usually on the chest and abdomen. In addition to the rash, some viral infections may cause mild cold symptoms and a fever. (Some viruses like chicken pox cause blisters instead of flat pink or red patches.) Most of these rashes are not itchy (except chicken pox) and do not cause any problems. Some viral infections that are known for the rash they produce are roseola and fifth disease (see Chapter 30, "Childhood Infections," for more information). Once-common causes of viral rashes such as measles and rubella (German measles) are rarely seen in the United States and other developed countries today because of the success of immunization programs. Some children who have received an MMR vaccine will develop red spots with or without a fever one to two weeks after receiving the vaccine. No treatment is needed for this rash. Viral rashes do not usually require any treatment, but if you are concerned, call the doctor.

Allergic reactions and hives. Similar in appearance to mosquito bites, hives are itchy pink or red raised bumps with pale to white centers. Hives are usually caused by an allergic reaction to food, medicine, insect bites, or some other substance in contact with the skin. Sometimes viral infections or other diseases cause hives. Hives can be limited to one area of the body or break out all over. Allergic reactions to foods usually occur quickly, but they can occur as long as several hours after eating the food. Rarely, hives are associated with swelling in the mouth and throat. In these cases, the child may have difficulty breathing and may wheeze (make a whistling or hissing noise when breathing out), vomit, cough, or become confused or disoriented. These symptoms indicate a medical emergency—seek emergency care (see Chapter 28, "First Aid and Emergency Care," for information about severe allergic reactions and anaphylaxis).

Drug reactions. Reactions to medicines can cause various types of rashes. Antibiotics (such as amoxicillin) are the most frequent cause of such rashes in children. The rashes can look like flat pink or red blotches or can be more serious and resemble hives. If your child develops a rash while taking a medicine, call your child's doctor.

Warts. For information, see Chapter 30, "Childhood Infections."

Impetigo. For information, see Chapter 30, "Childhood Infections."

Ringworm (tinea). For information, see Chapter 30, "Childhood Infections."

Lyme disease. For information, see Chapter 30, "Childhood Infections."

What You Can Do at Home
For itchy rashes:

- Keep your child in an environment with a normal room temperature. Heat makes some rashes worse and aggravates the itch.
- Dress your child in loose cotton clothing.

- Give oatmeal baths with slightly cool water; these can be soothing, particularly for chicken pox.
- Apply hydrocortisone 1 percent cream or ointment to help a child with an itchy rash feel better, but do not use it for chicken pox, ringworm, or impetigo.
- Place a cool moistened washcloth on the rash to help reduce itching.
- Ask your child's doctor about giving diphenhydramine (Benadryl) by mouth for severe itching. Most children feel sleepy when they take diphenhydramine, so using it at bedtime helps with both itching and sleeplessness.
- Ask your child's doctor about hydroxyzine (a prescription medication) if diphenhydramine does not work. Hydroxyzine may work better. Your child may also benefit from a prescription steroid cream or ointment.
- Encourage your child to resist scratching a rash. Areas of skin that are scratched open are more likely to get infected. (Keep your child's fingernails trimmed and clean to minimize the damage they can cause.)

To help prevent poison ivy:

- Teach your child what poisonous plants look like so he knows which plants to avoid touching.
- Dress your child in long pants and long sleeves when contact with these plants is likely.
- Have your child wash thoroughly with soap and water after coming in contact with the plant. The less time the oil from the plant is on the skin, the less severe the rash will be. Wash

all clothes, blankets, shoes, and pets that may have come in contact with the plant's oil. The rash itself is not contagious, but touching any remaining oil will spread the poison ivy.

For dry skin or eczema:

- Use mild soaps with no added perfumes, such as unscented Dove. Avoid regular Ivory and deodorant soaps that can lead to dry skin.
- Avoid giving your child long, hot, or frequent baths. These can lead to dry skin.
- Give your child short, lukewarm baths with three to four capfuls of mineral oil or baby oil added to the water; these can help restore some moisture to the skin.
- Pat (don't rub) your child dry after a shower or bath.
- Apply moisturizer generously to your child's skin immediately after the bath.
- Avoid products with lots of perfumes. These can cause allergic reactions in a child with dry, sensitive skin.

For allergic reactions:

- Make sure your child's caregivers and teachers are aware of your child's allergies. This is especially important if your child has a food allergy because children tend to share snacks and lunches at school and child-care centers.
- Usually mild allergic reactions can be treated with diphenhydramine (Benadryl).
- If your child has a severe allergy and your child's doctor has prescribed an EpiPen (a device for injecting

adrenaline to prevent a severe allergic reaction), make sure you have it with you at all times.

For warts:

- Warts usually respond well, but slowly, to over-the-counter products such as Compound W or special bandages with alpha-hydroxy acid on the pad. You should not expect the warts to disappear with only a week or two of treatment. If the surrounding skin becomes irritated, stop the treatment for a few days and try using petroleum jelly (Vaseline) to protect the skin surrounding the warts when you apply the medication.

For ringworm (tinea):

- Use an over-the-counter antifungal cream such as Lotrimin twice a day. Tinea (except in the scalp) generally responds well to this type of cream. It may take several weeks for ringworm to disappear. Continue to use the antifungal cream twice a day for a week after the ringworm has disappeared to ensure that the infection is gone.
- Treat scalp infections with a medicine taken by mouth and a shampoo that are prescribed by the doctor.

Sore Throat

(Note: Refer first to the section on Cough if the throat pain occurs only with coughing or if coughing is severe. Also, see Strep Throat/Sore Throat in Chapter 30, "Childhood Infections.")

Seek emergency care if your child shows any of the following signs:

- Leaning forward, drooling, and difficulty breathing
- Inability to drink or swallow own saliva

When to Call Your Child's Doctor

Call your child's doctor if your child shows any of the following signs:

- A sore throat that lasts more than a day, to see if your child should have a strep throat test
- Trouble drinking to the point that you are concerned about dehydration (see box on dehydration on page 579 in this chapter)
- So much throat pain that he's unable to fully open his mouth
- A muffled voice—as though your child's mouth were full of food

Sore throats are common in young children. Infants and toddlers who are too young to describe their throat pain tend to be more fussy than usual and do not want to eat even their favorite foods. A young child may drool more than usual because of pain with swallowing.

Sore throats have many different causes. Dry air in the home or nighttime mouth breathing due to blocked nasal passages can cause a scratchy throat in the morning that improves through the day. Colds and other viral infections may cause sore throats. A runny nose can also lead to throat irritation because of postnasal drip. The primary aim of treating a sore throat in a young child is to make the child comfortable and prevent dehydration, but some causes of sore throat need to be treated with antibiotics. These are the most common or important causes of sore throats:

Viral pharyngitis. Pharyngitis means "inflammation (irritation) of the throat." Some cases of pharyngitis are caused by bacteria, but the majority are caused by viruses. These sore throats are often accompanied by fever, a stuffy or runny nose, and cold symptoms. The pain tends to improve on its own in three to four days. Antibiotics do not work against viruses, so the goal of treatment is to keep your child comfortable.

Strep throat. For information, see Chapter 30, "Childhood Infections."

Hand, foot, and mouth disease (Coxsackie virus infection). For information, see Mouth Pain/Problems in this chapter.

Runny nose and sinusitis. The mere presence of a runny nose can cause a sore throat. Mucus from the nose running down the back of the throat (called postnasal drip) can be irritating. Treatment for a runny nose depends upon the cause. Most of the time, a minor viral infection is the culprit, and the sore throat will resolve in a few days. Sometimes the cause is a bacterial infection in the sinuses called sinusitis. A child with sinusitis usually has a persistent runny nose for at least two weeks, often with thick green or yellow nasal drainage. The child may also have low-grade fever. Mucus from the infected sinuses drips down the throat and causes irritation. Sinusitis can be treated with antibiotics. Sometimes a runny nose is due to an allergy to pollen, dust mites, pet dander, or molds (see Chapter 32, "Health Problems in Early Childhood," for more information about allergies). Children with allergies tend to have clear mucus from the nose, watery eyes, and itchy throats. If you think your child has allergies or sinusitis and is bothered by a runny nose or sore throat, call your child's doctor.

Croup. Croup is usually caused by a viral infection that affects the throat and area around the vocal cords and windpipe. Children with croup have pain with swallowing and may complain of a sore throat. (See information on croup in the Cough section under Respiratory and Breathing Problems in this chapter and Chapter 30, "Childhood Infections.")

Dry throat. Some children repeatedly wake up in the morning with a sore throat that gets better after they take a few sips of something to drink. The morning throat pain is usually caused by dryness of the throat due to breathing through the mouth during the night. (This is because air going through the mouth does not pick up extra moisture the way it does when traveling through the nose.) All children occasionally breathe through their mouths, especially when they have a stuffy nose. Dry throats in the morning can also be a problem in the winter when the air in the house tends to be drier. Setting the thermostat a bit lower at night and using a humidifier may help to some degree. If your child constantly breathes through his mouth, it could be due to enlarged adenoids (lymph glands located behind the nose), sinusitis, or allergies. If you are concerned about your child's mouth breathing, consult your child's doctor.

Epiglottitis. For more information, see Chapter 30, "Childhood Infections."

What You Can Do at Home
- Offer cool drinks and foods (like ice pops) that may help to soothe the mouth and throat.

- Offer soft foods that are easy to swallow and do not irritate the throat.
- Avoid spicy, salty, or acidic foods (like citrus fruits). These types of foods are especially painful when they come in contact with mouth sores or ulcers.
- Use acetaminophen (Tylenol) or ibuprofen (Motrin/Advil) to relieve the pain.

Stomach and Intestinal Problems
Abdominal Pain

Warning/Emergency Signs

Seek emergency care if your child shows any of the following signs:

- Continuous pain for more than one to two hours
- Inability to walk or difficulty walking because of the pain
- Abdomen that feels very hard or firm (and your child will not let you touch it without significant protest)
- Bloody or jellylike bowel movements
- Vomiting blood or material that is greenish-yellow (bile) or looks like coffee grounds
- Extreme lethargy or drowsiness
- Recent surgery or injury to the abdomen, or recent serious fall
- Swelling and redness in the groin or scrotum (the sack containing the testicles)
- Indication that your child may have swallowed some object, medication, household product, or unknown substance

- Repeated, sudden drawing of legs up to abdomen
- Irritability that gets worse when child is held or rocked
- Any signs of dehydration (See box on page 579.)

When to Call Your Child's Doctor

Call your child's doctor if your child shows any of the following signs:

- Refusal to eat or drink
- Vomiting that continues for more than two hours (if your infant is younger than six months old)
- Vomiting that continues for more than 12 hours (if your child is six months or older)
- Lethargy or irritability
- Crying in a way that is not usual for a colicky infant
- Abdominal pain that occurs frequently over several weeks
- Failure to gain weight or loss of weight over several weeks

Most causes of abdominal pain are not serious and symptoms will go away without treatment. Unfortunately, finding the exact cause of the pain is not always easy because the abdomen is a fairly complex part of the body involving many different organs. A stomachache can have a relatively obvious cause like overindulging in Halloween candy or a cause that seems unrelated to the abdomen, like emotional stress or a strep infection of the throat. A complaint of pain in one specific part of the abdomen is generally more cause for concern than the complaint of a vague bellyache. Here are some causes of abdominal pain:

Gastroenteritis. Commonly referred to as a "stomach bug," gastroenteritis can cause stomach pain, emotional discomfort, and a large mess in the bathroom (not to mention the rest of the house). Children often have nausea, vomiting, and diarrhea, although some symptoms can exist without the others (see Vomiting and Diarrhea sections in this chapter). These symptoms are caused by a variety of different infections (see Chapter 30, "Childhood Infections"). Often a child complains of a stomachache or not feeling well just prior to the onset of vomiting or diarrhea. The pain is usually crampy and diffuse (not located in one particular part of the abdomen). Pain usually gets better after the child vomits or has a bowel movement, but the relief is only temporary. Pain will often return in 30 minutes to a few hours, usually before a new round of vomiting or diarrhea. Vomiting usually lasts no longer than a day, but diarrhea may continue for two to three days or longer. It's important to make sure that your child does not get dehydrated during this type of illness. Young infants are more prone to dehydration and other complications with gastroenteritis.

Constipation. When a child is constipated, having a bowel movement may be difficult and painful. In addition, when the intestine contracts around a piece of stool that is difficult to move, it can cause pain or discomfort. Some children don't recognize this feeling as the need to have a bowel movement, or they resist having a bowel movement due to previous experiences with pain when passing stool. Fortunately, most constipation is not serious and will respond to changes in diet and routine (for more information on constipation, see Chapter 20, "Toilet Teaching").

Colic. Colic tends to start when an infant is about two weeks old and continues for about three to four months. For more information on colic, see Crying and Colic in Chapter 11, "Baby-Care Basics."

Food or formula intolerance. Everyone has eaten some food that didn't "agree" with them. Children can also have this problem. A child with food intolerance may develop stomach pain, gas, diarrhea, or a rash after eating certain foods. Babies can have an allergy to milk or soy protein and get cranky after feedings. Some children have reduced amounts of an enzyme (a type of chemical in the body) needed to digest lactose (the sugar found in cow's milk), so they may get gas, cramping, bloating, and diarrhea after eating foods containing lactose. Children with lactose intolerance may benefit from special milk or Lactaid tablets. (These tablets contain the enzyme the body is missing and help the child to digest lactose.) A few infants who appear to have colic actually have a formula intolerance or allergy, so if your baby is very fussy your doctor may suggest switching formulas. (Check with your child's doctor before changing formulas on your own.) If you are breast-feeding, your baby may react to things you have eaten. Caffeine and certain medicines get into the breast milk and can make a baby irritable, so check with the doctor if you are taking any medicine and plan to breast-feed. Speak with the doctor if you think your child has symptoms of food or formula intolerance or allergy.

Stress or emotional upset. Children react to stress in different ways. Some children are easygoing and nothing seems to bother them. Other children seem more sensitive and become easily upset over changes in their routine or stresses in their household. Children who tend to get stomachaches from stress are often serious, sensitive, and conscientious children. The pain in this kind of stomachache is usually vague and is not located in any particular part of the abdomen. These children do not have fever, vomiting, diarrhea, or other symptoms associated with their pain. This type of pain often occurs during traumatic events such as when a family is moving or a child is going to a new school. If you suspect this is the cause of your child's pain, sit down with your child in a quiet place where you can talk. Spend time talking to and listening to your child. Try to find out what is bothering your child and reassure him. Talk with your child's doctor if you have concerns or want suggestions to help your child cope with stressful situations.

Strep throat. Strep throat is caused by an infection with a type of streptococcus bacteria. The infection often causes abdominal pain and headache. For more information, see Chapter 30, "Childhood Infections."

Urinary tract infection. Most urinary tract infections are bacterial infections of the bladder (the hollow organ where urine is stored). For more information, see Chapter 30, "Childhood Infections," and Chapter 32, "Health Problems in Early Childhood."

Pneumonia. Pneumonia is an infection of the lungs (more information on infections can be found in Chapter 30, "Childhood Infections"). Children with pneumonia usually have a cough, fever, and trouble breathing. Some children with pneumonia will also complain of belly pain, usually in the upper part of the abdomen.

Appendicitis. Appendicitis is not a very common cause of abdominal pain, but it is one parents tend to worry about a great deal, and when it does occur it requires urgent medical attention. The early stages of appendicitis often resemble gastroenteritis. At first, the pain tends to be located around the belly button. As the illness progresses, pain usually moves to the right lower part of the abdomen and changes from intermittent to constant. The child may have nausea and vomiting and may not want to eat. He may or may not have a fever. A child with appendicitis often looks quite sick and has little interest in playing (or doing anything else). The child will stay fairly still because movement makes the pain much worse (and he will get very upset if you try to touch or push on his abdomen). It may be difficult to tell if infants or toddlers have appendicitis because children this young are not yet able to say exactly where it hurts. If you suspect your child may have appendicitis, do not give him anything to eat or drink until you speak with the doctor. For more information, see the information on appendicitis under Surgical Conditions/Procedures in Chapter 32, "Health Problems in Early Childhood."

Intussusception. Intussusception is a relatively uncommon cause of abdominal pain. It usually occurs in infants 6 to 24 months old. The problem in intussusception is that one part of the intestine slides into the part of the intestine right next to it (the way parts of a telescope slide into each other). This causes pain because it temporarily pinches off the blood supply to the intestine. The pain with intussusception is often colicky in nature (comes and goes). The infant cries and screams, pulls his legs up toward his chest, and then relaxes again. The child may seem fine between bouts of pain and act as if nothing is wrong. If these cycles of pain continue for a long time (several hours to a day), the child may pass bloody stools with clots that resemble jelly.

If your infant or toddler has these symptoms, call your child's doctor immediately or seek emergency care.

Testicular torsion and incarcerated hernia. Testicular torsion occurs when a testicle twists and cuts off its blood supply. This causes severe pain, swelling, and redness on one side of the scrotum (the sack that holds the testicles). Torsion may happen after trauma or there may be no obvious cause. Symptoms similar to those in testicular torsion occur when a child has an incarcerated hernia. A hernia occurs when a part of the intestine slips through a small opening or weak point in the groin or abdominal wall. Hernias can occur in many different parts of the body, but they are most common in the groin (inguinal hernia). A hernia may cause a bulge on one side of the scrotum. Normally, the intestine can move freely back and forth through the hole and does not cause any pain. If the intestine gets stuck (an incarcerated hernia), it can be very painful. An incarcerated hernia or testicular torsion requires emergency care.

Intestinal/bowel obstruction. A bowel obstruction is an unusual but serious cause of abdominal pain that occurs when there is a blockage in one part of the intestine. For more information, see Intestinal (Bowel) Obstruction under Vomiting in this chapter.

What You Can Do at Home

- Keep in mind that most abdominal pain is not serious and will often go away on its own.
- Encourage your toilet-trained child to try to have a bowel movement. This will help determine if the pain is due to mild constipation.

- Have your child lie down in bed or on the sofa and relax.
- Offer your child clear fluids to sip slowly.
- Avoid giving enemas, stool softeners, laxatives, or other medications without first consulting the doctor.
- Keep in mind that antidiarrheal medicines are not recommended for children. They may decrease the number of bowel movements, but this may allow the infecting agent (virus, bacteria, or parasite) to remain in the intestine for a longer time and may lead to serious complications.
- Remember that ibuprofen (Advil/Motrin) can irritate the stomach and make pain worse.
- If your child is vomiting, see page 581.
- If your child has diarrhea, see upcoming information.
- If your child is constipated, see page 575.

Diarrhea

Warning/Emergency Signs

Seek emergency care if your child shows any of the following signs:

- Signs of dehydration (See box on page 579.)
- Vomiting with diarrhea and inability to keep down clear liquids after three attempts (See Vomiting in this chapter for more on giving fluids to a vomiting child.)
- Extreme lethargy or drowsiness
- Severe abdominal pain that is constant for more than one to two hours or cramps that last for several hours and are not at least temporarily better after having a bowel movement

When to Call Your Child's Doctor

Call your child's doctor if your child shows any of the following signs:

- Blood or mucus in the stool
- Fever for more than two to three days
- More than five watery stools in one day (in an infant younger than six months)
- Ten or more watery stools in 24 hours (in a child older than six months)
- Diarrhea that does not seem to be improving after one to two days of dietary changes
- Diarrhea that begins after the child starts a new medicine
- Stools not back to normal after five to six days
- Stools that are chronically bulky, foul-smelling, or greasy looking
- Failure to gain weight normally or loss of weight over several weeks

Normal bowel patterns vary in infants and children, so diarrhea must be defined with these normal variations in mind. Early on, breast-fed infants may have a stool after every feeding, though later they tend to go less frequently. In breast-fed infants stools are typically small and loose. This pattern of bowel movements is normal and should not be cause for concern. Formula-fed infants typically have one to three pasty or seedy stools per day. If your infant or child is having more frequent or watery bowel movements than is usual for her, then she probably has diarrhea.

Diarrhea has a wide variety of causes including consumption of too much juice,

Signs of Dehydration

- Dry and sticky inside of the mouth
- Few or no tears when crying
- Eyes that look sunken into the head
- Soft spot (fontanel) on top of baby's head looks sunken
- Lack of urine or wet diapers for six to eight hours in an infant (or only a very small amount of dark yellow urine)
- Lack of urine for 12 hours in an older child (or only a very small amount of dark yellow urine)
- Dry or cool skin
- Lethargy or irritability

viral infections, and food poisoning. Diarrhea itself is not usually harmful, but dehydration due to loss of water and minerals in the stool can be dangerous. In general, the younger and smaller the child, the more likely she is to become dehydrated. (For tips on keeping your child hydrated during a bout of diarrhea see "What You Can Do at Home," page 580.) Here are some causes of diarrhea:

Gastroenteritis. Commonly referred to as a "stomach bug," gastroenteritis is one of the most common causes of diarrhea. Children with gastroenteritis often have nausea, vomiting, and diarrhea, although some symptoms can exist without the others. For more information, see Gastroenteritis under Abdominal Pain in this chapter.

Toddler's diarrhea. Toddler's diarrhea gets its name for an obvious reason—it affects toddlers. It tends to start when a child is about 12 months old and may last until the child is three or four years old. These children often have a normal stool in the morn-

ing and then have three to six loose bowel movements throughout the day. The children don't seem ill otherwise and don't have any belly pain or growth problems. Toddler's diarrhea usually goes away on its own. It can be made worse (or may sometimes be caused by) drinking juice. Juices contain a lot of sugar. The extra sugar attracts water into the intestine and makes stools loose. Try to limit juice to four ounces a day (or two diluted four-ounce servings of half juice, half water). Contrary to popular belief (and TV advertising), children do not need juice to grow up healthy, happy, and well adjusted. If your child is thirsty, she can drink water. Severely fat-restricted diets may also contribute to toddler's diarrhea.

Medicines. Diarrhea is a side effect of some medicines. Antibiotics (such as amoxicillin) often cause mild diarrhea, and other medicines can also have this side effect.

Malabsorption. In children with malabsorption, the intestine is not able to properly digest and absorb fat. As a result, there is extra fat in the stool. Stool that contains extra fat tends to be large, bulky, greasy, and foul smelling. (The new artificial fat Olestra is designed so that the body can't absorb it—this is how it can cause diarrhea. Diarrhea from malabsorption and from too much Olestra often look very similar.) Malabsorption is uncommon and can indicate the presence of a medical problem such as cystic fibrosis (see Chapter 32, "Health Problems in Early Childhood," for more information on this condition). Notify your child's doctor if your child's stool fits this description.

Lactose intolerance. Some children lack the enzyme needed to digest lactose (the sugar found naturally in milk), and gas, cramping, bloating, and diarrhea can result. For more information, see Food or Formula Intolerance under Abdominal Pain in this chapter.

Celiac disease. Celiac disease is a relatively uncommon cause of chronic diarrhea or recurrent diarrhea. For more information, see Chapter 32, "Health Problems in Early Childhood."

Inflammatory bowel disease. Inflammatory bowel disease (IBD) is a general term that includes both Crohn's disease and ulcerative colitis. These are uncommon causes of diarrhea in young children. Children with IBD may have abdominal pain, diarrhea, and poor growth. Their bowel movements may have blood or mucus in them. Problems with growth may appear months before any other symptoms appear. Call your child's doctor if you are worried about poor weight gain or if your child has diarrhea for longer than a week.

What You Can Do at Home

- If your child is vomiting, treat the vomiting as recommended in the section on Vomiting in this chapter.
- To prevent others in your household from getting diarrhea, make sure everyone washes their hands frequently, especially before eating.
- Remember that your goal in treating diarrhea should be to prevent your child from becoming dehydrated.
- If you are breast-feeding, continue to feed your child as you normally would and offer an electrolyte solution like Pedialyte between feedings to make sure your infant is getting enough fluid.
- If you are bottle-feeding, offer smaller amounts (one to three ounces) of formula in addition to an electrolyte solution like Pedialyte to drink. For older infants and children you can try electrolyte ice pops. These solutions are good because they provide enough sugar, salt, and water to replace what your child is losing. If your child will not drink an electrolyte solution, try a few ounces of a sports drink (like Gatorade).
- As the diarrhea improves, resume formula feedings in a bottle-fed infant. For infants and children taking solid foods, initially offer rice, crackers, toast, pasta, potatoes, yogurt, and chicken. Foods like these are easy for the body to digest, and feeding them to a child early in the illness has been shown to shorten the duration of diarrhea in most children. Avoid fried or fatty foods.
- Do **not** give only an electrolyte solution or clear liquids for more

than 24 hours. Your child will start to need more calories than these solutions can provide. If you feel your child is not getting better, call your child's doctor.

- Do **not** give your child boiled skim milk or other concentrated solutions. This can give the child too much salt, which can be dangerous.
- Do **not** give plain water to a child with diarrhea. It doesn't contain the minerals and calories the child needs to replace losses due to diarrhea, and giving plain water to an infant can cause a dangerous salt imbalance in the baby's blood.
- Do **not** use a medicine to stop the diarrhea. Antidiarrheal medicines may slow down the number of bowel movements, but they allow the infecting germ (virus, bacteria, or parasite) to remain in the intestine for a longer time and may lead to serious complications.

let you touch it at all), or the abdomen feels hard or firm
- Dizziness when standing up
- Unusual lethargy
- Extreme irritability or increased irritability when being held or rocked
- Disorientation or confusion
- Stiff neck
- Recovering from a recent head injury
- Indication that child may have swallowed some object, medication, household product, or unknown substance
- Inability to walk or difficulty walking because of pain
- Bloody or jellylike bowel movements
- Recovering from a recent surgery or injury to the abdomen, or a recent serious fall
- Swelling, redness, or pain in the groin or scrotum (the sack containing the testicles)
- Vomiting in association with hives or trouble breathing

Vomiting

Warning/Emergency Signs

Seek emergency care if your child shows any of the following signs:

- Signs of dehydration (See box on page 579.)
- Vomiting blood or material that looks like coffee grounds
- Vomiting greenish-yellow material
- Severe abdominal pain continuously for more than one to two hours
- Complaints of severe pain if you touch the abdomen (or child won't

When to Call Your Child's Doctor

Call your child's doctor if your child shows any of the following signs:

- Vomiting of clear fluids for more than three hours despite intake of only small volumes
- Any forceful vomiting (not just spitting up) in an infant younger than one week
- Vomiting that continues for more than two hours in an older infant
- Vomiting that continues for more than 12 hours in a toddler or older child

- Diarrhea for more than six hours along with vomiting
- Pain with urination, more frequent urination, or blood in urine

Spitting up and "wet burps" are common in babies and are usually no cause for concern. Episodes of more forceful vomiting also occur in infants and young children, most often because of infectious (usually viral) gastroenteritis. The vomiting that accompanies these "stomach bugs" usually doesn't last longer than a day. In a few cases, the vomiting (and the diarrhea that may accompany it) may cause a child to become dehydrated. Young infants are at greatest risk for this complication. In some cases, vomiting can be a symptom of a serious medical condition such as meningitis or an intestinal blockage. Here are some causes of vomiting:

Spitting up. Spitting up is extremely common in infants. Almost all infants have wet burps from time to time. Other children spit up more frequently because of a condition called gastroesophageal reflux disease (see Chapter 32, "Health Problems in Early Childhood," for more information about GERD). If the spitting up is effortless and your child is growing well and happy, it's more of a laundry problem than a medical one. There's little reason for concern. Most babies outgrow spitting up by six to nine months of age. If your child is not gaining weight normally or the spitting up is accompanied by a lot of coughing, gagging, crying, or fussiness, call your child's doctor.

Gastroenteritis. Usually caused by a viral infection, gastroenteritis symptoms can include vomiting, diarrhea, and stomach pain. For more information, refer to Gas-

troenteritis under Abdominal Pain in this chapter.

Food poisoning. Food poisoning causes symptoms similar to infectious gastroenteritis with vomiting and diarrhea. The foods that are most often to blame are cream sauces, pastries, and unrefrigerated meats. Beware of foods sitting around at picnics because these can spoil quickly on a hot day. Vomiting from food poisoning is treated the same way as vomiting from infectious gastroenteritis. Call your child's doctor if you are concerned your child is becoming dehydrated (for signs, see box on page 579).

Intussusception. Intussusception is a relatively unusual cause of abdominal pain and vomiting. See Intussusception under Abdominal Pain in this chapter.

Poisoning or ingestions. Toddlers and young children are naturally curious. They like to explore and taste every aspect of the world, from a fuzzball on the carpet to an interesting pebble outside. Swallowing certain medications, plants, or cleaning products can cause an upset stomach and vomiting as well as other symptoms related to poisoning. If you suspect your child has eaten something hazardous, call your child's doctor or the poison control center immediately (see Chapter 28, "First Aid and Emergency Care," for more information).

Stress or anxiety. Upset stomach associated with anxiety or stress is not unique to adults. Some children may vomit or experience abdominal pain under these circumstances. Call your child's doctor if you have concerns or need advice on managing the problem.

Head injury. One or two episodes of vomiting immediately after receiving a hard bump on the head is fairly common. Persistent vomiting or vomiting that starts several hours or days after the injury can be a sign of a more serious problem (see Chapter 28, "First Aid and Emergency Care," for more information about head injuries). If this happens to your child, seek emergency care immediately.

Urinary tract infection. A urinary tract infection is an infection in the bladder and/or kidneys and can sometimes be associated with vomiting. For more information, see Urinary Tract Infection in Chapter 30, "Childhood Infections," and Chapter 32, "Health Problems in Early Childhood."

Appendicitis. Appendicitis is not a common cause of vomiting, but it is one that needs prompt medical attention. For more information, see Appendicitis under Abdominal Pain in this chapter.

Pyloric stenosis. The pylorus is a muscle-walled channel located at the "exit" of the stomach that helps control the rate at which food moves from the stomach into the intestine. Sometimes in infants, the pylorus is too tight and does not let food out of the stomach. This problem usually occurs in babies ages two weeks to two months old. Formula or breast milk gets trapped in the stomach (because it can't leave through the tight pylorus), and the baby starts to vomit. The vomiting occurs after every feeding and becomes forceful. (This is the type of vomiting that can shoot across the room.) Immediately after vomiting, the baby seems hungry again. When feeding attempts are made, the vomiting recurs. This problem can be corrected with surgery that involves

making a cut in the muscle in the wall of the pylorus. Most babies can eat again within a few hours of the procedure. If your baby has forceful vomiting, call your child's doctor.

Meningitis. Meningitis is an infection of the covering of the brain. Irritation around the brain can cause headache and vomiting. More information on meningitis can be found under Fever in a Baby Younger than Three Months of Age in this chapter and in Chapter 30, "Childhood Infections."

Intestinal (bowel) obstruction. Bowel obstruction is an unusual, but serious, cause of vomiting. It occurs when a part of the intestine is blocked. There are many possible causes for blockage, but regardless of the cause, the symptoms are similar. A child with bowel obstruction will have severe abdominal pain and often will vomit greenish-yellow material. The child's abdomen may look swollen or distended (bloated and firm) and be painful if touched. Seek emergency care if your child has these symptoms.

Other causes. Certain medications, such as erythromycin, may irritate a child's stomach and cause vomiting. Vomiting may also occur in children with migraines or can be triggered by bouts of coughing associated with conditions such as asthma or sinusitis with postnasal mucous drip. As with adults, children may experience nausea and vomiting with motion sickness. Speak with your child's doctor about the management of vomiting from these causes.

What You Can Do at Home

- Offer your child frequent small volumes of clear fluids. Initially offer one-half ounce of clear fluids every five to ten minutes. Small amounts are more likely to stay down than large drinks. These are some fluids to give your child:

- Electrolyte solutions (like Pedialyte)—the best choice for infants
- Clear soups or broth
- Sports drinks (like Gatorade)
- Ice pops

- If your child vomits after drinking small volumes of fluid, give his stomach a 20- to 30-minute rest before trying to give more to drink.
- If your child doesn't vomit for three to four hours, gradually increase the volume of fluid offered to your child.
- Your child may be thirsty. Resist the urge to let him gulp large volumes of liquids. Large volumes are more likely to be vomited.
- If your child doesn't vomit for eight hours, gradually reintroduce food (and formula in bottle-fed infants). Start with bland, easy-to-digest foods, such as rice, crackers, pasta, potatoes, and yogurt. This is also a good initial diet for diarrhea, which often accompanies vomiting with infectious gastroenteritis.
- If you're breast-feeding, follow the same rule of small, frequent feedings. Limit feedings to five minutes on one breast. If the milk stays down, allow five minutes on the other breast. Gradually increase the time of feedings as your baby improves.
- Do **not** continue an infant or child on a clear-liquid-only diet for more than 24 hours.
- Do **not** give plain water to treat a child's vomiting. (It has none of the

minerals the child needs to have replaced.)
- Do **not** add salt to the fluids you give to your vomiting child.

Urinary or Genital Pain/Problems

Warning/Emergency Signs

Seek emergency care if your child shows any of the following signs:

- Bloody or red urine after a fall or other injury
- Inability to urinate or ability to urinate only in small dribbles
- No wet diapers for six to eight hours in a crying/irritable baby

When to Call Your Child's Doctor

Call your child's doctor if your child shows any of the following signs:

- Complaining of burning or stinging with two or more trips to the bathroom in the same day
- Crying during urination in a child who is too young to tell you where it hurts
- Very frequent urination
- Frequent wetting accidents after having learned to use the toilet
- Fever without other signs of illness to explain the fever (such as a runny nose or cough)
- Passing cloudy, foul-smelling urine
- Vaginal discharge that's foul smelling or associated with pain or itching
- Lack of a strong urinary stream in a newborn boy

As a general rule, one complaint of pain with urination from your child may not indicate a medical problem, but if your child continues to complain, call your child's doctor. Here are some urinary problems and their causes.

Urethral irritation. Irritation around the opening of the urethra (the tube through which urine leaves the body) is a common cause of urinary complaints, particularly in girls. The tissue around this opening is extremely sensitive. Soap, shampoo, and bubble bath can get inside the opening of the urethra and cause burning or discomfort during urination. Wet underwear or a wet bathing suit can rub against the area and cause pain that persists even after the wet clothes have been removed. A child can irritate the area by improperly wiping from back to front after going to the bathroom. (Children usually understand how to use the potty before they understand how to wipe properly.) Small pieces of toilet paper can get stuck when girls wipe, and if they are not removed they can cause irritation and pain. Sitting in a bath with warm water for five to ten minutes (without soap) three times a day for several days will usually clear up a simple irritation.

Urinary tract infections. Urinary tract infections result from bacteria getting into the bladder or kidneys. They are more common in girls than in boys. In part, this is because the urethra (the tube that carries urine from the bladder) is shorter in girls, and bacteria tends to enter the bladder by traveling backward through the urethra. A child with a urinary tract infection may complain of pain or burning while urinating and may make frequent trips to the bathroom but produce only a few drops of urine on each trip. A child who knows how to use the toilet may begin to have frequent wetting accidents and may also complain of abdominal pain. A child with a kidney infection may have back pain, fever, and vomiting. The urine may have a foul odor or appear cloudy. An infant is unable to describe symptoms but may be generally fussy and have a fever with no other symptoms. If your child has any of these symptoms, call the doctor. (See Urinary Tract Infection in Chapter 30, "Childhood Infections," and Recurrent Urinary Tract Infection in Chapter 32, "Health Problems in Early Childhood," for more information.)

Bedwetting (nocturnal enuresis). For information, see Chapter 20, "Toilet Teaching."

Vaginal irritation or discharge. The vagina is close to the urethral opening (the opening where urine leaves the body). Any irritation in the genital area can cause pain or burning with urination. Irritation in the vaginal area in young girls can be caused by soap, shampoo, or bubble bath; by the rubbing of wet underwear or bathing suits against the area; or by improper wiping when using the bathroom. Teach your child to wipe from front to back to prevent getting stool into the area of the urethra. Teach her to wipe gently and to make sure no pieces of toilet paper get stuck when wiping; these little pieces may go unnoticed until they cause a discharge or itching. (Other foreign bodies in the vaginal area can also cause discharge and itching.) Pinworms can also cause itching in the vaginal area. Pinworms crawl out of the anus and cause irritation there, but they sometimes travel toward the vagina and cause widespread irritation in the entire genital region, thus irritating the area around the urethra and causing urinary symptoms. If your child develops a vaginal discharge that smells foul or is associated with itching or pain, call your child's doctor.

Although vaginal irritation in young girls is usually due to improper wiping and hygiene problems, vaginal pain, discharge, or bleeding can also be signs of sexual abuse. Call your child's doctor if you have concerns about sexual abuse in your child. For more information about child abuse, see Chapter 32, "Health Problems in Early Childhood."

Labial adhesions. In some girls, the inner folds of tissue (labia minora) that surround the vagina may grow together across the vaginal opening. This condition, called labial adhesions, can occur in the first few months of life or, less commonly, when a child is older. Usually this causes the child no symptoms or problems; however, if the labial adhesions completely block the vaginal opening, vaginal secretions or urine may be trapped behind the fused tissue. This can lead to vaginal irritation, urination problems, or an increased risk of urinary tract infection. Labial adhesions are usually treated with a prescription cream containing the hormone estrogen that helps to separate the fused labial folds. If your child's labia appear to have grown together, speak with your child's doctor.

Diabetes. Children with untreated diabetes produce large amounts of urine and need to urinate more frequently. For more information on diabetes, see Chapter 32, "Health Problems in Early Childhood."

Posterior urethral valves. The presence of posterior urethral valves is an uncommon problem that is found in some newborn boys. The valves are little flaps of tissue in the urethra (the tube through which urine leaves the body) that partially block the flow of urine. If this problem is not corrected by surgery early on, back pressure in the urinary tract can eventually damage the kidneys. Infant boys with a normal urethra urinate in an arc (the kind of urine stream that shoots off of the changing table or threatens to hit you in the face or arm if you are not careful during diaper changes). Babies with posterior urethral valves don't have a normal stream because the urine flow is blocked—the urine dribbles out. If your newborn boy does not have a strong urinary stream, call your child's doctor.

What You Can Do at Home

- Wash your child's genital region with lukewarm water alone. Soaps that get into the opening of the urethra (the opening where urine leaves the body) can be irritating and cause a burning sensation during urination. Avoid bubble baths completely.
- Supervise wiping in a newly toilet-trained child. Teach your child to wipe gently from front to back to prevent bacteria in the stool from getting into the urethra, and check frequently that the child is still doing it properly. Girls can get pieces of toilet paper stuck using improper wiping techniques.
- Change wet bathing suits or underwear when your child is finished playing in water. The wetness can cause irritation.

- If your child has a urinary tract infection, offer plenty of fluids to help flush bacteria out of the bladder. Cranberry juice is a good choice because it contains a substance that inhibits the overgrowth of bacteria in the urinary tract. Fluids and cranberry juice alone are not enough to cure the infection, though. If your child has a urinary tract infection, antibiotic treatment is required—speak with your child's doctor.

Need More Information?

Check the Index and Appendix C, "Resource Guide." And of course, consult your child's doctor.

chapter thirty

Childhood Infections

*The facts about roseola, ringworm,
rheumatic fever, and more*

Index to Chapter

How to Use This Chapter

Sooner or later every child gets an infection, and most will have several each year as they grow up. That's especially true throughout the first few years of life, as your child is exposed to new bacteria and viruses. Soothing a feverish child, encouraging him to drink fluids, and cheerleading as he swallows an unpleasant-tasting medicine are all an inevitable part of parenting. Fortunately, the symptoms of most infections last only a few days, whether specific treatment is needed or not. Some, though, can be life-threatening or have long-term consequences. Some infections are common and can be expected to occur in almost every child. Some are extremely rare.

Immunizations, which are among the most important developments in the history of medicine, have controlled or wiped out diseases that used to claim or wreck millions of lives. More vaccines are on the way. (Be sure to read Chapter 16, "Immunizations.") Still, the majority of childhood infections can't be prevented by immunizations.

This chapter contains information about a wide range of infections that can occur in childhood. The information about each infection is structured in the same way: the name of the infection, its cause, the common symptoms, how it spreads, the length of its incubation period, how long its symptoms are likely to last, when to call your child's doctor, how the infection is diagnosed and treated (the doctor's treatment and things you can do at home to help your child feel better), how (if at all) it can be prevented, how long its contagious period is, and what complications might occur. Like the rest of *The KidsHealth Guide for Parents*, this chapter's focus is on the kinds of practical information you need to know as a parent.

Here are a few words about the concept of incubation and the contagious period. Length of incubation refers to the time between when a person first gets exposed to an infection and when symptoms of the infection finally appear. During that time, the germ is multiplying in the person's body. The person who is "incubating" the infection usually doesn't know he or she is about to get sick. Depending on the cause of the infection, the incubation period could be short (a few hours in some cases). With other causes, the incubation period can be a few weeks or even longer.

How about the contagious period? Isn't that just the same time that the person feels sick? Not exactly. In many infections, a person can be contagious (able to pass the infection to someone else) even before he has any symptoms or knows he is infected. Sometimes, a person is no longer contagious even though he isn't yet feeling completely back to normal or still has signs of the illness. With some infections, it's possible to remain contagious even after the illness seems to be completely gone.

We realize that it might be tempting to use this guide to diagnose your child's illness on your own. Don't. Different infections can have very similar signs and symptoms. And many noninfectious medical conditions can masquerade as infections, and vice versa. That's why it's important to consult your child's doctor whenever you think your child might have a significant illness. And remember that although we've written this chapter to be as up to date as possible, new treatments and ways to make diagnoses are constantly being developed, so be sure to get the latest information from your child's doctor.

Botulism

Cause Botulism is caused by the bacterium *Clostridium botulinum*. Infant botulism, which is seen in infants six months and younger, occurs when spores of the bacteria are consumed, grow in the intestines, and release a toxin that blocks the messages between nerves and muscles throughout the body, leading to paralysis. Food-borne botulism is caused by eating foods—such as contaminated home-canned foods—that contain the botulism toxin.

Symptoms Symptoms of infant botulism may include constipation, poor suck, increased drooling, lethargy, weak cry, and worsening muscle weakness. Food-borne botulism may include double vision, blurred vision, drooping eyelids, slurred speech, difficulty swallowing, dry mouth, and muscle weakness.

How It Spreads The bacteria live in soil and dust or may contaminate food, including honey (uncommon). The infection is not transmitted from person to person. Spores or the toxin must be consumed.

Incubation Period The incubation period of infant botulism is 3 to 30 days. With food-borne botulism, symptoms usually begin 18 to 36 hours after eating the contaminated food, but the period can range from 2 hours to as long as 8 days.

How Long Symptoms Last The average hospital stay is one month.

When to Call Your Child's Doctor Untreated cases can be fatal. Call your child's doctor immediately if your infant has trouble breathing, is drooling abnormally, or has trouble swallowing. Also see the doctor if your infant is not feeding well, cries weakly, has difficulty holding her head up, has poor muscle tone, or is constipated. Although it usually doesn't indicate any serious problem, check with the doctor if your child has not had a bowel movement for three days. Call the doctor immediately if your older child develops problems with vision, talking, or swallowing or if your child appears very weak or unable to move normally.

How the Diagnosis Is Made The doctor detects toxin in the stool or blood or finds the bacteria in the stool.

Treatment Botulism is treated with supportive care, usually in the intensive care unit. If diagnosed early, food-borne botulism may be treated with an antitoxin that blocks the effects of the toxin circulating in the blood. Doctors may also try to remove contaminated food by inducing vomiting or using enemas. Currently, antitoxin is not routinely given for treatment of infant botulism.

Prevention Most cases of infant botulism cannot be prevented, but children younger than one year should not be given honey. For food-borne botulism, people who do home canning should follow strict hygienic procedures. Because botulism is destroyed at high temperatures, consider boiling home-canned foods for 10 minutes to ensure safety. Oils infused with garlic or herbs should be refrigerated. Potatoes baked in aluminum foil should be served hot or kept refrigerated.

Complications Death is rare for patients who are hospitalized in the United States. However, some children may develop other complications, such as respiratory problems, pneumonia, or sepsis (blood poisoning).

After recovery, children appear to have an increased incidence of strabismus, a misalignment of the eyes ("wandering" or "crossing" eyes).

Bronchiolitis (Respiratory Syncytial Virus)

Cause An inflammation of the bronchioles, the lung's smallest air passages, bronchiolitis is usually caused by a viral infection. The most common cause, especially during cold-weather epidemics, is respiratory syncytial virus (RSV). Other causes include mycoplasma, parainfluenza virus, influenza virus, and some adenoviruses.

Symptoms Initial symptoms include congestion, runny nose, and mild cough for a day or two. These symptoms are followed by gradually increasing difficulty in breathing characterized by wheezing; rapid, shallow breathing (60 to 80 times a minute); rapid heartbeat; the sucking in of the skin over the neck and chest with each breath; and a cough. Fever may occur. Usually no vomiting or diarrhea occurs, although bouts of coughing may lead to vomiting.

How It Spreads Respiratory syncytial virus and other viruses spread easily through families, child-care centers, and schools, especially in winter. Children contract the viruses by coming in contact with the nose and throat secretions of others.

Incubation Period The incubation period is several days to a week, depending on the virus causing the infection.

How Long Symptoms Last Most cases last about a week, but in severe cases, coughing may continue for a few weeks even after the child appears otherwise well.

When to Call Your Child's Doctor If your child is having trouble breathing, contact your child's doctor immediately.

How the Diagnosis Is Made The doctor will listen to the child's lungs with a stethoscope and observe breathing. Rapid test for RSV is available to make the diagnosis.

Treatment Most cases are mild and can be treated at home. Cases in very young infants or those with other medical problems such as prematurity, lung disease, or heart disease may require hospitalization for oxygen, intravenous fluids, other treatment, and monitoring. Antibiotics are not helpful unless there is a secondary infection caused by bacteria.

Home Treatment Use a cool-mist humidifier during the dry winter months to keep air humid. (Clean every day to keep mold from growing.) Make sure your child gets enough fluids.

Prevention Try to get your child to wash her hands frequently and avoid contact with sick children. Bronchiolitis occurs more commonly in male infants three to six months of age who have not been breast-fed. Infants exposed to cigarette smoke are more likely to develop respiratory infections and have more severe symptoms. Some children become so ill from RSV infection that they need to be hospitalized, especially premature infants and those with lung or heart conditions. Synagis (palivizumab), a medication containing antibodies against RSV, is available to help prevent infection in these children. The drug is given as monthly injections during RSV season.

Contagious Periods Most infants infected with RSV can continue to spread the virus for 5 to 12 days after the start of symptoms. Bronchiolitis, especially from RSV, is spread very easily because the virus remains alive in nasal secretions and saliva outside the body for hours. Someone sneezing very close to someone else or touching a surface contaminated with secretions could therefore give someone RSV fairly easily. Therefore, good hand washing is extremely important to prevent outbreaks and rapid spread through child-care centers, schools, and hospitals.

Complications Complications from bronchiolitis include ear infections, and less commonly, secondary bacterial pneumonia. Sometimes, children with preexisting heart or lung conditions or who are born prematurely need hospitalization for oxygen or respiratory therapy. Up to 30 percent of children who develop bronchiolitis go on to develop some form of asthma, especially if there is a family history of asthma.

Cat Scratch Disease

Cause Cat scratch disease is caused by the bacterium *Bartonella henselae*, usually transmitted through a cat scratch.

Symptoms About one-half to three-fourths of children diagnosed have a cat scratch on their bodies. Within 3 to 10 days after the scratch, a blister or small bump develops. Usually within two weeks of the scratch, lymph nodes (glands) near the scratch swell. The nodes may be painful and surrounded by a larger area of swelling under the skin, which may be red. About one-third of children develop fever, fatigue, loss of appetite, and headache. In a few cases, the bump appears as a small sore on the conjunctiva (lining of the eye surface), with swollen nodes in the area around the ears.

How It Spreads It is transmitted by a scratch from an infected animal, most often a kitten. It is not spread from person to person.

Incubation Period It takes 3 to 10 days for a blister or bump to appear at the site of the scratch. Lymph node swelling starts about two weeks after the scratch, with a range of 7 to 60 days.

How Long Symptoms Last Usually nodes are swollen for one to two months, but swelling may last much longer.

When to Call Your Child's Doctor Call your child's doctor if your child has been scratched by a cat or kitten and develops swollen glands and a fever.

How the Diagnosis Is Made Exposure to a cat or kitten is the first clue. The doctor may order a blood test for cat scratch disease as well as other skin and blood tests to rule out other causes of swollen lymph nodes.

Treatment The doctor may or may not prescribe antibiotics. Even without antibiotics, the disease will go away in time.

Home Treatment The child does not have to be isolated from the rest of the family. Avoid injuring areas of the swollen lymph nodes. Moist compresses of salty water may help soothe painful nodes.

Prevention Teach children to avoid stray or unfamiliar cats. If your child is scratched by a cat or other pet, wash the area thoroughly with soap and water.

Contagious Periods For unknown reasons, cat scratch disease occurs more often in fall and winter. Kittens are more often infected with the bacteria than mature cats; once infected they carry the bacteria for months.

Complications A small number of children (less than 5 percent) develop seizures, bizarre behavior, or other neurologic symptoms several weeks after lymph node swelling appears.

Other Issues If you have a cat you believe has transmitted the disease, talk to your veterinarian. The cat does not have to be destroyed.

Cellulitis

Cause A spreading skin infection, cellulitis often begins in an area of broken skin like a scrape, cut, or scratch. It can be caused by many different bacteria; most common are group A *Streptococcus* and *Staphylococcus aureus*.

Symptoms Cellulitis typically appears on the face and lower legs. It begins as a small, tender, red, swollen area. As it spreads, the child may begin to feel ill. The child also may develop fever, sometimes with chills and sweating. Sometimes lymph nodes (glands) near the area become swollen.

How It Spreads It is not contagious.

Incubation Period Depending on the type of bacteria, it can take from hours to days to appear.

How Long Symptoms Last With antibiotic treatment it is usually cured within 7 to 10 days.

When to Call Your Child's Doctor Call your child's doctor whenever an area of your child's skin becomes red, warm, and painful, with or without fever and chills, especially if on the face. Call immediately if your child has a chronic illness like sickle-cell anemia or is receiving treatment that weakens the immune system.

How the Diagnosis Is Made Your child's doctor will examine the involved skin area. In some cases, blood tests will be ordered to check to see if the infection has spread to the blood.

Treatment Oral antibiotics are usually prescribed. In severe cases, your child will be hospitalized for intravenous antibiotic treatment. Usually your child's doctor will want to see your child a few days after the start of treatment to see if cellulitis has improved.

Home Treatment Heat or warm soaks can be applied to the affected area.

Prevention Wash any wound or scrape well with soap and water. Apply an antibiotic ointment and cover with an adhesive bandage or gauze. Check with your child's doctor if your child gets a large cut, a deep puncture wound, or a bite (animal or human).

Complications Cellulitis can occur very quickly after an animal or human bite, especially if the wound is deep.

Chicken Pox (Varicella)

Cause Chicken pox is an infection with the varicella-zoster virus.

Symptoms Characteristic blisters usually appear first on the trunk and face and can spread over the whole body. Blisters may also appear inside the mouth, nose, and vagina. Some children have a few blisters; others have hundreds. The blisters are about 0.2 to 0.4 inch wide, with a reddish base ("dew drop on a rose petal"). The rash is usually associated with moderate to severe itching. Some children have fever (usually mild), stomach pain, and a general ill feeling.

How It Spreads The virus is spread in nasal secretions and in fluid from inside the blisters. It is very contagious; epidemics are especially common in late winter and early spring. Ninety percent of all nonimmune children (those who haven't had chicken pox or vaccine) will catch it when exposed.

Incubation Period Typically, the incubation period is 7 to 21 days after exposure, with most cases appearing between 14 and 17 days.

How Long Symptoms Last Symptoms last for 7 to 10 days.

When to Call Your Child's Doctor If you are uncertain about the diagnosis or concerned about a possible complication, call your child's doctor. Call if there are signs that the skin blisters are infected (area around the blisters is swollen, red, or painful), the blisters are leaking thick pus-like fluid, or itching is so severe that it doesn't respond to treatment. Call your child's doctor immediately if your child is difficult to awaken or is confused, has trouble walking, has a headache, has a stiff neck, is vomiting repeatedly, has difficulty breathing, has a severe cough, or has eyes very sensitive to light. Also call immediately if fever rises above 103 degrees Fahrenheit.

How the Diagnosis Is Made Diagnosis is made through the appearance of the rash and other symptoms.

Treatment Because it is a viral infection, antibiotics are not useful unless there is a secondary bacterial infection. Children with a weakened immune system may be treated with the antiviral medicine acyclovir. Because it must be started within 24 hours of the first sign of pox and it is usually only mildly beneficial, it is not generally recommended for otherwise healthy children.

Home Treatment If your child is uncomfortable because of a fever (most children with chicken pox have only mild fever—less than 102 degrees Fahrenheit—and don't need treatment), use a nonaspirin medicine such as acetaminophen (Tylenol). Do not use aspirin because it can lead to Reye syndrome in infected children, which can harm the brain and liver. It is also best to avoid giving ibuprofen, as some recent studies indicate it may put children at risk for developing bacterial infections on top of the chicken pox sores. To relieve itching, use wet compresses or bathe your child in cool or lukewarm water every three to four hours. Calamine lotion may help. Trim your child's fingernails to help prevent tissue injury and secondary bacterial infection of the skin from scratching. For blisters in the mouth, avoid acidic or salty foods. If your child has sores in the genital area, ask your child's doctor or pharmacist about anesthetic cream.

Prevention The vaccine against chicken pox is 70 to 90 percent effective. Vaccinated children who contract the virus have a milder case. A single injection of the vaccine is recommended for children 12 months to 12 years of age who have not already had the disease.

Contagious Periods People with chicken pox are contagious from two days before blisters appear until all blisters are crusted over. Children with chicken pox should be kept out of child care or school for about a week; it's not necessary to wait until the scabs fall off to let the child out of isolation. People with certain chronic diseases or weakened immune systems and pregnant women should avoid contact with chicken pox. Once a child has had chicken pox, she will never get it again.

Other Issues Questions remain about how long the vaccine's protection lasts. Studies indicate that it should last for at least 10 years. It is not yet known if a booster is needed later in life.

Common Cold

Cause Dozens of viruses can cause infection of the upper respiratory tract, including rhinoviruses, coronaviruses, adenovirus, respiratory syncytial virus (RSV), enteroviruses, and the influenza and parainfluenza viruses. These can affect the nose, throat, sinuses, ears, eustachian tubes (fleshy tubes connecting the throat with the middle ear), trachea, larynx, and bronchial tubes.

Symptoms Symptoms include a tickle in the throat, runny or stuffy nose, and sneezing. Children may also have a sore throat, cough, headache, mild fever, fatigue, muscle aches, and loss of appetite.

How It Spreads It is spread by breathing in the virus spread through the air in secretions from sneezing or coughing, or by person-to-person contact. Children get more colds than adults do, especially through exposure in child care or school.

Incubation Period It takes two to five days for symptoms to appear after exposure to the virus.

How Long Symptoms Last Symptoms usually last 7 to 14 days.

When to Call Your Child's Doctor It is not necessary to call your child's doctor if typical symptoms (congestion, cough, sneezing, mild fever) are present, but call if there are other signs of concern. These include sore throat; coughing that produces green or gray sputum (mucus) or a cough that is getting worse or is not getting better over a three- to four-day period; fever lasting several days or higher than 101 degrees Fahrenheit; shaking chills; chest pain; shortness of breath, rapid breathing, or other signs that your child is working hard to breathe; or blue lips, skin, or fingernails. Other signs include difficulty swallowing, unwillingness to drink fluids, unusual fatigue, or enlarged lymph nodes (glands) in the neck. Also, call your child's doctor if your child has a very runny nose, especially with a green discharge, that lasts more than two weeks or if your child complains of headache or pressure behind the face.

Treatment Because a cold is caused by a virus, antibiotics are not helpful.

Home Treatment Infection resolves by itself; there is no cure. For relief of symptoms try saltwater drops in the nostrils to help relieve a stuffy nose, cool-mist vaporizer to increase air moisture, and petroleum jelly (Vaseline) on the skin under the nose to soothe rawness. Your child should get plenty of fluids and rest. For fever or headache, you can give your infant or child acetaminophen (Tylenol). Do **not** give a child aspirin; aspirin in children is associated with Reye syndrome, a rare but life-threatening disease. Over-the-counter decongestants and antihistamines are of questionable effectiveness, do not shorten the duration of symptoms, and can cause side effects potentially worse than symptoms from the cold itself, especially in infants and toddlers.

Prevention If possible, avoid contact with the person who has a cold for the first two to four days of symptoms. Usually, however, the person is contagious before he or she is aware of the infection. Children with colds should wash their hands thoroughly, especially after blowing their nose, and should be taught to cover their nose and mouth when coughing or sneezing.

Contagious Periods The contagious period depends on the virus causing the infection, but it is generally for several days after symptoms appear.

Other Issues There is no scientifically proven benefit to giving children megadoses of vitamin C (which can be toxic in high doses) to prevent or treat colds. Similarly, there is no evidence supporting the effectiveness of multivitamins, zinc, or chest rubs in children.

Conjunctivitis (Pinkeye)

Cause Conjunctivitis is caused by an inflammation of the conjunctiva, the thin membrane that covers the whites of the eyes and lines the inner surface of the eyelids. About 80 percent of infectious conjunctivitis cases are caused by bacteria, and the rest are caused by viruses. Allergies or exposure of the eyes to chemicals or other irritants can also be causes.

Symptoms Symptoms include discomfort or the sensation that something is in the eye, followed by redness and inflammation of the conjunctiva. After a day or so, there may be a discharge from the eye. In bacterial conjunctivitis, the discharge is thick and pus-like; in viral conjunctivitis, the discharge usually is watery. The eyelashes may be matted and stuck together when the child wakes in the morning.

How It Spreads It is spread through contact with discharge or secretions from the infected eye of someone else.

Incubation Period For bacterial conjunctivitis, the incubation period is a few days; for viral, it is up to a week.

How Long Symptoms Last Bacterial conjunctivitis lasts 7 to 10 days if untreated. Viral conjunctivitis can last as long as two weeks.

When to Call Your Child's Doctor If your child—particularly your newborn—has any of the symptoms of conjunctivitis, call your child's doctor. Also, call the doctor if your child complains of severe pain, a change in vision, or sensitivity to light, or if your child's condition does not get better in four to five days.

How the Diagnosis Is Made The doctor will examine your child's eye and in some cases may take a swab of the discharge for lab analysis.

Treatment Often infectious conjunctivitis will resolve by itself, but doctors usually prescribe antibiotic drops or ointment to decrease the possibility of spreading it to others. Drops are usually prescribed for a week, about four doses a day. Ointment, usually prescribed for infants, is given two times daily and can temporarily blur vision (to see an illustration of giving eyedrops to a child, refer to Chapter 29, "Signs and Symptoms"). Children with prolonged or repeated bouts of reddened, itchy, and watery eyes may benefit from treatment for allergies or removal of irritants (such as cigarette smoke) from their environment.

Home Treatment Warm compresses (a clean washcloth soaked in water) can help loosen crusts on eyelids and lashes. Gauze or cotton balls dipped in warm water can be used to carefully clean the infected eye.

Prevention Your child should wash her hands after touching the infected eye. Others touching the child's infected eye should also wash hands. Gauze or cotton balls used to clean the eye should be thrown away; child's towels, washcloths, and pillowcases should be washed in hot water.

Contagious Periods Children with bacterial conjunctivitis are contagious as soon as symptoms appear; the child will remain contagious as long as there is discharge or with bacterial conjunctivitis, until antibiotics have been given for 24 hours. Viral conjunctivitis is contagious before the onset of symptoms and for as long as the symptoms last. Children should not be in school or a child-care center while they have visible symptoms of conjunctivitis.

Complications Some bacteria can cause both conjunctivitis and middle ear infection (otitis media) at the same time.

Croup

Cause An inflammation of the upper airways, croup is generally caused by infection by one of several viruses, including parainfluenza virus (accounts for most cases), adenovirus, respiratory syncytial virus, influenza, and measles. It can also be caused by bacteria. Usually following a few days of cold symptoms, it most commonly occurs in late fall and winter.

Symptoms Symptoms include a loud cough that sounds like a seal barking, difficulty breathing, wheezing, or noisy breathing. With severe croup, there can also be a high-pitched squeaking sound called stridor when the child is breathing in. Some children have a fever. Symptoms are often worse at night or with crying.

How It Spreads The virus causing croup is spread through the air or on surfaces touched by those infected.

Incubation Period Symptoms appear two to five days after exposure.

How Long Symptoms Last Symptoms usually last five to six days.

When to Call Your Child's Doctor Most cases of croup don't require medical treatment, but your child's doctor may want to see your child to make sure there's no airway blockage or bacterial infection. Call 911 or take your child to the emergency room immediately if she is struggling to breathe and is making the harsh stridor sound, is drooling excessively or has difficulty swallowing or speaking, has difficulty bending the neck, shows signs of losing consciousness, has a high fever, looks very ill, or is beginning to turn blue around the mouth and fingers.

How the Diagnosis Is Made Diagnosis is made through the doctor's examination and sometimes an X-ray to look at the windpipe area in the neck.

Treatment No medication will kill the virus that causes croup, but sometimes your child's doctor will give your child steroid medicine, by injection or by mouth, to help lessen the airway swelling caused by croup to help your child breathe easier.

Home Treatment Moisture often relieves symptoms. Use a cool-mist vaporizer filled with water only, or mist up the bathroom with hot shower steam and sit with your child in the bathroom for 10 minutes. Sometimes taking your child into cool outside air for a few minutes can also help. If these measures don't improve your child's symptoms within 10 to 15 minutes, call your child's doctor. Note: No one should smoke in the house because this can make croup worse.

Prevention There is no form of prevention at present.

Contagious Periods With most viruses causing the infection, the child is contagious for several days after symptoms appear. Most children who are exposed will get an upper respiratory infection; only a small number will get croup.

Complications In some severe cases, a child may have to be hospitalized. Ear infection and pneumonia may occur as the croup symptoms are fading.

Diarrhea

Cause Diarrhea—frequent and watery bowel movements—can be caused by bacteria, viruses, or parasites that infect the stomach or intestines. The specific germs involved depend on the geographic area and the level of sanitation and hygiene.

Some Infections That Cause Diarrhea **Amebiasis.** Especially common in the tropics, this is an infection of the large intestine caused by the parasite *Entamoeba histolytica*, which is transmitted by contaminated food or drink or by direct fecal-oral contact. **Campylobacter.** The *Campylobacter* bacterium can cause diarrhea and is spread by drinking contaminated water, eating undercooked poultry or meat, or coming in contact with contaminated animals. **Cryptosporidium.** This parasite is a common cause of diarrhea outbreaks in child-care centers, and it can be spread by contact with infected animals—especially cows—or infected people or by drinking contaminated water. **E. coli.** Five classes of *E. coli* bacteria can cause diarrhea in children either by directly attacking the intestine wall or by producing a toxin that irritates the intestines. *E. coli* infections are usually spread through contaminated food or water. Undercooked beef in hamburgers can also be a source of *E. coli* infections. **Giardiasis.** Caused by the parasite *Giardia*, this is a common cause of diarrhea among diaper-wearing children, especially in child-care settings. It is spread through contaminated water supplies—especially at water parks, aquarium "touch tanks," and pools (it is resistant to chlorine)—and through human contact. **Rotavirus.** This virus is the most common cause of diarrhea in young children in the United States. It is spread through contact with infected feces, and outbreaks often occur in child-care centers and children's hospitals. **Salmonella.** These bacteria are responsible for 50 percent of food poisoning in the United States. Almost any food of animal origin, especially raw or undercooked meat, poultry, and eggs, can cause salmonella. **Shigella.** These bacteria are among the major causes of dysentery (bloody diarrhea) in the world and are spread by contact with contaminated feces. **Yersinia.** Contaminated water and meat products, especially chitterlings and other pork products, are a common source of infection with this organism.

Symptoms Symptoms usually include crampy abdominal pain followed by diarrhea. Some bacterial infections, including campylobacter, salmonella, *E. coli*, shigella, and yersinia also may cause blood in the stools. With salmonella, shigella, and yersinia, the stool may also contain mucus. Some bacteria may also cause fever, loss of appetite, nausea, or vomiting. All can potentially lead to dehydration and weight loss.

Incubation Period Times vary depending on the germ causing the infection. The incubation period for shigella is usually 16 to 72 hours. For a virus, incubation periods range from 4 to 48 hours. Parasitic infections usually have longer incubation periods; for example, giardia has an incubation period of one to three weeks.

How Long Symptoms Last In cases of mild diarrhea caused by a virus, the diarrhea resolves within a few days. With bacterial diarrhea, symptoms may last days to weeks. Parasitic infections may cause diarrhea lasting weeks or even months.

When to Call Your Child's Doctor Call your child's doctor if your child has a severe or prolonged bout of diarrhea with fever, vomiting, or severe abdominal pain, or if the stools contain blood or mucus. Call immediately if your child shows the following signs of dehydration: dry lips and tongue; pale, dry skin; sunken eyes; listless behavior; and decreased urination.

How the Diagnosis Is Made A stool sample may be tested in a lab to identify the specific cause of the infection.

Treatment First ensure your child receives enough fluids and minerals to replace those lost due to diarrhea (for more information, see Diarrhea under Stomach and Intestinal Problems in Chapter 29, "Signs and Symptoms"). Viral and some of the bacterial infections are not treated with antibiotics because children usually recover on their own. Those infections caused by parasites are treated with antiparasitic medicines.

Home Treatment Plain water should not be used to treat diarrhea in infants and small children. Your child's doctor may advise using a special drink called an oral rehydration solution (such as Pedialyte) that replaces salts and other nutrients lost with diarrhea and is available at drugstores or grocery stores. The Centers for Disease Control and Prevention recommends that these be kept in the home for treatment of bouts of diarrhea in young children.

Prevention Hand washing is the best way to prevent infections that are spread from person to person. Child-care personnel and parents should wash hands carefully after changing children's diapers. Bathroom surfaces should be kept clean. Wash fruits and vegetables thoroughly before eating. Wash kitchen counters and utensils that have been in contact with raw meat, especially poultry. Refrigerate meats immediately after bringing them home, and cook them until they are no longer pink. Refrigerate leftovers as soon as possible. Never drink from streams, lakes, or springs unless health authorities have said the water is safe for drinking. In developing countries it may be safer not to drink from the tap. Be careful when buying food prepared by street vendors, especially if no health agency oversees their safety practices. Keep pets' feeding areas separate from family eating areas. Never wash pet cages or bowls in the same sink where meals are prepared. Reptiles and amphibians such as iguanas and turtles may carry *Salmonella* bacteria and are not good pets for young children, who may fail to wash their hands adequately after handling them.

Complications Diarrhea accounts for 9 percent of hospitalizations in children younger than five years. It kills 300 to 500 children in the United States each year, most of them infants younger than one year. Worldwide, it accounts for the deaths of four million children each year.

Ear Infection—Ear Canal (Otitis Externa/Swimmer's Ear)

Cause An infection of the ear canal—the opening that carries sound from the outside to the eardrum—otitis externa can be caused by several types of bacteria and fungi.

Symptoms The major symptom is severe ear pain that gets worse when the ear is pulled. Sometimes there is an itching sensation in the ear before the pain begins. The outer ear may also become reddened. There

may be a slight fever or a greenish-yellow discharge from the ear opening, and hearing may be decreased. Otitis externa usually occurs in children whose ears are exposed to persistent moisture, especially when swimming. Chlorinated water can dry out the skin of the ear canal and make it easier for germs to attack. It can also occur when a child's ear canal has been scratched by a sharp object.

How It Spreads It is not contagious.

Incubation Period There is no set incubation period for an enfection of the ear canal, but ear pain often develops gradually over hours after the ear canal has been exposed to moisture, such as during swimming.

How Long Symptoms Last Pain may continue to increase for the first 12 to 24 hours after treatment begins. If treated with medication, it is usually cured within 7 to 10 days, but the child may have to stay out of the water longer than this.

When to Call Your Child's Doctor Call your child's doctor if there is pain in the ear with or without fever, loss of hearing, or discharge from the ear.

How the Diagnosis Is Made Your child's doctor will make a diagnosis by examining the ear with an otoscope.

Treatment For milder infections, your child's doctor will prescribe eardrops containing antibiotics, which fight infection, and sometimes corticosteroids, which reduce swelling. Eardrops are usually given several times a day for 7 to 10 days. If the opening of the ear canal is narrowed, the doctor may insert a cotton wick into the canal to help carry the drops into the canal. For more severe infections, oral antibiotics may be given.

Home Treatment Acetaminophen (Tylenol) or ibuprofen may be given to relieve pain. To protect the infected ear, the doctor will usually advise keeping your child's head out of water for 10 to 14 days, including covering the ear while bathing or showering. Shower caps or cotton earplugs coated with petroleum jelly—removed after bathing or showering—can be used for this purpose.

Prevention Children (and adults) should avoid putting straight stiff objects like cotton-tipped applicators or bobby pins in their ears. If your child doesn't have ear tubes or a hole in the eardrum, acid alcohol drops like SwimEar can be used after swimming to help keep the ear canal dry. Soft earplugs that easily mold to the shape of your child's ear canal can also be used while your child is swimming.

Complications Untreated, an infection can spread to the surrounding cartilage and bone.

Ear Infection—Middle Ear (Otitis Media)

Cause By age three, two-thirds of children have had at least one middle ear infection (otitis media). *Streptococcus pneumoniae* is the most common bacterial cause of the infection. Other bacteria, such as *Hemophilus influenzae*, *Moraxella catarrhalis*, and *Staphylococcus aureus*, and many viruses, including adenoviruses, rhinoviruses, respiratory syncytial virus, and influenza viruses, also can cause middle ear infections. Often otitis media occurs because of clogging and dysfunction of the eustachian tubes due to viral infection and inflammation. The eustachian tubes are channels that normally allow air pressure to equalize between the middle ear and the throat. If they become clogged, air flow is poor and bacterial infection then can easily occur within the middle ear with buildup of pus and fluid pressure behind the eardrum. This prevents the eardrum from moving and vibrating normally, resulting in pain and often temporary hearing loss.

Symptoms Symptoms include earache, fever, hearing loss, sometimes a discharge from the ear, and irritability. Infants and young children may grab or tug at their ears. These symptoms are often accompanied by signs of a respiratory infection, such as a runny or stuffy nose or a cough. Infections occurring in both ears are more likely to be viral; infection of only one ear is more often due to a bacterial infection.

How It Spreads A middle ear infection itself is not contagious; however, the bacteria and viruses that can cause otitis media are spread through direct contact with nose and throat fluids or airborne droplets.

Incubation Period The incubation period is uncertain. Otitis media often develops within a week of developing a cold.

How Long Symptoms Last There may be improvement within 48 hours even without treatment, especially if the cause of the infection is viral. Ear infections caused by bacteria are usually treated for 5 to 10 days with antibiotics; symptoms should subside within 3 days after starting the medication, although fluid may remain in the middle ear space for up to three months after treatment (see Complications).

When to Call Your Child's Doctor Call your child's doctor if your child has an earache with or without fever, has pus draining out of an ear, or cannot hear normally. In infants, persistent ear tugging, irritability, and unexplained fever are common symptoms.

How the Diagnosis Is Made Your child's doctor will examine the ear with an otoscope to see if the eardrum appears inflamed or bulging (due to the presence of pus in the middle ear). The doctor may also blow a puff of air into the ear canals to see whether the eardrums are able to move normally.

Treatment If the doctor believes that bacteria may be causing the infection, he or she will prescribe an antibiotic, usually amoxicillin. Although this usually cures the infection, your child may be switched to a different antibiotic if the symptoms persist for three days or more after starting treatment. In some cases, the doctor may pierce the eardrum with an instrument to let out the pus and relieve pressure. The procedure is called a myringotomy. Depending on the child's symptoms and the appearance of the eardrum, in some cases the doctor may choose not to start antibiotics (antibiotics are not effective in treating viral ear infections). Instead, he or she may recommend waiting to see if signs of a bacterial ear infection develop. Doctors and other health experts are concerned about the overprescribing of antibiotics, which has led to the emergence of more resistant (and difficult to treat) strains of bacteria causing otitis media and other infections in recent years.

Prevention Ear infections occur less frequently in breast-fed infants, which may be because immune cells and antibodies are passed on from the mother in breast milk and because the feeding position may be better for the functioning of the eustachian tube. If you are bottle-feeding, hold your child semiupright rather than letting him lie down flat. Don't let your child take the bottle to bed, which can increase the risk of ear infections as well as tooth decay. Exposure to cigarette smoke also seems to increase the risk of ear infection in children. A child's contact with large groups of children, such as in child-care centers, increases the likelihood of contacting the germs that cause colds and lead to ear infections. The pneumococcal conjugate vaccine—which is the newest of the immunizations given routinely to infants less than two years of age—will likely play a significant role in prevention of ear infections caused by *Streptococcus pneumoniae*, especially in younger children. This vaccine, and perhaps others in the future, is expected to change the ways doctors use antibiotics to treat ear infections.

Complications In some untreated cases of otitis media, the infection can spread to the skull bone located behind the ear called the mastoid, which may require surgical drainage. Some children develop otitis media with effusion—the presence of middle ear fluid for six weeks or longer after the initial acute infection. Ninety percent of such cases clear up within three months without additional treatment. Some children develop recurrent otitis media, with multiple bouts of ear infections requiring repeated courses of antibiotics. If the child goes for long periods with middle ear fluid, hearing loss sufficient to cause temporary delays in speech and language development and learning may result. Such children may be referred for evaluation by an ENT specialist for possible myringotomy and insertion of ear tubes to help restore hearing (see Chapter 32, "Health Problems in Early Childhood," for more information on myringotomy and ear tubes). In some cases, surgical removal of the adenoids may help. Recent studies suggest that most children with delays in speech and language development due to chronic ear fluid tend to catch up with their peers over time, when the fluid eventually clears with or without specific treatment. Therefore, the placement of ear tubes may not ultimately make a significant difference in long-term speech and language development in many of these children. Parents should discuss these issues with their child's doctor in making decisions about inserting myringotomy tubes.

Other Issues Children who have allergies and those with certain medical conditions such as Down syndrome and cleft palate are more likely to experience repeated ear infections. Boys tend to get otitis media more frequently than girls do, and Native Americans appear to be more prone to the infection, possibly because of differences in the shape of their eustachian tubes. Children younger than six months who develop ear infections may be more likely to have repeated ear infections throughout early childhood.

Encephalitis

Cause Encephalitis is an inflammation of the brain. Acute infectious encephalitis is most often caused by a virus. Enteroviruses cause about 80 percent of all cases. Arboviruses, transmitted by insects such as ticks and mosquitoes, can also cause encephalitis. West Nile encephalitis virus is an example. Measles, mumps, chicken pox, and mononucleosis can sometimes cause encephalitis, usually a mild case. Rabies can also cause encephalitis. Although rare, herpes simplex virus, the virus that causes cold sores, can cause a serious, life-threatening form of encephalitis. Tuberculosis, syphilis, and Lyme disease can also cause brain inflammation.

Symptoms In mild cases, the child may have a fever, headache, poor appetite, lethargy, sensitivity of the eyes to light, and a general "sick" feeling. Severe cases may involve high fever, severe headache, nausea and vomiting, stiff neck, seizures (convulsions), blurred vision, confusion, personality changes, problems in speech or hearing, hallucinations, difficulty moving limbs, involuntary movements, difficulty walking, loss of sensation in some part of the body, memory loss, drowsiness, and coma. In infants, look for vomiting, a full or bulging soft spot (fontanel), and persistent crying and irritability.

How It Spreads Depending on the type, a virus can be spread through airborne nose or throat fluid droplets or through direct contact with an infected person. Encephalitis caused by an arbovirus is not contagious from person to person but must be transmitted by the bite of an infected insect. Rabies is transmitted by a bite or scratch from an infected animal.

Incubation Period The incubation period depends on the cause. Enteroviruses have an incubation of four to six days.

How Long Symptoms Last For most types, the acute phase lasts several days to a week; recovery takes two to three weeks. In severe cases, such as those caused by herpes simplex encephalitis, the child must be hospitalized, and recovery may take several weeks or longer.

When to Call Your Child's Doctor Call your child's doctor immediately if your child has any of the symptoms described earlier, especially if your child is recovering from measles, mumps, or chicken pox and develops a high fever.

How the Diagnosis Is Made Your child's doctor may order blood tests and perform a spinal tap (lumbar puncture) to examine spinal fluid for evidence of infection. An EEG (electroencephalogram), which measures brain waves, and either an MRI or CT scan, which looks for swelling and other changes in the brain, may also be done.

Treatment In some mild cases, children can be treated at home, but others need to be treated and observed closely in a hospital. In most cases children with viral encephalitis will be given nonaspirin medicines to reduce fever and headache and will be placed in a darkened room away from noise and lights to enable comfort and rest. Those with herpes simplex encephalitis will be treated with an antiviral drug like acyclovir. Encephalitis caused by bacteria is treated with appropriate antibiotics.

Prevention Encephalitis caused by common childhood illnesses such as measles, mumps, and chicken pox can be prevented by getting the appropriate vaccinations. In areas with large numbers of mosquitoes during the summer months, keep children indoors from dusk to dawn when mosquitoes feed.

Dress your child in light clothing that covers the skin. If you have stagnant water around, get rid of it because it breeds mosquitoes. To prevent children from being bitten by a tick, make sure they wear long-sleeved shirts and long pants when walking through the woods. Tuck pants into socks. Regularly check for ticks on your child's body after the child has been outside. Make sure your pets are vaccinated for rabies.

Contagious Periods The contagious period varies according to the specific virus.

Complications Most children recover fully from viral encephalitis, but the outcome depends on the severity of the illness and the germ involved. Severe cases of encephalitis can cause damage to the nervous system that can result in epilepsy, hearing and visual problems, and impairment of intelligence and movement. Herpes simplex encephalitis is often fatal.

Epiglottitis

Cause Epiglottitis is an inflammation of the child's epiglottis, the flap of tissue that covers the windpipe, and is usually caused by the bacterium *Hemophilus influenzae* type B. Epiglottitis occurs most often in children age three to seven years, and it is more common in the fall and spring.

Symptoms Symptoms may develop very rapidly. The child may have symptoms of an upper respiratory infection. As the epiglottis becomes inflamed and begins to swell, the throat becomes sore and painful and the child's temperature may rise to 102 to 104 degrees Fahrenheit. The child may begin to drool because swallowing is painful. The voice may sound muffled. Within hours, the child may develop breathing difficulty. With each breath, the child may make a high-pitched squeaking sound (stridor). The nostrils may flare out as the child breathes. The child may appear anxious and want to sit up, holding the head and neck forward to help him breathe. The lips and fingertips may start to turn blue as less oxygen gets into the bloodstream. If not treated quickly, a child with this infection may die due to blockage of the windpipe by the swollen epiglottis.

How It Spreads The bacteria, found in nasal secretions, are spread when a person who may carry the bacteria without even being sick coughs or sneezes.

How Long Symptoms Last Symptoms usually improve quickly with treatment, but the child usually needs to stay in the hospital for several days to a week.

When to Call Your Child's Doctor Bring your child to the emergency room immediately if she shows the symptoms described. Epiglottitis can be deadly if not treated quickly.

How the Diagnosis Is Made Doctors suspect the diagnosis based on a child's symptoms. Your child is then usually taken to an operating room where a doctor will insert a lighted thin tube into the throat to see if the epiglottis is inflamed and swollen. It may appear cherry red. The swollen epiglottis can also be seen on an X-ray of the neck.

Treatment A specialist may insert a breathing tube into the windpipe to hold the airway open. Your child may then be placed on a ventilator (breathing machine) in the

hospital to help her breathe. Intravenous antibiotics are given to kill the bacteria causing the infection. When the infection and swelling of the epiglottis subside with treatment, the breathing tube can be removed.

Prevention The incidence of epiglottitis has decreased dramatically since the vaccine against *Hemophilus influenzae* type B was introduced. Infants should be immunized against this bacterium, which also causes meningitis and pneumonia. If your child develops epiglottitis, your child's doctor may recommend that anyone in the household not fully vaccinated (except pregnant women) receive a course of the antibiotic rifampin. The doctor may recommend the same for anyone not fully vaccinated at your child's school or child-care center.

Fifth Disease (Erythema Infectiosum)

Cause Fifth disease is caused by Parvovirus B19.

Symptoms Early symptoms include mild fever, headache, and cold symptoms. This is followed by a characteristic rash. Initially, redness and flushing of the face give the child a "slapped cheek" appearance. Then the rash spreads to the body and limbs. Following this, the reddened skin develops areas of clearing, making the rash appear "lacy." The rash then resolves on its own, but it may wax and wane over one to three weeks.

How It Spreads Fifth disease spreads from person to person through respiratory fluid droplets. The majority of cases occur in school-age children, especially in the late winter and spring.

Incubation Period The incubation period is from 4 to 28 days, with an average of 17 days.

How Long Symptoms Last The rash may come and go for up to three weeks. Sunlight, heat, exercise, or stress can cause the rash to flare up during this period.

When to Call Your Child's Doctor If you are uncertain of the diagnosis or if your child develops other symptoms that concern you, call your child's doctor.

How the Diagnosis Is Made The doctor observes the characteristic rash.

Home Treatment Fifth disease usually does not require treatment; however, nonprescription drugs such as acetaminophen (Tylenol) can be given to treat headache or reduce fever if your child is uncomfortable.

Prevention Usually children with fifth disease are no longer infectious by the time the rash appears; therefore, they should not be isolated or excluded from school or child care.

Hand, Foot, and Mouth Disease

Cause Certain strains of the Group A coxsackieviruses cause this disease.

Symptoms Symptoms include fever (usually mild) and malaise, followed by a characteristic rash: red bumps and/or blisters on the hands and feet, along with blisters and ulcers on the tongue and the inner linings of the cheeks. Most outbreaks occur during summer and fall.

How It Spreads It spreads person-to-person through stool and respiratory fluids.

Incubation Period The incubation period is four to six days.

How Long Symptoms Last Symptoms last four to seven days. Mouth pain is usually gone by about four days; mouth blisters are usually gone within one week.

When to Call Your Child's Doctor Call your child's doctor if your child develops a rash on the hands and feet and blisters or ulcers in the mouth. Call the doctor if your child will not eat or drink, shows signs of dehydration, or has fever for more than three days.

How the Diagnosis Is Made The doctor observes the characteristic rash and mouth lesions.

Home Treatment Nonprescription drugs such as acetaminophen (Tylenol) can be given to reduce fever or mouth and throat soreness. Do not give aspirin. Fluids such as water, ice chips, fruit ices, or cool gelatin can help relieve a sore mouth or throat. Avoid giving your child acidic, hot, or spicy foods that may irritate a sore mouth.

Prevention Encourage your child to wash his hands after going to the bathroom and blowing his nose and before and after eating. If changing the diaper of your child with the virus, make sure to wash your hands afterward. Also, wash your child's towels and sheets.

Complications A child can become dehydrated from inadequate fluid intake due to mouth pain. Inflammation of the brain (encephalitis) and membranes covering the brain and spinal cord (meningitis) can occur.

Hepatitis, Viral

Cause This inflammation of the liver is usually caused by infection with one of three hepatitis viruses: hepatitis A virus (HAV), hepatitis B virus (HBV), or hepatitis C virus (HCV). Viral hepatitis can also occur with cytomegalovirus (CMV), Epstein-Barr virus (the virus that causes infectious mononucleosis), and other viral infections.

Symptoms In the early stages of the illness, flulike symptoms are common in hepatitis A and hepatitis B and less frequent (less than 25 percent of cases) in hepatitis C. Symptoms may be very mild or may not occur in many children. These may include fever, malaise, muscle aches, loss of appetite, nausea, vomiting, and diarrhea. Jaundice (yellowing of the skin and whites of the eyes) may or may not occur in children with these infections. Tenderness over the swollen, inflamed liver (right upper abdomen) or swollen spleen (left upper abdomen) may be present. The urine may become dark ("tea-colored"), and the stools may become white or "clay-colored."

How It Spreads Hepatitis A infection occurs when a person touches or eats anything that has been contaminated with HAV-infected stool, such as water, milk, and foods (especially shellfish from sewage-contaminated waters). It spreads easily in overcrowded or unsanitary conditions and among young children who may not be suspected of having the illness because of mild or absent symptoms. Hepatitis B spreads through infected body fluids including blood, saliva, semen, vaginal fluids, breast milk, and urine. Infected infants usually have acquired the virus during the birth process from their HBV-carrier mothers. Hepatitis C usually spreads to children through transfused blood products, particularly with repeated blood product exposure as with chronic hemodialysis in a child with kidney failure. The virus may be passed from mother to infant, especially if the mother is also infected with HIV.

Incubation Period The incubation period for hepatitis A is 2 to 6 weeks; for hepatitis B, it's one to five months; for hepatitis C, it's 2 to 26 weeks.

How Long Symptoms Last Almost all previously healthy children with hepatitis A infection will recover fully within a few weeks or months. If symptoms develop with hepatitis B infection, they usually subside within six to eight weeks, but chronic infection with the virus can occur and can lead to liver damage and liver cancer. Chronic infection with the virus is particularly common (70 to 90 percent) in infants who acquire the infection from their mothers at birth and are not treated. Children with hepatitis C usually have no symptoms but are at risk for future liver damage due to chronic infection with the virus.

When to Call Your Child's Doctor Your child's doctor should be called for any child who develops jaundice or the other symptoms of hepatitis described earlier or who becomes very drowsy or confused. Also contact the doctor if your child has had contact with others with viral hepatitis or if your child will be traveling to an area where hepatitis infection is common.

How the Diagnosis Is Made The doctor suspects the diagnosis based on the child's symptoms; inflammation of the liver and infection with a specific hepatitis virus can be detected by blood tests.

Treatment Children with hepatitis who develop symptoms typically need no specific treatment other than specific supportive care—plenty of rest and adequate fluid intake to prevent dehydration. In a child with a poor appetite due to hepatitis, offering smaller, more frequent meals and fluids that are high in calories (like milk shakes) may help ensure that the child receives adequate nutrition while recovering. Some children whose symptoms are more severe may require hospitalization to receive IV fluids and other treatment.

Prevention The risk of exposure to hepatitis A can be reduced by following good hygiene—including hand washing—and avoiding crowded, unsanitary living conditions or drinking or swimming in contaminated water. Shellfish from sewage-contaminated waters should not be eaten. If someone in the household develops hepatitis, antiseptic cleansers should be used to clean any toilet, sink, potty chair, or bedpan used by that person. A hepatitis A vaccine is available, and it is recommended for children traveling to areas of the world where the risk of exposure to the virus is high. The staffs of child-care facilities, family members of infected persons, and sexual partners of someone with the infection are also candidates to receive the vaccine. Giving immune globulin within one to two weeks after exposure to the virus can prevent illness from developing in 80 to 90 percent of individuals. Hepatitis B infection from transfusions is very rare in the United States today because blood products are screened for the presence of the virus. Hepatitis B vaccine is now recommended for routine immunization of all infants and for adolescents who didn't receive the vaccine in infancy (for more information, see Chapter 16, "Immunizations"). Hepatitis B infection in infants and young children is usually the result of transmission of the disease at birth by an infected mother who carries the virus. Pregnant women should be screened for the virus, and if a woman is found to be a carrier, her infant should be given a dose of hepatitis B immune globulin (HBIG) at birth, followed by the recommended doses of the vaccine. In the United States, blood and plasma donors are screened for HCV infection. At present, there is no vaccine for the prevention of hepatitis C.

Complications Although children with HAV infection almost always recover fully without specific treatment, children with chronic HBV and HCV infections are at increased risk for the development of liver damage (cirrhosis), liver failure, and liver cancer as they get older. It is important that these individuals be followed medically for signs of these complications. New drugs, such as interferon alpha, may be helpful in some cases, and patients who develop liver failure may receive liver transplants.

Herpangina

Cause Group A coxsackieviruses are the cause.

Symptoms Usually there is a sudden onset of fever. Younger children are more prone to fever, and temperature may range as high as 105 degrees Fahrenheit. About one-fourth of children younger than five years have vomiting, and older children often complain of headache and backache. Small blisters appear in the back of the mouth and tonsil area. They enlarge over days and are usually surrounded by a ring. Most children get about five blisters, although some may get one or two, and others may get as many as fifteen.

How It Spreads It spreads through person-to-person transmission through stool and respiratory fluids.

Incubation Period The incubation period is three to six days.

How Long Symptoms Last Symptoms last for four to seven days.

When to Call Your Child's Doctor Call your child's doctor if any symptoms of herpangina occur.

How the Diagnosis Is Made The doctor will examine the child's throat.

Home Treatment Nonprescription drugs such as acetaminophen (Tylenol) can be used to reduce fever. Do **not** use aspirin. Fluids such as water, ice chips, fruit ices, or cool gelatin can help relieve a sore throat. Avoid giving the child acidic, hot, or spicy foods.

Prevention Encourage your child to wash her hands after going to the bathroom or blowing her nose and before and after eating. If changing the diaper of a child with the virus, be sure to wash your hands afterward. Also, wash your child's towels and sheets.

Complications The sudden onset of high fever can cause febrile seizures in some children. (For more information, see Epilepsy/Seizures in Chapter 32, "Health Problems in Early Childhood.") Herpangina is occasionally associated with viral meningitis, an inflammation of the membrane covering the brain and spinal cord.

Herpes Simplex

Cause The two types of herpes simplex generally cause different types of infections. Herpes simplex virus-type 1 (HSV-1) most often causes cold sores around the mouth. Herpes simplex virus-type 2 (HSV-2) usually causes genital herpes, which occur mainly in sexually active adolescents or adults.

Symptoms HSV-1: Blisters form on the lips and inside of the mouth and develop into ulcers. Gums become red and swollen, and the tongue may develop a white coating. The child may also have fever, muscle aches, difficulty eating, irritability, and swollen lymph nodes (glands) in the neck. HSV-2: Pain, tenderness, and itching in the genital area are accompanied by fever, headache, and a general ill feeling. Blisters appear on the penis in males or around the vagina in females.

How It Spreads The virus is spread by contact with sores from an infected person. HSV-1 can also be passed in the saliva (as with kissing) of an infected person; HSV-2 can be passed in the urine or genital fluid of an infected person. Infections can also be spread through the saliva or genital fluids of someone infected with the virus who has no symptoms.

Incubation Period Typically, the incubation period is 1 to 14 days; the average is 6 to 8 days.

How Long Symptoms Last Cold sores usually last up to a week. Genital ulcers usually
are most severe in the first five days. However, both infections can lay dormant and
recur months or years later, usually after
some type of stress, either emotional or
physical. This can include long exposure to
sunlight, tooth extraction, or a cold or
other infection.

When to Call Your Child's Doctor Call your
child's doctor if your child has a blister or
open sore around the mouth, fever, swollen
glands, or eating difficulties because of
mouth sores. A genital herpes infection in a
child or infant suggests that the infection
could have been transmitted by sexual abuse
(see Chapter 32, "Health Problems in Early
Childhood," for information about child
abuse). Pregnant women who have had
genital herpes should tell their doctor
before delivery.

How the Diagnosis Is Made The doctor can
do tests to identify the virus.

Treatment Your child's doctor may prescribe an antiviral drug such as acyclovir to
help shorten the course of the outbreak.

Home Treatment For cold sores, cold liquids
or frozen juice may help; avoid acidic juices
such as lemon or orange juice. Putting an
ice cube directly on the sore may also
relieve pain.

Prevention Herpes sores are contagious
until they are completely crusted over. The
saliva of someone with active sores is also
contagious. Children with cold sores should
not kiss others until the sores are fully
healed, and they should not be around anyone with immune system problems. Keep

your child's glass and utensils separate from
those of other members of the family, and
wash them thoroughly after use.

Complications In rare cases, HSV-1 can
cause meningitis, an inflammation of the
membrane covering the brain and spinal
cord. It is the most common cause of fatal
sporadic encephalitis, an inflammation of
the brain (see Encephalitis in this chapter).
A mother with genital herpes can pass on
the infection to her newborn, causing a
severe, potentially fatal infection in the
infant's central nervous system.

HIV/AIDS

For information about HIV/AIDS, refer to
Chapter 32, "Health Problems in Early
Childhood."

Impetigo

Cause This skin infection is usually caused
by *Staphylococcus aureus* or group A *Streptococcus* bacteria.

Symptoms Impetigo often appears in skin
areas already injured from a scrape, cut, or
rash. It can appear anywhere on the skin but
often attacks the area around the mouth in
children. When caused by group A *Streptococcus* it begins as tiny blisters; these eventually burst to reveal small, wet patches of red
skin that may weep fluid. Gradually, a tan or
yellow-brown crust covers the affected
area. Impetigo caused by *Staphylococcus* may
cause larger blisters containing fluid that is
first clear, then cloudy. These blisters are

less likely to burst. It is more common in hot, humid weather.

How It Spreads A child touching the infected area and then another part of the body can spread the infection. Playmates touching the infected skin can also become infected. Contact with the child's linens, towels, and clothing can also transmit the infection.

Incubation Period The incubation period lasts from a few days to several weeks. Usually, 7 to 10 days pass between the time of infection and the appearance of blisters.

How Long Symptoms Last Without treatment, most blisters go away within two weeks. If treated with an antibiotic, healing should begin within three days. A child should stay home from school or child care for at least 24 hours after antibiotic treatment has begun.

When to Call Your Child's Doctor Call your child's doctor if your child has signs of impetigo, especially if she has been exposed to someone with the infection. If your child is currently being treated, call the doctor if her skin does not begin to heal in three days. Also call the doctor if the child develops a fever or if the affected area becomes red, warm, or tender to the touch.

How the Diagnosis Is Made The doctor examines the skin or takes a culture of the infected area.

Treatment The doctor will prescribe an oral antibiotic for 7 to 10 days.

Home Treatment Wash infected areas gently with clean gauze twice a day using antisep-

tic soap. If the skin is crusted, soak it first in soapy water to remove layers of crust. To keep your child from spreading the infection to other parts of the body, cover the infected area with loose gauze and tape or a plastic bandage. Keep your child's fingernails trimmed.

Prevention Give your child a daily shower or bath. Keep injured areas clean and covered. If someone in the family has impetigo, use an antibacterial soap and make sure each person uses a separate towel. If necessary, substitute paper towels for cloth ones until the impetigo is gone. Keep the infected person's linens, towels, and clothing separate, and wash them with hot water.

Contagious Periods Sores are contagious until the child has been treated with antibiotics for longer than 24 hours.

Complications Blisters usually do not leave scars and rarely lead to complications.

Influenza (Flu)

Cause There are three types of influenza virus: Type A is usually responsible for large epidemics and is constantly changing with new strains appearing. Type B causes smaller, more localized outbreaks. Type C is less common and usually causes mild illness. Flu epidemics usually occur between November and March.

Symptoms Flu symptoms may be similar to those of the common cold, but they tend to develop quickly and are more severe. They can include fever (often sudden and high), chills, headache, muscle aches, dizziness, loss of appetite, cough, sore throat, runny nose, nausea, and weakness.

How It Spreads Flu spreads by virus-infected droplets coughed or sneezed into the air.

Incubation Period Symptoms usually appear one to four days after exposure to the virus.

How Long Symptoms Last Fever and most other symptoms subside within 5 days, but cough and weakness may persist. All symptoms are usually gone within 7 to 14 days.

When to Call Your Child's Doctor Children with mild cases usually don't need to see their doctor. Do call your child's doctor if your child has a fever of 103 degrees Fahrenheit or higher, if your child—especially your infant younger than three months—has a cough that does not get better over a three- to four-day period, or if your child is having difficulty breathing. A persistent cough, fever, increased breathing rate, or respiratory difficulty may indicate that your child has developed pneumonia as a complication of the flu.

How the Diagnosis Is Made The doctor will examine your child and listen to the lungs to determine whether any complications have developed, such as pneumonia. If pneumonia is suspected, a chest X-ray may be ordered.

Treatment Because the flu is caused by a virus, it is not treated with antibiotics unless there is a secondary bacterial infection. Some children with chronic medical conditions may require hospitalization. For a very ill child or one with other conditions that may predispose him to complications, a doctor may prescribe an antiviral medication to relieve symptoms; the medicine must be given within 48 hours of the onset of symptoms.

Home Treatment Children should rest in bed or play quietly. Give a nonaspirin medication such as acetaminophen (Tylenol) to relieve fever and aches. Do **not** give aspirin because it is associated with Reye syndrome, a rare but potentially fatal disease, especially if given to a child with influenza or chicken pox.

Prevention Try to keep your child away from crowds during an epidemic. Make sure that your child washes his hands thoroughly and doesn't pick up used tissues. The flu vaccine is not routinely recommended for children, except those with chronic heart or lung diseases (including asthma), sickle-cell anemia, diabetes, HIV, or other chronic conditions.

Contagious Periods The contagious period lasts from the day before to seven days after symptoms appear.

Complications Pneumonia (infection and inflammation of the lung), caused by the virus and/or a secondary bacterial infection, and otitis media (middle ear infection) are the most common complications. Myocarditis (an infection of the heart) and Reye syndrome are rare complications.

Kawasaki Disease

Cause The causes remain unknown, but the condition is strongly suspected to be due to an infection because (a) features of the illness include fever, rash, conjunctivitis, and swollen lymph nodes (glands); (b) it affects only infants and young children (suggesting that adults may have developed immunity); and (c) epidemics of the disease seem to occur periodically, as if a germ were being passed through the population. The disease occurs mainly in children five years and younger, most commonly in children ages 18 to 24 months. It affects boys more often than girls, and it is more prevalent among Asian children. The major threat that the disease poses for a child's health is related to its effects on the heart. The condition can cause inflammation of the coronary arteries and other blood vessels. Untreated, 20 to 25 percent of children will develop aneurysms (balloonlike enlargements) of the coronary arteries. In rare cases, this can result in the death of the child due to heart attack.

Symptoms The disease is characterized by fever, generally rising to 104 degrees Fahrenheit or more, for at least five days accompanied by (within a few days of the start of fever) several or all of the following: red, "bloodshot" eyes; redness and irritation of the mouth, tongue, and throat and red, cracked lips; a widespread red rash; swelling of the hands and feet with redness of the palms and soles; and swollen lymph nodes (glands), usually on one side of the neck. Irritability, loss of appetite, abdominal pain, diarrhea, and vomiting are also common. Peeling of the skin of the fingers, toes, and groin also frequently occurs in this phase of the illness.

How It Spreads Although it is still unknown whether the condition can be spread from person to person, siblings of a child with the disease are more likely than other children to develop it.

Incubation Period The incubation period is unknown.

How Long Symptoms Last Without treatment, the fever lasts for about 12 days. Loss of appetite and irritability may continue for two to three weeks.

When to Call Your Child's Doctor Call your child's doctor when you note persistent fever in your infant or young child, particularly if accompanied by the symptoms described earlier.

How the Diagnosis Is Made Doctors suspect the diagnosis based on fever and the other characteristic symptoms and findings on physical examination. There is no specific laboratory test for the disease, but blood tests may be helpful to support the diagnosis and rule out other causes of the symptoms. Because of the possible effects on the heart, if the diagnosis is suspected, the doctor will order an echocardiogram (ultrasound) imaging study to look for abnormalities in your child's coronary arteries.

Treatment Treatment with high-dose aspirin and intravenous immune globulin started within 10 days of the start of symptoms decreases the risk of developing coronary artery abnormalities and can also shorten the duration of fever and other symptoms. Once the fever comes down for several days, the aspirin dose is decreased and the child is continued on this for six to eight weeks to help prevent blood clots from forming in the coronary arteries. If coronary artery aneurysms are present, the child may be continued on long-term low-dose aspirin treatment.

Home Treatment Make sure your child takes adequate amounts of fluids to prevent dehydration during the initial phase of high fever, poor appetite, and sore mouth or throat. Aspirin should be given as prescribed by the doctor.

Prevention There are no known means of preventing the illness from occurring.

Contagious Periods There is no need to isolate the child from others because there is no evidence of person-to-person spread.

Complications In a few cases in which heart involvement is more severe, children may require treatment for heart failure or abnormal rhythm of the heartbeat. In all children with the condition, a follow-up echocardiogram to check for coronary artery aneurysms should be done six to eight weeks after the start of the illness. If abnormalities are present, the child should be followed closely by a cardiologist. Additional treatment with blood-thinning medications may be recommended to prevent blood clots. It is not yet known whether children who have had Kawasaki disease face a higher risk of heart attack as adults.

Lice

Cause Lice are tiny parasites that live among human hairs, draw blood from the skin, and lay eggs (called nits) on the hair shaft. The head louse, *Pediculus humanus capitus*, is the most common type that affects children, especially those in child care and school. The pubic louse, *Phthirus pubis*, mainly infects teenagers and young adults through sexual contact.

Symptoms Symptoms are itching of areas covered with hair.

How It Spreads Lice can pass from person to person on clothing, bed linens, combs, brushes, or hats.

Incubation Period Lice eggs hatch within one to two weeks after they are laid; newly hatched lice must have a blood meal within 24 hours of hatching to survive.

How Long Symptoms Last Medicated shampoos, creams, and lotions can end lice infestation immediately, but it may take five days for itching to stop.

When to Call Your Child's Doctor Call your child's doctor if your child is constantly scratching the scalp area or complains of continued itching. Check with your child's school or child-care center to see if other children have been treated recently for lice.

How the Diagnosis Is Made Look carefully on the nape of the neck or behind the ears in good light or with a magnifying glass. Head lice are about 1/10 inch, and pubic lice are smaller, 1/25 inch. They appear as small black or gray dots moving around. Nits look like white specks glued to the hair near the base of the shaft.

Home Treatment A shampoo, cream, or lotion containing permethrin (Nix) is the treatment of choice. Treatment should be repeated in 7 to 10 days. All household members need to be treated at the same time. Nits can be removed with a fine-toothed comb after a 1:1 vinegar to water rinse. Clothing and bed linens should be laundered in very hot water or dry cleaned. Brushes and combs should be discarded or coated with a louse killer for 15 minutes and then put in boiling water. Items that can't be washed can be sealed in plastic bags for two weeks to be made safe for reuse.

Prevention Your child should not share her combs, brushes, or towels or try on others' hats. If your child continues to get lice repeatedly after treatments, it's likely she is being reinfested from someone she has regular contact with or her clothing or linens still contain nits.

Lyme Disease

Cause Lyme disease is caused by the bacterium *Borrelia burgdorferi.*

Symptoms Some people have no apparent symptoms. A common, but not always present, early sign of infection is a red "bull's-eye" rash (erythema migrans), which appears as a solid red expanding rash or as a central red spot surrounded by clear skin and ringed by a red border. Flulike symptoms such as fever, fatigue, headache, achiness, and joint pain are also common. In a later stage (usually weeks to months later), the child may develop inflammation of a joint, commonly the knee. Rashes, headache, fatigue, enlarged lymph nodes, stiffness in the joints and neck, sore throat, sensitivity of the eyes to light, a facial paralysis (usually on one side), tingling or numbness in the hands or feet, irregular heart rhythm, and a mild fever may be present. Late-stage Lyme disease can include numbness in the arms, hands, legs, or feet; arthritis, especially in the joints of the arms and legs; and neurological problems such as memory lapses or difficulty concentrating.

How It Spreads Lyme disease has been reported in 49 states but is most commonly seen in the Northeast, upper Midwest, and northern California. The bacteria are spread by the deer tick, which is about the size of a sesame or poppy seed. The tick picks up bacteria from infected animals such as mice. It attaches to humans and transmits the bacteria into the bloodstream. Deer ticks are most active in the spring through late fall.

Incubation Period Infection occurs 24 to 72 hours after the tick attaches to the skin. Symptoms usually appear within a week of infection but may develop up to 30 days after the tick bite, if they develop at all.

How Long Symptoms Last Untreated, mild early stage disease symptoms usually subside in several weeks. In some people symptoms recur months later. If treated early, most children recover fully and have no recurrence of symptoms.

When to Call Your Child's Doctor Call your child's doctor if your child was bitten by a tick and has a bull's-eye rash or other symptoms such as swollen lymph glands near the area of the tick bite, general achiness, headache, sore throat, or fever. If you find a tick on your child and remove it, call your doctor to see if he or she wants it saved for identification.

How the Diagnosis Is Made Diagnosis is made by the appearance of the bull's-eye rash. If there is no characteristic rash but there are other symptoms, the doctor may order blood tests that show the presence of antibodies to the bacteria. However, the tests may indicate only that the child has been exposed to the bacteria at some point, perhaps years ago in some cases, so positive results may not mean that the child is infected currently. In the absence of other symptoms, the doctor may not prescribe antibiotics.

Treatment For early disease, treatment consists of oral antibiotics for three to four weeks. For later-stage disease, longer courses of oral or intravenous antibiotics may be used.

Prevention Deer ticks inhabit shady, moist ground cover and cling to tall grass, brush, shrubs, and low tree branches. Lawns and gardens, especially at the edge of woods, may also harbor ticks. When entering these areas, your child should wear enclosed shoes, long-sleeved shirts, and long pants. Tuck pants into shoes. Wear light-colored clothing to see ticks more easily. Use repellents sparingly on your child and never on babies. After an outing check yourself, your child, and your pets for ticks. Wash all clothes and bathe and shampoo the child. If you find a tick, use tweezers to grasp it and pull firmly until it lets go. Call your child's doctor to see if he or she wants you to save the tick for identification (you can put it in a jar of alcohol). Although it is being tested in children, the Lyme disease vaccine available for older teens and adults has not been approved for use in children younger than 15.

Contagious Periods The disease is not spread from human to human.

Complications Most later-stage symptoms associated with Lyme disease occur because the infection went undetected and untreated in the earlier stages. It's unclear what percentage of children develop late-stage neurologic Lyme disease, but it is considered rare.

Measles (Rubeola)

Cause Measles is a respiratory infection caused by the measles virus.

Symptoms The first symptoms, which usually last three to four days, are a runny nose, eyes that are red and sensitive to light, a hacking cough, and a fever as high as 105 degrees Fahrenheit. A rash with large, flat, red or brown blotches then appears, and the other symptoms, except the cough, usually disappear. Typically, the rash starts on the forehead and spreads downward over a three-day period. The child may also develop small, red irregularly shaped spots with blue-white centers inside the cheeks, called Koplik's spots.

How It Spreads Fluid from the nose and mouth spreads in airborne droplets.

Incubation Period The incubation period is 9 to 12 days from exposure to the virus to the onset of symptoms.

How Long Symptoms Last Symptoms usually last 10 to 14 days from the onset of first symptoms. It is usually safe for children to return to school or child care 7 to 10 days after the fever and rash are gone.

When to Call Your Child's Doctor Call your child's doctor if your child has any symptoms of measles. Also call if your child is an infant or has a weakened immune system and has been exposed to measles. If your child has measles, call your child's doctor if the child's temperature goes above 103 degrees Fahrenheit. Let the doctor know if your child has an earache, because this could be a sign of a bacterial ear infection. Call if there are signs of a lung infection (pneumonia), including breathing difficulty, a cough that brings up discolored mucus, or lips or nails that are bluish. Seek emergency care if your child has a severe headache, stiff neck, seizure, severe drowsiness, or loss of consciousness.

How the Diagnosis Is Made Generally, the diagnosis is made by the history of symptoms and the characteristic findings on physical examination.

Treatment A virus causes measles; antibiotics are not helpful unless used to treat a complicating bacterial infection.

Home Treatment Nonaspirin medications such as acetaminophen (Tylenol) may be used to help bring down fever. Do **not** use aspirin because it is associated with the rare but potentially fatal Reye syndrome. Make sure your child rests and drinks fluids. Use a cool-mist vaporizer to relieve congestion and other upper respiratory symptoms; clean it every day to prevent growth of bacteria and molds in the device.

Prevention The measles vaccine is given as part of the mumps-measles-rubella (MMR) shot, given at 12 to 15 months and then again at 5 to 6 years or 11 to 12 years. The measles vaccine is not usually given to infants younger than 12 months unless there is a measles outbreak. The vaccine should not be given to pregnant women or people with weakened immune systems. People who have had a very severe allergic reaction to eggs or to the antibiotic neomycin should not take the vaccine (for more information, see Allergies in Chapter 32, "Health Problems in Early Childhood"). Infants, pregnant women, or those with a weakened immune system can be protected from infection by an injection of gamma globulin within six days of exposure.

Contagious Periods Children are contagious from one to two days before the start of symptoms until four days after the appearance of the rash.

Complications Measles can lead to croup, conjunctivitis, myocarditis (infection of the heart muscle), hepatitis, or encephalitis. Measles can also make a child more susceptible to ear infection (otitis media) or bacterial pneumonia.

Meningitis

Cause An inflammation of the meninges, the membrane covering the brain and spinal cord, meningitis can be caused by bacteria, viruses, fungi, or parasites that enter into the cerebrospinal fluid from the blood. *Streptococcus pneumoniae*, *Neisseria meningitidis*, and *Hemophilus influenzae* type B are the most common bacteria causing the infection in children. Enteroviruses are the most frequent viral cause. Bacterial infections are generally more serious than viral defects of the meninges and are potentially life-threatening.

Symptoms Symptoms may include fever, severe headache, stiff neck, nausea, vomiting, irritability, sensitivity to light, seizure, rash, bulging fontanel (soft spot on top of the head) in infant, rash or bruise marks, confusion, or coma (unconsciousness).

How It Spreads The bacteria and viruses are usually spread by contact with infected feces or nose and throat drops. Typically, the infection begins in the respiratory system, but it can begin in other parts of the body, including the heart valves, bones, ears, nose, or teeth.

Incubation Period This varies with the organism. For enteroviruses, the incubation period is 3 to 6 days; other viruses may range from 4 to 21 days. Once the infection has entered the spinal fluid, symptoms usually occur rapidly.

How Long Symptoms Last The duration of symptoms varies according to cause. Once treatment begins, fever associated with bacterial infection usually resolves in 5 to 7 days, but fever longer than 10 days occurs in 10 percent of children. Viral infections usually are milder and symptoms last several days.

When to Call Your Child's Doctor Call your child's doctor immediately if your child has any of these symptoms: persistent vomiting, severe headache, stiff neck, lethargy or confusion, rash, or fever. In infants, also look for a bulging soft spot, irritability, poor feeding, and lethargy. If your child has had contact with someone with meningitis, consult your child's doctor.

How the Diagnosis Is Made A lumbar puncture, or spinal tap, is performed to examine the spinal fluid. Blood and urine tests may also be done.

Treatment Often antibiotics and intravenous fluids are given before the organism is identified, and the child is placed in isolation in the hospital. If the cause is a virus, the antibiotics will be stopped and the child may be given a pain reliever such as acetaminophen and, in some cases, intravenous fluids. If the cause is bacterial, antibiotics will be continued for up to several weeks; corticosteroids to relieve inflammation may also be given.

Prevention The *Hemophilus influenzae* type B vaccine, given to infants beginning at two months, is 70 to 100 percent effective in protecting against this cause of meningitis. Children younger than two years and children with weakened immune systems should be vaccinated against *Streptococcus*

pneumoniae. For children exposed to meningitis caused by certain bacteria, the doctor may prescribe the antibiotic rifampin to prevent infection.

Complications Most children completely recover from viral meningitis. Severe cases can result in seizures and intellectual, motor, hearing, visual, and psychiatric problems. In bacterial infections, the mortality rate in infants (after the newborn period) and children is 1 to 8 percent. Significant neurological and developmental problems occur in 10 to 20 percent of patients surviving the infection, including hearing loss, mental retardation, seizures, delay in speaking, visual impairment, and behavioral problems.

Molluscum Contagiosum

Cause This infection is caused by a harmless common strain of poxvirus (usually Type I).

Symptoms Small (two to five millimeters), dome-shaped skin bumps that are flesh-colored, smooth, and sometimes shiny in appearance occur with this infection. The lesions are harmless, involve only the skin, and resemble warts (but are not true warts). The lesions tend to occur most commonly in school-aged children and are generally located in small clusters (10 lesions or fewer) on one part of the body, usually on the face, neck, hands, or lower legs. They do not cause discomfort, except for mild itching. Occasionally, the lesions can be spread to other parts of the body by scratching (autoinoculation), and they may look cosmetically unappealing, especially if located on the face or neck. They sometimes also spread on the bodies of children with eczema or immune system problems.

Incubation Period The incubation period is approximately four to eight weeks.

How Long Symptoms Last The symptoms typically last six months to a year, sometimes longer, but usually remain in one area of a child's body.

When to Call Your Child's Doctor If the bumps look like they are spreading rapidly and look hot, red, painful, or oozing (rarely, they can become infected by bacteria if scratched or picked at), call your child's doctor.

How the Diagnosis Is Made Diagnosis is made by the typical appearance of the skin lesions.

Treatment The lesions disappear without treatment, but most of the time this takes about six months to a year. Sometimes treatment is recommended with chemicals or surgery (by scraping, laser, or cautery), which might leave slight scarring but will remove the lesions and could prevent spreading in some cases. Your child's doctor can help you to determine the best treatment option for your child.

Home Treatment There is no home treatment to make molluscum disappear faster. Keep your child from scratching or picking at the bumps (putting a plastic bandage over them may be helpful), and keep your child's nails trimmed and short. This will help keep the bumps from spreading or getting infected. For itching, a dose of oral diphenhydramine can be given as needed.

Contagious Periods Molluscum is considered only mildly contagious to others. A child with molluscum should not be kept out of child care or school.

Mononucleosis, Infectious

Cause More than 90 percent of infectious mononucleosis cases are caused by Epstein-Barr virus (EBV), a herpes virus; 5 to 10 percent are caused by other viruses such as cytomegalovirus, adenovirus, viral hepatitis, HIV, and possibly rubella virus, as well as *Toxoplasma gondii*, a protozoan. Studies have shown that most people are infected with EBV at some point in their lives and most develop no symptoms.

Symptoms The classic signs are fatigue, fever, sore throat, swollen lymph nodes or glands (usually in the neck, armpit, and throat), loss of appetite, enlarged spleen (the organ in the abdomen that functions as a blood filter and antibody producer) in 50 percent of cases and enlarged liver in 10 percent. Nausea, jaundice, headache, chest pain, and difficulty breathing also may be present. A widespread pink rash may also occur, especially in children who have been treated with the antibiotics ampicillin or amoxicillin; the reason for this is unknown. Younger children may have no symptoms or nonspecific symptoms like fever, fatigue, or loss of appetite.

How It Spreads It spreads through close contact with the saliva of an infected person, as with kissing.

Incubation Period The incubation period is 30 to 50 days.

How Long Symptoms Last Symptoms typically last two to four weeks.

When to Call Your Child's Doctor Call your child's doctor if there is a combination of fatigue, fever, sore throat, and enlarged lymph nodes.

How the Diagnosis Is Made Your child's doctor will examine your child, ask about the history of symptoms, and possibly do a blood test to check for EBV infection.

Treatment There are no specific antiviral treatments for this infection. Steroids are sometimes used to treat certain complications, such as the swallowing difficulty that occurs if the tonsils become extremely enlarged with the infection.

Home Treatment Bed rest and taking an antifever/pain relief medication such as acetaminophen (Tylenol) may help relieve symptoms. Do **not** give a child aspirin because it is associated with the rare but potentially fatal Reye syndrome. As soon as the child feels better, he can begin to resume ordinary activities. Because of the possibility of rupturing an enlarged spleen, your child should be cleared by the doctor before resuming any contact sports.

Prevention There is no vaccine against EBV. A child with mononucleosis should stay at home until symptoms subside enough to permit him to resume normal activities, but isolation and special precautions are not necessary.

Contagious Periods The length of the contagious period is uncertain, but people who are infected can probably pass on the infection for at least a few months after the symptoms have subsided.

Complications Possible rupture of the spleen is a concern, but this occurs in less than 0.2 percent of cases. Blood disorders such as hemolytic anemia (lowered number of red blood cells), inflammation of the heart muscle (myocarditis), involvement of the central nervous system (meningitis and encephalitis), and a paralyzing disorder called Guillian-Barrè syndrome are rare complications.

Mumps

Cause Mumps is caused by the mumps virus.

Symptoms Symptoms include pain and swelling of one or both of the parotid salivary glands, which produce saliva for the mouth, found toward the back of each cheek between the ear and jaw. The swelling usually peaks in one to three days and pushes the earlobes up and outward. The child will find it painful to swallow, drink, and eat. In some but not all cases, there may be a mild fever, headache, and loss of appetite. Other groups of salivary glands may also be swollen. In about 25 to 30 percent of cases, the symptoms are so mild that no one suspects the infection. The infection occurs more often in late winter or spring; however, the number of cases has dropped dramatically with the use of the mumps vaccine.

How It Spreads It spreads by contact with infected airborne respiratory secretion droplets, saliva, and possibly urine.

Incubation Period The incubation period is 14 to 24 days, with a peak at 17 to 18 days.

How Long Symptoms Last Symptoms usually last 10 to 12 days. It takes about a week for swelling in the parotid gland to go down.

When to Call Your Child's Doctor Possible parotid gland swelling should be discussed with your child's doctor in all cases—causes other than mumps may need to be considered. Also call your child's doctor if there are signs of complications, such as swollen testicles in a boy or abdominal pain. Call immediately if your child has any of the following symptoms: severe headache, stiff neck, seizures, extreme lethargy, or loss of consciousness.

How the Diagnosis Is Made Your child's doctor will examine your child and ask about the history of symptoms. A blood test can be done to specifically diagnose the disease if there is concern that some other condition is causing the parotid swelling.

Treatment There's no specific antiviral treatment for the mumps.

Home Treatment Acetaminophen (Tylenol) can be used to reduce fever and relieve pain. Do **not** use aspirin because it is associated with the rare but potentially fatal Reye syndrome. Warm or cold packs—whichever feels better—on the swollen parotid can also relieve pain. Serve a soft, bland diet that doesn't require chewing and doesn't include tart or acidic fruit juices that can make the pain worse. Make sure your child drinks plenty of fluids.

Prevention The mumps vaccine is generally given as part of the mumps-measles-rubella (MMR) immunization at 12 to 15 months and then again at 4 to 6 years or 11 to 12 years. It should not be given to pregnant women or those with cancer or weakened immune systems.

Contagious Periods Children may be contagious for up to nine days after the start of parotid swelling.

Complications About 10 percent of patients develop a mild form of meningitis, an infection of the brain and spinal cord covering. About 1 in 6,000 patients develop encephalitis, an infection of the brain itself, which is potentially life-threatening. Although it rarely occurs in preadolescent boys, one or both testicles may become very swollen. The pancreas may also become swollen and inflamed. Other rare complications include a swollen thyroid, infection of the heart muscle, deafness, visual impairment, and arthritis.

Osteomyelitis

Cause An infection of the bone and joints, osteomyelitis is usually caused by bacteria or sometimes a fungus. The bacterium *Staphylococcus aureus* is the most common cause; group A and group B *Streptococcus* and *Hemophilus influenzae* type B are also common causes. *Salmonella* bacteria can also invade the bone, especially in children with sickle-cell anemia.

Symptoms The area over the bone may become sore and swollen, and movement is painful. Most children have a fever, but symptoms may be harder to detect in newborns who may not appear ill and often do not have a fever. Pain usually worsens with movement and isn't relieved by resting, applying heat, or taking pain relievers.

How It Spreads The infection can be spread through the blood, by a penetrating injury (such as a broken bone that pierces through the skin or a nail or other contaminated object that penetrates the bone), or by an invasive surgical procedure. A sinus, tooth, or gum infection can sometimes spread to the surrounding jawbone. Frequently no source or cause of the infection can be found.

Incubation Period The incubation period depends on the organism and source of infection.

How Long Symptoms Last Once antibiotics are begun, symptoms generally subside within five to seven days.

When to Call Your Child's Doctor Call your child's doctor if your child has joint or bone pain with or without fever, if the area is red and swollen, or if your child resists moving a limb. If your child has an accident that involves a wound and possibly a broken bone, seek medical attention immediately.

How the Diagnosis Is Made In addition to performing a physical examination and taking a symptom history, your child's doctor may order a blood culture, other blood tests, and imaging studies such as an X-ray, ultrasound, magnetic resonance imaging (MRI), or bone scan to help make the diagnosis. The doctor may withdraw fluid from the infected area with a needle to culture

(grow) and identify the germ causing the infection.

Treatment Antibiotics, which may be begun intravenously, are usually given for a minimum of 10 to 14 days and may be required for up to four to six weeks. In some cases, especially for hip joint infections or when a foreign object is involved, surgery may be needed to help clear the infection. Your child will need bed rest, and an infected limb may be kept in a splint or cast; after several days, physical therapy may be required to prevent loss of normal motion of the limb or joint.

Prevention Prompt and appropriate treatment of infections that start in other parts of the body or of an accident involving a penetrating wound or bone break can help to prevent bone infection from occurring. Children who have artificial limbs or who have had bone surgery should be monitored closely for signs of infection.

Complications With prompt diagnosis and treatment, the outlook for complete recovery is excellent. Untreated, the infection can cause permanent disability, particularly in growing children. Infection involving the hip joint causes permanent damage to the joint in one-fourth to one-half of patients. A recurrence of the infection or development of a chronic infection of bone after treatment occurs in fewer than 10 percent of patients.

Pinworms

Cause A parasite, the worm *Enterobius vermicularis*, which measures about one-half inch in length, is the cause. The infection is also called "seatworm infection" or "threadworm infection."

Symptoms The child may have no symptoms. The most common symptom is itching around the anus, which is usually worse at night and caused by worms migrating to the area around the anus to lay their eggs.

How It Spreads The child ingests microscopic pinworm eggs. The eggs pass into the digestive system, hatch in the small intestine, move to the large intestine, and attach to the bowel wall. Two to four weeks later, adult females migrate to the area around the anus to lay eggs. If the child scratches the itchy anal area, the eggs are transferred to fingers and then onto other surfaces, including bed linens, towels, clothing (especially underwear and pajamas), toilets and bathroom fixtures, drinking glasses and eating utensils, toys, sandboxes, and food. Pinworm eggs are able to live on a surface for two to three weeks. In girls, pinworms may also spread to the vagina.

Incubation Period After the eggs are ingested, it takes two to four weeks for itching around the anus to begin.

How Long Symptoms Last One dose of medication will usually cure the infection and stop the itching within a few days.

When to Call Your Child's Doctor Call your child's doctor if your child complains of an itchy rectum or always seems to be scratching the anal-genital area. Also ask the doctor about a possible pinworm infection if your child has trouble sleeping.

How the Diagnosis Is Made If your child's symptoms lead your child's doctor to suspect a pinworm infection, he or she may ask you to place a sticky piece of tape against the child's anus when the child wakes up in the morning. The eggs will stick to the tape and can be seen under a microscope.

Treatment The medication albendazole, mebendazole, or pyrantel pamoate is given in one dose and then repeated two weeks later. Your child's doctor may recommend that everyone in the family be treated.

Prevention Remind your child to wash her hands after using the toilet and before eating. Make sure your child bathes regularly and changes her underwear every day.

Complications Pinworms are essentially harmless, but it is common for children, especially those in institutions, to become reinfected again and again.

Pneumonia

Cause Pneumonia is a general term referring to an infection of the lungs caused by viruses, bacteria, fungi, and parasites. In otherwise healthy children, viral pneumonia is most common. Viruses causing pneumonia include respiratory syncytial virus (RSV), parainfluenza, influenza, and adenoviruses. Among bacteria, *Streptococcus pneumoniae*, *Streptococcus pyogenes* (group A *Streptococcus*), and *Staphylococcus aureus* are the most common causes. Since the introduction of the Hib vaccine, *Hemophilus influenzae* type B is less often a cause. The sexually transmitted bacterium *Chlamydia trachomatis* can be passed on from the mother to the baby during delivery, leading to pneumonia. The microbe *Mycoplasma pneumoniae* also accounts for many cases of pneumonia, especially in older children and adolescents. In parts of California and the Southwest, the fungus *Coccidioides immitis*, found in the soil, can also cause the infection.

Symptoms Symptoms vary depending on the child's age and the cause of infection. They may include fever; chills; cough; unusually rapid breathing; making a "grunting" or wheezing sound with breathing; labored breathing that makes a child's chest wall skin suck in between the ribs and the nostrils flare; vomiting; chest pain; abdominal pain; decreased activity; loss of appetite or poor feeding; and bluish lips, tongue, and fingernails.

How It Spreads The viruses and bacteria are usually spread by nose and throat droplets passed along by coughing, sneezing, or coming in contact with the germ on utensils or used tissues. Although the person with the germ may not have pneumonia, the germ can cause pneumonia when passed on to the child.

Incubation Period The incubation period depends on the organism. Incubation for RSV is four to six days; influenza is one to four days; mycoplasma is one to three weeks.

How Long Symptoms Last With antibiotics, symptoms of most bacterial pneumonia will subside within the first 24 to 48 hours, although it may take several weeks before the lungs return to normal. Symptoms of viral pneumonia may last several days longer. With antibiotics, symptoms of mycoplasma pneumonia will improve over four to five days.

When to Call Your Child's Doctor Call your child's doctor if your child has any signs or symptoms of pneumonia, especially if he is breathing faster than usual, has a cough that is getting worse, has a fever of 101 to 102 degrees Fahrenheit or higher, or has signs of respiratory distress. Take your child to the emergency room if he is making a grunting sound when breathing; is struggling or gasping to breathe; has a bluish color of the lips, tongue, and fingernails; is lethargic or unresponsive; or pauses in breathing for longer than 15 seconds. Call your child's doctor if your child is being treated for pneumonia and symptoms have not improved within 48 to 72 hours.

How the Diagnosis Is Made Your child's doctor will ask about symptoms and listen to your child's chest with a stethoscope to hear where and how breathing is impaired; he or she may order a chest X-ray. The doctor may also take a blood test and a sample of mucus produced by coughing to see what organism is causing the infection.

Treatment In severe cases the child may be hospitalized. Bacterial or mycoplasma pneumonia is treated with antibiotics; the type used depends on the germ. Antibiotics are ineffective against viral pneumonia, and most patients recover with supportive care such as fluids, rest, and, if necessary, extra oxygen. If diagnosed within 48 hours of the infection, viral pneumonia may be treated in some cases with antiviral medication to reduce symptoms.

Home Treatment Use a cool-mist humidifier to increase air moisture. Encourage your child to drink fluids, especially with a fever. Ask your child's doctor before using cough suppressant medications because they can interfere with clearing mucus from the lungs, and this may be harmful in some cases of pneumonia.

Prevention Children younger than two years, those with weakened immune systems, and other high-risk children should be vaccinated against *Streptococcus pneumoniae*. The influenza vaccine is also recommended for high-risk children, including those with chronic lung or heart conditions that can make them more likely to develop pneumonia if they are infected with the virus. Pertussis (whooping cough), which can also lead to pneumonia, is the "P" part of the routine DTaP vaccine. The *Hemophilus influenzae* type B vaccine, given to infants beginning at two months, is 70 to 100 percent effective in protecting against infection with this germ. If someone in your house has pneumonia or a respiratory infection that could lead to pneumonia, keep your child away and practice good hygiene, keeping eating utensils separate and washing hands frequently.

Contagious Periods The contagious period depends on the organism.

Complications The mortality rate for children with bacterial pneumonia is less than 1 percent with antibiotic treatment. Almost all children with viral pneumonia recover without treatment, although RSV infections can be life-threatening, especially in infants younger than six weeks or those with heart or lung problems or a weakened immune system.

Rabies

Cause The rabies virus causes an infection of the nervous system. It is usually transmitted by an animal bite. Human cases are extremely rare in the United States; most years, there are no reported cases.

Symptoms The first stage usually lasts 2 to 10 days. Symptoms include fever, headache, muscle aches, loss of appetite, nausea, vomiting, sore throat, cough, and fatigue. There may be a tingling or twitching sensation around the area of the bite. The second stage, lasting 2 to 21 days, begins with a fever as high as 105 degrees Fahrenheit and any of the following: irritability; excessive movement or agitation; confusion; hallucinations; aggressiveness; muscle spasm; seizures; weakness or paralysis; extreme sensitivity to light, sounds, or touch; increased saliva or tears; and an inability to speak as vocal cords become paralyzed. In the last phases, there may be double vision, abnormal movements of the muscles that control breathing, and difficulty swallowing. Swallowing problems and increased saliva lead to foaming at the mouth.

How It Spreads The rabies virus is carried in the saliva of infected animals and is usually transmitted to humans through an animal bite. In rare cases, it can be spread when an infected animal's saliva touches mucous membranes, like the mouth or eyelids, or comes in contact with a cut or broken skin. In the United States the most common carriers are bats, raccoons, skunks, and foxes; cases have been reported with wolves, coyotes, bobcats, and ferrets as carriers. Animals not expected to carry rabies include small rodents, rabbits, and hares. In Central and South America, dogs are the main carriers.

Incubation Period The incubation period is usually 20 to 180 days, with the peak at 30 to 60 days.

How Long Symptoms Last Recovery is rare in humans who have developed symptoms.

When to Call Your Child's Doctor Call your child's doctor immediately if your child has any signs or symptoms of rabies, especially if he has been bitten recently by an animal. Call the doctor as well if your child has been bitten by an animal or has been exposed to a cat, dog, bat, or other animal that might have rabies. Also, call if you are planning a trip abroad where you might come in contact with infected animals.

How the Diagnosis Is Made The doctor will ask about recent animal exposure and look for symptoms.

Treatment There is no specific effective treatment once symptoms have developed. The person receives supportive care in an intensive care setting. Only a few individuals who have developed the disease have survived.

Prevention If your child is bitten by an animal, wash the area of the bite thoroughly with soap and water for 10 minutes and call your child's doctor, who will clean the wound thoroughly and check to make sure tetanus shots are up to date. You may also call the local animal control authorities to help find the animal that caused the bite. If the doctor decides to treat your child to prevent rabies, the treatment will involve shots of human diploid cell vaccine and human rabies immune globulin into a muscle, which should begin the day the child was bitten to be most effective. Part of human rabies immune globulin is usually injected near the bite area. Warn your child not to touch or feed stray animals, even dogs or cats. Report any stray animals to local health or animal control authorities, especially if they are acting strangely.

Reye Syndrome

Cause Reye syndrome is not caused directly by an infection but is the result of an infection-related injury to liver and brain cells. Nearly all cases are associated with a viral infection such as the chicken pox, flu, or an upper respiratory infection. The use of salicylates like aspirin to treat these infections appears to be linked to Reye syndrome.

Symptoms Symptoms are usually preceded by a viral illness and include nausea, vomiting, lethargy, confusion, and rapid breathing. In later stages, the child becomes comatose with dilated pupils. The liver may be enlarged, but there is no jaundice or fever.

How It Spreads The viruses that can lead to Reye syndrome are contagious, but the disorder itself is not.

Incubation Period Symptoms usually develop 1 to 14 days after viral infection, but they may begin as late as two months after the infection.

How Long Symptoms Last In mild cases, symptoms may disappear rapidly, but in the rarer severe cases, they can progress to death within hours. Progression of symptoms can also stop at any stage, with complete recovery in 5 to 10 days.

When to Call Your Child's Doctor Call your child's doctor immediately if, following a viral illness, your child shows symptoms of nausea, vomiting, or behavioral changes.

How the Diagnosis Is Made There is no single diagnostic test, but your child's doctor will check liver function with blood tests, and he or she may order a CT scan or MRI if he or she suspects brain swelling. A spinal tap (lumbar puncture) may be performed to rule out other conditions affecting brain function.

Treatment A child who is severely ill will be closely monitored in the intensive care unit, where the focus is on maintaining proper fluid balance and support of heart and lung function until problems in the brain and liver subside.

Prevention Aspirin and other salicylate-containing drugs should not be used in the treatment of chicken pox, flu, and other viral illnesses. Aspirin is not recommended to treat any routine illness in children younger than 12.

Contagious Periods The disease itself is not contagious. It occurs more frequently when viral diseases are more prevalent such as in the winter or following an outbreak of chicken pox or influenza B.

Complications Reye syndrome is still not well understood, but its incidence has fallen dramatically since the condition was first recognized in the 1960s, perhaps due to the decreased use of aspirin to treat symptoms of viral illnesses in children. Earlier diagnosis and treatment have reduced the mortality rate to about 20 to 30 percent. Children who progress to the late stages of the syndrome often have neurological problems.

Rheumatic Fever

Cause The features of rheumatic fever include inflammation of the joints, heart, and heart valves after an infection with group A *Streptococcus* bacteria. The condition is triggered by a strep infection in the throat that occurs one to three weeks prior to the onset of the child's rheumatic fever symptoms. The exact reason rheumatic fever develops is not completely understood. The condition is most common among children 5 to 15 years of age.

Symptoms Joint pain, fever, and fatigue are the most common first symptoms . One or more joints, particularly wrists, elbows, knees, or ankles, may become painful, red, warm, and swollen. Heart inflammation (carditis) may start at the same time as the joint pain, but there may be no symptoms of this at first. The doctor may hear a heart murmur (abnormal heart sound) through a stethoscope. The heart may beat rapidly, and the sac around the heart may become inflamed, causing chest pain. Heart failure may develop, the symptoms of which can include shortness of breath, nausea, vomiting, stomachache, and hacking cough. In some cases the child may also develop abnormal involuntary body movements, a rash, and painless bumps under the skin, usually on the knees, elbows, and spine.

How It Spreads Strep infections are contagious, but rheumatic fever is not.

Incubation Period Onset of symptoms is usually one to three weeks after a group A strep infection.

How Long Symptoms Last Symptoms usually last one to three months.

When to Call Your Child's Doctor Call your child's doctor if your child develops pain or swelling of the joints with fever.

How the Diagnosis Is Made No single lab test can confirm the diagnosis. The doctor will look for evidence of a previous streptococcal infection, usually by taking a throat culture and performing blood tests. Your child may also have several heart tests, including an electrocardiogram (a recording of the heart's electrical activity), a chest X-ray, and an echocardiogram (an image of the structures in the heart produced by ultrasound waves).

Treatment Antibiotics may be given to eradicate any remaining strep bacteria and prevent subsequent infections with the bacteria; aspirin is usually prescribed to relieve joint pain and inflammation. If the child has heart failure, your child's doctor may prescribe diuretics to reduce fluid retention.

Home Treatment Children with severe heart involvement may require bed rest for several weeks.

Prevention Treatment with antibiotics by one week after the start of strep symptoms prevents the development of rheumatic fever. If your child has had rheumatic fever, your child's doctor will also prescribe antibiotics to prevent strep infections, which can trigger further attacks.

Complications The heart valves may become permanently damaged, particularly if repeated attacks are not prevented, which can lead to chronic heart failure. Surgical replacement of damaged heart valves is necessary in some cases.

Ringworm (Tinea)

Cause Ringworm is not caused by a worm. It is a fungal infection caused by fungi called dermatophytes that can live on the dead tissue on the skin surface and on any structures that grow from the skin such as hair or nails. Three groups of fungi, *Trichophyton*, *Epidermophyton*, and *Microsporum*, are responsible for the various types of ringworm. One species, *Trichophyton tonsurans*, causes 90 percent of scalp ringworm in the United States.

Symptoms The infection starts as a round, reddish sore almost anywhere on the child's body. As the fungus grows, it spreads outward in all directions, causing the spot to become larger. The center of the sore usually heals, resulting in a reddish ring surrounding a clear area. The sore is often scaly and may be somewhat itchy. If ringworm is on the scalp, it invades the hair shafts, causing hair to break off, usually near the roots. The child develops bald patches that are usually circular. An area of the scalp may become inflamed, swollen, and red, oozing pus-like fluid; this is called a kerion. If the kerion is left untreated, permanent hair loss can result. Fungal infection on other areas of the body doesn't always look like a ring. It may remain as a solid reddish area, or it may form multiple rings. The sores may become crusted. When a fungus grows on the feet and between the toes, it is called athlete's foot. When it grows in the groin area, it is called jock itch. These forms are mainly seen in teens and adults.

How It Spreads Fungi can be acquired from the soil, from animals, or from humans, either by direct contact or indirectly from hair or clothing. A child can catch ringworm by sleeping in the same bed as an infected child. Combs, brushes, barrettes, telephones, and hats can transmit the fungi. Tight braiding and other hairstyles that expose or irritate sections of the child's scalp and gels and other sticky hair products may also make it easier for the fungus to grow. Ringworm is more prevalent in warm, humid regions. A minor break in the skin from an injury can set the stage for a fungus infection.

Incubation Period The incubation period varies.

How Long Symptoms Last Symptoms usually improve within days of treatment, but medications usually need to be given for weeks to completely eradicate the fungus. If left untreated, infections can become chronic.

When to Call Your Child's Doctor Call your child's doctor if your child's hair begins to fall out, if he develops sores like those described earlier on his body or scalp, or if his scalp continues to flake despite washing with an antidandruff shampoo. Call also if your child's sores do not begin to clear up within a week of starting treatment.

How the Diagnosis Is Made The doctor may take infected hairs or scrapings of skin to the lab for identification of the fungus causing the infection.

Treatment Ringworm of the scalp usually requires an oral antifungal medication, most commonly griseofulvin, given for eight weeks, and a special shampoo containing selenium sulfide. Corticosteroids

may be used to treat kerions. For most cases of ringworm on other parts of the body, a topical antifungal medication, such as miconazole or clotrimazole, may be used. Some are available over the counter; be sure to use the type your child's doctor recommends to cure the type of ringworm your child has.

Home Treatment Bathe your child every day and gently remove scabs and crusts. Wash your hands in hot soapy water before and after touching your child's skin and before and after applying cream. Try to keep your child from picking at the sores; this could spread the fungus or cause a secondary bacterial infection. If your child has ringworm on the body, loose-fitting clothes may be more comfortable.

Prevention Keep your child's hair and skin clean and dry. Make sure your child has and uses his own comb and brush. Teach him not to share grooming items, headphones, or caps. If your cat or dog shows signs of ringworm, call the veterinarian.

Contagious Periods A child is contagious as long as he has sores on his skin; however, he does not need to be kept out of school or from routine contact with other children while he is being treated. There is no need to shave the hair or cover the head with a cap in a child with ringworm of the scalp.

Complications If untreated, infections may linger for months or years. Secondary bacterial infections, sometimes requiring antibiotic treatment, may also occur if other germs invade the broken skin caused by the fungus infection.

Roseola

Cause Two common viruses, human herpes virus type 6 and type 7, cause the infection.

Symptoms At first the child may have a mild upper respiratory illness, then develop a high fever, from 101 to 105 degrees Fahrenheit. Some children become irritable and lose their appetites. Febrile seizures (see Chapter 29, "Signs and Symptoms," for information on seizures) may occur in 5 to 10 percent of children during this period. Some may also have a runny nose, sore throat, abdominal pain, vomiting, and diarrhea. The fever lasts three to five days and then goes away abruptly. A rash appears within 12 to 24 hours after the child's temperature drops. The rash is rose-colored and begins as small, slightly raised spots on the trunk. It usually spreads to the neck, face, arms, and legs. After one to three days the rash fades.

How It Spreads Unlike most other common childhood viral infections, roseola does not seem to be spread by obviously infected children, and outbreaks are uncommon. The virus-containing respiratory fluids or saliva of someone who has no obvious symptoms may be the source of the infection.

Incubation Period The incubation period is 5 to 15 days; 10 days is average.

How Long Symptoms Last Symptoms usually last for one week.

When to Call Your Child's Doctor Seek emergency care if your child has a seizure.

How the Diagnosis Is Made Doctors usually make the diagnosis based on the appearance of the typical rash after the fever is gone.

Treatment There is no treatment for roseola.

Home Treatment Acetaminophen (Tylenol) may be used to reduce the fever if your child is uncomfortable. Do **not** use aspirin because of the risk of the rare but potentially fatal Reye syndrome. Dress the child in lightweight clothing, and encourage him to drink fluids.

Prevention There is no known way to prevent roseola.

Complications Most children recover without any problems.

Rubella (German or Three-Day Measles)

Cause The cause is infection with the rubella virus.

Symptoms Lymph nodes or glands become swollen behind the ears and in the neck. About 24 hours later, a rash appears, beginning on the face and spreading quickly to the rest of the body. As the rash spreads downward, it usually clears on the face. In addition to discrete spots, there may be large areas of flushing. The rash may cause mild itching. The child may also have a fever (101 to 102 degrees Fahrenheit) for one to three days, a runny or stuffy nose, and mild inflammation of the lining of the eyelids. Some infected people don't develop any symptoms.

How It Spreads The virus is spread via droplets from an infected person's nose and throat fluids.

Incubation Period The incubation period is 14 to 21 days.

How Long Symptoms Last The rash and fever are usually gone in three days.

When to Call Your Child's Doctor Call your child's doctor if your child's symptoms seem more severe than the mild symptoms described previously. If you are pregnant and exposed to rubella, call your obstetrician immediately.

How the Diagnosis Is Made A blood test or growing the virus in a lab can confirm the diagnosis, although this is generally not necessary.

Treatment There is no specific treatment.

Home Treatment To relieve discomfort and fever you can give acetaminophen (Tylenol). Do **not** give aspirin because of the association with Reye syndrome. Pregnant (or possibly pregnant) women should avoid contact with a person who is infected with the rubella virus.

Prevention The rubella vaccine is usually given as part of the measles-mumps-rubella (MMR) vaccine given at 12 to 15 months of age. A second shot is given at 4 to 6 or 11 to 12 years of age. Pregnant women should not be given rubella virus vaccine, and women should not become pregnant for three months after being vaccinated.

Contagious Periods The contagious period is from one week before the rash appears until seven to eight days after it disappears.

Complications If a pregnant woman becomes infected with the rubella virus, it can cause a miscarriage or stillbirth. If the fetus survives, the child may have retarded growth, retarded mental development, deafness, and birth defects of the heart, eyes, or brain. An estimated 10 percent of women of childbearing age are still susceptible to rubella infection.

Scabies

Cause Scabies is caused by an infestation by the female mite *Sarcoptes scabiei*, which is about 1/50 inch long with four pairs of legs. The mite burrows in the top layer of human skin.

Symptoms Symptoms include itching, which may be worse at night or after a hot bath. The infection begins as small itchy blisters that break when the child scratches them. The itchy skin may become thick, scaly, and crisscrossed with scratch marks. The mite burrows can often be seen as short, dark, wavy lines on the skin surface. Arms and hands are most commonly affected, especially the webs between fingers, the inner part of the wrists, and the folds under the arms. If the infestation is severe, other body parts may be affected, including elbows, genitals, navel, and buttocks.

How It Spreads It spreads from person to person by close physical contact and by sharing the same bed, linens, clothing, or towels.

Incubation Period It takes four to five weeks for a mite to complete egg laying. The eggs hatch in three to five days. The mites are mature in two to three weeks.

How Long Symptoms Last Once treated, itching may persist for several days and sometimes weeks.

When to Call Your Child's Doctor Call your child's doctor if your child has an itch that doesn't go away, especially if it is worse at night and seems to particularly involve the wrists or webbed part of the fingers.

How the Diagnosis Is Made The doctor may take skin scrapings, which are examined under a microscope for signs of scabies.

Treatment A permethrin cream is applied from the neck down and left on the skin 10 to 12 hours. If necessary, it may be reapplied in one to two weeks. The entire family should be treated.

Home Treatment All clothing, towels, and bed linens need to be washed in hot water, and the child's toys must be washed.

Prevention Practice good hygiene: bathing or showering regularly, washing hands frequently, and wearing clean clothing. Encourage your child not to share clothes with friends.

Complications In some cases, a child may develop a secondary bacterial infection due to breakdown of the skin from scratching. This requires treatment with antibiotics.

Scarlet Fever

Cause It is caused by group A *Streptococcal* bacteria that produce a toxin that causes a rash in some but not all people.

Symptoms Onset of symptoms is rapid, with fever, chills, vomiting, headache, sore throat, and swollen glands in the neck. The tonsils and back of the throat may be covered with a whitish coating or appear red, swollen, and dotted with whitish or yellowish specks of pus. The tongue may have a whitish or yellowish coating; this sloughs

off, and the tongue turns deep red. The rash, tiny red bumps ("sandpaper" rash) that may be itchy, appears 12 to 48 hours later, usually appearing first on underarms, groin, and neck but then spreading to the rest of the body within 24 hours. Forehead and cheeks appear flushed, and the area around the mouth is pale. The fever may rise suddenly and peak at 103 to 104 degrees Fahrenheit on the second day.

How It Spreads Strep bacteria can be passed through contact with nose and throat fluids of someone who is infected or by contact with the infected skin of someone with strep impetigo.

Incubation Period The incubation period is one to seven days, with an average of three days.

How Long Symptoms Last Without treatment, temperature returns to normal within five to seven days; after penicillin treatment, fever is usually gone within 12 to 24 hours. The rash begins to flake and peel off toward the end of the first week and may last as long as six weeks.

When to Call Your Child's Doctor Call if your child suddenly develops a rash, especially if your child also has a fever, sore throat, or swollen glands.

How the Diagnosis Is Made The doctor may take a swab of throat secretions to test for the *Strep* bacteria, but often the diagnosis is made on the basis of the rash and accompanying symptoms.

Treatment The antibiotic penicillin is given for 10 days.

Home Treatment Soft food or a liquid diet may help a child with a sore throat. Children who are old enough can gargle with warm saltwater. Use a cool-mist vaporizer to add moisture to the air.

Prevention If your child is infected, keep her drinking glasses and eating utensils separate from the rest of the family's, and wash them thoroughly in hot soapy water. Wash your own hands frequently. Keep your child home at least 24 hours after beginning antibiotic treatment and until there has been no fever for 24 hours. Children with strep infections are no longer contagious after taking antibiotics for more than 24 hours.

Complications If scarlet fever is left untreated or inadequately treated with antibiotics, the child can develop abscesses on or around the tonsils or in nearby lymph glands. The bacteria can also cause ear or sinus infections. Untreated, the infection can also lead to rheumatic fever (see Rheumatic Fever in this chapter), which can cause an inflammation of the joints and permanently damage the heart.

Sinusitis

Cause Viruses that cause colds also can cause inflammation of the sinuses, the air spaces found in the facial bones around the nose. Acute bacterial infections of the sinuses around the nose are caused by the same germs that cause middle ear infections: *Streptococcus pneumoniae*, *Moraxella catarrhalis*, and *Hemophilus influenzae*. In chronic sinusitis, *Staphylococcus aureus* or multiple types of bacteria may be involved.

Symptoms Cough and nasal discharge are the most common symptoms of acute sinusitis. The cough occurs during daytime and often is worse when lying down for naps or at bedtime. Nasal discharge may be clear or cloudy. The child may have a sore throat as a result of postnasal drip, and the child may sniff, snort, or snore to clear the drainage. Viral upper respiratory infections usually clear up within 10 to 14 days. If symptoms persist without improvement for more than 10 to 14 days, bacterial sinusitis should be suspected. A more severe but less common form of sinusitis can occur in which the child develops a fever higher than 101 degrees Fahrenheit, a cloudy nasal discharge, headache, and eye swelling. In chronic sinusitis, cough, nasal discharge, and bad breath last for more than 30 days.

How It Spreads Bacteria and viruses are passed via throat and nose droplets.

Incubation Period The incubation period varies.

How Long Symptoms Last Viral infections resolve on their own within 10 to 14 days. With bacterial infections, once the child begins antibiotics, symptoms will usually subside within several days, but it may take several weeks for symptoms to completely disappear.

When to Call Your Child's Doctor Call your child's doctor if your child has a "cold" that lasts more than 10 to 14 days, if there are any symptoms of "allergies" that don't clear up with the usual allergy treatments, if she complains about a headache or pressure behind her cheeks or forehead, or if she has facial swelling.

How the Diagnosis Is Made The doctor will ask about symptoms, how long your child has had them, and where the pain and pressure is to try to distinguish whether the symptoms are caused by nasal allergies or viral or bacterial infection of the sinuses. X-rays or other imaging studies are sometimes used to diagnose sinusitis.

Treatment For viral infections, there is no specific treatment. For bacterial infections, antibiotics are given for 14 to 21 days. Decongestants may improve symptoms but do not clear the infection faster. Antihistamines are not helpful and may interfere with sinus drainage because they may cause thickening of secretions.

Home Treatment Acetaminophen, ibuprofen, and/or warm compresses may help reduce facial pain. Do **not** use aspirin because of the rare but potentially fatal Reye syndrome. If the child is old enough, saline nose drops can be used to help promote drainage of secretions and reduce swelling. A cool-mist vaporizer can help keep secretions moist so that the sinuses can drain more easily.

Prevention Encourage your child to cover her nose and mouth when she coughs or sneezes and not to share food or utensils. In the winter months, use a humidifier to keep home humidity at 45 to 50 percent; this will help make sinuses less of a target for infections. Avoid exposing your child to cigarette smoke—this can irritate mucous membranes and set the stage for sinusitis.

Complications In rare cases, the infection can spread out of the sinuses into other parts of the head, invading the bones (osteomyelitis) of the skull or spreading toward the eyes, causing an abscess (collection of pus) in or near the eye (orbital cellulitis). The infection can also invade the membranes surrounding the brain causing meningitis, which can be life-threatening.

Staphylococcal (Staph) Skin Infections

Cause *Staphylococcus aureus* bacteria can live harmlessly on skin surfaces, especially around the nose, mouth, genitals, and rectum. But when skin is punctured or broken, they can enter the wound and cause infections. Abscesses are collections of pus or fluid in tissues that result from an infection commonly involving staph bacteria. Specific types of abscesses include boils, folliculitis, and sties (see Eye Redness/Discharge in Chapter 29, "Signs and Symptoms"). Staph infections may also cause scalded skin syndrome, impetigo (see Impetigo in this chapter), and cellulitis (see Cellulitis in this chapter).

Symptoms Folliculitis is an infection of the hair follicles characterized by tiny, white-headed pimples at the base of the hair shafts, sometimes with a small red area around each pimple. Abscess of a hair follicle can lead to a boil, in which the infection spreads to the skin's oil glands or deeper tissue. The area may begin to itch or become mildly painful. Then it turns red and begins to swell over the infected area; the skin becomes very tender, and a white "head" may appear. The head may break open, and the boil may begin to drain pus, blood, or an amber-colored liquid. Scalded skin syndrome, a condition most often affecting newborns and children younger than five years, is a skin infection in which staph bacteria make a toxin that may affect the skin all over the body. The child has a fever, rash, and sometimes blisters. The rash often begins around the mouth, then spreads to the trunk, arms, and legs. As the blisters burst, the top layer of the skin peels off, and the skin surface becomes red and raw like a burn.

How It Spreads Fingers can carry staph infections from one area of the body to a wound or broken skin. Staph can spread through the air, on contaminated surfaces, and from person to person.

Incubation Period The incubation period is variable, depending on the skin injury and the age and health of the child.

How Long Symptoms Last Without treatment, folliculitis can either heal within a week or progress to the development of boils. Without treatment, boils may drain the pus they contain and heal in 10 to 20 days. Scalded skin syndrome may require treatment with intravenous antibiotics and management of the raw and vulnerable skin in a manner similar to that for burns.

When to Call Your Child's Doctor Call your child's doctor if your child has an area of red, irritated, or painful skin, especially if there are whitish or yellowish pus-filled bumps or "heads," or if your child has a fever. Call immediately if your infant develops blistered or peeling skin leaving raw, reddened areas. Also speak with the doctor if skin infections seem to be passing from one family member to another.

How the Diagnosis Is Made Folliculitis, a boil, or scalded skin syndrome is usually diagnosed by simply examining the skin. For severe infections, the doctor may take a fluid sample from the infected site and send it to the lab to identify the bacteria causing the infection.

Treatment Your child's doctor may cut and drain the boil and prescribe an antibiotic. For scalded skin syndrome, your child will be treated in a hospital and will usually be given intravenous antibiotics; the skin will be treated like a burn, and your child's body fluid balance will be monitored closely.

Home Treatment For folliculitis or a boil, remind your child not to touch the infected skin. Wash the skin with an antibacterial soap, apply an antibiotic ointment, and cover the skin with a clean dressing. To help relieve pain from a boil, use warm water soaks, a heating pad, or a hot water bottle applied to the skin for about 20 minutes three to four times a day. This also helps the boil drain the pus it contains sooner.

Prevention Wash hands regularly; keep child's skin clean with a daily bath or shower. Keep body areas that have been cut or injured clean and covered. To prevent the spread of an infection your child already has, use a towel only once when you clean an infected area, then wash it in hot water.

Complications With scalded skin syndrome, recovery usually occurs without complications, but excessive fluid loss, blood mineral imbalances, pneumonia, septicemia (blood infection), and cellulitis (see Cellulitis in this chapter) may occur.

Strep Throat/Sore Throat (Pharyngitis)

Cause Sore throats are most often caused by viruses, especially adenoviruses. Group A *Streptococcus* (the germ involved in strep throat) is the most common type of bacteria that cause sore throat; however, it accounts for fewer than 15 percent of all cases of sore throat. Typical strep throat is uncommon in children younger than two years.

Symptoms Symptoms for viral and bacterial infections overlap. Viral sore throat is often gradual in onset with fever, loss of appetite, and moderate throat pain. There may be red, irritated eyes, runny nose, cough, headache, vomiting, bad breath, and stomach pain. Lymph nodes (glands) in the neck may be enlarged, and the throat may be red and inflamed; sometimes there is pus on the tonsils. Strep infection symptoms in children three years and older include headache, stomach pain, and vomiting followed by fever as high as 104 degrees Fahrenheit. Hours later, the throat may become sore; the tonsils are enlarged in about one-third of cases. Children younger than three years with strep infection usually show fever and mucous discharge from the nose; there may also be irritability and loss of appetite.

How It Spreads It spreads through nose and throat droplets from an infected person.

Incubation Period For viruses, the incubation period is variable. For strep infection, it is usually between two and five days.

How Long Symptoms Last With viral illness, the sore throat may last fewer than 24 hours or as long as five days. In untreated strep throat, fever may continue for one to four days and sore throat for about three to five days; antibiotic treatment can shorten the duration of symptoms by several days.

When to Call Your Child's Doctor Call your child's doctor if your child has a sore throat that persists for more than a day, if you see pus on your child's tonsils or the back of the throat, if your child has a fever of 101 degrees Fahrenheit or higher, or if your child has a rash.

How the Diagnosis Is Made The doctor will examine the throat and ask about symptoms. If he or she suspects a strep infection, the doctor will take a swab of the throat to test for strep.

Treatment There is no drug treatment for a sore throat caused by a viral infection. For strep throat, an antibiotic such as penicillin or amoxicillin is usually prescribed for 7 to 10 days. Treatment with antibiotics by one week after the start of strep throat symptoms prevents the development of rheumatic fever.

Home Treatment Acetaminophen or ibuprofen may help to relieve symptoms. Do **not** use aspirin because of the rare but potentially fatal Reye syndrome. Gargling with warm salt water and using a cool-mist vaporizer may also may help relieve throat pain. Cool, bland liquids are usually tolerated better than solids or hot foods. Make sure your child drinks plenty of fluids.

Prevention Teach your child good hygiene, to cover his mouth when he coughs or sneezes, and to wash his hands before meals. If your child is sick, wash his utensils and glasses separately in hot, soapy water, and be sure to wash your own hands often.

Contagious Periods A child with strep throat is not infectious to others after antibiotics are taken for 24 hours, and he can go back to child care or school after this time if he is without fever.

Complications Most viruses cause no significant complications. Occasionally a child with strep throat will develop scarlet fever, in which the bacteria produce a toxin that causes a rash (see Scarlet Fever in this chapter). Particularly if strep throat is not adequately treated with antibiotics, the child can develop abscesses in the area of the tonsils or nearby lymph glands. Untreated strep throat can also cause rheumatic fever, which can involve inflammation of the joints and permanent damage to the heart (see Rheumatic Fever in this chapter). Another complication of group A strep infection is glomerulonephritis (see Chapter 32, "Health Problems in Early Childhood," for information about kidney diseases), a kidney problem that begins two to three weeks after the symptoms of strep infection began. Group A strep bacteria can also cause sinusitis (see Sinusitis in this chapter), ear infection (see Ear Infection in this chapter), pneumonia (see Pneumonia in this chapter), and skin infection (see Impetigo in this chapter).

Swollen Glands (Lymphadenopathy or Lymphadenitis)

Cause Located throughout the body, swollen glands or lymph nodes are signs that the body is (or was recently) fighting an infection or, rarely, that the child might have an inflammatory disease such as juvenile rheumatoid arthritis or cancer that involves or has spread to the lymph node tissue. Infectious causes of swollen glands include viruses, bacteria, protozoa, rickettsiae, or fungi.

Symptoms The glands are enlarged and may feel tender or painful to the touch. Sometimes the skin over the node looks red and feels warm.

How It Spreads Typically the infection has spread from a nearby skin, ear, nose, throat, or eye infection.

Incubation Period The incubation period varies, depending on the cause of infection.

How Long Symptoms Last Usually once the infection is treated the affected nodes slowly shrink over weeks.

When to Call Your Child's Doctor Call your child's doctor if nodes are enlarged or tender, with or without other symptoms of an infection such as fever, headache, general sick feeling, fatigue, or loss of appetite. Call if nodes are the same size or getting larger 10 to 14 days after treatment.

How the Diagnosis Is Made Usually the cause is an obvious nearby infection. In some cases, a biopsy (surgically removing the enlarged node or taking a piece of it to be tested in the lab) may need to be done.

Treatment If caused by a virus, the node will generally shrink on its own. If caused by bacteria, antibiotic treatment is usually given. Surgical drainage may be required if an abscess forms.

Home Treatment Warm compresses applied to tender nodes may help relieve the pain.

Prevention Good hygiene may help prevent many of the infections that can cause swollen glands.

Other Issues Enlarged nodes that continue to increase in size, do not decrease in size over 4 to 6 weeks, or do not return to normal size within 8 to 12 weeks can be a sign of a noninfectious disease. These may include autoimmune diseases such as rheumatoid arthritis, lupus, or dermatomyositis; cancers such as lymphoma or leukemia; and a variety of other conditions.

Tetanus (Lockjaw)

Cause Tetanus is caused by a toxin released into the nerves and muscles by the bacterium *Clostridium tetani*, which is found in soil, dust, and the feces of some animals. The disease occurs very rarely in the United States, in part due to the availability and routine use of the tetanus vaccine.

Symptoms It usually begins with muscle spasms in the jaw, along with headache, restlessness, and irritability, followed by difficulty chewing and swallowing and stiffness or pain in the muscles of the neck, shoulders, or back. The muscles of the face can lock into a characteristic smile with arched eyebrows. There may be a fever and chills. Spasms spread to muscles in the stomach, back, hip, and thigh muscles.

How It Spreads Most cases in the United States develop from a puncture wound or cut from a dirty object such as a nail, splinter, or fragment of glass. Neonatal tetanus occurs after a baby is delivered in unsanitary conditions, especially if the umbilical cord cut is contaminated with the bacteria and the mother has not been immunized against tetanus.

Incubation Period The incubation period is typically 2 to 14 days, but it can be as long as months after the injury. Symptoms of neonatal tetanus typically begin 3 to 12 days after birth.

How Long Symptoms Last Recovery usually takes at least four to six weeks.

When to Call Your Child's Doctor Call your child's doctor if your child gets a wound, especially if it is a puncture wound or an animal bite, and she has not been immunized against tetanus or you are unsure when she got her last tetanus booster; if your child develops any of the symptoms of tetanus; or if you are pregnant and unsure about your tetanus immunization status.

How the Diagnosis Is Made The diagnosis is usually made based on the history of symptoms and the doctor's physical examination of the child.

Treatment Tetanus is treated in the hospital, usually in an intensive care unit. The child receives antibiotics to kill the bacteria and an antitoxin to neutralize the toxin. Medications are given to control muscle spasms and to stop abnormal nerve activity that can cause disturbances in heartbeat, blood pressure, and body temperature.

Prevention Tetanus can be prevented by receiving the recommended routine immunizations with tetanus vaccine—usually as part of the DTaP (diphtheria-tetanus-pertussis) vaccine—at 2, 4, 6, and 15 to 18 months and again at 4 to 6 years. Boosters should be given thereafter at 10-year intervals. Although cleaning a dirt- or soil-contaminated wound is not a substitute for immunization, be sure to clean all wounds.

Contagious Periods The disease is not a contagious one.

Complications Death occurs in 5 to 35 percent of cases. With intensive care treatment, fewer than 10 percent of infants with neonatal tetanus will die; without it, more than 75 percent die. In some cases, children, especially infants, will suffer brain injury, resulting in cerebral palsy, mental retardation, or behavioral difficulties.

Toxoplasmosis

Cause This is caused by the parasite *Toxoplasma gondii*, which lives in warm-blooded animals, especially cats.

Symptoms Symptoms vary according to age and response of the immune system. With congenital toxoplasmosis, when a pregnant woman is infected, there is a 10 to 90 percent chance she will pass the infection on to her child, depending on the time of infection. Babies whose mothers were infected in the first trimester tend to have the worst symptoms. Although many children born with the infection have no symptoms early in infancy, others are born prematurely, have liver or bleeding problems, or may have severe birth defects. With infection in an otherwise healthy child, the child may have no symptoms or a few swollen lymph nodes (glands), usually in the neck. There also may be a general ill feeling, fever, sore throat, headache, or rash. The symptoms may resemble those of mononucleosis (see Mononucleosis in this chapter). With infection in a child with a weakened immune system because of AIDS, cancer, or other chronic disease, the infection may involve the brain and nervous system, causing swelling of the brain (encephalitis), fever, seizures, headache, confusion, bizarre behavior, and problems with vision, speech, or movement.

How It Spreads People can get toxoplasmosis through contact with infected cat feces or eating undercooked infected meat. Fetuses can get the infection from their mothers.

Incubation Period The incubation period is four days to three weeks.

How Long Symptoms Last Most people develop mild or no symptoms, but once someone is infected, the parasite remains in the body as a latent infection permanently.

When to Call Your Child's Doctor Call your child's doctor if your child develops symptoms, especially if she has a weakened immune system due to a chronic medical problem or is being treated with immunosuppressive medications. If you are pregnant, call the obstetrician if you develop swollen glands, especially if you have been exposed to cats or have eaten undercooked meat.

How the Diagnosis Is Made Lab tests can be done to check for parasites in the blood, spinal fluid, lymph nodes, bone marrow, amniotic fluid, and placenta of a pregnant woman. The doctor may order blood tests to check for levels of antibodies, part of the body's immune reaction to the parasite. Tests such as PCR (polymerase chain reaction) can be used to identify the DNA of the parasites.

Treatment For a congenital infection, if a pregnant woman becomes infected, she will be given antiparasitic medications that will reduce the chance of passing it to her child by about 60 percent. An infected newborn will be given similar drugs for one year. For an otherwise healthy child, antiparasitic drugs will be given for four to six weeks. Children with weakened immune systems may need to be hospitalized and given medications for at least four to six weeks beyond when signs of the infection disappear. Children with AIDS may need to take antiparasitic drugs for life.

Prevention Cook meats thoroughly. Wash hands after handling meat, and wash all kitchen surfaces and utensils. Wash all fruits and vegetables. If you own a cat, wash hands after changing litter and use detergent and hot water to clean the box. If you have a sandbox, keep it covered to keep cats from using it as a litter box. If you are pregnant, eat only well-cooked meat, let someone else change the cat litter, and avoid gardening, landscaping, or other activities involving contact with areas to which cats may have access.

Complications With congenital toxoplasmosis, aside from premature birth and low birthweight, infants are also at risk for eye damage involving the retina. Some have brain and nervous system abnormalities that can result in seizures, limp muscle tone, feeding difficulties, hearing loss, and mental retardation. They may be born with an unusually small or large head (see Chapter 32, "Health Problems in Early Childhood," for more information about hydrocephalus).

Tuberculosis

Cause Tuberculosis (TB) is primarily caused by the bacterium *Mycobacterium tuberculosis*, but other related mycobacteria may cause similar symptoms.

Symptoms Initially there are no signs of disease, except a positive tuberculin skin test, which indicates the child has been infected. The infection usually resolves on its own as the child develops immunity over a 6- to 10-week period. But in some cases tuberculosis can progress and spread throughout the lungs and to other organs. Symptoms include fever, night sweats, weight loss, fatigue, loss of appetite, and cough, sometimes with blood-tinged mucus. In other cases, more often in older children and adults, the infection remains dormant, sometimes for years, and then is reactivated when the immune system is weakened.

How It Spreads TB is spread by inhaling airborne fluid droplets from an infected person who sneezes or coughs. Young children with TB rarely infect older children or adults.

Incubation Period The time between initial infection and apparent disease is variable; early signs often occur within two to six months of infection with the germ, but they may not show up for years.

How Long Symptoms Last Tuberculosis is a chronic disease that can persist for years if not treated.

When to Call Your Child's Doctor Call your child's doctor if your child has a persistent fever or cough or if your child has come in contact with someone who is known to have or who is suspected to have TB.

How the Diagnosis Is Made A skin test (PPD), involving a small injection of test material under the skin, will tell if the child has been exposed to tuberculosis. If positive, the doctor may order a chest X-ray and examination of stomach fluid to look for the bacteria in swallowed mucus coughed up from the lungs.

Treatment Generally, children with a positive skin test but no symptoms will be given one drug. Those with active infection are given several, usually over a period of months. These may include isoniazid, rifampin, pyrazinamide, streptomycin, ethambutol, and others.

Home Treatment A child with TB needs adequate rest and nutrition. You need to make sure your child takes his medications as prescribed to ensure that the bacteria are killed.

Prevention Prevention depends on avoiding contact with those (usually adults) who have active disease, testing those who are at high risk for the disease, and promptly and adequately treating those with active infections to control spread to others. A vaccine called BCG can prevent TB in some situations, but it is not routinely given in this country due to the low likelihood of contracting the disease. It is recommended for children who are at high risk of long-term, close exposure to untreated or ineffectively treated adults.

Contagious Periods Someone infected with tuberculosis is very contagious to others because tuberculosis is spread through the air, by coughing or sneezing. TB bacteria can remain airborne for a period of time, long enough for an uninfected person to breathe them in. Anyone with active TB should not be around anyone with immune system problems such as someone with HIV or someone who is receiving chemotherapy.

Complications TB can spread to other organs, such as the kidney, liver, spleen, and brain, causing severe illness and requiring hospitalization. Untreated, TB can be fatal.

Other Issues It is important to perform screening skin tests on children at high risk for TB (see Chapter 14, "Health Screening Tests," for information about TB screening).

Urinary Tract Infection

Cause The bacteria *E. coli*, *Proteus mirabilis*, *Klebsiella*, and *Staphylococcus saprophyticus* are common causes of urinary tract infection. Viruses, especially adenoviruses, may also cause infections.

Symptoms Symptoms depend on the child's age and what part of the urinary tract is infected. With a bladder infection or cystitis, the child may have a burning sensation when urinating and a sense of urgency that leads to an inability to hold urine at times. The child may produce only a small amount of urine although feeling the need to go frequently. He may have low back pain or pain below the navel and above the groin (where the bladder is located). The urine may have a foul odor. Fever is not typical with cystitis. An infection of the upper urinary tract involving the kidneys (pyelonephritis) may be accompanied by fever, abdominal or lower back pain, fatigue, nausea, vomiting, jaundice (yellow skin) in newborns, and sometimes diarrhea. In infants, signs may be nonspecific and may include poor feeding, vomiting, irritability, and weight loss.

How It Spreads The infecting bacteria generally are present in the stool, living on the area surrounding the anus. They can then enter the bladder by traveling up through the urethra, the tube that carries the urine out. Bacterial urinary infections are not contagious. Urinary tract infections are much more common in girls, especially during toileting years. When boys or infants of either sex have a urinary tract infection, it may be due to an abnormality in the urinary tract system and may require further testing by your child's doctor.

Incubation Period The incubation period is variable, depending on the cause.

How Long Symptoms Last With treatment, symptoms should subside within 24 to 48 hours.

When to Call Your Child's Doctor Call your child's doctor if your child has fever, low back or abdominal pain, or pain when urinating; if your child begins to urinate frequently during the day or night; if the urine has a foul odor or is cloudy or discolored (pink, bloody, or tea-colored); or if your child was toilet trained and resumes bed-wetting or has accidents during the day.

How the Diagnosis Is Made A sample of urine is tested.

Treatment The type of antibiotic and length of time a child is on it depend on the type of infection and the child's age. Cystitis may be treated with trimethoprim-sulfamethoxazole, acephalosporin, or amoxicillin given for 3 to 5 days. For a kidney infection, a 14-day course of an antibiotic such as ceftriaxone may be used. If the child is younger than six months, he may be hospitalized and receive intravenous antibiotic treatment, especially if he is vomiting. If a child is having severe pain with urination, the doctor may prescribe a medication that numbs the lining of the urinary tract. This medication temporarily causes the urine

to have an orange color, which is of no concern.

Home Treatment Encourage your child to drink plenty of fluids, but avoid caffeine-containing beverages.

Prevention Encourage your child to wash frequently and drink plenty of fluids; discourage drinking carbonated and caffeinated drinks, which can irritate the bladder. When toilet training your daughter, teach her to wipe herself after a bowel movement from the front toward the back to prevent stool bacteria from spreading to the urethra or vagina. Buy loose-fitting cotton underwear instead of tight nylon. Change your child's diaper immediately when there is a stool.

Complications Recurrent or untreated kidney infections can scar the kidneys and ultimately interfere with kidney function (see Chapter 32, "Health Problems in Early Childhood," for more information about kidney problems and recurrent urinary tract infections).

Warts

Cause Four types of human papillomavirus (HPV) cause warts.

Symptoms Symptoms are hard bumps on the skin with a rough surface that often resembles a cauliflower. They may be white, pink, brown, or gray, and inside the wart are tiny spots that look like black hairs or specks. They can affect any part of the body, but most often they occur on the fingers, arms, feet, elbows, and knees. They are usually painless except when they are on the soles of the feet (plantar warts).

How They Spread They are spread by contact, either by touching someone's wart, by touching something that a person with warts touched, or by a person touching his own wart. Breaks in the skin and moisture help set the stage for infection by the virus.

Incubation Period The incubation period is one month or longer, depending on the HPV strain.

How Long Symptoms Last More than 50 percent of warts disappear spontaneously within two years. With treatment, warts can be removed quickly by a number of techniques but can return if all of the virus-containing tissue is not completely removed.

When to Call Your Child's Doctor If you have an infant or young child with a wart, call your child's doctor before trying to remove it with a commercial remedy. If your child has a wart on the face or genitals, call your child's doctor for treatment. Call your child's doctor if you are not sure the bump is a wart; if a wart becomes hot, red, or painful; if it begins oozing pus; or if the child's warts seem to be spreading.

How the Diagnosis Is Made The diagnosis is usually made just by observing the appearance of the wart.

Treatment Doctors may remove warts with strong chemicals not commercially available, freeze them off with liquid nitrogen, burn them off with electricity, numb the skin and then scrape the wart off, or use laser surgery. Within a few days the wart

usually falls off, but repeated treatments may necessary.

Home Treatment Nonprescription wart remedies are available, but check with your child's doctor before using them on your infant or young child.

Prevention You can encourage your child not to touch someone's warts or—if he already has some—his own warts to prevent them from being spread to other sites.

Complications Warts that are left untreated, especially those on the fingers, are more likely to spread. If a wart is scratched repeatedly, it can lead to secondary bacterial infection.

Whooping Cough (Pertussis)

Cause The bacterium *Bordetella pertussis* is the cause.

Symptoms It usually starts with symptoms similar to a common cold—congestion, runny nose, and low-grade fever. As these symptoms subside, coughing begins first as a dry, intermittent hack and evolves into coughing fits in which the child begins to choke, gasp, and flail arms and legs, with eyes watering and bulging and face turning red. Between coughing spells the child may gasp for air, making the characteristic "whooping" sound. The coughing may cause the child to vomit. Infants younger than one year who become infected are at particular risk for severe illness. They sometimes do not have the characteristic "whoop" at the end of coughing bouts— instead they may vomit, turn blue (due to lack of oxygen), and sometimes stop breathing. Severe coughing and vomiting may also interfere with an infant's ability to feed and gain weight normally.

How It Spreads It spreads via airborne nose and throat droplets from an infected person, usually an older child or adult with an undiagnosed infection.

Incubation Period The incubation period is 3 to 12 days.

How Long Symptoms Last The initial "cold" phase of the infection typically lasts two weeks; the coughing phase lasts two to four weeks, and the recovery phase typically lasts two to four weeks, but bouts of coughing can sometimes occur for months.

When to Call Your Child's Doctor Call your child's doctor if you suspect your child has whooping cough. Call if your child's coughing spells make him turn red or blue, if they are followed by vomiting, or if he makes the characteristic "whooping" sound at the end of a coughing bout. Call if your child has been exposed to someone with the infection, even if he has received the whooping cough vaccine.

How the Diagnosis Is Made Diagnosis is made by the history of symptoms and the physical examination and by taking a sample of respiratory fluids from the child for analysis. Blood tests and X-rays may also be done to help confirm the diagnosis and check for the presence of complications such as pneumonia.

Treatment Infants younger than three months are hospitalized; those three to six months of age may be hospitalized if coughing is severe. In the hospital, the infant's breathing and heartbeat will be monitored closely, and extra oxygen will be given if needed. Nutritional support is given, sometimes involving tube or intravenous feedings. The antibiotic erythromycin is given for 14 days, mainly to prevent the spread of the infection, because antibiotics don't change the course of the illness unless they are started in the early "cold" phase.

Home Treatment If you are treating your child at home, use a cool-mist vaporizer to help soothe lungs and breathing passages. Keep the home free of irritants that can trigger coughing, including tobacco smoke, aerosol sprays, smoke from cooking, and fumes from fireplaces and wood stoves. If your child is vomiting, give frequent small meals and encourage him to drink fruit juice and other clear liquids and soups. Watch for signs of dehydration: dry lips and tongue, dry skin, crying without tears, and infrequent urination.

Prevention Pertussis vaccine is part of the DTaP (diphtheria-tetanus-pertussis) combination vaccine routinely given in five doses, starting at age two months (see Chapter 16, "Immunizations," for more information). Those who have been exposed to someone with pertussis, even those who have been immunized, should be treated with erythromycin to prevent the development of whooping cough.

Contagious Periods An untreated child with pertussis can spread the infection throughout the initial "cold" phase and active coughing phase of the illness. Close to 100 percent of family members not vaccinated against pertussis will get the infection if they are exposed.

Complications Complications can include pneumonia, seizures, brain damage, and death. Infants younger than six months are especially vulnerable.

Yeast (Candida) Infections (Thrush, Diaper Rash)

Cause A yeast infection appears in the mouth (thrush) or as diaper rash in infants and is caused by candida, a yeastlike fungus. The majority of infections are caused by one species, *Candida albicans.* Oral thrush occurs in 2 to 5 percent of normal newborns and a higher percentage of low-birthweight babies. Diaper dermatitis is the most common infection caused by candida. Older children who have been treated with oral antibiotics or who have a weakened immune system are also prone to yeast infections.

Symptoms Oral thrush appears as white cheeselike areas in the mouth that may bleed if the white material is scraped off. The baby may have a sore mouth and be fussy with feedings. A diaper rash that lasts longer than three days despite frequent diaper changes and use of irritation-preventing diaper ointments may be due to candida infection, especially if there are small, round, red areas called "satellite lesions" around the borders of the red rash in the diaper area. Thrush and candida diaper rash often occur together in an infant.

How It Spreads Some babies are infected by coming in contact with the yeast from the mother's vagina during delivery. Babies can get thrush from close contact with people who carry the yeast on their hands.

Incubation Period For newborns infected at birth, thrush may develop in the first 7 to 10 days after birth.

How Long Symptoms Last With treatment, it generally takes 7 to 14 days for the infection to clear up completely.

When to Call Your Child's Doctor Call your child's doctor if your baby has patches of cheesy white material on the inner cheeks and tongue (that doesn't wipe off easily like milk) or a diaper rash with the characteristics described earlier.

How the Diagnosis Is Made The diagnosis is made by examining the baby's mouth or diaper area.

Treatment For oral thrush, treatment of mild cases may not be necessary. The most commonly prescribed medication is nystatin, a topical fungicide. For diaper rash, a prescription topical antifungal ointment may be needed to clear up the rash.

Prevention If bottle-feeding, make sure nipples are sterile. Wash your hands before feeding your infant.

Complications Persistent thrush can be a sign of abnormalities in the body's immune system. Candida infections in people with weakened immune systems can range from minor to life-threatening sepsis (infection of the blood).

ⓘ Need More Information?

Check the Index and Appendix C, "Resource Guide." And of course, consult your child's doctor.

chapter thirty-one

Medications and Alternative/ Complementary Care

A guide to treatments

Medicines are tools that can correct, cure, or prevent a medical problem; they can also be used to make your child feel more comfortable by relieving symptoms. But like any tool, medicines must be used correctly to work properly. In this chapter, we'll help you understand how medicines work, how you can choose the right medication for your child, and how to give your child medicine (this can be a real challenge sometimes—especially with toddlers!). We'll also explain how to store medicines properly and safely.

In addition, we'll discuss what you should know about alternative and complementary health care before choosing it for your child. There's been explosive growth in a wide range of treatment options, and we'll arm you with the information you need to make educated—and safe—choices for your child.

Using Medications with Care

Sometimes the best remedy is no medication at all. For many common illnesses, such as colds, children do not need any medicine. No over-the-counter (OTC) product or prescription medicine will make your child's cold run its course any faster, and any possible relief of symptoms that your child might experience may be outweighed by side effects of the drug. For colds and other common viral illnesses, your child's doctor may recommend that you try some nonmedicinal remedies first to help your child feel better—extra fluids, rest, saline (saltwater) nose drops, or a cool-mist vaporizer, for example. This is a better first approach than automatically reaching for the medicine bottle. Giving medicine as a reflex response to every sniffle or minor ache or pain may only make the situation worse because virtually all medicines have side effects. And setting this example may result in your child adopting a "feeling bad? . . . take a pill" attitude later in life.

After trying some nonmedicinal remedies, you may decide that your child needs some sort of medication—but which kind? The many medicines that are available for children can be divided into two major categories: prescription medicines, which must be ordered by your child's doctor or other licensed prescriber, and over-the-counter (OTC) medicines, which can be bought without a prescription. Whatever you choose, you should always check with your child's doctor or pharmacist about proper dosage and how long your child will need to take it. Don't assume that just because you used a certain dose a few months ago that it's still the correct dose for your child today—children grow quickly, and a little extra weight from recent growth may mean that your child now needs more. And you should never give any medicine to a child younger than two years of age without first consulting with your child's doctor or pharmacist.

If your child's doctor recommends an OTC product for your child, ask the pharmacist on duty to help you make the right selection for your child. He or she can recommend an appropriate product and also help you make sure you're not overmedicating your child by choosing a product that contains more than you need.

Also, make sure that the doctor and pharmacist know about any drug allergies or significant reactions to medications your child has had in the past, or other med-

KidsHealth Tip

Don't Do It in the Dark

It's the middle of the night and your child needs his medication. You stagger out of bed and stumble down the darkened hallway, spoon and bottle in hand. Back in bed again, you start to worry: "Did I give the proper amount?" Never give your child medicine in the dark or without wearing your glasses or contact lenses. Giving the wrong dose or medication could have serious consequences.

KidsHealth Tip

What's in a Name?

Which should you buy, the expensive name brand or the less-expensive store brand? When it comes to over-the-counter medications and vitamins, price may be the only difference. Often the same companies make the national brands and the store brands. Consumers who buy the more expensive versions may be paying extra for packaging and advertising. Compare the labels of several brands, and ask your pharmacist for advice.

ications (prescription or OTC) your child is taking that have been prescribed by another health care provider.

One more caution: Never give aspirin to your child without your child's doctor's approval. Aspirin has been linked to Reye syndrome (a serious and sometimes fatal disorder), especially when given to children with the flu or chicken pox. Aspirin can also interfere with the way your child's body handles other medicines. Be aware that aspirin can be "hidden" in many medications such as Pepto-Bismol, Excedrin, Alka-Seltzer, and others. Read the label on any medication you plan to give your child.

How to Give Your Child Medicine

There are a few safety tips you should follow before you put that medicine spoon into your child's mouth. Keep these in mind:

- Before leaving the pharmacy, make sure you have the right prescription by checking the name and the dosage against your child's doctor's instructions. If there are any discrepancies, ask the pharmacist for clarification.
- Read the instructions carefully to find out if the medicine should be taken with or without food, how many times a day it should be given, and if it needs to be refrigerated or shaken.
- Read the entire label each time you are going to give your child a dose.
- Ask about any common side effects that your child might experience.

- If you have any questions, ask the pharmacist before you leave the store, or call your child's doctor or pharmacist after you've returned home.
- If your child's liquid medicine contains a dropper, wash it with hot, soapy water after every use before putting it back in the bottle. If you have more than one child, you might want to keep separate OTC liquid medicines for each.
- Check the expiration date of all medicines before you buy them and before giving them to your child. Throw away all OTC medicines that have expired or prescription medicines that are more than one year old (flush away all old medications so your child cannot get the medicine out of the trash).
- If you are having trouble getting your child to take medicine, check with your pharmacist for suggestions. Although most liquid medicines are now flavored, some medicines can be mixed with chocolate or maple syrup.
- Do not put liquid medicine (or crushed pills) into a bottle for your baby; if he doesn't finish the bottle, he won't get all the medicine.
- When measuring liquid medicine, use a proper dosage spoon or an oral medication syringe (these can be purchased at most pharmacies). If you must use a household spoon, use cooking measurement spoons.
- If you accidentally give your child too much medicine, contact your child's doctor or pharmacist right away and follow his or her instructions. If you can't reach someone immediately, call your local poison control center.
- Most OTC medicines are to be used on an as-needed basis. But most prescription medicines (especially antibiotics) should be taken until the full course is finished. Don't stop them early even if your child seems better. If

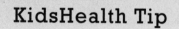

KidsHealth Tip

No Candy in the Medicine Cabinet

Never tell your child that pills are candy or that they taste like candy. Pills' colors and shapes often look like candy, and your child may just decide to help herself. Accidental poisoning from medications can be fatal, so be sure that your child knows that pills—even vitamin pills—aren't treats.

you have any questions about how long to give your child a medicine, consult your pharmacist or your child's doctor.

- Nearly all medicines can have some side effects, so you should watch for adverse reactions and report them immediately to your child's doctor. Be sure to tell him or her if your child is taking more than one medicine at a time because some medicines react with each other, creating a potentially dangerous situation.
- Never try to diagnose your child's problem yourself or use leftover prescription medicine from a previous illness or medicine that was prescribed for someone else.
- Keep medicine in a cool, dry place. The high moisture level in bathrooms makes the "medicine cabinet" a poor choice because moisture can seep into many medicines and make them less potent. It's better to keep medicines in a hall closet or kitchen shelf—unless they need to be refrigerated.
- For your child's safety, always keep all medicines in childproof containers and out of the reach and out of sight of your child.
- If any problems persist or your child is not feeling better after taking the medicine for the recommended time, call your child's doctor. He or she may need to reexamine your child and may prescribe a different medicine or treatment.

It's particularly important that you talk to your child's doctor or pharmacist if you're going to give a child younger than two years an OTC medicine because no recommended dosage is given on OTC labels for children in this age group. Infants and toddlers should not be given a child's dosage, and children should not

KidsHealth Tip

Down the Hatch

It's not always easy to give a baby liquid medication; parents often find that their baby balks at swallowing, and the medicine ends up everywhere but down his throat. To ensure that your baby swallows all of his medicine, put the medicine in his mouth and blow gently on his face. He will blink and swallow as a reflex action, and the medicine will go down.

KidsHealth Tip
Make the Medicine Go Down

When kids already feel under the weather, the taste of strong antibiotics can make the situation even more unpleasant. Check with your pharmacist to see if your child's liquid antibiotic must be kept at room temperature. If it doesn't have to be at room temperature, try chilling it in the refrigerator. This will take away some of the bitter taste and may make the medicine go down a little easier.

be given an adult's dosage. Make sure you—and your child's doctor and pharmacist—know how much your child currently weighs.

Alternative Medicine and Your Child

The phrase "alternative (or complementary) medicine" may conjure up images of pungent herbal teas, poultices, chanting, or meditation. In fact, herbal remedies and meditation, as well as dozens of other treatments, fall under the heading of complementary and alternative medicine (CAM). Although there is no strict definition of alternative medicine, it generally includes any healing practices that are not part of mainstream medicine—that means any practice that is not widely taught in medical schools or frequently used by doctors or in hospitals.

But the boundaries of alternative medicine in the United States are constantly changing as different types of care become more accepted by doctors and more requested by patients. A few practices (such as acupuncture and hypnosis) that were once dismissed as nonsense are now considered helpful therapies in addition to traditional medicine. As alternative remedies become more accepted, the question becomes, can alternative medicine help your child?

Types of Complementary and Alternative Care

The National Center for Complementary and Alternative Medicine at the National Institutes of Health recognizes five general areas of alternative care. Within these areas are some practices that have been put through rigorous scientific testing, and many that have not.

1. Complete alternative medical systems, such as traditional oriental medicine, are increasingly popular in the United States today. These complete health care systems generally fall outside our conventional medical system of doctors and hospitals and have been widely practiced as the primary medical care system in other countries for hundreds or even thousands of years. Some of the more common alternative medical systems now available in the United States include these:

   - Traditional oriental medicine. This centuries-old system, also called traditional Chinese medicine (TCM), focuses on establishing the proper balance of *qi* (pronounced "chi"), or energy, in the body; qi imbalances are thought to lead to illness. Through acupuncture, herbal medicine, oriental massage, and energy therapy called *qigong*, practitioners try to rebalance qi.
   - Ayurveda. This traditional system of medicine in India focuses on restoring harmony between a person's body, mind, and spirit. Through

---

KidsHealth Tip
Avoiding Medication Mistakes

With more than 8,000 drugs available in the United States today, it's not surprising that medication errors occur. Help protect your child from such errors:

- Use only one pharmacy. Select your pharmacy in the same way you would choose a doctor.
- Make sure that the pharmacist has a complete record of your child's allergies and knows which nonprescription medicines your child takes regularly.
- Don't rush the pharmacist. Give the pharmacist time to fill the prescription safely and accurately.
- Ask your pharmacist for written information about medications.

diet, exercise, herbs and oils, meditation, exposure to sunlight, and breathing exercises geared to rebalance a person's unique body type, practitioners try to heal the body and prevent future illness.

- Homeopathy. Practitioners of homeopathy—which started in the West—believe that large buildups in the body of certain elements such as zinc can result in illness. They use very small amounts of that same built-up substance to try to rebalance the body, heal it, and prevent future illnesses.
- Naturopathy. This comprehensive system of care doesn't treat diseases. Rather, it focuses on restoring the natural processes that the body normally uses to keep itself well; restoration results in healing. Practitioners use diet, homeopathy, acupuncture, spinal and soft tissue manipulation, herbal medicine, and other treatments.

2. Mind-body intervention therapies are used by practitioners who believe that they can facilitate the mind's ability to change bodily processes, control symptoms, and fight off disease. Meditation, hypnosis, dance, music, art therapy, prayer, and mental healing are some examples of mind-body interventions used by practitioners in the United States.

3. Biological-based therapies include herbal, dietary, orthomolecular, and individual biological therapies. These practices often overlap with conventional medicine's use of drugs and nutritional supplements. For example, herbal therapies—which are widely available at health food and drug stores today as teas and pills—use chemicals in plants to bring about healing reactions in the body. Special diets, such as the Pritikin low-fat diet, are believed by many to promote healing in the body. Orthomolecular therapies use special concentrations of chemicals and megadoses of vitamins, such as vitamin C, to facilitate healing. And biological therapies include the use of special natural substances such as shark cartilage and bee pollen to treat certain diseases.

4. Manipulative and body-based therapies used by chiropractors, massage therapists, and some osteopathic physicians are based on the belief that bone and muscle structure and function—especially in the spine—can significantly impact overall health. They believe that an imbalance in one area of the body can negatively affect another area and cause illness. These practitioners use bone and soft tissue manipulation techniques to realign bones and muscles.

5. Energy therapies deal with manipulating the "electrical" energy fields within the body (biofields) or outside the body (electromagnetic fields). In some therapies, such as qigong, reiki (a Japanese energy therapy), and therapeutic touch, practitioners try to manipulate biofields through touch, pressure, placing their hands within these fields (which have not yet been scientifically

proved to exist), and channeling the spiritual energy of the practitioner to the patient.

There are many resources you can use to learn more about the complementary and alternative therapies available today, including books and Web sites. For more information about evaluating health information on the Web, see Chapter 34, "Finding Health Information on the Web."

How Does Alternative Medicine Differ from Traditional Medicine?

Alternative therapy is frequently distinguished by its holistic methods, which means that the doctor or practitioner treats the "whole" person and not just the disease or condition. In alternative medicine, many practitioners address patients' emotional and spiritual needs as well. This "high-touch" approach differs from the "high-tech" practice of traditional medicine, which tends to concentrate on the physical illness.

Most alternative practices have not found their way into mainstream hospitals or doctors' offices, so you or your child's doctor may not be aware of them. However, new centers for integrative medicine offer a mix of traditional and alternative treatments. There, you might receive a prescription for pain medication (as you might get from a traditional health care provider) and massage therapy to treat a chronic back problem. Such centers usually employ both medical doctors and certified or licensed specialists in the various alternative therapies.

Despite recent explosive growth in the field, the majority of alternative and complementary therapies are not covered by medical insurance. This is largely because few scientific studies have been done to prove whether the treatments are effective (unlike traditional medicine, which relies heavily on studies). Rather, most alternative therapies are based on long-standing practice and word-of-mouth stories of success. Be sure to ask your insurance provider about what's covered before you commit to an alternative treatment plan. If it's not covered, make sure that you fully understand the projected length of treatment and expected costs.

What Are the Risks?

The lack of scientific study means that some potential problems associated with alternative therapies may be difficult to identify. What's more, the studies that have been done used adults as test subjects; there is little known about the effects of alternative medicine on children. Although approaches such as prayer, massage, and lifestyle changes are generally considered safe complements to regular medical treatment, some therapies—particularly herbal remedies—might pose serious health risks.

Unlike prescription and over-the-counter medicines, herbal remedies are not rigorously regulated by the FDA. They face no extensive testing before they are marketed, and they do not have to adhere to a standard of quality. That means that when you buy a bottle of ginseng capsules, for example, you might not know what you're getting. The amount of herb can vary from pill to pill, with some capsules containing much less, much more, or none of the active herb indicated on the label. Depending on where the herb originated, other plants, even drugs like steroids, may be mixed in the capsules. Herbs that come from developing countries may be contaminated with toxins like pesticides or heavy metals.

Natural does not necessarily equal "good" or "safe," and many parents don't consider the possibility that herbal remedies can actually cause health problems for their children. Medicating your child without consulting your child's doctor could result in harm. For example, certain herbal remedies can cause high blood pressure, liver damage, or severe allergic reactions:

- Ephedra (often sold as the Chinese herb *ma huang*) has been linked to several deaths in people with heart problems.
- Alone and in combination with prescription drugs, several dietary supplements—such as chaparral, comfrey, germander, and ephedrine—have been linked to severe illness, liver damage, and even death.

Parents might also give their children much more of an herb than recommended, thinking that because it's "natural," higher doses won't hurt. But many plants contain potent chemicals; in fact, approximately 25 percent of all prescription drugs are derived from plants. In addition, if your child is already taking medication—even something as common as an OTC allergy medication—there may be unknown chemical reactions between the herb and the medication.

Choosing a practitioner can pose another problem. Although many states have licensing boards for specialists in acupuncture or massage, for instance, there is no federal organization in the United States that monitors alternative care providers or establishes standards of treatment. Basically, almost anyone can claim to be a practitioner, regardless of training. Research the credentials of any care provider you are considering—don't hesitate to ask detailed and aggressive questions, because you are considering trusting your child's health to this person.

Perhaps the greatest risk, however, occurs if traditional medical treatment is delayed or rejected in favor of an alternative therapy. Illnesses such as diabetes and cancer require the care of a doctor. Relying entirely on alternative therapies for any serious chronic or acute conditions will jeopardize the health of your child.

Can Alternative Care Help Your Child?

Many parents turn to a cup of chamomile tea or ginger as a first line of treatment against the flu or nausea. Anxious children can learn to relax with the help of meditation or yoga. Such alternative therapies complement traditional care, and they can help your child feel better.

If you want to try alternative medicine for your child, you should first discuss the proposed treatment with your child's doctor or talk to your pharmacist to make sure it is safe and will not conflict with any traditional care your child receives. Your child's doctor can also give you information about treatment options and perhaps recommend a reputable specialist. By coordinating alternative and traditional care, you don't have to choose between them. Instead, you can get the best of both.

Need More Information?

Check the Index and Appendix C, "Resource Guide." And of course, consult your child's doctor.

PART SIX

When Your Child Has a Health Problem

chapter thirty-two

Health Problems in Early Childhood

A parent's desk reference

Index to Chapter

How to Use This Chapter

Fortunately, most children go through childhood with health problems little more serious than an occasional earache, a few cuts and bruises, and a case or two of the flu. When these happen, they're uncomfortable for your child and can be worrisome for you. But they do get better. That's not true for all medical problems. Some children have more serious or chronic (long-lasting) illnesses that can be limiting or disabling and may require treatment with medications, special diets, surgery, hospitalization, and visits to medical specialists.

This portion of *The KidsHealth Guide for Parents* is intended to be a "mini-encyclopedia" of a number of health conditions seen in young children. Some of these are common, such as asthma, which affects about 1 in 10 children at some point in their life. Others are relatively rare, such as phenylketonuria (PKU), a metabolic disorder that occurs in about 1 in 16,000 births. Others you may never have heard of, such as fragile X syndrome—one of the most common genetic causes of mental retardation. The overall fraction of children who will have a medical condition requiring special care is more than 15 percent.

The entries in this chapter include a brief overview of the condition with a definition, causes (when known), symptoms that might be seen, how a diagnosis is made, what treatments exist at this time, and—in general—what can be said about the outlook for a child with the condition. Where appropriate, we also comment on prevention, and for those conditions that might run in families or have a genetic basis, we include information about prenatal testing and counseling.

Although this section contains plenty to read, it's far from comprehensive—either in the number of conditions we could include or what we say about each. In fact, we've created a three-volume reference encyclopedia (*Human Diseases and Conditions*, Charles Scribner's Sons, 2000) that describes many of these conditions in more detail. You may also want to check out our Web site, www.KidsHealth.org, to see if we've posted something new about your topic of interest.

Some additional thoughts as you read this section: Advancement in the understanding and treatment of medical conditions is progressing rapidly. There is ongoing research involving virtually every one of these conditions—so be sure to check with your child's doctor for updates on diagnosis and treatment.

And speaking of treatment, you might ask, "Which doctor do I go to to get my child the best treatment for a condition described here?" In general, we can say that the less common the condition, the less familiarity a primary care doctor may have with its diagnosis and treatment. Often the care of a complex medical condition requires not just a specialist physician, but a whole team of specialized health care personnel that may include nurse-practitioners, dietitians, social workers, various therapists, and educators. That care may take place in a "multispecialty" clinic, which is usually based either at a children's hospital or at a medical center with a larger pediatric department. (For more information, see Chapter 27, "The Health Care System for Children.")

Some children have complicated ongoing needs requiring significant medical and technical support including specialized therapies and equipment. See Chapter 33, "Caring for Your Child with Special Health Care Needs," for additional information.

Medical Conditions

Allergies

An allergy is a reaction of the immune system to a substance that is typically harmless to most people. In a person with an allergy, the body treats the substance, called an allergen, as an invader. Some of the most common allergens are pollen, dust mites (tiny bugs that live in household dust particles), molds, cockroaches, animal dander (especially cats and dogs), and foods such as peanuts, egg whites, wheat, fish (including shellfish), soy, citrus, and dairy products (milk products). Insect bites or stings can also cause allergic reactions. Allergy symptoms can be seasonal, occurring only when the allergen (such as pollen) is in the air, or chronic, such as an allergy to dust mites.

With most common allergies, the person's immune system produces antibodies against the particular allergen involved. When the person is exposed to the allergen, the "attack" mounted by the immune system against this substance triggers the release of certain body chemicals that cause the symptoms associated with allergies.

About 50 million Americans, including 2 million children, have some type of allergy. The tendency to develop allergies is inherited. If one parent has allergies, the child has a 25 percent chance of developing allergies, and the risk is even greater if both parents are allergic.

Symptoms and Diagnosis The type and severity of allergy symptoms vary from allergen to allergen and from child to child. They can be mild or life-threatening.

Food allergies can cause mild to severe symptoms that may include itchy mouth and throat, general itchiness, hives (raised welts) or rash, runny and itchy nose and eyes, nausea, vomiting, or diarrhea. More severe, life-threatening reactions can include swelling in the mouth, throat, and airways, which can interfere with breathing or may indicate the onset of anaphylaxis.

Symptoms of allergies to inhaled particles, such as molds, pollen (hay fever due to ragweed pollen, for example), animal dander (especially cats), chemicals, and perfumes can include sneezing, clear runny nose, itchy or stuffed nose, itchy or runny eyes, and fatigue. Symptoms of asthma (cough, wheezing, or shortness of breath) may also occur (see Asthma in this chapter).

Some people can suffer a potentially life-threatening whole-body allergic reaction called anaphylaxis in which there is a sudden onset of symptoms that may include breathing difficulty; swelling of the lips, tongue, and throat; vomiting; dizziness; and collapsing. Allergies to stinging insects (such as bees and wasps), peanuts, tree nuts, and seafood are among the most likely causes of anaphylaxis. (For more information about anaphylaxis, see Chapter 28, "First Aid and Emergency Care.")

In many cases, a child's history of symptoms that develop when exposed to a particular allergen is sufficient to diagnose an allergy. For example, cold symptoms that last for more than two weeks or a "cold" that seems to occur at the same time every year may actually indicate an allergy.

To determine the cause of an allergy, a doctor may perform skin tests. In these tests, a drop of a purified liquid form of an allergen is dropped on the skin and the area is pinched with a small plastic device, or a small amount of the allergen is injected just under the skin. After about 15 minutes, if the area becomes reddened, the test is positive. Special blood tests are also sometimes used in diagnosing specific allergies.

Treatment and Outlook The primary method of allergy treatment is the avoidance of whatever substance causes the allergic reaction. If that isn't possible or if it doesn't sufficiently control the symptoms, antihistamines may be prescribed. These drugs block the effects of allergy-symptom-producing chemicals released by the body in response to an allergen. Newer types of antihistamines approved for children have fewer side effects (such as drowsiness and behavior changes) than previously available types. Nasal steroid sprays may also be recommended for children with allergic rhinitis (sneezing and itchy, runny nose).

If a child's allergy symptoms are more troublesome or severe and they can't be controlled adequately with allergen avoidance and medications, immunotherapy (allergy shots) may be recommended. This treatment, used for children as young as four or five years, involves giving the child a series of injections with increasingly stronger solutions of the purified form of the allergen that is triggering the child's symptoms. This process actually causes the child to experience fewer or less severe symptoms by "desensitizing" the child to the offending allergen. The injections cause the child to develop "blocking" antibodies that interrupt the immune system "attack" against the particular allergen.

Immunotherapy is most effective in controlling symptoms related to inhaled allergens (such as pollen) and insect venom allergies. The shots are usually given over a

period of several years and should be administered under the supervision of an allergist or other doctor specifically trained in this form of treatment.

With environmental changes that reduce exposure to the allergen along with proper medical treatment, most allergies can be successfully controlled throughout life.

Anemia, Hereditary

Anemia refers to a condition in which the number of red blood cells (RBCs) or amount of hemoglobin (the protein that carries oxygen) in the RBCs is below normal. Inherited abnormalities in hemoglobin may cause anemia; it may also result from nutritional problems (see Anemia, Iron-Deficiency, in this chapter for more information), blood loss, and various other medical conditions. Two of the most common hereditary forms of anemia are sickle-cell anemia and thalassemia.

Sickle-Cell Anemia

Also called sickle-cell disease, sickle-cell anemia is an inherited disorder in which the RBCs are sickle shaped. Normal RBCs are round and disc shaped, and their flexibility enables them to flow easily through the blood vessels and capillaries (the smallest blood vessels) to deliver oxygen. But the presence of a faulty gene that produces an abnormal form of hemoglobin (called hemoglobin S, or HbS) can cause RBCs to become the shape of a sickle or crescent. Because these sickle-shaped cells are rigid and brittle, their flow through narrow vessels is hindered; they can clog the flow of blood and break apart. This can deprive the body tissues of oxygen and can cause pain and damage to tissues.

Sickle-cell anemia is an inherited disease. A child receives genes in pairs: one from the father and one from the mother. If a child inherits one faulty hemoglobin S gene, he has what is known as sickle-cell trait. With few exceptions, people with sickle-cell trait are healthy and will never develop symptoms of sickle-cell anemia. But if a child inherits faulty genes from both the father and mother, he will have sickle-cell anemia.

Sickle-cell is found most frequently in Africa, where in some locations, up to 40 percent of the population has at least one sickle-cell gene. Among people of African ancestry in the United States, about 8 in 100 carry at least one sickle-cell gene; about 40,000 people carry two copies and have sickle-cell anemia. The gene is also found in people in the Mediterranean and Middle Eastern areas and among groups in India, Latin America, and the Caribbean. It is believed that sickle-cell trait (one copy of the gene) provides some protection against malaria; two copies of the gene do not, however.

Symptoms and Diagnosis The symptoms of sickle-cell anemia vary but may include those common to all anemias: fatigue and feeling of faintness, pale skin, and shortness of breath on mild exertion. Typically, patients with the disease experience episodes known as sickle-cell crises in which sickle-cells clump together and block the blood supply to body tissues. These crises may be triggered by infection, exercise, dehydration, high altitudes, or general anesthesia. The symptoms may include severe pain and swelling around the bones and joints, particularly of the hands and feet in young children; stomach pain; and chest pain and shortness of breath.

All babies, regardless of ethnic background, are tested for the presence of hemoglobin S associated with sickle-cell anemia. This test is part of the newborn disease screening tests performed throughout the United States. Early diagnosis of sickle-cell anemia can help doctors prevent and treat serious complications of the condition that can occur in early infancy.

Treatment and Outlook Some sickle-cell crises are potentially fatal, and medical help should be obtained immediately. Hospital treatment is often necessary for managing a crisis. The child may be given intravenous fluids, pain relievers, antibiotics if there is an underlying infection, and oxygen if necessary.

Because fever may be a sign of life-threatening infection in children with sickle-cell anemia, all fevers should be brought to the attention of a doctor promptly. Infants and young children should receive ongoing treatment with penicillin to help prevent serious infections until they are about five years old. It's also very important that children with the disease be fully immunized.

Those with recurrent crises or those with other severe complications of the disease may benefit from receiving blood transfusions from healthy donors. In some cases, bone marrow transplantation from a suitable donor has enabled patients with sickle-cell disease to begin producing hemoglobin and red blood cells in a normal manner. Research continues on the development and testing of hydroxyurea and other drugs that can improve hemoglobin production in sickle-cell patients.

Prevention and Prenatal Testing Genetic testing and genetic counseling are available for sickle-cell anemia.

Thalassemia

Thalassemia refers to a group of inherited blood diseases characterized by absent or decreased production of normal hemoglobin. In the thalassemias, faulty genes cause an imbalance in the production of one of the two types of protein chains (called alpha and beta) that make up hemoglobin. Thalassemias are categorized according to the protein chain affected. The two main types are alpha-thalassemia (four genes are involved; one or more of the four alpha chain genes fails to function properly) and beta-thalassemia (two genes are involved; one or both of the beta chain genes fail to function properly).

Depending on the number of genes inherited that do not function properly, a person with thalassemia may have no symptoms, mild symptoms, or a life-threatening anemia. Fetuses with four defective alpha chain genes will die before birth.

The thalassemias are seen in areas where malaria is common, such as Asia and Africa. In some regions of Southeast Asia, up to 40 percent of people have one or more thalassemia genes. From 3 to 8 percent of Americans of Italian or Greek ancestry and 0.5 percent of African Americans carry a beta-thalassemia gene. About 25 percent of African Americans carry one of the genes for alpha-thalassemia.

Symptoms and Diagnosis The symptoms of alpha-thalassemia are usually undetectable or mild; however, moderately severe anemia can occur. If a child has inherited defective genes for beta-thalassemia from both parents, the symptoms of severe anemia may appear between four and six months of age, including pale skin, breathing difficulty or shortness of breath, and swelling of the abdomen because of an enlarged spleen and liver.

Thalassemia will be suspected if a child has symptoms of the condition or if a routine blood test shows signs of anemia. When this is the case, a child's doctor will order a blood test specifically for thalassemia if more common causes of anemia such as an iron deficiency (see Anemia, Iron-Deficiency, in this chapter) are not present.

Treatment and Outlook If a child has mild thalassemia, he may only need to take folic acid supplements to support the production of red blood cells. If a child has severe thalassemia, he may require lifelong blood transfusions. In some cases, removal of the enlarged spleen may be helpful. Although the procedure carries significant risks, bone marrow transplantation has resulted in a cure in some patients with thalassemia.

Growth and sexual development are usually delayed in children with severe beta-thalassemia. The bones of the skull and face may thicken as the bone marrow expands in an attempt to form more blood cells. To prevent the damaging buildup of iron in organs that can result from repeated blood transfusions, the child may need continuous treatment with a drug that helps the body excrete iron through the urine.

Prevention and Prenatal Testing Genetic testing and genetic counseling are available for thalassemia.

Anemia, Iron-Deficiency

Iron-deficiency anemia is a condition in which the body produces too little hemoglobin (an iron-containing protein in the red blood cells that carries oxygen) due to a lack of iron. Although iron deficiency has long been considered the major cause of anemia in childhood, the condition has become much less prevalent in the United States over the past 20 years, primarily due to iron-fortified infant formulas and cereals.

Full-term babies are born with enough iron stored in their bodies to supply their needs for about the first four months of life. After this period, infants depend on a steady supply of iron from their diets to meet their needs as they grow rapidly. This is why infants who don't receive adequate amounts of iron are likely to develop anemia between six months and two years of age. Infants who are born prematurely or who are small at birth for other reasons, and those who lose excessive amounts of blood during the birth process, have smaller stores of iron and therefore may develop anemia earlier than age six months. Infants fed cow's milk before age 12 months tend to lose blood (and the iron it contains) into their stools, causing them to be at higher risk for iron deficiency and anemia. Similarly, infants or older children who lose blood through chronic bleeding or acute hemorrhage from any cause may also develop the condition.

Most children with iron deficiency do not eat enough foods containing iron such as meat, vegetables, beans, and iron-fortified formulas and cereals.

Symptoms and Diagnosis Children with mild iron deficiency may have no symptoms. Those with moderate or severe deficiency are pale, irritable, and easily tired; they may show delays in reaching developmental milestones. Recent research indicates that iron deficiency, even if mild enough not to cause anemia in a child, may have negative effects on a child's behavior and intelligence.

If doctors suspect iron deficiency based on the child's dietary history, symptoms, or physical findings, they will usually perform blood tests to confirm the diagnosis.

Treatment and Outlook In most cases of iron deficiency in infants and children, the doctor will prescribe an iron supplement to be given orally, usually in liquid form. Depending on the severity of the iron deficiency, the child's anemia will resolve within a few weeks on this treatment. It's important to continue the iron supplement for several months after the anemia has been corrected, however, to replenish the child's stores of iron. The child's diet should also be modified to ensure adequate intake of iron-containing foods so that iron deficiency doesn't recur.

Prevention For most infants and children, iron deficiency is entirely preventable by ensuring that the child's diet includes adequate amounts of iron. Breast-fed infants should be given iron supplements to prevent anemia. Babies should not be fed cow's milk before age 12 months to avoid blood (and iron) loss in the infant's stools.

Asthma

Asthma is a chronic inflammatory lung disease that causes the airways to tighten and narrow, resulting in coughing and breathing difficulties. The sensitive airway linings become inflamed (swollen and filled with mucus). The muscles in the walls of the swollen airways tighten and constrict, making the air passages even more narrowed and obstructed, so that it becomes difficult to move air in and out of the lungs.

Doctors and scientists don't know the exact cause of asthma, but they do know that the tendency to develop asthma is often inherited. Allergies, an infection such as a cold or sinus infection, smoke, air pollution, or exercise can trigger an asthma attack. Not every child with asthma has allergy-triggered asthma, but about 80 percent of people with asthma have some type of allergy. Even if a child's primary triggers are colds and other respiratory viral infections (the most common triggers for young children) or exercise, allergies can sometimes play a role in aggravating the condition (see Allergies in this chapter for more information).

Asthma is a common condition, affecting about 10 percent of children at some point in their lives. This figure is higher for certain high-risk groups, such as inner-city children from low-income families—the occurrence of asthma among these children may be greater than 20 percent.

Symptoms and Diagnosis In asthma, air passages are narrowed due to inflammation, excess mucus, and tightening of the muscles in the walls of the air passages. This makes it difficult to move air in and, particularly, out of the lungs. During an asthma flare or attack, children may experience coughing, wheezing (a hissing or whistling sound in the chest when breathing), a feeling of chest tightness, increased heart rate, sweating, and shortness of breath. Parents may notice that the child is breathing faster than usual, that the child's stomach is moving up and down with breathing, and that the skin covering the chest is being sucked in between the ribs or below the "Adam's apple" in the neck with each breath. A severe asthma attack can be life-threatening. Uncontrolled asthma may cause coughing, wheezing or heavy breathing with exercise, exercise avoidance, nighttime awakenings or poor sleep due to coughing and breathing difficulties, decreased appetite, and pro-

longed or severe coughing or congestion with colds. For many children, coughing is the only or the predominant symptom.

When considering a diagnosis of asthma, a doctor first tries to exclude other possible causes of a child's symptoms. He or she asks questions about the details of the child's symptoms and the family's history of asthma and allergy and performs a physical exam. With this information, doctors can diagnose most cases of asthma. The diagnosis is often aided by observing how the child's symptoms respond to asthma medication. Other tests such as a chest X-ray may sometimes be helpful to rule out other causes for the cough or wheezing.

In older children, if the diagnosis is not clear from the history and physical exam, an asthma specialist, such as a pulmonologist or allergist, can perform breathing tests using a spirometer, a machine that does a detailed analysis of a child's airflow through the airways in the lungs. A spirometer can also be used to see if the child's breathing problems can be reversed with medication—a hallmark of asthma.

Treatment and Outlook Every child with asthma needs a doctor-prescribed individual asthma-management plan to treat and prevent symptoms and attacks. This plan usually includes identifying and controlling asthma triggers (by avoiding, if possible, known allergens and irritants such as cigarette smoke), anticipating and preventing asthma attacks, and taking medications as prescribed to prevent or treat symptoms.

There are two main categories of asthma medications: quick-relief and long-term preventive ("inflammation preventing" or "controller") drugs. Inhaled medications such as cromolyn sodium and corticosteroids (not related to "bodybuilding" steroids) are often prescribed to prevent or control symptoms. For most children with moderate or severe asthma, proper use of prevention medicines and avoidance of asthma triggers can significantly reduce or eliminate symptoms and prevent attacks. If a child has symptoms more than two times per week despite adequate control of the triggers in the child's environment, then adding or increasing the use of prevention medicines is recommended. Besides just helping a child with asthma to feel better, adequate use of asthma prevention medicines significantly reduces the need for emergency room visits or hospitalizations and decreases the risk of death from a severe attack.

Acute asthma flares or attacks are treated with bronchodilator medications such as albuterol, which open the airways, and sometimes a short course (about five days) of oral corticosteroids (such as prednisone). The occurrence of asthma attacks may indicate the need to increase the level of prevention medicines used. Over-the-counter medications, home remedies, and herbal combinations are not substitutes for prescription asthma medication. They are less effective, and using them can lead to dangerous delays in getting more appropriate treatment.

If specific allergies are identified, the best treatment is to avoid exposure to allergens whenever possible. Getting rid of allergens in the home can be an important step in accomplishing this. When avoidance isn't possible, antihistamine medications may be prescribed. Nasal steroids (inhaled into the nose) may be given to block allergic inflammation in the nose, which can trigger attacks in some individuals. In some cases, an allergist may prescribe immunotherapy, a series of allergy shots that gradu-

ally block the body's reaction to specific allergens.

Untreated or inadequately treated asthma can be life-threatening and may lead to permanent lung damage. The incidence of asthma has been rising in the past several decades, especially in the inner city among African Americans and Latinos. Poverty, substandard housing, exposure to certain indoor allergens such as cockroaches, lack of education about the disease, failure to take medications, and lack of access to adequate health care contribute to the risk of having severe or poorly controlled asthma and its complications. Although the frequency of attacks and severity of asthma tend to decrease as most children get older, children with poorly controlled asthma miss more school, are less likely to exercise, and may suffer from long-lasting emotional, behavioral, and psychological problems due to their condition.

Attention Deficit/Hyperactivity Disorder (AD/HD)

Attention deficit/hyperactivity disorder (AD/HD) is diagnosed in children who consistently display certain characteristic behaviors over time. The most common features include inability to sustain attention to tasks, impulsiveness, and hyperactivity. These behaviors must be beyond the usual distractibility and impulsive behavior of children. Boys are more likely than girls to have the disorder, which afflicts an estimated 5 percent of the U.S. population.

The causes of AD/HD are not fully understood. Many scientists believe that the condition results from an imbalance of chemicals called neurotransmitters that affect how the brain works. There is much evidence that AD/HD runs in families, which suggests genetic factors play a role. Some research indicates that the use of alcohol or drugs during pregnancy may affect the baby's brain development and in some cases result in AD/HD.

Most experts do not believe that the condition is caused by poor parenting, family problems, poor teachers or schools, or too much TV. Nor do food allergies, food additives, or excess sugar appear to play a major role in the development of the condition. The results of one study indicated that eating a diet low in refined sugar and food additives seemed to help only about 5 percent of children with AD/HD, mostly very young children or those with food allergies. However, too much caffeine (found in coffee, tea, and some sodas) may trigger or exacerbate hyperactive behaviors in children with AD/HD. (For information on discipline and hyperactivity, see Chapter 19, "Temperament, Behavior, and Discipline.")

Symptoms and Diagnosis Some common symptoms of AD/HD include the following: often failing to give close attention to detail or making careless mistakes, having trouble keeping to tasks, not seeming to listen when spoken to directly, or failing to follow instructions completely or carefully. Other typical AD/HD behaviors include losing or forgetting important things, feeling restless or fidgeting with hands or feet, and running or climbing excessively. Children with AD/HD may also show impulsive behavior such as blurting out answers before hearing the whole question and having difficulty waiting for a turn. Not all children with AD/HD have all of these symptoms. Many affected children are not overactive or hyperactive, for instance, but may appear dreamy and absentminded.

There are three subtypes of AD/HD:

1. An inattentive subtype with signs that include being easily distracted, being unable to pay attention to details, not following directions, and losing or forgetting things like toys or homework
2. A hyperactive-impulsive subtype with signs that include fidgeting, squirming, blurting out answers before hearing the full question, having difficulty waiting, and running or jumping out of a seat when quiet behavior is expected
3. A combined subtype with signs that include those from both of the other subtypes and can be seen with or without hyperactivity

To diagnose a child with AD/HD, these behaviors must have appeared before age seven and have continued for at least six months. The behaviors must also be creating difficulties in at least two areas of the child's life, such as school, home, or social settings.

A primary care doctor who suspects a child has AD/HD usually will refer the child to a psychologist, psychiatrist, neurologist, or developmental pediatrician for further evaluation based on observation, achievement and ability tests, and in-depth discussion with the child's parents. Other problems that can complicate the condition or produce similar symptoms should also be excluded, such as depression, anxiety, hearing problems, a seizure disorder, obstructive sleep apnea, or learning disabilities.

An added difficulty in diagnosing AD/HD is that it often coexists with other problems. Mood disorders, such as depression, are commonly seen in children with AD/HD. Many children with AD/HD also have a specific learning disability, which means that they might have trouble mastering language or other skills when they get older, such as math, reading, or handwriting. Nearly half of all children with AD/HD (mostly boys) also have oppositional defiant disorder, which is characterized by stubbornness, outbursts of temper, and acts of defiance.

Treatment and Outlook Treatment of AD/HD should be comprehensive and individualized. In many cases, medications are helpful for managing the condition, but treatment should also include counseling or therapy to help the child learn coping skills and how to modify certain behaviors. Parents, teachers, and other adults who play a major role in the child's life have to be involved in the treatment plan. The child with AD/HD often has low self-confidence and low self-esteem because of repeated frustration or failure; this too must be addressed in a supportive treatment plan.

Medications used include stimulant medications such as Ritalin, Dexedrine, and Adderall, which have been shown to be of benefit in as many as 90 to 95 percent of cases. It is thought that these medications act as gatekeepers, helping the brain regulate the manufacture, storage, and flow of neurotransmitters. Other medications may also be used. Side effects of stimulant medications include loss of appetite, trouble sleeping, or a temporary slowing of growth. If these effects occur, the medication may be changed or the dosage adjusted.

There has been much debate in recent years about whether stimulant medications are overprescribed. Some argue that many children who do not actually have AD/HD may be given stimulant drugs inappropriately in an attempt to control difficult behaviors due to other causes. However, a study conducted by the American Medical Association published in 1998 did not find that this was a widespread problem.

A person probably does not outgrow AD/HD, but about half of children with the disorder appear to function well as adults. Others continue to have symptoms and require medication and behavioral coping strategies throughout life. It's important to maintain lifelong medical follow-up.

Autism

Autism is a brain disorder that affects the ability of a child to communicate with and relate to other people. The cause of this disorder is unclear, but research suggests that autism may be the result of abnormalities in brain chemicals and perhaps the structure of the brain itself. Studies have shown that certain areas of the brain in people with autism may be different in size from those in the brains of people without autism. Other studies have demonstrated abnormal levels of neurotransmitters, the chemicals that allow nerve cells to communicate with each other, in autistic children. Also, if one identical twin has autism, there is an 80 percent chance that the other will have the condition, too, suggesting genetic factors play some role in the condition. Certain chromosomal abnormalities are also more common in families with autism. Autism is not caused by bad parenting.

About 3 to 4 children in 10,000 have autism, and the disorder affects males three to four times more often than it affects females. Autism usually develops before the child is two and one-half years old. Many children with autism are also mentally retarded, and some have seizures. About 10 percent also have fragile X syndrome associated with mental retardation.

The term *pervasive developmental disorders* (PPD) is applied to children with autism, but it also includes children with similar but milder disorders that do not meet the criteria for the diagnosis of autism. For example, children with Asperger syndrome have problems interacting socially and may show several types of unusual behavior; however, they have normal or above average intelligence and do not have the language difficulties that are characteristically seen in children with autism.

Symptoms and Diagnosis Some children show signs of autism from birth, such as arching the back to avoid contact with people who try to hold them or banging their head against the side of their crib. Others appear to develop normally until about 12 to 18 months of age, when they may develop a range of symptoms.

Symptoms of autism include the following: failure to develop normal speech, including not speaking, not being able to sustain a conversation, or repeating nonsense words or sounds; absence of normal facial expression and body language; lack of eye contact; being withdrawn and spending long hours in play alone; inability to make friends; a need for sameness in play and other rigid routines; and a heightened awareness to some stimuli (such as loud noises) and a dulled awareness to others.

There is no single test for autism, and because the symptoms vary widely, it can be difficult to diagnose. The doctor will rule out other conditions that may be associated with similar symptoms such as hearing loss, speech problems, mental retardation, and other brain disorders.

Treatment and Outlook Presently there is no cure for autism. Children with autism and their families often need a variety of support services. Therapy for the very young child usually focuses on speech and language, special education, and sometimes medications to relieve specific symptoms. Behavior modification can help replace abnormal behaviors with more normal ones. Occupational therapy may help improve an autistic child's physical and sensory skills.

Some individuals with mild autism are capable of living independently, but most cannot. Often, they need a supervised environment throughout their lives.

Birthmarks and Moles

Birthmarks are marks on the skin that are either present at birth or develop shortly thereafter. Vascular birthmarks, which are composed of clusters of blood vessels in the skin (which are responsible for the color of the birthmarks), include the following:

- Hemangiomas—a common type that can either be red and raised (strawberry hemangioma) or that appear bluish-red beneath the outer layer of skin (cavernous hemangioma)
- Salmon patches—faint reddish birthmarks that are also called "stork bites" when they appear on the back of the neck or "angel's kisses" when they appear on the forehead
- Port-wine stains—birthmarks that appear maroon in color on the surface of the skin, usually on the face or neck

Moles are typically raised collections of pigment-producing cells that appear brown, black, or blue in color and are sometimes called "beauty marks" or "beauty spots." Some moles may be flat or skin-colored.

Although some moles are present at birth (called congenital nevi), most will usually appear on the skin by early adulthood. Everyone has moles—sometimes more than 40 of them. Moles may enlarge with time or darken with exposure to the sun, and some may sprout hairs.

Symptoms and Diagnosis A doctor can diagnose a vascular birthmark by performing a physical examination looking for a pink, red, or bluish-red discoloration of the skin.

A doctor can diagnose a mole by performing a physical examination looking for roundish, perhaps raised areas of the skin that are brown, black, or blue in color (although some moles may be flat and have the same coloring as normal skin). Most moles don't cause health problems, but changes in their appearance should be brought to the attention of the child's doctor.

Treatment and Outlook Most birthmarks do not require treatment, but a doctor should evaluate them on a regular basis. Some hemangiomas will shrink or disappear on their own by the time a child is five years old—and almost all strawberry hemangiomas will disappear by age nine. Cavernous hemangiomas sometimes disappear on their own, as well. However, large birthmarks on the face (such as port-wine stains) or hemangiomas that interfere with a child's vision, hearing, or breathing may be treated with laser surgery and/or steroid medication.

Hemangiomas may bleed if they are injured. In this case, the area should be cared for by applying gentle pressure to the area and by cleaning with soap and water, then following with the application of a gauze bandage. If bleeding persists for more than 10 minutes, the child's doctor should be contacted.

Most moles do not require any treatment or pose any threat to a child's health, but they should be monitored regularly for abnormal changes, such as an irregular border, a color change, or growth (moles that become wider than a standard pencil eraser should be checked by a doctor). These changes increase the likelihood that the mole may be or may become cancerous. Moles that may be cancerous are surgically removed and examined.

Moles and often birthmarks may also be covered with cosmetics designed to conceal blemishes, or they may be removed for cosmetic reasons. Most moles will not grow back, but those that do should be brought to the attention of a doctor.

Blindness/Visual Impairment

Many conditions can cause visual impairment. The most common in children is amblyopia. Amblyopia, sometimes called "lazy eye," is the loss of vision in one eye that can occur when the eye is used less than the other during infancy and early childhood. Development of normal vision in both eyes requires that the brain receive stimulation from each eye during the first several years of life. If one eye gets less use for any reason, the part of the brain connected to that eye gets inadequate stimulation, and permanent vision loss may result if not corrected early. This can result from several eye problems including cataracts or other abnormalities of the eye that block light from entering or passing through the eye, as well as strabismus ("crossed" eyes), a condition in which the eyes are misaligned and not working together properly—see Strabismus in this chapter.

Vision loss can also result from glaucoma (rare in childhood), a disorder in which fluid pressure builds inside the eye and damages the optic (visual) nerve. Physical, chemical, or heat injuries to the eye can also cause visual impairment or blindness.

Some children are born with conditions that can cause blindness, such as cataracts, which cloud the lens in the eye. Cataracts present at birth can result if a pregnant woman is infected with rubella (German measles) or toxoplasmosis, a parasite that can be contracted from eating raw or undercooked meat or exposure to animal (especially cat) feces.

If a child is born prematurely, he will be checked by an ophthalmologist (eye specialist) for retinopathy of prematurity, a disorder in which the blood vessels in the retina, at the back of the eye, develop abnormally. In the most severe cases, the retina may detach from the back of the eye, leading to vision loss.

Vision problems can also result from a number of birth defects involving the structures of the eye, the optic nerves, and the areas of the brain involved with vision. Birth defects such as hydrocephalus ("water on the brain"—see Hydrocephalus in this chapter) can also cause blindness.

Rare inherited disorders such as retinitis pigmentosa, in which the retina slowly degenerates, can also cause visual loss, as can tumors in the eye such as retinoblastoma, a cancer of the retina.

Symptoms and Diagnosis There are a number of signs that may indicate that a child is having visual difficulties or has a disease that may affect vision. These include excessive tearing; sensitivity to light; "crossed" eyes or eyes that don't move together; holding the head in an abnormal or tilted position; frequent squinting; drooping eyelids; pupils of unequal size; persistent eye rubbing; eyes that "bounce" or "dance"; inability to see objects unless held very close; cloudy cornea (the outer part of the eyeball); and, in newborns, redness, swelling, crusting, or discharge in the eye.

The child may complain of double vision, frequent headaches, dizziness, nausea after doing close-up work, an inability to see clearly, or itching or burning of the eyes.

Unless there are known birth defects or other problems that would raise immediate concern about vision, your child's doctor will examine the eyes at routine checkups to be sure that your child's eyes and vision are developing normally. If an eye or vision problem is suspected, your child will be referred to an eye specialist.

Treatment and Outlook There are no specific treatments for some causes of blindness, such as birth defects or retinitis pigmentosa; however, others can be effectively treated. Strabismus can usually be corrected with eyeglasses, eyedrops, or surgery. If surgery is needed, it is usually done between 6 and 18 months of age.

Children who have strabismus may need to wear a patch over the more used eye intermittently to force use of the other eye (and the part of the brain connected to it) to prevent amblyopia from developing. If the condition is not treated in the first few years of life, vision in the underused eye can be permanently lost.

Glaucoma and cataracts can be treated with surgery.

Children with significant visual impairment or blindness should receive services including special training and stimulation programs, educational support, and assistive devices and technology that are necessary to help support their developmental progress, social and emotional adjustment, educational achievement, and attainment of their full potential as they grow into adulthood. Parents should work closely with their child's doctors and other health care professionals to ensure that these needs are met.

Prevention and Prenatal Testing To help prevent vision loss in their babies, pregnant women should make sure that they have been successfully immunized against rubella (German measles) before becoming pregnant. They should also avoid handling cat litter or eating raw or undercooked meat.

To prevent eye injuries, keep all chemicals out of reach; watch for sharp, pointed objects or toys; keep children away from darts and air rifles; teach children how to handle scissors and pencils properly; keep children away from lawn mowers, which can hurl stones or other objects; and don't let children near when you are lighting fires or using tools. Children who are nearby when adults are using hammers or power tools should wear goggles. Tell children not to look directly into the sun, even with sunglasses. Never allow a young child near fireworks.

For information about vision, see Chapter 15, "Hearing and Vision."

Celiac Disease

Celiac disease is a digestive disorder in which there is damage to the small intestine that interferes with absorption of nutrients from foods. It is an autoimmune disease, meaning that the body's immune system attacks some of the body's normal tissues. People with celiac disease, also known as celiac sprue, nontropical sprue, and gluten-sensitive enteropathy, cannot tolerate a protein called gluten, found in wheat, rye, and barley. When people with the disease eat foods with gluten, their immune system responds by attacking and damaging the small intestine. The normal small, fingerlike protrusions called villi on the lining of the small intestine, through which nutrients from food are absorbed into the bloodstream, are lost. Without enough villi, a person may become malnourished, regardless of the amount of food eaten.

Celiac disease runs in families and is the most common genetic disease in Europe. Recent studies have suggested that celiac disease is underdiagnosed in the United States. Sometimes the disease is triggered or becomes active for the first time after surgery, infection, emotional stress, pregnancy, or childbirth.

Symptoms and Diagnosis Symptoms directly involving the digestive system may or may not occur. Irritability is one of the most common symptoms in children. Other symptoms include recurring abdominal pain; bloated belly; chronic diarrhea; weight loss or slow weight gain; pale, foul-smelling stools; unexplained anemia (low red blood cell count); gas; behavior changes; decreased muscle mass; fatigue; and delayed growth/short stature (height).

Some people develop symptoms as children, others as adults. One factor thought to play a role in when and how the condition appears is whether and how long a person was breast-fed: In general, the longer the person was breast-fed, the later the symptoms of the disease appear. Other factors include when the person began eating foods with gluten and how much gluten is in the person's diet.

Celiac disease can be difficult to diagnose because some of its symptoms are similar to other diseases, such as irritable bowel syndrome, inflammatory bowel disease (Crohn's disease, ulcerative colitis), and intestinal infections. To diagnose the disease, doctors test blood to measure levels of antibodies to gliadin (a part of gluten) and antibodies to intestinal tissues. The doctor may also biopsy (remove a small piece of) the lining of the small intestine to check for damage to villi. A repeat biopsy showing improvement after 6 to 12 months on a gluten-free diet can confirm the diagnosis.

In Italy, where the disease is common, all children are screened by age six, and Italians of any age are tested whenever they show symptoms. As a result, the time between when symptoms appear and when the disease is diagnosed is two to three weeks. In the United States, where many doctors are unfamiliar with the disorder, the time between first symptoms and diagnosis averages about 10 years.

Treatment and Outlook The treatment for celiac disease is a gluten-free diet. Usually children will show dramatic improvement in their symptoms within one to two weeks of starting the diet. Recovery may take longer in children who were more ill and malnourished before beginning treatment. The condition is lifelong, so children must continue following the diet into adulthood to remain healthy.

Malnutrition can be a severe complication of celiac disease. Particularly if untreated for years, the disease also puts a person at increased risk for lymphoma and adenocarcinoma (two forms of cancer that can develop in the intestine), osteoporosis (in which the bones become brittle and weak), and short stature.

Because genetic factors seem to play a role in the development of celiac disease, closely related family members of people with the disease should be tested.

Cerebral Palsy

Cerebral palsy (CP) is a condition involving dysfunction of the nervous system stemming from damage to or a defect of the developing brain. It's one of the most common congenital disorders. There are 10,000 new cases diagnosed each year in the United States. The overall incidence is rising because premature babies who once would have died are surviving; about 5 percent of premature infants are diagnosed with the condition.

The causes of most cases of CP are unknown; most are the result of problems during pregnancy in which the brain is either damaged or doesn't develop normally. Problems during the birth process are the cause of CP in fewer than 10 percent of cases. Infections and other maternal health problems during pregnancy, birth defects of the central nervous system, premature birth, low birthweight (especially infants weighing less than two pounds at birth), multiple births (twins, triplets, etc.), and lack of oxygen reaching the fetus' or infant's brain have been associated with an increased risk of CP. Injury to the brain in infancy or early childhood can also cause CP.

Symptoms and Diagnosis Cerebral palsy is a condition characterized by poor muscle control, spasticity, paralysis, and other problems of nervous system function.

Cerebral palsy is classified into three types. Spastic cerebral palsy (the most common type) involves muscle stiffness and difficult movement. Children with athetoid cerebral palsy have uncontrollable slow, writhing movements. In ataxic cerebral palsy the child mainly has difficulties with balance and coordination.

Children with CP have widely varying degrees of physical disability and may have associated medical problems such as seizures, speech or communication problems, learning disabilities, and mental retardation. Other medical problems may include visual impairment or blindness, hearing loss, bladder and bowel difficulties, feeding and nutritional problems, aspiration (inhaling of food or fluid into the lungs), vomiting, tooth decay, sleep disorders, and behavior problems.

The diagnosis may be made early on in infants at high risk for the condition, especially those born prematurely who developed bleeding inside the brain or severe lung problems. In babies without known risk factors, CP may be more difficult to diagnose in the first year of life. A delay in reaching normal developmental milestones, such as not reaching for toys by four months or sitting without support by eight to nine months, may raise concerns. Other signs include the following: poor muscle tone, poorly coordinated movements, and the failure of infantile reflexes such as the Moro (startle) reflex to fade at the ages expected. If the delay in development is mild, however, the diagnosis of CP may not be made until the child is 12 to 15 months or older.

Treatment and Outlook Cerebral palsy can be managed with a variety of therapies and support. As soon as a child is diagnosed with CP, he can begin therapy aimed at maximizing movement, speech, hearing, learning, and social and emotional development. Medication, surgery, and leg and lower body braces may also be used to help the child attain as much movement and muscle function as possible.

Providing the child with adequate nutrition can be a particular challenge in children with CP who have problems with swallowing and aspiration. Feedings

through a tube passed into the stomach through the nose or through a tube inserted surgically through the abdominal wall directly into the stomach can be helpful in these situations. Parents and children with the condition must work closely with their doctors, therapists, psychologists, nurses, social workers, and teachers.

Laws exist affirming the right of children with disabilities to a public education. With appropriate support and accommodations, many children with CP can receive their education in a regular classroom setting with their peers.

The child's family plays a key role in managing the child's condition and providing the support necessary for the child to reach his full potential. It's important for parents to become as informed as possible about their child's condition and to take advantage of available resources for support in caring for their child and coping with the challenges involved.

There is no cure, but CP is not a progressive condition—it will not get worse over time. About 90 percent of children with CP live to their 20s or beyond. However, children with quadriplegic (affecting all four limbs) CP and severe mental retardation have a lower survival rate, with only about 70 percent reaching their 20s. Respiratory failure due to problems such as pneumonia and aspiration is the chief reason for early death in these children.

Prevention and Prenatal Testing Controlling diabetes, anemia, hypertension, and nutritional deficiencies during pregnancy will help reduce the possibility of a baby being born prematurely and thus reduce the risk of CP. A premature baby's risk of having CP is 50 times higher than that of a full-term baby. There is no test for CP before birth.

Child Abuse (Physical and Sexual)

Each year, approximately 1 million children are abused (injured, neglected, or emotionally mistreated) in the United States, and 1,000 to 1,300 U.S. children die as a result of physical abuse. Those who survive may suffer emotional trauma that lasts long after the bruises have healed.

In the United States, one out of every eight boys and one out of every four girls is sexually abused before reaching age 18. In 90 percent of these cases, sexual abuse occurs in the home, particularly when younger children are involved. A child who knows the abuser (about 90 percent of cases) usually senses that the abuse is wrong, but she may feel trapped by the affection she feels for the person or fearful of the power the abuser has over her, so she doesn't tell others about what happened.

The following actions can be considered physical abuse if they are done intentionally to harm a child: hitting, throwing, kicking, choking, biting, shaking, beating with an object, burning (with a match, cigar, or cigarette), scalding with hot water, pushing and holding a child underwater, and tying up a child.

The following actions can be considered physical neglect: starving or failing to provide food for a child, not providing adequate housing or warm clothing in cold weather, locking a child in a closet or room, leaving a child alone for extended periods of time, not providing medical care when a child is sick or injured, and placing a child in a physically dangerous situation.

These actions can be considered sexual abuse: fondling, touching, or kissing a child's sex organs; making a child touch someone else's sex organs; having sex with a child; showing a child pornographic material; showing sex organs to a child; forcing a child to undress; forcing a child to have sex with someone; making a child pose or perform for pornographic pictures or videos; and telling "dirty" stories to a child.

Shaken baby/shaken impact syndrome is a specific form of child abuse. It's the leading cause of death in child abuse cases in the United States. Most shaking incidents last just 5 to 20 seconds, but that's enough time to cause sufficient brain damage to kill a baby. In some cases, a blow to the head accompanies the shaking.

Symptoms and Diagnosis There's no one telltale sign that a child is being abused. Unexplained injuries such as bruises, black eyes, and broken bones or findings such as vaginal discharge or bleeding in an infant or young girl are certainly clues, but other signs are less obvious. Children who have been abused may behave differently. They may have nightmares or trouble sleeping. They may also:

- Have a poor self-image
- Be unable to love or trust others
- Be aggressive or disruptive
- Display intense anger or rage
- Act out sexually
- Be self-destructive or self-abusive
- Feel sad, passive, withdrawn, or depressed
- Show a fear of certain adults

Children who witness abuse but are not victims themselves may also display some or all of these symptoms. It's important to note that these symptoms are all nonspecific, meaning they could result from a number of causes—not just child abuse. Children who are under stress for a variety of reasons—including parental separation, divorce, and visitation and custody issues—may show similar symptoms.

The American Academy of Pediatrics Committee on Hospital Care recommends that suspected abuse victims be brought to a hospital, where the initial diagnosis can be made and treatment, if necessary, can be given. Hospitals can provide several services for abused children, especially battered children who may need medical examination, X-rays, or cultures for a diagnosis to be made. X-rays can show broken bones (from both recent and old injuries), which may be the only sign that infants and young children have been physically abused, as they often can't or won't speak of the abuse themselves. If the child's injuries are severe or if there is significant concern about the risk of further injury if the child is returned home, the child may be admitted to the hospital for treatment and monitoring, and to allow social workers and child protection agency personnel to begin an evaluation of the child's environment.

Treatment and Outlook If your child tells you about an abusive experience, remain calm and let him know that you believe him. Your reaction can either help him begin to recover or further traumatize him. Here are some tips:

- Listen carefully and calmly, no matter how upset you are. You'll need to remember what your child tells you. And let your child know he's being heard.
- Assure your child that you're glad that he told you of the abuse, that it was in no way his fault, and that you will make sure it doesn't happen again.
- Encourage him to tell you everything, but avoid asking too many specific questions—they may mislead or confuse your child, or

they may be asked in a way that prompts a particular answer. Later, this may seriously affect the ability of investigators to find out exactly what did or did not happen.
- Don't say anything negative about the suspected perpetrator, who may be someone your child truly cares for. If you make threats, your child may feel the need to protect the person and may not be as forthcoming with details.
- If you think that your child wants to say more but is afraid, speak with your child's doctor or a social worker, or call a child abuse hotline for further advice and assistance.

Your child will need medical care if he has been sexually molested or physically injured. Even if signs of abuse are not evident, it's best to err on the side of caution and take him to the doctor anyway. Above all, keep your child in safe environments and assume the allegation is true until proved otherwise. Psychological help is also strongly recommended. Without it, children who have been abused tend to repeat the pattern of abuse with their own children. As adults they may have trouble establishing and maintaining close relationships, and they are at greater risk for anxiety, depression, substance abuse, medical illness, and problems at work.

Cleft Lip/Palate

A cleft lip is an opening in the upper lip that occurs on one or both sides of the lip. Cleft palate is an opening in the roof of the mouth either at the midline or on one or both sides. (The palate extends from the top of the upper teeth to the uvula, the little piece of tissue that hangs at the back of the throat. There is a bony hard palate, just behind the teeth, and a muscular soft palate, behind the hard palate.) Clefts can occur in just the lip or just the palate. Formation of the lip and palate are linked, however, and in many cases children are born with both.

These openings are present normally during the early part of fetal growth but usually close by the third month of pregnancy. Three developing areas must close together to form the face. The pieces that form the palate usually come together properly, but when the growth process is disturbed, the area doesn't close, leaving a cleft.

Cleft palate and lip probably occur as the result of a number of factors. In some cases, genetics appear to play a role. It's likely that the susceptibility for developing the condition is inherited, probably through several different genes. Factors to which the fetus is exposed early in pregnancy may also be involved. Recent research indicates that binge drinking (five or more drinks at one time) of alcohol during the first three months of pregnancy increases the risk for a cleft defect in an infant. Some cases occur as a part of a syndrome involving additional birth defects.

Symptoms and Diagnosis A cleft lip is a highly visible birth defect that is immediately noticed and diagnosed. Infants with cleft palate may have difficulty sucking from the breast or bottle because they can't latch on to the nipple in the airtight manner necessary for sucking effectively. A cleft can also allow food or milk to leak out of the nose during feeding. These problems will alert the baby's medical providers to check for palate problems. Some children with clefts have associated birth defects or other problems such as congenital heart disease, growth disorders, or learning difficulties.

Treatment and Outlook Initially, feeding is the main problem that needs to be addressed when an infant is born with a cleft lip or palate. Special nipples and artificial devices that temporarily plug the opening in the palate are used to allow the infant to suck and feed successfully.

Cleft lip usually is closed by a plastic surgeon when the baby is about two to three months old if the infant is otherwise healthy and has had satisfactory weight gain. Around nine to twelve months, cleft palate is usually closed with a single operation unless the cleft is wide, in which case the child may require a second procedure later.

As the child grows, other surgeries may be needed. Around age three to four years, some children will need additional surgery on the palate, especially if their speech continues to sound nasal.

Many children with this condition have dental problems such as missing jawbone tissue, missing or malformed teeth, and top and bottom teeth that do not fit together properly, called malocclusion. Left uncorrected, these problems interfere with chewing and cause more facial deformity. Surgery on the upper jaw may be required if there is severe malocclusion, although if possible this is delayed until the child's growth has been completed. Final lip and nose surgery may be required when the facial structures have reached maturity, between ages 17 and 21.

Because a cleft palate allows liquid to get into the sinuses and ear (eustachian) tubes, children with cleft palate are also more prone to ear and sinus infections. To help manage ear problems related to this, the surgeon may insert tubes in the eardrums to drain fluid and allow air to enter and leave the middle ear. The child will need to have his hearing checked regularly. He will also have to work with a speech therapist to learn how to train his palate muscles to work properly.

With appropriate medical care, children with cleft palate or lip have a normal structural, functional, and cosmetic outcome. Speech and orthodontic development need close supervision, but the outlook for normal development is good.

Uncorrected clefts can cause abnormal growth of the face and significant difficulty in developing normal speech. When a person speaks, sounds are made by directing air through the nose or the mouth. A cleft palate lets air escape out of the nose all the time, resulting in unusual sounds. A normally formed upper lip is also required to make certain sounds.

Uncorrected, cleft lip or palate can also lead to social and self-esteem problems.

Prevention and Prenatal Testing To help prevent cleft palate and lip (and other birth defects), pregnant women should avoid drinking alcohol, and they should make sure they are getting proper nutrition and prenatal care. Prospective parents who have cleft lip or palate should be aware that, in some cases, their children might have a significantly increased risk for the condition. Parents who have a child with a cleft lip or palate, particularly if the child has additional birth defects, should seek counseling about the possible increased risk of cleft or other defects for future pregnancies.

Congenital Heart Disease

Congenital heart disease includes a number of birth defects of the heart, the blood vessels that feed into it, or the vessels that carry blood out from it. The causes of most of these defects are unknown. Genetic factors play some role, and the risk of a child having a heart defect increases if a parent or sibling has one. In one large study, 12 percent of the cases of congenital heart malformations were related to a chromosomal defect such as Down syndrome (see Down Syndrome in this chapter), and 8 percent occurred in infants who had multiple congenital abnormalities (birth defects). Some children with congenital heart disease have an identifiable single gene defect, such as Marfan syndrome, a hereditary connective tissue disorder.

About 3 percent of cases are associated with a disease the mother had during pregnancy, including diabetes, lupus, rubella (German measles), or phenylketonuria (PKU), a disorder involving the enzyme that processes the amino acid phenylalanine. Certain drugs taken during pregnancy, such as lithium, ethanol (alcohol), warfarin (a blood thinner), thalidomide, antimetabolites (such as some cancer chemotherapy drugs), and anticonvulsant (seizure) medications are also associated with an increased incidence of congenital heart defects.

The most common defects are holes in the walls that separate the heart into the left and right sides. Atrial septal defects occur between the upper chambers of the heart, which receive the blood entering the heart. These account for 6 to 8 percent of all heart defects. Ventricular septal defects occur between the lower chambers, which pump blood out of the heart to the lungs and the rest of the body. These represent about 25 to 30 percent of all heart defects. In both of these abnormalities, some of the blood returning to the heart from the lungs is not pumped out to the body normally—it is sent back to the lungs instead.

As a result, the amount of blood in the lungs' blood vessels increases, causing extra work for the heart and sometimes problems in the lungs.

A third common defect is patent ductus arteriosus, which occurs in about 7 percent of infants with heart defects. The ductus arteriosus is a blood vessel connecting the aorta, the large artery that carries oxygen-rich blood to the body, and the pulmonary artery, the artery that carries oxygen-depleted blood to the lungs. The ductus allows blood to bypass the lungs in the fetus, because the fetus gets oxygen from the placenta and doesn't breathe air. However, at birth blood must flow to the lungs to receive oxygen. Normally, the ductus closes within a day or two after birth. But if the ductus remains open, blood intended for the rest of the body may return to the lungs, sometimes causing abnormal stress on the lungs and heart.

Narrowing (stenosis) of valves (one-way openings into the heart that keep the blood from flowing backward) is also not uncommon. Valves that are narrowed do not permit normal blood flow.

Symptoms and Diagnosis Some children may show signs of a heart defect in the first few days after birth; others may seem completely healthy until they are a few weeks old or until later in childhood. Generally, signs of significant heart disease in infants may include rapid breathing; shortness of breath; blueness of the lips, tongue, and under the nails; tiring out easily with feedings; and failure to gain weight normally.

Children with large ventricular septal defects are at risk for repeated respiratory infections, other lung complications, and heart failure.

Children with atrial septal defects usually have less obvious symptoms.

There are usually no symptoms with a small patent ductus arteriosus, but a large defect will lead to heart failure and failure to grow normally.

The doctor will listen to the child's chest with a stethoscope to hear if there is an abnormal sound, called a heart murmur, that might indicate blood is not flowing through the heart and blood vessels properly. It is important to note that some heart murmurs may be present at birth and disappear with time, and others may not appear until weeks or more after birth. Most heart murmurs are benign ("innocent") and do not mean there is heart disease or affect a child's health. The doctor will also feel for pulses to see if blood is being circulated through all parts of the body normally.

If the child's symptoms or if the findings from a physical examination are of concern to the doctor, he may order further evaluation. This may include blood tests, a chest X-ray, electrocardiogram (EKG), or echocardiogram (ultrasound imaging study of the heart).

If a more significant heart defect is suspected, particularly of a type requiring surgical correction, the heart specialist (usually a pediatric cardiologist) may perform a cardiac catheterization study. In this procedure, a thin tube is inserted into a blood vessel in the child's leg or arm and then passed into the heart. Doctors can then measure the pressures and oxygen content of the blood in various chambers of the heart and large blood vessels, and also inject dye that can be seen on X-rays to get a detailed look at the pattern of blood flow and the structure of the child's heart.

Treatment and Outlook Treatment for heart defects depends on the type and severity. Some heart defects, such as small ventricular septal defects, may resolve on their own, requiring nothing more than careful follow-up and watchful waiting.

Certain forms of congenital heart disease can actually be treated by installing patches onto holes in the heart through a heart catheterization procedure or widening narrowed heart valves by pulling a balloon on the tip of the catheter through the obstructed area; these procedures can avoid or delay the need for open heart surgery.

Other heart defects may require surgical correction, with timing of the procedures and techniques used depending on the severity and type of the defect.

Before, and sometimes after, surgery is performed to treat a heart defect, a variety of medications may be used to support the child's heart function or control other problems associated with the child's condition.

Most children with congenital heart defects are at greater risk for developing a serious bacterial infection of the lining of the heart or heart valves. This is of particular concern with certain procedures, such as some types of dental work, that cause germs to be shed into the child's bloodstream where they can be carried to the heart. Parents should speak to their child's doctors about the need for antibiotic treatment before such procedures to prevent infection of the heart.

The long-term outlook for children with congenital heart disease varies widely depending on the type and severity of the defect, treatments available, and other health problems the child may have.

Prevention and Prenatal Testing The heart of the developing fetus is most susceptible to damage during the first three to seven weeks of pregnancy. Because more than half of all pregnancies are unplanned and the fetal heart may suffer injury before a woman knows she is pregnant, careful attention to risk reduction is important in all women who are planning to become pregnant. This includes avoiding drinking alcohol and taking certain medications. Before getting pregnant, a woman should discuss with her doctor what medications are safe for her to take during pregnancy. If she has a chronic disease such as diabetes, she should discuss with her doctor the best way to manage it both before and during pregnancy. Rubella (German measles) also puts a woman at risk of having a baby with a heart defect. A woman planning a pregnancy should be sure that she has immunity against rubella—if she doesn't, she should be vaccinated. However, it is recommended that a woman should not become pregnant for three months after being vaccinated, and pregnant women should not be given live rubella virus vaccine.

Parents who have a child with congenital heart disease and who are planning another pregnancy may wish to seek genetic counseling about the risk of congenital heart disease occurring in subsequent children.

Congenital Hypothyroidism

Hypothyroidism occurs when the thyroid, a butterfly-shaped gland located in the front of the neck, cannot produce enough thyroid hormones. These hormones control the rate at which many of the body's chemical functions (metabolism) take place. Thyroid hormones are necessary for bone growth and critically important for normal brain development in infants and young children.

Congenital hypothyroidism—meaning the child is born with an absent, underdeveloped, or inadequately functioning thyroid gland—usually occurs in infants with no known family history of the condition. Approximately 1 in 3,000 infants born in this country have the disorder. Some (nearly 10 percent) of these infants have a hereditary disorder affecting the ability of the thyroid gland to produce hormones, but most are born with absent or underdeveloped thyroid glands. The developing thyroid gland of the fetus can be damaged or destroyed, resulting in congenital hypothyroidism, if the mother herself is treated with radioactive iodine for a thyroid condition during pregnancy. A temporary form of hypothyroidism can result if the mother was treated with antithyroid drugs during pregnancy or was exposed to excessive amounts of iodine.

Symptoms and Diagnosis Newborns with congenital hypothyroidism often have few or no symptoms or abnormal findings on physical examination at birth. Signs that may develop over the first days and weeks of life may include the following: prolonged newborn jaundice (yellow skin), poor appetite, constipation, a hoarse cry, sluggishness, breathing problems because of an enlarged tongue, nasal stuffiness, and slow growth.

Early detection of congenital hypothyroidism is extremely important because adequate levels of thyroid hormone are critical for an infant's brain development. If the condition is not diagnosed and treated within a few weeks of birth, hypothyroidism can result in developmental delay and irreversible mental retardation. For this reason, newborns have their thyroid hormone levels routinely measured by a blood test within the first few days of life as a part of the newborn screening programs established in every U.S. state and most developed countries worldwide.

Treatment and Outlook The treatment for congenital hypothyroidism is oral thyroid hormone replacement medication. The child must be followed closely; adjustments of the medication dosage are made based on periodic tests of the levels of thyroid hormones in the blood.

If diagnosed and treated promptly, children with the condition usually will grow and develop normally both physically and mentally.

Prevention and Prenatal Testing A woman who has hyperthyroidism (overactive thyroid gland) should not receive radioactive iodine treatment for the condition if she is pregnant or suspects she may be pregnant. This treatment can damage or destroy the developing thyroid gland of the fetus.

Cystic Fibrosis

Cystic fibrosis (CF) is an inherited condition in which the body produces excessively sticky mucus. Mucus is needed to lubricate the lungs, trap dust and bacteria inhaled through the nose, and protect the lining of the intestines from the acids needed to digest food. But the mucus produced by a person with CF clogs the lungs, liver, pancreas, and intestines, leading to a host of medical problems and complications.

Cystic fibrosis is caused by mutations in a gene on chromosome number 7. One mutation (delta-F508) accounts for approximately 50 percent of the cases of CF. A variety of other mutations account for the rest of the cases. These mutations result in the production of an abnormal protein that does not allow normal passage of chloride across cell membranes. The effect of this on the body is the production of mucus that is much thicker and stickier than normal. Because this abnormal mucus and debris cannot be cleared from the lungs, the child is very susceptible to lung infections, and the resulting chronic inflammation (irritation) in the lungs leads to progressive, permanent lung damage. In the pancreas, the thick mucus blocks the channels that would normally carry enzymes to the intestines to digest foods. Thus the child can't process or absorb nutrients properly, especially fats. The child has trouble gaining weight, even with a normal appetite and food intake.

Symptoms and Diagnosis The major symptoms of CF result from problems in the lungs and digestive organs and can vary in severity. Doctors may suspect CF soon after birth if a baby becomes ill with repeated respiratory infections and fails to gain weight despite a normal appetite.

Some children with the disease have symptoms at birth and may be born with a condition called "meconium ileus." All newborns have meconium, a thick, dark, puttylike substance that usually passes out through the baby's intestinal system in bowel movements in the first few days of life. But in children with CF, the meconium is too thick and sticky to pass through and can block the intestines.

More common, babies born with the condition have no immediate problems but fail to thrive despite a good appetite and milk intake. The abnormal mucus blocks pancreatic enzymes from entering the intestines, so nutrients pass out of the body unused. Poor fat absorption makes the child's stool appear oily and bulky and increases the risk of deficiencies in the fat-soluble vitamins A, D, E, and K. The unabsorbed fats may also cause excessive gas, an abnormally swollen belly, and abdominal pain.

Because the condition also affects cells in the sweat glands, children with CF may also have a salty "frosting" on their skin or taste salty when kissed. They may also lose large amounts of salt from their bodies when they sweat on hot days.

Nasal congestion, sinus problems, wheezing, and asthmalike symptoms are also common in children with CF. As the symptoms progress, the child may develop a chronic cough that produces thick, heavy, discolored mucus. The child may also suffer from repeated lung infections like pneumonia and bronchitis. As chronic infections reduce lung function, the person may begin to feel short of breath all the time. Lung disease is a common cause of disability and shortened life span in people with CF.

The diagnosis of CF is usually made before a child is three years old, although about 15 percent of children with CF are diagnosed later in life. A sweat test is generally used to diagnose the disease. It measures the amount of salt in sweat, usually collected from a child's forearm. The level of salt in sweat in people with CF is higher than in unaffected people. Generally at least two sweat tests are performed to confirm the diagnosis. Other tests may be used to monitor a child's disease, including chest X-rays, blood tests to check for signs of malnutrition, pulmonary (lung) function tests to measure the effects of the disease on the child's breathing, and bacterial cultures to guide treatment of lung infection with antibiotics.

Genetic testing can also be used to confirm the diagnosis in many cases.

Several states now include a test for CF in the battery of screening tests routinely performed on newborns.

Treatment and Outlook The basic daily care of a child with CF usually includes treatments to maintain lung function, such as chest physical therapy, in which the back and chest are thumped to help loosen and clear mucus from the lungs. The child usually eats a modified diet with vitamin and mineral supplements and may take daily doses of pancreatic enzymes by mouth to help him digest foods better. Children with CF may also need oral or inhaled antibiotics to treat lung infections and medications to thin mucus. Some of the medicines used to treat asthma are also frequently used for treating respiratory symptoms in patients with CF.

In the past, CF almost always caused death in childhood due to lung damage. But treatments in recent decades have allowed many children with CF to live into adulthood and have productive, active lives. Average life span is now about 30 years.

Prevention and Prenatal Testing It takes two copies of a CF gene, one inherited from each parent, for a child to have the disease. People born with only one CF gene—inherited from only one parent—and one normal gene are CF carriers. They do not show symptoms but can pass the problem gene to their children. It is estimated that about 12 million Americans are currently CF carriers. If two CF carriers have a child, there is a one in four chance the child will have CF.

So far, scientists have identified at least 600 mutations in the CF gene that are capable of causing the disease. The most common mutation, delta-F508, can be detected in children by genetic testing, both before and after birth.

In some circumstances, the test can also be useful for adults considering having children who want to know whether they carry the mutant gene.

Deafness/Hearing Impairment

There are several types and causes of hearing impairment.

With conductive hearing impairment, sound waves are not transmitted completely from the outer and middle ear to the inner ear. This can occur when an eardrum is damaged as a result of an object being placed too far inside the ear, ear infections, a head injury, a sudden or extreme change in air pressure against the eardrum, or an explosion or gunshot. Conductive hearing problems can also occur because of abnormal development or growth of the ossicles, the tiny bones in the middle ear that work together to transmit sound from the eardrum to the inner ear.

In sensorineural hearing impairment, the cochlea—a tiny snail-shaped organ in the inner ear filled with liquid and covered with tiny hairs called cilia that stimulate nerves connected to the brain—is damaged or destroyed, or there is a problem with the nerve connection from the cochlea to the brain. About 50 percent of cases of sensorineural deafness are the result of genetic disorders. The condition may also be caused by a viral infection of the inner ear. Cytomegalovirus (CMV) is the most common infectious cause, but bacterial meningitis can also lead to deafness, as can mumps, rubella (German measles), and measles. Hearing loss can also occur in an infant if the mother takes certain medications early in pregnancy such as certain cancer chemotherapy drugs, diuretics (water pills), or aminoglycosides (a class of antibiotics) or if the child is exposed before or after birth to quinine, lead, or arsenic. Traumatic injuries and exposure to loud noise (whether prolonged exposure or one exposure to extremely loud noise) can also cause this type of hearing loss.

Mixed combined conductive-sensori-neural hearing impairment also occurs.

Symptoms and Diagnosis Hearing loss that is present from birth is usually first noticed by parents when the baby doesn't react to sounds, or later on when the child has a delay in speech development. Signs in older children may include needing to turn up the TV louder than normal, not understanding what people are saying, not hearing the doorbell or phone, or slurred or indistinct speech.

Because of the importance of hearing to normal speech development, the earlier hearing problems are identified and addressed, the better. In fact, at the time of this writing, many states are in the process of passing legislation mandating routine hearing screening of all newborns. Many hospital nurseries have already instituted such programs. By school age, all children should have had their hearing tested either by a doctor or in school. Most children can cooperate for a routine hearing screening test around age four years.

There are several tests used to diagnose hearing loss. In babies, hearing can be tested by putting the infant in a soundproof booth and observing the child's behavior in response to sounds. Techniques such as OAE (otoacoustic emission testing) and ABR (auditory-evoked brainstem response) that don't require cooperation by the child can also be used to evaluate hearing in infants.

Treatment and Outlook Treating ear infections with antibiotics and sometimes surgery (insertion of tubes into the eardrums) can reverse or prevent worsening of some forms of hearing loss. Surgery to repair damaged eardrums or the bones in the middle ear is also possible in some cases. Some children can benefit from special amplification systems used in the school classroom. Hearing aids that fit behind or in the ear can amplify and clarify sounds. A procedure called a cochlear implant that captures sound waves and transmits them to a receiver that is surgically placed inside the skull can be effective in some cases. For others, learning sign language and/or how to read lips allows them to live full, successful lives in all respects—educational, social, and vocational.

Prevention and Prenatal Testing Ensuring that ear infections are promptly diagnosed and properly treated is one way to help prevent hearing loss. Exposure to extremely loud noises should also be avoided. Pregnant women should check with their doctor to make sure that any medications they might take are not harmful to the developing fetus.

For information about your child's hearing, see Chapter 15, "Hearing and Vision."

Developmental Delay/Mental Retardation

Typically children reach certain basic physical, intellectual, and social milestones within certain age ranges (see Chapter 17, "Growth and Development"). A child who does not reach developmental milestones within the expected ranges is said to have a developmental delay.

In most cases, the delay has no obvious cause. But in others, the delay is a sign of an underlying condition. For instance, children with cerebral palsy or who are blind will have trouble with movement. Hearing problems may lead to a delay in speech and language development. Attention deficit/

hyperactivity disorder (AD/HD) may make it difficult for a child to develop fine motor skills or socialize with other children.

The diagnosis of mental retardation is made if a child's developmental delay leads to a permanent state of subnormal intelligence confirmed by difficulties with communication, learning, and general living skills.

Three of the most common recognizable syndromes associated with mental retardation are Down syndrome, fetal alcohol syndrome, and fragile X syndrome.

Down syndrome is caused by an extra chromosome in the cells (see Down Syndrome in this chapter).

Fetal alcohol syndrome occurs when the mother drinks alcohol during pregnancy (see Chapter 26, "Medical Issues in Adoption," for more information about fetal alcohol syndrome).

Fragile X syndrome, which is associated with mental retardation mainly in boys, is caused by the presence of abnormal genes on the X chromosome.

Mental retardation also can result from problems that occur during pregnancy, delivery, or early infancy, such as the following:

- Malnutrition or exposure to radiation during pregnancy
- Maternal infections, such as rubella (German measles) or toxoplasmosis
- Metabolic or hormonal disorders such as phenylketonuria (PKU), galactosemia, and hypothyroidism if not diagnosed early and treated adequately
- Disruption of the oxygen supply to the baby during delivery
- Prematurity (Babies born prematurely have a higher risk for developing mental retardation,

especially if the baby weighs less than three pounds at birth.)

Problems after birth, including lead or mercury poisoning, severe malnutrition, severe head injuries, or an interruption of the oxygen supply to the brain such as occurs with near drowning, can also cause mental retardation. Diseases such as encephalitis (inflammation of the brain) or meningitis (inflammation of the lining covering the brain) can also lead to mental retardation.

Symptoms and Diagnosis There are four levels of mental retardation, defined as having an intelligence quotient (IQ) of 70 to 75 or less compared to the normal average of 100.

Most mentally retarded people are mildly retarded, with IQs of 55 to 69. They are usually slower to walk, talk, and reach other developmental milestones. But they may go undiagnosed until they reach school age. They can learn to read, do math, and other practical skills up to a fourth- to sixth-grade level. Mildly retarded adults can usually develop social and job skills and live on their own.

Children with IQs ranging from 40 to 54 are considered moderately retarded. These children show noticeable delays in developing speech and motor skills. They can learn basic communication, some health and safety habits, and other simple skills. They cannot learn to read or do math. Usually, moderately retarded adults cannot live independently.

Children with IQs of 20 to 39 are severely retarded. They are usually diagnosed at birth or soon after. By preschool age, they show delays in motor development and little or no ability to communicate. With training they may learn some skills such as how to feed and bathe themselves. They usually learn to walk and gain some understanding of speech. As adults, they need to live in a protected environment.

Profoundly retarded children have IQs of 0 to 20. These children often have other medical problems and need nursing care. They show delays in all aspects of development. With training they may learn to use their legs, hands, and jaws. They may learn some speech and how to walk. They cannot take care of themselves and need complete support.

In children who are subsequently diagnosed as mentally retarded, developmental delays, such as being slower to walk or talk than other children, are usually noticed by parents, or other signs may be noted by the doctor at routine checkups. The doctor may arrange for special tests to investigate other causes for developmental delay, such as a hearing or vision test, or order blood tests to check for genetic or metabolic disorders.

Treatment and Outlook In some cases, specific developmental delays can be treated by addressing an underlying disorder or disease—such as treating recurrent middle ear infections, which may lead to temporary language delays.

There is no cure for mental retardation, but many children can be taught skills that allow them to live as independently and fully as possible. Schools in all states are required to provide appropriate education for children with mental retardation up to age 21.

Prevention and Prenatal Testing Prenatal tests such as amniocentesis, chorionic villus sampling (CVS), and ultrasound can help detect inherited metabolic and chromosomal disorders linked to mental retardation.

Vaccinations can prevent pregnant women from getting diseases such as rubella that can injure the brain of the fetus. Avoiding alcohol and not eating raw meat or handling cat feces—associated with toxoplasmosis—during pregnancy can also prevent brain damage.

Screening blood tests at birth can detect disorders such as hypothyroidism and PKU, allowing for early treatment to prevent brain damage.

Infants and young children also need to be protected from lead poisoning and head injuries.

Diabetes Mellitus

Diabetes is a condition that affects how the body handles glucose, a sugar released from the foods we eat. Glucose is an important energy source for the body, especially for the brain. Blood levels of glucose are controlled by the hormone insulin, which is produced by cells in the pancreas. Normally, soon after a person eats, these cells, called beta cells, secrete insulin into the bloodstream to help the body handle the glucose absorbed into the blood from digested food. The insulin allows glucose to enter the body's cells for use as fuel and directs the conversion and storage of extra glucose in fat cells (as fat) and in the liver (as glycogen).

When children develop diabetes, it's usually because the pancreas stops producing enough insulin. This is called insulin-dependent diabetes mellitus, Type 1 diabetes, or juvenile diabetes. The child's own immune system attacks and destroys the beta cells in the pancreas. Although children with diabetes inherit the susceptibility to develop diabetes in their genes, their immune systems appear to need some sort of trigger to set off the beta cell destruction. The exact triggers are still not known, although some research suggests that viruses may be involved.

Type 1 diabetes is usually diagnosed before age 19 years. About 500,000 to 1 million Americans have Type 1 diabetes. Their bodies make little or no insulin on their own, and they depend on insulin injections to stay alive.

More than 14 million Americans have Type 2 diabetes. This form of diabetes is most common in adults older than 40 years, particularly in those who are obese. In Type 2 diabetes, the pancreas still produces insulin, but cells in the body do not respond to the insulin in the normal way. In many cases it can be controlled by losing weight, exercising, and eating a healthy diet; however, treatment with oral medications, and sometimes insulin, is often necessary. In recent years, the incidence of Type 2 diabetes has been increasing in children, which may be related to rising obesity rates.

Symptoms and Diagnosis Classic symptoms of diabetes are being abnormally thirsty, needing to urinate frequently, and losing weight despite a normal appetite. Blurred vision and lack of energy can also occur. There can be other symptoms, such as bedwetting in a child who had been dry at night. Girls may develop a discharge and vaginal itching due to a yeast infection.

Once insulin-producing beta cells are destroyed, the child's pancreas cannot replace them. As beta cells die, insulin levels drop and glucose can no longer enter the body's cells to be used for energy. Without insulin, the body's cells "starve" for glucose fuel, even as glucose levels rise higher and higher in the blood. The body reads the message from its hungry cells and low insulin levels as signals that the child is starving, so appetite increases and the child eats more. In a further attempt to increase energy supplies, the body also activates other hormone systems to begin breaking down stored fat and muscle to produce even more glucose.

As excess glucose from the blood leaves the body through the kidneys, large amounts of urine are produced and the child needs to urinate frequently. As she loses more body water, the child begins to become dehydrated and very thirsty.

As the child's body breaks down fats for energy, by-products called ketones build up in the blood. In severe cases—called diabetic ketoacidosis—rising levels of ketones can trigger episodes of rapid, deep breathing and give the child's breath a fruity smell. She may have nausea or abdominal pain and may vomit. As the child's blood fills with abnormally high levels of acid, the brain cannot work normally, and the child may become very sleepy and even go into a coma if not treated promptly.

Usually, a urine test is the first diagnostic test a doctor will perform if a child's symptoms suggest diabetes. A special strip of paper treated with a chemical is dipped in a sample of the child's urine. If the strip shows glucose is present, the doctor will do a blood test to see if there are high levels of glucose in the blood.

Treatment and Outlook Children with diabetes must supply their bodies with the correct amount of insulin every day. Insulin comes in a liquid that must be injected into the body. Most children take insulin by injecting it through a needle inserted into the layer of fat under the skin. Most inject insulin two or more times a day on a schedule coordinated with meals.

Some people with diabetes use an insulin pump, a device the size of a beeper containing insulin. The insulin is automatically pumped into the body through a small tube attached to a needle inserted into the skin. The insulin is pumped at a slow rate day and night and at a higher rate before meals to help the body handle incoming sugar.

Researchers are experimenting with other ways to get insulin into the bloodstream, such as eyedrops, nasal sprays, and inhalers. There is also much ongoing research involving the transplantation of the pancreatic cells that make insulin into the bodies of people with diabetes so that their bodies can once again produce insulin.

Children with Type 2 diabetes, who are usually overweight, may be able to control their blood sugars without insulin injections through weight loss, exercise, and the use of oral diabetes medications.

Children with diabetes must check their blood glucose levels several times a day by testing a small blood sample, usually with chemical test strips and a glucose meter. The results of these tests are used to make adjustments in the child's diabetes management plan. These children must also follow a balanced diet and exercise regularly to help control blood glucose levels. This is necessary to avoid symptoms caused by abnormal blood sugar levels, to ensure normal growth and pubertal development, and to reduce the risk of long-term (occurring more than 10 to 15 years after diagnosis) complications of diabetes, such as eye and kidney problems and heart and blood vessel diseases. Studies have shown that good control of blood sugar levels can help prevent or lessen the severity of these long-term complications in people with diabetes.

By following a proper diabetes management plan—often with the guidance of a team of diabetes health professionals including doctors, nurses, dietitians, educators, psychologists, and social workers—children with diabetes can participate fully in school, sports, and other activities, and can grow into well-adjusted, successful adults.

Prevention and Prenatal Testing Some studies suggest that breast-feeding may help protect a child from developing Type 1 diabetes. Avoiding obesity may help prevent or delay the development of Type 2 diabetes in children and adults.

Down Syndrome

Down syndrome is one of the most commonly occurring conditions associated with a chromosomal abnormality. Normally, there are 46 chromosomes—23 pairs—with one of each pair inherited from each parent. Chromosomes contain all the genetic information needed for the cells in the body to function properly. Most children with Down syndrome have cells that contain not 46 but 47 chromosomes. About 95 percent of Down syndrome cases occur when an infant is born with three rather than two copies of chromosome 21. In most of the remaining 5 percent of people with Down syndrome, the genetic material from the extra chromosome 21 is attached to another chromosome. This extra genetic material disrupts the child's physical and mental development.

Exactly why these chromosomal abnormalities occur is unknown. Women ages 35 and older have a higher risk of giving birth to a child with Down syndrome. The risk of a 25-year-old woman having a baby with Down syndrome is about 1 in 2,250. By age 45, the risk is about 1 in 30. However, because more young women have children, there are more babies with Down syndrome born to younger women.

Symptoms and Diagnosis Typical features of a baby with Down syndrome include a flattened face, up-slanted eyes, low-set ears, a protruding tongue, a short neck, a single straight skin crease across the palms, short arms and legs, and poor muscle tone (the infant seems unusually "floppy" when held). Children with Down syndrome are also mentally retarded, ranging from mild to severe.

About one in three children with Down syndrome also has an abnormality of the heart, usually a hole in the wall that separates the main chambers of the left and right sides of the heart (ventricular septal defect).

These children are also at increased risk for leukemia, cancer of the white blood cells. Children with Down syndrome can have abnormalities in the digestive tract, causing the intestines to be narrowed or blocked. They are at increased risk for otitis media (middle ear infection) and have a higher risk of developing hypothyroidism (underactive thyroid gland). They may also develop eye problems due to abnormalities in their corneas and lenses.

Most women are offered a blood test to screen for Down syndrome during the early weeks of pregnancy (discussed later). Sometimes, however, Down syndrome is not diagnosed until the baby is born. The condition is usually recognized by the distinctive appearance of the infant's face. An analysis of a sample of the baby's blood to look for the extra chromosome 21 will confirm the diagnosis. Other tests may be done to look for some of the birth defects and problems that can occur with the syndrome.

Treatment and Outlook Physical therapy, speech therapy, and special education programs can help children with Down syndrome develop to their fullest potential.

Some children can learn to read and write and may be able to work later in life. However, most are not able to live independently as adults and need long-term supervision either at home or in a residential facility.

Surgery may be necessary to help correct heart or digestive system abnormalities. Children with the condition need to be followed closely for diagnosis and treatment of repeated ear infections, and they should have regular eye examinations to monitor for changes in the cornea or lenses.

Although most people with Down syndrome survive into middle age, about 20 percent of children with Down syndrome die in childhood, usually because of congenital heart disease.

Prevention and Prenatal Testing There are several ways to screen for Down syndrome before a baby is born. The triple screen test and alpha-fetoprotein (AFP) test, usually done at 16 to 18 weeks of pregnancy, measure the amount of certain substances in the mother's blood that might indicate the fetus has Down syndrome. But if a test is positive it doesn't necessarily mean the baby has Down syndrome. Rather, it means that more tests should be done to confirm whether the baby has the condition.

Similarly, the tests can yield false negative results, meaning that the test results do not indicate Down syndrome even though the fetus has it. Low levels of a substance called alpha-fetoprotein in the mother's blood suggest the possibility of Down syndrome, but the test detects only 35 percent of cases. The triple screen test, which measures three different substances, is correct about 60 percent of the time.

Pregnant women older than 35 years and those with positive results from screening tests can be tested by amniocentesis or chorionic villus sampling (CVS), in which samples are taken from the tissue or fluid surrounding the baby. The chromosomes from the tissue are then examined. These tests can give a definitive answer, although there is a small risk of miscarriage associated with having either procedure. Chorionic villus sampling is usually done between 8 and 11 weeks of pregnancy; amniocentesis is usually done between 14 and 18 weeks.

Eczema/Atopic Dermatitis

Eczema refers to a number of different skin conditions characterized by itchy, red, dry, scaly, irritated skin that may become moist and oozing, and sometimes crusted and thickened. Eczema is sometimes called "the itch that rashes" because the dermatitis is triggered by scratching. The two major types are atopic dermatitis and contact dermatitis.

Atopic dermatitis, sometimes called infantile eczema, is a common form of this condition, affecting 10 to 12 percent of children. Typically, symptoms appear within the first few months of life, and they almost always appear before age five. The word *atopic* describes conditions that occur when someone is overly sensitive to substances and other factors in their environment. Although atopic dermatitis is not necessarily caused by allergies, it often appears in infants and young children who have (or will develop) allergies, hay fever, or asthma or who have a family history of these conditions. Environmental allergens such as pollens, molds, dust, animal dander, certain foods, and other factors (such as exposure to cold, heat, soaps, rough fabrics, or emotional stress) can trigger or aggravate atopic dermatitis. Foods that most often trigger eczema are egg whites, dairy prod-

ucts (milk products), wheat, tree nuts, peanuts, seafood, and soy.

Contact dermatitis is an allergic reaction or irritation that results from direct skin contact with a substance, such as a plant (poison ivy), metal, medicine, or soap.

Symptoms and Diagnosis Between two and six months of age, infants with atopic dermatitis may develop itchy, red, oozing skin behind their ears and on their cheeks, forehead, and scalp. Children often try to relieve the itching by rubbing the affected areas with a hand, pillow, or anything within reach. The rash may spread to the arms and trunk, and red, crusted lesions may appear on the face, scalp, arms, or legs. In toddlers and older children the rash usually becomes drier, involving the neck, wrists, ankles, and the creases in the elbows and behind the knees. With persistent scratching the affected skin becomes thickened and darker in color.

The itching and rash tend to worsen and improve over time, with flare-ups occurring periodically. In some children, the condition may improve by the age of five or six and then resurface at the onset of puberty, when hormones, stress, and irritating skin products or cosmetics are introduced. Some will experience some degree of dermatitis into adulthood.

A doctor's diagnosis of eczema is based mainly on the scaly rash's appearance and distribution pattern and on the length of time it has been present. A family history of allergic diseases (such as asthma, allergies, or eczema) can also be an important clue. There's no test available to diagnose the condition definitively.

The doctor will also want to exclude other diseases and conditions that can cause skin irritation. He or she may recommend allergy testing to find out if the rash is an allergic reaction to a certain substance. Your child's doctor may also ask you to eliminate certain foods from your child's diet, change detergents or soaps, or make other changes for a certain period of time to find out whether your child's rash is being triggered by a particular food or substance. If your child's doctor is uncertain of the diagnosis or if the symptoms are severe, he or she may also refer your child to a pediatric dermatologist.

Treatment and Outlook Because susceptibility to atopic dermatitis is believed to be inherited, there's no way to prevent a person from having the tendency to develop the condition. However, because specific triggers may tend to make it worse, flare-ups may be prevented or controlled by avoiding excessive heat, cold, sweating, emotional stress, contact with wool and other rough fabrics, and harsh soaps and detergents. It also helps to make sure the skin is not allowed to become too dry. Other substances to be avoided if they are aggravating the condition include skin care products, tobacco smoke, chemicals, foods, and other known allergens or irritants. Also, curbing the tendency to scratch the rash can prevent the condition from worsening and progressing to cause more severe skin damage.

Moisturizers, corticosteroid ointments, and antihistamines can provide relief of itching and other symptoms. Using mild soaps for bathing, avoiding frequent long hot baths, and routinely using moisturizing creams is helpful in preventing flare-ups and controlling the condition. Sometimes raw, moist areas of skin can become infected by bacteria. In this situation, the doctor may prescribe a course of topical or oral antibiotics. The child's fingernails should be kept short and clean to help prevent skin damage

and infection. If scratching at night is a problem, having the child wear gloves to bed may be helpful.

In almost all cases, eczema is controllable with proper care. Most children grow out of this condition, but some will have chronic eczema throughout life.

Epilepsy/Seizures

Epilepsy is a condition of the central nervous system characterized by recurrent episodes (seizures) that temporarily affect a person's awareness, movements, or sensations. The cause in most cases is unknown. However, there are certain factors or conditions that may be associated with epilepsy, including the following: infection or illness in the mother that affects the developing fetus during pregnancy, injuries during the birth process, brain tumors, head injuries, environmental toxins such as lead, infections such as meningitis (inflammation of the covering of the brain) or encephalitis (inflammation of the brain), abnormal brain development, a number of genetic conditions, metabolic disorders causing imbalances of various substances in the blood, or heart rhythm abnormalities.

Epilepsy is usually not genetically inherited, although a susceptibility to seizures may run in families, and seizures may occur as a feature in a number of inherited conditions.

Symptoms and Diagnosis Seizures occur when bursts of abnormal electrical activity occur in the brain and the person's consciousness or actions are altered for a short period of time. When the brain's electrical activity returns to normal, the seizures stop. Seizures may be triggered by repetitive sounds, flashing lights such as strobe lights, touch to certain parts of the body, hormonal changes, hunger, exhaustion, or lack of sleep. Some people with epilepsy are aware of the factors that trigger their seizures or can sense in advance that a seizure is about to occur. Usually, however, seizures occur without warning and without the person's awareness of what is happening. Some people with epilepsy will have months or years without a seizure; others will have many a day.

Having a seizure is not necessarily a sign of epilepsy. For example, an infant or young child whose body temperature rises rapidly with a fever may have what is known as a febrile seizure. These seizures are very brief (a few seconds or minutes), result in no harm, and usually do not indicate that the child has epilepsy. Febrile seizures generally stop occurring before the child reaches school age.

Epileptic seizures have different characteristics depending on where the seizure begins in the brain and how the abnormal electrical activity spreads across the brain. Seizures can be classified into two major categories: generalized and partial.

Generalized seizures affect nerve cells throughout the cerebral cortex (the outer part of the brain) or the entire brain. The most common types of generalized seizures are these:

- Tonic-clonic, or grand mal, seizures. In the first phase of this type of seizure, children often lose consciousness, drop to the ground, and suddenly cry out. In the next phase, the child's muscles may stiffen all at once or in a series of shorter rhythmic contractions, causing a thrashing motion. Usually this kind of seizure lasts for a few minutes and is followed by a period of sleepiness

and sometimes a headache. Loss of bladder and bowel control is also common during this type of seizure.
- Absence, or petit mal, seizures. Symptoms include staring blankly, rapid blinking, and chewing movements. Facial or eyelid muscles may jerk rhythmically.

Partial seizures are those contained within one region of the cerebral cortex. These are the most common types of partial seizures:

- Simple partial seizures. The child is awake and alert. Symptoms vary depending on what part of the brain is involved. They may include jerking movements of one part of the body, emotional symptoms such as unexplained fear, nausea, or smelling nonexistent odors.
- Complex partial seizures. In this type, the child loses awareness of surroundings and is either unresponsive or only partially responsive. There may be a blank stare, chewing movements, repeated swallowing, or other random activity. Following the seizure, the child has no memory of it. The child may become confused or begin to fumble, to wander, to pick at his clothes, or to repeat inappropriate words or phrases. It is similar to an absence seizure, but it is followed by these random activities.

To diagnose epilepsy, a doctor will ask about how long the child's seizures last, how frequent they are, what (if anything) seems to trigger them, and what the seizures look like. The doctor will examine the child and may order several tests including an electroencephalogram (EEG). By showing the patterns of electrical activity in the brain, the EEG may reveal abnormalities indicating the presence and type of epilepsy. Computerized tomography (CT) and magnetic resonance imaging (MRI) scans are sometimes used to detect abnormalities of the brain that might be the cause of the child's epilepsy. Blood tests may also be done to exclude chemical imbalances that can result in seizures.

Treatment and Outlook Most cases of epilepsy can be partially or completely controlled by treatment with one or more of a number of available anticonvulsant (antiseizure) medications. These drugs may have side effects such as drowsiness or hyperactivity and weight gain. Blood tests may be done periodically during treatment to look for other evidence of drug side effects.

Following a ketogenic diet (a diet that is high in fat and low in carbohydrates) may help children with difficult-to-control seizures. By creating ketosis, a condition in which the body primarily burns fat for energy instead of glucose (sugar), seizures stop or are better controlled. This type of diet must be prescribed and monitored by a doctor.

If medications or other treatments don't control the seizures adequately, some patients may be candidates for a surgical procedure that removes the abnormal or damaged brain cells that are triggering the seizures.

Gastroesophageal Reflux Disease (GERD)

Gastroesophageal reflux disease (GERD) occurs when food from the stomach moves backward (refluxes) into the esophagus.

This can occur if the lower esophageal sphincter (the muscle that connects the esophagus with the stomach) relaxes or is weak.

It's normal for babies to occasionally spit up small amounts of formula or breast milk after a feeding, particularly when being burped or during periods of movement. For babies with GERD, however, breast milk or formula regularly refluxes into the esophagus and sometimes out of the mouth. Sometimes babies regurgitate forcefully; other times they experience something like a "wet burp." Most babies outgrow the condition by the time they are one year, and it's uncommon for a child to have GERD beyond age two.

GERD can cause a number of complications. Because stomach acid accompanies the food as it moves back up the esophagus, the esophagus can become irritated, resulting in esophagitis. Infants with GERD can develop pneumonia if the stomach contents are refluxed to the level of the trachea (windpipe) and then into the lungs. Babies with GERD may also experience choking or extended pauses in their breathing pattern (apnea), which can be life-threatening in a few cases. Some infants with GERD may fail to gain weight and grow normally due to persistent vomiting and feeding difficulties.

Symptoms and Diagnosis Signs and symptoms of GERD in infants include these:

- Pain, irritability, or constant or sudden crying (signs that may be mistaken for colic) after feedings, which may be worse if baby is held in a horizontal position after a meal
- Frequent spitting up or vomiting after feeding or that continues after the first year

- Inability to sleep soundly
- "Wet burp" or "wet hiccup" sounds
- Weight loss or poor weight gain

Other, less common signs include constant eating and drinking, inability to eat certain foods, refusing food or accepting only a few bites despite hunger, swallowing problems (such as gagging or choking), hoarse voice, frequent sore throats, frequent respiratory problems (such as pneumonia, bronchitis, wheezing, or coughing), bad breath, and excessive drooling.

The most common test used to diagnose GERD is an X-ray called a barium swallow. If the doctor orders this test, the child will be given a small amount of a chalky liquid (barium) to swallow. If the child has GERD, the X-ray will show this liquid refluxing into the esophagus from the stomach. It may also show whether the esophagus is irritated or whether there are any other abnormalities in the upper digestive tract.

A more sensitive test called the 24-hour pH-probe study is considered the most accurate way to diagnose reflux. A thin, flexible tube is placed in the esophagus with the tip resting just above the esophageal sphincter. The tube is connected to a device that monitors the acid levels in the esophagus. High acid levels in the lower esophagus indicate the refluxing of stomach acid, as occurs in GERD.

Upper gastrointestinal tract endoscopy also can be used to diagnose esophagitis and GERD. This procedure uses a narrow, tubular fiber-optic scope to view the child's esophagus and stomach.

Treatment and Outlook Babies with GERD should be fed in a vertical position and burped frequently. After meals, the child should be kept in a seated position or held upright. Meal size may have to be reduced, and spicy, fatty, and acidic foods (like citrus fruits) may need to be limited or avoided.

Doctors usually recommend that parents slightly thicken their baby's formula or breast milk with rice cereal so that less reflux occurs after feedings. Some babies may benefit from special formulas.

Doctors may also prescribe medicines to reduce the amount of reflux or to lower the levels of acid in the stomach. If medicine and other treatments aren't successful, a surgical procedure called fundoplication may be recommended. This procedure creates a valve at the top of the stomach by wrapping a portion of the stomach around the esophagus. Fundoplication is successful in eliminating reflux in more than 90 percent of cases. However, there are possible complications and side effects, including a gagging sensation during meals, feeling full more quickly, and an inability to burp or vomit.

Because a child with GERD loses nutrients from spitting up and also may have a decreased desire to eat, proper nutrition is sometimes a concern. If a child is not gaining weight as expected or is losing weight, the doctor should be consulted.

Growth Disorders

A growth disorder is any problem in infants, children, or teens that prevents them from meeting realistic expectations of height and/or weight. These disorders can result in "failure to thrive" in infancy and short stature or failure to gain height and weight appropriately in childhood, and they may involve delayed sexual development in teens. There are many causes of disordered growth including genetic, hormonal, and nutritional problems. A variety of chronic medical conditions can also interfere with growth in children. (True growth disorders also must be distinguished from normal variant patterns of growth seen frequently in children—familial, or genetic, short stature and constitutional growth delay. For more information on these patterns and other aspects of your child's growth, see Chapter 17, "Growth and Development.")

Although it's common for newborns to lose a little weight in the first few days, some infants continue to show slower than expected weight gain and growth, a condition known as failure to thrive. Failure to thrive is most common in children younger than three years and is usually the result of a feeding problem that causes inadequate food intake. Failure to thrive may also be a symptom of a number of chronic medical conditions. Child neglect or abuse may also be associated with failure to thrive. (For more information on failure to thrive, see Chapter 17, "Growth and Development.")

Chronic infections, metabolic disorders, and certain diseases of the nervous system, kidneys, heart, gastrointestinal tract, lungs, and other body systems can impair growth. Although other symptoms in these children usually point to the underlying diagnosis, poor growth may be the first sign of a problem in some of these conditions.

Endocrine diseases, which involve a deficiency or excess of hormones, can cause growth failure during childhood. Growth hormone deficiency is a disorder that involves the pituitary gland (the small gland at the base of the brain that secretes several hormones, including growth hormone). A damaged or malfunctioning pituitary gland may not produce enough hormones for normal growth. Hypothyroidism is a condition in which the thyroid gland fails to make enough thyroid hormone, which is essential for normal bone growth. Excessive amounts of glucocorticoids in a child's system—

whether due to the body's overproduction of these hormones or the result of treatment with steroid medications (such as prednisone)—can also impair growth.

Symptoms and Diagnosis Growth disorders are suspected in children if they fail to grow at a normal rate or if they are unusually small for their age. These assessments should be based on accurate measurements performed in the doctor's office that are plotted on standard growth charts (see Appendix B). If a problem is suspected based on the child's growth pattern, additional testing will usually be done.

Your child's doctor or the pediatric endocrinologist (to whom your child might be referred for further evaluation) looks for signs of the many possible causes of short stature and growth failure. Blood tests may be performed to look for hormone and chromosome abnormalities as well as to exclude other diseases associated with growth failure. A bone-age X-ray is frequently done to assess how the child's skeleton is maturing, and magnetic resonance imaging (MRI) or computerized tomography (CT) scans of the head are sometimes done to check the pituitary gland and brain for abnormalities associated with growth problems.

To measure the ability of a child's pituitary gland to produce growth hormone, the doctor may perform a growth hormone stimulation test. This involves giving the child certain medications that cause the pituitary gland to secrete growth hormone and then drawing several small blood samples to check growth hormone levels over a period of time after the medications are given.

Treatment and Outlook Although the treatment of a growth problem is usually not urgent, earlier diagnosis and treatment of some conditions may help children achieve more normal adult heights.

If an underlying medical condition is identified, specific treatment of the problem may result in improved growth. Growth failure due to hypothyroidism, for example, is usually simply treated by giving the child oral thyroid hormone replacement therapy.

Growth hormone injections for children with growth hormone deficiency and certain other conditions, such as chronic kidney failure and Turner syndrome, may help them reach a more normal height. Human growth hormone is generally considered safe and effective, although treatment usually takes many years, and some children will not respond to it as well as others will. The treatment can be quite expensive (approximately $20,000 to $30,000 per year), although most health insurance plans will cover the costs.

Although their growth patterns are considered a variation of normal, children diagnosed with familial short stature or constitutional growth delay may face social problems because they are short or don't enter puberty when their classmates do. These children should be reassured that they do not have a disease or medical condition that poses a threat to their health or requires treatment. However, children who are small or who grow more slowly than others their age for any reason may need extra support in coping with teasing by their peers and positive reinforcement regarding their abilities and talents to help them maintain a positive self-image.

Hemophilia

Bleeding disorders, characterized by a tendency to bleed easily or excessively, may result from defects in the blood vessels or from abnormalities of the blood clotting system. Hemophilia is the most common severe inherited bleeding disorder.

When a person is injured, tiny blood cells called platelets stick together to form a small plug at the point of bleeding. Platelets release chemicals that aid in the formation of fibrin, a hard substance that helps stop bleeding by forming a stable clot at the injury site. Fibrin can be produced only with the aid of substances in the blood called clotting factors. Hemophilia is caused by a deficiency of clotting factors and is one of the most common X-linked (meaning the gene is carried on the X chromosome) genetic diseases. The condition almost always affects boys—it affects approximately 1 in 10,000 males. The boy inherits the gene for the disease on the X chromosome he receives from his mother. (Because women have two X chromosomes, the carrier mother doesn't have the disease herself because she has a second X chromosome that doesn't carry the abnormal gene, so she can produce normal amounts of clotting factors.)

There are two major types of hemophilia. In hemophilia A, clotting Factor VIII is deficient. This interrupts the clotting process, so blood from a wound continues to flow. Hemophilia B, which is less common, is caused by a Factor IX deficiency.

Symptoms and Diagnosis The primary symptoms of hemophilia are excessive, poorly controlled bleeding, easy bruising, and swelling in the joints or muscles from internal bleeding. Hemophilia varies in severity. Children with the most severe form have less than 1 percent of the normal amount of clotting Factors VIII or IX. They can bleed internally without having been injured. Bleeding into the muscles can damage nerves and blood vessels. Neck, tongue, and throat hemorrhages can obstruct breathing. A head injury can cause bleeding in the brain, which can be life-threatening.

Those with moderate hemophilia have excessive bleeding associated with major injuries, surgical procedures, or tooth extractions. People with mild hemophilia may not even be aware they have the condition until they experience excessive bleeding associated with an operation later in life.

The diagnosis of hemophilia is made by testing the ability of the child's blood to clot in the laboratory. If this test is abnormal, the levels of the specific clotting factors are measured.

Treatment and Outlook Minor bleeding episodes can often be treated with routine home care—ice and pressure applied to the wound. Children with moderate or severe hemophilia may often need to be given doses of the blood clotting factors they lack, which can be infused through a vein. How often infusions of clotting factors are needed depends on how severe the condition is or how often the child is injured. A medication called DDAVP (desmopressin) can sometimes help control bleeding by increasing Factor VIII levels in children with mild or moderate hemophilia A.

Bleeding into muscles and joints is one of the most common problems that people with hemophilia face. Hemorrhage into the joints causes pain and limitation of movement. Repeated bleeding into the joints can eventually lead to arthritis, inflammation, and deformities of the joints. Therefore, orthopedic surgeons are frequently involved in managing these joint problems.

Infusions of clotting factors may be given before dental procedures or other surgeries to help control bleeding during and after the procedure.

Life for children with hemophilia has improved significantly in recent years with the availability of clotting factors for transfusion. Although most are restricted from participation in contact sports, many are able to participate fully in school, social, and other activities. Parents can help by encouraging their child to participate in low-impact physical activities and by controlling the tendency to limit or overprotect the child.

Prevention and Prenatal Testing DNA tests can be done on a woman or her fetus to see if she is a carrier of a hemophilia gene or if her baby has inherited it. The sons of women who carry the gene for hemophilia have a 50 percent risk of having the disease.

Hip Dysplasia/Dislocation in Infancy

In this condition, the hips at birth are rarely dislocated but are "dislocatable"; that is, the rounded head (top) of the femur (thighbone) easily pops in and out of the socket of the hip bone. The condition usually occurs in newborns, and the reasons for this abnormal development (dysplasia) of the hip joint are not completely understood. Genetic factors may play a role, because there is a family history of the disorder in about 20 percent of cases. The condition may also be related to the effects of the hormones that relax the mother's own ligaments for labor and delivery.

About 1 in 250 babies is affected. Girls are affected nine times more often than boys are. About 60 percent are firstborns, and about 40 percent were in the breech position (buttocks first) in the womb.

Symptoms and Diagnosis Signs and symptoms of hip dysplasia/dislocation may include asymmetrical (not the same on both sides) creases in the skin on the back of the infant's thighs, an inability to move the affected thigh outward fully at the hip, shorter appearance of the affected leg, and limping when the child is older.

The doctor will check the baby's hips shortly after birth and then at routine checkups until he is walking normally. In mild cases, the hip joint moves excessively when manipulated. In moderate cases, the thighbone, or femur, slips out of the hip socket when manipulated but can be put back in. In severe cases, the head of the thighbone remains outside of the hip socket.

If the doctor suspects the problem may be present, he or she may order X-rays of the hips or an ultrasound scan to aid in making the diagnosis.

Treatment and Outlook Treatment depends on the age of the child when the condition is discovered and the severity of the problem. Less severe forms may correct themselves during the first few weeks of life. If not, in young infants, the hip joint may be positioned with a harness that holds the head of the thighbone in the socket for 8 to 12 weeks. In an older baby, the hip may be held in place using a cast for as long as six months. If this treatment is unsuccessful, surgery may be necessary.

If the condition is recognized and treated early, most children will experience normal development of the hip joint and have no problems later on. However, if the disorder is left untreated until the child is older, permanent hip problems may result, and the child may have difficulties walking.

Prevention and Prenatal Testing There is no known way to prevent the disorder. Parents should be aware of the increased risk (20 percent) of the condition in their children if there is a family history of congenital hip dislocation.

HIV/AIDS

Human immunodeficiency virus (HIV) is spread when an infected person's body fluid (blood, semen, vaginal fluid, breast milk, or any body fluid containing blood) enters the bloodstream or contacts the mucous membranes of another person. Infected mothers may pass the virus on to their babies during pregnancy, childbirth, or breast-feeding. During the 1990s, nearly 90 percent of existing AIDS cases and almost all HIV infections among children in the United States could be attributed to transmission of HIV at birth.

HIV can lead to acquired immune deficiency syndrome (AIDS), in which the body's resistance to diseases is lowered, resulting in infections and a number of other health problems. It is possible to be infected with HIV and not have AIDS. Some people are infected with HIV for years before they get sick.

HIV infection leading to AIDS has been a major cause of illness and death among children. By the end of 1998, AIDS had killed 5,000 children younger than 15 years in the United States and more than 3 million worldwide.

Symptoms and Diagnosis When a baby is born to an HIV-infected mother, there is no immediate way to know whether the baby is infected. The most commonly used test, which looks for HIV antibodies in the blood, will be positive even if the baby has not been infected with the virus because babies will have their mother's antibodies for as long as 18 months. Uninfected babies will gradually lose their mother's antibodies during this time, whereas infected infants will continue to have antibodies in their blood. By using more recently available tests such as polymerase chain reaction (PCR) or the p24 antigen test, the diagnosis can be made in the first few months of life. Although there are no immediate physical signs of HIV infection at birth, children with HIV can develop infections in the first months of life with germs that usually don't cause problems in uninfected infants, like pneumocystis carinii pneumonia (PCP). Infections like PCP occur because of the baby's weakened immune system and used to be a major cause of death in HIV-infected infants. Now all HIV-infected infants are routinely treated with antibiotics to reduce the risk of PCP infection.

Other possible symptoms of HIV infection in infants include low birthweight, poor weight gain, persistent thrush (a yeast infection in the mouth or diaper area), frequent fevers and diarrhea, enlarged lymph nodes, enlarged liver and/or spleen, neurological problems and developmental delay, and a variety of infections.

Treatment and Outlook There are currently three categories of medications used to control infection with HIV: nucleoside antiretrovirals, such as AZT; protease inhibitors, such as indinavir; and nonnucleoside reverse transcription inhibitors, such as nevirapine.

Because these drugs work in different ways, they are usually prescribed in combination. If the treatment regimen is not followed precisely, the virus becomes resistant to the drugs, thus reducing treatment options for the child.

Parents need to work closely with the child's doctors—usually part of a team of health care personnel led by an infectious-disease specialist—to prevent, recognize, and treat complicating bacterial infections with antibiotics. The child should receive appropriate vaccines to help prevent the special problems he may develop if he contracts these infections. Supporting the child's nutritional needs is also important. Providing a loving environment also goes a long way in helping to achieve a better life for children with the condition. Because the infection usually has been passed from mother to infant, the child's mother may be ill and the family will need additional support to care for the child.

If a family seeks health care in an emergency room or other health facility, parents should be sure to let health care providers know that the child has HIV infection because this may affect how the child's care will be managed.

Overall, HIV appears to be minimally contagious from a child to another person. There are only a handful of reported transmissions, and these involve direct blood contact in a family setting. There have been no reported transmissions of the HIV virus within a school or child-care setting.

There is no known cure for AIDS. Current treatment advances can slow the progression of the disease and improve quality of life, however.

Prevention and Prenatal Testing Drug treatment of an infected mother and her infant can significantly decrease the likelihood of infection in the baby. Pregnant women with HIV infection may be given AZT during their second and third trimesters. The baby is then given a six-week course of oral treatment with the drug. Studies have shown that this treatment can reduce the risk of transmission of the infection to the baby from 30 percent (untreated) to less than 2 percent. Delivering the baby by cesarean section may also reduce the risk of transmission to the baby.

Hydrocephalus

Hydrocephalus (also known as "water on the brain") is a central nervous system disorder that can cause enlargement of the head in newborns and infants, brain damage, and neurological problems. Hydrocephalus is characterized by an excessive accumulation of cerebrospinal fluid (CSF) in the brain. Normally, CSF (which protects the brain and spinal cord by acting as a cushion) flows through the central nervous system much like oil flows through a car's engine. A membrane in the brain produces CSF, which travels down the spinal cord and back again to the brain, where structures in the brain reabsorb it. Under normal circumstances, this flow pattern keeps a healthy amount of CSF surrounding the brain and spinal cord. If the brain does not properly reabsorb the CSF or something in the brain blocks the normal CSF flow, the amount of CSF and the pressure within the head increase, which may damage brain tissue and result in hydrocephalus.

Hydrocephalus may be caused by prenatal exposure to an infection such as rubella (German measles), herpes virus, cytomegalovirus (CMV), or toxoplasmosis. Children born with spina bifida (see Spina Bifida in this chapter) and premature infants who have had hemorrhage (bleeding) in their brains often develop hydrocephalus.

Meningitis, brain tumors, or a head injury may also cause the condition.

Symptoms and Diagnosis In newborns and infants, symptoms of hydrocephalus include an enlarged head or rapidly increasing head size, delayed development, and lethargy. The doctor may note that the child has abnormally prominent scalp veins, thinned scalp skin, and poor head control. A CT scan or MRI study can reveal a buildup of CSF in the brain, evidence of increased pressure in the head, and abnormalities in the brain that may be the cause of hydrocephalus.

Treatment and Outlook Some forms of hydrocephalus require close monitoring but no treatment; other forms require the surgical implantation of a shunt, which is a tube that is inserted through the skull to drain some of the CSF out of the head and into the bloodstream or to where the fluid can be reabsorbed into the bloodstream by the body. This surgery can relieve the pressure on the brain and prevent further injury to the brain, but it cannot reverse any brain damage already present.

Typically, a neurosurgeon will place a ventriculoperitoneal (VP) shunt in a child's brain. This is a tube inside the body that will connect a child's ventricles (the CSF reservoirs in the middle of the brain) to his peritoneal cavity (the space in the abdomen that contains the stomach and other organs). The excess CSF will flow down into the peritoneal cavity, where the cavity lining absorbs it. This helps restore the normal balance of CSF surrounding the brain.

Once a VP shunt is in place, the child can engage in normal activities. However, occasionally complications may occur that will interfere with proper shunt functioning. If the shunt becomes blocked, disconnected, or infected, the child may experience headaches, lethargy, irritability, and vomiting. If this happens, the doctor will surgically replace or repair the shunt with a procedure called a shunt revision.

Most children who are born with hydrocephalus survive provided they receive treatment, but about 50 percent have mental or physical disabilities.

Juvenile Rheumatoid Arthritis

Juvenile rheumatoid arthritis (JRA) is a condition involving inflammation and stiffness in one or more joints lasting longer than six weeks in a child 16 years or younger in whom other causes of arthritis have been excluded. There are three types of JRA: pauciarticular, in which four or fewer joints are affected; polyarticular, in which five or more joints are affected; and systemic, which may affect internal organs, such as the liver and spleen, and the tissues covering the heart and lungs.

Juvenile rheumatoid arthritis is an autoimmune disorder, which means that the body mistakenly identifies some of its own tissues as foreign matter. The immune system begins to attack healthy cells and tissue, leading to redness, warmth, pain, and swelling. Researchers are still unsure exactly why children develop JRA. Scientists believe that there probably is something in the child's genetic makeup that makes her susceptible to JRA. Factors from the child's environment, such as a virus infection, may trigger the condition in a genetically susceptible child.

Symptoms and Diagnosis The most common initial symptoms of JRA are persistent joint swelling, stiffness that is typically worse upon awakening in the morning or

after a nap, and pain that is usually worse later in the day. The child may show limited movement, although she may not complain of pain. The knees and joints in the hands and feet are commonly affected in JRA. One of the earliest signs may be limping in the morning because of an affected knee.

With the systemic form of JRA, children may have bouts of high fever and a light pink rash, which may appear and disappear very quickly. The condition may cause lymph nodes (glands) in the neck and other areas to swell.

There is no single, specific test that can be used to diagnose JRA. A thorough medical history, physical examination, and laboratory tests can be used to look for other conditions that cause joint pain and inflammation, such as physical injury, bacterial infection, Lyme disease, lupus, some forms of cancer, and other disorders.

Treatment and Outlook The goals of treatment for JRA are to relieve pain and inflammation, slow down or prevent the destruction of joints, and restore use and function of affected joints in order to promote optimal growth, physical activity, and the social and emotional development of the child.

A combination of medication, physical therapy, and exercise is used to treat JRA. The child's health care providers, including her primary care doctor, rheumatologist, and physical therapist, should work together to develop the best plan of treatment.

Nonsteroidal anti-inflammatory drugs, such as ibuprofen and naproxen, are often the first types of medication used to treat JRA symptoms. Medications called disease-modifying antirheumatic drugs, such as hydroxychloroquine, are also used. Methotrexate, a drug also used to treat cancer, can be used as well, although children receiving this drug must be carefully monitored for liver damage. Corticosteroids such as prednisone may be added to control severe inflammation; however, prolonged treatment with these drugs is associated with slowing of growth and many other side effects. Recently, new medications have been developed that can effectively reduce inflammation in the joints of patients with JRA without causing the side effects associated with many of the other drugs used to treat the disease.

Depending on the severity of the disease and the joint involved, the growth of bones in affected joints may be too fast or too slow, causing one limb to be longer than the other. Joints may also grow unevenly and become distorted or deformed. Overall growth may be slowed as well.

Eye inflammation (uveitis) is a potentially severe complication that sometimes occurs in children with pauciarticular JRA. These children need to be checked regularly by an ophthalmologist (eye specialist).

At present, about half of all children with JRA continue to have active disease with physical limitations lasting into early adulthood. However, with early diagnosis and proper treatment, most children with JRA can expect to lead full and productive lives.

Kidney Disorders

The kidneys filter the blood to remove waste products and excess water from the body. The waste products and water leave the body as urine after passing through a system of hollow tubes and ducts known as the urinary tract. The kidneys also play important roles in the regulation of blood pressure, the stimulation of red blood cell production, and the body's handling of vitamin D and minerals necessary for the growth and maintenance of bone. A number of kidney and urinary tract disorders affect children and may need treatment. Some of these conditions can result in problems with kidney function or, in some cases, lead to kidney failure.

Birth defects—or congenital malformations—of the kidneys are relatively common. Fortunately, most of these abnormalities do not interfere with kidney function or produce other symptoms or health problems. Children can be born with a single kidney or two kidneys connected at their base to form a single horseshoe-shaped kidney. One or both kidneys may be abnormally positioned in the abdomen or pelvic region. In some cases, birth defects of the kidneys or urinary tract may be part of a syndrome (a group of congenital defects that tend to occur in a characteristic pattern). As long as the child has one functioning kidney, health problems usually do not result; however, in this situation it becomes more important to protect the single kidney from injury due to recurrent urinary tract infections (see Recurrent Urinary Tract Infection in this chapter) or trauma.

Glomerulonephritis

Glomerulonephritis, a condition in which the filtering units of the kidneys called the glomeruli become inflamed, may be acute or chronic. Acute disease can occur as a reaction to a drug or as a complication of certain infectious diseases. In children, it usually follows an inadequately treated strep throat infection. An acute form called pyelonephritis results when bacteria causing a urinary tract infection ascend the urinary tract and infect the kidneys. Chronic glomerulonephritis may be associated with an autoimmune disorder such as systemic lupus erythematosus, in which the immune system attacks the body's own tissues. This can result in inflammation and abnormal function of several organs, including the kidneys.

Symptoms and Diagnosis Signs and symptoms may include blood-tinged, tea-colored, frothy, or cloudy urine; puffiness of the face, with swelling around the eyes; swollen feet and legs; fever; weakness; shortness of breath; poor appetite; and sometimes pain in the side or back. In the early stages of chronic glomerulonephritis, there may be no symptoms.

If the condition is suspected, the doctor will perform blood and urine tests. In some cases, a kidney biopsy (removal of a small piece of kidney tissue for laboratory examination) will be done to guide treatment by learning more about the exact cause of the problem.

Treatment and Outlook If the cause of the glomerulonephritis is a bacterial infection, such as with pyelonephritis, antibiotics are prescribed. If the cause is an autoimmune disorder, then it may be treated with corticosteroids or other immune system suppressing drugs. Medications and a low-salt diet may be necessary to control high blood pressure and excess fluid accumulation in the body. Depending on the cause, glomerulonephritis may resolve on its own with supportive care, or it may continue to cause inflammation and damage to the kidney. If kidney failure develops, the child may require dialysis (use of an "artificial kidney" to filter waste and remove excess fluid from the blood) or a kidney transplant.

Hydronephrosis

An abnormality of the urinary tract present at birth can cause hydronephrosis. This is a swelling of the kidney due to a blockage of the urinary tract that can be caused by a narrowing of the ureter, the tube that takes urine from the kidney to the bladder. The enlarged kidney may be detected as a mass in the abdomen of a newborn.

Symptoms and Diagnosis A child may show no symptoms, or there may be pain in the abdomen or lower back and nausea and vomiting. Because blockage of the flow of urine frequently leads to infection, fever may also occur.

To diagnose hydronephrosis, the doctor will order an ultrasound study or other imaging tests that can also help to locate the blockage in the urinary tract. Blood and urine tests to see how well the kidneys are functioning will also be done.

Treatment and Outlook Surgery may be required to relieve the obstruction to urine flow, and antibiotic therapy will be given if an infection is present. The long-term function of the involved kidney (or kidneys) depends on how much damage to kidney tissue occurred before the blockage was corrected.

Nephrotic Syndrome

Nephrotic syndrome is a kidney disorder resulting from damage to the glomeruli that causes loss of protein into the urine and swelling of body tissues due to the accumulation of excess fluid. In children, the condition occurs most commonly between ages 18 months and four years and more often in boys than in girls. Although it can result from a reaction to a drug or from glomerulonephritis, the cause in most childhood cases is not understood.

Symptoms and Diagnosis Signs and symptoms may include loss of appetite, a generally sick feeling, puffy eyelids, abdominal pain, bloating and tissue swelling, and frothy urine.

Urine and blood tests can confirm a diagnosis of the syndrome, and the doctor will perform additional tests in the attempt to discover its underlying cause. In some cases, the doctor may also take a small sample of kidney tissue (a biopsy) to help make the diagnosis and guide treatment.

Treatment and Outlook Usually children with nephrotic syndrome will be treated with steroid medications initially, which help the disease subside and reduce the loss of protein into the urine. Fluid and salt restriction and sometimes additional medications may be needed to control the balance of body fluids. Children with nephrotic syndrome are more prone to certain bacterial infections and may require treatment with antibiotics because of this. Although in most children the disease eventually resolves over months or years, relapses may occur—particularly after colds or other infections—making repeated courses of treatment necessary in some cases.

Polycystic Kidney Disease

Polycystic kidney disease is an inherited disorder in which the kidneys have a honeycomb appearance because of numerous fluid-filled cysts. The genetic defect that causes the disease may be dominant (adult form) or recessive (infantile form). That is, a person with the disease has either inherited a dominant gene from one parent or a recessive gene from both parents. Those with dominant gene inheritance usually have no symptoms until adulthood; those with recessive gene inheritance have severe illness in childhood.

Symptoms and Diagnosis In the infantile form, because of kidney enlargement, the doctor may notice a lump or mass in the baby's abdomen or side. The doctor can confirm diagnosis with an ultrasound study.

Treatment and Outlook Eventually kidney failure occurs, and the child will need dialysis or a kidney transplant. A severely affected newborn may die soon after birth. Genetic counseling can help people with the disease understand the probability of their children inheriting the condition.

Recurrent Urinary Tract Infection

Recurrent urinary tract infection in infants and children may be associated with reflux (or backflow) of urine from the bladder into the ureters, the tubes taking urine from the kidneys to the bladder. If the infection moves up the ureter into the kidneys, an infection of the kidney(s) called pyelonephritis can result. Repeated infections of this type can lead to scarring and damage to the kidney, in some cases resulting in kidney failure. The tendency for ureteral reflux can run in families, suggesting a genetic factor in some cases.

Symptoms and Diagnosis Symptoms of recurrent infection are the same as those of common urinary tract infection (for more information on urinary tract infections, see Chapter 30, "Childhood Infections"), which may include fever, vomiting, diarrhea, irritability, or drowsiness. Older children may complain of the frequent, urgent need to urinate, a burning sensation when urinating, and pain in the lower abdomen or side, and they may experience bedwetting or daytime accidents after having been dry.

A urine sample is checked for evidence of infection, and the child is given an antibiotic if indicated. An ultrasound or other type of scan may be done to look for scarring in the kidneys or other abnormalities or blockage of the urinary tract, and a special X-ray to check for urinary reflux may be done.

Treatment and Outlook Prophylactic (preventive) antibiotic therapy may be given in children with repeated infections, and surgery may be required to correct reflux or other abnormalities of the urinary tract causing the recurring infections.

Wilms' Tumor (Nephroblastoma)

Wilms' tumor, or nephroblastoma, the most common form of kidney cancer in children, is usually diagnosed between birth and age five years. The cause is unknown, but it sometimes runs in families. Children with certain birth defects (or who have family members with these defects) such as the absence of irises (the colored part of the eye) or overgrowth of one side of the body have an increased risk of developing Wilms' tumor. Children with this tumor are also more likely to have birth defects of the heart and urinary system, such as an undescended testicle [see Undescended Testicle (Cryptorchidism) under Surgical Conditions/Procedures in this chapter].

Symptoms and Diagnosis Signs and symptoms may include a lump or mass in the abdomen or side, abdominal pain, fever, poor appetite, nausea, and vomiting. Blood appears in the urine in about 20 percent of cases. If a tumor is suspected, the doctor may order blood tests and an ultrasound, computerized tomography (CT) scan, or magnetic resonance imaging (MRI) for diagnosis.

Treatment and Outlook The treatment involves surgery to remove the involved kidney and tumor tissue that may have spread through the abdomen. Depending on the appearance of the tumor and if and how much it has spread at the time of diagnosis, surgery, radiation, and chemotherapy may be used. Wilms' tumor is curable in about 90 percent of cases.

Lead Poisoning

Lead is a naturally occurring metal that is found in ore deposits in the ground. It has been used in the manufacture of household plumbing materials and water service lines, lead-based paints, gasoline for motor vehicles, older ceramic dishes and lead crystal, and the plastic of certain nonglossy vinyl window blinds. The wicks of some candles may also contain lead.

Young children, who are likely to put things in their mouths, are exposed to lead most often when they eat chips of lead-based paint and lead-containing dust. Eating as little as $1/10$ of a square inch of paint daily for 15 to 30 days can result in a blood lead level of 10 mcg/dL, the level that indicates cause for concern according to federal health guidelines.

The vulnerability of the developing brain to injury from the toxic effects of lead puts young children at particular risk from lead poisoning. The tendency of children to absorb a greater percentage of the lead they ingest further heightens their risk from environmental lead exposure. The health effects of lead poisoning include developmental delay, hearing problems, learning difficulties, anemia, and, in severe poisoning, seizures, coma, and even death. Lead poisoning can also affect a fetus carried by a woman who has been exposed to high levels of lead during pregnancy.

Since 1971, the elimination of leaded gasoline and the ban of paints containing 0.06 percent or more of lead have helped reduce average U.S. blood levels of lead. Still, lead poisoning remains a threat to children's health, particularly urban children from low-income families, most often because of exposure to lead-based paint in older homes. More than 80 percent of homes built before 1978 contain lead-based paint, which has also been used to cover playground equipment in schools and public parks.

Symptoms and Diagnosis Symptoms of lead poisoning, if they occur, can resemble those of other illnesses, making the condition difficult to detect. Some early signs include fatigue or overactivity, irritability, loss of appetite, weight loss, difficulty sleeping, and constipation.

Still, even children who appear completely healthy may have damagingly elevated blood lead levels, which is why the U.S. Centers for Disease Control and Prevention (CDC) recommends routine testing of children considered to be at high risk for lead poisoning (see Chapter 14, "Health Screening Tests") at 9 to 12 months and possibly again at two years. In addition, many states have regulations requiring that all children be screened around 12 months of age.

Treatment and Outlook Once lead poisoning has been detected, the first step is to remove the source, which can mean removing or sealing off lead-based paint in the child's environment, treating water sources, and making dietary changes if necessary. Children who are properly nourished and eat at least three meals a day will absorb less lead, and foods rich in iron and calcium can also help reduce lead absorption.

Medications (called chelating agents) that bind lead in the body so that it can be removed via urine or stools may be prescribed if blood tests reveal high levels of lead.

Because lead can remain in the body for a lifetime and a young child's developing nervous system is vulnerable to permanent damage from lead exposure, early detection of lead poisoning and prompt treatment are essential.

Prevention These tips can help you decrease your family's risk of lead exposure:

- Check with your public water company for assistance and information about lead levels. If you have a private well, have your water tested by a local laboratory.
- If your private well has high lead levels, consider a water treatment device. If lead levels are still high, consider using bottled water.
- When you use water for cooking or drinking, use cold tap water only.
- Let tap water run for about one minute in the morning before you drink it.
- Do **not** drink from lead crystal on a daily basis, and do not store liquids in lead crystal bottles or glasses.
- Do **not** store food or liquids in antique or collectible dishes or in dishes made by hobbyists, especially if the dishes are brightly decorated, metallic-coated, or imported from foreign countries.

- Remove all flaking or peeling paint from areas in the home and vacuum dust from floor surfaces and carpets using a special high-powered vacuum cleaner.
- If your home has high lead levels, replace painted items, cover painted surfaces with sealant or gypsum wallboard (a temporary solution), or have the lead-based paint professionally removed.
- Do **not** burn candles with lead wicks.
- Due to the production of lead-contaminated dust and waste, do **not** allow infants and children to stay in the home during the lead removal process or during renovation of an older home that might contain lead-based paint.

If you are concerned that your home may contain high amounts of lead because of old lead-based paint, call the National Lead Information Hotline and Clearinghouse at (800) 424-LEAD.

Leukemia

The term *leukemia* refers to cancers of the white blood cells (WBCs, also called leukocytes). When a child has leukemia, large numbers of abnormal white blood cells are produced in the bone marrow. These abnormal cells crowd the bone marrow and may flood the bloodstream. As leukemia progresses, the cancer interferes with the body's production of other types of blood cells, including red blood cells and platelets. This results in anemia (low numbers of red cells) and bleeding problems, in addition to the increased risk of infection caused by white cell abnormalities. Initially, abnormal leukemia cells appear only in the bone mar-

row and blood, but later they may spread elsewhere, including the lymph nodes, spleen, liver, and brain.

In general, leukemias are classified into acute (rapidly developing) and chronic (slower developing) forms, although in children, about 98 percent of leukemias are acute. Childhood leukemias are also divided into acute lymphocytic leukemia (ALL) or acute nonlymphocytic leukemia (ANLL), depending on whether the cancer involves specific white cells called lymphocytes. ANLL is also called acute myelogenous leukemia (AML).

ALL generally occurs in children ages two to eight, with a peak incidence at age four. It's more common among Caucasian children than among those of other racial backgrounds, and it affects boys more often than girls. AML can be seen in infants during the first month of life, but then it becomes relatively rare until the teenage years.

For both ALL and AML, children have a 20 to 25 percent chance of developing leukemia if they have an identical twin who was diagnosed with the illness before age six. In general, nonidentical twins and other siblings of children with leukemia have two to four times the average risk of developing this illness.

Children who have certain genetic disorders, such as Down syndrome, have a higher risk of developing leukemia, as do children who are treated with drugs that suppress the immune system after organ transplants. Children who have received prior radiation or chemotherapy for other types of cancer also have a higher risk for leukemia, usually within the first eight years after treatment.

Symptoms and Diagnosis Because infection-fighting white blood cells are defective in children with leukemia, these children may experience more fevers and infections. They may also become anemic as leukemia affects the bone marrow's production of oxygen-carrying red blood cells. This makes them appear pale, and they may become abnormally tired and short of breath while playing. They may also bruise and bleed easily, have frequent nosebleeds, or bleed for an unusually long time after even a minor cut, because leukemia can interfere with the bone marrow's ability to produce clot-forming platelets.

Other symptoms of leukemia may include pain in the bones or joints; swollen lymph nodes (glands) in the neck, groin, or elsewhere; an abnormally tired feeling; and poor appetite. In about 12 percent of children with AML and 6 percent of children with ALL, spread of leukemia to the brain causes headaches, seizures, balance problems, or abnormal vision. If ALL spreads to the thymus gland inside the chest, the enlarged gland can crowd the trachea (windpipe) and important blood vessels, leading to breathing problems and interference with blood flow to and from the heart.

A doctor will perform a physical examination to check for signs of infection, anemia, abnormal bleeding, and swollen lymph nodes. The doctor will also feel the child's abdomen to see if there is an enlarged liver or spleen. A complete blood count (CBC) will measure the numbers of white cells, red cells, and platelets in the child's blood. A blood smear will also be examined under a microscope to check for specific types of abnormal blood cells.

Further diagnostic measures include removing samples of marrow cells for laboratory examination, a lymph node biopsy, and possibly a sample of spinal fluid obtained through a lumbar puncture (spinal tap) to examine for the presence of abnor-

mal cells. Bone marrow and lymph node samples will be examined to help determine the specific type of leukemia. More evaluations are also generally done, including genetic studies and other tests to distinguish among specific types of leukemia.

Treatment and Outlook With ALL, children are usually classified as either standard-risk or high-risk patients before treatment begins. Risk is used to determine the likelihood that the leukemia will return or won't respond well to current treatment. Standard-risk patients include all those between ages one and nine who have a white blood cell count of less than 50,000 per microliter at the time of diagnosis. All other children with ALL are considered to be high-risk patients. Although all patients are treated with chemotherapy, standard-risk patients usually receive two- or three-drug regimens. High-risk patients usually receive more complex regimens of four or more drugs.

To decrease the chance that leukemia will invade the central nervous system, standard-risk patients receive intrathecal chemotherapy (administration of drugs into the cerebrospinal fluid surrounding the brain and spinal cord). Radiation treatments may be used in addition to intrathecal chemotherapy for certain high-risk patients. Once a child with ALL has entered remission (tests no longer show evidence of the disease), maintenance chemotherapy continues for two to three years.

To treat AML, children usually also receive chemotherapeutic drugs. Some form of central nervous system treatment, usually intrathecal chemotherapy with or without cranial radiation, is also given in most treatment plans. Once remission has occurred, most treatment plans include trying to prolong the remission state by using either bone marrow transplantation or maintenance chemotherapy.

After standard treatment, more than 80 percent of standard-risk ALL patients and approximately 60 to 65 percent of high-risk ALL patients will be cured of their disease. The cure rate for AML patients is about 50 percent with chemotherapy alone, but this rises to 70 percent if chemotherapy is followed by bone marrow transplantation from a compatible donor.

Prevention and Prenatal Testing In most cases, neither parents nor children have control over the factors that trigger leukemia, although current studies are investigating the possibility that environmental factors may predispose a child to develop the disease.

Most leukemias arise from noninherited mutations in the genes of growing blood cells. Because these errors occur randomly and unpredictably, there's currently no effective way to prevent or predict most types of leukemia.

Close medical follow-up can spot early signs of leukemia in the relatively rare cases where this cancer is linked to certain genetic conditions, prior cancer treatment, or treatment with immunosuppressive drugs for organ transplants.

Metabolic Diseases (PKU, Galactosemia)

There are a number of uncommon conditions affecting children that are the result of an abnormal gene that causes a disturbance in the chemical processes of the body. These hereditary disorders are called inborn errors of metabolism. More than 200 inborn errors of metabolism have been identified, but most are rare. Most of these

conditions are inherited when a child receives two copies of a faulty gene, one from each parent.

Two of these conditions—phenylketonuria (PKU) and galactosemia—are of particular importance in that, if they are not diagnosed and treated early in life, they can cause damage to an infant's brain and result in mental retardation.

PKU, which affects about 1 in 16,000 infants, is an inherited genetic disease in which the enzyme needed to metabolize phenylalanine, an amino acid, is missing or deficient.

Galactosemia, which affects 1 in 60,000 infants, is caused by the lack of an enzyme needed to metabolize, or break down, the sugar galactose found in milk and other foods.

Symptoms and Diagnosis Inborn errors of metabolism produce diseases that can range from mild to lethal. Many can be detected in the newborn period or shortly thereafter. Infants with metabolic disorders are usually normal at birth, but symptoms may develop as early as a few hours of age. Infants may vomit; begin to lose weight or not gain weight; show developmental delays; or have elevated blood or urine levels of particular body substances, a peculiar odor to the urine, an enlarged liver, and other signs and symptoms.

There usually are no symptoms of PKU in the newborn. Affected infants tend to have lighter hair, skin, and eyes than family members without the disorder. Some develop a rash, and their urine may smell musty. Vomiting may be an early symptom. Developmental delay may develop gradually and may not be evident in the first months. If left untreated, PKU will usually result in severe mental retardation. Other symptoms in children with undiagnosed or untreated PKU include seizures and hyperactivity with purposeless movements. A small head (microcephaly) and other growth abnormalities may also occur in untreated infants.

Like those with PKU, infants with galactosemia seem normal at first, but within a few days or weeks, they lose appetite, vomit, have a yellowish color of the skin and eyes (jaundice), may develop hypoglycemia (low blood sugar), and stop growing normally. They are also at risk for developing life-threatening bacterial infection in the newborn period. The liver becomes enlarged, and over time, if untreated, children with galactosemia grow poorly and become mentally retarded. They will also develop cataracts and chronic liver failure. Girls often have nonfunctioning ovaries, resulting in infertility.

Lab studies are performed to determine which enzyme is missing or not functioning properly due to the genetic defect. Knowing whether other family members have had a specific metabolic disease can also help a doctor determine the diagnosis.

Blood tests for PKU and galactosemia are included in the battery of tests routinely performed on newborn infants in U.S. hospitals in most states to diagnose conditions in which early recognition and treatment can prevent serious health problems. (For more information, see Chapter 14, "Health Screening Tests.")

Treatment and Outlook With PKU, children are put on a special diet that includes low-phenylalanine formula, low-protein foods, and fruits and most vegetables. High-protein foods (which contain phenylalanine) such as meat, fish, poultry, dairy products, baked goods, and eggs must be avoided. Recent studies show that when

children are diagnosed early and stay on the special diet throughout life, most will have normal intelligence as adults.

Children with galactosemia have to eliminate all milk and milk products, the major source of galactose, as well as some fruits and vegetables, from their diets. If adequately treated, most do not become retarded, but their intelligence is usually lower than their siblings', and they frequently have speech problems.

Prevention and Prenatal Testing Subsequent infants born to parents who have had a child with either PKU or galactosemia have a one in four risk of having the disease. It is possible by amniocentesis or chorionic villus sampling (CVS) to detect the abnormality in the fetus.

Pregnant women with PKU who are not on a low-phenylalanine diet have a higher risk of miscarriage. Their infants also have a higher risk of being mentally retarded and being born with heart abnormalities.

Muscular Dystrophy

Muscular dystrophy refers to a group of degenerative muscle diseases characterized by gradual weakening and deterioration of skeletal muscles and sometimes the heart and respiratory muscles. Most children with muscle diseases are born with abnormal genes that cause their muscles to function improperly. The most common types of muscular dystrophy (such as Duchenne, Becker, myotonic, and limb-girdle) result in dramatic physical weakness, so children lose the ability to do things like walk, sit upright, breathe easily, and move their arms. The increasing weakness often leads to other serious complications and, for many, a shortened life span. Other forms can result in relatively minor physical disabilities or develop late in life, allowing fairly normal life spans and activity levels.

Muscular dystrophy is caused by a genetic abnormality. Some types of muscular dystrophy, including Duchenne (the most common and severe type, affecting 1 in 3,600 boys), are X-linked, which means that the abnormality is carried on the X chromosome. A girl receives two X chromosomes, one from each parent, whereas a boy receives a Y chromosome from the father and one of the mother's two X chromosomes. As a result, it's usually boys who develop symptoms. Even if a girl inherits an X chromosome with the abnormal gene from her mother, she also receives an X chromosome from her father that doesn't contain the muscular dystrophy gene. The presence of a normal gene on that chromosome prevents the girl from developing the disease; however, she is a "carrier" of the condition. Sons of women who carry the abnormal gene have a 50 percent chance of receiving the X chromosome with the abnormal gene and developing muscular dystrophy.

Symptoms and Diagnosis Many parents first learn of a potential problem from a teacher who notices that their child isn't as active as other children are. Typical symptoms of Duchenne muscular dystrophy include toe-walking, waddling gait, and difficulty walking up stairs. These symptoms usually appear between the ages of two and five.

Toddlers may develop a swayed back to compensate for weakening hip-area muscles, and some children may struggle to get up from a sitting position. Many children also develop enlarged calf muscles, a condition called calf pseudohypertrophy, as muscle tissue is destroyed and replaced by non-muscle tissue.

Symptoms can first appear from early childhood through late adult life, depending on the type. For example, symptoms of Becker dystrophy are similar to Duchenne, but they may start during the school-age years and are less severe. In contrast, Duchenne dystrophy begins during early childhood and causes fairly rapidly progressing weakness.

The condition also affects the brain and nervous system, and this may result in lowered intelligence. Although only about 20 to 30 percent of children with the condition are mentally retarded, most have some learning difficulties.

In addition to a clinical history and a physical exam, a doctor who suspects muscular dystrophy will perform tests to measure blood levels of serum creatine kinase, a muscle enzyme that's released into the bloodstream when muscle fibers are deteriorating in the body. If a child is found to have a high level of this enzyme, the next test may be a DNA test or a muscle biopsy. The DNA test is used to check for gene abnormalities, whereas the muscle biopsy is used to examine a muscle tissue sample for patterns of muscle deterioration and abnormal levels of dystrophin, a protein building block of muscle that is deficient in the disease. These tests can reveal the type a child has.

Treatment and Outlook Muscular dystrophy is treatable but not curable—children with the disease are now living longer and having a better quality of life because of new treatments that can improve muscle and joint function, slow muscle deterioration, and keep children comfortable, active, and independent for a longer time.

A team of medical professionals is usually involved in the treatment of a child with muscular dystrophy and may include a neurologist, orthopedist, pulmonologist, physical and occupational therapists, psychologist, nurse-practitioner, and social worker. Depending on the type of disease and the severity of symptoms, treatment may include physical therapy, joint-bracing techniques, and prednisone, a steroid medication that may slow muscle deterioration.

Physical therapy can help maintain muscle tone and reduce the severity of the joint contractures, which can occur when muscles attached to a joint have unequal strength (the stronger muscle pulls and bends the joint into a locked and nonfunctional position). Physical therapists also use bracing techniques to prevent contractures and to enable children to use weakened muscles and joints more effectively.

Because their capacity for exercise is limited, children with muscular dystrophy may need nutritional guidance to help them avoid obesity—excess weight can strain their already weak muscles.

Children with Duchenne or Becker dystrophy may develop scoliosis, which is an abnormal curvature of the spine that develops when the back muscles are too weak to hold the spine erect. Spinal fusion, surgery that involves placing a pair of metal rods down the length of the spine and fusing the vertebrae (bones of the spine) together, can help children to sit upright, breathe better, and be more comfortable.

Many children with muscular dystrophy also develop weakened heart and respiratory muscles. Because children can't cough out mucus from their lungs well due to weakened respiratory muscles, they sometimes develop respiratory infections that can quickly become serious. Receiving good general health care and vaccinations against the germs that can lead to pneumonia is especially important for children with muscular dystrophy to help prevent these infections.

Assistive devices, such as wheelchairs, ramps, and computerized equipment, can help children with muscular dystrophy maintain their independence and mobility as their muscles weaken.

Prevention and Prenatal Testing People with a family history of muscular dystrophy can have a blood DNA test to determine whether they are carrying the abnormal gene. Prenatal testing can also detect the presence of the abnormal gene in a fetus.

Obesity

Obesity is the medical term for the presence of excessive amounts of body fat. More than half of American adults and more than 30 percent of American children are overweight or obese. Although causes are still unclear, genetics seems to be a factor, as obesity tends to run in families. But lifestyle factors such as high-calorie, high-fat diets and lack of adequate physical exercise also appear to play an important role. In rare cases, obesity is caused by a hormonal disorder, or it may be associated with taking certain medications.

Symptoms and Diagnosis The presence of obesity is determined by measuring body mass index (BMI). BMI equals a person's weight in kilograms divided by height in meters squared (BMI = kg/m^2). This formula has been shown to be a relatively good indicator of body fatness. (See Appendix B for standardized BMI growth charts for children ages 2 to 20 years.)

Plotting a child's growth over time on standard growth charts allows a doctor to see if a child is growing in a consistent, healthy way. If a child's BMI is greater than the 85th percentile for age or is rising abnormally rapidly, this should alert the doctor and parents to review the child's eating habits and physical activity.

Treatment and Outlook In most cases, the treatment of obesity in childhood is centered on changing eating habits and increasing physical activity. Generally, the nutritional objective is to modify food choices, mainly by decreasing the amount of calorie-dense, high-fat, high-sugar, nutritionally "empty" foods and increasing the child's intake of fresh fruits, vegetables, whole grains, and lower-fat dairy products. For most overweight children, the focus should not be on achieving weight loss but instead on slowing the rate of weight gain or maintaining the same weight as the child grows taller—allowing the child to "grow into his weight." Children, particularly infants, should never be put on a diet without a doctor's supervision. The child's exercise habits must be addressed as well, to ensure that the child is burning calories through physical activity in addition to limiting intake.

As with adults, diets for children sometimes improve weight in the short term, but unless eating and exercise habits are changed over the long term, the child's weight problem will return.

Parents should also be aware that excessive weight gain in some children can be triggered by emotional stress. Problems at home, at school, or with peers may need to be addressed before or along with attempts to control weight.

Children have fewer immediate health problems from being overweight than adults have. But they may suffer from self-esteem problems and fear of teasing from other children. Some children may also have higher blood pressure and higher blood cholesterol levels. The greatest health concern, however, is that they often grow into obese adults who have a higher risk for the development of heart disease, stroke, diabetes, and a number of other medical problems.

Prevention Parents may help their children avoid becoming overweight by establishing good eating patterns and exercise habits from the start. The USDA nutrition guidelines (for more information, see Chapter 22, "Healthy Eating") outline the components of a healthy, balanced diet, calling for no more than 30 percent of the diet coming from fat and promoting a good balance of fruits, vegetables, and grains. The guidelines also recommend that a child should engage in at least 60 minutes of moderate exercise (walking, biking, skating, etc.) on most days.

Some research studies suggest that the increasing prevalence of weight problems among children in the United States is due in part to too many hours in front of the TV or the computer. Not only is the child sedentary, he is also more likely to eat junk food while engaged in these activities. Helping a child pick healthy foods, limiting junk food intake (drinking water rather than soda, juices, and other calorie-filled sweetened drinks is particularly important), keeping TV and computer time to a minimum, and making sure he has time each day for active play can go a long way toward preventing weight problems. It will also establish good habits for maintaining health over his lifetime.

For more information about obesity, see Appendix C, "Resource Guide."

Orthopedic Conditions of the Legs and Feet

Common orthopedic conditions of the lower limbs in early childhood include bowed legs, flatfeet, and intoeing.

Bowed Legs

Many newborns appear to have bowed legs (or bowlegs) after birth because of the usual position of the fetus's legs in the uterus—crossed and wrapped around the front of the body. The legs typically begin to straighten once children begin to walk. However, pronounced bowing of the legs that persists beyond age two may be an indicator of an underlying disorder of the bones, such as rickets (which can be caused by a lack of vitamin D in the diet or by a genetic abnormality) or Blount disease (a deformity of the top of the tibia bone near the knee).

Symptoms and Diagnosis Bowed legs are present if the child's knees don't touch when a child is standing with feet together and ankles touching. Doctors diagnose the condition by performing a physical examination of the child. X-rays and blood tests may be performed if a bone deformity or disorder is suspected.

Treatment and Outlook Most cases of bowed legs do not require treatment, as the legs usually begin to straighten once walking begins. Bowing from Blount disease may require bracing or surgery between the ages of three and four.

If bowed legs are caused by rickets due to deficiency of vitamin D, the condition can be successfully treated by adding vitamin D to the child's diet. Although fairly uncommon today, children in certain high-risk categories are more likely to develop rickets. Black or dark-skinned children (darker skin pigmentation prevents sunlight from penetrating the skin where it helps the body produce vitamin D) who are breast-fed without receiving vitamin D supplements or who don't drink vitamin D–fortified formula or milk are particularly at risk for the condition. Rickets may be diagnosed before age two because the child's rate of growth is usually slow. Other features related to abnormal bone growth, such as thickened wrists, may also be noted in children with the condition.

Flatfeet

Infants and young children tend to have a flat arch due to the normal looseness of the ligaments connecting the bones of the foot. In most cases a normal arch will develop over time. In children with persistently flatfeet, the arch of the foot never fully develops (usually this diagnosis can't be made until the child is of school age or older), and the bottom of the foot appears flat. Flatfeet are so common (one in seven adults has flatfeet) that they are considered to be a normal variation of human anatomy.

Symptoms and Diagnosis Signs and symptoms of flatfeet include a flat appearance of the bottom of the feet (which can also be observed when the child's bare feet make footprints on the floor, dirt, or sand) and ankle pronation (an inward turning of the ankles). Pain in the feet or lower legs may be reported by some children, but this is not common. Doctors diagnose this condition by performing a physical examination of the child. X-rays are usually unnecessary unless the flatfoot is rigid and a bone deformity or other abnormality is suspected.

Treatment and Outlook Flatfeet usually do not require treatment, but if pain is present, a child may be given orthotics (shoe inserts that will help support the arch of the feet). Orthotics may help relieve the pain, but they will not correct the flatfeet. Most children with flatfeet do not experience any problems—they have as much athletic potential as other children and usually do not require any special footwear.

Intoeing

Infants and toddlers with intoeing (or "pigeon toes") have feet that turn in, which is usually the result of the normal positioning of the fetus' legs and feet in the cramped uterus—crossed and wrapped around the front of the body. In most cases, intoeing is not a significant problem and will usually correct itself in time. Intoeing in an infant or child may be the result of an inward curve of the front portion of the foot (called metatarsus adductus), a twisting of the tibia bone of the leg (called internal tibial torsion), or a twisting of the femur bone in the thigh (called excess femoral anteversion).

Symptoms and Diagnosis Parents may notice a curvature in their child's feet or lower legs during infancy or an inward twisting of the legs and/or thighs after the child is walking. Doctors can usually diagnose the cause of the intoeing by physical examination alone. X-rays may be performed in cases where an underlying deformity or other abnormality of the bones is suspected. *Clubfoot* is a term used to describe a combination of rigid foot and ankle deformities that usually includes an inward curving of the foot. This deformity does not resolve on its own, and treatment beginning soon after birth is required.

Treatment and Outlook Most cases of intoeing require no treatment, as the child will usually grow out of the condition. In the past, foot stretching exercises, special shoes, splints, and braces have been used for correction, but these techniques alone have not been proved to speed up the body's own natural correction of the condition. In the few cases in which the child's foot or leg deformity is rigid (such as with clubfoot), or if the problem does not resolve sufficiently over time, specific treatment with casting or surgery may be necessary. Children with intoeing that persists usually do not experience any physical problems—they can participate in sports and have as much athletic potential as other children.

Precocious Puberty

Precocious puberty is defined as the appearance of any of the physical changes associated with puberty in a girl younger than age eight or a boy younger than age nine and a half.

Normally, puberty begins when a part of the brain known as the hypothalamus sends signals to the pituitary gland (which is located just beneath the brain), which in turn releases hormones into the bloodstream that stimulate the gonads (ovaries in girls; testicles in boys) to make sex hormones (estrogen in girls; testosterone in boys). These gonadal sex hormones cause the physical changes of puberty.

In most cases when the changes of puberty begin too early, no specific underlying cause can be found—the child's internal "puberty clock" just seems to be running ahead of the usual time schedule. Usually there are no other family members with the condition; however, in about 5 percent of boys with precocious puberty, the disorder is inherited.

In some cases, precocious puberty may occur in association with certain medical problems such as a brain tumor or other condition causing irritation or pressure in or around the brain or a tumor or other disorder affecting hormone production in the ovary, testicle, thyroid, or adrenal gland. A child may also show signs of pubertal development if exposed to sex hormones by ingesting birth control pills or other hormone-containing medications or foods.

For those children with precocious puberty who have no underlying medical problem, there are two major concerns: growth and psychological issues. When a child's growth spurt occurs at an abnormally early age, the skeleton matures too rapidly. If left untreated, this will cause the growth regions of the bones to fuse closed too soon, leading to a shorter-than-expected adult height for the child. Significantly premature sexual maturation can also result in teasing by the child's peers and psychological adjustment difficulties.

Symptoms and Diagnosis The symptoms of precocious pubertal development are the early appearance of the physical changes of puberty. This includes breast development and menstrual bleeding in girls and enlargement of the testicles and penis, muscular development, facial hair, and deepening of the voice in boys. In both girls and boys, the hormones of puberty also stimulate the growth of pubic hair and underarm hair and trigger the spurt in height growth that accompanies sexual maturation.

Many children who show early signs of pubertal maturation have what is known as "partial" precocious puberty. Some girls, usually beginning between the ages of six months and three years, may show breast development that subsequently disappears or may persist without other associated physical changes of puberty. Similarly, some girls and boys may experience early growth of pubic and/or underarm hair that is not associated with other changes in sexual development. Children with "partial" precocious puberty may require a medical evaluation to rule out "true" precocious puberty, but they generally need no treatment and usually will show the other expected signs of puberty at the usual age.

The doctor will confirm the presence of precocious pubertal development by physical examination of the child. The medical history and physical examination of the child may also reveal evidence of one of the associated medical problems discussed earlier. The child's growth records may show an accelerated growth rate. Laboratory studies for diagnosis of precocious puberty may include the measurement of blood hormone levels, X-rays to assess skeletal maturation, and in some cases imaging studies of the brain (MRI or CT scan) or ultrasound examination of the ovaries or adrenal glands.

Treatment and Outlook If an underlying medical cause for the child's precocious puberty is discovered, the condition may require specific medications or surgery to treat the problem. Those children with no associated medical problems can be treated with injections of an LHRH analog (a synthetic hormone medication), which is usually successful in arresting the progression or causing regression of the child's pubertal development. If this therapy is started before pubertal changes have progressed very far, significant shortening of the child's adult height may be prevented. Regression in the physical changes of puberty, such as breast development or menstrual bleeding in a girl, can also help relieve the emotional or psychological stress that sometimes occurs with these changes. When the child has reached the age that most other children experience puberty, the medication is stopped and the child is thus allowed to finish pubertal development and growth.

Spina Bifida/Myelomeningocele

Spina bifida and myelomeningocele are neural tube defects. The neural tube, which develops along the back of the fetus in about the third week of pregnancy, later becomes the brain, the spinal cord, and their coverings (the meninges). If this tube fails to close completely, defects result.

Neural tube defects sometimes run in families, suggesting a genetic role. Not getting enough folic acid, a B vitamin, at the time of conception or in the early weeks of pregnancy is linked to a higher risk of having a child with spina bifida. Mothers who have diabetes or who have taken certain drugs to treat epilepsy also have a higher risk of having a baby with the condition.

Symptoms and Diagnosis Spina bifida occurs when the sides of the neural tube do not join together properly, leaving an open area. Spina bifida occulta is the mildest form of spina bifida, and in many cases the gap in the spine is never detected. A dimple, a birthmark, or a patch of hair may be visible on the skin over the gap.

Spina bifida manifesta includes two forms of spina bifida, which occur in about 1 in 1,000 babies born in the United States: meningocele and myelomeningocele.

Menigocele occurs when the meninges —membranes that cover the brain and spinal cord—create a sac filled with cerebrospinal fluid. The sac, which bulges out like a blister through the vertebrae (bones of the spine), isn't associated with nervous system problems unless the nerves of the spinal cord are involved, which can affect movement and bladder control. The condition accounts for about 4 percent of children born with spina bifida manifesta.

About 96 percent of infants born with spina bifida manifesta have myelomeningocele, the most severe type of spina bifida. As in meningocele, the meninges bulge out through a gap in the spine, but in this type, the spinal cord bulges out too. The sac may be covered with skin, or the nerves may be exposed.

Children with myelomeningocele may have many health problems, the severity of which depends on where the defect occurs in the spine and the extent of the defect. A gap higher in the spinal column generally will be associated with more problems than a gap in the lower back.

Usually there is paralysis (loss of movement) below the level of the spinal defect. The most severely impaired children cannot walk or control their bowels or bladder. Many children born with this condition also have hydrocephalus, a buildup of the fluid surrounding the brain. If not treated, the excess pressure in the skull can cause blindness and brain damage.

If a baby is born with a neural tube defect, an MRI or CT scan is usually done to assess the severity of the defect.

Treatment and Outlook Children with less severe forms of spina bifida usually live normal lives with no significant impairment.

Myelomeningocele and meningocele require surgery within 48 hours of birth to close the gap in the vertebrae to protect the spinal cord and prevent infection. If there is hydrocephalus, this must also be treated by surgically inserting a device called a shunt to drain the excess fluid and relieve the pressure on the brain.

Even with aggressive treatment, the mortality rate for children with this condition is 10 to 15 percent, with most deaths occurring before age four years. Children often have multiple problems resulting from their spinal cord defects, including an inability to control their bowels and bladders. Urinary catheters are used to drain urine from the bladder and help prevent recurrent urinary tract infections. Many children also have trouble walking and need crutches or wheelchairs. In addition, although most surviving children have normal intelligence, many have learning disabilities that require special educational support.

Management of the condition is best done through a multidisciplinary team approach including a variety of physician specialists and therapists.

Prevention and Prenatal Testing To reduce the risk of spina bifida, it is recommended that all women of childbearing age take 400 micrograms of folic acid daily. This is recommended because by the time a woman knows she's pregnant, the damage might have already occurred if she didn't get enough of the vitamin. Folic acid is found in fresh, dark, leafy green vegetables, fruits, liver and other organ meats, and dried yeast. Breads and cereals are also fortified with folic acid. Multivitamin supplements are another source.

During pregnancy, women are offered a blood test called the maternal serum alpha-fetoprotein (AFP) test at 16 to 18 weeks to screen for severe neural tube defects. If the AFP level is high, the test is repeated. If it is still high, an ultrasound or amniocentesis procedure or both will be performed to confirm the diagnosis.

For more information about spina bifida, see Appendix C, "Resource Guide."

Tic Disorders/Tourette Syndrome

Tics occur when a muscle or group of muscles contracts repeatedly and uncontrollably. The condition most often affects the facial muscles but may also cause uncontrolled movements of the limbs and sounds such as grunts and throat clearings.

Tourette syndrome, an uncommon but severe tic disorder, is believed to be caused by an abnormality in the brain's neurotransmitters, chemicals that carry signals from one nerve to another. One neurotransmitter that is affected is dopamine, which controls movement. Tourette syndrome appears to run in families; boys are affected three to four times more often than girls.

Symptoms and Diagnosis Many children have simple tics, which seem to be merely habits that disappear over time. The symptoms can vary but may include rapid uncontrolled blinking, twitching of the muscles in the face, shrugging of the shoulders or jerking movements, grunting, barking sounds, or inappropriate bursts of speech.

The tics in Tourette syndrome are more complex. A child may repeatedly move his head from side to side, blink his eyes, open his mouth, and stretch his neck. He may hit and kick, grunt, snort, and hum. He may call out an obscenity for no apparent reason or repeat words immediately after hearing them.

Treatment and Outlook Because most simple tics disappear within a few weeks, treatment is not necessary, but early diagnosis is helpful so that parents can be reassured that the behavior isn't voluntary. The tics of some children with Tourette syndrome may make learning and social interactions difficult. Drugs such as haloperidol may suppress the tics, although they can have side effects. These children may also suffer from emotional problems and certain phobias or fears. Special help with school and psychological counseling may be helpful.

Surgical Conditions/Procedures

Most childhood health problems either resolve on their own or can be treated or controlled with medications. However, there are a number of childhood conditions that require surgery. Some of the more commonly occurring surgical conditions and procedures include the following:

Appendicitis

Appendicitis is an inflammation of the appendix, a hollow, fingerlike pouch of tissue that connects to and opens into the beginning of the large intestine. The condition is uncommon in children younger than two years. Symptoms of appendicitis include abdominal pain, nausea, vomiting, and fever. Suspected cases of appendicitis should be evaluated by a doctor immediately because surgery to remove the inflamed appendix is necessary before it perforates (breaks open) and spreads bacteria throughout the abdomen. A doctor will determine whether surgery is necessary based on the patient's history of symptoms and physical examination findings, as well as blood tests and sometimes X-rays or other imaging studies.

An inflamed appendix is usually removed through a small incision in the abdominal wall. If the appendix is removed before it perforates, complications are rare.

The child's hospital stay is usually two or three days. If the infected appendix perforates, it must still be removed surgically, but a longer hospital stay is needed so that antibiotics can be given to kill bacteria that have spread through the abdominal cavity.

Hernia

An inguinal hernia occurs when a loop of intestine or other abdominal contents push through an opening or weak area in the wall of the abdomen. Although they can occur at any age, inguinal hernias are most commonly diagnosed in the first year of life and are four times more likely to occur in boys than in girls. An inguinal hernia usually appears as a lump or swelling in the groin or scrotum (the sac containing the testicles) in boys or in the labia (the folds of skin surrounding the opening of the vagina) in girls. In infants, the first sign of a problem may be that parents observe the baby to be fussy or uncomfortable. Inguinal hernias usually don't cause symptoms, but they can pose a problem if the protruding tissue becomes trapped (incarcerated), which can cut off the blood flow to the organ involved. Surgical repair involves closing the opening in the abdominal wall through an incision made in the groin area. The procedure is usually done on an outpatient basis, and a child may go home within a few hours after the surgery. Acetaminophen may be given for pain, but most children are able to resume normal activities within a few days.

An umbilical hernia is present when the wall of the abdomen surrounding the navel does not fully close before birth, allowing part of the intestine to protrude through the opening. (For more information about umbilical hernias, see Chapter 5, "Common Newborn Medical Conditions.")

Hypospadias

Hypospadias is a fairly common (it occurs in about 1 in 300 boys) birth defect in which the opening of the urethra—the passage that carries urine from the bladder to the outside of the body—develops on the underside of the shaft of the penis instead of at the tip. Most commonly the opening develops near the end of the penis, but in severe cases it can occur at the base of the penis where it joins the scrotum. Hypospadias may run in families, suggesting a genetic factor in some cases.

Doctors diagnose the condition by performing a physical examination. The foreskin of boys with hypospadias is hoodlike and doesn't cover the underside of the head of the penis as it normally should. Abnormal bands of tissue may also extend from the underside of the penis to the scrotum, causing the penis to assume a downward curve. Boys with hypospadias are more likely to have other abnormalities of the urinary tract and genitals such as inguinal hernia and undescended testicle (cryptorchidism). The doctor may order special imaging studies to look for associated abnormalities of the bladder or kidneys.

The treatment of the condition involves a surgical procedure to move the urethral opening to the normal position at the end of the penis. Because this surgery often uses the foreskin tissue to accomplish the repair, boys with hypospadias should not be circumcised before they have been fully evaluated by the surgeon. The surgery is usually done in one stage, and it should be performed before 18 months of age. If the condition is not treated early, the boy will

need to sit down to urinate. Mild cases that will not interfere with urinary or sexual function do not require surgical treatment unless the cosmetic appearance of the penis is an issue.

Myringotomy (Ear Tube Surgery)

Surgical insertion of a tiny hollow tube through an incision in the eardrum, or myringotomy, is often used to treat recurrent or persistent problems related to middle ear infection (otitis media). Most children will develop one or more ear infections during the first few years of life; however, these infections usually respond well to antibiotic treatment and result in no long-term effects on hearing or other complications (for more information about ear infections, see Chapter 30, "Childhood Infections"). Myringotomy is usually considered for treatment of children with frequently recurring bouts of otitis media despite antibiotic therapy or for children with a persistent (lasting more than three months) collection of fluid behind the eardrum, particularly if the fluid is impairing the child's hearing. Blockage of the eustachian tube (the canal connecting the throat and middle ear, which normally allows air to flow in and out of the middle ear) is usually the cause of chronic ear fluid collection.

During the myringotomy procedure, small plastic tubes are inserted through an incision made in the eardrum during surgery and left in place, which allows air to enter the middle ear. This equalizes the pressure between the middle and outer ear, which can help eliminate the collected fluid, restore normal hearing, and decrease the likelihood of repeated infections. Children younger than three months or with complicating medical conditions may stay in the hospital overnight after the procedure, but other children usually go home within a few hours of the surgery. There is generally no need for further surgery to remove an ear tube. Generally, the tube stays in the ear for up to two years before falling out on its own. Although the procedure is usually effective in clearing up middle ear fluid, about 25 percent of children who require ear tubes before the age of two need to have tubes inserted again at a later time. With proper treatment and follow up, most children with recurrent or chronic ear problems will maintain hearing at a level sufficient to permit normal speech and language development.

Pyloric Stenosis

Pyloric stenosis is a condition in which the pylorus—the muscle that controls the rate at which food moves from the stomach into the small intestine—is too tight, resulting in forceful vomiting after feedings. (For more information on pyloric stenosis, see Chapter 29, "Signs and Symptoms.")

Strabismus ("Crossed" Eyes)

Strabismus (or "crossed" eyes) is a misalignment of the eyes, in which an eye may turn in (esotropia), out (exotropia), up (hypertropia), or down (hypotropia). If an eye is chronically misaligned and not used by the child to see, weak vision (amblyopia or "lazy eye") may result. Most children with strabismus are otherwise healthy, but the condition appears with greater frequency among children with conditions involving the brain such as cerebral palsy and hydrocephalus. Strabismus may be caused by muscle weakness, eye injury, other eye diseases, or, rarely, a tumor. Symptoms of strabismus include "crossed" eyes, squinting or tilting of the head to see things, headache, eye rubbing, tearing, and double vision.

Amblyopia can be prevented by patching the eyes alternately, forcing the child to use and develop vision in both eyes. Patching must be done in the first few years of life to prevent vision loss. In some cases, corrective eyeglasses can be used to prevent amblyopia and properly align the eyes.

Often surgery on the muscles that control eye movement is necessary to achieve proper alignment. The procedure involves tightening or weakening eye muscles to create a correct balance between the pairs of muscles that help control the position of the eyes. This surgery can usually be performed on an outpatient basis. In some cases, more than one operation may be needed to achieve proper eye alignment.

Tonsillectomy and Adenoidectomy

The tonsils are fleshy lumps of tissue located on either side of the back of the throat. Some children require a tonsillectomy (surgical removal of the tonsils) because the tonsils have become enlarged and partially block the airway, which can cause sleep apnea (prolonged pauses in breathing with interruption of normal sleep) and chronic stress on the heart and lungs. In some cases, children who have very frequent infections of the throat and tonsils may benefit from a tonsillectomy; however, the procedure is performed much less frequently today for these symptoms than it was in the past.

The adenoids are lumps of tissue similar to the tonsils located behind the nose and hidden from view by the palate (roof of the mouth). They are usually removed if they block the nasal passages or the eustachian tubes, which connect the middle ears to the throat. Such blockages can play a role in persistent ear or sinus infections. In addition, enlarged adenoids may produce symptoms such as difficulty breathing through the nose, noisy breathing, speech problems, snoring, and sleep apnea.

Depending on a child's symptoms, a tonsillectomy, adenoidectomy, or both (also known as a "T&A") may be recommended. T&A is the surgical removal of the tonsils and adenoids. This procedure is usually performed by an ENT (ears, nose, and throat) specialist. The child is usually able to go home within hours of the surgery with a prescription for pain medication. White patches may appear in the child's throat where the tonsils were, but these will disappear in time.

Undescended Testicle (Cryptorchidism)

Undescended testicle, or cryptorchidism, is a condition in which, during development of the fetus, one or both (both in 10 to 20 percent of cases) testicles do not fully descend from the abdomen, where they form, into the normal position in the scrotum (the sack holding the testicles). About 3 percent of term infant boys and as many as 30 percent of premature boys have this condition. In about two-thirds of cases, an undescended testicle moves down into the scrotum on its own within the first six months of life—those that do not move down usually need treatment. The future sperm-producing tissue in the testicle becomes progressively damaged if an undescended testicle is not brought down into

the lower-temperature environment of the scrotum early in life. This increases the risk of infertility—especially if both testicles are undescended.

Doctors usually diagnose the condition by physical examination at birth or at a checkup during early infancy. True cryptorchidism must be distinguished from a benign (needing no treatment) condition common in young boys called retractile testis, in which the muscle attached to the testicle temporarily pulls it up into the groin or abdomen when the boy is stressed or undressed or when the genital area is touched or exposed to cold. Repeated examinations may be necessary to determine whether the testicle is indeed undescended. Undescended testicles are also often accompanied by inguinal hernia (see Hernia in this chapter).

If the testicle does not come down, the condition should be treated by about 12 to 15 months of age to minimize damage to the testicle. In some cases, hormone therapy may be given in an attempt to move the testicle into the scrotum, but this is not often successful. Standard treatment is a procedure called an orchiopexy, which involves surgically bringing the testicle into the scrotum and fastening it there. The procedure, performed in one or two stages, is successful in the large majority of cases.

After treatment, boys develop normally (the male-hormone-producing tissue of the testicle is not significantly affected by the condition), and sexual function is unaffected. If one testicle is involved and treated, 85 percent of boys with the condition will be fertile later on. If both testes are involved, the fertility rate is lower—approximately 50 percent. Boys with undescended testicle have an increased risk of developing cancer of the testicle (1 in 40 to

1 in 80) as young adults, whether they are treated or not. They should be taught testicular self-examination (as should all teen boys) and have regular examinations of their testes performed by a doctor through adulthood.

Need More Information?

Check the Index and Appendix C, "Resource Guide." And of course, consult your child's doctor.

chapter thirty-three

Caring for Your Child with Special Health Care Needs

Being your child's best advocate

A child is considered to have special health care needs if he requires more or different health services than children generally do. This covers children with a wide range of physical, developmental, behavioral, or emotional conditions. Chronic illnesses and disabilities in children vary in severity from the relatively minor, such as mild asthma, to the more serious—sometimes life-threatening—conditions that require complex or intensive treatment and support. For example, an infant born extremely prematurely with severe lung, nutritional, and nervous system problems might need treatment with multiple medications; long-term follow-up care from several physician specialists; physical, occupational, and speech therapy; home-nursing support; special formula and feeding supplies; devices such as wheelchairs, braces, and breathing equipment; and special developmental stimulation and education services. The parents of such children face considerable challenges, as they must not only learn to care for their child at home and ensure that all needed services are provided, but they also must coordinate all of these treatments and activities while attempting to maintain a reasonably normal life for the family.

After the initial shock and heartbreak you may experience in learning that your child has a chronic illness or disability, you'll need to set about the task of providing what your child needs to have the healthiest, happiest, and most successful life possible. Caring for your ill child with a chronic illness may involve frequent hospitalizations and doctor visits, exhausting caretaking duties, battles with health insurance companies, financial worries, and relationship strain. But your load can be lightened if you gather knowledge and support from health care providers, social workers, advocacy and support groups, clergy, friends, and family. This chapter is intended to give you an overview of some of the challenges you may face and some suggestions on how to best manage the care of your child with special needs.

Parenting Your Child with a Chronic Condition

Parenting a child with a chronic condition can be different from parenting a healthy child in several ways. You may need to explain difficult medical concepts to your child, or you may struggle with helping your child become as independent as possible. Whatever the challenges, the cornerstone of your parenting philosophy should be to treat your child as you would if he did not have a chronic medical condition.

Talking About Your Child's Illness

Explaining complicated medical information and technology to a child can be difficult, but by keeping your child informed, you help her to feel she is in control and to understand the purpose of her various treatments.

Communicate medical information clearly and honestly in an age-appropriate manner. With an infant or young child, reassurance or a soothing tone of voice can help your child feel more comfortable and relaxed. If your child is older and has verbal skills, use correct medical terms so she can talk about her concerns and be understood by medical professionals. A forthright approach may seem frightening to a parent, but to a child with limited context, the words *malignant* or *cancer* are just medical words.

Earn your child's trust by explaining her treatment, where it will take place, who will be there, and the discomfort she may feel. If a procedure or treatment will be painful or uncomfortable, don't lie to your child; say exactly how it will feel and then reassure her that you will be there for support.

If you need to have a private conversation with your spouse or partner, either to talk about your child's treatment or to discuss your own emotions, be sure to do it far away from little ears. Children can sense despair, anger, or resentment, too—you are not a bad parent for having these feelings, but just be sure that the feelings don't unnecessarily upset your child.

Coping with Your Child's Emotions and Feelings

Your child may go through a range of emotions as he faces coping with a long-term illness. Mostly, your child probably just wants you to listen to his fears and concerns. Refrain from offering explanations or reassurance right away—simply be a good listener and let your child get it all out. Ask questions about how he feels about specific treatments, discomfort, and limitations.

Although you can't always promise that everything is going to be fine, you can allow your child to acknowledge the reality of the situation and reassure your child that you're always there if he needs you. If your child finds it difficult to talk about his emotions, other modes of expression like music, drawing, or writing may give you a view of what he is thinking.

Your child needs to hear you say that he is not responsible for his illness. He may feel guilty for causing the disease and for its impact on the family. Say loud and clear and often, "This problem is not your fault."

Dealing with Your Ill Child's Behavior

Even though your child needs extra physical care and emotional support, the need for daily discipline is just as important as it would be for any other child. Once you've established a normal routine and expectations, set limits on unacceptable behavior and avoid overindulgence. You shouldn't feel guilty about setting limits; spoiling your child can not only lead to personal difficulties with self-control, but

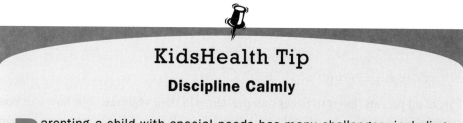

KidsHealth Tip

Discipline Calmly

Parenting a child with special needs has many challenges, including discipline. If your child refuses to comply with your requests to get dressed, for example, try not to show your frustration—that will only show your child that yelling or refusing to do something gets a reaction from you. Instead, proceed with the task calmly and offer your child as much control as possible (such as choosing what socks to wear).

it can also cause your child to feel that she is more ill, disabled, or limited than she actually is. Some children may even be frightened if they receive special treatment because they may think that you are sending the message that they are near death.

Getting a Head Start on Education for Your Chronically Ill Child

Under the federal Individuals with Disabilities Education Act (IDEA), your child has the right to a public education. But your child will probably benefit if you, as a parent, take the initiative to seek out special services, equipment, and technologies necessary for him to be educated in the most appropriate environment.

Educational intervention begins long before your child starts school. IDEA early intervention programs for children from birth to three years of age are designed to maximize family involvement and help you better understand and meet your child's educational needs. Check with your state's board of education to find out exactly what programs and services your child may be eligible for. Individualized education plans (IEPs) can also be developed for your child through your local school district. Contact your local board of education and explain your child's condition to find out if he is eligible for free evaluation and services.

> ### The Voice of Experience
>
> *"Never let your child hear you say that he can't do this or that because of his 'condition.' It can become an excuse for him not to try things he should be able to do. Treat your child as 'normally' as possible. What he accomplishes may surprise you."*
>
> —FROM THE KIDSHEALTH PARENT SURVEY

Fostering Independence in Your Child

Part of all parents' job is to foster independence in their children. But how can you accomplish that when your child with special needs is so reliant upon you and on health professionals? Here are a few guidelines:

- Give your child the tools he needs to express himself. By helping your child understand medical terminology and procedures, you enable him to explain to health professionals himself how he is feeling and what his medical concerns are.

- Encourage your child to do what he can. Even if your child has physical limitations, he may still be able to dress himself, keep his room neat, and decide how to spend his allowance.
- Teach your child responsibility. A major part of independence is learning responsibility, and by teaching your child to be responsible for himself and his words and actions, you are helping him develop independence.
- Encourage your child to develop relationships with health care professionals, siblings, and friends. These relationships will give your child a sense of individual identity and help him develop a positive self-image.

Tips for Helping Your Child Manage Stress

- Encourage your child to develop her own support group. Ask friends from school or playgroups to visit at the hospital or at home. Help your child go online to Web sites for children with chronic illnesses, such as Band-Aides & Blackboards (http://funrsc.fairfield.edu/~jfleitas/contents.html).
- Help your child continue her normal activities. If your child with cancer loves to play basketball and has to miss a season, allow her to follow professional or college basketball on TV, send someone to videotape her team's performance, or give her a videotape that allows her to study fundamentals, even if she can't practice them yet.

KidsHealth Tip

Exercise Together

Children with disabilities need exercise, too. It may not be possible to go running or play tennis, but it's important that your child remains as active as possible. If time is an issue, try combining your workout schedule with your child's by going for a walk or splashing in a pool together, for example.

- All children need to continue their learning process by attending school or receiving home instruction. Help your child adjust by reading to her or encouraging her to study with a friend or sibling.
- Make an effort to let your child know she is still an important part of the family. Establishing normalcy through family activities and routines takes the focus off your child's illness and places it on the well-being of the entire family.
- Continually listen to and reassure your child.

Caring for Your Child Dependent on Medical Technology

To care for your child effectively, you'll need to familiarize yourself with the specific medical technology used to keep your child healthy. Because medical technology is constantly advancing, you may find it difficult to keep up with new research and new methods of treatment.

Although every child will have individual needs, here are several basic pieces of medical technology that you may encounter in your child's care and treatment.

Tracheostomy A tracheostomy (trach) permits the insertion of an artificial airway, essentially a tube, through an opening made in a child's neck. This tube allows ventilator equipment to be easily attached. The tube must be changed regularly, a procedure that you will need to learn. It's essential that a clear airway be maintained at all times.

Ventilator The ventilator, which attaches to the tracheostomy tube, performs mechanical breathing. Valves on the ventilator are set to combine air and oxygen from a separate tank into a precise mix at a pressure level and rate that is adjusted for each child.

Manual Resuscitation Bag This is a breathing device that can be used in an emergency. The bag is worked manually like a small bellows. A manual resuscitation bag should be nearby in case the ventilator fails.

Suction Machine A suction machine may be needed to clear the tracheostomy tube if a child cannot cough to clear his own airway. Suctioning is done by inserting a tiny tube, about ⅛ inch in diameter, into the tracheostomy opening.

Catheter A catheter is a thin, hollow tube that can be inserted into the body to withdraw or inject fluids. A child may have what's called a Foley catheter to help drain urine from the body. Usually the catheter is connected to a plastic bag into which the urine drains.

Feeding Equipment Children who cannot eat may have feeding tubes inserted into their bodies. A gastrostomy tube goes through the skin at the abdomen, directly into the stomach; a nasogastric tube is inserted through the nose and down the throat into the stomach. For children who cannot be fed through their gastrointestinal tract, nutrient-rich fluids can be fed through a central line, which goes directly into the bloodstream through a large vessel in the chest, neck, or groin. These alternative modes of feeding require special care, particularly with a central line, which must be kept very clean because of the risk of infection entering the bloodstream.

Bringing Your Child Home

Even if your child is dependent on medical technology, she may not have to stay in the hospital. You and your child's health care team may decide that she could receive better physical and emotional support at home. Once you've made the deci-

KidsHealth Tip

Getting Through in an Emergency

If you have a child who is dependent on medical technology, you must have a working telephone nearby in case of emergency. But did you also know you could notify your phone company that your child is on life support? If you do so, your phone company will have on record that your phone lines must be working at all times in case of medical emergency and will respond to your service requests immediately. For further backup, have a cellular phone available, and don't forget to keep a list of emergency phone numbers by each phone in your home.

sion to bring your child home, however, you have a lot to prepare for and consider.

Quality home care depends on family caregivers and a backup team always being prepared and well informed. You and your family must be organized at planning ahead for supplies and technical needs. For example, your child's room must be equipped with the proper equipment, sufficient electrical outlets, and a backup power supply from a battery or generator. Also, you must have a telephone for emergencies and keep emergency numbers nearby. It's a good idea to notify your local ambulance corps of your child's special medical needs in case of emergency.

Some advanced in-home medical equipment requires a trained caregiver to operate it. All caregivers should be chosen and trained well in advance of your child's arrival home and should receive ongoing education. The caregivers should be trained in and demonstrate their skills in monitoring and use of your child's equipment, knowledge of your child's medical problem, detection of medical problems, emergency procedures, and machinery maintenance.

Your Family's Needs

Try to maintain as normal a family routine as possible. Siblings should continue to attend school and should be encouraged to participate in their normal extracurricular activities. Schedule regular family time together, even if it's as simple as a family meal several times a week.

Spend individual time with your other children every day. Even if it's only 10 minutes a day, your other children need to feel like special individuals. During individual time, make sure that the focus is on the child and that he helps decide how you spend the time together.

Involve siblings in the treatment process. By visiting the hospital, meeting medical personnel, and asking questions, your children can develop understanding and alleviate their fears of the unknown. It might be a good idea to discuss your child's treatment with the entire family so that everyone can ask questions and any confusion or fears can be addressed.

Inform school personnel of your family's situation, and ask your children's teachers to be on the lookout for any signs of stress. Your child may react to stress by acting angry, sullen, resentful, fearful, or withdrawn. Frequent fighting or problems with schoolwork are also common in kids who have a chronically ill sibling. Pay close attention to any changes in your children's behavior, and, if necessary, talk to your children's doctor or mental health professional about the situation.

Your other children may feel jealousy and resentment toward your child with chronic illness. Ask siblings to explain how they feel, and make it clear that you understand, but remind them that physical or verbal abuse will not be tolerated.

Your partner also needs attention and normalcy. Even though it may be difficult, carve out quiet time together, whether it's after your children have gone to bed, on a special date night, or on the occasional weekend away from home. Remember, your relationship with your spouse is important to your child's health care, too—a loving home can go a long way in making a child feel comfortable and secure.

Developing a Support Network

Every caregiver needs some help or someone to lean on at times. You can help reduce stress and do a better job of caring for your child if you develop a support network. Here are a few tips:

- Don't hesitate to call on helpful family members or friends when you feel overwhelmed, need to run an errand, or need to attend to a family emergency unrelated to your child's illness. This kind of support will alleviate any guilt you feel when you need to take care of yourself or your family and can't be with your child.
- Find a support group in your area for parents of children with chronic illness. Your hospital social worker or case manager may be able to refer you to groups that meet at the hospital or in local community centers. A Web search for support groups will usually turn up multiple group listings. If you live in an area where support groups are hard to come by, try starting one yourself! Or go online to bulletin boards and Web sites where parents of children with chronic illnesses can post their questions, concerns, and encouragement.
- Develop working relationships with health care professionals. You are an integral part of your child's treatment and care, and by finding out all you need to know about your child's illness, you will be better able to make informed decisions. Ask your child's doctor about places you can go for additional infor-

mation, and clarify your questions with nurses, health care staff, and physicians.

- Rely on your partner for support. Your child's illness affects no one more than your child, you, and your partner. If you are the primary caregiver, be sure to share all information and decisions about your child's care with your partner so that he or she feels included. Try to realize that everyone handles stress differently, so if you and your spouse have different worrying or coping styles, talk about them together.

Managed Care and Your Child with Special Needs

Managed care plans place limits on the amount, type, and frequency of health care, and this may create problems in your attempt to meet your child's health care needs. (For more information, see Chapter 27, "The Health Care System for Children.")

Even if you have no battle to wage with a managed care company, health plan literature can be confusing and intimidating. But arming yourself with the knowledge of your child's benefits will help you to be prepared.

In many cases, enrollment in a managed care plan actually benefits a child with special health care needs. Advantages may include better coordination of care, availability of special educational and specific chronic disease management programs, fewer out-of-pocket expenses, and (sometimes) a wide network of providers.

> ### The Voice of Experience
>
> *"I've learned that it's OK to ask others for help. I guess I was afraid of looking weak or inadequate if I needed help, but instead I found that I'm human just like everyone else."*
> —FROM THE KidsHealth PARENT SURVEY

But unless you take an active role in choosing a health plan (if you have a choice) and selecting your child's primary care doctor, you won't be guaranteed that certain benefits will come your way. So ask as many questions as you need to and don't settle until you have all the answers. Here are some tips:

- Make a list of every doctor and specialist your child uses. Include the office address and phone number for each provider, and indicate how often your child visits each provider. Note which providers are most important for your child's care.

- Make a list of all therapies, medications and prescriptions, treatments, or special programs your child needs.
- Make a list of all of the supplies and equipment your child uses and the companies or pharmacies that manufacture or supply these items.
- Before meeting with a benefits counselor or service representative, write down any questions you have about the plan's benefits, health care provider network, or policies.
- As you talk to a representative or case manager of the insurance company, refer to your questions and take detailed notes of any answers you are given. Be sure to always get the full name and title of the person you are speaking with to refer to later. If the service representative gives you any verbal commitments (such as, "You can continue to use that experimental therapy for your child and it will be covered"), ask if he has the authority to make such a commitment, and then have him or his superior put it in writing. Always follow up your conversations with a written summary that is dated and signed.
- Record keeping is key for your success in dealing with the health care system. Keep an up-to-date file of your child's care history, and carry it with you to appointments.

KidsHealth Tip

Plan Ahead for Babysitters

When leaving pertinent information for babysitters, such as the telephone numbers for poison control centers or your child's doctor, write down your family's health insurance information. If the sitter needs to bring your child to the hospital, this information will help things progress more quickly and smoothly. Include the name of the insurance provider, the group and ID numbers, and which parent's employer provides the coverage.

Financial Considerations

Although many families believe that their health plan will cover all or most of their child's medical expenses, they are often wrong in this assumption. Hospital care, surgical procedures, doctor visits, and laboratory tests are separate services, and some or all of them may not be covered by the plan. Other costs such as missed time at work, special transportation needs, and increased utility bills can also contribute to financial strain. Here are some suggestions:

- Use the resources available within your child's hospital, such as a financial counselor or hospital business office, for answers about your child's medical expenses.
- Ask to have a case manager, a person who helps coordinate the care of a child with medically complex needs, assigned to your child. If the hospital has none on staff, ask your insurance company.
- Make your child's health care providers aware of your plan's benefits and limitations. They can become your partners in coordinating care with your health plan.
- Negotiate fees with your child's doctors, clinics, and hospital, and set up realistic payment plans.
- Organize! Keep a journal and files to record doctor visits, services performed, and fees so that detailed information about your child's health care is easily accessible.
- Know your rights as a health consumer. If your insurance company denies coverage for certain expenses, appeal the decision. (Make sure you know about the plan's appeal policies and procedures.)
- Contact your state's department of insurance if you encounter unresolvable problems with your child's health care coverage.

It might be difficult to ask for help, but your friends and family may be willing or even enthusiastic about helping you out. In addition, some private and government agencies, such as charitable foundations, disease- or disability-related organizations, civic or social welfare agencies, or churches and community groups, may have financial or other aid available.

Two government programs are available to supplement the health insurance of chronically ill children: Medicaid and Supplemental Security Income (SSI). Talk to your child's case manager or social worker, the Medicaid office, or your local health department about eligibility for these programs.

Getting a Second Opinion and Trusting Your Instincts

You may need to make some tough decisions regarding her health care providers and recommended treatments. Never forget that you are in charge of all decisions about your child's medical care. If you have any doubts about your child's treatment or the treatment recommended to you, seek a second opinion.

If you do not agree with your child's doctor, you may choose not to follow his or her recommendations. In some cases, you may disagree with only one point of treatment. Whatever the case, make your feelings known. Your child's doctor cannot treat your child without what's known as your informed consent—that is, he or she must explain to you the risks and benefits of any treatment or test and must get your permission beforehand.

Never feel guilty about wanting a second opinion. After all, you know your child and his needs better than anyone else, and you are ultimately responsible for the care he receives. Be honest and open with your child's doctor—explain why you are getting a second opinion, and try to get one as soon as possible so that any treatment your child needs is not delayed.

Need More Information?

Check the Index and Appendix C, "Resource Guide." And of course, consult your child's doctor.

PART SEVEN

Finding High-Quality Health Information

chapter thirty-four

Finding Health Information on the Web

Whom do you trust?

Picture this typical scenario from a few years ago: Parents are concerned about symptoms their child has been experiencing, so they make an appointment with their child's doctor. Before the day of the visit, the parents talk to their family, friends, and neighbors about their child's problem. But, except for what bits of advice and comfort they glean from these conversations, the parents decide to place their trust in their child's doctor to find out what's wrong.

How is this so different from the parent-doctor relationship today? Well, most parents still ultimately trust their child's doctor. And parents today still get advice while talking over the backyard fence. But now they can look much further than their own backyard and circle of family and friends. In fact, now they have the entire World Wide Web at their fingertips.

Increasingly, families are turning to the Web to find all kinds of information, purchase products, or locate services. Although it's only about a decade old, the Web has revolutionized numerous industries: health care, banking, travel, and news delivery, to name just a few. Yes—there is plenty of hype about online technologies, but the Web is truly changing the way we get information. The Web can provide interactive, up-to-date information 24 hours a day, seven days a week —usually at little or no cost. So the problem today is not that we lack information—it's that there's too much information to sort through, and not all of it is accurate.

The Web and Health

The Web is filled with health-related information. It can be used to learn more about specific medical conditions, locate doctors and hospitals, purchase products and medications, and find sources of emotional and financial support. Most doctors report that an increasing number of their patients arrive in their offices armed with pages printed from the Web. Sometimes the information is of excellent quality and it helps families understand problems and evaluate treatment options. Other times, it's confusing, outdated, or dangerously inaccurate. The challenge is finding reliable, accurate, up-to-date information among those thousands of sites.

> ### The Voice of Experience
>
> *"Dear KidsHealth,*
> *I would like to thank you not only for the information, but also for the way it was presented. I do not have a medical background, so it was nice to be able to read your article and understand it . . . at least now I will understand half of what the doctor is saying. . . . Again, I thank you, and please keep up the excellent work."*
> —FROM THE KidsHealth PARENT SURVEY

Although we can't review all of the Web sites that contain health information about babies and young children, we do have some thoughts that you might want to consider as you browse the Internet. These thoughts are based on our experience as the creators of KidsHealth.org, one of the oldest, largest, and most-visited Web sites devoted to children's health.

Here are a few questions worth keeping in mind as you evaluate the quality of a site's health information:

- Does someone make sure information on this Web site is accurate? There's no official Web information approval office that's "in charge" of making sure everything that gets posted on the Web is accurate. Anyone can have a Web site, and, in many ways, that's good because it capitalizes on the power of free speech. But this also means that you need to be a critical user, carefully evaluating the accuracy of each site you visit.
- Can you judge a site by its appearance? A professional-looking Web site doesn't necessarily mean it contains accurate information. It may simply mean that there's a good Web designer involved or that it's well funded.
- Is the site's goal to educate—or is it to sell a product? Sometimes it's hard to tell a commercial message from objective content. Unlike news magazines or

other printed sources of medical information, many Web sites don't have a clear division between their information and their advertisements. Many sites, particularly the dot-coms, exist primarily to sell products or services. There's nothing inherently wrong with that; it's just that editorial policies can be unclear and driven by biased agendas. For example, a site that offers information on diaper rash and its treatment may encourage you to buy its own ointment. Even the most respectable sites need to have advertising—after all, expenses need to be paid to support the publication's existence. In reputable sites, however, there is often a clear division between the editorial and advertising departments. Certainly advertisers should not unduly influence or distort the content. Many Web sites do not clearly observe that ethical boundary—their main goal is to sell more health insurance, ginkgo, or wrinkle reducer. Does that mean their information is not accurate? Not necessarily—but let the buyer beware.

- Do you know who creates the Web site? If you know who creates the site, you can better judge its reliability. Your best bet is to find sites that come from a recognized authority, such as a medical school or a health-related foundation or society, or from a reputable health agency like the U.S. Centers for Disease Control and Prevention. How can you do that? Often the source is in the three letters after the dot. Sites that end in ".gov" indicate that they are from a government source. Sites that end in ".edu" indicate that they come from colleges and universities. Sites that end with ".org" used to mean that they came from a nonprofit organization, but that is no longer necessarily the case. Sites that end in ".com" are commercial, business-related sites. Whatever the end of the site—be it ".com," ".org," ".gov," or ".edu"—the creator should make it crystal clear who the publisher is.

- Are the editors and writers qualified to give health information? You'll need to look at the site credits to judge this. Usually, sites have a description of how the content is created and reviewed. Of course, having a medical degree attached to the creator's name doesn't guarantee quality (or even that the person really is a medical doctor)—nor does its absence mean there's a lack of quality.

- Is the site regularly updated? Are review dates posted? Are articles reviewed on a reasonably frequent basis (say, every 12 to 18 months or more often)? Many sites include the day's date at the top or the bottom of the articles, but this does not always mean that the content was reviewed for accuracy or posted that day.

- Does the site present a balanced viewpoint? Some sites are little more than someone's axe to grind. The person behind the site might feel injured, disrespected, or excluded by the "powers that be." Sometimes that axe is wielded not by an individual but by a whole group. The Web can be an effective way to voice an alternative opinion, but you have to be wary of this kind of content. Beware of sweeping claims, miraculous cures, hints of conspiracy, and overreliance on personal testimonials.

Online Support Groups and Chat Groups

The development of online support groups has been a positive outgrowth of the Web. A support group is composed of families (or individuals) with a common concern, such as a specific medical condition. These groups often provide vital emotional support and guidance to families who might otherwise feel isolated. In addition, support groups serve as important sources of education, disseminators of information about new developments, and resources for hard-to-find products. The Web has enabled support groups to form more easily while helping to eliminate many geographic and time barriers.

Aside from all the positives, we're skeptical about the value of unsupervised chat groups. Chats are often confusing—and sometimes irresponsible. In many cases, people are typing away with little understanding about what's being said. Even more disturbing is when misinformed individuals are misinforming others. False claims may be made and repeated so often that it can be easy to start believing that they are true. Confidentiality can also be a problem with chats.

Some chat sites offer the service of mailing lists and newsletters to further help you stay in touch and share information. Some communicate about medical conditions through on-site bulletin boards that allow readers to post comments. The most valuable are those that are moderated—that is to say, experts determine what comments get posted and may make comments of their own. At their best, bulletin boards can provide interesting reading and useful tips. But do you really want to take medical advice from strangers?

Beware of Online "Experts"

Some sites claim to be able to make medical diagnoses from afar—whether free or by charge card. Some of these sites dish out a "diagnosis" based on information

Fourteen Health Activities on the Web

The Web has many health-related opportunities for parents, including these:

1. You can learn about conditions, diseases, and treatments.
2. You can find support groups.
3. You can purchase health care goods and services.
4. You can obtain prescription medications.
5. You can buy nutriceuticals (vitamins, dietary supplements, herbs, and so on).
6. You can gather information on health care providers and health plans.
7. You can make health care transactions.
8. You can use interactive personalized health tools (body mass index calculators, pregnancy calendars, and so on).
9. You can store and access personal medical records.
10. You can participate in online patient care management (diabetes-care management, and so on).
11. You can use Web-enabled diagnostic tools.
12. You can ask for personal medical advice from physicians.
13. You can chat with others, including professionals.
14. You can watch Webcasts and videos of various medical procedures.

you supply on their form. Others let you ask a doctor a question and then send you the response by email. Despite the appealing nature of these concepts, we'd recommend caution. Good medical care generally requires personalized, interactive discussion; an examination of your child's medical history; and a careful physical examination. These are lacking or limited via a Web site. In some of the sites we've looked at, the "expert" is a medical student or first-year resident. In our opinion, this is not the person you want directing the health care of your child. At least for the time being, use the Web as a potentially terrific source of supplementary information, not as a sole source of health care.

About KidsHealth.org

We love the Web, not just as big-time users of that vast, multimedia library—but as long-standing creators of Web content. As you probably know, this book was written by members of the team at The Nemours Center for Children's Health Media, creators of the KidsHealth.org Web site. The Center was established in 1993 and is funded by The Nemours Foundation—the largest accumulation of assets in the nation devoted to the direct health care of children. We develop high-quality print, video, and online educational material for families. Our site, KidsHealth.org, has been on the Web since 1995—and is the most-visited and linked-to children's health Web site. We're pleased that it has received dozens of top, juried awards for its reliable, entertaining content.

KidsHealth.org is really three sites in one, with separate articles for parents, kids, and teens. The massive site contains thousands of original articles, features, animations, parent-friendly research updates, and even games.

One of the unique things about KidsHealth.org is the content created for kids and teens. That's a rarity on the Web. We've found that kids and teens who understand their bodies, illnesses, and themselves feel empowered and less afraid—and may be more likely to do what they need to do to get better—and stay healthy. As Emily, a 14-year-old KidsHealth reader, wrote us: "This is the best Web site I have seen that relates to this kind of stuff. While reading through some of the articles, I could put myself into some of the situations. It makes me glad to know that I'm not alone. Thank you for boosting my confidence and my self-esteem. You really made my day."

Children's Health Information on the Web

A number of Web sites have health information about infants, children, and teens—as well as information about more general parenting concerns. Some of these sites cover a broad range of topics (such as KidsHealth.org); others are focused primarily on one topic or therapy. No doubt you've noticed that more and more organizations are including their Web site addresses in their literature and ads to help you find them. Here are a few examples of the different sorts of sites you'll find out there. Some have a remarkably narrow focus of interest, such as a French site (also in English) devoted to a specific complication of bone marrow transplantation called Graft versus Host reaction (www.perso.infini.fr /gvhd/us/general_us/frameset1_us.html). Another "flavor" of narrow focus is The Triplet Connections (www.tripletconnection.com), providing information, support, and resources to families who are expecting triplets, quadruplets, quintuplets, or more.

Some sites are disease- or condition-oriented, such as Children with Diabetes (www.childrenwithdiabetes.com). This site is a focused resource with information about the latest research, family support, educational materials, events, and more. Families of individuals with spinal muscular atrophy, a relatively rare disorder, can find a site (www.fsma.org) devoted to them, which provides background information, late-breaking news, and practical advice.

Families of children with rare conditions often feel isolated and unsupported. The Web is particularly useful in connecting those families to hard-to-find resources and other similarly affected families. One outstanding site, created by the National Organization for Rare Disorders (www.rarediseases.org), is an excellent place to start your information search.

Foundations devoted to specific health concerns, such as that of the National Childhood Cancer Foundation (www.nccf.org) and the American Cancer Society (www.cancer.org), are well represented on the Web. Educational institutions also sponsor helpful sites. Try the database for lay readers on the New York Online Access to Health (NOAH) site (www.noah-health.org) or Tufts University Nutrition Navigator (www.navigator.tufts.edu).

The U.S. government sponsors many sites such as Health.gov (www.health.gov) and the U.S. Centers for Disease Control and Prevention's site (www.cdc.gov). This latter site, incidentally, is an excellent source of the latest immunization recommendations for would-be travelers, health advisories, and tobacco and drug information, among other things. The U.S. government also provides a general health portal, Healthfinder (www.healthfinder.gov), which can direct you to scores of useful health sites. You might also check out the Medline Plus database sponsored by the National Library of Medicine (www.nlm.nih.gov).

Private industry devotes efforts to providing educational and entertaining information regarding their area of interest. Dole, for example, has their well-known 5 A Day site (www.dole5aday.com) created with support from the National Cancer

Institute. Another example is the National Dairy Council's Family Food Zone at (www.familyfoodzone.com).

Pharmaceutical firms, too, have their own sites; some are devoted to the company in general, such as Abbott Laboratories' site (www.abbott.com). Many have separate sites for specific products.

Speaking of medications, it's possible to purchase or refill medications on the Web, sometimes at a considerable discount. Drugstore.com (www.drugstore.com) was created for the Web, and traditional "brick and mortar" stores such as Eckerd (www.eckerd.com) are there, as well.

For the latest (and usually reliable) information on alternative and complementary medicine, you can start with the site sponsored by Dr. Andrew Weil (www.drweil.com).

How to Use General Search Tools

Sometimes you'll want information but won't know the specific uniform resource locator (URL) . . . you know, the address for the Web site. In these cases, you can find what you need by using one of the many Web search tools. There are a number of ways to find what you seek.

The Web has many general search tools, such as Excite, Yahoo!, LookSmart, Lycos, and Google. The browsers (Netscape and Internet Explorer) have built-in search buttons. A search using these tools and a specific keyword will give you plenty of sites to choose from—usually too many. If you put in a general term like "asthma," you'll be overwhelmed with several hundred possible sites. In general, it's best to be specific.

Most of the search tools, such as Yahoo!, now have specific topic areas, such as "health." If you go to the health section, you may also find subsections, such as "children's health." Search engine site editors have gathered their choices to make your job easier. How well they do their job, however, is variable—and sometimes the recommended sites have an economic partnership with the search sites to ensure that they get "top billing" for searches.

There are a few sites that are specifically health search tools, such as PEDINFO (www.pedinfo.org), which was created primarily for pediatricians—but is useful for the general public as well.

The Web and Confidentiality

Medical confidentiality is an important feature of doctor-patient relationships—but it may not be adequately protected on a Web site. Theoretically, information transmitted on the Web can be adequately encrypted and securely stored. That's how banks do it. But security and privacy are what banks are all about. Simple health sites may not be as sophisticated or be willing or able to spend the money necessary to keep out prying eyes, despite the laws requiring that they do so. Our advice: Be cautious about sharing personal health information over the Web. Know with whom you're sharing your personal information—and check out their confidentiality policy before you hit the "submit" button.

Need More Information?

Check the Index and Appendix C, "Resource Guide." And of course, consult your child's doctor.

Preparing Your Child's Health Record

Keeping your own record of your child's health information is a good idea. It can help in an emergency, if you're traveling, or if you have to see a new doctor—in fact, anytime a medical issue arises and your child's medical records are not immediately available. (Besides, when your child is grown, his health record can be one more, albeit slightly offbeat, memento of childhood. Someday it will look quaint.)

Creating a health record is easy. Keeping it up to date and easy to find is more difficult. To make sure you have it when you need it, it would be ideal to keep one copy at home, one in each parent's car or office, and one in each parent's bag or wallet. Give a copy to your child's day-care center or babysitter. Take it along to medical appointments, and update it on the spot, then update or replace all the copies. Have it on hand when you call the doctor's office for medical advice.

A health record should include the following information:

- Your child's full name and date of birth
- Your name and phone number
- The name and phone number of your child's doctor
- Your child's height and weight measurements (This information can be useful for doctors who are calculating medication doses. Because these measurements change over time in a growing child, date these entries and update them regularly.)

- Your child's allergies (Include allergies to medications, both prescription and nonprescription, as well as allergic reactions to insect stings and bites and allergies to foods. This information often can help medical personnel diagnose your child's problem more accurately, administer the correct treatment, and avoid prescribing a medication that could possibly harm your child. If your child has no known allergies, note that as well.)

- Medications currently being taken (List prescription and nonprescription medications and anything else your child takes, including herbs. Include the doses and the times of day the medications are taken. Be sure you keep this entry up to date. In an emergency or certain other situations, it may affect what medications your child will be given. This is particularly important if your child is taking multiple medications for a chronic or complex medical problem. Because drugs can interact with each other in the body, adding a new medication could throw a medical condition out of control or possibly cause a life-threatening reaction. If your child takes no medications, note that as well.)

- Preexisting illnesses or conditions (Note any chronic illnesses like asthma, seizures, or diabetes and conditions like heart murmurs or other heart abnormalities. Preexisting illnesses can greatly affect the kinds of tests or treatment your child needs.)

- Hospitalizations and operations (For each time your child was hospitalized, list why, when, where, and who the attending physician was if it wasn't your child's regular doctor. List any operations and the names of the surgeons.)

- Other major illnesses or injuries (List illnesses or injuries that were serious enough to need treatment or visits to the doctor. These might include chicken pox, broken bones, or recurring ear infections. Include dates and any medication or other treatment given.)

- Immunizations (Keep an updated record of all your child's immunizations. If you lose track, the staff at your child's doctor's office can assist you. If your child ever had a serious reaction to an immunization, such as seizures, high fever, or severe discomfort, be sure to note that. If your child has not received the recommended vaccines because of religious or other reasons, be sure you include that information.)

A Note on Blood Type

It usually doesn't matter whether you list your child's blood type, despite what many people think. In an extreme emergency requiring immediate blood transfusion, only universal donor blood (type O negative) would be given, which is generally safe for all people to receive. In less urgent circumstances, your child's blood would be typed by the hospital laboratory, even if you have that information on hand. Because making a mistake in blood type can be extremely dangerous, medical personnel generally will not rely on a parent or outside medical records for this information.

Your Child's Health Record

Child's full name_____

Parent's name_____ Phone number_____

Doctor's name_____ Phone number_____

Birth Information

Date_____ Weight_____ Mother's age_____ Length of pregnancy_____

Complications, if any_____

_____

_____

Weight and Height Measurements

Date	Weight	Height

Allergies

Prescription medications _____

Nonprescription medications _____

Other allergies_____

Family Medical History

Allergies/Asthma_____ High blood pressure_____

Heart disease_____ Tuberculosis_____

Diabetes_____

Other_____

Child's Chronic Illnesses or Conditions

Note any chronic illnesses like asthma, seizures, or diabetes, and conditions like heart murmurs or other heart abnormalities._____

_____

_____

_____

Hospitalizations and Surgeries

Date	Reason/type of surgery	Where	Physician/surgeon

Immunizations

The recommended age or age range for each immunization appears in **bold**. Write the actual date of your child's immunization in the space provided.

KEY	
DTaP = diphtheria, tetanus, and acellular pertussis (whooping cough) vaccine	MMR = measles, mumps, and rubella vaccine
Hep B = hepatitis B vaccine	PCV = pneumococcal conjugate vaccine
Hib = Hemophilus influenzae type b vaccine	Td = tetanus/diphtheria booster
IPV = inactivated poliovirus vaccine	Var = varicella (chicken pox) vaccine

Immunization Chart

Birth–2 Months	2 Months	1–4 Months	4 Months
Hep B #1_____	DTaP #1_____	Hep B #2 _____	DtaP #2_____
	Hib #1_____	(given 1 month after first dose)	Hib #2_____
	IPV #1 _____		IPV #2_____
	PCV #1 _____		PCV#2_____

6 Months	6–18 Months	12–15 Months	12–18 Months
DTaP #3_____	Hep B #3_____	Hib #4_____	Var_____
Hib #3_____	IPV #3_____	MMR #1_____	
PCV #3_____		PCV #4_____	

15–18 Months	4–6 Years	11–12 Years	
DTaP_____	DTaP_____	Td_____	
	MMR #2_____		
	IPV_____		

Vaccinations not given, and reason: _____

_____

_____

_____

Medications Taken

Medication	Dosage	How often	Dates taken	Reason taken/ reactions, if any

Major Illnesses and Injuries

List illnesses or injuries that required treatment or visits to the doctor.

Date _____ Diagnosis _____

Symptoms _____

Medications _____ How long given? _____

Other treatment _____

Drug reactions? _____

Complications? _____

Date _____ Diagnosis _____

Symptoms _____

Medications _____ How long given? _____

Other treatment _____

Drug reactions? _____

Complications? _____

Date _____ Diagnosis _____

Symptoms _____

Medications _____ How long given? _____

Other treatment _____

Drug reactions? _____

Complications? _____

Date _____ Diagnosis _____

Symptoms _____

Medications _____ How long given? _____

Other treatment _____

Drug reactions? _____

Complications? _____

Date _____ Diagnosis _____

Symptoms _____

Medications _____ How long given? _____

Other treatment _____

Drug reactions? _____

Complications? _____

Date _____ Diagnosis _____

Symptoms _____

Medications _____ How long given? _____

Other treatment _____

Drug reactions? _____

Complications? _____

Date _____ Diagnosis _____

Symptoms _____

Medications _____ How long given? _____

Other treatment _____

Drug reactions? _____

Complications? _____

Growth Charts and Body Mass Index Charts

G rowth is one of the most important indicators of a child's health. The pattern of a child's weight gain and growth in height can be affected by a number of specific growth disorders as well as by many nutritional problems and chronic medical conditions (see Chapter 17, "Growth and Development," and the entry for Growth Disorders in Chapter 32, "Health Problems in Early Childhood"). For this reason, at periodic health visits your child's doctor will weigh and measure your child and plot the measurements on standard growth charts.

The set of growth charts contained in this appendix is reproduced with permission from the National Center for Health Statistics. These charts represent the most recently published (June 2000) standards for U.S. children. Plotting your child's measurements on these charts will allow you to compare your child's growth patterns with data collected on thousands of U.S. children. In all cases, there are separate charts for boys and girls. The standard charts included are these:

- For children ages birth to 36 months (three years):
    - Weight for age, pages 770 and 771
    - Length for age, pages 772 and 773
    - Head circumference for age, pages 774 and 775
    - Weight for length, pages 776 and 777
- For children ages two to twenty years:
    - Weight for age, pages 778 and 779
    - Stature (height) for age, pages 780 and 781

- Weight for stature (height), pages 782 and 783
- BMI (body mass index) for age, pages 784 and 785

How to Use and Interpret These Growth Charts

- All of the charts in this set show "percentile" lines for comparison with the general population of children at any given age. The 50th percentile line represents the average value for age. The lowest line shown is the 3rd percentile line (3 percent of children will be at or below this value), and the highest line is the 97th percentile (3 percent of children will be at or above this value).
- Growth data are of little value if the measurements are not performed properly. In general, you should plot on these charts only those measurements that have been obtained in your child's doctor's office or by a person skilled in proper techniques using an accurate measuring device. Home measurements (as well as those done in a doctor's office hastily or with an uncooperative child) are frequently inaccurate.
- Length and height are not the same. Only length (lying down) measurements should be used for all children younger than two years old and until they can cooperate for a height (standing) measurement. Height measurements are often an inch or more less than length measurements in the same toddler or preschool child.
- Head circumference should be measured by encircling the child's head at the widest point with the tape measure just above the eyebrows.
- The rate or pattern of a child's growth over time is a much more important indicator than a single measurement when considering a possible growth problem. For example, a child whose height drops from the 50th percentile to the 10th percentile on the growth chart is more likely to have a problem than a child who is growing steadily along the 5th percentile line. Consult your child's doctor about any concerns you have about your child's growth or for assistance in interpreting your child's growth data.
- Both the weight for stature (height) and the BMI (body mass index) charts can be useful for assessing (but not directly measuring) body fat in children two years and older; however, the U.S. Centers for Disease Control and Prevention have stressed that the recently released BMI charts are preferred for this purpose.

- Children who fall below the 5th percentile on either of these charts are considered underweight. Children at or above the 85th percentile are considered overweight (and at risk for obesity), and those at or above the 95th percentile are considered to be obese.
- To calculate a child's BMI (body mass index), if using metric measurements (kilograms and meters), the formula for calculating BMI is: BMI = weight/(height)^2 *or*

  1. Multiply the child's height (in meters) times itself.
  2. Divide the child's weight (in kilograms) by the result in number 1.

  If using English measurements (pounds and inches), the formula for calculating BMI is: BMI = weight/(height)^2 × 703 *or*

  1. Multiply the child's height (in inches) times itself.
  2. Divide the child's weight (in pounds) by the result in number 1.
  3. Multiply the result in number 2 times 703.

  Note: Because of the manner in which BMI is determined, accuracy in measuring the child's height is very important—a small error in height measurement can result in a large error in the BMI result.

- Consult your child's doctor with any concerns you have about your child's growth or for assistance in interpreting your child's growth data.

CDC Growth Charts: United States

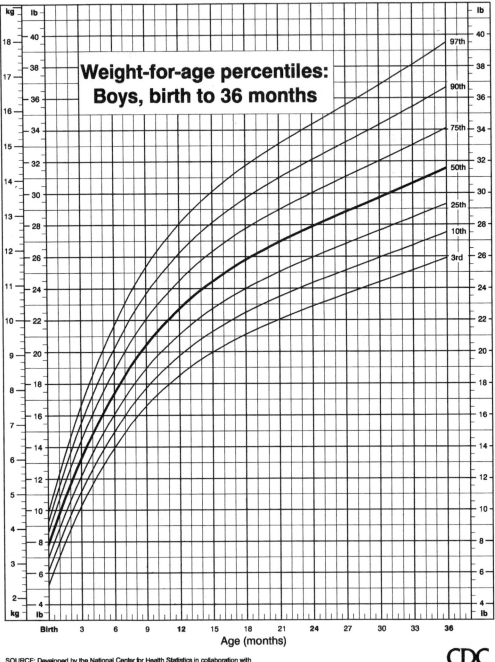

Weight-for-age percentiles: Boys, birth to 36 months

SOURCE: Developed by the National Center for Health Statistics in collaboration with the National Center for Chronic Disease Prevention and Health Promotion (2000).

CDC Growth Charts: United States

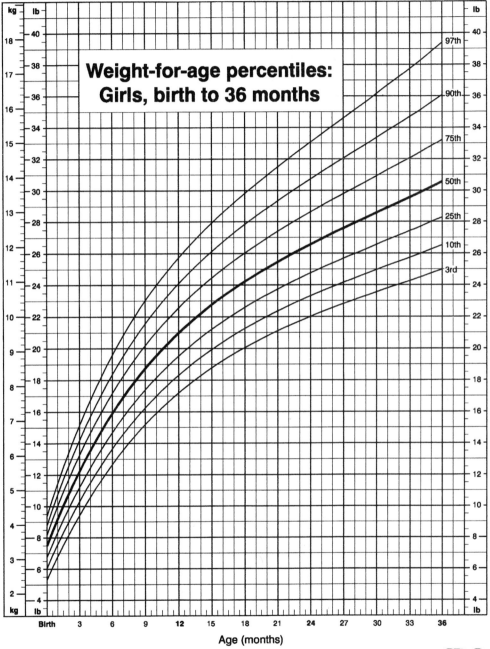

**Weight-for-age percentiles:
Girls, birth to 36 months**

Age (months)

SOURCE: Developed by the National Center for Health Statistics in collaboration with
the National Center for Chronic Disease Prevention and Health Promotion (2000).

CDC Growth Charts: United States

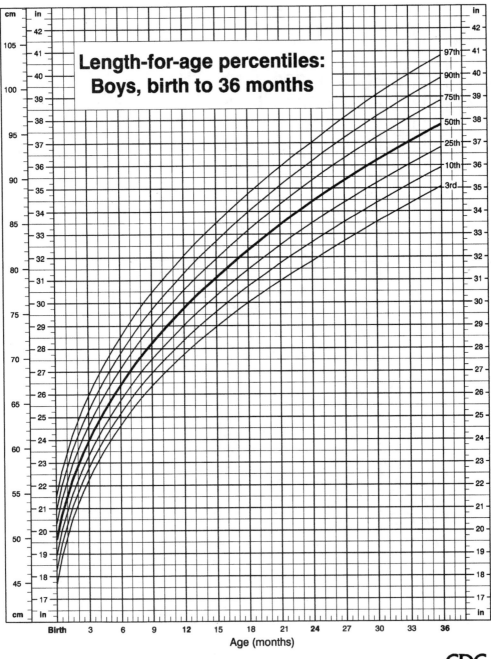

Length-for-age percentiles:
Boys, birth to 36 months

SOURCE: Developed by the National Center for Health Statistics in collaboration with
the National Center for Chronic Disease Prevention and Health Promotion (2000).

CDC Growth Charts: United States

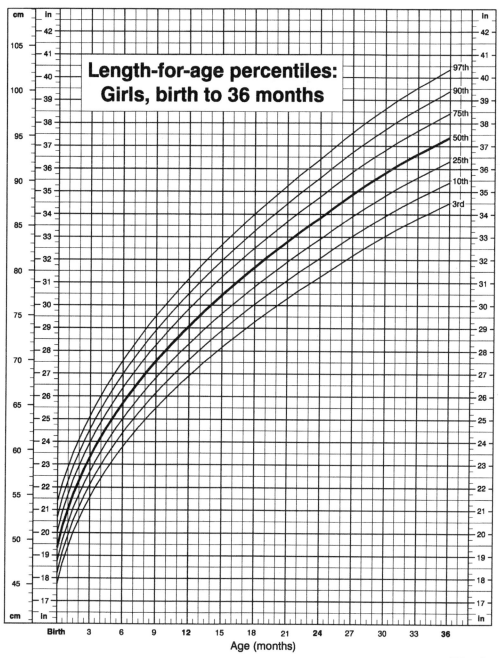

Length-for-age percentiles: Girls, birth to 36 months

Age (months)

SOURCE: Developed by the National Center for Health Statistics in collaboration with the National Center for Chronic Disease Prevention and Health Promotion (2000).

CDC Growth Charts: United States

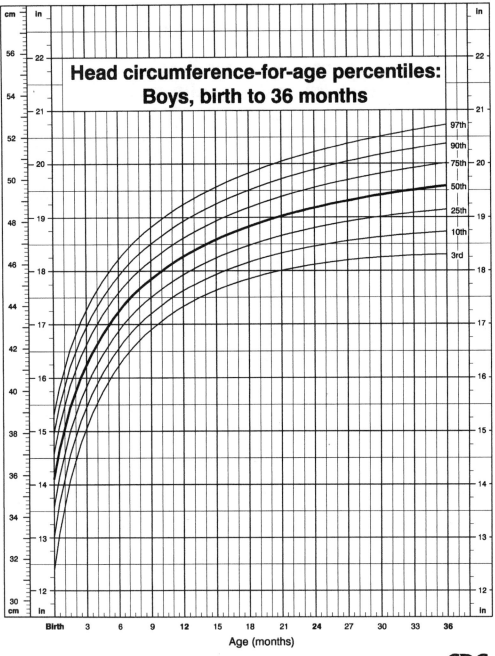

Head circumference-for-age percentiles: Boys, birth to 36 months

Age (months)

SOURCE: Developed by the National Center for Health Statistics in collaboration with
the National Center for Chronic Disease Prevention and Health Promotion (2000).

CDC Growth Charts: United States

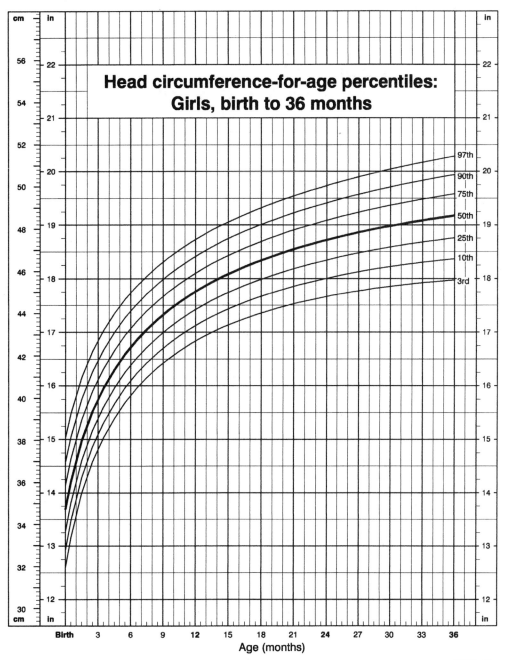

Head circumference-for-age percentiles: Girls, birth to 36 months

Age (months)

SOURCE: Developed by the National Center for Health Statistics in collaboration with
the National Center for Chronic Disease Prevention and Health Promotion (2000).

CDC Growth Charts: United States

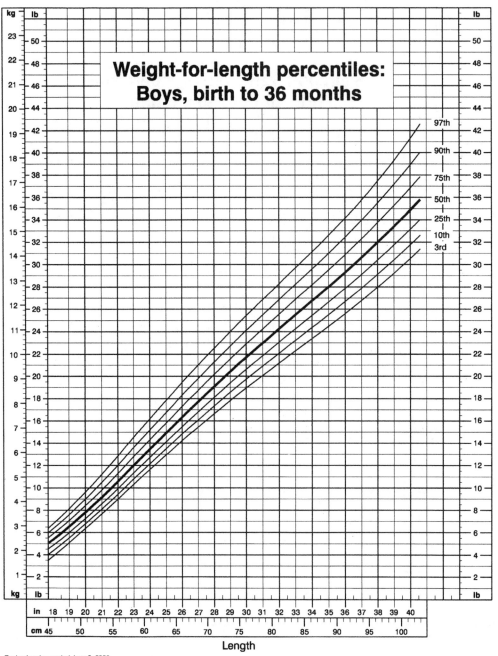

Weight-for-length percentiles: Boys, birth to 36 months

Length

Revised and corrected June 8, 2000.

SOURCE: Developed by the National Center for Health Statistics in collaboration with
the National Center for Chronic Disease Prevention and Health Promotion (2000).

CDC Growth Charts: United States

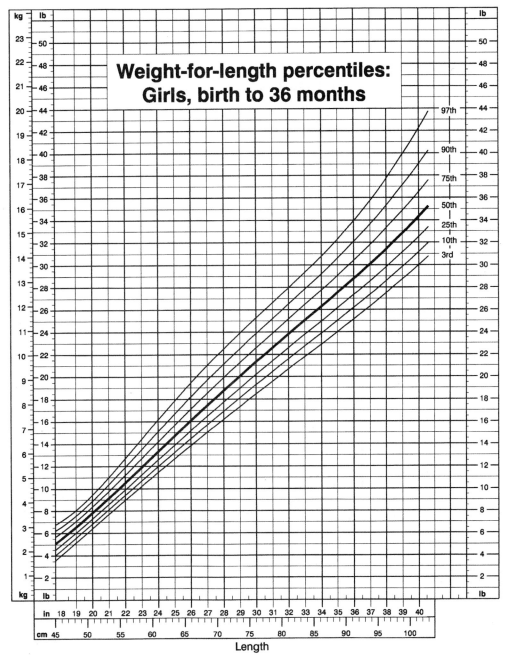

Weight-for-length percentiles: Girls, birth to 36 months

Length

Revised and corrected June 8, 2000.

SOURCE: Developed by the National Center for Health Statistics in collaboration with the National Center for Chronic Disease Prevention and Health Promotion (2000).

CDC Growth Charts: United States

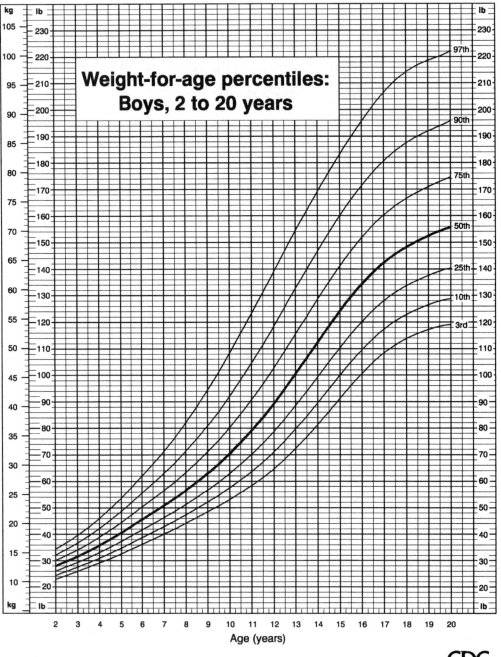

Weight-for-age percentiles:
Boys, 2 to 20 years

Age (years)

SOURCE: Developed by the National Center for Health Statistics in collaboration with
the National Center for Chronic Disease Prevention and Health Promotion (2000).

CDC Growth Charts: United States

Weight-for-age percentiles: Girls, 2 to 20 years

Age (years)

97th
90th
75th
50th
25th
10th
3rd

SOURCE: Developed by the National Center for Health Statistics in collaboration with
the National Center for Chronic Disease Prevention and Health Promotion (2000).

CDC Growth Charts: United States

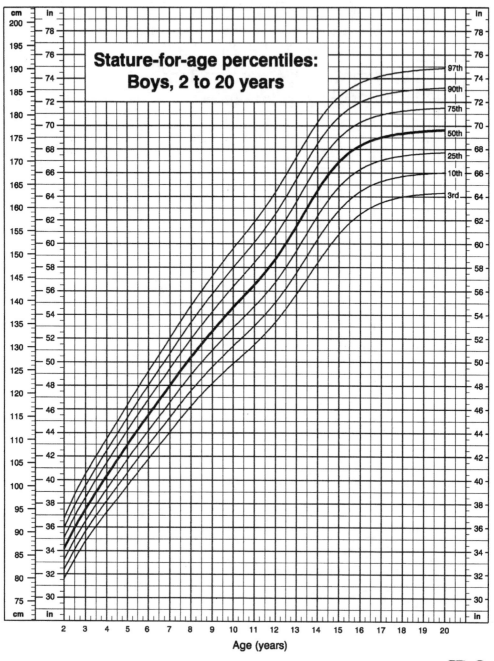

Stature-for-age percentiles:
Boys, 2 to 20 years

SOURCE: Developed by the National Center for Health Statistics in collaboration with
the National Center for Chronic Disease Prevention and Health Promotion (2000).

CDC Growth Charts: United States

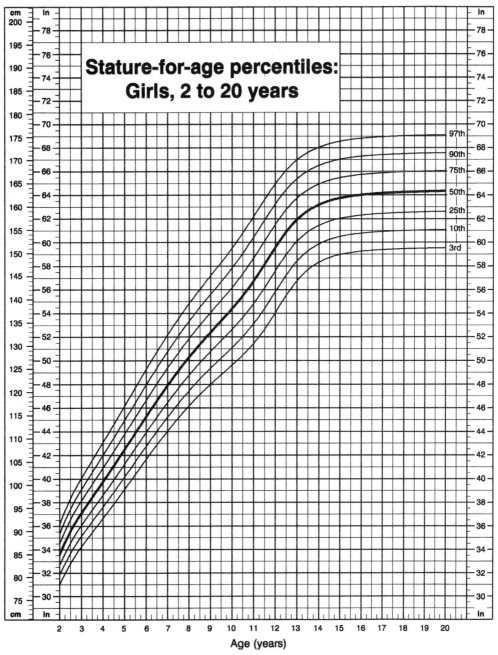

Stature-for-age percentiles:
Girls, 2 to 20 years

SOURCE: Developed by the National Center for Health Statistics in collaboration with
the National Center for Chronic Disease Prevention and Health Promotion (2000).

CDC Growth Charts: United States

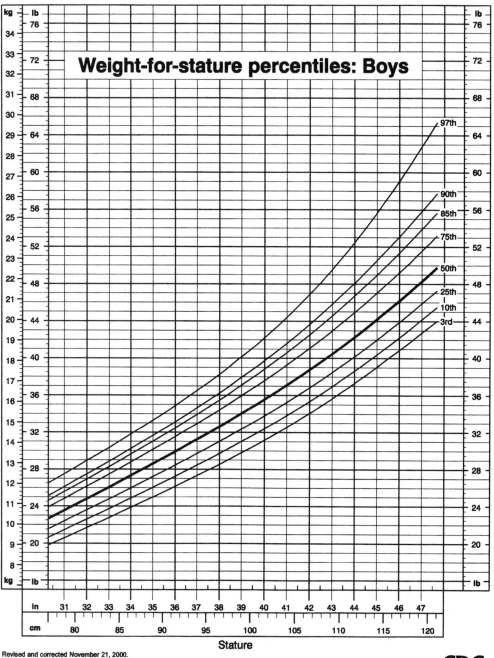

Weight-for-stature percentiles: Boys

Stature

Revised and corrected November 21, 2000.

SOURCE: Developed by the National Center for Health Statistics in collaboration with
the National Center for Chronic Disease Prevention and Health Promotion (2000).

CDC Growth Charts: United States

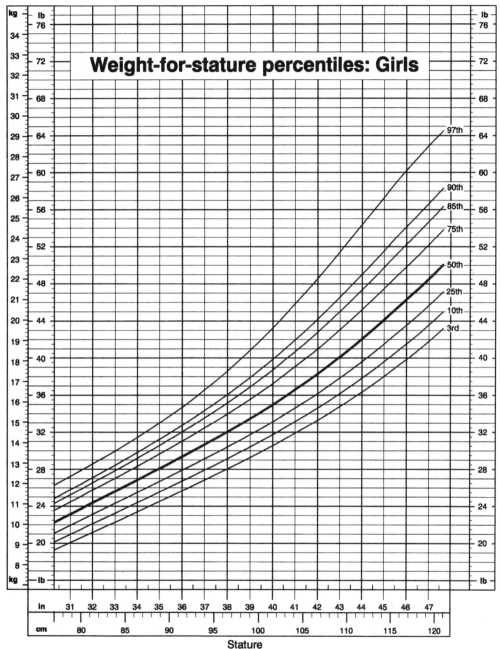

Weight-for-stature percentiles: Girls

Revised and corrected November 21, 2000.

SOURCE: Developed by the National Center for Health Statistics in collaboration with
the National Center for Chronic Disease Prevention and Health Promotion (2000).

CDC Growth Charts: United States

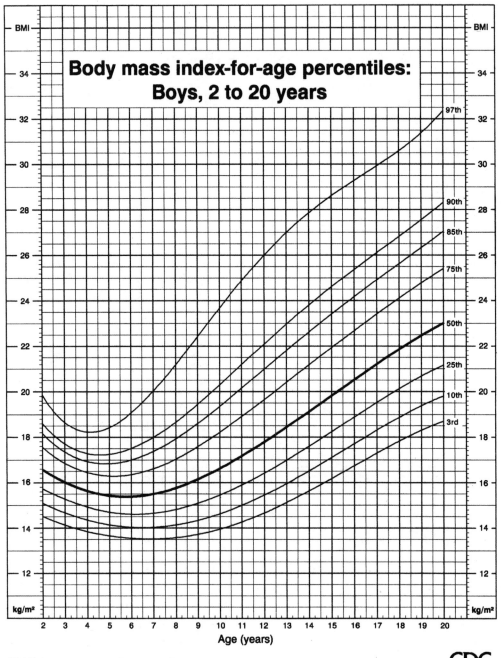

**Body mass index-for-age percentiles:
Boys, 2 to 20 years**

SOURCE: Developed by the National Center for Health Statistics in collaboration with
the National Center for Chronic Disease Prevention and Health Promotion (2000).

CDC

CDC Growth Charts: United States

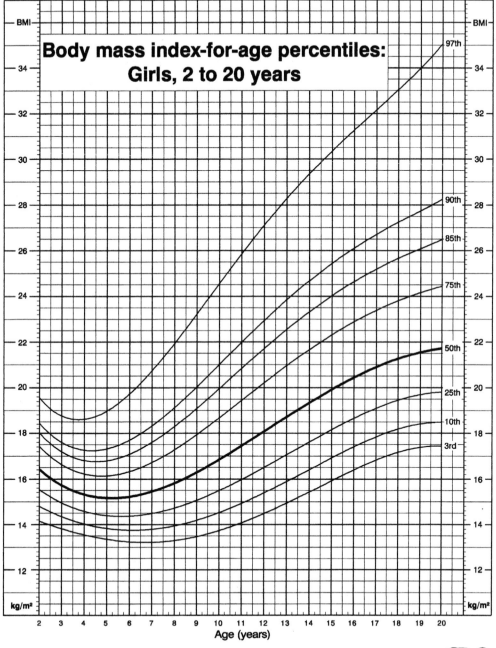

Body mass index-for-age percentiles: Girls, 2 to 20 years

SOURCE: Developed by the National Center for Health Statistics in collaboration with the National Center for Chronic Disease Prevention and Health Promotion (2000).

Resource Guide

Organizations

The Administration for Children and Families
Department of Health and Human Services
370 L'Enfant Promenade SW
Washington, DC 20447
Phone: (202) 401-9215
Web: www.acf.dhhs.gov

Administrators in Medicine (AIM)
Web: www.docboard.org

Agency for Healthcare Research and Quality (AHRQ)
2101 East Jefferson Street
Suite 501
Rockville, MD 20852
Phone: (301) 594-1364
Email: info@ahrq.gov
Web: www.ahrq.gov

The Alan Guttmacher Institute
120 Wall Street
21st Floor
New York, NY 10005
Phone: (212) 248-1111
Web: www.agi-usa.org

American Academy of Pediatric Dentistry
211 East Chicago Avenue
#700
Chicago, IL 60611-2663
(312) 337-2169
Web: www.aapd.org

American Academy of Pediatrics (AAP)
141 Northwest Point Boulevard
Elk Grove Village, IL 60007-1098
Phone: (847) 434-4000
Web: www.aap.org

American Association for Premature Infants
P.O. Box 46371
Cincinnati, OH 45246-0371
Web: www.aapi-online.org

American Association of Oriental Medicine
433 Front Street
Catasauqua, PA 18032
Phone: (610) 266-1433
(888) 500-7999
Fax: (610) 264-2768
Web: www.aaom.org

American Board of Medical Specialties Public Education Program
47 Perimeter Center East
Suite 500
Atlanta, GA 30346
Certified Doctor Verification Service:
www.abms.org/verify.html
Certified Doctor Locator Service:
www.abms.org/search.asp

American Cancer Society
1599 Clifton Road NE
Atlanta, GA 30329
Phone: (404) 320-3333
Web: www.cancer.org

American Cleft Palate Association
104 S. Estes Drive
Suite 204
Chapel Hill, NC 27514
Phone: (800) 24-CLEFT
(919) 933-9044
Web: www.cleftline.org

American Dental Association
(online resource to find a dentist in your area; contact through Web site only)
Web: www.ada.org

American Diabetes Association
Attn: Customer Service
1701 North Beauregard Street
Alexandria, VA 22311
Phone: (800) DIABETES
Web: www.diabetes.org

The American Fertility Society
2140 11th Avenue South
Suite 200
Birmingham, AL 35205-2800

American Holistic Health Association (AHHA)
P.O. Box 17400
Anaheim, CA 92817-7400
Phone: (714) 779-6152
Web: www.ahha.org

American Lung Association
1740 Broadway
New York, NY 10019-4374
Phone: (212) 315-8700
Web: www.lungusa.org

American Medical Association Doctor Finder
Web: www.ama-assn.org/aps/amahg.htm

American Red Cross (ARC)
National Headquarters
c/o Public Inquiry
431 18th Street NW
Washington, DC 20006
Phone: (202) 639-3520
Web: www.redcross.org

American Speech-Language-Hearing Association
10801 Rockville Pike
Rockville, MD 20852
Phone: (800) 498-2071
(301) 897-5700
Web: www.asha.org

The Arthritis Foundation
1314 Spring Street
Atlanta, GA 30309
Phone: (800) 283-7800
Web: www.arthritis.org

Association for Children and Adults with Learning Disabilities
4900 Girard Road
Pittsburgh, PA 15227-1444
Phone: (412) 881-2253

Association for Children with Retarded Mental Development
162 Fifth Avenue
New York, NY 10010
Phone: (212) 741-0100

Association for Neuro-Metabolic Disorders
5223 Brookfield Lane
Sylvania, OH 43560-1809
Web: www.kumc.edu/gec/support/neurome.html

Asthma and Allergy Foundation of America
1233 20th Street NW
Suite 402
Washington, DC 20036
Phone: (800) 7-ASTHMA
Web: www.aafa.org

Birth Defect Research for Children (BDRC)
930 Woodcock Road
Suite 225
Orlando, FL 32803
Phone: (407) 895-0802
Web: www.birthdefects.org

Breastfeed.com
Web: www.Breastfeed.com

C. Everett Koop Institute at Dartmouth
HB 7025 Strasenburgh Hall
Hanover, NH 03755-3862
Phone: (603) 650-1450
Fax: (603) 650-1452
Web: www.koop.dartmouth.edu

Cancer Information Service
National Cancer Institute
NCI Public Inquiries Office
31 Center Drive, MSC 2580
Building 31, Room 10A03
Bethesda, MD 20892-2580
Phone: (800) 4-CANCER
Web: www.cancernet.nci.nih.gov

Centers for Disease Control and Prevention
1600 Clifton Road NE
Atlanta, GA 30333
Phone: (404) 639-3311
Web: www.cdc.gov

Childbirth.org
Web: www.childbirth.org

Clearinghouse on Disability Information
Web: www.ed.gov/OFFICES/OSERS

ClinicalTrials.gov
ClinicalTrials.gov provides easy access to information on clinical trials for a wide range of diseases and conditions.
Phone: (888) FIND-NLM
Web: www.clinicaltrials.gov

Consumer Information Catalog
Pueblo, CO 81009
Phone: (888) 8-PUEBLO
Web: www.pueblo.gsa.gov

Cystic Fibrosis Foundation
6931 Arlington Road
Suite 200
Bethesda, MD 20814
Phone: (301) 951-4422
(800) FIGHTCF
Web: www.cff.org

drkoop.com Drug Checker
Web: www.drugchecker.drkoop.com/apps
/drugchecker/DrugMain

Emergency Medical Services for Children (EMSC)
National Resource Center
111 Michigan Avenue NW
Washington, DC 20010-2970
Phone: (202) 884-4927
Fax: (202) 884-6845
Web: www.ems-c.org

Epilepsy Foundation of America
4351 Garden City Drive
Landover, MD 20785
Phone: (301) 459-3700
(800) 332-1000
Web: www.epilepsyfoundation.org

Federation for Children with Special Needs, Inc.
1135 Tremont Street
Suite 420
Boston, MA 02120
Phone: (800) 331-0688
(617) 236-7210
Web: www.fcsn.org

Food and Nutrition Information Center (USDA)
Web: www.nal.usda.gov/fnic/

Genetics Society of America
9650 Rockville Pike
Bethesda, MD 20814-3998
Phone: (301) 571-1825
Web: www.faseb.org/genetics/

Gluten Intolerance Group of North America
15110 10th Avenue SW
Suite A
Seattle, WA 98166
(206) 246-6652
Web: www.gluten.net/default.htm

Healthfinder
Web: www.healthfinder.gov

Health-Mart.net
Phone: (601) 362-9900
Fax: (601) 362-9905
Web: www.health-mart.net

Hospital Select
Web: www.hospitalselect.com

Human Growth Foundation
997 Glen Cove Avenue
Glen Head, NY 11545
Phone: (800) 451-6434
Web: www.hgfound.org

Immunization Action Coalition
Web: www.immunize.org

International Childbirth Education Association, Inc.
P.O. Box 20048
Minneapolis, MN 55420
Phone: (952) 854-8660
Web: www.icea.org

The Juvenile Diabetes Foundation
120 Wall Street
New York, NY 10005-4001
Phone: (800) JDF-CURE
Web: www.jdrf.org

The Kempe Children's Center
1825 Marion Street
Denver, CO 80218
Phone: (303) 864-5252
Web: www.kempecenter.org

KidsHealth
Web: www.KidsHealth.org

La Leche League International
1400 North Meacham Road
Schaumburg, IL 60173-4048
Phone: (847) 519-7730
Web: www.lalecheleague.org

The Leukemia and Lymphoma Society, Inc.
1311 Mamaroneck Avenue
White Plains, NY 10605
Phone: (914) 949-5213
Fax: (914) 949-6691
Web: www.leukemia.org

The Lyme Disease Foundation, Inc.
1 Financial Plaza
18th Floor
Hartford, CT 06013-2601
Phone: (800) 886-LYME
(860) 525-2000
Web: www.lyme.org

March of Dimes Birth Defects Foundation
1275 Mamaroneck Avenue
White Plains, NY 10605
Phone: (888) 663-4637
(914) 428-7100
Web: www.modimes.org

Maternal and Child Health Bureau
5600 Fishers Lane
Parklawn Building, Room 18-05
Rockville, MD 20857
Phone: (301) 443-2170
Web: www.mchb.hrsa.gov

Maternity Center Association
281 Park Avenue South
New York, NY 10010
Phone: (212) 777-5000
Web: www.maternity.org/index.html

MayoClinic.com Drug Information
www.mayoclinic.com/home?id-sp5.7

MedicAlert Foundation U.S.
2323 Colorado Avenue
Turlock, CA 95382
Phone: (800) 432-5378
(209) 668-3333
Web: www.medicalert.org

MEDLINEplus Drug Information
www.nlm.nih.gov/medlineplus/druginformation.html

The National Association for Home Care
228 Seventh Street SE
Washington, DC 20003
Phone: (202) 547-7424
Fax: (202) 547-3540
Web: www.nahc.org

National Association for the Visually Handicapped
22 West 21st Street
Sixth Floor
New York, NY 10010
Phone: (212) 889-3141
Web: www.navh.org

National Center for Chronic Disease
Prevention and Health Promotion
Division of Reproductive Health
4770 Buford Highway NE
Mail Stop K-20
Atlanta, GA 30341-3717
Phone: (770) 488-5372
Web: www.cdc.gov/nccdphp/drh

National Center for Homeopathy
801 North Fairfax Street
Suite 306
Alexandria, VA 22314
Phone: (877) 624-0613
(703) 548-7790
Fax: (703) 548-7792
Web: www.homeopathic.org

National Center for Natural and
Holistic Health (NCCAM)
Clearinghouse
(Division of National Institutes of Health,
or NIH)
P.O. Box 8218
Silver Spring, MD 20907-8218
Phone: (888) 644-6226
Fax: (301) 495-4957
Web: www.nccam.nih.gov

National Center for the Blind
1800 Johnson Street
Baltimore, MD 21230
Phone: (410) 659-9317
Web: www.blind.net/bonw3000.htm

National Child Abuse Hotline
(24-hour hotline)
Phone: (800) 422-4453

National Child Care Information
Center (NCCIC)
243 Church Street NW
Second Floor
Vienna, VA 22180
Phone: (800) 616-2242
Fax: (800) 716-2242
Web: www.nccic.org

National Clearinghouse on Child
Abuse and Neglect Information
330C Street SW
Washington, DC 20447
Phone: (800) 394-3366
(703) 385-7565
Web: www.calib.com/nccanch

National Committee for the
Prevention of Child Abuse
Publishing Department
332 South Michigan Avenue
Suite 950
Chicago, IL 60604-4357

National Council on Alcoholism and
Drug Dependence
20 Exchange Place
Suite 2902
New York, NY 10005
Phone: (212) 269-7797
Web: www.ncadd.org

National Diabetes Information
Clearinghouse
1 Information Way
Bethesda, MD 20892

National Digestive Diseases
Information Clearinghouse
Box NDDIC
2 Information Way
Bethesda, MD 20892
Phone: (301) 468-6344
Fax: (301) 907-8906

National Easter Seal Society
230 West Monroe Street
Suite 1800
Chicago, IL 60606-4802
Phone: (312) 726-6200
Web: www.easter-seals.org

National Eye Institute (a division of National Institutes of Health)
(Free pamphlets, brochures, and educational materials are available.)
2020 Vision Place
Bethesda, MD 20892-3655
Phone: (301) 496-5248
Web: www.nei.nih.gov

National Family Caregivers Association
10400 Connecticut Avenue
#500
Kensington, MD 20895-3944
Phone: (800) 896-3650
Fax: (301) 942-2302
Web: www.nfcacares.org

National Hemophilia Foundation
116 West 32nd Street
11th Floor
New York, NY 10001
Phone: (212) 328-3700
Web: www.hemophilia.org

National HIV/AIDS Hotline
Phone: (800) 342-AIDS
SIDA: (800) 344-7432 (Spanish)
(800) 243-7889 (Hearing impaired)
Web: www.cdc.gov

National Hydrocephalus Foundation
12413 Centralia Road
Lakewood, CA 90715
Phone: (562) 402-3523

National Information Center for Children and Youth with Disabilities
P.O. Box 1492
Washington, DC 20013-1492
Phone: (800) 695-0285
(202) 884-8200
Web: www.nichcy.org

National Institute of Child Health and Human Development
Public Information and Communication Division
P.O. Box 3006
Rockville, MD 20847
Phone: (301) 496-5133
Web: www.nichd.nih.gov

National Institute of Diabetes, Digestive, and Kidney Diseases
National Institutes of Health
31 Center Drive
Building 31, 9A04
Bethesda, MD 20892-2560
Phone: (301) 496-3583
Web: www.niddk.nih.gov

National Kidney Foundation, Inc.
30 East 33rd Street
New York, NY 10016
Phone: (212) 889-2210
Web: www.kidney.org

National Organization for Rare Disorders, Inc.
P.O. Box 8923
New Fairfield, CT 06812-8923
Phone: (203) 746-6518
Web: www.rarediseases.org

National Safe Kids Campaign
1301 Pennsylvania Avenue NW
Suite 1000
Washington, DC 20004
Phone: (202) 662-0600
Web: www.safekids.org

National Safety Council
1121 Spring Lake Drive
Itasca, IL 60143-3201
Phone: (800) 621-7615
(630) 285-1121
Web: www.nsc.org

National Sickle-Cell Disease Program
National Heart, Lung, and Blood Institute
National Institutes of Health
Federal Building, Room 508
7550 Wisconsin Avenue
Bethesda, MD 20892
Phone: (301) 496-6931

The National Women's Health Information Center
8550 Arlington Boulevard
Suite 300
Fairfax, VA 22031
Phone: (800) 994-9662
Web: www.4woman.gov

New York Online Access to Health (NOAH)
Web: www.noah-health.org

Nursing Mothers Counsel
P.O. Box 50063
Palo Alto, CA 94303
Phone: (650) 599-3669 (national referral line)
Web: www.nursingmothers.org

Pediatric AIDS Foundation
2950 31st Street
#125
Santa Monica, CA 90405
Phone: (310) 314-1459
Web: www.pedaids.org

Planned Parenthood Federation of America
810 Seventh Avenue
New York, NY 10019
Phone: (212) 541-7800
(800) 829-7732
Web: www.plannedparenthood.org

PottyTrainingSolutions.com
Web: www.pottytrainingsolutions.com

Preemies.org
Web: www.preemies.org

Sexuality Information and Education Council of the United States
130 West 42nd Street
Suite 350
New York, NY 10036
Phone: (212) 819-9770
Web: www.siecus.org

Sickle-Cell Disease Association of America, Inc.
4601 Market Street
Second Floor
Philadelphia, PA 19139
Phone: (215) 471-8686
Web: www.sicklecelldisease.org

Society for Autistic Citizens
8601 Georgia Avenue
Suite 503
Silver Spring, MD 20910

State Children's Health Insurance Program (SCHIP)
Insure Kids Now
Phone: (877) KIDS-NOW
Web: www.insurekidsnow.gov
www.hcfa.gov/init/children.htm

Stuttering Resource Foundation
123 Oxford Road
New Rochelle, NY 10804

United Cerebral Palsy
1660 L Street NW
Suite 700
Washington, DC 20036-5602
Phone: (202) 776-0406
(800) USA-5-UCP
Web: www.ucp.org

U.S. Consumer Product Safety Commission
Washington, DC 20207
Phone: (800) 638-2772 (outside Maryland)
(800) 492-8104 (in Maryland)
(800) 638-8270 (TDD)
(301) 504-0580
Web: www.cpsc.gov

U.S. Department of Health and Human Services
Administration of Children, Youth, and Families
Child Care Bureau
330 C Street SW
Switzer Building, Room 2046
Washington, DC 20447
Phone: (202) 690-6782
Fax: (202) 690-5600
Web: www.acf.dhhs.gov/programs/ccb

U.S. National Library of Medicine
8600 Rockville Pike
Bethesda, MD 20894
Phone: (888) FIND-NLM
(301) 594-5983
Web: www.nlm.nih.gov

U.S. National Library of Medicine—MEDLINEplus
Web: www.nlm.nih.gov/medlineplus

U.S. Pharmacopeia (USP)
12601 Twinbrook Parkway
Rockville, MD 20852
Phone: (800) 822-8772
Web: www.usp.org

Visiting Nurse Associations of America
11 Beacon Street
Suite 910
Boston, MA 02108
Phone: (617) 523-4042
Fax: (617) 227-4843
Web: www.vnaa.org

Workingmom.com
Web: www.workingmom.com

Publications

The ABC's of Safe and Healthy Child Care (online handbook)
Web: www.cdc.gov/ncidod/hip/abc/abc.htm

The Birth Partner: Everything You Need to Know to Help a Woman Through Childbirth
By Penny Simkin, P.T.
Published by Harvard Common Press

Bottlefeeding Without Guilt: A Reassuring Guide for Loving Parents
By Peggy Robin
Published by Prima Publishing

Building Healthy Minds: The Six Experiences That Create Intelligence and Emotional Growth in Babies and Young Children
By Stanley Greenspan, M.D., with Nancy Breslau Lewis
Published by Perseus Book Group

Building the Healing Partnership: Parents, Professionals, and Children with Chronic Illnesses and Disabilities
by Patricia Taner Leff and Elaine H. Walitzer
Published by Brookline Books

A Child Is Born
By Lennart Nilsson
Published by Bantam Doubleday Dell

The Complete Book of Breastfeeding
By Marvin S. Eiger and Sally Wendkos Olds
Published by Bantam Books

Directory of Physicians in the United States
To order, call American Medical Association
(800) 621-8335

Dr. Mom's Guide to Breastfeeding
By Marianne Neifert, M.D.
Published by Plume

Easing Labor Pain: The Complete Guide to a More Comfortable and Rewarding Birth, Revised Edition
By Adrienne B. Lieberman
Published by Harvard Common Press

The Enchanted Broccoli Forest
By Mollie Katzen
Published by Ten Speed Press

The Everything Get Ready for Baby Book
By Katina Z. Jones
Published by Adams Media Corporation

Feed Me, I'm Yours
By Vicki Lansky
Published by Meadowbrook Press

Guide to Your Child's Nutrition
By the American Academy of Pediatrics
Published by Villard

Health Benefits Under COBRA (government pamphlet)
Phone: (800) 998-7542 to order
Web: www.dol.gov/dol/pwba

Infants and Mothers: Differences in Development
By T. Berry Brazelton, M.D.
Published by Delacorte Press

Mothering the Mother: How a Doula Can Help You Have a Shorter, Easier, and Healthier Birth
By Marshall H. Klaus, Phyllis H. Klaus (Contributor), and John Kennell (Contributor)
Published by Perseus Press

The Nursing Mother's Companion
By Kathleen Huggins, R.N., M.S.
Published by Harvard Common Press

Nutrition and Your Health: Dietary Guidelines for Americans, Fifth Edition (2000)
Copies are available for $4.75 each from the Consumer Information Center (Item 147G).
Order online at www.health.gov/dietary guidelines/ or call (888) 878-3256 (M-F, 9 A.M. to 8 P.M. eastern time).

One Bite Won't Kill You
By Ann Hodgman
Illustrated by Roz Chast
Published by Houghton Mifflin Co.

Preemies: The Essential Guide for Parents of Premature Babies
by Dana Wechsler Linden, Emma Trenti Paroli, and Mia Wechsler Doron, M.D.
Published by Workman Publishing

The Pregnancy Book
By William Sears, M.D., and Martha Sears, R.N.
Published by Little Brown & Co.

Right from Birth: Building Your Child's Foundation for Life
By Craig T. Ramey and Sharon L. Ramey
Published by Goddard Press Inc.

The Scientist in the Crib: Minds, Brains, and How Children Learn
By Alison Gopnik, Andrew N. Meltzoff, and Patricia K. Kuhl
Published by William Morrow & Co.

The Thinking Woman's Guide to a Better Birth
By Henci Goer
Illustrated by Rhonda Wheeler
Published by Perigee

What to Expect When You're Expecting
By Arlene Eisenberg, Heidi E. Murkoff, and Sandee E. Hathaway, B.S.N.
Published by Workman Publishing

Your Guide to Choosing Quality Health Care: Summary (pamphlet)
Consumer Information, December 1998
Agency for Health Care Policy and Research, Rockville, MD
Web: www.ahrq.gov/consumer/qntool .htm

Index